'EVERY MOTHER'S SON IS GUILTY'

Dr Chris Owen is a historian and Honorary Research Fellow in the School of History at the University of Western Australia. He has been researching Aboriginal history since the late 1990s and worked with Noongar Aboriginal people to establish their native title in the South West of Western Australia. He has published in peer-reviewed journals. His research interests, utilising primarily archival state records, include colonial policing (specifically the Kimberley), Aboriginal policy and governmental administration and the social conditions at the frontiers of colonisation in Western Australia. He lives in Perth, Western Australia with his wife and twin daughters.

'EVERY MOTHER'S SON IS GUILTY'

Policing the Kimberley
Frontier of Western Australia
1882–1905

CHRIS OWEN

UWAP

First published in 2016 by
UWA Publishing
Crawley, Western Australia 6009
www.uwap.uwa.edu.au
UWAP is an imprint of UWA Publishing

THE UNIVERSITY OF
WESTERN AUSTRALIA

a division of The University of Western Australia

National Library of Australia Cataloguing-in-Publication entry
Creator: Owen, Chris, author.
Title: 'Every mother's son is guilty...' : policing the Kimberley
frontier of Western Australia 1882 - 1905 /
Chris Owen.
ISBN: 9781742586687 (paperback)

Notes: Includes bibliographical references and index.
Subjects: Criminal justice, Administration of—Western
Australia—Kimberley Region—19th century.
Police—Western Australia—Kimberley Region—History.
Frontier and pioneer life—Western Australia—Kimberley Region—History.
Pioneers—Western Australia—Kimberley Region—History.
Kimberley (W.A.)—History—19th century.
Kimberley (W.A.)—Social conditions—19th century.
Dewey Number: 994.1403

Typeset by J & M Typesetting
Cover design by Upside Creative
Cover image: 'Group of prisoners in neck chains, Wyndham, Western Australia', circa 1898–1906. Courtesy State Library of Victoria, MS13867/65.
Printed by McPherson's Printing Group

The author and UWA Publishing gratefully acknowledge the Australian Academy of the Humanities and the Western Australian History Foundation for their financial support in the production of this book.

Warning: This book contains the names and images of Aboriginal people now deceased.

 uwapublishing

CONTENTS

FIGURES

PREFACE

This is a marvellous contribution by Chris Owen to the under-standing of the role the Western Australian police force played in the colonial expansion into the Kimberley district of Western Australia. The context and imperatives of how that policing affected the lives of the various Aboriginal tribes in the Kimberley, from the period of 1882 to Dr Walter Roth's controversial investigation *The Report of the Royal Commission on the Condition of the Natives* in 1905, is treated in a balanced and fair manner.

This encroachment stems clearly and regrettably from the dictates of a colonial settler society steeped within its own internal tensions and preoccupations, and oblivious to the rights of the Aboriginal people as original owners of the land or, even, as British subjects. Owen sheds light on activities and dynamics that might make some uncomfortable. He certainly positions the role of the police within a far broader context of colonialism, the rise of state sovereignty, and the demands of colonists in industries concerned only for the economic success of their endeavours. And all the while the reader witnesses Aboriginal people moving from self-confidence and self-reliance to subjugation, confusion, despair and indifference. Those police who rode on horseback through the Kimberley did not always understand the manifestation of these dynamics; they were, however, the agents of the untold and uncountable deaths of many innocent Aboriginal people.

Owen illustrates with details from reports written by the police themselves from their outposts in the isolation of the Kimberley to the authorities in Perth. These reports are indicative of the daily activities of the police in a particular district and describe the topography, its suitability for pastoralism or other industry, and the characteristics of the settlers of the region. Owen uncovers these stories with great skill and highlights the interconnection between how land was taken from the Aboriginal people and the dependency of the police on the local colonists for resources and civil and social respite. Police were, in a real way, co-dependent upon such people. The resourcing of the police and their capacity to remain independent to uphold the law is a theme that also shapes the characteristics of the frontier society in which Aboriginal people were pushed to the margins or extinguished from its presence.

It is hard to imagine the impact of the environment on individuals and their ability to undertake their responsibilities while remaining sane in such circumstances. These were English, Irish and Scottish men who were often poorly trained and poorly paid to uphold British law in the harsh conditions of the Kimberley. They were also caught amid tensions between the role of the government resident and the officer in charge of police. Their mandate to protect Aboriginal people was often compromised by the demands for justice, legitimate or otherwise, by colonists; their job made more difficult by the colonial pastoralists and pearlers who wanted police to turn a blind eye to their activities with Aboriginal people.

As the British government's responsibility diminished within the colony of Western Australia following the granting of self-government in 1890, the notion of the rule of law became almost synonymous with preventing Aboriginal people from interfering

in the colonists' possession of the land. It was not their concern what happened to the Aboriginal people in the wake of
their dominance and occupation of their lands. Owen clearly
exposes this reality based upon archival and historical records and
Aboriginal oral history. Indeed, a vast array of records is utilised,
including the extensive documentation by police themselves of the
killing that went on during police patrols. In addition, eyewitness
accounts of the shooting and burning of Aboriginal people make
this an especially important chronicle of colonisation.

Owen contrasts the pressures brought upon the policing role
and functions with the expansion of the colonists into the pearling
and pastoral industries. Pastoralists disregarded Aboriginal land
ownership and demanded police prosecute Aborigines for cattle
losses when they were not responsible. Colonists wanted them
removed, managed and prevented from impeding their expansion
over lands that they considered theirs. And police did turn a
blind eye and allowed what amounted to slavery, exploitation and
cruelty to the Aboriginal people – by pearlers especially. Owen
brings clarity to the discussion of what the internal challenges
were for the policemen involved.

The actions of Jandamarra cannot be underestimated amid the
growing paranoia that the Aboriginal people were going to rise
up and rid the Kimberley of white colonists. The 'solution' was
to force Aboriginal people to submit to the imported law of the
colonists. Owen pieces together Jandamarra's pivotal story with
the same analysis and clarity evident throughout the rest of this
book. In the post 1900 period, as Western Australia entered the
Australian Federation, we see how control of Aboriginal people
gradually progressed to mass arrest and increasingly punitive legislation that sought to control them – the damaging effects of which
endure to this day. This book is a substantial contribution to our

knowledge of Kimberley policing during this time and also sheds light on the key factors regarding contemporary policing that has resulted in such a chronic over-representation of Aboriginal people in custody and the ongoing mistrust of police.

Senator Patrick Dodson
Yawuru Elder

ACKNOWLEDGEMENTS

I owe a debt of thanks to Charlie Fox, Andrea Gaynor and David Barrie for supervising the PhD on which this book is based, and especially to Charlie for assistance with final editing of this book. Great thanks go to the historians whose work inspired this research and who gave me assistance and advice: Geoffrey Bolton, Andrew Gill, Cathie Clement, Neville Green, Fiona Skyring, Christine Choo, Howard Pedersen, Malcolm Allbrook, Mary Anne Jebb, Russell McGregor, Steve Kinnane, Peter Conole and Don Pashley. Thanks to Ronald Morgan and the Balanggarra Aboriginal Corporation, and Sarah Yu and Pat Dodson at Nyamba Buru Yawuru Ltd. My thanks go to the staff at the State Records Office of Western Australia for assistance with accessing records. My gratitude for help along the way to Mike Donaldson of Wildrocks Publications, Mark Finnane, Robert Foster, Henry Reynolds, Jane Lydon, Amanda Nettelbeck, Jonathan Richards, and Mark Chambers. My appreciation also goes to my father, Geoff Owen, and his wonderful book collection, and my mother, Margaret Owen, for her assistance in editing and general encouragement. Richard Bosworth, Frank Broeze, Tom Stannage and Ian Brash gave me early inspiration to study history along the way. Massive thanks to Terri-ann White, Kate Pickard and the staff at UWA Publishing. And, finally, thanks and appreciation to my wife, Gretta Little, and my twin girls, Edi and Olive, who put up with me beavering away for years and who like to ask about the 'olden days'.

I have included material I authored from C. Choo and C. Owen, 'Deafening Silences: understanding frontier relations and the discourse of police files through Kimberley Police Records', in C. Choo, and S. Hollbach (eds), *Studies in Western Australian History: History and Native Title*, no. 23, 2003. An article that forms part of chapter 10 has been published as C. Owen, '"The Police Appear to Be a Useless Lot Up There": law and order in the East Kimberley 1884–1905', *Aboriginal History Journal*, vol. 27, 2003.

Cover image: 'Group of prisoners in neck chains, Wyndham, Western Australia', circa 1898–1906. Courtesy State Library of Victoria, MS13867/65.

INTRODUCTION

The cover photograph, titled 'Aboriginal bathing gang in Wyndham', was published on 18 February 1905 in the weekly Western Australian newspaper, *Western Mail*.[1] It shows nearly one hundred Aboriginal prisoners chained at the neck in the port town of Wyndham, from where cattle were exported, in the East Kimberley district in the far north of Western Australia.[2] The photograph was published after the release of Dr Walter Edmund Roth's *The Report of the Royal Commission on the Condition of the Natives* (Roth Report).[3] This investigation was instigated after nearly two decades of allegations of abuse of Aboriginal people in the Kimberley and North West districts. The photograph was intended to be a response to these claims and show that treatment of Aboriginal people in the Kimberley was not harsh, but orderly and humane.

The Roth Report was the first independent inquiry into the workings of the Western Australian police force since the foundation of the Swan River Colony, later the city of Perth, as a British colony seventy-five years earlier in 1829. Roth took testimony from forty-two witnesses and provided valuable insights into a unique policing culture and the associated judicial process that led to Aboriginal imprisonment.[4] These practices were not widely known outside the North West and Kimberley districts and were largely unknown in the major cities and overseas.

In January 1905 the Roth Report was tabled in the Western Australian parliament. The entire report was serialised and reported on, not only in Perth newspapers, but also all over the nation and overseas to significant national and international controversy.[5] The Perth *Daily News* declared 'Council of Churches, Horror-Stricken and Sorrowful'. *The W.A. Record* announced 'A Shocking State of Affairs'. *The Sydney Morning Herald* proclaimed 'Blacks Brutally Treated', 'Western Australian Sensation', 'Horrible Cases of Cruelty'. The Perth *Sunday Times* was damning, declaring 'Congo Cruelties Paralleled' referring to the millions of Africans who died as a result of exploitation and disease in the African Belgium Congo under King Leopold between 1885 and 1905.[6] London newspapers were more restrained, although headlines there included 'Australian Scandal' and 'Australian Race Problem'.[7]

One of the police witnesses interviewed was Wyndham Police Constable (PC) John Inglis who, along with PC Jack Wilson, was stationed at Halls Creek Police Station, 322 kilometres south of Wyndham. On 11 November 1904 Inglis responded to Roth's questions regarding the arrests of Aboriginal people suspected of killing cattle on various Kimberley pastoral stations.[8] Inglis responded with brevity that belied the true scope of police activities that went like this.

On a journey that would take anywhere from weeks to several months, armed police on horseback, with the aid of armed Aboriginal men called native assistants, tracked and located the Aboriginal groups believed responsible. Sometimes these patrols would take place after a complaint had been received from a pastoralist alleging that Aboriginal people were killing his cattle and a warrant for arrest had been issued.[9] Usually, though, they occurred without a formal warrant and without any instruction or information from the pastoralist concerned.[10] Evidence of human footprints was sufficient to identify suspects. In a morning raid, where there may or may not have been shooting of people allegedly resisting arrest, known as a 'dispersal', men and, at times, children as young as ten would be detained, arrested and charged with the criminal offence of cattle killing.

At times the groups contained up to thirty-three Aboriginal men. After arrest the accused would be neck chained and chained together at a distance of just 61 centimetres apart.[11] Neck chaining was considered the most effective and humane way of restraining prisoners as it left their hands free, though it was rarely used on non-Aboriginal prisoners. Police regulations issued in 1898 regarding chaining Aboriginal people stipulated that only those from the 'bush' or 'desperate characters' were to be neck chained and the practice should not be used if it could be avoided.[12] That stated, all Aboriginal prisoners in the Kimberley, regardless of their crime, were neck chained.[13] By contrast Aboriginal people from the 'southern areas' of Western Australia were generally not neck chained.

Following a directive from senior police, Aboriginal women, although part of the same group, were never arrested. Instead, women, wives and relatives would be brought in as witnesses, not for the defence of the accused but as witnesses for the prosecution. Despite having no charge against them and with no legal authority, they, too, were ankle or neck chained. The group would then be forced to walk up to 24 kilometres a day, sometimes as far as 400 kilometres. At night, with the addition of ankle chains, they would be chained together around a tree and watched over by native assistants.

The prisoners would finally arrive at Broome, Halls Creek or Wyndham where, in groups of five or ten, they would be charged with the same offence and face court. A magistrate or justice of the peace (at times the JP who owned the property) would charge them. At Halls Creek the police officer in charge of the police station would charge the prisoners.[14] As PC Inglis testified the men, who he recognised speared cattle because their traditional food sources had been displaced by stock, would invariably plead guilty and could be found summarily guilty. They were then gaoled for up to three years with or without a whipping.

Kimberley gaols were crude and harsh. Wyndham gaol, for example, was a galvanised iron shed, and, as the Kimberley experienced subtropical conditions and oppressive heat at times in the mid-40s degrees Celsius (110 F), conditions were stifling. At night prisoners were chained at the ankle to ring bolts in the floor but the neck chains were not removed.[15] While police regulations allowed ankle chains there were no such regulations regarding neck chains. And they would remain on the prisoners for the period of their gaol sentence despite there being no legal authority allowing the practice. This was, one senior government witness said, an informally accepted practice of the last thirty years.[16] The neck chains were usually fastened with 'single cuff' locks, though prior to 1905 prisoners from Wyndham had their neck chains fastened with 'iron split links' that were extremely difficult to remove.[17] The links were not police issue but purchased privately from an ironmonger in Perth.[18] They could only be opened with 'a hammer and a chisel with the prisoners head on a blacksmiths anvil',[19] a process that would take up to ten minutes. In addition the neck chains used at Wyndham weighed 2.4 kilograms, which was over twice the weight of the chains used in other Kimberley locations. This added 'security' was to cater for what was considered a more aggressive and fearsome type of Aboriginal prisoner in the East Kimberley.[20]

There were critics of these practices that included the new magistrates to the district. In 1904 the new resident magistrate and district medical officer in Wyndham, Dr Dodwell Brown, fiercely criticised the judicial system and the practices of police, arguing Aboriginal people were gaoled on insufficient evidence.[21] Other witnesses declared that the prisoners did not understand what they were being charged with or why they were being punished. The gaoler at Broome stated that 'not one' Aboriginal prisoner knew why they were in gaol.[22] The gaoler at Wyndham admitted 'grave blunders' had been made in identifying people and as a consequence the wrong Aboriginal people were gaoled for periods of up to two years.[23] In a practice Roth called 'carelessness almost amounting to criminality' prisoner's names would be mixed up and one prisoner would be charged with another's crime and receive the incorrect sentence.[24] One witness described the whole criminal justice system as a 'perfect farce'.[25]

Near the end of Roth's examination of PC Inglis he asked him a question: Was this informal, possibly unlawful yet widely accepted, arrest and gaoling system, where regulations regarding arrest and rules of evidence were so lax, a 'rather one-sided justice' for Aboriginal people? Inglis admitted as much remarking, 'It's a queer country where I am. Every mother's son is guilty.'[26]

This is the untold history of policing the Kimberley district of Western Australia from 1882 until 1905. The opening date indicates the establishment of police in the Kimberley while the closing date marks the release of the Roth Report.[27] The Kimberley was the first part of the Australian continent to be occupied by Aboriginal people, and was possibly the last frontier of the continent to be colonised by Europeans.[28] At the time of colonisation, the Kimberley district, with its unique environmental and geographic conditions, was home to an estimated twenty-seven different Aboriginal language groups, with a population somewhere between 10,000 and 30,000 people.[29] This represented possibly a quarter of the total number of Aboriginal people in Western Australia, but this pre-contact Aboriginal population significantly decreased after the arrival of Europeans. Figures from an early 1900s police annual report quoted the Aboriginal population of the Kimberley as 'approximately' 5000.[30]

In contrast with other Australian colonies, the state of Western Australia, due to its sheer size, experienced an extended period of colonialism. European expansion began in Albany (King George Sound) on the far south coast in 1826 and continued into the North West in the 1860s and 1870s, and the Kimberley district in the 1880s and the 1890s. The Kimberley police jurisdiction was part of the largest jurisdiction in the world and, coupled with an extremely small number of police, would be extremely difficult to police. The commissioner of police and the Western Australian government administered the Kimberley police force from Perth, 3218 kilometres to the south, so far away that it was in another climatic zone. The isolation and lack of authority was in many ways responsible for the unique culture of not only the police but also of the colonists.

Initially colonisation in the Kimberley occurred in the late 1870s for guano mining in and around the North West and northern coastal islands. What would bring Aboriginal people into contact and conflict with colonists was the establishment in the early 1880s of pearling on the coast and gold mining inland. The most pervasive and enduring enterprise, however, was pastoralism, in particular cattle farming on the enormous expanses of open-range cattle country. Pastoral enterprises were established in 1881 and expanded all over the Kimberley. By 1905 pastoral expansion was complete and spanned the length and breadth of the district on what was traditional Aboriginal *country*.[31]

The first European colonists viewed Western Australia through the prism of the doctrine of *terra nullius*, as 'unoccupied', despite the obvious presence of Aboriginal people.[32] In the early period of colonisation of Western Australia in 1836, a treaty with the local Aboriginal people regarding the use and purchase of their land was discussed by the government of the day, though it was ultimately rejected and no provisions were made to regulate dealings between them and the colonists.[33] The decision to classify the colonies of Australia as settled, rather than conquered or relinquished, meant that the colonists brought with them the general body of English law, including criminal law.

For most of the nineteenth century there was deep uncertainty within the government, judiciary and the colonist populations about how criminal law should be applied to Aboriginal people. Although by the time the Kimberley was colonised most of these problems had been resolved, there was considerable confusion about how criminal law should be policed. And policing was complicated. The statutory role of police was a dual one: to enforce criminal law equally among colonists and Aboriginal people and to protect the latter as British subjects from the worst excesses of European colonisation. There is extensive evidence that at first police did attempt to protect Kimberley Aboriginal people under the law, but this changed considerably as European expansion progressed over the *country* of very large (and to the Europeans, largely unknown) Aboriginal language groups. Using an extensive range of police and government records this book reveals the evolution of the Kimberley police force from a relatively benign one in 1882 to a semi-militarised and profoundly violent one in the later 1890s and then something different again after 1900.

The findings of the Roth Report, which will be discussed in chapter 12, were based on very limited information due to both the time Roth was given to complete the investigation and the difficulties in examining witnesses over such a vast and inhospitable area. Roth stated as much in the opening paragraph, that his commission only dealt with 'occurrences taking place' from 1901 to 1904, thus effectively excluding any investigation of the Kimberley during the previous eighteen years.[34] If he had examined reports from the earlier period he might have discovered a considerable body of evidence describing dubious policing and legal practices, extensive violence towards Aboriginal people and a colonial culture that not only tolerated this violence but one that often encouraged it. In Western Australia reports of Kimberley violence were sporadically reported (to government or newspapers) but were not often acted upon as violence towards Aboriginal people was usually justified and accepted as part of the colonising process. Aboriginal people, however, refer to this time as the 'killing times'.[35]

Reconsidering the Kimberley

In what follows we shall reconsider the history of the Kimberley police. Studies of policing tend to view West and East Kimberley districts as discrete entities with particular histories. Histories of the West Kimberley are usually associated with stories of Aboriginal criminality or resistance to colonisation, typified by the well-known mid-1890s story of Jandamarra (or 'Pigeon' as he was earlier known) and the Bunuba (earlier spelt as Punuba) people (for more on Jandamarra see chapter 1).[36] Histories of the East Kimberley tend to suggest that conflict between police and

Aboriginal people was the random and sporadic result of overly aggressive policing on an uncontrolled frontier.[37] However, as we will see, East and West had much in common. Recent histories of the Kimberley tend to view the police as axiomatically punitive, in permanent and oppressive opposition to Aboriginal people, often acting without authorisation and having considerable independence due to their isolation from the centre of police administration in Perth. Other writers have suggested that 'violence was endemic from the very beginning' of European colonisation.[38] Certainly the preceding evidence from the Roth Report tends to support this view; however, the history is far more complex. We will see that for all the police who became notorious for being aggressive towards Aboriginal people there were others who would seek to protect them and investigate wrong-doing.

Violence against Aboriginal people was not endemic from the very beginning, indeed the most significant conflict occurred over a decade after Europeans first arrived. Evidence from police and government records from the early period of European colonisation shows that in the 1880s European violence against Aboriginal people was the exception rather than the norm. Additionally the style of police and policing was profoundly different from that instituted later. Police Sergeant Patrick Troy, an Irish migrant, was one of the first police officers sent to the Kimberley frontier. In October 1883, in his first police reports from the district near Derby, Troy described his new, vast jurisdiction in considerable descriptive and evocative detail. Initially he was bewildered by the environment, the heat and flies – 'weather was hot and flies were troublesome' as he put it. He also recounted moments of first contact with the local Aboriginal people, remarking that they showed no fear of him and that through mutual exchange of goods, trust was established.[39] A certain naivety is revealed in his early reports;

being sent to such a harsh, oppressive and isolated environment must have been a shock and he must have soon realised that his job would be to impose British law on Aboriginal people who neither understood nor recognised it. His naivety stands in stark contrast to the brutal cynicism displayed by police in later police records.

Certainly police faced great difficulties and many could not cope. Of the first deployment of police to the district, PC Lemon was transferred back to Fremantle in late 1884.[40] PC Buckley was speared in an attack at Halls Creek in 1888.[41] In the same year Lance Corporal Payne, who had returned to the district and was promoted to sergeant, was implicated in a case regarding the murder of Aboriginal people. PC Sherry stayed on and was promoted to sergeant, but in 1891 at Wyndham was demoted and reprimanded for constantly being in 'a maudlin state of drunkenness'.[42] PC Lee resigned from the police force shortly after arriving and completing his first bush patrol because the 'climate does not agree with my health'.[43]

In the early years of colonisation, police such as Troy thoroughly and conscientiously investigated allegations of abuse of Aboriginal people by colonists. For instance in 1884 Troy investigated the killing of Aboriginal boy Julemar, alias Dan, by a colonist in Derby.[44] In late 1886 he investigated a particularly repellent case where an ex-policeman by the name of John Eatch had murdered a young Aboriginal station servant named Charcoal by kicking him to death.[45] In this early period police seemed prepared to prosecute the law equally.[46] It is clear, however, that by the time of the Roth Report investigation in 1904 this earlier protective role had transformed into something altogether different.

Aboriginal responses to the colonists had changed too. In the late 1880s and into the next decade there were concerns at the highest level of government that Europeans might be driven out of the Kimberley, and these concerns grew as years passed. In 1893 local Aboriginal people were said by one newspaper to be 'threatening Wyndham with absolute annihilation'.[47] In late 1894 Premier John Forrest considered the Aboriginal groups around Wyndham in the East Kimberley to be more aggressive than any others, claiming that: 'A sort of warfare was going on there between the whites and the blacks.'[48] Another report from the East Kimberley in March 1895, at the time when Jandamarra was declared an outlaw, stated: 'The natives here are more ferocious than those giving such immense trouble in West Kimberley at present.'[49] Overall police killed far more Aboriginal people in the East than in the West, as they tried to stem stock losses allegedly caused by Aboriginal people (stock losses dominated reports from the period, where arrests for cattle killing accounted for 90% of Aboriginal crime), remove Aboriginal people from pastoral lands and drive those who remained into subservience.[50]

To track this change in the history of Kimberley policing we require an examination of complex political, social and environmental issues unique to Western Australia. The first factor shaping the history of Kimberley policing was the political and constitutional changes in Western Australia. The colony and, later, the state went through three distinct political phases that would profoundly influence the policing of Aboriginal people. The first was as a British colony from 1829 to 1890. During this time the *Aborigines Protection Act 1886,* designed to provide protection for the Aboriginal people of Western Australia, was legislated. The second was the period of responsible government from 1890 to 1901 and the third was the period after 1901 when the colony of Western Australia became a state and entered the Commonwealth of Australia.[51]

Western Australia was the last colony in Australia granted responsible government by the imperial government in London in 1890, because of its enormous area and relatively low and dispersed population. Most other colonies achieved responsible government in the 1850s. There was also deep concern in the British government about the treatment of Aboriginal people. After Western Australia gained responsible government, the legislature introduced many oppressive laws and regulations aimed at controlling Aboriginal people. Under direction from the Western Australian government police actions changed, with the period of greatest conflict coinciding with the concerted Aboriginal resistance to colonisation and the decentralisation of Western Australian police in late 1894. This period can reasonably be called a war such was the level of conflict across both the East and West Kimberley districts between Aboriginal groups, police and colonists, and considering the large numbers of Aboriginal people killed. After Western Australia entered Federation the treatment of Aboriginal people became a national concern.

The second factor was the diversity of the Aboriginal groups of the Kimberley. While the Jandamarra episode is crucial to the history of policing in the Kimberley, it is best understood as a local conflict within the much broader West and East Kimberley conflict. Many other Aboriginal groups were involved in conflict, utilising the enormous semicircle of ranges and hills along the Napier Range (or the Barrier Range as colonists called it) from Derby in the West Kimberley (including the Napier and King Leopold ranges) to Wyndham in the East Kimberley (including the Durack Ranges). From Derby, groups that included the Warwa, Nyikina and Unggumi peoples tracked along the Robinson River at Oobagooma and along the Fitzroy and Lennard River districts. The Worla, Kija and other language groups of the East

Kimberley saw conflict around the Durack and Ord rivers. Indeed, Aboriginal people killed more Europeans in acts of resistance on Warwa, Nyikina, Unggarangi and Worowa *country* in the West Kimberley and on Kadjerong and Yiitji *country* in the East Kimberley than in the area in and around Bunuba *country* where Jandamarra was fighting.[52] This conflict emerged as a result of a specific set of factors, primarily the unregulated expansion of the pastoral industry and the associated loss and destruction of Aboriginal food sources.

With the arrival of the Europeans life for Aboriginal people was irreversibly altered. Many, although not all, worked on pastoral stations, some by choice, some under duress, others out of sheer necessity. Others stayed on country, following their own traditions where possible, living on traditional food sources but also, as their sources of food dried up, spearing and taking the introduced food source: cattle. At first there was an uneasy accommodation between some groups and the colonisers appropriating their *country* but later, as colonisation intensified, conflict became much more widespread and police were instrumental in subordinating Aboriginal people to pastoral stations. By the end of our period of study, resistance fell away as Aboriginal people seemed to recognise their newly subordinate position.

The colonists described Aboriginal people through a conceptual scheme which classified them depending on their place in or outside the pastoral workforce: those who worked on pastoral stations they called 'station blacks' or station workers, while those untouched by European contact they called 'wild', 'bush blacks' or 'hill natives'. In the East Kimberley, 'bush blacks' were referred to as 'myalls'.[53] Underpinning these labels was another conceptual scheme that described Aboriginal people in terms of their adoption of European civilisation, thus some were referred to as 'civilised', others as 'half-civilised' and others as 'uncivilised'. Many observers tend to see policing in the Kimberley as a conflict between 'uncivilised bush blacks' and police; however, such conflict was not axiomatic. For example, the first recorded killing of a European in the district was not by a 'bush black' but rather by an Aboriginal pastoral worker. Many Aboriginal people worked with or for Europeans and became acculturated to aspects of the European lifestyle. Jandamarra himself was such an individual, having first worked as a station hand then as a police assistant before turning against the Europeans. Colonisers soon recognised the conflict between themselves, police and those station Aborigines they called 'half-civilised'. The idea of the 'treacherous native' who had betrayed attempts to civilise him arose out of these conflicts.

The third set of factors shaping the nature of policing was environmental, geographic and demographic. Coupled with isolation were the unusually harsh environment and the subtropical weather patterns, the monsoonal 'wet and dry'; torrential rain flooded the major rivers, such as the Fitzroy and the Lennard, juxtaposed with the 'dry' of scorching heat. For police, the country in the 'wet' was extraordinarily difficult to traverse. They also had to journey through some of the most challenging landscapes in Western Australia, for example the long and high Napier Range and King Leopold Ranges separating the East and West Kimberley. The police often could not access the rugged and high limestone areas where Aboriginal people would find safe haven. The most well-known refuge for Aboriginal people was the Windjana Gorge, or Devil's Pass as it was known. Sites such as these have stories attached to them and have profound religious and ceremonial significance to Aboriginal groups.

The fourth factor was the social context in which colonists and police operated. While both the East and West Kimberley were colonised primarily for pastoral-based industries, the nature and background of the colonists in the East and West were quite different, which produced a different social context in which the police operated. Perth-based pastoral interests that initially invested in sheep farming, and later cattle, took up land mainly in the West Kimberley. By contrast the East Kimberley was colonised generally by those called 't'othersiders': cattle farmers from the eastern colonies who drove their cattle overland to the Kimberley, the most prominent of those being members of the Durack family from New South Wales and Queensland. These colonists came from colonies where pastoralists had openly killed Aboriginal people on their 'runs'. The Queensland government used the notorious native police to quell Aboriginal resistance and this background profoundly influenced the attitude of colonists to Kimberley Aboriginal groups.[54]

Police in the Kimberley had to work in the context of social expectations that interfered with norms and conventions of policing. Local social 'understandings' exercised considerable influence on the patterns of policing. Colonial authority was so distant both physically and psychologically that it held little sway with Europeans. The remoteness and lack of government and legal authority encouraged pastoralists and others to do what they liked with Aboriginal people, exploiting and using violence against them, taking the law into their own hands by punishing and killing them in what they euphemistically called 'summary justice'.

Pastoralists believed that police should act in their interests, protecting their stock, punishing people they called cattle killers and returning runaway Aboriginal workers to their stations. They certainly did not believe that police should act in the interests of Aboriginal people and they became extremely angry when they seemed to do so. And, of course, pastoralists held great political power in the Western Australian parliament, using their positions to call for more vigorous policing. Some of the most oppressive pieces of legislation to control and punish Aboriginal people in the history of the colony were passed through the parliament at the behest of these groups.

The fifth factor shaping Kimberley policing is a largely unstated aspect of Western Australian policing: the model of policing utilised. The Western Australian police force acted under the authority of the *Police Ordinance Act of 1849,* which was amended in 1861 and which granted police only civil, not military, powers. The *Police Act 1892* reinforced this civil status.[55] While Western Australian frontiers followed a similar but not identical pattern to those of New South Wales, Victoria, Queensland, South Australia and the Northern Territory, Western Australia differed in not instituting a paramilitary native police force of the kind that had proved so devastatingly effective in subduing Aboriginal resistance in other colonies. Indeed, Western Australian government authorities refused to implement one. Western Australian authorities had, therefore, to come up with a different model of policing. This model included innovations such as the use of native assistants or armed Aboriginal trackers and, at times, the swearing in of special constables.

A recurrent theme in the history of policing in Western Australia is that the government always considered policing extremely expensive. For example, in the early 1900s expenditure on policing in Western Australia was the highest of all of the states and more than twice that of the most populous state, New South Wales. This was largely due to the enormous distances involved and the large numbers of small settlements. Tasmania, by contrast, expended the least on policing.[56] Policing was measured in 'cost per head' of white population. The proportion of police to the population they policed in Western Australia was extraordinarily low. In 1898 it was one to 41,149 people, and the cost per head was 12s 3d. As a consequence few police were sent to the Kimberley, where there were so few European colonists;[57] in mid-1887 there were a total of just twenty-three police constables with four supervising officers (and seventy-one horses) for the entire Kimberley district.[58]

Historical Records Utilised: The Police Records

The collection of written records of the Western Australian Police Department (WAPD) held in the State Records Office of Western Australia (SROWA) is the main source of evidence. In contrast to many other Australian frontiers, police and government records relating to the Kimberley during the period under study are vast, detailed (albeit often difficult to decipher) and frank, particularly on the levels and circumstances of violence. Police were required to write and process daily written reports detailing their actions and they were accountable to superior officers, superior officers' superiors and then to the governor. The police records, depending on the year and location, contain great narrative detail about police actions, often with up to twenty and sometimes fifty pages of detailed description about the preparation, travel, action in engaging any sought-after Aboriginal group and eventual return.

Prior to the advent of the telegraph these police records, including journals and diaries, from the Kimberley district were the only way in which the senior police in Perth could obtain information about what was going on. These records are some of the only means we now have of finding out about interaction between European and Aboriginal people on this frontier. Police, at the vanguard of contact, came to know a great deal about Aboriginal custom. Police records are replete with descriptions of land usage or *country* and of Aboriginal boundaries. Police records also documented the transition of Aboriginal people into colonial life as station workers. Thus one finds that the WAPD records contain some of the most detailed and, at times, vivid depictions of the first European interaction with Kimberley Aboriginal people.[59] Archival police records show in frank detail what the frontier of the Kimberley was like: harsh, unforgiving and exceptionally violent. Aboriginal society was not excluded from this situation as groups did engage in internecine conflict. Injury and death through violence, such as from spearing to resolve disputes, revenge or matters of honour, were common.

The official records police left illustrate a range of attitudes to their role and the people they policed: some police sought to learn Aboriginal languages;[60] generally they became knowledgeable about the more observable aspects of Aboriginal culture, such as hunting and gathering for food, weaponry and body scarification; and they knew broadly of different 'tribal' areas. They characterised Aboriginal groups generally by the location that they inhabited, or by their *country*. There were, for example, 'Fitzroy River', 'Barrier Range' and 'Ord River Natives'. Police categorised different language groups according to temperament. Troy regarded the 'hill natives' (those whose country was on the ranges and hills) and the 'coastal natives' as being far more 'hostile and treacherous' than 'the plains and pindan natives' whom he regarded as 'the most tractable and of a better disposition altogether'.[61]

Surveying the police records the reader is struck by the matter-of-fact narrative describing how Aboriginal people were dispatched by firearm. Most records relating to the Kimberley are scattered and research involves the painstaking reconstruction of events from disparate records. However, in the case of Jandamarra research is relatively easy. Most of the hundreds of records around the Jandamarra episode were collated under order of the commissioner of police in the 1930s to help Ion Idriess write his book *Outlaw of the Leopolds*.[62] Helpfully for researchers they are all in the one archival location,[63] which is one reason why this aspect of policing in the West Kimberley gets more attention than in the East Kimberley.

All letters and reports from any district destined for transmission to the superintendent or commissioner of police were to be forwarded through the officer in charge of the district, except in cases of 'exceptionally grave outrages', which had to be sent to the commissioner with 'urgency'. Written reports were to be kept in occurrence books and a copy was to be made each week on the occurrence sheets that were then transmitted through the district officer to the commissioner. *The Police Gazette*, the official publication of the police force, was issued weekly with new regulations and circular orders included which were 'to be promptly filed'.[64] Copies were inserted into the occurrence books alerting police to new rules and regulations.

Senior police or sub inspectors furnished reports on the day-to-day running of stations. With the establishment of different districts, reports were forwarded to the relevant inspectors. The police records, which were considered 'confidential and the proceedings of the police were not to be generally known' were of the following main types: general orders, circular orders, codes of behaviour, and duties and responsibilities.[65] These were constantly revised or added to by the commissioner of police.

The police in the field responded with letterbooks containing correspondence between police stationed in the Kimberley and Perth regarding directives on locations to patrol and instructions, including changes to police numbers and police regulations and circular orders. The letters were transcribed into these books down the left-hand column while any response was written on the right-hand side. Letterbooks were generally written by senior police or inspectors and contained information about junior police and activities in the district, and also reported on complaints from pastoralists about the extent of stock depredations and the general condition of the 'natives'. As we will see, pastoralists did not always appreciate the findings of these reports.

Occurrence books were a day-to-day journal of police activities. A nominated police officer recorded the activities of all police, assistants and horses. For example, it might describe one sergeant in charge, one constable on horse and stable duty, one constable on town duty and one out on patrol. Occurrence books, according to police regulations, were required to record details of individuals: 'the arrivals and departures of persons, the movements of the criminal classes', which referred to a social class regarded as 'habitual' or 'professional criminals', but also a wide range of other matters:

> reports of articles lost or found, inquests, accidents, affrays, meetings and their object, public entertainments, openings of new inns or stores or manufactories and by whom; in country places, states of roads, complaints by settlers and others, manner in which public houses are kept...no idle gossip is to be entered – nothing but what is authentic.[66]

These records were the bane of the head office in Perth. Officers in Perth were constantly critical of the content, or lack thereof, in occurrence books. Occurrence books were mandatory but were often poorly written with little of the specified material required. They were to be copied onto 'occurrence sheets' and forwarded to Perth each week. Police were expected not only to record matters of police business but also to be the eyes and ears of the force, for 'their object is to keep the Head of the Police thoroughly posted up in what is taking place all over the colony'.[67]

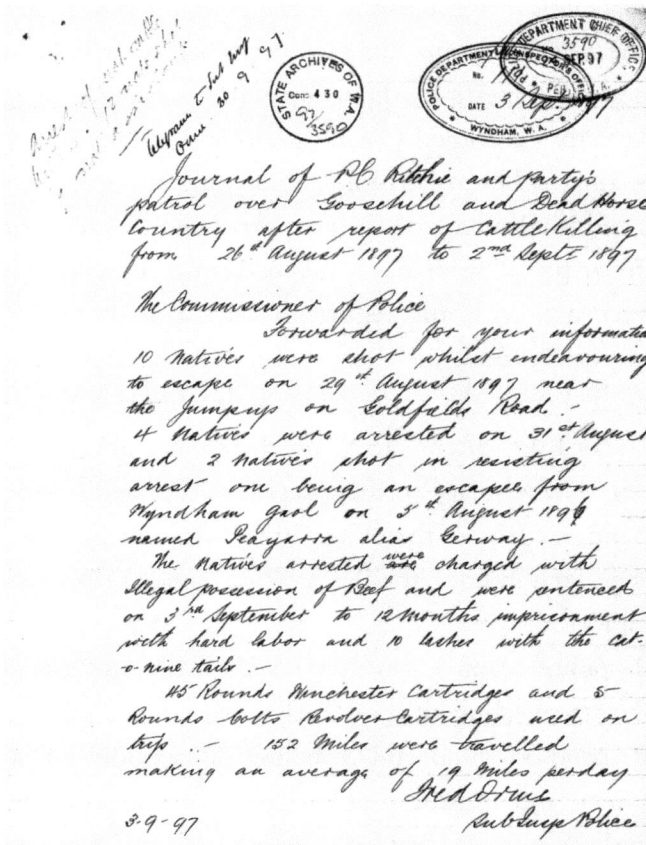

Figure 0.1. Example of a report of a bush patrol. WAPD, 'East Kimberley District. Wyndham Station. Journal of PC Ritchie and Party. August 26 to September 2, 1897', SROWA, Cons. 430, AN 5/1, File 3590/1897.

21

The most contentious of all these reports were the police journals or diaries of patrols from stations, in which police were required to keep a daily record of their activities. Police went on bush patrol for many reasons, for example, for the collection of census material or agricultural statistics or to deliver letters, but primarily they went in pursuit of Aboriginal people accused of stealing or disturbing stock. Varying in length, detail and content, the reports of these patrols became one of the most contested sources of information for the head office, senior police and the highest echelons of the Perth establishment. At times they might record the fact that police tediously travelled for weeks over several hundred kilometres without apparently seeing a soul, while at other times they recorded violent arrests and 'dispersals'.

The men who undertook these journeys were generally experienced 'bushmen' and their reports were usually written on return from patrol from notes taken during the trip. The only things recorded with any regularity on patrol were the names of police, native assistants, horses and a declaration of how far they travelled each day. However, as this book will show, the written record was often 'silent'; much was left unsaid and much unwritten. The veracity of these reports depended solely on the honesty and integrity of the officers who wrote them. The reports were, when forwarded to the Perth office, signed off and approved by a senior officer.

Early police records, mostly from the early 1880s and stored under the unrevealing title of 'Early Police Dept Files', contain some of the most vivid and revealing descriptions of both the new country and European colonisation of the Kimberley, particularly the nature of first contact between Aboriginal people and the police. These records were far from the glib, terse and violence-filled police records that came later. At the request of the police commissioner who asked that police report in detail, they are written in a descriptive narrative form that tended to drop off in the police records after 1883. Mention must be made of the telegram as a valuable historical record. We shall see how the telegraph was used to devastating effect in the mid-1890s. Orders and correspondence, usually of a very frank nature, were transmitted via telegram and this provided a far superior and faster mode of communication for police authorities.

Research using police records is made difficult by the fact that many records are neither comprehensive nor complete, while others are not always housed in chronological order. This is a frustration for researchers as the historical record is fragmented with many of the thousands of entries from original indices (police and colonial secretary's office) either destroyed or lost.[68] Gaps exist in almost all police station or camp records, assumed lost, removed, damaged or destroyed. Environmental factors can be blamed for the loss of many records, particularly given that those men delivering mail had at times to swim over flooded rivers, resulting in the mail being soaked.[69]

The absence of certain archival records appears more than random or coincidental, however. There is a very curious correlation between the absences of records and an area known to have had a large number of police involved in 'dispersals'. Thus Fletcher Creek Outstation records do not appear to have survived. The occurrence books for Halls Creek Station are missing from 1893 to 1900 and only a few bush patrol records are available.[70] There are no station records from Fitzroy Crossing Police Station, from where notorious officer Sergeant Richard Henry Pilmer operated (see chapter 11). Wyndham police records are missing for pivotal periods of East Kimberley policing in 1894 and 1895, although some significant events involving large-scale killings of fifty Aboriginal people at a time near Wyndham are recorded in newspapers.[71] Fortunately the private notebook of Sergeant Wheatley, found in the Battye Library, fills in for the missing evidence (described in chapter 10) at a time of another of the biggest single dispersals of Aboriginal people by police on patrol in Western Australian history.[72] Files from the Colonial Secretary's Office (CSO; series 675, consignment 527) are missing from late 1894 (curiously when the Jandamarra episode started) through all of 1895, as are files from the Aboriginal Protection Board for the same period.

The police patrol journals of PCs Thomson and Hill working out of Argyle police camp – where in late 1901 there were detailed reports of shootings and burnings of Aboriginal people – were also initially thought to be missing from the SROWA. Again, fortunately, uncatalogued copies discovered at the Western Australian Police Service in early 2004, and now in possession of this author, reveal some alarming claims of corruption regarding the activities of certain colonists and pastoralists, which are detailed in chapter 10.[73] More baffling still, in early 2013 it was discovered that these particular files were indeed housed in the SROWA yet they had been omitted from the physical index, making discovery almost impossible.[74] Who could have altered indices cannot be known, although the correlation between contentious contents and archival absence is too great to be put down to coincidence.

The categories under which the police records are housed are as follows: all police station records are indexed by Archive Note 5 (AN 5) under various accession numbers, which contain all occurrence books, letterbooks, and bush patrol reports that have survived and made it to SROWA. Consignment 430 contains the individual reports (correspondence) that were *sent* to Perth.[75] They should, in theory, be a verbatim record of the

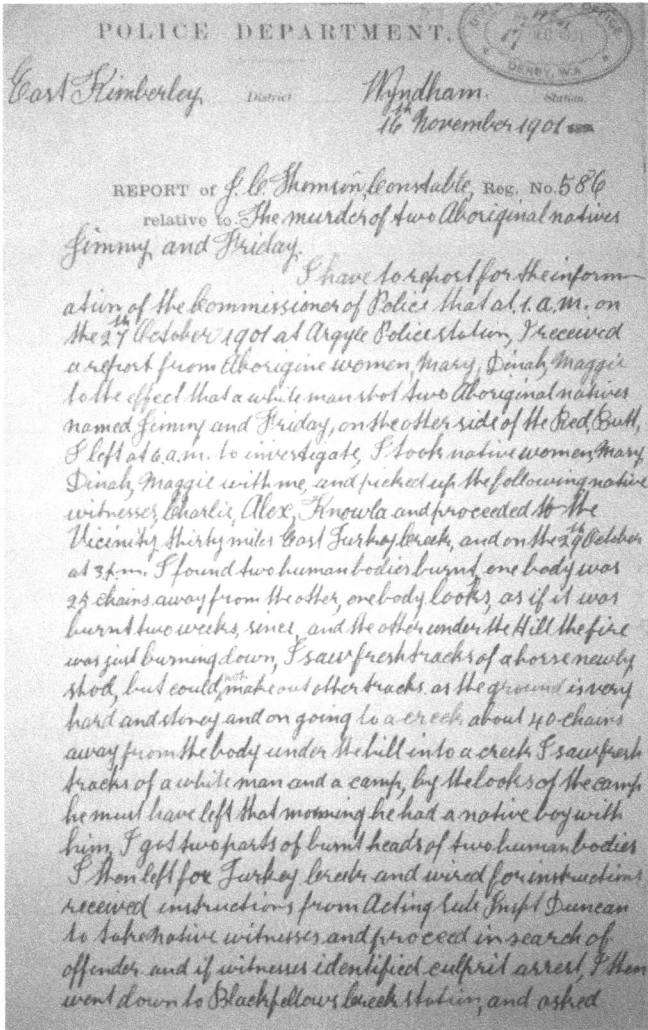

Figure 0.2. 'Alleged Murder of Two Natives by Thomas McLoughlin [sic]', WAPD, AN 5/2, Cons. 430, File 1382/1905. Courtesy SROWA.

police station records. The Perth reports are generally far superior in quality, writing style and presentation compared to the district police station records. However, not all these police records are catalogued.[76] Furthermore it is difficult to get a sustained and coherent reading from police records given the rapid turnaround in personnel in the force. Some officers wrote much more detailed reports than others. After 1896 police records were forwarded to decentralised substations rather than to the Perth office.

There are many thousands of pages of the various police records of the period in SROWA. Some are water and mud stained, some written in a barely legible scrawl and some in clear, fluid and descriptive prose. This is both a reflection of the environment and the quality of policemen who went to the district. Kimberley records are the poorest of all records from the Western Australian police force for this period in terms of writing, style and content. Despite instruction from police authorities that 'no personal information is to be included', aspects of policemen's personalities are evident. What they put in, what they left out, the language used, their notion of justice and propriety, the writing style and how they wrote about the Aboriginal population all provide insights into informal social hierarchies and relationships in Kimberley colonial society. The records also reveal that police were at times terrified, hopelessly under-equipped and poorly trained. Police records are usually devoid of emotion towards Aboriginal people. The few signs of empathy or concern in police records are seen in the attitudes of police to their horses, which were possibly their closest companions and, of course, crucial to their survival.

The content of these records reveals a great deal about the men who wrote them, the times in which they lived and how they went about their work. Aboriginal names (if given) are often spelt in several different ways in the same report. There are few examples of police reporting on other police – not surprising given that it was an activity with potentially fatal consequences in such an environment. However, the records studied show that disputes between police were far more common than has been acknowledged in previous writing. One thing is clear: police reports themselves indicate that, with noted exceptions, police operated under the assumption of the justice of British law or the rhetorical necessity at least of reporting as if the British law applied.[77]

Other Sources Utilised

Other colonial records utilised include those produced by the Colonial Secretary's Office. These often contain a wealth of information, particularly on the interaction between the Perth administration and the Kimberley police. Importantly they also contain large volumes of correspondence from colonists. Like the police records, unfortunately, an enormous number of CSO files are missing. The original index displays thousands of entries relevant to the police, however, in many cases the original file is not archived. Files and annual reports of the Aborigines Department and the Aborigines Protection Board, particularly the reports of the travelling inspector for the Kimberley, George Marsden, which appear in 1896, are very valuable. Marsden was one of the few independent observers in the district.

The Police Gazette contains detailed names of Aboriginal prisoners and provides dates of entry and departure of police officers, as well as all promotions, demotions and dismissals. Fortunately the reasons for these are sometimes to be found in another kind of source: Western Australian newspapers, such as the conservative *The West Australian* and the more radical *The Sunday Times*. These were typically scathing when it came to stories about police movements, usually attributing them to whether or not the officer in question had links to the Perth colonial elite. Northern Western Australian newspapers utilised are *Nor-West Times and Northern Advocate, Northern Public Opinion and Mining and Pastoral News* and *Eastern Districts Chronicle*. These papers, as their names might suggest, do not contain disinterested editorials. Australian and overseas newspapers are also utilised (see the Bibliography for a full list of newspapers and periodicals referenced).

The books, records and memoirs of colonists are valuable as they describe the working life of their stations, express anxiety about Aboriginal attacks and sometimes show how they were caught between wanting to tell their story and needing to keep it quiet. Such was the fear of 'northern' Aboriginal people on the frontiers of Western Australia that books such as H.G.B. Mason's *Darkest Western Australia: A Treatise Bearing on the Habits and Customs of the Aborigines and the Solution of 'The Native Question'* found a ready audience. This *Guide to Out-Back Travellers*, published in 1909, reads as a textbook for prospectors on how to survive amongst Aboriginal people in the 'interior'.[78] For example, on encampments: 'Camps should be selected in open country on rising ground...';[79] on camping alone: 'Always keep moving, if possible, never sleep twice in the same place...';[80] and on protection: 'Do not use a muzzle loading gun – if none other, [n]ever fire both barrels in succession unless otherwise armed.'[81] Mason's account also provides insights into the virulent attitude and social values of many colonists on Aboriginal *country*: 'Treatment of Natives: In no instance is the adage about "familiarity breeding contempt" better exemplified than the nigger. The more you give him the more he wants.'[82] Mason's solution to the 'native question', as indicated in the title of the book, was emasculation and/or castration followed by forced indenture to colonists.[83]

The memoirs of G.H. Broughton reveal late-nineteenth and early-twentieth-century attitudes to Aboriginal people in the Kimberley.[84] Lurid details of how matter-of-factly colonists killed Aboriginal people can be found in Keith Willey's account of cattleman Matt Savage's experiences in the Kimberley in *Boss*

Drover.[85] Memoirs of explorers in the Kimberley, such as Alexander Forrest, Frank Hann, David Carnegie and Aeneas Gunn, and early 'overlanders', like Gordon Buchanan and Gerard Lamond, provide insights into racial attitudes to Aboriginal people. Hann and Gunn outline conflicts and shootings at 'bush blacks' and of European 'nigger hunting' parties.[86] Buchanan and Carnegie describe the practice of capturing and chaining Aboriginal people whilst feeding them salt to dehydrate them until they would reveal water sources.[87] Carnegie took a particular interest in and had genuine respect for Aboriginal weapons, noting that Kimberley spears were so sharp they could pass straight through cattle.[88]

Personal memoirs and pioneer diaries held in archives are the most revealing sources of information on Kimberley social life. They reveal what the colonists viewed as the 'realities of settlement' and the frontier culture of the Kimberley. These records, many written with an assumption that colonial authorities would not see them, contain very frank accounts of life in the Kimberley. It is abundantly clear that many colonists saw themselves in a state of war with the Aboriginal inhabitants. The writings of Doug Moore, Richard Allen and Thomas Wheatley are utilised in this study. Memoirs from police who served in the Kimberley are scarce. In fact police, like colonists, rarely wrote down exploits they regarded as 'outside the law' lest they incriminate themselves.

Cathie Clement and Peter Bridge have presented an annotated and edited version of the colourful memoirs of Richard Henry Pilmer, one of the more infamous West Kimberley policemen. Pilmer saw his police role as a positive nationalist white 'civilising force', 'dispensing justice' towards Aboriginal people by punitive means with his duty 'to teach the wild Australian Blackfellow the rights of property in the great unfenced'. Pilmer freely admitted to 'doing away', or shooting, 'desperate characters'.[89] He was so notorious for shooting Aboriginal people that in Aboriginal oral history accounts of the Kimberley his name, sometimes seen as 'Bilimur', became synonymous with 'police' and the two are often used interchangeably, particularly in relation to massacres of the period, even though Pilmer did not serve in the East Kimberley.[90] Clement and Bridge's editorial work also includes *Kimberley Scenes*, a collection of very frank memoirs, stories and letters from the Kimberley frontier.[91]

The Problem of Historical Silences

The East and West Kimberley have been popularised in literature that has shaped many later historical accounts. Ion Idriess' 1952 historical novel *Outlaw of the Leopolds* deals with the West Kimberley and retells the story of Jandamarra. In the East Kimberley Mary Durack's popular 1959 family history, *Kings in Grass Castles,* and the sequel, *Sons in the Saddle,* told the story of the establishment of the Durack pastoral dynasty.[92] These narratives celebrated European exploration, pioneering, colonisation and conquest. Aboriginal people were part and parcel of the environment: an element to be overcome by force if necessary, along with drought, wild animals, hunger and thirst. Unspoken in these accounts is the detail of the extreme violence between colonists, police and Aboriginal people, what J.S. Battye in his *History of the Northwest of Australia* euphemistically called the 'difficult aspects' of colonisation.[93] Durack makes many references to violent interactions involving the killing of Aboriginal people in her published works, though events are spoken of in euphemisms (the term 'dispersal' being the most obvious) or clouded under a veil of allusion.

Mary's father, Michael Patrick (M.P. 'Miguel') Durack, one of the first colonists of the East Kimberley in 1882, was less circumspect and wrote in 1932: 'It should be added that the black-fellow on the whole was never given a chance, and the coming of the whites meant the going of the blacks.'[94] How 'the going of the blacks' occurred is not explained, although Durack does directly admit that, following the spearing of 'Big' John Durack in November 1886, punitive expeditions occurred and 'a lot of the blacks were shot'.[95] Mary Durack also wrote of the spearing and refers to the punitive expedition (discussed in detail in chapter 6) but downplays it in these quixotic terms:

> After the death of Big Johnny Durack a chain of fires blazed defiance from range to range. Lucanus [friend and ex-native police trooper from South Australia] marshalled his forces and rode the countryside and slowly the fires went out.[96]

What is lacking, of course, is detail. These events are clearly sensitive issues for a writer who would be implicating people, including family members, in murder. Curiously the most recent biography of Mary and Elizabeth Durack, by Brenda Niall and published in 2012, appears to acknowledge this fact and, perhaps reflecting changing sentiments since Mary Durack's 1959 telling, airbrushes the account from history by claiming the punitive expedition 'failed to find them' [Aboriginal people].[97] This topic and the issue of 'pioneer silences' are explored in more detail in chapter 3.

While historians have focused their attention on the West Kimberley, overall there is a more diverse historical record and far more significant and varied Aboriginal oral history accounts of the colonisation of the East Kimberley. In them unrecorded killings is a common theme. These accounts, much like other traditional stories, are passed through generations of families from Elders. Unpublished oral histories from the East Kimberley area are found in the work of Helen Ross and Eileen Bray, who interviewed East Kimberley Elders and recorded their stories of the 'killing times', the *kartiya* as they were known, when Europeans were colonising the district.[98] Some accounts detail the practice of killing and burning Aboriginal people (including women and children) by piling the bodies up (after, it appears, the condemned had gathered the wood for the fire) and incinerating them with kerosene.[99] Police records corroborate accounts of this nature. Cathie Clement has provided a detailed historical summary to complement these oral histories.[100] Published works include the biography of 'black tracker' Jack Bohemia,[101] and a range of works by Bruce Shaw and Mary Anne Jebb.[102] Jebb's nuanced history of Aboriginal integration into the pastoral industry in *Blood, Sweat and Welfare* covers much of the time after the period covered in this book.[103]

Bruce Shaw has edited the extraordinarily detailed life story of Gadjerong man and stockman on Durack pastoral stations Jack Sullivan, who recounts his integration into the pastoral economy. This is possibly one of the few published challenges to European written history presented by writers such as Mary Durack. Veronica Ryan edited a collection of stories titled *From Digging Sticks to Writing Sticks: stories of Kija women,* which contains valuable oral accounts of many of the Bedford Downs massacre stories.[104] Other oral histories that record Aboriginal people's experiences in integrating into station life are found in the works of Ambrose Chalarimeri, Joyce Hudson and Pat Lowe.[105]

Other oral histories from the West Kimberley describe other accounts of Aboriginal countrymen being burnt after being killed.[106] Steve Hawke and Michael Gallagher in *Noonkanbah:*

whose land, whose law recorded Aboriginal oral histories that detail these events. Here Noonkanbah Elder Ginger Nganawilla talks about the conflict in the 1890s directly referencing Jandamarra and PC Pilmer.[107] Nganawilla also provides accounts of the notorious 1926 Forrest River massacres, discussed later in this book in the Postscript, which corroborate allegations of Aboriginal shootings and subsequent burning of bodies.[108]

Deborah Bird Rose's account of the Aboriginal people of the Victoria River district, just across the border in the Northern Territory, is chilling in its detail and reveals stark similarities to the Kimberley.[109] Rose argues that the arrival of Europeans involved 'mass killing, introduced diseases, huge displacement of people, increased ecological and social pressures within available refuge areas and increased competition for women'.[110] Additionally, policing illegal behaviour by colonists, such as those engaged in 'cattle duffing' and those who took the law into their own hands and killed Aboriginal people, was difficult as they 'resented bitterly any police interference' in such practices.[111] Travelling further east across northern Australia, Tom Roberts has documented similar accounts of punitive expeditions and frontier policing using a native police force over the newly established pastoral industry in the 'Gulf Country' of the Northern Territory from 1881 to 1900, which dispossessed the Aboriginal inhabitants and caused the deaths of at least 600 people.[112]

The history of policing the Kimberley is a challenging one to research and write. On one hand there is an extraordinarily rich and detailed historical record; on the other hand we have to question some of the details contained in these records, including the numbers of Aboriginal people killed, particularly during pivotal periods in the mid-1890s. Police records must be read with the understanding that they were not disinterested reports or confessionals. They were, in effect, testimonials to the competence of the officer involved. Police were sometimes held to account over their reports. As will be shown in subsequent chapters, police could (and some did) face internal investigations or criminal charges based on the information contained in their reports. Generally, however, bush reports were written in a way that justified police actions. Police officers learnt, indeed were instructed, to write them in such a way so as to avoid investigation of their actions. For instance, violence in the historical record is written about in two ways: violence when used by Aboriginal people was 'savagery and treachery', but when used by colonists and police was an 'instrument of justice'. Reading the evidence for the gaps, silences and rhetorical tropes is very necessary indeed.

During the period under study Aboriginal people had little to no opportunity to speak for themselves. Whilst attempts have been made to incorporate Aboriginal evidence in the form of oral history, this presents extremely difficult methodological challenges. The few pieces of written evidence from Aboriginal people were often witness statements or evidence given in court under duress and as a consequence the material utilised is limited. That stated, it is usually quoted in full in this book, such is the power of this rarely seen non-European perspective. The spelling of Aboriginal names is based on police records and newspaper reports and invariably will differ between different sources.

Throughout the text references to 'the Kimberley' (also known as 'Kimberleys') mean the East and West Kimberley districts unless specified. Indigenous people of the Kimberley are referred to as Aboriginal people throughout. The 'Aborigines Protection Board' was also referred to as the 'Aboriginal Protection Board' and the terms were used interchangeably. Non-Aboriginal people of the

Kimberley are referred to as colonists and owners of pastoral stations are referred to as 'pastoralists', although they may have been known as 'settlers' or 'squatters' in the historical record. The lowest ranks of mounted police constables, particularly in the East Kimberley, were colloquially referred to as 'troopers' in the historical record. These terms remain when used in a historical source that is quoted.

For terminology regarding Aboriginal people, *'country'* describes land and sea areas belonging to different language groups. The complexity of Aboriginal society across the Kimberley was unknown to colonists at the time and it included up to seven different types of social organisation concerning kinship systems, marriage divisions, and classificatory 'Sections' also known as 'skin names'.[113] The prevailing assumption was that Aboriginal people lived and moved in defined areas and possessed a 'tribal structure' that shared a common language and culture. This perception was reflected in later anthropology and the term 'tribes' was used extensively up until the 1950s to describe what are now generally known as language or dialect groups that consisted of smaller 'bands', 'hordes' or clans. Aboriginal people could also often speak a variety of dialects of the same language and their identity was not fixed. For example a person may be from 'coastal' Warwa *country* but have affiliations with another location. The term 'tribe' is used if quoted in a historical source. Similarly 'mob' was extensively utilised to describe anything from 'tribes' to family groups.

This book contains historical extracts with often derogatory and offensive terms for Aboriginal people that were common to the time. To ignore or delete these would be to airbrush the past, to present a censored view of Kimberley history and do a disservice to the historical record. It also includes the names of deceased Aboriginal people from various historical records. The author apologises and states that no offence is intended by the inclusion of this material.

Chapter 1

'SCHOOLING THE UNRULY ABORIGINAL INTO OBEDIENCE'

Historiography and Literature Review

Until relatively recently there were few histories of Australian policing and very few histories of the policing of Aboriginal people. Early institutional histories that refer to policing Aboriginal people, generally speaking, focused on the formation and role of the colonial forces and the problems associated with organisation, training and administration. They were written with a self-conscious nationalism in the context of the history of British colonisation. The act of colonising was described in terms of foundational narratives where the rule of law was established to create order and police enforced the law justly and courageously. This perspective is apparent in A.L. Haydon's 1911 history, *The Trooper Police of Australia*.[1] In references to the Western Australian police, Haydon was possibly the first to comment on 'Pigeon' (Jandamarra) in the Kimberley in the 1890s.[2] In keeping with the temper of the times, Haydon's police were 'picked men'. Their examination 'on entry into the force is a severe one, for only the best are wanted'.[3] Haydon described the police as an enduring, if romantic, symbol of authority:

The day is far distant when he will not be seen riding over the plains on his solitary patrol, an emblem of that authority which has made itself respected and feared by

the white transgressor of the law, and which is schooling
the unruly aboriginal into obedience.[4]

Western Australian historians such as J.S. Battye saw the role
of police in relation to Aboriginal people in similar terms. In
his 1912 narrative of institutional and economic progress, Battye
wrote on the founding of Western Australia:

> One of the principal duties of the force was to pro-
> tect colonists from the depredations and attacks of the
> natives, a duty they carried out with severity, but at all
> times with justice.[5]

In 1960 G.M. O'Brien published a long account of the history
of Australian police in *The Australian Police Forces*.[6] O'Brien, a
Victorian police public relations officer, depicted police as 'pre-
serving peace and good order' and as 'society's shield and safeguard
against anarchy'. Western Australian police, he wrote, had the task
of 'protecting the settlers from predatory bands of blacks roaming
the territory'.[7] O'Brien described police using punitive force on
Aboriginal people as enforcing criminal justice. His argument
was coupled with an idealisation of the 'frontier spirit', exploration, triumphalism and the strength of the Australian character
overcoming the natural environment of which Aboriginal people
were a part.[8]

Changes in Australian historiography during the late 1960s
and early 1970s, which followed a general world historiographical
trend in the reassessment of European imperialism, saw a revision
of the history of colonisation and the role of police in this process.[9] Contemporary historiography, often with a more regional
focus, has positioned the police at the vanguard of Aboriginal

pacification and dispossession on all frontiers in Australia. In the new historiography, Aboriginal actions are given motive and conceptualised more as acts of resistance than as crimes. But these undoubted advances have created new problems and the result has been a more complex, nuanced historiography that draws heavily on advances in other forms of policing history.

This chapter reviews the literature on policing both in and relevant to Australia. It surveys the changes in associated histo-riographical perspectives regarding policing over the twentieth century. It explores the different models of international policing and the origins of Australian policing, and examines Australian innovations such as the Australian native police. Moving from the general to the particular, it explores Western Australia and Kimberley historiography including personal memoirs and Aboriginal oral histories. Finally it presents a summary of the historiographical argument and an account of its contribution to the history of policing in Australia.

Imperial Policing in the United Kingdom and Colonies

The first histories of British policing were Whiggish in character, charting a history of progress from divided, localised and ineffi-cient policing to a centrally controlled, professional force working to impose order on chaos in British society. They describe how Robert Peel and the *Metropolitan Police Act 1829* established the principles that shaped modern English policing, amongst other things, promoting the preventive role of police as a deterrent to urban crime and disorder.[10] Police in this modern police force were referred to as 'Bobbies' after Robert (Bobby) Peel.[11]

Later historians of policing in England, Ireland and Scotland have substantially revised this historical writing.[12] They show that significant reforms in police and policing systems in Dublin under the *Dublin Police Act 1808* predated Peel's police force as the first modern police force of the British Isles.[13] And the even earlier *Dublin Police Act 1786* established a unified hierarchical command that would later become common to the modern civil police force.[14] In his seminal studies published in the mid-1970s, Robert Storch argued that modern policing in the industrial districts of northern England in the mid-nineteenth century came about through consensus amongst the propertied classes.[15] He proposed that before the establishment of the modern police, the aristocracy and gentry interpreted, and in some cases laid down, rules for the orderly functioning of society. Storch notes that what came to be called the 'modern police' represented a major shift away from the notion of communal policing and the traditional institution of village constables: the old parish constable system was increasingly perceived as 'worse than useless' and unsuitable to meet the needs of a class-based, capitalist society. The propertied classes, he argues, wanted to 'create a professional, bureaucratically organized lever of urban discipline' to insert into the heart of working-class communities. These police were regarded by these working-class communities in particular as a 'plague' that used their coercive and surveillance powers over them instead of protecting them.

Charles Edwards' work takes a similar line. He contextualises the creation of the London modern police in demographic changes during the early nineteenth century when large numbers of urban rich held wealth in property and land.[16] This new middle class feared the new urban poor. However, the poor saw the creation of a 'police force' as yet another tool to oppress them while the landed gentry (who had their own policing in the form of bailiffs and servants) saw that their taxes would be used to pay for the force.[17] Control of local police was maintained through a centralised, semi-military organisational structure with the authority of the English constable deriving from three official sources: the Crown, the law and, in theory at least, the consent and cooperation of the citizenry.[18] This model of policing became the basis for the creation of police forces in most countries, such as the United States and colonies of the British Empire, although with some important distinctions.

Scholars of policing show that different kinds of police forces came into existence in the nineteenth century, influenced by the *Metropolitan Police Act 1829*, including a range of law-enforcement bodies in the United States and Canada.[19] In Canada the Toronto police department was founded in 1834 and was one of the first municipal police departments on that continent, followed by police forces in Montréal and Québec City, both founded in 1838.[20] In the United States, the first organised police service was established in Boston in 1838, followed by New York in 1845. While the *Metropolitan Police Act 1829* influenced these forces, they were functionally distinct from each other in their operations.

Clive Emsley and, later, Jonathan Richards have shown how in Germany, Italy and France an older tradition of police called the *gendarmerie*, literally a group of *gendarmes* (a word derived from the French for cavalry), came into operation during the middle of the eighteenth century.[21] This military model of policing of civilian populations was so effective it evolved into a paramilitary style of policing that is in existence to the present day.[22] Emsley notes that many English politicians rejected the European model as too centralised and uncontrollable by local magistrates and as such it was unlikely to be extended to British colonies.[23]

David Anderson and David Killingray characterise the emergence of colonial police forces in the British Empire in terms of their visibility as the most public symbol of colonial rule.[24] Policing was an integral part of expanding the empire because police were often the colonial state's first line of contact with the majority of the population.[25] They also point out the significant problems police faced in maintaining the authority of the Crown on colonial frontiers such as Australia. As they argue, to enforce the 'thin blue line' in a frontier environment and hostile country over people who had no concept of British law required a 'conjuring trick of enormous proportions'.[26] Other historians have pointed out that many colonial forces were based on the paramilitary Irish police model because of the effectiveness of the model in policing local indigenous populations.[27] In Ireland armed police, organised in detachment form, lived in fortified barracks, policed the local inhabitants and were responsible for the suppression of occasional riots and rebellions.[28]

There is considerable debate, however, as to whether colonial police forces owed their origins solely to the Irish and metropolitan police forces. Anderson and Killingray argue that the colonial police forces took on a distinctive local character and their diversity cannot be reduced to a single origin.[29] Superficially the Australian police forces on the frontier shared many similarities with the Irish forces of the 1820s and the 1830s, which themselves were based on the Royal Irish Constabulary. They were invariably paramilitary in organisation and were concerned with rural disorder. But Ireland was heavily policed whereas the Australian colonies were not. Furthermore the Irish police were organised to combat agrarian violence and protest whereas the Australian model was designed to both pacify the frontier and control bushranging. Colonial police in general and Australian police in particular, therefore, while owing much to the Irish model, took on a dynamic particular to the location they policed.

As discussed, older historical representations of police tend to suggest they were simply instruments required 'to enforce the law as laid down by parliament and the courts on behalf of the community'.[30] Later perspectives include studies that stress the complex relations between police and the wider society and show how particular forces reacted and performed in their social and physical environment.[31] Australian historians of policing Mark Finnane and, later, Jonathon Richards both note that explanations for the diversity in policing across the globe can be found by examining the social context in which police functioned.[32]

Finnane has written authoritative studies on the function and associated cultures of Australian policing.[33] He casts doubt on the traditional representation of police and notes that histories of the formation of colonial policing generally fall into two different accounts.[34] The first is the 'Whiggish' view that colonial police were essential to the running of an increasingly urbanised and modern society.[35] Here police act in a unifying role responding to the rising crime associated with growing colonial societies. The second suggests that police forces are products of unequal societies, particularly class-based colonial societies such as those in Australia.[36] Police then are 'instruments of dominant social forces', dedicated to upholding an unequal social order and maintaining the 'thin blue line' between order and chaos.[37] Historians taking this more radical position, such as Connell and Irving, suggest that police played a central role 'as agents of the central government when cultural intervention became necessary in the period of working class mobilisation'.[38]

Finnane argues that neither of these positions is sufficient to understand the development of Australian policing. The second model disregards individual police attitudes and practices, ignores the fact that policing often cut across class lines and implies a degree of control over police amongst the propertied classes that simply did not exist.[39] With Steven Garton, Finnane has argued that the 'social order' is a complex and amorphous idea, the dynamics of which preclude easy arguments about its relationship with policing.[40] They argue that some authors have underplayed these social forces and the way they act and interact with police.[41] Rather the Australian police role was characterised by a regulatory rather than a prohibitive function. While it still maintained and defended an unequal social order, its role was more concerned with maintaining particular kinds of social relations. Although police were given the role of preventing crime, the ordinary policemen on the beat often took a pragmatic approach to policing, turning a blind eye to certain behaviours such as drunkenness or prostitution as long as they did not undermine harmonious social relations.[42]

It is clear then that while police regulations prescribed certain actions it did not follow that these happened 'on the ground'. Police in local communities 'tolerated specific illegalities, solved particular local conflicts and sometimes actively sought community sympathy and support even to the point of ignoring orders from centralised authorities'.[43] This, as Finnane and Garton note, suggests that police were 'managers of the social order'.[44] However, implying a fluid non-problematical form of negotiating relationships between various social groups – as if police were the 'oil' that smoothed social relationships between competing interest groups – is an inadequate way of explaining the relationship between police and society. Relationships between police and vested interest groups involved complex and competing interests. Fundamentally they were based on an uneven distribution of power between politicians, police authorities, local interests and, of course, in colonial societies, Aboriginal people. Furthermore police forces were never united or harmonious. As Finnane and Garton rightly note, conflict between the centralised police authorities and the local police officer 'on the beat' is a central dynamic in the history of policing.[45]

Of course there were other problems that police had to face, one being the public perception of them, often as inveterate drunks, and studies of this issue present another historiographical tradition.[46] Chris McConville has argued that men chose to become police officers because of the twin certainties of a regular salary and the prospect of orderly promotion.[47] However, as in England and elsewhere, for the nineteenth-century Australian police on the beat, the dour reality was that they were objects of derision and low social status. Police enforced laws that many resented and were often seen as agents of surveillance who would monitor trade union activity, drinking, gambling, potential political activities and a whole range of social activities.[48] Russel Ward wrote in his seminal work *The Australian Legend* that 'dislike and distrust of policemen, at least partly merited, has sunk deeply into the national consciousness'.[49] He noted that nineteenth-century police in general were viewed with 'hatred and contempt'[50] and that this attitude was not only held by the 'less wealthy class' but by most people who saw the police as 'corrupt, besotted, cowardly, brutal and inefficient'.[51]

Native and Other Specialised Police

Almost all studies of the emergence of the new police forces in the nineteenth century, whether in Britain or North America, India, Australia or any of the other colonies, emphasise the difficulties in building a disciplined and effective force.[52] High turnover of personnel often contributed to the poor quality of officers, and low pay and often extremely harsh and isolated conditions led to poor morale.[53] One solution was to utilise Aboriginal men as aides, trackers, troopers and as police. In Australia native police were utilised on frontiers from 1837 in the Port Phillip District of New South Wales (now Victoria) as well as in Queensland, South Australia and the Northern Territory. The Queensland native police force was by far the largest and longest lasting, operating from 1848 under the control of Captain Frederick Walker and comprising fourteen Aboriginal troopers, and persisting in different and more extensive forms to at least 1897 and possibly up to 1920.[54] The native police, supported by colonists, were 'instrumental' in breaking Aboriginal resistance to colonisation.[55]

Why did Aboriginal men join the native police? Were they coerced into the role? Marie Fels' history of the native police in the Port Phillip district from 1842 to 1852 is distinctive in its approach.[56] Rather than representing the native police as hapless victims of colonising white policies, Fels argues that they actively collaborated for the benefits and power it gave them. Joining the native police corps was, Fels argues, 'best seen as a strategy in the direction of sharing power and authority in the Port Phillip District'.[57] Evidence from the Kimberley native assistants also suggests a strong cultural change occurred amongst young Aboriginal men who were socialised through the colonisation period. Their highest ambition, one observer stated, was to become a police tracker wielding power over others. He became 'a king amongst his people. He intimidates and does what he likes with them, because of what he has learnt from the whites.'[58] These perspectives do, however, tend to deny the social position of Aboriginal people as colonised and subjugated individuals with restricted options. Indeed Kimberley Aboriginal oral history accounts suggest that if a tracker didn't do what his police officer said, or they accused the police of a crime, they would get 'beaten up'. If they did it twice they would be 'shot'.[59]

Leslie Skinner's earlier history of frontier policing in the eastern colonies focuses on the then northern part of New South Wales and a body of men he describes as 'tangible evidence of the final bankruptcy of frontier policing'.[60] Skinner argues that the official rhetoric of humanitarianism was hopelessly outweighed by the practicalities of the Australian frontier that 'precluded peaceful cohabitation'.[61] In addition the actions of native police, Skinner suggests, were hidden from the official records.

Jonathan Richards challenges this convention in his more recent book, *The Secret War: a true history of the Queensland native police*.[62] Richards asserts that, contrary to received wisdom, many records of the Queensland native police are indeed extant; historians just assumed that they had all either vanished or been destroyed. Richards' thesis substantially revised the historiography of native and colonial policing in general, and is the most detailed and authoritative study yet completed. As the title of his book suggests, Richards concludes that 'a secret war' was being conducted, largely by the native police. At least eighty-five different native police barracks were established at different points between 1859 and 1898 depending on the needs of the time. The Queensland government condoned this war as one of 'cruel necessity', but because there was never a direct order to kill Aboriginal people it avoided scrutiny.[63] He also argues that the style of policing of Aboriginal people in Queensland was 'standard colonial practice' across the empire rather than particular to Queensland.[64]

Gordon Reid, Bill Wilson and, more recently, Robert Foster and Amanda Nettelbeck have described aspects of the native police force that was utilised in South Australia from 1852 to 1857 and in the Northern Territory between 1884 and 1900.[65] A large portion of the Northern Territory bordered the Kimberley district and thus was subjected to similar tropical environmental effects.[66] Indeed some pastoral stations straddled both districts creating jurisdictional issues as a native police force would police South Australia while a purportedly civil force policed the Kimberley. With stark similarities to the Kimberley, Wilson notes the period of 1884 to 1898 was 'one of institutionalised violence' towards Aboriginal people with the expanding Northern Territory pastoral industry being a major driver of police placement.[67]

Constable William Willshire, of the South Australian and later Northern Territory native police force, was a central figure who represents the duality of policing during the late 1880s and 1890s. Willshire became notorious for killing very large numbers of Aboriginal people yet was celebrated by local colonists for his effectiveness whilst operating 'with a violent and legally flexible model of frontier policing'.[68] Much like Richard Henry Pilmer in the Kimberley, Willshire justified his brutality in the name of the evolving white nationalism of the period and saw himself as an 'agent of civilisation'.[69] It should be noted that Pilmer was as notorious for being brutal to Aboriginal people as he was for prosecuting colonists for ill-treating Aboriginal people.[70]

Other historians have shown that most British colonies in the nineteenth century utilised native or indigenous police in a range of army and police roles. Indigenous men were first used as guides, for example for early explorers and colonists, then as native police, who might then be trained as soldiers and frontier guards in areas such as Africa and India.[71] Native police were not only familiar with local geography, customs and languages but they also could live off the land without the debilitating and often fatal health problems that affected Europeans. British migrants, for example, would have suddenly found themselves in an unfamiliar, usually harsh tropical environment. Indeed British soldiers in tropical locations suffered more casualties from medical problems than conflict.[72] As we shall see, in Australia, too, the effect of the environment on European police in some areas was, at times, catastrophic.

Historians have also shown that a significant benefit of utilising native police was financial.[73] Policing was one of the more costly colonial government departments and native forces were paid less, if at all, so their overall cost to colonial administrators was much less than that of European police. Most European powers used formations of native troops and native police in their colonies. Native police forces under British officers defended country borders and enforced colonial law throughout India during the nineteenth century.[74] Locally recruited indigenous troops called *sepoys* worked with British troops and were able to control most of the subcontinent.[75] In 1857 the British East India Company employed an army of 300,000 *sepoy* troops of whom 96 per cent were native to India.[76] European colonial powers in Africa often used indigenous mercenary armies.[77] French colonial expansion in West Africa was assisted by indigenous colonial infantry from Senegal. Indeed these Senegalese troops, which were formed in the 1850s, were used during the First and Second World Wars and until the early 1960s.[78] Established in 1873 the Canadian Northwest Mounted Police was intended to be a native police force composed of indigenous troopers called *métis* and commanded by European officers.[79] The name of the force was later changed to the well-known Royal Canadian Mounted Police.

Although Australian forces were based on European models, some particular forces were administratively, culturally and in their performance quite different from the other empire police forces. Michael Sturma's comparative study of nineteenth-century frontier policing in Australia, Britain and America is a useful introduction to how Australian conditions affected the creation of specific police forces. He argues that as European colonisation spread over the continent a unique style of Australian policing developed. A small and extremely dispersed population made policing difficult, especially in environmentally oppressive areas. The solution was the development of highly mobile mounted police forces.[80] These, he argues, 'profoundly affected the pattern of law enforcement in Australia'.[81]

Of course, Sturma notes, the mounted police force was not an Australian innovation; it existed in Britain and elsewhere as early as the eighteenth century. Where Australian mounted police differed was the degree of responsibility they bore for policing the frontiers of colonisation, particularly the Aboriginal population and, in other parts of the continent, local bushrangers. These mounted police were an example of the variety of different colonial forces: as well as the establishment of the native police there were specialised police forces created in Western Australia, such as the Goldfields police (1885) and the Imperial Water police (1851–1876).[82] These were police who performed a very different function from the 'cop on the beat' in the city.[83] The history of the native police is important because, when the Kimberley began to be colonised, the Western Australian government, so conscious of what had occurred in the self-ruling eastern colonies and under the watch of the British imperial government over the treatment of Aboriginal people, refused to create a native police force. This then left it with the problem of how to police Aboriginal people, an issue that will be explored in subsequent chapters.

The Australian Frontier

The particular history of Australian colonisation was one in which Aboriginal resistance perennially posed the question of the responsibility of colonial governments in regulating the conditions of colonisation. Charles Rowley shows how the question was answered or, more accurately, not answered on Australian frontiers. European occupation of almost all outlying areas of the Australian colonies progressed beyond the boundaries of government authority; Europeans explored and claimed land well before colonial authority established police forces. These simple yet crucial facts had critical consequences for the character of social relationships on the frontier, particularly the relationships between colonists and Aboriginal populations. The frontier, as the term implies, is where government authority had yet to be imposed. Law and order depended on the government taking charge of exploration, colonisation, labour trade and then establishing order – the rule of law.[84] As Rowley points out, this rarely, if ever, happened in Australian colonial history.

Instead exploration, colonisation and trade invariably commenced prior to the establishment of government authority and were, in fact, a necessary requirement in establishing government revenues. Police, when finally established in any particular area, were posted to locations after complaints from the new locals about 'trouble with the blacks'. Police, therefore, were called in to establish 'law and order', which invariably meant punitive administration of the law. Rowley was one of the first to present this interpretation but he also gave a voice to Aboriginal experiences. Indeed he was also one of the earliest to describe the extreme violence of the Australian frontiers.[85] Others who followed, such as Henry Reynolds and later Raymond Evans, Richard Broome, Lyndall Ryan and Noel Loos, have been prominent in the new historiography, while more recently Robert Foster and Amanda Nettelbeck have been exploring the history of the South Australian frontier.[86]

Typifying much of this historiography Reynolds noted how the advance of the pastoral frontier was a major determinant of colonist and Aboriginal conflict in Australia.[87] And, despite whatever colonial administrators dictated, colonists on Australian frontiers often considered themselves in a state of war with local Aboriginal groups.[88] By taking an Aboriginal perspective in his work, the perception of the police role necessarily had to change. Police were no longer described as the bearers of order and justice, rather they were depicted engaging in repression and dispossession. Aboriginal people were now described as people who joined together to resist European colonisation in defence of their *country*.[89]

While the new historiography has brought to life many aspects of a previously unexamined Aboriginal response, it has also tended to produce something of a standard historiographical narrative that might be called the 'dispossession–resistance model', in which police have little more than a repressive role. Some historians have asserted that there were great differences between Aboriginal communities and their responses to colonisation, that Aboriginal–colonist violence had been overstated and that it ignored the equally common issues of Aboriginal accommodation and co-dependence.[90] Bob Reece raised the former issue in an article entitled 'Inventing Aborigines'. Using the establishment of the Swan River Colony in 1829 as an example, he argued that rather than Aboriginal people being a politically unified entity, 'the Aborigines', there were in fact hundreds of different and discrete language groups across the continent.[91] Others such as Derek Mulvaney and Ann McGrath argued that the resistance model dominated Australian history to such an extent that the net result being the historical period being reduced to a battle between 'good and bad'.[92] To the contrary, McGrath argues, the frontier was a place where Aboriginal people and colonists met and intermingled and Aboriginal people moved backwards and forwards 'on both sides of the frontier'.[93] Other historians such as John Hirst have suggested intra–Aboriginal violence has been understated, if not ignored altogether, in recent literature, and argues some historians have attributed anachronistic sensitivities to many colonists, suggesting they could have acted outside of their social context.[94]

Historians have reassessed the roles of police too. They have explored the impediments that police faced in prosecuting colonists who committed crimes, including murdering Aboriginal people. Colonist populations invariably had a very different understanding of the role of police and often placed significant obstacles in front of them.[95] Foster and Nettelbeck's history of the South Australian 'frontier wars' acknowledges the 'complicated network of difficulties' police faced on the frontiers of colonial expansions outside the 'settled areas'.[96] This history has strong parallels to that of the Kimberley in that the South Australian authorities sought to prevent the violence that had occurred in the earlier colonised areas and to provide protection under law to the local Aboriginal people. The reality bore little resemblance to this intent as the 'tyranny of distance' encouraged 'a margin of flexibility in the interpretation of the law' over a people who did not readily submit to it.[97] The authors note the remoteness and lack of police resources 'seemed to almost inevitably produce a hidden culture of settler reprisals against Aboriginal people', a situation with clear parallels to the Kimberley.[98]

In examining the cultural conditions of policing, Judith Allen's *Sex and Secrets: crimes involving Australian women since 1880* took a new perspective by examining crimes against women. Allen's analysis of the gendered nature of crime reveals that historians have often focused on bushranging, convicts and the penal period.[99]

According to Allen history writing in Australia has a tendency to focus on the 'masculine monopoly of public politics and culture' that permitted the 'construction of a masculinist social formation in which women were presented as dependent parasites'.[100] The writing of Australian criminal history is masculinist in nature dealing as it predominantly does with crimes mostly committed by men, such as larceny, drunkenness and crimes against property. The writing about crimes of infanticide, abortion and sexual and domestic violence are secondary, if not non-existent. This is partly because evidence such as criminal statistics and court records will inevitably be a flawed way of finding out anything meaningful about the often hidden crimes committed against women.[101] This is particularly pertinent on Australian frontiers. In the Kimberley, an area where European women were a minority, police, by ignoring or 'turning a blind eye' to criminal activity, often were facilitators of crimes against Aboriginal women. The taking of Aboriginal women or the rape of Aboriginal girls by European men was often not defined as a crime. The role of Aboriginal women as sexual partners, in what Ann McGrath noted was referred to as 'black velvet', was recognised as a cause of a great deal of conflict yet, although it was reported, it was hardly policed, if at all.[102]

Keith Windschuttle has issued a challenge to all recent historiography of the frontier. In late 2000 he published in *Quadrant* magazine a series of articles in a polemical style entitled *The Myths of Frontier Massacres in Australian History,* with the first part called 'The Invention of Massacre Stories'.[103] Influenced by the work of Western Australian journalist Rod Moran, who disputed claims put by Neville Green regarding allegations of a massacre in the East Kimberley, Windschuttle began denouncing much of contemporary Australian historiography.[104] Two of the three examples in this essay dealt with well-known incidents in Western Australian history. The first concerned what is known as the Battle of Pinjarra in 1834, and the second the 1926 Forrest River massacre in the East Kimberley. Both of these incidents have been subject to considerable historical debate.[105] On Pinjarra (discussed in chapter 2) some historians contend that the event was a massacre of unarmed Noongar people, including women and children, by an overpowering military force. Windschuttle argues it was 'a real battle between warring parties, with casualties on both sides, rather than a massacre of innocents' and that those who argue otherwise use it 'to question the legitimacy of the British occupation of the Australian continent and of its commitment to the rule of law and civilised values'.[106]

Windschuttle's goal is clearly less an examination of historical events and more an attempt to reassert the reputation of British colonisation and thus sovereignty over Australia. On the Forrest River massacre (see Postscript), where reports of the murder and burning of eleven Aboriginal men in 1926 let to a Royal Commission, Windschuttle argues that the absence of direct evidence undermines the case entirely.[107] Windschuttle also attempted to refute claims of a massacre at Mistake Creek in 1915 in the East Kimberley. Cathie Clement, using a combination of archival records and the oral history of Gija [Kija] elder Peggy Patrick, has comprehensively shown how Windschuttle misrepresented his evidence.[108]

Windschuttle aggressively criticises recent historical scholarship arguing that it ignores the scholar's basic duty to empiricism, that is, being 'objective' and true to the evidence. He then outlines what he sees as the requirements of historical evidence and the appropriate methodology for writing history:

> Historians should only accept evidence of violent deaths, Aboriginal or otherwise, where there is a minimum amount of direct evidence. This means that, at the very least, they need some reports by people who were either genuine eyewitnesses or who at least saw the bodies afterwards. Preferably, these reports should be independently corroborated by others who saw the same thing. Admissions of guilt by those concerned, provided they are recorded first-hand and are not hearsay, should also count as credible evidence.[109]

This tendentious argument sets up an impossible burden of proof for historians of frontiers where violence was used as a means of control and colonists had vested interests in keeping it hidden from colonial authorities. Significantly his argument also means dismissing Aboriginal oral history as a viable historical source. In volume one of a proposed series on Australian frontiers, Windschuttle asserted that Aboriginal people were not engaged in resistance to or 'guerrilla warfare' against British colonisation but rather were engaged in acts normally regarded as criminal behaviour, such as theft and plunder.[110] The violence used by colonists, he argued, was merely self-defence.[111]

Sparking a very public debate, which was a prominent part of 'the history wars', Windschuttle sought to reinterpret and defend British colonisation of Australia by asserting that historians of the 'orthodox school', who he framed as 'left wing', had overplayed the effect of colonisation, and overemphasised violence and the incidence of massacres.[112] Historians (including archaeologists) of the past thirty years were the main targets of his attack.[113] This was hardly a fair or reasonable critique. Stuart Macintyre, amongst others, noted that Windschuttle had misread the historians he castigates.[114] Bain Attwood noted that Windschuttle's 'interpretations bore little relationship to the work they purported to describe'.[115] Certainly, as seen earlier in this chapter, Mulvaney for one has been critical of the existing consensus regarding Aboriginal attitudes on Australian frontiers and as such is hardly orthodox. Windschuttle's interpretations have been heavily criticised elsewhere for his 'pitiless' representation of Aboriginal Australians.[116]

Windschuttle also controversially argued that massacres could not have occurred or have been as widespread as claimed because colonists adhered to the humanitarian principles of the European Enlightenment, the nineteenth-century evangelical revival and the British doctrine of the rule of law. These, he argues, had a profound effect on colonial policy and behaviour, which was humane and just.[117] Reynolds has suggested that this claim is 'truly extraordinary'.[118] Certainly in relation to colonial frontiers in Australia, Windschuttle's claim flies in the face of vast and overwhelming evidence to the contrary.[119]

Reynolds, and later Broome, whilst acknowledging it was extremely difficult to come up with exact numbers, estimated that a figure of up to 20,000 Aboriginal people had been killed across Australia during colonisation.[120] More recent studies in 2014 by Evans and Robert Ørsted–Jensen suggest over 60,000 were killed in Queensland alone.[121] By no means were all the killings by police. By way of comparison Evans suggests, in relation to the Queensland frontier, that while the native police corps was a notoriously 'destructive institution', 'private settlers, alone or in vigilante parties' (also known as punitive expeditions) ignored the rule of law and killed more Aboriginal people than the native corps by a factor of at least two to one.[122] Evidence produced in what follows reveals that the rule of law meant very little to many colonists apart from the fact that they knew they could be prosecuted for murder so hid the evidence of illegal activities. Indeed, as discussed in chapter 3, colonists believed that the rule of law was so desperately inadequate that it provided the very justification for taking the law into their own hands.

Western Australian Historiography

There are few academic studies of Western Australian police. These include P.W. Nichols' thesis *Police Powers in Western Australia 1829–1970* and John McArthur's dissertation on the early Swan River Colony, which dealt with the years 1829 to 1850. There is also the unpublished work of Andrew Gill.[123] For Nichols, police powers were unproblematically punitive in nature and Aboriginal people were 'coerced in peacefulness'.[124] McArthur identifies the significance of the Western Australian police in the consolidation and legitimisation of the role of government in what was a 'capitalist, private venture' where returns on investment were an inducement to colonisation.[125] For McArthur, police were an arm of the colonial government essential for the protection of new investment in the colony.

Mollie Bentley's social history of the development of the Western Australian police force from 1829 to 1889 describes the early development of policing in the fledgling colony.[126] Bentley sympathises with the extreme difficulties the colonists faced and identifies a central issue in the history of the development of Western Australian policing: the limited government finances available to establish police over an enormous territory.

One of the more recent publications is former police officer A.R. (Don) Pashley's documentary summary of Western Australian police stations.[127] Another is Peter Conole's ambitious, Whiggish narrative history that sees the Western Australian police force developing as a product of the economic development of the emerging state.[128] Conole's detailed history personalises police and presents some valuable insights into the background of policing in particular periods, but it contains some curiously ill-considered polemical statements regarding historical methodology that detract from the text.[129] Conole does not engage in an analysis of policing of Aboriginal people, viewing the police role in Aboriginal dispossession as an inevitable part of 'the great age of imperial expansion in the nineteenth century'.[130] Conole acknowledges police did kill Aboriginal people, particularly during the mid-1890s, but he views this as police 'acting within the law'.[131] Following Windschuttle, Conole also dismisses Aboriginal oral history accounts and denies that massacres of Aboriginal people occurred in the case of the Forrest River and Mistake Creek incidents.[132]

Other earlier Kimberley-specific police histories examine aspects of the policing of Aboriginal people. The first academic work to highlight the role of police in controlling Aboriginal people on the Kimberley frontier was Andrew Gill's seminal 1977 essay 'Aborigines, Settlers and Police in the Kimberleys 1883–1905'.[133] In introducing his thesis Gill bemoaned the fact that neither historian Paul Hasluck in *Black Australians* (1942) nor Peter Biskup in *Not Slaves, Not Citizens* (1973) had 'come satisfactorily to grips with the nature of day-to-day relationships between the European and Aboriginal sections of Western Australian society'.[134] Gill stated that his study was an 'attempt to assemble a picture of some of the relationships between Aborigines, police and settlers'.[135] He very successfully interrogates aspects of social relationships in the Kimberley and examines police practices, revealing that police often 'shot dead' Aboriginal people. He questions whether police reports of these events 'depict a full and truthful picture of police actions'.

In Western Australia there was no wholesale practice of 'dispersal' of Aboriginal people as existed in Queensland, where Aboriginal people were excluded from pastoral leases and associated settlements and native police enforced this by shooting.[136] Russell McGregor's 1985 dissertation, *Answering the Native Question: the dispossession of the Aborigines of the Fitzroy District, West Kimberley, 1880–1905*, goes some way to answering the questions Gill did not.[137] McGregor shows how Aboriginal groups from the Fitzroy were progressively stripped of their rights as British subjects and their rights to their *country* through 'a facade of legality' and observes parallels to the situation in Queensland.[138] Proclaiming Aboriginal people as British subjects precluded the official conquest of their *country* so police were used in a de facto military sense to compel Aboriginal people into subservience. In a 1993 article McGregor expands on this theme and in a comparative study of the West Kimberley and North Queensland argues that the 'colonial police forces played a key role in subjugating the Aborigines'.[139] He observes that the line between police as agents of conquest or agents of the law was thin, if not indiscernible.

In 'Monotony, Manhunts and Malice: East Kimberley law enforcement' Cathie Clement argues that what distinguished the Kimberley from most other regions, and distinguishes hers from perspectives of writers like Gill and McGregor, was the 'web of interdependence' between police, colonists and Aborigines. Unlike Gill she argues that these relationships were often characterised by complementary and mutual interests, and although often violent it was not endlessly antagonistic. Clement suggests the police, although engaged in widespread shootings, paradoxically did 'contribute to the ultimate survival of the Aborigines in the East Kimberley'.[140] That is, police played a mediating and surveillance role over colonists in this district.

Neville Green's influential and pioneering investigations into killings in *The Forrest River Massacres* contains an introductory narrative on nineteenth-century policing including a version of the police pursuit of Jandamarra.[141] Green denies the varying role of the police in the Kimberley that Clement favours. Instead he places the police, largely divorced from their political context, in permanent opposition to the Aboriginal population. Indeed he saw the police in the mid-1890s as being 'a law unto themselves. They were wild cannons....'[142] Green tends to overstate the case for police as an independent military force involved in 'pro-active swashbuckling roles'.[143]

Kevin Moran, a former police officer, has been the first to attempt to write a comprehensive history of policing in the Kimberley. His *Sand and Stone* set of social history books could have made a substantial contribution to Kimberley historiography.[144] However, he portrays Aboriginal people and their actions in resisting colonisation as criminal acts to which the police, of necessity, reply. Yet he has done valuable research in identifying large numbers of new Aboriginal people involved in resistance during the period and he has included previously unrecorded names. Clearly influenced by Windschuttle, Moran purports to utilise a 'Rankean empiricist' methodology. Unfortunately this claim is undermined by an absence of references for quotations and sources in all volumes. Puzzlingly Moran also attacks 'academic historians' who he claims use 'fabrication and elaboration' to write history.[145]

This survey of Kimberley policing historiography requires an account of the many histories of 'Pigeon' or Jandamarra (variations include Sandimarra,[146] Gendamurra[147] and Tjangamarra[148]). On 3 November 1894, when Jandamarra was acting as an informal native assistant to the police at Lillamaloora police station, he killed his officer William (Bill) Richardson, released thirteen Aboriginal prisoners just arrested for stock killing, and escaped and hid in Windjana Gorge, the natural hideaway of Tunnel Creek in the Napier (or Barrier) Range.[149]

The period between November 1894, when Jandamarra killed Richardson, and April 1897, when Jandamarra was killed, was well documented by police and colonists and accounts appeared in contemporary newspaper articles, for example in *The West Australian* and *Golden Age*.[150] These accounts were subsequently reported on widely in Australia and overseas at the time.[151] Headlines such as 'Outrage of the Blacks', 'Mutiny', 'Bushranging' and 'Cannibalism' appeared, sparking alarm that Kimberley Aboriginal people were turning against the European colonists. After the turn of the century more florid accounts appeared, such as the 1912 article 'The Niggers of the North; A Massacre Feared'. One of the police officers involved in the pursuit, Richard Henry Pilmer, raised fears of a mutiny if the 'blacks' discovered another leader such as Jandamarra under whom 'they could rise and annihilate the few whites'.[152] Hyperbole like this came to typify descriptions of the period.

The Jandamarra story was researched in the 1930s by author Ion Idriess and in 1952 was published as a semi-fictionalised story.[153] Idriess went on patrol with police in the Kimberley to get experience in police duties.[154] He then completed the research for his book with extensive help from the Commissioner of Western Australian Police Cecil Treadgold who, in mid-1932, obligingly provided details of police involved in the conflict. Idriess told him that 'I think I have got my finger fairly well on the pulse of the public's fancy'.[155] *Outlaw of the Leopolds* told the story of how Pigeon held police at bay for several years and led to a series of books by Idriess about the Kimberley.[156] Idriess described this period as one in which 'a gang of Aboriginal outlaws terrorised the north west of the continent'.[157]

Pigeon cursed the trackers, then gasped, "Give—me—cartridges—and I'll—fight—you—you . . .!'

Figure 1. I. Idriess, 'The Battle Of Wingina [sic] Gorge', The Sunday Herald, 28 December 1952.

Outlaw of the Leopolds was well in keeping with themes of the triumphalism of European colonisation; in much contemporary writing it celebrated police and popularised and romanticised the period for a European audience. It also moved the Jandamarra stories into historical fiction. Idriess' account was later serialised in journals and Australian newspapers such as the Sydney newspaper *The Sunday Herald* (see figure 1.1) and, in 1956, *The Countryman*.[158] These stories contained conflicting accounts of the episode, were often wildly inaccurate and exaggerated and usually attributed simplistic explanations to Jandamarra's motives, emphasising outlawry, murder and 'treachery'.[159]

Critiquing modern accounts of the Jandamarra story is difficult for many reasons. Jandamarra holds an important place in many Kimberley Aboriginal communities where he has become a hero who stood up for Aboriginal rights and protection of *country;* indeed he has become a metaphor for resistance against white colonisation.[160] Accounts of this period have, however, perhaps irreversibly, become fused with historical allegory.

In later literature Pigeon becomes Jandamarra and is lionised as a resistance fighter leading Aboriginal people of the Kimberley to drive white colonists out. This perspective is epitomised in Howard Pedersen and Banjo Woorunmurra's 1995 revisionist history *Jandamarra and the Bunuba Resistance.*[161] Pedersen and Woorunmurra's version provided valuable new insights into Jandamarra's history. Woorunmurra, as 'custodian of the Pigeon story', adds vivid detail via oral history that forms the basis for much of the narrative.[162] The authors bring life to aspects of Aboriginal culture, agency and what they see as collective resistance, presenting what they view as a concerted attempt by Jandamarra and the Bunuba people to drive Europeans from the district. Ironically, however, the *Jandamarra and the Bunuba Resistance* narrative veers perilously close to simply inverting Idriess' characterisations.[163] This book is lightly referenced and with Woorunmurra's voice passive in the narrative, it is not possible to establish which component of the story comes from oral history and which does not.[164] This is important, as there are discrepancies in the narrative that go well beyond debates around interpretation.[165] Additionally the authors make no mention of the numerous accounts that have informed this story.[166]

The subject of resistance is one of the most significant issues in recent literature on Jandamarra. Pedersen and Woorunmurra construct a narrative of a coordinated resistance under the leadership of Jandamarra with conflict between different Aboriginal groups and colonists from all over the Kimberley incorporated into their retelling. By contrast Green views the actions of Jandamarra and other Aboriginal groups during the mid–1890s as 'uncoordinated' and 'random or impulsive actions of individuals or the concerted protest of small and vulnerable bands'.[167] How realistic was an organised and unified Aboriginal resistance to white colonisation as suggested by Pedersen and Woorunmurra? Certainly the language groups, in the pre-contact period at least, were regarded more often 'hostile' to each other than united.[168] As shall be shown, the resistance theme in narratives of the Jandamarra story is better viewed as a series of localised responses by various Aboriginal groups to the expansion of pastoralism rather than as a large-scale rebellion led by an individual. Ironically, the notion of a rebellion was created by colonists and police who believed that Aboriginal people would unite against them.

To finalise this chapter it is necessary to place what follows within a historiographical setting. In summary: early Australian and Western Australian police histories that view police as 'preservers of peace and good order' and 'the thin blue line between order and chaos' will no longer do. Later histories that propose that police were unproblematically agents of the colonial state and ruling class will not suffice either. This book rejects descriptions of the period in terms of reductionist binary oppositions that posit good/bad dichotomies between Aboriginal people, colonists and police. A better way of looking at the history of the period is to follow an approach developed by Mark Finnane, which examines the complex web of relations in which police were embedded and the social context in which police operated.[169]

This book situates policing in the Kimberley in terms of broad colonial encounters, but recognises considerable diversity in policing. It also recognises the importance of local circumstances to patterns of policing, including the unusually harsh environmental conditions in which police worked. As shall be shown, individual police could have a profound effect on patterns of policing and as such there is a need to recognise their relative autonomy, especially on colonial Australian frontiers. In the context of histories of policing in the Kimberley, this book follows in the footsteps of, and builds on, the small-scale or localised histories produced by Gill, Clement, Green and the unpublished work of McGregor.

There are some particular points to note in relation to the wider historiographical context. While Kimberley police were like police in other Australian colonies in that they were a specialised mobile and mounted force, they were different in that, despite repeated efforts by interested parties, a native police force was never implemented; Western Australia never embraced the native police idea in the way that New South Wales and Queensland did. But what option did this leave it with? Clearly it was left with a civil police force operating against a people who, in part, acted in opposition to the European presence.

This book goes further. It recognises the wider conceptual issues of policing Aboriginal people in the context of debates around Aboriginal resistance and frontier warfare. These are not simple concepts, nor is Kimberley policing easily reducible to such categories. Firstly it argues that it is not possible to define Aboriginal actions in the Kimberley simply as criminal acts, and police responding as police do to criminal acts, as Windschuttle suggests. Secondly it shows that it is not possible to describe Aboriginal actions over the period under study as a unified form of resistance to white occupation, thus it rejects the standard dispossession–resistance narrative. We will see how police adapted and were ordered into roles depending on the period and the circumstances. In the years before 1890 police seemed to take seriously their duty to protect Aboriginal people from the violence of the colonists, but in the post-1890s period protection was replaced by growing punitive violence, merging into warfare. In this sense there are apt parallels to Foster and Nettelbeck's account of the earlier colonised South Australia.[170] There authorities sought to avoid the calamitous violence towards Aboriginal people of the earlier colonised parts of eastern Australia by providing Aboriginal people with equal legal status as British subjects. This in itself created an impossible bind with the realities of the frontier precluding peaceful colonisation – as Aboriginal people did not willingly concede their *country* – and police caught in the dual duty of protection and prosecution of Aboriginal people. Police would inevitably have to defer to the latter course of action to assist in controlling and managing successful colonisation.

This chapter has surveyed the historiography relating to policing and Aboriginal people. It has examined and rejected two dominant historiographical traditions in the study of Australian policing, what might be called the Whig version and the dispossession–resistance model. Instead it has advocated a more complex model of policing which explores the historical and environmental context, historical change, the notion of relative autonomy and the variety of policing strategies and Aboriginal responses. Yet it does not shy away from labelling police behaviour as violent and, in certain circumstances, the relationship between police and Aboriginal people as a form of warfare. The next chapter begins to explore the origins of Western Australian policing, then places this model in the context of the physical and commercial environment in which the Kimberley police worked.

Chapter 2

'THE ONLY REMAINING PORTION OF THE LARGE CONTINENT OF AUSTRALIA HITHERTO UNOCCUPIED'

Setting the Scene

This chapter sets out part of the historical, political, demographic and commercial background to the later analysis of Kimberley policing.[1] It charts the establishment of Western Australian policing in the Swan River Colony and the statutes that shaped the makeup and model of later Kimberley policing. It then outlines the Kimberley environment in which the colonists, including police, would operate. It details the Aboriginal language groups and their *country* in the Kimberley district and then details the 'first contact' between these groups and European explorers. Then follows an analysis of commercial enterprises that the colonists established on Aboriginal *country* and a description of the conflicts of interest of those who had commercial investments in the Kimberley yet were also members of the Western Australian government.

Early Western Australia Policing

Unlike Australian colonies that were founded as convict settlements, the Swan River Colony, later to become the colony of Western Australia, although a Crown colony was not a British imperial enterprise.[2] It was a private, speculative and high-risk free venture devised by Captain James Stirling. As a consequence funding to run the colony relied for the most part on funds drawn from local colonists and available revenue rather than from the

British government, which would supply only occasional parliamentary grants.[3] Colonists were granted lots of land, on what was Noongar *country,* in proportion to the value of assets and labour they brought to the colony, and were not given full title to the land until it had been sufficiently 'improved'. However, as most of the land was 'unimproved' little revenue could be gained from farming or trade.[4] The strained financial position of the fledgling colony limited police numbers, which were always minuscule relative to the area of land they had to cover. Western Australia was not only the largest police jurisdiction in Australia, but one of the largest in the world, encompassing an area of some 2.5 million square kilometres.

The first civil police presence in Western Australia consisted not of a formalised police force but rather a group of constables.[5] This term did not signify rank but legal authority. Though technically Stirling had no formal legal authority, seven months after colonisation, in December 1829, he appointed justices of the peace and constables that were responsible to magistrates.[6] Their primary role was to deal with instances of petty theft, drunkenness and violations of indentured servants.[7] The police were to be one of the main sources of information on 'the state and conditions of the natives'. The harsh social and environmental factors of the Swan River Colony profoundly affected police and policing. Europeans were manifestly unequipped to cope with the local conditions and the English model of policing had not been created with the local Noongar in mind.

The British government had proclaimed Aboriginal people as British subjects with the same rights to protection under law as any colonist.[8] Officially it insisted upon a strict policy of non-interference with the traditional laws and customs of 'the natives' with the expectation that the colonists would gradually subordinate them to British law. How this was to be achieved was not spelt out, though clearly there was an assumption that the police would themselves create some form of order.[9] Stirling was largely unsympathetic to Noongar rights to their land despite the British government's assertion.[10]

By the early 1830s Aboriginal people who continued to assert their own laws were, according to lawyer, landowner and advocate general George Fletcher Moore, becoming 'troublesome' and had committed 'many acts of outrage and plunder'.[11] Problems arose when Noongar people took European property and food sources. The colonists regarded this as theft even though the Noongar were engaging in a system of reciprocity in return for the use of the land. A colonist named Mckenzie was speared, then a colonist named Entwistle was killed by Noongar leaders Yagan and Midgegooroo.[12] In 1831 Stirling, who had become the colony's governor, proclaimed that the colony was 'on alert for the Aborigines who were considered an enemy'.[13] It is very clear in the early literature that Noongar people who showed resistance, such as Yagan who related his thoughts to the colonists, felt robbed of their hunting grounds, aggrieved that their food resources were destroyed and angry that they were attacked by colonists or the military if they took European produce.[14]

The colonists, in turn, were advised that the military would not be called out against Noongar people 'except in the case of a systematic attack'. It was widely believed at the time that all Noongar people might unite against the colonists and as a consequence the role of protection fell to the police. In late 1831 Stirling engaged Edward Barrett Lennard as commanding officer of a citizens' militia of Middle Swan residents who were instructed to warn colonists 'to keep the natives at a distance firmly and resolutely, and avoiding all contact with them'.[15] Clearly not distant enough, for in May 1832 Yagan speared a man named Gaze.[16] In the same year a petition from 139 colonists to the secretary of state for the colonies requested an increase in militia to protect them from attacks.[17] Colonists also reported that Noongar people were driving cattle away from farms and had killed up to 200 pigs on the Swan River.[18] Agriculturists and other colonists gathered in Guildford to pressure and petition the government 'to protect life and property' and threatened to 'abandon the colony' if they did not receive protection.[19] Even Moore, who was known to be sympathetic to the plight of Aboriginal people, stated he would, through desperation, take the law into his own hands if provoked enough. On 21 June 1832, on finding six of his pigs missing and two wounded, he wrote to his family stating:

> "Ardet inexcita *Ausonia* atque immobilis ante." My war-like propensities are so much excited that I have arranged my affairs, as the phrase goes (thinking of you to the last), and am preparing to watch and attack the natives, and kill, burn, blow up, or otherwise destroy the enemy, as may be most practicable.[20]

In February 1832 an Executive Council and a Legislative Council met for the first time, but Stirling, as governor and the supreme political figure in the colony, presided over both bodies and other colonists, despite the presence of the Legislative Council, had no say in government. Six months later the name of the Swan River Colony was changed to Western Australia and the model of policing also changed. It had become a small semi-military mounted police corps situated in Perth under the command of the Superintendent of Native Tribes Theophilus Tighe Ellis.[21] European expansion to find 'pasturable' areas south of Perth was being increasingly hindered by Noongar groups who were antagonistic to the Europeans claiming their land and killing Noongar people. In late April 1883 Yagan's brother Domjum was shot in the head by a colonist whilst robbing a store and later died. In payback killings Yagan speared two more colonists, Thomas and John Velvick. An enraged Yagan inflicted 'upwards of one hundred spear wounds'.[22] Yagan told colonists he was going to 'the Canning [district near Perth] to spear the white man'.[23] Yagan and Midgegooroo were classed as outlaws of British law. Midgegooroo was caught and, without a trial or hearing, illegally executed by soldiers in a firing squad in Perth in May 1833.[24] Two months later Yagan was killed by two boys.[25] More conflict ensued: on 16 April 1834 a colonist named Budge was killed by Noongar people, and three months later on the 23 July 1834 a soldier, Private Nesbitt, was killed.[26]

In 1834 colonists sent a petition to London stating that they wanted self-rule of the colony via a more representative Legislative Council.[27] Secretary of State for Colonies in London, Lord Glenelg, decided that the colony was not ready and rejected this motion.[28] The actions of the Western Australian police force were profoundly influenced by demands from influential colonists, who expected police to subdue the Noongar populations and assert control over land the colonists saw as theirs.[29] There were exceptions, of course, such as Reverend Dr Louis Giustiniani and Robert Menli Lyon, both of whom advocated for Aboriginal people.[30] Lyon argued resolutely for a treaty because colonists had stolen Aboriginal land, until he was driven from the colony.[31] Certainly, from the earliest days of the Swan River Colony, public opinion as expressed in the local newspaper, *The Perth Gazette*, tended to see the police less as a law enforcement body and more as a force for dealing with 'the native'.[32] This new model, employing ex-soldiers, was an experiment in the policing of Aboriginal people that even the editorial writer noted was 'a new era in the Colony, and we hope it will work'.[33] Significantly, many of the new police were discharged soldiers from the previously utilised military forces who were 'inured to the bush' and knew 'the different haunts of the natives'.[34]

Stirling's plan to create a settlement south of Perth at Pinjarra was thwarted by the 'Murray tribe'.[35] He told the colonial office that they 'threatened to destroy all the whites in the district' and argued that if a 'check' was not made on them, they may 'tempt other tribes to pursue the same course, and eventually combine together for the extermination of the whites'.[36] The 'check' occurred on 28 October 1834 when Governor Stirling and twenty-four soldiers and civilians cornered the Murray tribe, an estimated eighty men, women and children, in what has become one of the most infamous punitive expeditions in Western Australian history. An indeterminate number of people were killed, the event itself created political controversy and, later, historians debated whether the 'check' was legal, a 'just battle' or a 'massacre'.[37]

Stirling's own words on this matter were explicit and suggested the massacre description was apt. In his report to the colonial office he declared that he had set out to punish the whole tribe and that his intention was to instil fear in the Aborigines and break their resistance.[38] The only way to deal with Aboriginal people, he wrote, was to 'reduce their tribe to weakness' by inflicting 'such acts of decisive severity as will appal them as people'.[39] *The Perth Gazette* reported on an uncompromising warning to the survivors that if there were any more trouble 'four times the present number of men would proceed amongst them and destroy every man woman and child'.[40] Lord Glenelg responded to Stirling's reports with alarm, suggesting his actions were more a form of warfare than enforcement of British law and reiterating that Aboriginal people were British subjects protected under British law.[41]

In February 1835 complaints about the cost of keeping a police force arose and a second petition from eighteen prominent colonists (including landowners, merchants and tradespeople) to the secretary of state for the colonies was raised, this time on a different matter. The petition requested that the mounted police corps be disbanded and replaced again by a militia, as police were 'burdensome on the resources of the colony'.[42] The tenuous financial position of the early colony, unable to support an outlay of even three or four men, had seen this force cut back by 1835 so that funds could be freed up for exploration and the building of roads.[43] Stirling himself rejected this proposal and insisted that a mounted police corps was 'indispensably requisite for the mutual protection of the white and black populations against each other's encroachments' and the proposed reductions in mounted police 'will be received by his majesty's government as a departure from their line of policy in regards to the natives.'[44] Stirling went on to state what clearly was the reality of the situation, that:

> unless a police corps be established and maintained for the purpose of protecting, controlling, managing, and gradually civilising the aboriginal race of this country, there will be a fearful struggle between the invaders and the invaded, which will not cease until the extermination of the latter be accomplished, to the discredit of the British name.[45]

While Stirling had acted aggressively at Pinjarra he also espoused moral arguments on the need to protect the Noongar people. This apparent contradiction between policing as domination and policing as protection would remain unresolved at a political and administrative level for the next hundred years, bedevilling police and Aboriginal relationships. But this was only one of the significant issues arising in the early period of colonisation that would later have profound consequences for Aboriginal people.

Even at this early period the colonists, Stirling and the Executive Council were well aware that Noongar people held custodianship over their own tracts of *country*. The 'native interpreter' and missionary Francis Armstrong published articles in *The Perth Gazette* outlining the existence of Aboriginal rights to land, social rules and laws:

> The rights to property is well recognized among them, both as to land as to their moveable effects…Land appears to be apportioned to different families and is not held in common by different tribes… land is beyond doubt inheritable property and they boast of having received it from their fathers' father, etc, to an unknown period back.[46]

This issue provoked considerable local debate, particularly in light of agreements that were being discussed in other colonies, such as between John Batman and the Wurundjeri people at Port Phillip Bay in early 1835.[47] G.F. Moore sought to absolve the colonists of legal responsibility and stated that, while he agreed that the Noongar people should get compensation, that it was the responsibility of the British government and not the 'poor struggling settlers', particularly when the provision of such compensation was not a condition that they had agreed to before emigrating.[48] In

1836 colonists, independent of the Executive Council, raised the idea of a treaty or purchasing Noongar land as a way of appeasing aggrieved Noongar groups, and some, such as merchant and businessman George Shenton (Sr), had already done so.[49]

Stirling followed Richard Bourke, the Governor of New South Wales, in rejecting the 'Batman treaty' and explicitly vetoed the idea, publishing a proclamation in *The Perth Gazette* to the effect that colonists could not enter into a treaty with the local Noongar people or buy land, and any agreements signed on Crown land would be invalid.[50] In September 1836 the Executive Council would have final say on the notion of Noongar land rights by stating there would be no negotiation:

> After some conversation it appeared more advisable to inform the natives that it was not the wish of the government to deprive them of any part of their land beyond that which is or may be required by the white inhabitants of the territory and upon which they are not to trespass or commit any theft.[51]

Clearly both the British government and the colonists wanted to retain their ability to control the alienation of land. Any proposal to acknowledge *country* or compensate Aboriginal people would have meant a loss of the already tenuous economic position. The lack of formal recognition of Aboriginal *country* was a legacy that would continue into the next century. Instead of negotiating agreements over land with local Aboriginal people, the colonial criminal law and a police force would be used to control people who were committing 'trespass' and 'theft'.

In late 1838 and into 1839, in an attempt to find a solution to rising numbers of Aboriginal prisoners and the inadequacy of the 'roundhouse' gaol at Fremantle, the offshore island of Rottnest was annexed as a prison.[52] In the same year more police were required because hostilities between the new colonists and the Noongar people escalated and a woman and child were killed at York.[53] Governor John Hutt, Stirling's successor, created a 'native police force' under the command of Inspector John Nichol Drummond, consisting of three European officers and Aboriginal assistants.[54] Hutt was a reformer considered far less militant than Stirling and, along with Moore, developed close relationships with local Noongars, recording some of the first languages in Western Australia.[55] Hutt sought to educate and protect Aboriginal people and their rights by creating 'Aboriginal Protectorates'.[56] Thus the new police force assisted the newly created 'protectors of Aborigines', whose role was to 'civilise and protect the natives'.[57] This force would work alongside the civil police force and its Aboriginal members came to be called 'native assistants'. This native police force was not the same as in Queensland and New South Wales: it was a small body of men charged with reducing attacks on European property, protecting the colonists, preventing intra-Noongar conflict, prosecuting colonists for abuses of Aboriginal people and preventing colonists from taking the law into their own hands.[58] They were intended to be a temporary force.

In 1849, to satisfy colonists that the law could be used to protect their interests in this expanding frontier, Western Australian local magistrates, sitting with one justice of the peace, were given special powers to summarily try Aboriginal people in certain cases. *An Ordinance to Provide for the Summary Trial and Punishment of Aboriginal Native Offenders* explicitly stated that it was 'expedient' to give penalties of up to two dozen lashes and a six-month term of imprisonment for most non-capital offences.[59] This was intended to bring Aboriginal people under British jurisdiction and to prevent colonists from inflicting their own punishments. But it also effectively, as Ann Hunter notes, gave Aboriginal people a different legal status.[60]

In the period after the 1850s recorded incidents of Aboriginal and colonist conflict in the southwest of Western Australia lessened although, according to Neville Green, twenty-three colonists, four soldiers, two police and ninety-five Aboriginal people were recorded killed, with possibly many more deaths unrecorded.[61] After 1857 the role of protectors and the special office for Aboriginal people lapsed and until 1886 there was no special office concerned with Aboriginal matters. Indeed it was during the governorship of Hutt's successor, Charles Fitzgerald (1848–1855), that it became more common to use criminal jurisdiction as the means of 'civilising the Aborigines'.[62] The role of mediating colonist and Aboriginal conflict and protecting commercial development would fall on the police.

Police Ordinance Act 1849

In 1849 the Western Australian police force was given a legislated organisational structure under the first *Police Ordinance Act*. This Act established a formal police force with a chief of police.[63] Following this, in 1853 the first published Code of Rules and Regulations governing the Western Australian police force appeared, outlining a new administrative structure and regulations.[64] The police force became centralised under the command of Superintendent J.A. Conroy, who reported to the governor.[65] From 1829 to 1853 police were employed on a local, 'as needed' basis. From 1853 onwards foot police and mounted police were formed into a unified police force, then in 1861 a more detailed Police Ordinance was passed which spelt out the administrative structure, powers, roles and responsibilities of officers and the range of offences they had to deal with. The police force at this time consisted of a superintendent, an inspector and sub inspectors, 'Serjeants' [sic], corporals and constables. Applications to join the force were made to the superintendent: if the testimonials presented were satisfactory and the person was found to be 'duly qualified', then he was noted on a list of candidates and a written communication to that effect was sent to him. When the services of that candidate were required, he was summoned to attend.[66] The qualifications for the police force expressly were minimal and stated that the candidate was:

> to be under 40 years of age; to be able to read and write; to be free from any bodily complaint calculated to interfere with his duties, and, to be generally intelligent.[67]

As European colonisation expanded following private commercial opportunities, and towns were established around industries such as agriculture, pastoralism and mining (to the east and north during the 1860s and 1870s and later the Kimberley region), police continued to be used in a pacifying and punitive role, as if it were a regular and proper role for a civil police force.

During this time there was again growing local interest in establishing elective self-government and thus more control over the colony. In 1870 Governor Frederick Weld oversaw the establishment of representative government in Western Australia, which was largely symbolic as the governor still retained executive control of the colony and only men who owned property of a certain value were allowed to vote.[68] This issue would continue to cause tension because the executive and legislative arms of the colonial government remained divided. Members of the

Legislative Assembly would continue to lobby the governor and executive for greater control. Other colonies such as New South Wales, Victoria, Tasmania and South Australia had achieved responsible government and independence in the early 1850s, while Queensland attained self-rule in 1859.

'Bring Them to Subjection by Force of Arms'

The limits of government authority in Western Australia would have devastating outcomes for Aboriginal people in the remote areas of the colony. There was confusion around lines of authority over police, and intolerable and unresolved tensions remained around the treatment of Aboriginal people. As European colonisation expanded into the Northern, Gascoyne, Murchison and Kimberley districts many more Aboriginal language groups were encountered. In the absence of any treaty the government expected the colonists to utilise and 'civilise' the Aboriginal people whose land they had taken, while the colonists expected the government to provide protection as they were paying rent for the land.

On the one hand many colonial authorities and pastoralists infantilised and brutalised Aboriginal people, describing 'the blacks' as 'children' needing 'civilising', 'advancement' and 'improvement'. This was to be achieved through corporal punishment and floggings at the behest of the white man – as that 'was the only language they understood'.[69] On the other hand representatives of the Crown, such as magistrates, members of the judiciary, government residents and certain colonial secretaries, insisted that British law be followed and that Aboriginal people had equal privileges and rights with the white man. This debate was neither new nor particular to the Kimberley.

Indeed Ann Hunter notes these debates about Aboriginal policy in the Swan River Colony in 1834 and it is clear that the issue remained unresolved some fifty years later.[70] But what did it mean to say that Aboriginal people had rights as British subjects? Before the expansion of Europeans north into the Murchison and Gascoyne districts, there was much resistance regarding instructions from the colonial office that Aboriginal people were to be treated the same way as any other British subject. Local pastoralists voiced opposition and suggested that those far away in London and even in Perth had little understanding of the local conditions. Conflict had largely ceased in the southern areas by this time but became a pressing issue again with colonisation into the northern areas.

In parliament debates between Governor Weld and colonists in the north of the state became more acerbic. In mid-1871 an angry debate ensued when, in Roebourne, a colonist by the name of Lockier Clere Burges killed an Aboriginal man he caught stealing his saddle. Burges was charged with manslaughter and gaoled for five years.[71] The central issue raised in his defence was whether a white man 'in the north district far beyond the bounds of settlement' could shoot an Aboriginal person in 'self-defence' as punishment or deterrence without being required to account for these actions before a legal tribunal. The pastoralists' primary desire was that 'their life and property be protected' in an area where there was no police presence and almost no legal measures guaranteeing them protection.

Governor Weld, being of a liberal persuasion, sought to prosecute the law equally and insisted that in such cases the perpetrator be tried for murder, much to the chagrin of over 300 petitioners including prominent pastoralists, farmers and men who would be future members of the Western Australian parliament: John Forrest (Premier), George Shenton (Colonial Secretary), Septimus Burt (Attorney General), William Marmion (Commissioner for

Crown Lands) and Harry Whittall Venn (Commissioner for Railways). They demanded Burgess' release because he had not done anything 'morally wrong'.[72]

The expanding Gascoyne and Murchison pastoral industry, coupled with these ongoing unresolved 'native policy' issues, would lead to increasingly urgent and direct appeals to the governor to provide a solution to stem what some viewed as catastrophic stock losses and frequent Aboriginal attacks. There was prodigious public debate over these issues[73] and on 18 May 1882 a deputation of prominent parliamentarians and land owners, including J.G. Lee Steere (Member Legislative Council), Maitland Brown (MLC), S.E. Burges, J.H. Monger, Dr Hope, Robert Sholl and Alexander Forrest, petitioned Governor Robinson calling for more police protection 'in view of the aggressive and hostile attitude of those natives' in these districts.[74] The colonists claimed the further north they ventured the more hostile the Aboriginal people were. Brown boldly suggested:

> the simplest and most effectual way to settle our own native difficulty, would be to declare war against them, and bring them to subjection by force of arms; but, of course, that sort of thing could not be done now, though it was done, with very satisfactory results, in the early days of the colony.[75]

Whilst the government was seeking independent rule it had to be seen to be treating Aboriginal people justly and could not, as Stirling had done in 1834, launch punitive expeditions against Aboriginal people. Instead the government insisted upon utilising the rule of law: policing, arrest and judicial process as a mechanism for establishing peaceful relations. One of the immediate consequences of this approach was a tripling in the numbers of Aboriginal prisoners or 'ringleaders' sent to Rottnest prison from 1882 onwards.[76]

The government emphasised the role of Robert Fairbairn's parliamentary investigation into conditions in the Gascoyne and Murchison districts; however, when Fairbairn's report was tabled it was not favourable to the views of those demanding action. In the Gascoyne district Fairbairn found the practice amongst pastoralists of attributing all stock losses to Aboriginal people was common even when the losses were by other means. He found that 'civilised station blacks' and 'bush blacks' communicated and that there was no simple demarcation between them. Indeed many stock losses were the station workers giving stock to family and kin groups on *country* in order to survive.[77] He also found that the keeping of Aboriginal women was the main reason for attacks on pastoralists and not, as pastoralists argued, 'innate treachery'.[78] He concluded that 'the native question' or the aggression of Aboriginal people 'had been exaggerated' and it was up to pastoralists to 'bring about a better state of affairs with the natives not the government'.[79]

Fairbairn's report would bring up issues regarding the use of force against Aboriginal people that would characterise the entire region for the next half a century. For during this time there were many requests from pastoralists that the government 'shut its eyes' for a period and in effect make the district free from British law so they could sort out 'the native problem' themselves through use of force which, as shall be shown, often occurred.

The 'Narratives of Peril' Defence

It is clear then that while Aboriginal people were British subjects, their legal status was ambiguous with the situation at the time creating a range of subversive colonist behaviours. Aboriginal people could not legally be killed as there was no official war against them. The fact that the law clearly provided that murder was an offence punishable by death did not preclude violence towards them by colonists, including police. This grey area offered a most convenient cover for all manner of brutal actions and Aboriginal people were murdered with impunity. If there were no independent witnesses to these events and no evidence of a crime taking place then police would be reluctant to lay formal charges against suspects; the prevailing view was that no crime had occurred.[80] In the rare cases where charges were laid magistrates or judges would often defer to colonist accounts. Evidence from Aboriginal witnesses and accounts were rarely tendered. Cultural and linguistic differences made it very difficult for a cogent account of an infraction by a colonist against an Aboriginal person to be put before a court; evidence from white colonists did not suffer from the problems faced by aggrieved Aboriginal people. On the other hand Aboriginal attacks on colonists were viewed as criminal acts which were invariably successfully prosecuted.

The precedents were found in the early colonisation of Australia where a colonist would simply state that the death of an Aboriginal person was an act of self-defence or for the protection of their property, which was enough to silence any further inquiries. The assumption was that a form of natural law underpinned colonial and Aboriginal violence and that the violence was necessary. Colonists, they would argue, were provoked into violence by Aboriginal actions. This is what Lisa Ford calls the 'narratives of peril' defence whereby the colonist would broadly describe the mortal danger they were in and how they were provoked and acted in self-defence.[81] The narrative-of-peril defence related to not only the individual but also the wider European community, which was by implication also imperilled and thus the violence was justified.[82] The judicial system tolerated this culture of colonist violence. It would also tolerate a culture of violent policing.

New Country

The Kimberley would be colonised in much the same fashion as the earlier areas and ultimately police would be deployed, but in a starkly different environment from that which had been experienced further south. The Kimberley district, named after Lord Kimberley, the British Secretary of State for the Colonies, was gazetted in 1880. Prior to that it was considered part of the North West (an area that would later be called the Pilbara) of Western Australia. The Kimberley was officially partitioned in 1883 into the West and East districts in a demarcation that followed natural geographic features. The importance of describing these and other geographic features is that they define both East and West Kimberley Aboriginal language group (and sociocultural region) boundaries, and identify terrain used by Aboriginal people to hide from police. These features and locations are explored in subsequent chapters.

The West Kimberley is bound on the north and west by the Timor Sea and the Indian Ocean and has precipitous cliffs dotting the coastal areas around the entry to the main port of Derby through King Sound (see Appendix 1). The West Kimberley joins the East Kimberley around the Durack Ranges and extends from the port town of Wyndham at the north of Western Australia south along the corridor of the fertile Ord River valley and its many tributaries in and around Halls Creek. To the south it is bound by the Great Sandy and Tanami deserts. The eastern boundary was the then South Australian border (now the Northern Territory). Environmentally the Kimberley has more in common with northern Queensland and the Northern Territory than the southern regions of Western Australia. The seasons are characterised by monsoonal patterns of the 'wet' and the 'dry'. Between December and March 'wet' tropical conditions prevail and monsoon rains flood many plains along major rivers such as the Fitzroy and the Ord. The environmental and geographic conditions of the Kimberley dictated Aboriginal land usage patterns and seasonal travel. They also determined European land use patterns as they sought the most fertile pastoral land along the river plains. Between April and November is the 'dry', with months of extreme heat in which lack of water caused the deaths of many colonists unfamiliar with the land. The dry periods after May meant that Aboriginal groups could travel again and conduct ceremonial business. It was also the season when police would travel on patrols.

The Fitzroy and the Ord rivers carry the greatest volume of water in all of Australia.[83] The Ord River, some 320 kilometres long, cuts through two large ranges, the Carr-Boyd and Dixon, and discharges into the Indian Ocean in the Cambridge Gulf.[84] The river has thirty-five tributaries; pivotal among these is the Lennard River, which flows into the King Leopold Ranges and in a westerly direction through the Lennard River Gorge and the Windjana Gorge before merging with the Meda River.[85]

Enormous limestone gorges and ranges run through both districts, partitioning the country between north and south and east and west. Perhaps the most well-known geological feature is Windjana Gorge (or Devil's Pass as it was known in the 1880s). The Lennard River, cutting through the Napier Range, created this gorge, 3.5 kilometres long and in places 100 metres high. In the wet season the Lennard and Fitzroy rivers often flooded and enormous volumes of water travelled through.[86] Along the

Kimberley rivers where the water meets the land are very large areas of mudflats and mangroves.

Figure 2.1. Kimberley Languages. Courtesy AIATSIS.

The Napier Range runs about 250 kilometres from the north-west to the southeast in the West Kimberley and is approximately 3–5 kilometres across. The King Leopold Range stretches from the West Kimberley coast at Collier Bay in an enormous semicircle, passing the Fitzroy River and meeting up with the East Kimberley at the Ord River. From there the range joins the Durack Ranges and carries on up to Wyndham. The Margaret River, an Ord tributary, cuts through this range. One police officer described the King Leopold Ranges as 'something beyond conception, it is nothing but a succession of cliffs and precipices'.[87]

The Aboriginal language groups within the Kimberley are numerous, with natural geographic features such as rivers and mountain ranges demarcating *country*.[88]

Figure 2.2. Wandjina rock painting. Courtesy Mike Donaldson, 2007.

Archaeological finds at Lake Gregory near Halls Creek show the existence of stone tools dated at 50,000 years old, which is some of the oldest evidence of human activity in Australia.[89] The Kimberley district had been subject to some of the earliest explorations by non-Aboriginal people in Australia. Rock paintings such as the Wandjina rock paintings (generally on Worowa, Ngarinyin and Wunumbal *country*) or the older *Gwion Gwion* (also earlier known as the 'Bradshaw Paintings' following recording by Joseph Bradshaw in 1891), primarily in the North Kimberley, can be dated up to 17,000 years old and include representations of visitors who came before official European colonisation of the district.[90]

Trade routes, and economic and ceremonial networks called the *Wurnan* spanned a number of language groups in the Kimberley and beyond. The *Wurnan* operates at both small and larger scale inter-group levels.[91] The social groups are the clans and the *moieties* (a form of social organisation in which most people are divided into two classes or categories). In the Kimberley *moieties* are named and are often associated with special totems or animals. Another aspect of the *Wurnan* is the idea that the totemised animal and plant species depicted in cave paintings are linked to specific clans so that the ordering of humans is extended to nature.[92] *Moiety* affiliation would have implications for the ordering and performance of rituals, for example in determining camping and seating arrangements.[93]

Aboriginal oral history accounts recount stories of visitors arriving in boats.[94] Dutch explorer Abel Tasman was the first European to make a confirmed landing on the Kimberley coast in 1644. One of Tasman's accounts recorded that near Carnot Bay he came upon an Aboriginal group, likely Bardi people:

> They once came to the number of fifty, double armed, dividing themselves into two parties, intending to have surprised the Dutch, who had landed twenty-five men; but the firing of guns frightened them so, that they fled. Their proas are made of the bark of trees; their coast is dangerous; there are few vegetables; the people use no houses.[95]

In 1688 William Dampier, with up to ninety shipmen, visited on the ship *Cygnet* and spent several months on the east side of King Sound.[96] Dampier recorded that the local people, likely Bardi or

Djawi people, sustained themselves by collecting 'cockles, mussels, and periwinkles' and maintaining stone 'wares' that trapped small fish in tidal inlets.[97] They lived in companies of twenty or thirty men, woman and children and the 'old people' and 'tender infants' waited their return upon which all food was shared.[98] In 1699 Dampier returned in the ship *Roebuck* to La Grange Bay. He was engaged in a 'battle', which would later be called a 'skirmish', and he wrote that he came under attack and shot one man.[99] Of the first visit he wrote the now infamous passage that was reproduced in a 1697 publication *A New Voyage Round the World* where he stated that 'the inhabitants of this country are the most miserablest people in the world'.[100]

From 1750 Makassan fishermen from Sulawesi, an island now part of Indonesia, visited the Kimberley coast from Broome to Cape Leveque to collect and process *trepang*, also known as bêche-de-mer or sea cucumber.[101] Crews of up to thirty would travel in the wet season, to take advantage of the seasonal wind patterns, in boats called *perahu* or *praus*. Aboriginal oral traditions describe these fleets' visits and provide narratives of events associated with their stay.[102] Another critical implication of these visits was that the Makassans would later introduce the devastating disease smallpox to the North West and Kimberley.[103] Later European explorers included Phillip Parker King who, in 1819, on the ship *Mermaid,* was the first European to sail into the Cambridge Gulf in the East Kimberley.[104]

The first European explorer to reach inland Kimberley was twenty-five year old George Grey, 150 years after Dampier, in January 1838. Another expedition followed a year later in February 1839.[105] Although inexperienced, Grey's aim was to explore the 'North west', as it was called, and find what was thought to be a great inland river or inlet.[106] Grey discovered what would later be named the Fitzroy River. His journeys, recorded in his journals in vivid detail, are replete with tales of near death experiences due to lack of water, intolerable heat, mosquitoes, flies and near impenetrable countryside.[107] Near Hanover Bay on the Prince Regent River, Grey was speared twice by those he called 'an old enemy' (likely Worora people) who had been following the party for months.[108]

Grey encountered groups of 200 men, women and children and he also was the first European to see and record Wandjina images, copying many of the rock art sites he came across.[109] He described Wandjina art as being 'far superior to what a savage race could be supposed capable of'.[110] These explorer accounts are characteristic of most reports of those visiting the continent: the tendency was to extrapolate localised experiences, usually of the first people they met, to describe the nature and character of people of entire districts if not the whole country. Typically, as Dampier in particular exemplifies, they were derogatory observations. The perceptions of these early explorers and writers were shaped by their own culture, and began with the assumption of primitiveness and lack of development, inadequacy and weakness of the people they observed. As amateur scientists these mercantilists and traders were also concerned with what they considered were the fundamental issues of humankind and civilisation, such as belief in the existence of a god, belief in an after-life, a system of morality, social structure and a system of government.[111] That the inhabitants appeared not to farm or trade goods merely confirmed their presumed backwardness.

Figure 2.3. 'Alexander Forrest's 1879 Kimberley Expedition'. Left to right standing: James Carey, John Campbell, Matthew Forrest, Arthur Hicks. Sitting: Tommy Pierre, Fenton Hill, Alexander Forrest, Tommy Dower. Courtesy State Library of Western Australia, 066175PD. Photographer unknown.

Later explorers were to come to a better understanding of the character of different Aboriginal groups and the existence of an identifiable culture in the Kimberley. One such explorer was Alexander Forrest, who would also be one of the pioneers of the Kimberley pastoral industry. In early 1879, the twenty-nine year old Forrest asked the colonial secretary to allow him to lead an expedition to the district (figure 2.3).[112] Forrest's journey from his starting point on the De Grey River was demanding and his opinions on the worth of the country varied. On 27 February 1879, he wrote that the area consisted of 'spinifex country' of 'wretched description'. Near Collier Bay and 'Mount Hopeless' (one of the many landmarks named that indicated his despondency) he wrote of the country, 'I only hope I may never see it again, or anything approaching its character'.[113] However, glowing descriptions followed in October 1879 when he discovered what he considered millions of acres of fertile plains and good land along the Fitzroy River, well suited to 'sheep, cattle and horses'. He advised that the whole district should be opened up for pastoral and agricultural settlement',[114] 'The natives', he wrote, 'were friendly all through our journey and are, I imagine, unlikely to provide a source of any annoyance to future settlers.'[115]

Forrest's record is an extraordinary account of first contact with Aboriginal people. It is notable for his descriptions of meetings with various groups in different parts of the country who fed, found water for and guided the group through their own territory. As Forrest travelled he found evidence of group boundaries or boundaries of *country*, befriending groups who then left him at the end of their *country*. Continuing further he met with new groups where the process of observation, wariness, approach and trust was again established.[116] Forrest wrote of how he met groups of twenty to thirty en route and while some initially responded to their presence in 'abject terror', eventually he became friends with them all.[117] On his trip, aided by his Aboriginal guides, Forrest met Njaangamarda Kundal and Bardi people and travelled through many different language groups into Nyikina, Bunuba, Unggumi, Warwa and Ngarinyin *country* and into what would become the East Kimberley at Kija.[118] So far did he travel in difficult terrain that he nearly died from exhaustion, although he fared better than later explorers, such as men on the Calvert expedition, who died of dehydration.[119]

Forrest went on to map the country he explored, naming many features of the Kimberley district.[120] His expedition exposed several social issues that would escalate in coming years. Local groups were initially friendly and curious and engaged in the reciprocal exchange of goods, indicating trust. They also had clear boundaries of their *country* and would protect that *country* if necessary.[121] Forrest's knowledge and experience of the country was unsurpassed and he would become a pivotal figure in the development of the Kimberley pastoral industry.

The Selling of the Kimberley

Following Alexander Forrest's positive reports to the Western Australian government detailing the promise of the Kimberley of 'some twenty-five million acres' of potential pastoral land, the government invited applications for leases of blocks of land.[122] Applications were received from all over Australia.[123] Perth-based interests applied primarily for West Kimberley leases where the land and climate were considered more amenable, after having experienced the already depressed sheep market of the south-west.[124] The first conflict of interest was that many of those who purchased these leases were members of the proudly parochial and conservative land-owning classes of the Western Australian parliament. Applications for the East Kimberley leases were made by 't'othersiders' or non-Western Australians primarily from Queensland, New South Wales and Victoria. This was due, in part, to the fact that available leaseholds on the east of the continent were vanishing quickly as wealthy monopoly interests consolidated leases that did exist. Droughts in Queensland in the early 1880s only added to the appeal of the new district.[125] These smaller scale squatters, often following scant advice, were willing to take enormous risks both personally and financially to search for new pastures thousands of kilometres away. Their risks were rewarded when they acquired much of the East Kimberley.[126]

James Sykes Battye and, more recently, Geoffrey Bolton and Cathie Clement have documented the dubious manner in which these leases were allocated.[127] They show irregular acquisition of leasehold land occurred prior to the establishment of regulations which would decide who could stock the land.[128] Because of the unexpected number of applications for blocks in the district, the Secretary of State for the Colonies, Lord Kimberley, put in place strict stocking regulations relating to leases.[129] His concern was that there be an incentive to stock the land otherwise it would lie idle and 'unproductive'. Blocks that abutted a watercourse were highly sought after and the regulation for such pastoral land was that it had to be three times as deep as the length bordering the river. The theory was that this would prevent monopoly interests from gaining all the best land. Blocks of less than 50,000 acres (200 square kilometres) in size had leases at 10 shillings per 1000 acres and these expired in 1893. Pastoralist leaseholders were required to stock with 'twenty sheep or two large head of stock' for every 1000 acres held. Failure to comply would mean doubling of the rent or forfeiture of the land.[130] There were numerous protests at these conditions particularly since the cost of establishing a station was extremely high in such a remote area.[131]

Because of the suggestion of impropriety in the way leases were granted, the Western Australian government placed a moratorium on the selection of pastoral leases north of the 19th parallel. It was not until late 1880 that the government agreed on the land regulations – though Aboriginal people were not mentioned in them – that would prevent acquisitions through illegal means and were designed to encourage rapid colonisation of the district.[132] Even so the process by which leases were allocated was ad hoc and biased. Applications for land were submitted and were all to be opened on the same day, 1 February 1881.[133] If two or more applications were for the same land then the decision was to be made by ballot. However, there was no limit on applications that one could submit or on the acreage applied for, nor was there any requirement of guarantee that the applicant could pay rent on these leases.[134]

Hundreds of submissions, mostly from Western Australian interests, arrived with many containing multiple applications.[135] Surveyor General Malcolm Fraser (who would in 1883 become the Western Australian Colonial Secretary), in an attempt to rectify this anomaly, circumvented the procedures already in place and suggested that the Land Office allot adjacent vacant lands to applicants if someone else had already taken part of the lands they wanted.[136] The result was that the ballot was circumvented by cartels, which included prominent Western Australian politicians.

George Shenton (parliamentarian and, following representative government in 1890, the first colonial secretary) won three leases from twenty-four applications. One cartel consisted of William Edward Marmion (member for Fremantle in the Legislative Council), his brother-in-law Richard Gibbons, Dr Charles Henry Elliott and the three brothers, William Silas Pearse (member for North Fremantle in the Legislative Assembly), George Pearse and Samuel Pearse. William Paterson of the Murray Squatting Company sat in the Legislative Council for the Murray and Williams districts in 1889 to 1890 and, in the period 1890 to 1895, he represented Murray in the Legislative Assembly supporting Sir John Forrest.

Marmion with Edward McLarty, member of the Legislative Council, would form the Kimberley Pastoral Company, run and operated by his brothers, and would be shareholders in this company along with Alexander Forrest, W.S. Pearse, Robert Sholl and G. Pearse.[137] Edward's son, Sir Ross McLarty, would become member of the Legislative Assembly for the district of Murray and the future premier of Western Australia. Between them, these individuals lodged 160 of the 448 applications in the ballot.[138] This cartel, by duplicating and overlapping each other's applications in an attempt to secure the richest segments of the Fitzroy and Meda river valleys, secured one-third of the first 102 Kimberley pastoral leases. They lodged at least eleven applications in four different names to win six adjoining blocks totalling 300,000 acres on the north bank of the Fitzroy River and won other blocks on the Meda River where the notable stations Liveringa and Meda were established.[139] Of the 102 leases approved by ballot in February 1881, sixty-one lapsed when the rent was not paid at first instance. Of the forty-one leases on which rent was paid, twenty belonged to members of the cartel whose land had frontage to the Fitzroy or Meda rivers. Shenton's lease did not end up constituting a viable pastoral station. After paying a total of £300 in rent he let his lands revert to the Crown. The new lessee to take over the land was Alexander Forrest.[140]

A large number of leasehold applications were received in 1882 and 1883 from the eastern colonies. Some applicants acquired enormous tracts of land.[141] By 1883 some 51,289,080 acres of land had been leased. However, with most leaseholders being in Perth, Victoria or Queensland, very little of the land, with the few noted exceptions, had even been sighted. The lack of detail did not stop others entering the Kimberley and at least attempting to stock the district well before anything resembling a police force existed.

The Western Australian government had deemed that 'no protection or Government establishment' would be established in the Kimberley until it was financially viable. Indeed revenues from the leases of land were needed to fund such expenditure, thus there were no police or police stations or government residents north of Roebourne, some 800 kilometres south of the Kimberley, until 1883. This situation would have crucial ramifications for the police when they sought to impose British law on both the colonist populations and Aboriginal people, as both groups had already established social interactions that operated well outside of British law.

Complaints about the onerous nature of the regulations regarding stocking and high rents came from parliamentarians such as Marmion, who had interests in two pastoral stations, pearling interests around Broome and shipping interests.[142] There was also concern expressed by members of the Western Australian government about the fact that many of the leases were being taken up by non-Western Australian interests. There was also anxiety about the overall lack of detail about almost all aspects of the Kimberley, including the nature, extent and number of the Aboriginal 'tribes'. One of the few first-hand accounts came from Forrest's expedition. To rectify this situation John Forrest, accompanied by Alexander Forrest in a private capacity, ventured forth as surveyor general to explore the district and get more detailed information on the conditions. John Forrest organised the first large-scale survey of the Kimberley district with geologist E.T. Hardman.[143]

John Forrest was by this point already an established and respected explorer and had between 1869 and 1874 undertaken three very notable expeditions.[144] He had also had significant personal experience in coming into contact with Aboriginal groups hostile to his group's presence. In June 1874 at Weld Springs Forrest had shot Aboriginal people himself when about 'forty to sixty natives' came 'running towards the camp, all plumed up and armed with spears and shields'.[145] These experiences would inform Forrest's later judgements and opinions.

Figure 2.4. Samuel Calvert, Sketches in the Kimberley District of Western Australia, 26 June 1886, Melbourne David Syme and Co. 18, Courtesy of the State Library of Victoria, Cons. IAN26/06/86/100-101, Image No. mp010352.

In late 1883 Forrest visited Windjina Gorge, naming it Devil's Pass due to the difficulty in traversing it.[146] He realised that the Kimberley was exceptionally harsh environmentally and that it was profoundly different from the cooler forested areas of the southwest of Western Australia.[147] Commenting on Alexander Forrest's report from 1879, John Forrest declared that the district was overrated as pastoral country and that the 1879 report had 'a very high if not exaggerated idea of the value, richness...of the Kimberley district'.[148] This opinion did not influence others as the rush for the Kimberley had already started.

The West Kimberley: Arrival

The first pastoralist to enter the West Kimberley was Julius George Brockman, who in late 1879 landed 300 sheep at Beagle Bay in Nyul Nyul people's *country*.[149] Other individuals followed soon after: in 1880, Alexander Richardson of the Murray River Squatting Company sailed from Fremantle on a small vessel laden with sheep and also landed at Beagle Bay.

With William Paterson, his brother George S. Elliot and Hamlet Cornish they established Yeeda Station on Warwa *country* about 45 kilometres from Derby.[150] George Canler Rose and Edwin Rose would also arrive with stock and later take over Yeeda Station.[151] In 1881 the McLarty brothers, John and William G., followed Alexander Forrest's trekking route through Beagle Bay and attempted to land. Most of the sheep were lost on the trip. This property, owned by the Kimberley Pastoral Company, became Liveringa Station on Nyikina *country*.[152] As we have seen, the principal shareholders were the notable figures Alexander Forrest, William Marmion and Robert Sholl.

Two other firms associated with Julius Brockman and Alexander Richardson ignored the regulations contained in *The Waste Lands Unlawful Occupation Act 1872* and took sheep there. A Victorian pastoralist who would become notable in the early 1890s during the time of conflict around Jandamarra was William

Forrester of King Sound Pastoral Company's Lillamaloora Station;[153] he ventured to the district in 1883.[154] On these main early areas of colonisation of Warwa and Nyikina *country* the new arrivals lived in makeshift camps with stock under the control of Aboriginal shepherds.

Stations on the Meda River were established from 1882 when Marmion and Thomas Lavender's Meda River Pastoral Company was established.[155] In the same year William Lukin and J.H. Monger arrived with 1800 sheep for the Lennard River Station on Ungumi *country*. Most of the 4500 sheep they started with at Fremantle were lost, either on the way or when trying to land the sheep at Beagle Bay.[156] The area of pastoral occupation expanded from its 1884 limits on the lower Fitzroy, Meda and Lennard rivers to the area from Oobagooma on the northwest on Warwa *country* to Gogo (also known as Margaret Downs) on Gooniyandi *country* in the southwest to Jurgurra Creek in the south by the end of the decade. Further south lay the semidesert of the Great Sandy Desert. These limits on pastoral occupation or 'unlocking the land' were to remain virtually unchanged until the turn of the century.

The early land speculation ensured that much of the West Kimberley remained undeveloped until 1885. The two years after 1885 brought considerable change in the pace and extent of pastoral expansion in the Fitzroy district. Until this time speculative investors held large tracts of potential pastoral land. Many leases expired, as the land was never stocked in the allotted time and the leaseholds were forfeited, sold at auction and made available to other lessees.[157] From 1885 to 1887 Kimberley Pastoral Company had established more stock on the upper Liveringa, and in 1885 Solomon and Isadore Emanuel had established sheep on Noonkanbah Station on the border of Nyikina and Walmajarri *country*.[158] Cattle runs on Yawuru *country* were taken up around Broome by 1887 and complemented the pearling industry in that area. By 1886 there were eight station holders employing fifty-two Europeans in the West Kimberley.

In June 1886 one of the longest and largest droving expeditions in Australian history came to an end when Fossil Downs Station on Gooniyandi *country* was established. Commencing on the 26 March 1883 from Goulburn in New South Wales, Charles and William Neil MacDonald travelled 5600 kilometres with 'overlanding' beef cattle to establish the station which, at around 1 million acres, was then the largest privately owned cattle station in Australia.[159] This station was situated at the junction of the Victoria and Margaret rivers and became one of the most profitable pastoral concerns in the Fitzroy district. Typically on these enormous treks the organisers relied on small numbers of highly skilled Aboriginal stockmen to muster the stock. Cattle farming would eventually replace sheep farming as the major industry in the Kimberley as cattle were more amenable to the harsh pastoral conditions than sheep and required less attention. They also required less in the way of infrastructure, such as fencing and enclosed paddocks, which was difficult to establish in such a remote area. But cattle were also far more expensive to transport and significantly more valuable than sheep, especially the breeding stock, some of which were speared by Aboriginal people. Additionally, as we shall see, colonists also stole cattle. Cattle were also far more destructive of the vegetation and had a greater effect on native animals on which Aboriginal people relied.

John Forrest returned to the Kimberley and between 29 March and 11 May 1886 explored the Cambridge Gulf at the very north peak of the Kimberley on Yitji and Kadjerrong *country*. There he promoted proposals for new land regulations and founded the town of Wyndham in 1886.[160] The Legislative Council considered Forrest's amendments to the land regulations during mid-1886, and as a result the requirements for stocking were reduced by half.[161]

From 1887 to 1890 established companies such as Rose Brothers and Emanuel and Sons limited pastoral expansion along the upper Fitzroy River due to the Australia-wide economic depression. There were other failed attempts to develop stations, including two attempts made by Victorian companies to form sheep stations in the north Kimberley. In 1885 the Cambridge Downs Company introduced 3000 sheep on 20,234.5 square kilometres of the western side of the Cambridge Gulf. In late 1886 the settlement was abandoned due to poor management and because the sheep succumbed to heat and disease. The remaining sheep were sold to the Victoria Squatting Company.[162]

Solutions to the problems that stations suffered in the Kimberley were found partly in the amalgamation of pastoral interests. Alexander Forrest amalgamated with the brothers, Isadore and Sydney Emanuel, to become the largest pastoral holders in the West Kimberley. Bolton shows how, in 1893, of 14,080,000 acres leased in the entire Kimberley district, 4,376,000 acres were held under mortgage and all of it in the West Kimberley.[163] The period between 1890 and 1896 confirmed the shift to cattle production along with sheep, which was taken up on new land along the Lennard River and south towards the Edgar Range. Sheep were confined to a smaller area of land along the Fitzroy River and around Liveringa Station.[164]

It was not until the late 1890s that stations were established at Leopold Downs and Mount House in the area north of the Napier and King Leopold ranges. In 1898 Queenslander Frank Hann, with his Aboriginal assistant 'Talbot', located a passage through the King Leopold Ranges, which had previously formed a physical barrier to European expansion.[165] And on 9 May 1901 Frederick Drake-Brockman and a party of eleven men explored the last of the previously uncharted areas of the North Kimberley, subsequently recommending new stock routes.[166]

The West Kimberley was difficult to access by boat. Initially stock was imported from Cossack near Roebourne. Derby Port was constructed in 1885, although navigating through the islands of the Buccaneer Archipelago was exceptionally difficult. Steering ships required considerable skill not least because of the extraordinary tidal range exceeding 11 metres, which would leave many ships dry on the mudflats. At high tide rips and whirlpools also created enormous steering difficulties. Prior to the establishment of the port at Derby, wool bales for export were carted from the shore onto waiting boats. In one instance in mid-1883, noted by Bolton, all the wool bales waiting for pick-up were lost in a tsunami caused by the eruption of the volcano Krakatoa.[167]

The East Kimberley

New South Welshmen and Queenslanders made some of the first incursions into the East Kimberley to form pastoral stations. In late 1882 and early 1883 New South Wales born Michael 'M.P.' Durack explored the upper Ord River in the East Kimberley and established the Durack family pastoral empire, which continued for the next fifty years on Miriuwung, Doolboong and Gajirrawoong *country*.[168] In 1883 William O'Donnell and William Carr–Boyd explored under charter from the Cambridge Downs Pastoral Association.[169] The substantive difference between the East and West Kimberley districts was the stock. Nathaniel 'Nat' Buchanan introduced cattle into the East Kimberley. In June 1884 he 'overlanded' 4000 cattle from Queensland for J.A. Panton and W.H. Osmand and formed the Ord River Station on Kija and Malngin *country*.[170] In late 1884 Michael Durack and Tom Kilfoyle, who also drove cattle from Queensland, formed Lissadell Station and Patrick Durack formed Argyle Station, each with 2000 cattle (also both on Malngin and abutting Kija *country*). These settlements followed on from the establishment of cattle stations at Wave Hill, Victoria River Downs and Auvergne in the Northern Territory. Two years later Tom Hayes and J.J. Durack established Rosewood Station and Francis Connor, with Denis Doherty, established Newry Station in South Australia. Further north the Duracks established Ivanhoe Station and Carlton Hill Station on Miriuwung *country* in 1893. The Connor and Doherty company (storekeepers and packers) was established in 1893 and facilitated trade by acting as a shipping agent in the Kimberley.[171] Weeks and Stretch of Sturt Creek arrived in 1885.[172]

The main areas of European colonisation in the East Kimberley districts were along the Ord River valley. The district itself extended from the port town of Wyndham at the north of Western Australia, south along the corridor of the fertile Ord River valley and its many tributaries to around Halls Creek. The East Kimberley joined the West Kimberley district around the Durack Ranges and its eastern boundary was in and around what was then the South Australian border. Settlement patterns were affected by the existence of goldfields. Following on from a gold-seeking expedition by Phillip Saunders and Adam Johns in 1881 and a government-sponsored second expedition in 1883 by geologist Edward T. Hardman, gold was discovered in the Elvire valley in 1884. These events led to a rush of gold seekers from all over Australia involving an estimated 10,000 men.[173]

Halls Creek was named after one of the first prospectors, Charlie Hall, who discovered gold in 1885 in the heart of traditional Kija and Jaru *country* and right in the middle of trade routes between different groups. Miners and prospectors poured into the port of Derby on their way to the goldfields.[174] Geographically the enormous East Kimberley pastoral leases from Wyndham along the Ord River valley formed a pattern of boundaries over long-established Aboriginal land and language groups: the lands of the Miriuwung, Doolboong, Gajirrawoong, as well as the Kija right down to the Jaru. Their other activities traversed the entire area. The telegraph line from Wyndham to Halls Creek cut a line straight through the *country* of the Kija and Jaru people. The importance of this will be detailed in chapter 10.

Alexander Forrest

Alexander Forrest had a leading role in the acquisition and allocation of pastoral leases in the Kimberley and he deserves special attention for the scope of his influence. By late 1881 he had left his surveying work and had established an agency that specialised in Kimberley leases. Using his contacts in the eastern colonies Alexander Forrest met with Queensland speculators Patsy and Michael Durack and Solomon Emanuel.[175] He also met with Melbourne-based investors John Panton and George Poulton.[176] In 1882 Alexander Forrest, as an employee of the survey department, received a land grant of 5000 acres for his services in exploring the district in preparation for colonisation. On the expedition with his brother John in 1883, he conducted early negotiations with three pastoralist interests around Derby and the King Sound area in relation to the potential shipment and selling of stock.[177] Perhaps as a result of his near-death experiences in exploring the Kimberley, Forrest left the survey department but there may have been other reasons.[178]

Bolton suggests that Forrest found the conditions and subsequent restrictions on who could acquire land too onerous.[179]

Governor Robinson had issued instructions to the effect that public officers of the government were not allowed to purchase or lease any land without written approval and no survey department staff member was permitted to have any interest directly or indirectly in land for sale.[180] Forrest set up a business in Perth as 'consulting expert' and 'licensed surveyor' for prospective investors in the Kimberley. Placed advertisements in the Perth daily newspaper *The Inquirer,* detailing his '11 years' experience' in Crown land transactions and associated tasks that related to this business; he also emphasised his experience of the Kimberley.[181] Of the Aboriginal inhabitants of the Kimberley, Forrest suggested to the Duracks, according to Mary Durack, that 'I should think them decidedly less warlike, probably more backward, than the Queenslanders' with whom the Duracks were familiar.[182]

Alexander Forrest lent money to the cartel controlling the Kimberley Pastoral Company and purchased shares in both the company and one of the vessels that it used to ship sheep to the Kimberley. Forrest also acted as the Western Australian agent for Englishman James Aylward Game, who commenced his long-term acquisition of Kimberley land by purchasing Yeeda Station from Alexander Richardson and his associates. Alexander Forrest installed George Canlar Rose as the manager of the station, whom he knew as a family friend in the Australind district just south of Perth.[183]

Forrest acted as an 'agent of absentee' for many of the larger companies from the eastern colonies who were seeking larger lease holdings.[184] The degree of his influence is revealed by the fact that he actually selected the lands for many of the most prominent names of the Kimberley. He selected land for the Duracks and Emanuels, Osmand and Panton of Ord River Station, the MacDonalds of Fossil Downs Station and J.A. Game of Yeeda

Station.[185] As well as acquiring prime lands for these interests he acted as a shipping agent in the capital of the colony, Perth, and an intermediary for the sale of stock.[186] Alexander Forrest was also a consultant for the Duracks, the Emanuels, the MacDonald brothers, the Buchanans on behalf of Osmand and Panton, as well as many others who by 1883 had taken up in total over 51 million acres of Kimberley pastoral leasehold.[187] When cattle stock levels had reached a marketable point Alexander Forrest, as stock agent, sold some of Yeeda Station's cattle to the Perth market. This was the start of the West Kimberley cattle industry.[188]

The massive influx of individuals seeking their fortune saw the Western Australian government deem the Kimberley as a district that needed parliamentary representation in the Legislative Council. In 1887 Alexander Forrest was chosen as the inaugural member for the Kimberley district and he would later, when seeking re-election, boldly broadcast his influence in protecting voters in his Kimberley electorate from the 'depredations' of Aboriginal people.[189] In late 1887 Forrest, who was an ardent opponent of Federation, promoted protectionism for local interests in the parliament, and succeeded in moving for increases in the duties on imported meat, livestock, and grain, thus insulating local producers against competition from the eastern colonies. When responsible government was established in 1890 he represented West Kimberley in the Legislative Assembly.[190]

By 1907 when the pastoral expansion was complete critics remarked that monopoly interests had taken control of the finest portions of pastoral lands in the Kimberley and thus the Kimberley meat market.[191] Parliamentarians came under intense pressure for what many rightly saw as outrageous conflict of interest. The 'meat ring' as they were called, of just one hundred people, held an extraordinary 40 million acres of land. Allegations were made that among the principal lessees many 'were dummies for opulent plutocrats' to hide their true investment in the properties whilst shielding their name from public scrutiny.[192]

This chapter has served a dual purpose. It has set out the origins of policing in Western Australia, as a backdrop to discussion of Kimberley policing in the next chapter; the general shape of Aboriginal social organisation; and the process of discovery and colonisation of the area by European pastoral interests, to provide contexts for the development of pastoral politics in the Western Australian parliament and the subsequent history of the region. The pastoral industry was a high-risk economic and physical venture that the Western Australian government encouraged to promote growth in the colony. The establishment of the industry was on Aboriginal land and affected a people who, initially at least, were not hostile to the European presence. The next chapter begins a full-scale analysis of Kimberley policing.

Chapter 3

WEATHER HOT, FLIES TROUBLESOME...
Arrival

On 18 November 1881 the Superintendent of the Western Australian Police Force, Mathew Skinner Smith, wrote to the colonial secretary regarding the provision of police to what was then called the 'Fitzroy River district' in the West Kimberley. He wrote that 'the natives of that locality are numerous and inclined to be troublesome', but, significantly, he included the caveat that police were to uphold British law for all people and 'it is as necessary to make provision for protecting the blackman as the white'.[1] It was not until nearly a year later on 31 October 1882 that Smith invited thirty-one-year-old Lance Corporal Patrick Troy to head the Kimberley police force. If Troy took the appointment he would automatically become a sergeant. One sergeant and four constables would commence from 1 January 1883 with one sergeant and two constables stationed on the Fitzroy River and two constables at Beagle Bay (figure 3.1).[2] The sergeant, who would be responsible to the resident magistrate, would reside in the Fitzroy Station and have charge of the district: this was the early criminal justice system for the new district.[3]

This chapter examines the introduction of police to the Kimberley and the way their superiors perceived their role, particularly with regard to Aboriginal people on *country*. It explores the early interaction between Aboriginal people and the developing commercial industries. It examines the limits geography imposed and explores the social milieu in which police found themselves and the barriers this milieu put in the way of the kind of policing the superintendent imagined.

Figure 3.1. Patrick Troy (right) and unknown. Courtesy Don Pashley. Photographer and date unknown.

At the time of his appointment Patrick Troy was working as a lance corporal patrolling the Lyons River in the Gascoyne district some 1050 kilometres north of Perth. Such was the distance that the letter had to travel and the mode of delivery, by sea then horse and cart, that Troy did not receive the letter until 5 December 1882. Troy replied stating he would indeed like the job, and thanked the superintendent for 'giving him the substantial rise in the force'.[4] Directed to join Troy in establishing the Kimberley police force were police constables Edward Lemon, David Buckley, James Sherry, Wheatley Lee and Lance Corporal

Charles Payne. Payne was commissioned on a temporary basis until Troy's arrival.[5]

Establishment

The other officers who were to join Sergeant Troy in the Kimberley left on 4 April 1883 from Fremantle on the *Amur*.[6] On board was timber to build the Kimberley and Roebuck Bay police stations and a house for the government resident.[7] Also on board were four native assistants, eleven police horses, seven survey horses, twenty-three surveyors, sheep, the clerk W. Ord and the resident magistrate for the new district, R.M. Fairbairn.[8] The voyage, as described by LC Payne, took three weeks and the police reached King Sound and anchored near Mary Island on 26 April 1883.[9] Once lodgings and a rudimentary police camp were established in King Sound Station (later to move and become Derby Police Station), police commenced their duties on the *country* of the Warwa and Nyikina people. These involved patrolling the newly established police jurisdictions on 'town and station duty' and undertaking 'bush patrols' on the pastoral stations. LC Payne's first patrol from King Sound Station from 2 June 1883 encompassed the colonised districts of the Kimberley on the May and Meda rivers.[10] His report reveals that social changes within the Aboriginal groups were already occurring as many came to work on the new pastoral stations.

On these early bush patrols the police reported on the nature of the Aboriginal populations, stock numbers and the organisation of the station labour forces. LC Payne recorded that 'a native came to the camp who seemed very friendly'.[11] The man told Payne that his name was Jacob, a name he received from Mr Theo Lowe, one of William Lukin's workers on Lennard River Station on Warwa *country*. Jacob informed LC Payne that 'the natives around here were *Libe* (good) and those high up the river were *Meta Libe* (no good)'. Payne's party gave him food and he stayed at camp all night.[12] On the next day, 3 June, Payne visited Meda Pastoral Company's station on the May River which Mr Coucher managed. Payne recorded that there 'were 8 white persons and one half caste employed on this station'.[13] Payne was told they had 2900 sheep, which were very bad with the sheep disease 'scab'.[14]

They reported that 'they had only seen 8 natives since their arrival' and that 'they were armed with flint headed spears and came to them in a suspicious manner but when seen by them and ordered to lay down their spears they at once obeyed and shortly after went up the river'.[15] At this point Payne made the first official report about the character of the colonists. Payne noted that the seven 'whites' employed 'appear a lazy, dilatory lot of men and do not seem to look after their own interests'.[16] This practice of reporting on the character of the colonists would become a major cause of friction between police and the colonist population.

For the next few weeks Payne was joined by pastoralist George Poulton and patrolled and reported on several more stations including William Lukin's Lennard River Station. He reported stock suffering from poisoning from native grasses and getting diseases from other stations' stock.[17] The pastoralists reported to Payne that they had only seen a handful of 'bush blacks'.[18] He also stated that it was 'very rare to see a female native about the station'.[19] This is a critical point that was to have ramifications in later years. Later in his patrol Payne travelled along the Yeeda, Fitzroy and Minnie rivers.[20]

George Rose at Yeeda Station had about '25 Fitzroy Natives' and, in contrast to Lennard River Station, there were both males and females working for him. He saw at Egan's camp '4 male natives, 4 female natives and 2 children (male and female) all Fitzroy Natives'.[21] They were:

> all said to be very good at minding sheep more especially the females minding lambs. They appeared very friendly and happy. He asked them if they would Corroboree for them and they at once ornamented themselves with pelican feathers and commenced their various performances. The young men were very smart fine made men, the females were also well proportioned and tall. One he saw he considered measured 5ft 10 in height.[22]

George Rose informed Payne that about two or three weeks previously six sheep were stolen from 'Ward's flock on the Fitzroy River but he sought no police help with the theft'.[23] Payne thought that 'native dogs took them as they are very numerous in this district and will go into the flock in broad-daylight'.[24] Payne noted that 'the specimen of natives of the Fitzroy which he had seen and from what he had heard of their conduct that he considered that with good and kind treatment they would in the course of time become very useful to the settlers'.[25]

During the early 1880s the Western Australian government was blind to events in the 'outlying areas of settlement'. Very few people, including those who had purchased leaseholds, had even visited the Kimberley. As a consequence the government drew information from the few reports that were available, including those from explorers such as Alexander and John Forrest. It also had to rely on individual commissions whenever it wanted information about Aboriginal groups. Two notable examples were the *Fairbairn Commission*, 1882, and *The Commission to Inquire into the Treatment of Aboriginal Prisoners of the Crown,* 1884. In the first of these, Government Secretary and Resident Magistrate Fairbairn investigated pastoralists' complaints that Aboriginal groups were killing stock in the Gascoyne district just south of the Kimberley.[26] The second inquiry investigated the treatment of Aboriginal prisoners, including on Rottnest Island. John Forrest, now commissioner of Crown lands, chaired this commission which made a raft of recommendations for the support of Aboriginal people including the establishment of missions and, significantly, the creation of an unnamed 'board' that would be responsible for 'all matters' concerning Aboriginal people. It also recommended funds from the lease of lands 'originally possessed by its native inhabitants' be devoted to Aboriginal welfare.[27]

Police reports, which documented a diverse range of topics relating to European colonisation, would become one of the most valuable and up to date accounts of what was occurring in the Kimberley. They also formed a fundamental link with the imperial government. Police reports were published in *Votes and Proceedings of the Western Australian Parliament* and were often also published verbatim in Perth newspapers. They were both valuable sources of information on progress in the colony and the lens though which policing of the Kimberley was understood. These and other police reports revealed a lot more than social relationships. They discussed how Europeans adapted to the environment and the transplantation of British law. They revealed prevailing social and moral codes regarding individual behaviour and social mores. They narrated tales of social and environmental interaction in the late nineteenth century. The police were 'discovering' the land for themselves – the terrain, the heat, the conditions – and reporting their findings to their superiors. Reports like those of Patrick Troy (who also performed touring inspector roles termed 'special service') and to a lesser extent his younger brother, Sergeant

Richard Troy, were so detailed that the government regarded them highly.[28] Police provided similar reports on the new districts in the East Kimberley goldfields, where they often travelled over 560 kilometres.[29] They included details such as the best tracks to take, best land, where to find water, the attitude of the Aboriginal people whose *country* they were traversing and the treatment of Aboriginal people by colonists. Such details would be published in Perth newspapers for the benefit of those wishing to 'try their luck' in the new districts.[30] Additionally the Western Australian government used these reports to make decisions about expenditure and development.[31] The Aborigines Protection Board used Troy's reports in its official reports to the Western Australian Legislative Council.[32] In terms of policing Troy reported primarily not about police roles of 'maintaining law and order' but, rather, on the utility of the land in the Kimberley and the people inhabiting it. Police in this regard were positioned at the vanguard of reporting on the development potential of the district.

Patrick Troy Arrives

When Sergeant Troy arrived his first order from the superintendent was similar to that of LC Payne, to report on the 'status of settlement and report on the conditions of the natives'.[33] In his first report on 3 October 1883, after the trip – approaching the end of the dry season – he described how, with PC Lee and an unnamed native assistant, he left the newly established Derby Police Station (merely a tent at this stage) on horseback to travel to Roebuck Bay. Troy described how he travelled through Pindan (wooded country) full of 'coarse grass' and at 14 kilometres he passed a native well on the side of a dry swamp. He then found a 'nice swamp with lots of fresh water' and camped for the night. Here he found a group of thirty-four Aboriginal people camped, likely either Jukun or Yawuru. One man told Troy the group were called 'Mimikijarra'. Troy noted that 'they have twelve young children with them'. Troy said 'they seemed friendly enough we gave them some tobacco and a little damper with which they seem much pleased'.[34]

The following day they passed 'Nobby's Well' where they saw a couple of colonists working on well construction and several pastoralists from the newly established Kimberley Pastoral Company's Yeeda and Fraser River Country stations on Nyikina *country*. Troy travelled 32 kilometres that day and noted that there were 'splendid soils around'. On Sunday 9 September he reached the Fitzroy River. Here he saw George Riley who was in charge of a small flock of sheep belonging to Mr Daley. Troy noted that the sheep looked well and that Riley had said that the Aboriginal people gave 'no trouble'. Further on he saw a flock of sheep belonging to Yeeda Station under the charge of a 'Fitzroy Aborigine' called 'Lame Jimmy' with three 'bush natives' in his company.[35] By this he meant that station worker Lame Jimmy would have been with his extended family group still living on *country*.

On Monday he decided to travel slowly as the condition of the horses was 'very poor'. Troy observed the profusion of Kimberley wildlife. There were 'thousands' of pigeons here, he noted, so many that his native assistant shot seventeen with two shots. He wrote that the 'feathered tribe' were numerously and variously represented there: emus, native companions [brolgas], turkeys, ducks, pigeons, doves and other kinds.[36] PC Lee contracted a 'fainting illness', which was probably sunstroke and dehydration, and 'continued unwell' through the night. The only remedy Troy had to give him was a dose of fruit salt. The next day was very hot and they travelled about 34 kilometres. Troy observed that 'no natives had shown themselves', but as there were several bushfires about he thought there would be some in the neighborhood. There were numbers of what Troy thought were 'large vampire bats' there; Lee shot one with a wingspan of almost 1 metre. Fourteen emus came in to the water, but they were very shy. He noted that the 'weather was hot and flies were troublesome'.

On Saturday 15 September Troy wrote:

> We camped at the native well and just after doing so heard a native hail us, we answered him and four men came to us, one being a very old man whose hair was perfectly white. As none of our party could speak a word of their language, we could hold but very little communication with them, they made us understand they had seen Elliott and Cornish. We gave them enough flour to make a damper. And a couple of half sticks of tobacco with which they were very pleased and seemed to think we were very good fellows. I noted that these natives possess some sense of decency, each of them had their privates covered.[37]

With regard to the country they traversed on this trip Troy described it to the superintendent as 'abundantly grassed', though coarse, 'which would doubtless improve by stocking and burning'. In his opinion the country was very suitable for 'paddocking' and 'could not be surpassed for cattle'. Troy noted that the 'Pindan' was well grassed, had the 'advantage of shelter for stock and was similar to a good deal of the country that carried sheep in the southern districts of the colony'.[38] The main 'objection to settlement', Troy observed, would be the climate, which he feared would be 'rather trying' for Europeans. 'There has occurred already about 9 or 10 cases of fever and ague amongst a population of about 60 souls.'[39]

Troy's and Payne's narratives in these early records are revealing. They show that pastoralists were prepared to assist police in their daily duties. The nature of the relationship between pastoralists and the local Aboriginal groups was generally more curious than hostile. Police viewed and described Aboriginal people in terms of their utility to European colonisation and commercial development and not yet as problems related to law and order. Evidently there were so few pastoralists over such a vast country that even seeing any Aboriginal people was rare, although some worked on stations. LC Payne's belief that 'with good and kind treatment' Aboriginal people would become useful would become a critical issue.

In terms of their surveillance role police were required to furnish information about the population and 'habits and customs of the natives' to the government, but they were also directed locally by the government resident to inquire into how the pastoralists treated Aboriginal people. This role was the first of several which would turn the pastoralists against the police because it could result in pastoralists being charged with criminal offences. In August 1884 the Government Resident of the West Kimberley, Robert Fairbairn, sought this information and Sergeant Troy reported that there were no issues relating to mistreatment reported.[40] PC Lemon also investigated and reported back 'no complaints from the natives about anyone'.[41]

The historical record shows that Kimberley groups did not believe that the newcomers were there to stay permanently. Because there were so few pastoralists and only small numbers of stock arriving, and the rate of their arrival was staggered over many years and over such vast areas, the impact on Aboriginal people was neither immediate nor large scale. Traditional food sources were not initially threatened and stock was, for the most part, left alone. In the early period a cautious accommodation between the two cultures existed. The social structure of family and language groups and their districts would become apparent to police as the years progressed. However, in this early contact period, pastoralists had little knowledge or (possibly) desire to understand the people whose land they were on. Early contacts in the West Kimberley were marked by mutual ignorance and, as neither party could comprehend the other, they often resorted to gestures.[42] As the police role was primarily one of reporting rather than of prosecuting, Aboriginal groups were not yet fearful of them. Certainly, in these early days, there were no police procedures for the management of the Aboriginal populations, although police activities in late 1884 and early 1885 would soon involve arresting those Aboriginal people who absconded from their employment.

As the pastoral industry slowly became established a central policy issue was the question of who was responsible for the Aboriginal people whose land had been appropriated. Was it the pastoralists or the Western Australian government, which was drawing revenue from use of the land? Certainly the manner in which the Kimberley was colonised did not promote the welfare of Aboriginal people. They were perceived in accordance with prevailing notions of racial thought: their future was preordained. They were considered a 'dying, doomed race'.[43] As in other colonised areas of Western Australia, little provision was made for their way of life. The virtues of colonisation, or 'opening up the new country', were not open to debate and Aboriginal groups were expected to accommodate themselves to and integrate into a new way of life.

Aware of emerging reports of ill-treatment, religious orders sought to enter the district. A temporary Christian mission lead by Father Duncan McNab to evangelise, educate and train Aboriginal people in the Kimberley had been established on the Dampier Peninsula near Derby at Point Cunningham between 1884 and 1887. And with help from the outspoken humanitarian Bishop Mathew Gibney the first permanent Catholic mission was established in 1890 on government-granted land at Beagle Bay on Nyul Nyul *country* by Trappist monks from France. Bishop Gibney supported this concept and supplied funds along with small government grants.[44] Another Trappist mission was established, with help from Bishop Gibney, at Disaster Bay in King Sound in 1896, though this would close in 1905. However, overall the missions were underfunded and under-resourced to deal with such large populations and, as families were split up, would contribute to the breakdown of Aboriginal families. Other missions were established in the West Kimberley at Lombadina (1892) and Broome (1895). In 1899 Sydney Hadley established the non-denominational school at the Sunday Island Mission. In the East Kimberley the Protestant Forrest River Mission was established in 1896.[45]

Regulations outlined in imperial land legislation sought to protect Aboriginal people. The governor had powers to set aside Aboriginal reserves under the *Waste Land Act 1842* (Imperial) 'for the use or benefit of the Aboriginal inhabitants of the country' and this was restated in land regulations acts from 1872.[46] In the North West and Kimberley the size of the reserves were enormous, frequently over 1 million acres (about 4045 square kilometres).[47] In the late 1890s ideas were floated to house every Kimberley Aboriginal person on native reserves. According to an Aborigines Protection Board official this was considered impractical, because 'it would take years to collect them; when collected it would take a large staff to hold them; there would be interminable bloodshed with warring tribes in the same place'.[48] In practice the reserve system was a futile concept as it rested on the belief that Aboriginal people were wandering nomads who could, and would want to, move from their *country*. Pastoralists would also oppose large reserves for Aboriginal people in the Kimberley as they would then be outside their own control and the reserve land would no longer be available for use.

Aboriginal Labour

The intrusion of pastoralists brought Europeans into contact with numbers of Aboriginal people, many of whom came to work on their stations. Men and women would work in a variety of roles including shepherding, shearing, cleaning, winding and scouring wool, fencing, as teamsters (cart drivers), stock-hunting and drawing water. Women would also act as domestic helpers in the main station house. In the early period of European colonisation Aboriginal people were paid no wages but received what became 'standard issue' of a blanket and clothing in addition to a supply of limited rations: mutton or beef, perhaps from a 'killer' (stock killed for farm use), sometimes tea, flour and sugar, and a stick of tobacco a week. They would supplement this with traditional bush food.

In the Kimberley a good (and loyal) labour source was essential for a productive property. Indeed Aboriginal labour was essential to the establishment, running and survival of the pastoral and farming industries not only in the Kimberley but over all of Western Australia.[49] Colonists took up the land believing in their own moral and technological superiority. However, from the earliest period it is evident that colonists needed Aboriginal help for many reasons: to explore the lands colonists had claimed and to prevent them from getting lost; to help find water and food; and to work their properties. The use of convict labour was prohibited north of the Murchison district so Aboriginal labour was essential.[50] Colonists did not just want Aboriginal help, they absolutely needed it.

The way in which Aboriginal labour was utilised was not consistent across the Kimberley. Early pastoralists in the West Kimberley followed the tradition established on all pastoral stations up through the Gascoyne and Murchison districts, using the Aboriginal populations whose *country* they had claimed as a labour force. Often the entire workforce was Aboriginal. However, West Kimberley pastoralists employed up to ten times more workers than those in the East Kimberley, primarily because the open range method of stocking cattle practised by Queenslanders meant that less labour was required. Also East Kimberley pastoralists, especially in the early years of pastoral establishment, brought their own labour with them. The 1891 census notes 231 Aboriginal men and women employed in the West Kimberley and only thirty in the East. By 1901 the figures were 659.[51]

Due to the 'wet' and 'dry', work was predominantly seasonal. However, Aboriginal people did not stay on the stations all year around, rather they travelled in traditional seasonal patterns that often meant they were travelling during shearing. Aboriginal people who went on cultural business, known as 'pinkeye' (the Kimberley equivalent of 'walkabout'), were often punished for leaving their station.[52] Conversely Aboriginal workers were not required all year round and became an expense to the pastoralists when they stayed on their stations expecting to be fed. Certainly it is clear that once Aboriginal people had commenced work on a station some of them, not surprisingly, expected to stay.

The primary reason for using Aboriginal labour was financial. In fact it was widely understood that pastoralism in the North West and Kimberley could not have succeeded if owners had to pay for labour.[53] But Aboriginal labour was a sensitive issue. One particularly blunt observer suggested that 'the only reason natives were not improved off the face of the earth' or exterminated was because of the value of their labour.[54] Station owners only needed a certain number of Aboriginal people to run their stations. The remainder were simply not required and, in fact, created problems, often by their presence, as well as when they killed stock for food. In addition pastoralists would prefer Aboriginal people live as traditional a lifestyle as possible as this would not only largely absolve them of the expense of feeding them but also absolve them of responsibility for their welfare. Neither government nor pastoralists addressed the question: what would become of them?

Figure 3.2. 'Domestic staff, Derby, 1898'. Back row, left to right: Charlie, Jack, Paddy, Terry, Dubadub, Pompey, Spoof and Ike, Banjo, Lumpy; Front row: Rosie, Ouida, Fanny, Lilkie, Lulu, Button, Polly, Polly, Kitty, Lassie, Judy. Courtesy State Library of Western Australia, 026322PD. Photographer Walter Henry Snell Martin.

It took time but Aboriginal lifestyle, tradition, law and custom were profoundly changed after the arrival of Europeans. The extent of the changes depended on the extent that Aboriginal people accommodated or resisted the new arrivals. Some groups 'sat down' or willingly joined up as pastoral workers, some were drawn into station work as other family members joined up, but others resisted living a life that involved contact with the new arrivals.

However, the nature of the relationship between the pastoralists and the Aboriginal people was not a simple case of exploitation. For many Aboriginal people it was often a complex relationship and involved a significant spiritual and cultural element. Within the *Wurnan*, the system of exchange and sharing of resources, Aboriginal people tended to see pastoral bosses and their families as 'strange relatives', giving them a comparable status to non-local Aboriginal people, thus creating distant kin obligations and reciprocity, as well as rights and associations. Because they were still on their own *country*, Aboriginal station workers considered themselves to be the land owner and considered the white bosses as the land managers.[55]

The number of Aboriginal people officially employed by colonists on the early stations, as recorded by police in the district, was quite small. Of the eight stations that existed in 1884, only three employed any local Aboriginal people. Thomas Lavender, manager of Meda Station, employed four; George Rose, manager at Yeeda Station, employed four; while J.P. McLarty of Liveringa Station employed 'a good many of the natives of the district'. By the 1890s, however, as stock numbers massively increased, Aboriginal labour would become critical to the survival of stations.

As the stations were located on the *country* of the Aboriginal groups, extended families of station workers lived in 'blacks' camps' on the stations but away from the station homestead. People from these camps provided occasional additional labour and received rations to supplement traditional hunting and gathering.[56] The Aboriginal groups who did not join up as labour, who stayed on *country* and who generally kept out of the way of the new colonists and their livestock, were termed by colonists 'bush blacks'.

The migration from 'traditional' Aboriginal life to pastoral life with the associated social changes was to cause ruptures in Aboriginal social structures, yet these should not be overstated. In the historical record the categories 'bush blacks' and 'station blacks' were created by police and colonists, but there is an extensive oral history tradition recording the entry of Aboriginal people into station life which shows that those Aboriginal people who 'came in' as 'bush blacks' and became 'station blacks' retained many aspects of traditional culture including kinship relationships.[57] Tensions did develop between the Aboriginal people supplying their labour willingly and those who actively (and passively) resisted. Evidence indicates paybacks and murders occurred when Aboriginal people informed on each other for stock thefts, and this had ramifications throughout extended family groups. The following case provides an illustration.

Yeeda Station on Warwa *country* was the first place on which an Aboriginal man killed a colonist. This man was working as a station hand and was not a 'bush black'. On 12 December 1882, partner and shareholder in the station Anthony Cornish was killed by a man named Guerilla who was working with Cornish woodcutting or fencing. The killing was done with Cornish's own axe.[58] A man called Loffgut (in the employ of Rose at Yeeda Station) informed LC Payne that about four weeks previously while at Bung-arrow-gate on the Beagle Bay Road he was beaten with a large stick by natives 'Dabber Dab' and 'Bedab' because he assisted in the tracking and capture of Guerilla.[59]

Informally pastoralists in the Kimberley treated Aboriginal labour as a commodity, similar to land and stock to be bought and sold. William Lambden Owen, a warden in the Cossack district, described it in these terms:

How many acres? How many miles of fencing? How many niggers? The niggers always went as part of the stock. If there were no niggers, or not enough, the sale was off or the price was dropped. Many a squatter was a JP [Justice of the Peace], so he could sign on a neighbour's blacks.[60]

A significant problem for police was how to police these informal practices. Dr Walter Roth, who investigated Aboriginal labour in the Roth Report, called the principle that you did not employ another station owner's natives a 'code of honour'.[61] Similar arrangements existed in the pearling industry. When the pearling 'plant' was sold the Aboriginal people working the boats went with it; it was believed the boat would be worth three times as much when the Aboriginal pearl divers were included in the sale.[62] Diverse reports exist supporting the prevalence of this practice: John Cowan observed, 'The transfer of natives increases its price. There are abundant instances which must be known to the government authorities.'[63] Other sources corroborated these reports and added details of how station workers and pearl divers were branded 'on the fleshy part of their body' with a letter representing the station they 'belonged' to.[64] In the early period it was these unregulated and exploitative relationships in which Aboriginal people and their labour were viewed as a free commodity that caused friction between police and colonists. This perverse fiefdom in which the pastoralists believed they owned and controlled the Aboriginal people whose *country* they had colonised, would in many ways define social relations in the Kimberley pastoral industry.

In the early period of European colonisation of the Kimberley, Aboriginal people were not employed through any legally binding contracts. The Western Australian government attempted to legislate, and thus control, work conditions of the Kimberley through the use of the *Masters and Servants Act*. Absconding from pastoral service while under agreement or contract was a serious offence and police regularly issued warrants for offenders. Curiously, though most Aboriginal workers on stations were not employed under contract, police were still called on and, indeed, instructed to arrest absconders. This went on for the entire period under question but was simply illegal and represented no less than a system of involuntary indenture or a form of servitude. But what then was the role of police? While police were expected to protect colonists from Aboriginal people and, in effect, assist them, they were also to protect Aboriginal people from exploitation by colonists, and to prosecute any colonists caught ill-treating Aboriginal workers. This contradiction within police duties caused enormous confusion and anger among European colonists. Pastoralists often expected police to be at their bidding and not interfere with the operation of their stations.

Aboriginal workers were expected to work on stations and receive rations. If they absconded, pastoralists expected police to both arrest and return them to the station. However, when their work was done they were expected to go back to their *country*. The acting attorney general raised this point in parliament, suggesting that some employers signed up Aboriginal workers 'simply in order to have some hold upon them and to secure the services of the police to fetch them in when required'.[65] Police found themselves caught between enforcing the law and being pressured by pastoralists to do the pastoralists' own work for them.

The role of justices of the peace was pivotal in sentencing those considered cattle thieves and also in signing up Aboriginal workers. The *Masters and Servants Act* stipulated that an employee was liable to imprisonment with hard labour for breaking a labour contract, so after Aboriginal people were signed onto an agreement, which they often signed without knowing what it meant, they could be pursued and imprisoned if they left their employment or their station.[66] The 'unwritten rule of the north', that one 'did not employ another man's natives', meant that recaptured Aboriginal station workers were ordered by the local magistrate or station owners to return to their station and were punished, often severely.[67] Those who refused to return were labelled 'troublesome' and were often subject to ill-treatment.[68] Reflecting the ad hoc judicial system, many pastoralists were also justices of the peace who would adjudicate on cases involving their own workforce.[69] Punishment for other misdemeanours was harsh. Leslie Marchant refers to a case where Harry Whittall Venn, who was a member of the Legislative Council, branded an Aboriginal worker on the forehead with a letter 'T' for allegedly stealing from him.[70]

In many respects these informal social understandings far outweighed understanding or appreciation of colonial laws. When Sub Inspector Troy visited the lower Gascoyne regions in early 1889 to investigate allegations of cruelty towards Aboriginal people, he found that the practice of kidnapping Aboriginal people for pearling had ceased from the district.[71] The reason had more to do with prevailing custom towards Aboriginal people than with changes in the law regarding Aboriginal labour: the land from where Aboriginal people were being taken was now pastoral land and taking Aboriginal workers meant stealing another man's 'natives'. George Marsden discovered that it 'is considered a gross breach of "bush etiquette" even to order another man's boy [Aboriginal worker] to do anything for one except through one master, and I might mention that settlers are very jealous of anybody interfering with their boys'.[72]

Policing the Pearling Industry

During the early 1880s the police focus was not on the pastoral industry but rather on another critical commercial industry: the burgeoning and lucrative pearling industry. Aboriginal people along the West Kimberley coast collected the large and shining pearl shell for use in rituals and ceremonies and it was the most widely distributed item in Aboriginal Australia, traded across two-thirds of the continent as well as with colonists for rations and goods.[73] With the arrival of European pearlers, both male and female Aboriginal people were utilised by pearlers to obtain pearl shells, as their skills in diving to great depths were renowned.

Official government records show that as many as 549 Aboriginal people were officially employed on pearling vessels at the peak of the industry in 1884.[74] Unofficially the numbers would have been much larger, with many workers not registered or employed under contract. Evidence exists that some of these workers, who were described as 'little boys' as young as ten years old, had been indentured to pearlers. None were paid wages.[75]

Pearling was a very large and profitable industry, made more profitable by free Aboriginal labour. Europeans 'recruited' Aboriginal divers around the towns of Broome and Cossack. The way these workers were recruited provoked conflict between Aboriginal people and pearlers as well as police and pearlers because it involved kidnapping Aboriginal people, in a practice that was carried out all over Australia and was known as 'native hunting', 'nigger-driving' or 'blackbirding'.[76] Certain pastoralists in the West Kimberley assisted this illegal practice by keeping the Aboriginal people on their station until they were 'picked up' by pearlers. That Aboriginal people were often not from coastal areas and could not swim appeared immaterial to the blackbirders.[77] Police were required to investigate allegations of kidnapping as part of their duties.

The history of blackbirding goes back well before the official colonisation of the Kimberley and efforts to police the practice reveal the limits of police authority. During the 1860s and 1870s, as the pearling industry spread north from Exmouth Gulf to the Kimberley around Cossack, Broome and Beagle Bay, there were attempts to legislate and control illegal labour practices such as blackbirding.[78] In 1871 Governor Weld introduced the *Pearl Shell Fisheries Act* and associated regulations concerning the legal hiring of Aboriginal divers and prohibiting the use of Aboriginal women as divers.[79] However, due to the distance from Perth and the lack of local authorities overseeing employment they were effectively ignored. This shows how fundamentally weak and unenforceable the legislation was. There were also those holding government positions that had vested interests in the industry. The Government Resident and Chief Magistrate of Roebourne, Robert Sholl, was directly involved in the lucrative pearling industry with his two sons.[80] In a police report on conditions in the North West in 1873 Sub Inspector Piesse reported to Governor Weld on a litany of illegal and corrupt behaviour. 'The natives fear Mr Sholl will put them in prison if they refuse to serve his sons who are pearlers... native men and women are kidnapped...and practically taken into slavery'.[81] Piesse corroborated earlier reports that Aboriginal divers were traded and increased the value of the sale of a boat. Additionally if they tried to escape 'they would be shot'. Piesse could not get sufficient evidence to prosecute because 'the whites will not give evidence against each other'. Governor Weld reported that Sholl's abuse of his position and authority was 'a disgrace to the British name'.[82]

From 1873 to 1880 further legislation was enacted and in 1881 an inspector of pearl shell fisheries was appointed to see that regulations were followed.[83] These legislative changes had minimal effect as reports of abuses in the Kimberley continued well into the late 1880s.[84] Much of this legislation, which by now was well over ten years old, continued to be ignored, as it was difficult to enforce, and blackbirding continued without any attempt to disguise it. Indeed some of the people involved in the practice were members of the Western Australian parliament. In one of the first police reports of the time, LC Payne reported that a notorious blackbirder from Cossack by the name of Thomas Mountain was coming to the West Kimberley in the employ of William Marmion's company. Marmion was a member of the Legislative Council representing Fremantle. Mountain was well known as a professional blackbirder and, along with two other men called Sharp and Alfred Rouse, had allegedly 'publicly advertised to procure and put niggers aboard at £5 a head for anybody or shoot them for the government for half a crown a piece'.[85]

Payne noted 'for the record' that watch would be kept on Mountain's movements.[86] He gathered other evidence from local Aboriginal men that pearlers from Cossack had been coming to the Fitzroy and Meda rivers, kidnapping the Aboriginal people and chaining them by the neck until they got them to the port.[87] Payne finalised his report by stating that as soon as any pearlers were known to be in the district a strict watch and inquiry would be kept on their movements.[88] Critically for relations between police and colonists, this new police force and its investigations interfered with blackbirding. Police were not only taking evidence from Aboriginal people but also actively defending them. One result of this was that those involved in or associated with blackbirding would give the police little or no information. LC Payne noted that the pearlers 'were very careful not to inform the police of any more than they are compelled'.[89]

The evidence of blackbirding, systematic kidnapping, coercion, cruelty and murder on the pearling fields was vast.[90] Police took evidence from Aboriginal witnesses, although it was evident that they could do little more than report it happening. Payne noted the 'natives stated that they do not like pearling because the whites treat them so badly'.[91] On one patrol PC Lemon's party had met with a white man at Julius Brockman's old house, Beagle Bay, named Charles Clifford. Clifford had been charged the previous year with the manslaughter of an Aboriginal man by the name of Thackabiddy at Gascoyne. He was found not guilty of this charge despite the victim having been 'chained to a horse and dragged for a mile'.[92]

Later police patrols confirmed allegations that pastoralists both kidnapped and cooperated with pearlers who kidnapped Aboriginal people. Sergeant Troy reported that John Pollard and J.P. McLarty of the Emanuel-owned Kimberley Pastoral Company station Liveringa participated in kidnapping expeditions with Captain Tuckey of the schooner *Argo* by collecting groups of Aboriginal people 'from the bush' and keeping them at his station until the pearlers collected them.[93] McLarty was the brother of Edward McLarty, landowner, justice of the peace and member of the Legislative Council in the 1890s.[94] On 8 November 1884, over a year after the first patrol occurred, PCs Lemon and Buckley and Native Assistant Charley patrolled the Fitzroy River investigating J.P. McLarty and the very same blackbirder's troupe.[95] Lemon's party 'came upon a lot of natives who were in the river but could not get down to them'. After some time he induced four of the group to come up to them. 'They were very frightened', Lemon wrote. He asked them why they were afraid and they answered that 'white men were no good'.[96] They also told him that a lot of other Aboriginal people had run away frightened, thinking we were 'Yandegeburra (boat) white fellows'.[97] Later that year PC Sherry, with PC Adlam and Native Assistant George, reported that whilst out collecting returns of pastoralists and stock on the Fitzroy River and Yeeda stations they came across thirteen Aboriginal people who had fled the ship *Argo*. They said they ran away because 'they did not get enough to eat' and were forced to go up the rigging and remain there nearly all the night as punishment for not getting enough shell.[98]

It is very clear that the activities and practices of the black-birders were the origins of later conflicts between Aboriginal people and colonists. A Derby correspondent to *The West Australian* newspaper reported in August 1885:

> The resistance offered was due in a great measure to the action of the pearlers. When they wanted to get natives for pearling, before the diving dresses became general, or wished to get ashore for water and thought the natives hostile, they used to fire their guns over their heads to frighten them. This instead of having the desired effect, made the natives think that the white men were aiming at them but were such bad shots that they could never hit one, and hence they began to regard the 'white fellow' as a rather despicable foe.[99]

Some local colonists also supported the claims made by police. David Carley, who arrived in Roebourne in 1872 and worked on the coast at LaGrange Bay in the Kimberley, made many public allegations of cruelty of Aboriginal people in the North West. Carley had reported the notorious Flying Foam massacre of between February and May 1868 at Nickol Bay in the North West where he claimed local pastoralists John Withnell and Alex McRae led a party each, authorised by Resident Magistrate Robert Sholl, with the result being 'sixty natives, men, women and children shot dead'.[100] This was following the killing of PC Griffis and his native assistant and two colonists by local Yaburara people. Griffis was speared for allegedly abducting and raping a local Aboriginal woman.[101]

Carley agitated from 1872 until the 1880s to local magistrates in Roebourne and in Perth and enraged local and Perth authorities by writing directly to the secretary of state.[102] His allegations of slavery in the North West were publicised widely and reported on in inflammatory terms to the point where it was suggested that the 'North-West coast of Western Australia is steeped to its neck with murder, rapine and slavery'.[103] Carley's reputation was impugned and his evidence questioned because he was an ex-prisoner.[104] However, his cause was taken up by the London Aboriginal Protection Society and was discussed in the House of Commons.[105] Locally the Methodist Reverend John Gribble, who in 1885 had established a mission on the Gascoyne River, supported and reported his claims and suggested actions that would, as shall be shown, have significant ramifications for the colony.[106]

For other Roebourne colonists, such as 'Bengallee' who commented publicly on affairs (albeit under a pseudonym), harsh treatment of Aboriginal people was fully justified, though it was couched in terms of expediency. While the allegations of slavery made by Gribble were 'amusing', 'ridiculous nonsense' of the 'insane ravings of the Gascoyne missionary', it was quite appropriate for 'a few niggers to be chained to wheelbarrows' to work.[107] 'Let anyone try to keep a nigger', the writer stated, without them being secured in some way, 'especially on or near his own country', and they would leave.[108]

In 1886 LC Payne returned to Roebourne where he attempted to prosecute European pearlers for illegal activities. The new Government Resident, Colonel Edward Angelo, was 'appalled by the system of organized slavery in the north' and supported him. In one case Payne charged John Wells with killing an Aboriginal man, 'Charlie'. Unfortunately he came up against impossible obstacles. Despite having six witnesses who could corroborate his evidence that John Wells and the owner of the pearling boat *Dawn*, Duncan McRae, 'beat Charlie all day [on the head] with a rope' and 'forced him to stay up on the rigging if he got less than 10 or 12 shell', they could not sustain the prosecution against the opposition of the local justices of the peace hearing it, who were involved in the pearling industry.[109] Payne reported that the Aboriginal witness gave both pearlers 'a very bad name' for cruelty and said that 'very little reliance can be placed on [the pearlers'] defence testimony'.[110] Payne's exasperation shows in his report. 'I would also beg to submit that this case be tried at Perth as justice can never be got here the whole of the justices being against Col Angelo GR [Government Resident] and all of them being more or less interested in pearl fishing.'[111] In later reports in December 1886 Payne reiterated his observations.

It is almost impossible to get any white evidence in these cases. The feeling being so strong against the police for taking any steps against the pearlers in favour of the natives. And if any justices sit with the government resident it is impossible to get a conviction as all the honorary justices are very deeply interested in the pearling and native question. I would be very grateful for some instruction in the matter. In the mean time I will use every endeavour to get any further evidence in the matter.[112]

Soon afterwards Angelo was removed from his office for what Robert Sholl described as overzealousness and 'ill-advised fussiness' towards Aboriginal people.[113] Payne's complaints were important well beyond the apparent corruption of the legal process. Police who would later investigate stock losses in the Kimberley were the very same police who had observed Europeans such as J.P. McLarty engage in 'blackbirding', but could neither arrest nor prosecute them. These limits on police power meant their authority and thus effectiveness was severely compromised.

In 1888 Payne would return to the East Kimberley district as a sergeant. At this point it became clear that the inability of police to effectively prosecute criminal cases against pastoralists was severely affecting morale and therefore the desire to use police powers. In late 1888 at Goose Hill in the East Kimberley, PC Graham informed Sergeant Richard Troy that Aboriginal people had been murdered by colonists who were out with the police and that nothing was ever said about it. According to Graham, when he reported this matter to Sergeant Payne, he was told 'they had better keep it quiet as there would only be a row about it if it was known', and advised him not to report these Aboriginal deaths. It was, he suggested, often better to do nothing than be seen to be ineffective and that alerting authorities to the killings would only complicate matters in their locality.[114] Evidence such as this suggests these colonial police who attempted to uphold British law on the Kimberley frontier often did little more than make their own life extremely difficult. How do we explain this?

The police in these districts were dependent on pastoralists not only for social acceptance and approval but also for rudimentary and essential items such as food and water. If police on bush patrol did not do what many pastoralists wanted they would not receive food and assistance. It appears that it often became easier for police to 'turn a blind eye' to illegal activity than investigate it. It also appears that ignoring these events prevented animosities between the colonists and police. The fact that Aboriginal people had 'no voice', their evidence was rarely utilised and they could rarely defend themselves in a court contributed to this situation.

The preceding summary reveals some severe limits to police authority. While there were police enquiries into blackbirding and ample evidence that it took place, no men were arrested or even prevented from engaging in this practice. Many European men whom the police identified as engaging in illegal behaviour were also the men who ran many of the pastoral stations in the early period of the West Kimberley. Police had nothing to gain by arresting any of the few Europeans in the district when that could turn the whole community against them. Typically police documented the transition from an unpoliced to a policed society in Western Australia. That, in the early years of the opening of the Kimberley, they watched and reported rather than punished is typical of the history of Western Australian policing as European colonisation expanded into new territories. Soon, however, the police role changed to protecting commercial interests and criminalising Aboriginal activities.

The Aborigines Protection Act 1886

One of the consequences of the flow of information about the Kimberley was a significant piece of early legislation: the *Aborigines Protection Act 1886*. The debates around this act reveal tensions between the colony of Western Australia, which was seeking independence from Britain, and the British government, which sought to protect Aboriginal people. This Act was necessary as the treatment of Aboriginal people was one of the key obstacles to Western Australia attaining responsible government, and it was intended to act as a buffer between the colonists of Western Australia and British philanthropists known derisively locally as the 'Exeter Hall types'.[115] There was a wide gulf between how the imperial office thought Aboriginal people should be treated and how the fiercely parochial and defensive Western Australian government saw it.

During this period there was a distinct British foreign policy towards native or indigenous people of the British Empire that was informed by being signatory (along with fifteen other nations) to an Act that sought to regulate the colonisation of Africa. In early 1885 this Act was signed at a meeting known generally as the Berlin Conference. The Act included Article 6 that guaranteed that colonising countries 'bind themselves to watch over the preservation of the native tribes, and to care for the improvement of the conditions of their moral and material well-being, and to help in suppressing slavery, and especially the slave trade'.[116]

Between 1886 and 1888, when negotiations to establish responsible government in Western Australia were taking place, the British colonial office insisted that the administration and control of Aboriginal people remain vested with the governor. The British government was suspicious that its 'black subjects' were not being treated fairly.[117] The government in Perth needed to show that Aboriginal people were not being abused and exploited, particularly in light of the controversy surrounding David Carley's allegations from the 1870s and new allegations by Reverend John Gribble. Gribble's allegations of mistreatment of Aboriginal people and the taking of Aboriginal women for 'immoral purposes' by white colonists was published in 1886 in London as *Dark Deeds in a Sunny Land, or, Blacks and Whites in North-West Australia*, and circulated widely in newspapers in Australia and in London, generating, as Sue Hunt shows, 'a tone bordering on hysteria by the Perth community'.[118] Gribble's allegations were so inflammatory that he was ridiculed and mocked in Perth newspapers; a petition for his removal was circulated; and he was assaulted and threatened with death by 'hanging, drowning or shooting' for daring to interfere with 'their natives'.[119] In mid-1887 Gribble, attempted to sue *The West Australian* for libel after the paper called him 'without exaggeration' a 'lying, canting humbug' and accused him of making Western Australia 'notorious' for his comments on colonists in the North West.[120] Gribble lost the case with Chief Justice Brown stating that the defendants, represented by solicitor Richard Septimus 'R.S.' Haynes, 'were fully justified in using the epithets complained of'.[121] That Gribble was a t'othersider from New South Wales and had the temerity to comment on Western Australian affairs only added to the outrage and he was subsequently removed from his posting. Tellingly, Septimus Burt, who was then acting Attorney General, refused to act in defence of Gribble and almost nothing was done to investigate his claims.[122] Haynes, on the other hand, became outspoken on Aboriginal welfare issues in Perth and would, as shall be shown, make public claims of large-scale killings of Aboriginal people.[123] Finally, revealing the disturbing and malicious extent of the social ostracisation of Gribble was the magnitude of what was called 'black-balling.' John Gribble's wife later reported such was the contempt with which Gribble was held when their three-year son became gravely ill with 'convulsions' no local doctor would treat the boy because 'it was our child' and the boy subsequently died.[124]

From 1 January 1886, following the advice of a British select committee, the administration of Aboriginal affairs was removed from the Western Australian colonial secretary and delegated to the Aborigines Protection Board as a statutory authority under control of the governor.[125] This issue around the governance of the Board being out of colonial control would reverberate well into the next decade. In addition the state treasury was to fund the Aborigines Protection Board the figure of £5000 (or 1% of gross revenue should revenue exceed £500,000 per annum) annually towards the welfare of the Aboriginal population. The intent was to guarantee funds to supply food and clothing to Aboriginal people and to promote the education of Aboriginal children.[126] The *Aborigines Protection Act 1886* was the first of a series of Acts that were designed to 'protect' Aboriginal people from the worst excesses of colonisation and to give legal protection from physical and economic abuse. Police officers were to become an integral part of this apparatus. In the course of their duty they were now legally required to act as protectors and inspectors for the Aborigines Protection Board and other agencies if and when the need arose. They were also responsible for distributing rations. In 1897, for example, the police distributed rations to 611 'sick and infirm' Aboriginal people, 2192 blankets and 3896 'gifts'.[127]

The Aborigines Protection Board consisted of five members and a secretary, all of whom were nominated by the governor without the advice or consent of the Western Australian Executive Council.[128] John Forrest was appointed to the Board in April

1890 although there is no record of his attendance.[129] The Board oversaw the activities of protectors who were empowered to institute court proceedings and to enforce judgments for or on behalf of any Aboriginal person. The Board did not have any staff to begin with, and in practice the role of 'protectors' fell to justices of the peace, ministers of religion, resident magistrates and police. Section 36 of the Act related to the creation of the protector of Aborigines. It allowed for resident magistrates to make any 'Aboriginal or part-Aboriginal child' an indentured servant or 'apprentice', and legalised the 'detention and custody of Aboriginal Native Prisoners beyond the limits of a common gaol'.[130] Under the Act contracts between workers and their bosses had to be in a prescribed format to show the age of the employee, the nature of work to be performed, the period and payment. By 1892 the Aborigines Protection Board had appointed one paid full-time protector, and by 1896 one of three full-time protectors was stationed in the Kimberley.[131] Aboriginal protectors who worked in the Kimberley were firstly C.M. Straker, then George Marsden and C.A. Bailey for the east goldfields region.

Protectors who were not full-time employees of the Board were not paid for their work and it is clear they did not relish the position. More concerning was the fact that some individuals who were appointed protectors were the very people accused of murder and ill-treatment of Aboriginal people.[132] The powers of protectors were limited, which rendered them all but ineffective, although, critically, most protectors did have the power to report what was going on in the Kimberley, so provided an alternative to the police reports the Board had hitherto used.[133]

The Aborigines Protection Board was widely detested by the colonial community because it represented interference by Britain in Western Australian affairs, but in the Kimberley pastoralists believed that it also interfered in commercial operations, particularly regarding the control and treatment of Aboriginal labour. George Marsden noted with some understatement that 'the Aboriginal Protection Board is not popular amongst the settlers in the Kimberley District'.[134]

'Up in the North Men Kept their Mouths Shut'

As shown earlier, in 1886 LC Payne found it 'almost impossible to get white evidence' of crimes against Aboriginal people and could not get written statements from colonists. Some nineteen years later, Corporal Goodridge reported a similar situation in the 1905 Roth Royal Commission:

> There is a sort of Freemasonry among bush people and it is impossible to get written statements from them, as one of the station managers said to me that they might as well leave the district at once if they gave a white man away [report a murder] as there [sic] horses and cattle would be turned adrift and things made very unpleasant for them generally.[135]

In the Kimberley, relationships developed between colonists that could be termed 'bush agreements' or simply 'understandings'. These were frontier 'covenants' between the white colonists that arose out of the nature of the contact between Europeans and Aboriginal people. Whilst the deliberate killing (including shooting, poisoning and burning) of Aboriginal people was illegal, it was accepted within sections of the European colonist community in the Kimberley, and most northern frontiers across the border and into Queensland, from the time of first colonisation apparently right up until the 1920s and possibly later.[136]

It is clear that many if not most Kimberley colonists regarded the Kimberley as so isolated, the small police forces as so ineffectual and the laws as they stood so unsuitable that they not only felt free to take the law into their own hands but felt justified in doing so. As shall be shown there were many notable massacres and punitive expeditions in the Kimberley region in the time leading up to and within the period under study. Earlier massacres recorded in the North West, such as the aforementioned Flying Foam massacre at Nickol Bay in 1868, reveal these incidents as not just single events but having occurred over weeks or months.[137] Historian Peter Gifford has described how the punitive party 'harried the Yaburara mercilessly, killing indiscriminately for weeks on end until the Resident Magistrate who had licensed this retribution, Robert John Sholl, now sickened by it, put an end to it'.[138]

Colonists engaged in these activities avoided investigation, learning from previous legal cases where individuals had been prosecuted for crimes against Aboriginal people. Between 1829 and 1886 Western Australia had sought to prosecute more colonists for crimes against Aboriginal people than any other Australian colony.[139] Colonists would not write anything down that might incriminate themselves or others, and would make sure the event was not reported. There is, however, a body of literature that confirms these events and corroborates Aboriginal oral history accounts. Richard Allen, a Kimberley pioneer, wrote in his reminiscences:

> Hundreds of men, women and even children were shot down in this period. Where once natives roamed in hundreds only 40 odd years ago, hardly any survive, and you can ride in these ranges for days and never see a sign of natives let alone tracks.[140]

Another Kimberley local, in describing the West Kimberley 'river tribes', stated that 'one man with a reliable revolver on a good horse could disperse a whole tribe as long as it was light'.[141] Other commentators referred to the type of 'cut-throat' men for whom the 'taking of a nigger's life was of no more consequence than the drowning of a superfluous kitten'.[142] Another stockman, Keith Willey wrote: 'Most blacks were fairly docile and when they did become cranky a belt over the ear was usually enough to settle them down. I never found it necessary to shoot any of them; though others did.'[143]

Typically allusion abounds in the description of killings. Clearly the writers had no wish to incriminate themselves or others in murder. As shall be shown in chapter 6, telling police or any investigating authority that killing Aboriginal people was an act of self-defence was enough to prevent further enquiries. European historical accounts of hostile interactions, which included killings, are often written up with euphemisms such as 'a run-in' or 'fell-upon' groups of Aboriginal people. The use of the euphemism 'dispersal' also implied killings. 'Dispersals' have been part of the European cultural lexicon in Australia since 1788. Theoretically dispersal meant the physical breaking up of groups considered hostile so that they would no longer be a danger. In practice 'dispersal' included killings on a very large scale and over a long period of time. Western Australian police authorities referred to not only 'dispersals' but also as 'giving a punishment' or 'teaching a lesson' as if they were normal and acceptable instructions to a civil police force. That this was occurring was an open secret in the highest echelons of the Western Australian government. Officials from the Aborigines Protection Board wrote about it in these terms:

It is strange that if a tribe in India or Africa is trouble-some an expedition is organised and the natives are 'taught a lesson'. If individuals are troublesome here (for there are no tribes) he is 'taught a lesson', it is murder but it is called 'dispersing the natives.'[144]

The code of silence that precluded police from prosecuting crimes against perpetrators was widespread across the Kimberley. Gordon Broughton, a young Sydney man who tried his luck as a stockman in the Kimberley, described the bond between male European colonists, the 'mateship', as a form of 'bush masonry'. As some of the few white men in a vast expanse of country, the 'ties that bound them' became very strong.[145] These men were usually there on their own, without women or wives, and were there to make money rather than 'make a home'. Broughton stated:

The basic philosophy of men living in the Kimberley was that the cattlemen had battled their way into the empty land with great hardship and at high cost in lives and money; that they were here to stay and if the wild blacks got in the way – in other words speared men or killed and harassed cattle – they would relentlessly be shot down. It was as simple and brutal as that.[146]

Broughton regarded most colonists as 'good men' but knew others who 'would shoot a black man as readily as they would shoot a black snake, for no other reason than he was a 'bloody *munjung*' (wild man)'.[147] Broughton noted the attitude to Aboriginal people:

Native life was held cheap, and a freemasonry of silence among the white men, including often the bush police, helped keep it that way. In far off Perth, clerics and various 'protection' societies tried to get at the truth of stories of native killings, sometimes spilled by a drunken bushman on a spree in the city, but up in the north men kept their mouths shut.[148]

Donald Swan described the Kimberley 'bushman's code of honour' on shootings in punitive expeditions thus: 'Either stand in with the mob and keep your mouth shut or refuse to stand in and also keep your mouth shut. In either case you will be respected and no more will be required of you in the matter.'[149] In this statement there is the suggestion that a colonist could be killed for reporting or 'opening his mouth'.[150] Another illuminating example was explorer Aeneas Gunn's observation that: 'It is considered a breach of northern etiquette to ask a man whether or not he shot a blackfellow or not.'[151] This is revealing, both in the sense that it was deemed acceptable, but also that it was considered bad manners to talk about it.

Europeans developed several ways to justify this position. A.R. Richardson, Member for De Grey (and owner of Yeeda Station), likened the shooting of Aboriginal people to war. In defending the actions of colonists engaged in the Flying Foam massacre, he said they were:

as justified in obeying orders as British soldiers when they shot at either Kaffirs, Zulus, Abyssinians, or any other inferior race, and for which they are frequently decorated with medals, iron crosses etc and their names sounded forth as heroes and brave soldiers, the pride of the nation. There was nothing in the nature of 'massacre'.[152]

They also believed that if the government was not going to protect them then they would protect themselves. Gordon Buchanan, son of 'Nat' Buchanan, wrote of frontier justice after a killing: 'They held their own inquest. In those days there were no police within three hundred miles [483 kilometres]. Every man was his own policeman: and the letter of the law was often ignored in favour of summary justice.'[153] He went on to justify his actions by admitting that, although these killings occurred, the treatment of Aboriginal people 'compared favourably with white methods all over the world. Imprisonment for cattle killing was quite impracticable and if no punishment was inflicted it would have been impossible to settle the country.'[154] Thus, killings were justified in the name of British colonialism.

Isolation and what Buchanan called being 'removed from the restraint of formal law' allowed men to engage in any activity that was conducive to claiming the land.[155] That they were the only white men in a hostile land and amongst a hostile people was a justification for killing as self-defence. And that the people thousands of miles away did not understand or sympathise with their plight was a further reason to keep events silent. Jim Durack, brother of Big John, wrote a poem summing up this 'northerners perspective' justifying the killings and damning the 'southerners' for not understanding them after his brother was killed.[156] Of course, not all Europeans were involved in the killings but those who were not, as shall be shown in subsequent chapters, would, in much the same way as Reverend John Gribble, be shunned, 'black-balled', threatened or worse for reporting ill-treatment and killings of Aboriginal people. Thus, the code of silence was maintained.

Cattle Duffing

There is a well-known inscription on a Boab tree on the banks of the Ord River. It was done by Jim Patterson, manager of the large Ord River Station from 1910 to 1914:

> Oh heavenly father if you please,
> We pray to thee on bended knees
> That thou and Thy Dear son, Our Lord,
> Will keep the 'Cockies' off the Ord.
> O Paralyse the duffer's hand
> When he lifts up his flaming brand;
> Keep poddy-dodgers from the glen
> For Jesus Christ sake, Amen.
> Now Oh God, forgive our sins,
> And may every cow on Ord have twins.[157]

This poem is an ode to a very common issue in the Kimberley: cattle theft. A question that must be asked is where did the smaller scale pastoralists get their stock from?[158] Lacking the money or resources of the 'bigger' pastoral companies to ship the stock from Perth or Darwin required to start a station, many duffers (also known as 'poddy dodgers') resorted to stealing or cattle duffing from the larger firms.[159] The historical record is largely silent on the extent of cattle duffing contributing to overall stock losses in the Kimberley but these losses would have been enormous. One observer noted a 'leading Kimberley grazier told me that the cattle-duffing by unscrupulous whites caused him far more losses than the depredations of the niggers'.[160] Another man named only as 'H.T.H.' (Hely-Hutchinson), who overlanded cattle to Lissadell Station, stated that the crime was so prevalent that the 'two principal industries on the East Kimberley side are cattle rearing and cattle duffing'.[161] As will be shown in chapter 10, up to six stations around the Ord River, where cattle losses were blamed solely on Aboriginal people, were said to have been established by cattle duffers.[162]

Cattle duffing went on in both the West and East Kimberley, though perhaps more so in the East. From as few as one hundred to 300 cattle 'duffed', a herd of 3000 to 7000 could be developed within 'a few years'.[163] Often the duffer was an employee of the larger stations who then might sell the cattle back to the very pastoralist from whom he had stolen them.[164] Some large-scale Kimberley cattle duffers, such as Ben Bridge who was cattle duffing for over seven years in the 1890s, became quite notorious.[165] However, overall it was very difficult if not impossible to stop or to police the practice. H.T.H. reported a conversation with an unnamed representative of one of the 'largest firms' in the East Kimberley as to why cattle duffers were rarely arrested:

'What is the use?' replied the squatter. 'The first thing is to catch the thief, and even when that is done — and it is a most difficult thing to do — you cannot find a jury to convict him; and, then, again, the law for the prevention of cattle stealing is all in favour of the thief; in fact, one would think the law had been framed by men given to duffing their neighbour's cattle.'[166]

But why was policing this so difficult? It was probably for a variety of reasons. Ironically perhaps, it was the peer pressure of men not reporting on other 'fellow men', least of all to police. Men in the 'north' simply did not incriminate other men. Perhaps most importantly, however, cattle duffers were tolerated because of the lack of stockmen over vast areas of country. Cattle duffers served a useful purpose in that their characteristically brutal presence on *country* kept the 'bush blacks' away from the majority of stock.[167] Other evidence suggests cattle duffers didn't consider stealing cattle a crime as long as it was from the 'large, wealthy stations'. But why so? Because they believed wealthy pastoralists started their stations by cattle duffing themselves.[168]

This chapter has detailed some of the complexities of early Kimberley policing. The initial role of the police was a multifaceted one. Their many duties included reporting on the frontiers of European colonisation and supporting an informal (and illegal) role, facilitating the supply of Aboriginal workers to pastoral stations by returning absconding workers. Policing in a commercial environment and attempting to protect the rights of Aboriginal people made the lives of police extremely uncomfortable as they were inevitably ostracised. We have seen how police worked in a culture in which local social conventions, such as regarding Aboriginal people as personal property and the 'conspiracy of silence' regarding killings and stock thefts, worked against the effective administration of justice. The virulent responses to individuals such as the Reverend Gribble, who sought to publicise the mistreatment of Aboriginal people in the Kimberley, were testament to the powers of the commercial interests and their connections with state power.

Chapter 4

'SHOW CIVILITY AND A READINESS TO ASSIST'

Issues and Innovations in Kimberley Policing

This chapter continues and broadens the analysis of Kimberley policing. It describes Kimberley police administration, rules and regulations and the social background and character of the Kimberley force. It details the innovations employed to counter problems specific to the Kimberley, such as isolation, the enormous distances between the Kimberley and police headquarters in Perth and the limited number of police expected to cover such a vast area. It also looks at some of the solutions, including the use of native assistants and special constables. Finally it examines the autonomy of Kimberley police and the contradictions between the freedom this gave them and the expectations of them articulated in official rules and regulations.

During the 1850s and 1860s there was pressure in all colonies, except Tasmania, to coordinate colonial forces, to improve their efficiency and the standard of recruits and to raise their standing in the community.[1] By the second half of the nineteenth century the dominant model of policing in Australia was a centralised, bureaucratically organised police force responsible to the local governor and therefore substantially autonomous of political control.[2] The colonial legislative acts that created Australian police forces specified that the police were to be headed by one responsible officer, variously titled superintendent, commissioner, chief commissioner or inspector-general. In Western Australia the responsible officer's title was superintendent up to January 1887 and commissioner thereafter. This officer was to administer the police, subject to the direction of the governor. Officially, the Australian police were administered from the capital of each colony.[3] With the exception of Tasmania, from 1863 until 1898 all Australian police forces were organised around the principle of a centralised model.[4]

Australian policing, unlike that of Britian, Canada or America, was organised on a colony-wide jurisdiction.[5] South Australia was the first colony to embrace the centralised policing system in 1844, followed by Victoria in 1853, Western Australia in 1861, New South Wales in 1862 and Queensland in 1863.[6] The formation of the centralised police forces was driven by various factors: large convict and ex-convict populations, an Aboriginal population that was often thought to be aggressive, tumults caused by gold discoveries creating enormous flows of itinerant fortune seekers, and the rise of the Australian bushranger.[7]

Administratively, police establishments were paid out of general government revenue rather than by local authorities so police were an extension of the colonial state. These centralised police forces were the key agents of the emerging colonial states in establishing and maintaining order and, in theory, were independent, free from local influences and thus impartial enforcers of the law. Of course, the practice was quite different as police were subject to social and political pressures that influenced their actions and, as we shall see, were often widely disliked.

This central control of police created enormous problems in the bigger colonies: it made it exceptionally difficult to impose regulations and discipline far away from where the force was headquartered.[8] But control of police through the centralised, hierarchical organisation did have certain benefits over a localised police force. The decision to vest authority in a single commissioner, subject to the direction of the colonial secretaries and governors, excluded local magistrates and other officers of the judiciary from direct control over police administration.[9] As a consequence, the commissioner of police was the most important figure in policing.

While administratively police in the Kimberley were under the direct command of the commissioner of police, they also received orders from government residents who lived in the district and who were effectively representatives of the governor. Before the establishment of responsible government in 1890 (after which the position was abolished) government residents had substantial powers and they became an important local mediating authority over police. They were responsible for appointing justices of the peace and also acted as agents for the government, transmitting official correspondence and instructions between the colonists and the government. They were also responsible for a farrago of administrative duties: vetting land regulations, registering births, deaths and marriages, and addressing civil disputes and 'native troubles'.[10] In theory only they held control over the police force and the judiciary and were responsible for 'keeping the peace' in any district in Western Australia. In practice their power was limited as the commissioner of police could override them. This was perverse in the Kimberley context as these government residents lived in the district that was policed and thus saw what was needed whilst the commissioner of police was situated over 2400 kilometres away.

The government residents in the Kimberley during the period covered by this book were highly educated men who were respected, at least at the government level. Robert Fairbairn was the first government resident and he had come to the Kimberley by boat with Lance Corporal Payne and the other police officers.[11] Fairbairn had furnished the Western Australian government with reports from two commissions of inquiry: *The Fairbairn Commission* in 1882 and *The Commission to Inquire into the Treatment of Aboriginal Prisoners of the Crown* in 1884 (see chapter 3 for more detail). In 1882, Fairbairn, acting as special magistrate, toured the Gascoyne and Murchison districts for the government and his findings, as we have seen, had profound implications for the Kimberley, as he went on to become resident magistrate of the district.

In October 1885 the English-born Dr Thomas Henry Lovegrove replaced Fairbairn when the Kimberley goldfields were declared. His first position in Western Australia commenced in 1867 at Bunbury as resident medical officer.[12] Lovegrove was a member of the Royal College of Surgeons of England and, after this, was appointed by the imperial government as a medical officer in the Western Australian Convict Service. Later he was appointed police magistrate for the Blackwood district and became a justice of the peace. By 1885 he was the resident magistrate and chairman of the court of petty sessions in the Kimberley. He also officiated as warden.[13]

Lovegrove is a significant figure as his actions, as detailed in chapter 5, reveal the confusion around chains of command and limits to authority between the government resident, the commissioner of police and the colonial secretary of Western Australia. His clear sense of propriety, his education and background and the fact that he was also a member of the social elite evoked resentment. Government residents also came to be known as resident magistrates although, confusingly, some government residents were not magistrates but were appointed justices of the peace. Each acted as a chairman of the court of general sessions in the district over which they presided.[14]

Much of the confusion detailed in subsequent chapters over chains of authority can be explained by the manner in which the police force was established in Western Australia. In the early Swan River Colony period Governor Hutt saw the government resident as having the 'eyes of the Governor' (or 'Governor in miniature') in remote areas.[15] The local magistrate was the person in command of the police in his locale. When the local police forces were amalgamated under Superintendent Conroy's Police Ordinance of 1853, the magistrates lost the authority to direct police in terms of orders and duties. However, police rules stipulated that police were required 'to obey the orders of any single magistrate or bench of magistrates *in their magisterial capacity*', so police were still expected to carry out the duties of the court. Magistrates 'were not permitted to interfere with the internal or executive arrangements of police', although there was sufficient scope in interpreting police rules that they often did. Magistrates could, if they suspected 'felonious attempt upon life or property' or any threat to public safety, call upon the police 'as they deem necessary'. During this time the police officer was to act under the magistrate's orders 'so long as he is present'.[16]

As far as police were concerned, an order from the government resident was to be taken very seriously. The superintendent of police instructed that they 'should be attended to at once'.[17] The social position of the government resident and magistrates created problems particularly as police were sometimes summoned (at the whim of the residents) to carry out mundane activities such as cooking for them and providing police escorts. This caused considerable resentment.[18] A final complication was that in other districts, such as the East Kimberley goldfields, the police received orders from police officers and government residents who were classed as 'wardens'.

We will now look at the administration of the commissioner's orders particularly as they related to the Kimberley. Senior police advised the commissioner on what action should be taken in response to the behaviour of Aboriginal people. Commissioners, rhetorically at least, strove to maintain British law, 'civility' and professionalism in the force, but senior police faced the practical realities of the Kimberley frontier where Aboriginal groups were resisting white colonisation. The police commissioner's orders were commands to be followed, and the commissioner was constantly issuing new general orders, circular orders, codes of behaviour, duties and responsibilities which were, for the most part, driven by advice from senior police in the district. However, police rules were also constantly affected by the interaction between the commissioner or superintendent of police, the police in the district, the government resident overseeing the police and the people whom they policed.

Police Act 1892

A significant change in police legislation appeared in the form of the *Police Act 1892*. This was a consequence both of European expansion during the 1880s into the North West and the Kimberley, and the granting of responsible government in Western Australia in 1890. Prior to this Act the police ordinances were a medley of imperial enactments.[19] The *Police Act 1892* made provision for local conditions and a new set of 708 police regulations was published, the most expansive yet.[20] These measures codified regulations and were an attempt to enforce the authority of the commissioner of police. They reiterated the strict rules that police were expected to abide by, as well as laying out, in minute detail, the chain of command that was to be followed without deviation. Police were expected to familiarise themselves with all these regulations and they could be reprimanded for not following one of them. Failure to follow regulations correctly indicated that they had not read the regulations closely enough.[21] The rules themselves were indicative of the attempt to impose authority through a hierarchical system within a police force dispersed over an extremely large area.

General uniformed police came under the control (in order) of the commissioner of police, chief inspector, inspector, sub inspector, senior sergeants, sergeants, corporals, first-class constables and second-class constables. The lowest ranked were the probationary constables.[22] Official police rules dictated that all officers received and had to obey direct commands from the commissioner as well as from their immediate superiors.[23] Applicants for the police force in the 1890s had to apply personally to the chief inspector of police in Perth. They were required to be 'over twenty-one and under thirty years of age, to be able to read and write and be mentally, physically and constitutionally fit for service.' Candidates for the mounted police could not be 'less than 5 feet 10 inches [1.7 metres] nor more than 11 stone 7 lbs [73 kilograms] in weight' but 'able to ride well'. Aboriginal assistants, or native assistants as they were known, were allowed 'where desirable'.[24] There is little evidence to show how the application criteria were applied during this period although it appears, in contrast to the official regulations, that entry to the police force was often very informal. A young Irish migrant, James Twigg, described the application procedure in the early 1890s. He decided to join the police force after failing to make a living labouring for '£1 a month and tucker'.[25] He 'sent in his name' to the commissioner of police in Perth who in turn wrote to the inspector in Bunbury, where Twigg was staying, who then offered him a position. Twigg wrote:

> I went in and passed a rough exam and a stiff medical one. I had to pay the medical myself 10s.6d for the certificate. The Inspector said that I would probably have to

go to Perth and get sworn in almost immediately but I have not got orders yet. The pay is about £7 per month but you have to grub it yourself (£1 a week out here). I wish I was on the force…I am sure to be sent North where the niggers are committing great depredations. They chained up a copper the other day and sacked the station.[26]

Who Were the Police?

Patrick Troy's career, which would involve moving to locations all over Western Australia, was typical of many who joined the force.[27] While his frequent movement was typical, the records he left were not, and his intelligence and sympathy are evident throughout. Born in Ireland in 1851, he arrived in Western Australia with his parents in June 1853. He became a policeman in 1873.[28] Articulate, loyal and respected, Troy was a lance corporal in the Gascoyne district, then became sergeant in the new Derby and West Kimberley District in 1883, and in June 1886 he became a sub inspector in charge of the West Kimberley Gulf Force and a year later in charge of the Kimberley Police. He left the Kimberley in March 1888, transferred to Bunbury, then in 1899 went to the 'Northern districts' as a junior inspector.

From 13 December 1894 Troy was part of the decentralisation of the Western Australian police when he took on the senior role of travelling inspector of police, a role designed to provide some assistance to the commissioner of police by inspecting police stations across the vast areas of Western Australia. This office would change names over the years to titles such as chief inspector (1898) and superintendent (1900).[29] Troy left this role in June 1896 for unknown reasons, although it is possible that he found the conflict occurring in the Kimberley at this time not to his liking, and became relieving warden at Coolgardie. A year later he became the warden and resident magistrate for the Murchison district.[30] His final appearance, as we shall see, was when he investigated an alleged rape at Isdell Police Station in the North Kimberley in 1905.[31]

The Western Australian police force was not considered a career choice of skilled 'white collar' workers, but became a choice vocation for low-skilled men. Historical antipathy to the police in Australia, described by Russel Ward, was a factor,[32] and joining the police force was a last resort for many men, but it held out the prospect of progressive promotion, regular pay and a way out of poverty. Western Australian police were, however, poorly paid. Despite the addition of the district allowance for serving in the Kimberley placing them at the top range of police salaries in the colony, constables were paid between £125 and £135 per annum.[33] To put this in perspective, shepherds employed by local pastoralists received £80 per annum plus clothing and rations so it is little wonder many police left, particularly when they were placed in very dangerous positions.[34]

Some joined and left the force several times depending on their fortunes elsewhere whilst others made a career of it, and there was a preponderance of Irish men in particular in the Australian police forces. Historian Patrick O'Farrell observed that basically Irish migrants had three choices: 'The three P's of the Irish Catholic – priest, publican or policeman.'[35] In the historical record one finds whole migrant families who joined up and whose surnames are still recognisable today as serving officers.

According to Andrew Gill, between 1885 and 1893, 1046 men applied to join the Western Australian police force but, because of the limited financial capacity of the government of the time, only a quarter of these applicants were able to be employed.[36] The occupations of those who wished to join fell into five broad categories. The first category was unskilled workers or 'labourers'; the second, men from police forces in other parts of Australia or from overseas; and the third was those with a military background. The importance of those police with military backgrounds is an under-acknowledged component of Kimberley police that shall be detailed later. During 1902 Commissioner Frederick Hare received 219 applications from local men to join the police force but also nearly 200 applications from Great Britain and South

Figure 4.1. Western Australian police, PC Richard Troy (middle). Courtesy Peter Conole. Photographer and date unknown.

Africa (those who had fought in the Boer War).[37] The fourth category was those whose trade or calling was 'not given'.[38] These four categories made up 96% of all applicants with the remaining 4%, the fifth category, identifying as 'clerical' or 'skilled'.[39] Some 22% of 'unskilled' applicants were born in Ireland, 22% in England, 38% in Australia, 8% in 'other countries' and 7% apparently had 'no birthplace'. Of those successful unskilled applicants, 28% were Irish, 17% were English and 43% were Australian born.[40] Most of these new officers were not born in Australia and came from a European climate far removed from where they would ultimately serve.

The Application of Police Rules in the Kimberley

As police regulations stipulated, discipline in the Western Australian police force was very strict. An officer was as likely to be reprimanded for not filing circular orders correctly as he was for a breach of firearm regulations. When it came to the attention of Sergeant Patrick Troy that certain police in Wyndham had 'been in the habit of frequently entering public houses' he had to remind Sergeant Houlihan, who was in charge, that these were issues of 'gross misconduct' as were swearing, drinking, billiard playing and 'gaming'.[41] Those officers caught drinking could be charged under section 9 of the Police Ordinance.[42] There were rules relating to being on town duty dictating that the police were to turn out 'clean with the uniform in good order' and rules pertaining to practical issues such as not 'overexerting your horse'. The local enforcement of rules and regulations was monitored by senior officers or inspectors, although often extremely infrequently, for example twice a year. Penalties for breaches of the rules ranged from reprimands to demotion and even dismissal from the force.

Kimberley Gaols

Prisoners in the Kimberley were held in neck chains that varied in weight at different locations, from 2 pounds (1 kilogram) at Broome to 5.25 pounds at Wyndham where presumably a heavier gauge was required.[43] There were idiosyncratic police regulations (No. 647) on the chaining of Aboriginal people. This read:

- in escorting native prisoners, the practice of chaining by the neck must not be resorted to except in cases where the prisoners are of desperate character or have been arrested a considerable distance in the bush; or when travelling by sea they are near the land to which they belong and it is necessary to adopt special measures to secure them, even then this practice must not be adopted if it can be avoided.[44]
- they must be chained at night by the leg.[45]
- the police should caution persons travelling in the Kimberley and Roebourne districts not to place too much confidence in the natives with whom they come into contact.[46]

Chaining by the neck for individuals under arrest was illegal in Western Australia as of 1878 except in the case of 'bush natives', although the practice was widely used even on Aboriginal children as young as ten and elderly Aboriginal people (figure 4.2). Gaols that housed the prisoners were built as required in the towns of Roebourne, Derby, Wyndham, Broome and Halls Creek. Until the gaol was established at Broome in late 1894 prisoners 'were kept in a cow-shed together with the police horses'.[47] Prisoners were held in ad hoc arrangements of neck and leg chains (sometimes riveted on) that were left on and often bolted to the floor or wall.[48] As we have discussed, some neck rings were secured with 'split links' that would be removed with 'a hammer and chisel with the prisoners head being placed on a blacksmiths anvil'.[49] Some prisoners were sent to Carnarvon gaol (1931 kilometres to the south) where they were chained together at the neck and wrist and then 'shackled at both ends to permanent mooring stones in the gaol yard'.[50] At Wyndham gaol prisoners would be chained in threes and be released under armed supervision of warders to build roads and walls and any work the town required. To wash they would be directed to the nearby coast and, still chained together in threes, wash in the ocean.[51]

Figure 4.2. 'Aborigines in Chains', circa 1901, Courtesy State Library of Western Australia, 004648D. James McClure Thomson.

There were reports of mistreatment in prisons. One witness reported in one instance that police at Roebourne were transferring fifty prisoners in neck chains to Ashburton, a distance over

482 kilometres, at some 55 kilometres a day without water. One prisoner became 'raving mad from thirst' at which point he was allegedly 'shot through the head, unchained from the rest then buried in the sand'.[52] Depending on the charge, if the accused was found guilty they may have been sent to Rottnest Prison in the far colder south of the colony. For many prisoners, used to hot and humid weather, the cold was intolerable and caused many deaths.[53] In addition it appears prisoners were poorly fed at times, merely on 'bubble-bubble' that was a mixture of flour and water.[54]

Methods of Control: Firearms, Native Assistants and Special Constables

The firearms used by police in the Kimberley were initially the single shot Snider-Enfield rifles, which fired an enormous .577 inch cartridge, although by the late 1890s they were considered too old, complicated and prone to becoming clogged with sand. The Winchester Carbine rifle, which was known as a 'repeating rifle', could fire many shots before having to be reloaded and was considered a superior weapon; it became the weapon of choice through the mid-1890s.[55] The side arms used were Webbley revolvers until replaced by Smith and Wesson colts.[56] One of the most contentious rules related to the appropriate legal use of these firearms.

Originally, the Western Australian police force acted under the authority of the *Police Ordinance Act of 1849,* which was amended in 1861 and which provided that police had only civil, not military powers. The *Police Act 1892* reinforced this civil status.[57] Police regulations dictated that:

- the police should always remember that they are a civil and not a Military force, and it is under the exceptional circumstances existing in Western

Australia that they are armed with deadly weapons
to be used on rare and exceptional occasions.[58]

While this regulation may seem clear-cut, additional regulations
introduced an element of interpretation:

- a constable seeing a person running away with
  goods is not justified in shooting at such person…
  unless he *knows* that he has committed a felony in
  taking such goods.[59]
- if a person having committed a felony will not suffer
  himself to be arrested but stands on his own defence
  or fly so that he cannot possibly be apprehended
  alive by those who pursue him with or without
  warrant from a magistrate the constable in pursuit
  would be justified in firing upon him.[60]
- it is to be particularly impressed upon all officers of
  police that the above rules apply to cases of arrest
  and pursuit of aboriginal natives as well as other
  criminals.[61]

Official police regulations, as stipulated in 1863 and repeated
in 1898, prescribed the police role as 'the prevention of crime'.[62]
Theoretically this appears clear-cut but at a practical level for
police dealing with Aboriginal populations it was dangerously
ambiguous. Police were required not only to enforce the law but
also to compel Aboriginal people to obey the law: a law that was
imposed on them without their knowledge.[63] Aboriginal people,
as we have seen, were British subjects and thus entitled to the same
protections as any subject of the Crown. It is evident, however, that
there was a vast gulf between official rhetoric and police practices,

particularly during the mid-1890s. As shall be detailed in chapter 5, the rules regarding lawful firing on Aboriginal people would be widened to strengthen police powers and compensate for the small number of police officers.

We have seen how the cost of policing in Western Australia was the highest in Australia partly due to the enormous size of the state. The expedient solution to having inadequate numbers of police was found in complementing them with native assistants and, at times, the swearing in of special constables. In the Kimberley, each police officer would have one or sometimes two or three native assistants, effectively doubling or tripling police numbers. The role of native assistants in the Western Australian police force is an aspect of policing that has not received sufficient attention in the literature on this period. Their practices often went unrecorded but their impact in aiding police in the Kimberley was enormous.

Native assistants were Aboriginal men who often were recruited for their skills in bush craft, tracking, knowledge of *country,* tending to horses and use of firearms. Regardless of their age they were infantilised and known as 'the boys'. Critically they acted as interpreters for the police, often gaining information from those arrested about movements of different Aboriginal groups.[64] Police were basically rendered ineffectual without the tracking abilities of their assistants, as most Europeans could not navigate the harsh terrain themselves.

Native assistants were especially useful in tracking and apprehending the 'bush blacks'. They were known in many cases to be able to 'identify all the natives in that part' of the Kimberley, and some could even identify individuals by their footprints.[65] At times they acted as negotiators with local groups for safe passage of the police through *country* known to be dangerous. In police correspondence it is clear that police regarded native assistants as more important than the actual officers and certainly the remote police camps were considered no good without them.[66] Police attributed native assistants' skills to 'native instinct'. In one patrol in late 1893, when Sergeant Brophy's Native Assistant Micky avoided a spear, his 'innate skills' saved him.[67]

Native assistants received no pay from the police force but their officers received a 'credit' allowance, typically of 2 shillings a day, for their upkeep that would pay for their food rations.[68] In effect they 'belonged' to the police officer although they were 'lent' to other officers when the officer agreed. The wives of trackers often also worked for the police as cooks and general hands.[69] In 1886 Acting Commissioner Phillips issued a circular order drawing attention to the untidy appearance of some native assistants and asking for police to 'dress them as neatly as the means of their disposal will permit'.[70] Curiously, however, native assistants were not under the official authority of the commissioner and were not employed under any contract but rather were responsible to their officer. As was revealed in the Roth Royal Commission of 1905, the then Commissioner Captain Hare was not even aware that the native assistants were not employed under contract.[71]

There are very few photographs of native assistants and in the historical records they are usually named only by a single alias. The name of a native assistant was usually a European name given by the police officer in charge of the person or a bastardisation of his real name. Native assistants generally were selected from areas outside of those being policed. Being a member of a local group was likely to limit their ability to apprehend people to whom they may have been related by blood or marriage, so police attempted to ensure that native assistants would not identify with alleged offenders and thereby sabotage their policing. Police also learnt from the case of Jandamarra ('Pigeon') in which his family and kinship obligations affected his loyalty to the police officer he was serving. Native assistants were often handpicked by a police officer from prisons, including Rottnest Island. Generally these assistants came originally from the Murchison or the Gascoyne regions. The first two native assistants in the Kimberley were handpicked by LC Patrick Troy in March 1883. Originally from the Murchison district, they were acquired from Rottnest prison. They were named Mardachalgo, aka 'Monkey', and Belbager, aka 'Michael'.[72]

Some were also brought over as long-time 'special assistants' from other colonies. In 1895 Sub Inspector Drewry had plans for all native assistants to be 'Queensland boys' and not local.[73] By 'Queensland' they meant from the east of Western Australia including the then South Australia (Northern Territory) where a formalised native police operated.

The deaths of a number of native assistants in 'skirmishes' were the direct result of the police patrols having them in the 'front line' of attack, with responsibility to track and apprehend alleged offenders. It may also have been a deliberate strategy by Aboriginal groups to remove native assistants on whose tracking abilities the police depended. Between 1895 and 1904 at least six native assistants were killed by Aboriginal people.[74] Native Assistant Willy was killed in July 1896 when on patrol with Constable Inglis.[75] In mid-1899 'Dicky', a prominent native assistant in many of the police attacks outlined in chapter 10, was killed by an Aboriginal 'outlaw' named Nalmurchie and most likely targeted to cripple the police tracking.[76] After 1900 native assistants were also killed by escaping prisoners to prevent them being tracked.[77]

The exact legal status of the native assistant was extremely vague. This ambiguity was a convenient grey area, aiding police practices by effectively placing them outside the law and with no accountability. Clearly this is a situation that suited both the police and government – if no one knew what they were doing, as senior authorities often indicated, then nothing could be held against them. Police utilised this to their advantage. Unlike police officers, native assistants were not required to keep records and as they told few stories almost nothing was recorded of them. Contrary to police regulations, native assistants carried and used firearms without supervision from their police officer, though under what legal criteria they were allowed to is unknown and remained so for decades into the 1930s and 1940s.

PC William Armitage's native assistant, Jerry, referred to his rifle as a 'killaman', indicating that native assistants were used to shoot people.[78] In this sense we see similarities with the Queensland model of a native police force, especially when large-scale shootings occurred and no prisoners were taken. They were not permitted to arrest, shoot or kill Aboriginal people although in practice they did.[79] Keith Willey claimed that 'they did most of the official killing'.[80] Police could effectively 'use' them to do their 'dirty work' and not be held responsible. And they were responsible to an officer whose reputation rested on their skills. They were almost invisible in a bureaucratic sense so rarely did they appear in the records, but the Kimberley police force simply could not have functioned without them.

To finalise this survey of the make-up of the Kimberley police force we need to comment on the position of the 'special constable'. On some of the bigger police raids, especially to track down those who were alleged to have killed colonists or police, the police were assisted by special constables, men who were appointed, sworn in and paid for their services from police funds for a particular raid. In 1901 they were paid 10 shillings a day for their service, five times more than the allowance allocated for native assistants.[81] The decision to swear in special constables lay beyond the power of the local police – it was entrusted to the local magistrate and government resident under the Police Ordinance 1861, 'in order for the suppression of any tumult, riot, or affray, or on any other emergency, for the preservation of public peace and the due execution of justice'.[82]

This Police Ordinance remained in force in the *Police Act 1892* although in a modified form. Under section 36 of the Act the commissioner of police had the power to swear in special constables and they had 'all of the powers, duties and obligations that a police officer or a member of the Police Force has under any written law other than this Act'.[83] In the Kimberley special constables were usually local pastoralists, station workers and others who volunteered for a particular raid. Special constables and native assistants had a significant role to play in these raids and were often less disciplined than members of the police force. Their use was controversial as special constables were often associates and friends of the victims. Their use also effectively raised the number of armed men as police by a factor of up to ten. Special constables played a pivotal role in significant massacres of Aboriginal people.

'The Whole of Kimberley is Miserably Horsed'[84]

Police movement around the large districts of the Kimberley relied almost totally, and out of necessity, on horses. In fact there were far more police horses than police. The number of regulations outlining rules for care and maintenance of horses demonstrates their importance. Indeed horse stealing (or 'horse sweating' as it was known) was considered a very serious offence.[85] Police regulations stipulated 'that no horse is to be hard ridden or over 6 miles [9.6 kilometres] p/h except in emergency' and police were disciplined for this act. In mid-1893 at Derby Station, for example, Constable Handly was reprimanded 'for extraordinary conduct' when he galloped his horse 'unnecessarily'.[86] Officers were personally responsible for their horses' upkeep and general welfare. Although horses were an invaluable resource (and also companion) in such a district, they were constantly described as being 'knocked up', that is fatigued, and they suffered from lack of water that led to ailments such as the 'mad staggers'.[87]

Flies and mosquitoes plagued both man and horse alike and there were tips issued in police regulations on how to prevent horses becoming ill.[88] Horses would constantly be overworked simply because there was such a limited number of 'good' horses in the district, particularly towards the end of the patrol 'dry' season. Unless they were shod correctly their shoes would fall off on the harsh rocks 'every day', necessitating the onerous task of walking for all parties.[89] If all the horses were 'knocked up' and there were simply no horses to ride, then police could not visit stations at all. Sergeant Lavery described his police horse, Cataract, losing a shoe as 'a calamity'.[90] At the start of the 'Pigeon affair' in the West Kimberley and the ensuing conflict, so many horses belonging to police and colonists were 'speared by the natives' that they struggled to find any horses at all.[91] Because of this situation police had to at times hire horses from pastoralists. As Sub Inspector Drewry noted in October 1892, the police horses were a 'disgrace' and the pastoralists knew it and charged 'at great expense'.[92] This, no doubt, was less of an issue than the fact that police horses were seen as 'a subject of jest amongst the inhabitants'.[93]

Dependence on pastoralists further compromised police independence. Police were in the invidious position of having to humiliate themselves by asking for help from the colonist population that disliked them, but they were also expected to produce results, as they were unofficially beholden to those who assisted them. A final impediment to maintaining sufficient and dependable police transport was the lack of decent feed for horses in the district, a point noted by Sir John Forrest in the Western Australian parliament. Even if there were several good horses for every officer there was not a guarantee that enough feed (and often water) would be available to supply their needs.[94]

As policing was considered a very expensive public service there was much resistance to hiring more officers. There was public debate from 1882 about moving police from certain locations, typically 'southern areas' of the colony to areas where they were needed, typically 'northern areas'.[95] Commissioner Phillips repeatedly questioned police on their spending and directed that they try to reduce it. The commissioner directed his sub inspectors, such as Francis Wheatley Lodge and Patrick Troy, to be expedient to minimise costs. That they did so was illustrated by police having to pay for rudimentary police items, such as secure chains for prisoners, themselves.[96] When police numbers were reduced in early 1888, Sergeant Farley requested that Commissioner Phillips allow him more native assistants to compensate. Phillips replied that if he wants one 'he has to pay for him himself'. Later accounts reveal police were forced to buy their own horses and firearms given the standard issue by the police department was so substandard.[97]

During the mid–1880s, systems of rationing and relief, as outlined in early Aboriginal 'protective' legislation that police administered, were already being established in Kimberley towns such as Fitzroy Crossing, Derby and Wyndham. One consequence of creating relief depots where 'old and decrepit natives' could get a supply of rations was that hundreds of Aboriginal people gravitated towards towns. That Aboriginal people were in towns inflamed tensions with white townspeople and police were often called on to drive Aboriginal people out of the towns, away from the 'settled districts' under section 43 of the *Aborigines Protection Act 1886*. In this case police were caught between requirements of the same Act, unable to please anybody. Distributing rations was not officially part of a police role but it was given to them because they were some of the few government officials in the district.

Here we see, while the police regulations outlined police duties in detail, the actual duties of police once they were in a particular district were ambiguous and frequently far exceeded the scope of the regulations. Sergeant Farley from Halls Creek Station claimed that between 15 and 19 August 1889, as well as performing his duty as a police officer, he did the work of a magistrate's clerk, registrar and postmaster, delivered mail and repaired the telegraph line after arresting those he caught damaging it.[98] Furthermore he had to act as an escort for the local mining warden who demanded a police escort whenever he travelled.[99] Undertaking duties outside their main role took up time that could be used for policing and also complicated police funding. If police collected agricultural or pastoral statistics (police were required to count and submit sheep and cattle numbers in various districts) or were placed on mail duty or similar, the police department was not reimbursed for this. At times police would have to perform these tasks at the same time as they were arresting and escorting prisoners.[100] Clearly the Western Australian government used police in a variety of roles normally performed by other officers, in order to lower costs.

One of the more curious police roles was that of collectors of Aboriginal cultural material. During 1889 and 1890 John

Forrest was an avid collector of Aboriginal physical and cultural objects or 'curios', as they were known, including weapons such as spears, *wommeras* (spear throwers), *kileys* (type of boomerang), food-making items, water-carrying bowls, and various Aboriginal ornaments and dresses. Intriguingly he did not collect these himself but rather utilised over thirty-three different police in different regions of Western Australia through his friend Commissioner Phillips. Known as the Forrest collection they were shipped to the Victorian Museum with the profits from the sale of the items to the museum (generally £2) going back to the constables.[101]

The Problem of Prosecution

The diverse roles police performed were complicated by an equally difficult duty. Besides pursuing and apprehending Aboriginal people who disturbed and killed cattle, police had to pursue, arrest and aid in the prosecution of Aboriginal people who killed or assaulted other Aboriginal people in what were known as *inter se* offences. This duty was fraught with difficulty due to the problems police had in identifying Aboriginal people and because those they arrested often did not know what they were being arrested for. The issue of Aboriginal people engaging in customary activities that caused injury and death to others in their groups highlighted the inconsistency in the application and attitude of British law. This issue remained unresolved in the 1890s despite repeated attempts by governments to resolve it since colonisation of the Swan River Colony in 1829.[102] Some Aboriginal people who killed other Aboriginal people would be prosecuted for murder while others who did would not be. In September 1886, for example, several Aboriginal people were convicted of manslaughter after they had 'split open a native woman's head with an axe' and in another case that the court regarded as a traditional 'tribal fight', the penalty, again for manslaughter, was three months' gaol.[103] Colonists in the regional outlying areas clearly did not view the killing of an Aboriginal person as equivalent to the killing of a European.[104] For police this was yet another aspect of their role marked by confusion. Were they to arrest and prosecute offenders? And if they did could the evidence be sustained in a court with people who could not speak English and who did not understand the charge against them?

In 1885 the Western Australian judiciary would often sentence Aboriginal people convicted of murdering other Aboriginal people to a term of imprisonment at Rottnest Island rather than sentence them to hanging.[105] In 1886 Governor Broome made attempts to enforce and regularise the penalties although the secretary of state for colonies did not endorse this. He suggested that the governor, as he had done in the past, exercise his discretion.[106] A year later Broome tried introducing a draft bill to make 'tribal murder', defined as 'the killing of an Aboriginal native in the pursuance of a native custom or superstition', a felony with severe punishment of up to life imprisonment. The draft bill was never endorsed.[107] Local circumstances and expediency would outweigh legal procedures in regard to Aboriginal people in almost every case. As a consequence the status quo remained. A colonist's death remained far more important and was investigated and prosecuted to the fullest extent whilst an Aboriginal person's death remained altogether less worthy of investigation.

Another impediment to police effectiveness was problems with successful prosecution. A particularly egregious example of this was reported in November 1894, just at the start of 'the Pigeon Affair', wherein police were said to have performed well and arrested fifty-nine Aboriginal people in the course of their patrols in the West Kimberley over the previous few months.

However, '59 were arrested on suspicion of murder but were discharged by the magistrate as none could be identified'.[108] This example illustrates how difficult it could be to prosecute Aboriginal people in a formal court of law. But this was only part of the difficulty. The rules and regulations guiding Western Australian police were drafted with different environmental conditions in mind, principally the southwest where there were fewer Aboriginal people, who were also thought to be less agressive than the Kimberley peoples.

Life on the Stations

The environmental conditions, remoteness and makeshift nature of police facilities such as housing in the Kimberley did little to foster feelings of security. Sergeant Wheatley's Denham River Police Camp police quarters was made of paper bark. 'I am daily afraid it will burn down', he told his superior officer.[109] Such was the size of the Kimberley that police could often visit certain colonists and pastoralists just once or twice a year. Towns were not much help. The provision of resources was rudimentary – a 'general store', a wheelwright and blacksmith perhaps, a 'public-house' or hotel definitely, and later, a police station.[110]

Such was the despair of some who lived in isolation in the district that there were at least ten suicides during the late 1880s and 1890s.[111] In terms of the health of police officers, environmental factors affected them in different and profound ways. Diet, drunkenness, distance, climate and isolation, incrementally and in combination, exhausted and crippled some police unused to the environment. Resulting medical afflictions were difficult to treat, if treatment was available at all. The police records document myriad medical complaints from moderately severe yet common malaises such as sunstroke, dehydration, sandy blight (a severe and painful eye infection that impaired vision), delirium, fever or 'ague' (evidently treated with 'quinine and rum taken in prodigious quantities') to potentially fatal ailments like 'bilious diarrhea', dysentery (often treated with a dose of whisky), 'Barcoo Rot' (a form of scurvy caused by vitamin deficiency), malaria and typhoid.[112]

The nutritional intake of officers was poor with most subsisting on a diet of salted meat, tea and damper or 'Johnny cakes'. Fruit and vegetables were near impossible to obtain let alone buy. Indeed, in March 1889 Sergeant Keen died from scurvy at Halls Creek Police Station.[113] By comparison the diet of Aboriginal people, derived from the natural environment, was far superior and contained the necessary nutrition to avoid such ailments. Some police reported painful diet-related physical afflictions that made riding their horses intolerable. Sergeant Cadden resigned from the force explaining: 'My reason being I have suffered so severely from piles my life has been a misery to me during the last ride down from Halls Creek with prisoners I lost seven nights sleep and twenty pounds in weight.'[114] The suffering involved in riding a horse with such a condition can only be imagined.

The chains of command in the Kimberley were often ineffective. Following centralised commands was difficult because of distances from the administrative centre of the colony. Communicating with the Kimberley often took months as mail had to come via sea and then overland on horse and spring cart to reach the sub-settlements and the police station, which may have been a canvas tent or a 'paper mache hut with fly'.[115] Morale was very poor and police in the more unforgiving districts often ignored directives from the commissioner who, they said, had no idea of the conditions of the district. Drinking was rampant and visiting hotels was common, which is not surprising given that they were often the only places for social gathering.[116] Colonial authorities and senior police would always 'prefer a man of temperate habits' but in reality drinking and drunkenness was endemic to the area, especially in the East Kimberley goldrush areas. Much of the social interaction that colonists engaged in involved drinking.[117] In April 1893 Constable Mitchell of Broome Station was given a 'second and last warning' regarding 'the drink question' by Sub Inspector Drewry, who declared 'I will not have men in my district who constantly obfuscate their brains with drink.'[118]

Police also encountered difficulties socially, for example when they arrested 'sly-grog' sellers (those who smuggled in and provided cheap alcohol to the townspeople) they further alien-ated themselves from the colonist community. As police were unpopular in the towns and were considered a lower class than pastoralists they were often isolated. Pastoralists felt that they could rebuke and berate them for enforcing the law. As we will see in subsequent chapters, this created a great schism between them.[119]

Kimberley police had a great deal of autonomy as a result of their geographical distance from the police headquarters in the south: there might only be six police in any one district the size of the state of Victoria. The nature of their policing, therefore, was to a large degree dependent on the character of the policemen. One policeman might be 'a good bushman, handy in shoeing horses and steady and sober'.[120] Another might be 'idle, untrustworthy' and 'a confirmed soaker'.[121] Yet another could be 'no horseman, no bushman' and, most damning of all, an inexperienced officer or 'new chum' might be 'useless'.[122]

Police records reveal that finding men suitably qualified and competent to operate in Kimberley conditions was an enormous problem. At an estimate, for every police constable who went to the Kimberley another two were unsuited and termed 'useless'. These men were described as 'more of an encumbrance to other officers than any assistance and cannot stand the climate and the hardships attached to patrol duty'.[123] Colonists complained that police were sent to the Kimberley 'who could not even ride a horse'.[124]

The introduction of police to the Kimberley affected Western Australian police policy on promotions, which was based not solely on experience but whether or not an officer would serve in a particular district. Police were often reluctant to serve in the northern districts due to the harsh conditions. Because of a lack of suitable police in the Kimberley, the Western Australian government published an advertisement in the *Government Gazette* of 1888 detailing the required attributes. A person had to be:

> an active and able bodied single Western Australian born man, aged between 20 and 26, of not less than 5 feet 6 inches tall, be able to read and write, be a good rider and accustomed to bush life.[125]

In October 1888 a special allowance had to be created to entice men to serve in the North.[126] Despite demands from the commissioner of police encouraging senior police to train and 'break the new men into the ways of the bush', many men simply did not, and could not, remain.[127] There is ample evidence of police requesting transfers from the district.[128] It would be fair to say that the idealised version of police behaviour as envisaged by the colonial police authorities', 'to show a ready and cheerful obedience to all orders they may receive' and 'to show civility and a readiness to assist', was somewhat different from the reality of life in the Kimberley police force.[129] Nevertheless, the police who did stay in the district were, or became, 'good bushmen'. These were police officers who were 'good with horses, good with guns, used to bush life and had experience with dealing with the natives'.[130]

The characters of police and their behaviours are evident when studying the police records. One officer might be under the watch of the commissioner of police for the manner of his administration.[131] One might exhibit understanding towards Aboriginal people, another violent contempt, and the language in the reports reflects these attitudes. One policeman might be somewhat educated and another might be barely literate or might write with a hand struggling with delirium tremens.[132] All these individual factors meant that policing in the Kimberley was more varied than we might expect. All police officers, however, were expected to be able to competently undertake a bush patrol.

Anatomy of the Bush Patrol

In the Kimberley, 'bush patrols' or 'bush work' would become the most contentious aspect of policing though it would be the model of patrolling that would endure well into the 1930s and 1940s.[133] In the earlier periods, as we have seen, bush patrols were long though relatively benign affairs. By the late 1880s and into the 1890s they became extremely dangerous and evidence suggests that many new and inexperienced police did not like them – for good reason. Bush patrols effectively became hunting parties. Police, theoretically with warrants but usually without, would leave on horseback in search of offenders with their 'plant', including rations and chains for prisoners, and with native assistants and trackers.[134] Information relating to Aboriginal movements and 'depredations' on pastoral leases was generally anecdotal – a message from a carrier or teamster, a complaint from a pastoralist about the alleged activities of the local Aboriginal people at a particular location. This might be something like 'the blacks are killing cattle down the back of my run'. When warrants for the arrest of those believed to be responsible were finally issued, if at all, it might be many weeks or months or up to a year before a police party was organised and dispatched.

'Good bushmen' (as opposed to 'new chums') were police who could camp out in the Kimberley landscape for weeks or sometimes months on end – known in the local parlance as a 'long pull'.[135] They were familiar with horse work, useful with guns and, most importantly, were experienced in dealing with Aboriginal people, especially those they called 'bush blacks'. Police constables worked closely with their native assistants, who were often sent ahead to find tracks and other evidence of the presence of Aboriginal people, for example abandoned camps and fires. Often trackers could identify individual Aboriginal people by their footprints and knew whether they had passed by weeks, days or hours before. Once the alleged offenders were located and theoretically identified, the police and their trackers would attempt an arrest.

If the group was not considered 'troublesome' the police announced themselves, walked up and arrested 'wanteds'. If the particular group included those whom police considered to be 'treacherous', they ambushed the camp. Armed police and their native assistants camped at a distance and waited, usually until dawn. When they approached the camp, a native assistant would lead the way, and often all the officers removed their shoes to silence their walking. They then ambushed the camp en masse. The camp dogs often woke the sleeping families and the chaos that ensued often led to extreme violence. People would fly in all directions and the police would order them to stand with an Aboriginal word for 'stop'.[136] Police often tried to identify 'ringleaders': those who appeared strong, aggressive or who 'would show fight when cornered'.[137] Anyone who attempted to escape risked being shot and if they threatened or attacked an officer they would certainly have been shot. At times police would engage with Aboriginal people gathered together in very large numbers, when they were probably engaged in ceremonial business and other communal activities.[138] Once the battle was over, spears were usually destroyed but sometimes kept as mementos. Police were also required to shoot dogs under the *Dog Act 1883*.[139] Dogs hold a special place in Aboriginal culture and that police would shoot all but the one dog Aboriginal people were allowed under the Act caused considerable grief.

The number of Aboriginal people wounded by police shootings on bush patrols in the Kimberley is largely unknown and curiously under-reported in police records. This was despite a requirement from late 1888 to report numbers wounded.[140] For comparison, Raymond Evans, citing evidence from the Queensland frontier, suggests a ratio of a minimum of three woundings to one killing, and likely much higher when police were operating on patrols.[141] This ratio does not appear unreasonable given police and native assistant shooting, often being on horseback shooting moving targets. The extraordinary under-reporting of wounding of Aboriginal people in police records was possibly due to the obligation it would place on an officer to care for a wounded prisoner who might not be able to walk back to a town centre. Furthermore, walking long distances 'on the chain' was a prerequisite for an Aboriginal prisoner.

Captured Aboriginal people, including children and those taken as witnesses, were brought back to town, in groups of anywhere between three and forty, on foot. Men were put 'on the chain' around the neck, with women and children following behind.[142] From the 1890s native trees called Boabs, some up to 1500 years old with enormous girths of over 12 metres and hollow interiors, were utilised as makeshift overnight gaols to hold prisoners (both inside and chained outside) on these long treks. One was near Derby and one near Wyndham 40 kilometres away on the King River road. The Derby Boab prison tree is far more well known though the Wyndham prison tree, known as the 'Hillgrove lockup', was used far more at the time (see figure 4.3).[143]

Figure 4.3. 'Men in Front of Boab Tree', Wyndham. Courtesy State Library of Western Australia, 006056D. Photographer unknown.

The accused, often whole groups, would then stand trial in the local court at Wyndham, Derby or Broome before a resident magistrate, although if the charges were sufficiently serious they were referred to the Roebourne Court. Many of those convicted of murder were sentenced to death though most sentences were commuted to terms of imprisonment on Rottnest and prisoners were often released after as little as two years.[144] Sometimes these journeys to court took several weeks, covering distances in excess of 400 kilometres.[145] As Gill observed, the act of arrest, no doubt terrifying to the pursued, and the subsequent neck chaining and being forced to walk out of their *country* for these extraordinary distances appears to have been part of the punishment in itself.[146]

What actually occurred at these bush raids depended on the historical period, locations, personalities of the individual police involved and the nature of the original complaint, that is, whether the raid was related to cattle killing or to the killing of a European. On some of the bigger raids organised to track down those who were alleged to have killed colonists, the police were assisted by special constables. Certain police officers established a degree of infamy regarding their bush patrols and were sometimes sought out by their superiors for undertaking this work as they were considered 'good bushmen'.

This finalises the summary of Kimberley police and policing, highlighting the developments and changes made to the force to accommodate the environmental conditions and limited number of police. We have seen how the Kimberley police force was administered from the capital of the colony, Perth, and how distance and financial constraints meant that very few police were recruited relative to the size of the region. Expediency would prevail. Innovations such as native assistants and special constables were employed to inexpensively bolster numbers. Front-line police faced profound challenges of distance, confusion over lines and limits of authority and power, as well as the everyday difficulties of their work. But there were also demands imposed by the inordinately harsh conditions of an isolated and socially and environmentally hostile district. This included policing a colonist community that was often contemptuous of and operated outside the law, and an Aboriginal people who had become subjects of a law that they neither knew nor understood. The next chapter begins the detailed examination of early policing in the West Kimberley.

Chapter 5

'THESE PUERILE ATTEMPTS AT ARREST'
Early West Kimberley Policing, 1882–1890

This chapter examines policing in the West Kimberley from 1882 until the granting of responsible government in Western Australia in 1890. It describes the changes in policing related to commercial activities, the actions of Aboriginal people and divergent claims from both colonists and police about what was occurring. It explores the developing tensions at the political level, not only about the precise role of police but also about the role of the judiciary and the government resident. Policing, to say the least, was performed in a range of very difficult circumstances.

After the establishment of the West Kimberley pastoral industry, Western Australian government services and industry assistance remained poor, so on 3 April 1885 representatives formed the Kimberley Pastoral Association. Its members included influential West Kimberley pastoralists William Lukin, William Forrester, Isadore Emanuel and J.P. McClarty.[1] The Association voiced its concerns on a range of issues, one of which was the 'native question'. Other issues were government support for jetties, the appointment of local justices of the peace and the reduction of lease rents.[2] From mid-1885 editorials in Perth newspapers aired these complaints.[3] Similar complaints were raised and aired in Perth newspapers by East Kimberley pastoralists independent of the Association: lack of government help, 'excessive mining taxes', 'outrages' of the Aboriginal populations and having 'four police' in an area the size of England. They threatened that, if help was not offered, they would secede and 'it will be necessary for us to petition the Home Government to separate these districts from Western Australia and form another colony'.[4]

The main reason for the escalating political activity was that the Kimberley pastoral industry began to struggle. Between 1883 and 1887 the number of leases had fallen from 487 to 133 and the amount of land occupied fell by over a third from 51,289,080 acres (207,560 square kilometres) to 16,831,080 acres.[5] This abandonment of leases was caused by what many pastoralists saw as the onerous nature of the land regulations relating to the stocking requirements (many being unable to provide the required numbers of stock per acre) and high rents.[6] Part of the difficulty in stocking was that many who attempted to ship stock to the Kimberley lost the great majority on the journey. Environmental hazards, primarily flooding and drought, also led to stock losses. In addition living conditions were extraordinarily hard and, to compound matters, prices for wool were low. Many of the pastoralists were struggling financially and relying on advances from the banks to survive.[7]

While the changes to the lifestyle and culture of Aboriginal people were of little concern to many of the early pastoralists, their presence on the land was not. An early concern was the well-documented Aboriginal practice of 'firing the grass'. This was a land management practice, thousands of years old, whereby in the dry season areas of *country* were set on fire to drive native game out and to regenerate vegetation for food.[8] The practice not only destroyed essential grasses and feed on which the stock fed but also distressed and sometimes killed the stock. It was not a new problem either. In 1839 colonists in the Swan River Colony had 'promised rewards' to the Noongar people if they would 'avoid setting fire to the bush' to no avail.[9]

In early 1884 Sergeant Troy received several complaints from pastoralists in the Lennard River area 'about all the country being burned by the natives'.[10] In August 1884 a coalition of West Kimberley pastoralists put in a request to the government resident at Derby that police put a stop to this practice.[11] In May of the following year, J.P. McLarty, now chairman of the Kimberley Road Board, wrote another letter suggesting the practice be banned, naively commenting that 'there was plentiful food such as fish available' for them to subsist on.[12]

Provisions in the early imperial land regulations protected Aboriginal people as they included the obligation to accommodate (and not exclude) Aboriginal ways of life on leasehold properties.[13] This provision, which was preserved in legislation in 1865, 1872, 1878 and 1887, enabled Aboriginal people 'the full right' of free entry at 'all times to enter upon any unenclosed or enclosed but otherwise unimproved part' of the country for the purpose of seeking their subsistence in 'their accustomed manner' for hunting, foraging and other traditional activities.[14] Being imperial decrees the Western Australian government, lacking self-rule, could not simply change this legislation. The details of these regulations were relayed from Colonial Secretary Malcolm Fraser to the government resident in the West Kimberley, who informed leaseholders, though the issue remained unresolved for several more years.

The government resident had particular power and influence at this time. At a meeting of the Kimberley Pastoral Association in 1885, William Lukin motioned that the law for punishing Aboriginal servants should be altered so that flogging could be used as a punishment for absconding from their employers.[15]

Government Resident Robert Fairbairn did not endorse the colonist's claims for greater powers and argued successfully against it.[16] Fairbairn again raised the recurring and unresolved question of who was responsible for Aboriginal people on the country being colonised.[17] Pastoralists, however, had other ideas: Frank Wittenoon suggested to Fairbairn that the police be withdrawn and the colonists be left to deal with the Aboriginal people suggesting that if 'half a dozen of the worst ringleaders be shot' it would solve the situation of stock losses.[18]

In the first few years of police presence in the district, pastoralists made many requests to the government for more police with greater powers. The main focus of concern about Aboriginal people was their effect on stock but few articulated the impact of the environmental conditions. Sheep shearing would commence after the wet season around March. Similarly, cattle 'fattened up' quickly after the wet season and pastoralists learnt that this was the best time to get cattle to market as they were in peak condition. However, the Kimberley seasons often involved catastrophic environmental events. On 28 February 1885, during the wet season, destructive rains flooded the Fitzroy and Lennard rivers and all the plains country along their banks 'to an extent unknown since the settlement of the district'.[19] Sergeant Sherry could not visit any pastoralists on the south side of the Fitzroy due to the flood. He wrote, 'The country in the vicinity of the Mount Winnie had the appearance of an inland sea.'[20] Stock losses were enormous and pastoralists were reported to be on the verge of starving.[21] After the floods pastoralists resumed farming but it is clear that stock losses placed a significant financial burden on their businesses.

By early 1886 allegations of stock losses caused by Aboriginal people were being reported to police more frequently and with more urgency. What was not clear was how to get the evidence required of who, or what, killed the stock. It became evident to police that stock wandered away from their flock, drowned, were killed by native animals or possibly stolen or 'duffed' by other colonists.[22] In one instance McLarty, the manager of the Liveringa Station, alleged to PC Ritchie 'that natives had killed about ninety sheep on his station since last shearing time'.[23] However, Sergeant Troy found all the losses were a result of sheep being 'lost in the bush and killed by wild dogs', adding that it was 'the practice of station managers to attribute all losses to the depredations of the natives'. Sergeant Troy had, some three years earlier, made damning observations about pastoralists doing this when inquiring into the cause of stock loses in the Gascoyne district. He reported:

> settlers in their reports to the newspapers ascribe the whole of their losses to native depredations whereas they have lost largely from drought, neglect and other causes. But they carefully avoid saying anything about this.[24]

While both police and pastoralists' reports were published in Perth newspapers, the police reports would later cause both anger and outrage among the pastoralists.[25] Along with reports of stock losses pastoralists frequently complained about Aboriginal aggression and general behaviour, including petty thefts of valuable rations such as flour.[26] Especially worrying to the pastoralists were the groups called the 'Hill Tribes' or the Bunuba, Worla and Kija groups along the King Leopold Range and the Lennard River.

However, colonisation was reducing the size of Aboriginal groups. Introduced diseases such as influenza and measles that Aboriginal people had no resistance to took a devastating toll. For example, in early 1885 police recorded a measles epidemic in the West Kimberley travelling 'some forty miles [64 kilometres] up the Fitzroy' and killing many.[27] The government resident ordered pastoralists to provide food and shelter to those affected.[28] The cost was to be borne by the government.[29] Overall, it is difficult to ascertain the numbers of people who died through introduced disease.

Imposing British Law

Early attempts by police to impose British law on Aboriginal people are well documented and revealing. On 13 December 1885 Sergeant Sherry with PC Adlam and Native Assistant Tommy left Derby Station to travel along the Lennard River to 'the Hills' below the King Leopold Ranges to explain to the Aboriginal people what they were required to do under law.[30] Finding it impossible to travel by horse they went on foot and came across 'some friendly natives', most likely Unggumi people. Sergeant Sherry asked if 'some of the old men' could be brought down to talk. Here Sherry 'fully impressed upon them the punishment to which they would be subjected if they interfered with the whites or meddled with their rations'.[31] Sherry surmised that, given time, the police would be able to bring Aboriginal people under British law.[32]

However, the behaviour of Aboriginal groups in relation to the police presence was not as expected. Clear opposition to European colonisation took the form of overt and covert attacks on property and stock and the theft of European goods. This resistance was small scale, sporadic and reported from all over the West Kimberley. Often, however, the complaints from pastoralists arose out of fear rather than actual attacks. In February 1886 there were reports to Derby police that stockmen 'were in fear of their lives'.[33] McLarty of Liveringa Station claimed to have been told 'by an old native in his service that the blackfellows were making plans to kill the whites'.[34]

Figure 5.1. Windjana Gorge. Courtesy Mike Donaldson,
Wildrock Publications, 2004.

Many early reports of stock losses, threats and thefts centred around William Lukin's and J.H. Monger's Lennard River Station, William Forrester and James Munro's King Sound Pastoral Company's Lillamaloora Station, and at the McLarty-run and Emanuel-owned Liveringa Station.[35] Lillamaloora station bordered Lennard River Station on the north boundary and was divided by the Napier Ranges. The police often called it the 'Barrier Station'. It abutted Windjana Gorge and Forrester had constructed sheep yards near the entrance to the gorge. There had been a series of incidents over many months where stockmen had come into conflict with armed men; on one occasion Forrester wounded a man named Jilbara in the leg. The result was that in April 1886 during the start of the dry season PC McAtlee and others left Derby to investigate.[36] On 14 May they visited the King Sound Pastoral Station where William Forrester gave information that one of his station hands named Cairns at Lillamaloora had been attacked and Cairns had fired on the attackers.[37] Ellemarra, (or Ellamurrah) was suspected of staging this attack.[38] Ellemarra, who was Jandamarra's uncle and who many would later claim influenced Jandamarra to kill PC Richardson, was one of the first of the so-called outlaws of the West Kimberley.[39]

McAtlee wrote that Forrester, Cairns and Gunn had gone the next day to follow the attackers and 'had gone about half way through the pass [Windjana Gorge] when they saw about twenty natives who appeared hostile and seemed to dispute the way Mr Cairns and Mr K. Gunn crossed the river'.[40] Forrester said 'he fired two shots into the air with a view to scare the natives away but they at once scrambled up the rocks and began pelting rocks down upon Cairns and Gunn who were below them'.[41] On 21 May the police party travelled along the Napier Ranges where they heard 'natives coeey'.[42] Their unnamed native assistant:

> pointed out some natives on a cliff flourishing their spears and making other hostile gestures. I sent our native up on a cliff above us to parley with them and try and get them to come down and they told him they would come into Mr Forrester's station when we were gone but till then they would stay where they were. I moved in towards them and they at once disappeared.[43]

Critically, these police patrols on Aboriginal groups caused the conflict to spread to other stations. In the next police patrol in August of the same year Constable Ritchie shot and killed a man named Nuglay.[44] Not surprisingly this antagonised local groups. George Poulton, a newly arrived pastoralist from Melbourne on the Robinson River, wrote to his partner Nichols 'in haste' in August 1886 outlining his outright panic:

The shepherds are in real fear of blacks as two painted men have been seen in the vicinity of stations each carrying a plentiful supply of spears. I followed them to the range but did not see them myself, however expect an attack shortly as by the large numbers of smokes extending from NW to SE both yesterday and this morning and presume there are lots of blacks collecting. Can you send me assistance? Also could you send word to Lavenders that Finnerty may know our position the sooner.[45]

Nichols' letter mirrored Poulton's concerns: 'It is evident that the natives intend mischief probably in retaliation for the visit of the police the other day', he wrote. 'Squatting will become impossible.' He added that 'there were only six white people on the Robinson River now.'[46]

'Most of the Danger is in his Imagination...'

After these events, Kimberley Government Resident Thomas Lovegrove wrote a letter to the colonial secretary justifying the killing of Nuglay:

The shooting of the native [Nuglay] appears to have been quite justifiable...the natives about Poultons and up in the neighbourhood of the Bents Pass will do mischief yet unless they receive a severe check from the police. Ritchie informs me that the absconder 'Ellamurrah' tells the blacks that white fellow is no good, black fellow used to be afraid of them. I am of the opinion that a strong police force should be sent as soon as possible.[47]

194

Acting Police Superintendent Phillips then wrote to the colonial secretary to endorse strengthening the police force as there were reports that 'the natives were assembling in force to attack Grant, Anderson and Edgar's and Poulton's stations'. Inspector Finnerty, a friend of Phillips who had arrived from Roebourne to assist and only stayed in the position for a short time, confirmed this, writing that 'the settlers on the Lennard and Robinson Rivers stated that they are expecting a general raid by the natives'.[48] Finnerty wanted two additional mounted constables at Derby and even bought another rifle privately as the force simply did not have enough.[49] Phillips responded that provisions had been made in next year's estimates for three 'foot constables' and two probationary constables for the district.[50]

In September 1886 Finnerty added some observations of his own. He visited the stations himself to 'personally ascertain what grounds the settlers had for their fears'.[51] He observed that Poulton's and Nichols' station, where most of the reports had come from, had 'no' Aboriginal people on it. They had 'retreated into the ranges about 100 miles distant'. Of Nichols' concerns he wrote: 'He is new to this life and I consider that most of the danger was in his imagination.'[52] However, the reports from the Leopold Ranges of sheep that the pastoralists had put in paddocks being killed were of great concern. Several warrants were taken out and Finnerty intended for police to make arrests. 'These natives being range natives will probably show fight when cornered.'[53] Finnerty wrote:

> as far as I can tell the natives are very scarce on the plains.
> On and about the Barrier Ranges they are numerous
> and courageous. But I cannot see the settlers being in
> a more dangerous position than other settlers in new

country. The settlers here are for the most part placing their sheep in paddocks and thus the natives have every chance of killing sheep without detection.[54]

The next police patrol, when PC Ritchie went on patrol with special constables to search for offenders including Ellemarra, is a pivotal point in the history of police and Aboriginal relations. His journal is extremely long and detailed, suggesting that he was anxious to explain and justify his actions: few subsequent police records went into as much detail. On 14 September 1886 he came across the Aboriginal group:

> we called upon them to put down there [sic] spears in their own language...Ellammurah was amongst them and was determined to arrest him if possible. I galloped up close to them with my revolver in hand thinking it would frighten them and they would throw away there [sic] spears but instead of doing as I thought one of them through [sic] a spear at me which narrowing escaped my horse. I then fired two shots at him with my revolver but missed him. He then put his hands up having two spears in them still saying 'meta, meta' which means 'no, no' at this time he was making for an ant-hill...I heard PC Farrell call to them to throw away their spears but one answered in English 'whitefellow no good, *Wemba Marlow Genkel Cathem'* which means Native no spear threw away...[55]

On 27 September 1886 PC Ritchie reported in his journal of again visiting Lukin and Monger who had reported stock killing.[56] On 3 October the police party came upon a group that had been camped: 'as soon as they saw us they took up their spears and showed fight'. Ritchie wrote that he was 'remonstrating with the group for 15 minutes to try and get them to put their spears down which they would not do'. The police party left the area and returned 'two hours' later at which point an 'old man' threw a spear at Ritchie and the police party all shot at him, killing him. The other Aboriginal people saw this and returned to the top of the ranges 'shaking their spears' at the police party who left the scene.[57] The next day Ritchie again tried to negotiate although he reported that they kept shouting *'Wok, Wok'* which he believed to be 'their war cry'. Here PC Powell 'shot him [Lambnada] through the head'.[58] Ritchie wrote that this action was 'fruitless' and, not wishing to shed more blood, the party decided to go back to camp and issue warrants for the rest of the suspects.[59]

On 5 October the patrol went to Windjana Gorge to search for Aboriginal people who had killed stock. They were met with a barrage of rocks thrown by Aboriginal people above and there was 'no shifting them unless with a rifle and that means a lot of men'. They returned to Derby where they found that an unnamed Aboriginal man had come to the police station and told Gunn (Forrester's replacement) that as soon as the police leave the area 'the Leopold Range natives are coming down to kill them'.[60] It is clear that Aboriginal people had quickly learnt to avoid police patrols.[61]

The immediate reason for this escalating conflict stemmed from the government's declaration that the track from Derby to Devil's Pass (the name John Forrest gave Windjana Gorge) would now constitute a main road and thus Europeans would be travelling in greater numbers through the *country* of Aboriginal people and through significant spiritual sites around Windjana Gorge.[62] Importantly the Halls Creek goldrush had begun and men were travelling from Derby Port through the area on the way to the Halls Creek goldfields.

Figure 5.2. East End Windjana Gorge. Courtesy Mike Donaldson,
Wildrock Publications, 2004.

Meanwhile, Government Resident Lovegrove perused Ritchie's report of shootings on 11 September 1886 with great alarm and forwarded his concerns to the Perth office. The 'administration of the native question in the West Kimberley is the subject of great and grave responsibility', he wrote, 'and that as the chief officer of the government at Derby I am entitled to and must receive any information and assistance I may require from police'.[63] There were now significant differences between Lovegrove and police as to what action to take. Inspector Finnerty defended the police and Lovegrove defended the rights of Aboriginal people and described the shootings as outside the scope of lawful action. Lovegrove wanted more, not fewer, police on patrol, so they could arrest suspects instead of shooting them. Indeed he threatened that he would not issue warrants, stating forcefully that 'these puerile attempts at arrest' by the police only resulted in 'useless if not unjustifiable taking of life'.[64]

After another patrol by PC Ritchie the issue had not been resolved. In a carefully worded memo to the commissioner of police, Lovegrove reiterated his position regarding police shootings, stating that the shootings did not compel Aboriginal people to observe the law, in fact quite the opposite. He suggested, again, that larger police forces be sent so arrests could be made on warrant. Furthermore, sending junior officers, he said, was inviting trouble. 'Ritchie is a good man', he wrote, 'but it is unfair towards him that he be placed in such a position'.[65] It was becoming apparent that the disjunction between the financial constraints of the government and the reality of what was occurring on the frontiers of the Kimberley was exacerbating the other factors pushing encounters towards violence.

A New Commissioner of Police

A significant change in policing occurred in early 1887 when Superintendent M.S. Smith died in office. In April of that year Colonial Secretary Malcolm Fraser appointed George Braithwaite Phillips as police commissioner.[66] Three months later, due to financial restrictions imposed by the Western Australian government, Phillips retrenched a number of serving officers, which significantly affected police numbers in the Kimberley.[67] This was all the more unfortunate as around this time Sub Inspector Troy had argued the need for more competent 'bush police' to be sent there. Many who were already there were considered largely 'useless'.[68]

In November 1887 Troy visited all the stations in the West Kimberley and reported that the travellers whom he met complained that 'the natives along the Fitzroy were getting bold and unfriendly'.[69] Troy had now been in the Kimberley for several years and had become more familiar with Aboriginal people. His reports had become more detailed, almost in the mode of an amateur ethnographer, and he was able to describe the nature and characteristics of all the different groups in the entire region.[70] He also had to report the continuation of arrests of Aboriginal people under warrants and the wholesale arrests of large groups of people without warrant.

In May 1888 the Kimberley Pastoral Association petitioned the government requesting that two troopers each be put on the Lennard and Fitzroy rivers. Phillips' response was to reiterate that there was simply an 'insufficiency of men and funds at my disposal' and that the only thing he could do was to move some police from other stations.[71] Then perhaps reflecting his naivety and inexperience he suggested 'buying presents for the natives' to 'restore some sense of civility' and getting a 'better class of officer' who would be able to effect change.[72]

During May to October, the dry season, the matter of Aboriginal people 'firing the grass' became a pressing issue again with colonists. Colonial Secretary Fraser again emphasised and endorsed the rights of Aboriginal people on their land as outlined in imperial legislation.[73] However, as Lukin observed, 'the framers of this clause had no idea that firing the country was one of the principal modes of hunting for six months of the year'. By this time Lukin claimed to have lost 230 sheep and all his fences to fire.[74] Lukin was known as being sympathetic to the plight of the Aboriginal people but his correspondence clearly displayed his exasperation. After catching a group 'firing the grass' just outside his property, he wrote that because of the clause in the law he did not have 'even the power to demand him to desist from doing so'.[75] In July 1888 Lukin suggested to Governor Frederick Broome that 'firing the grass' for hunting could occur, but only on the areas 'outside his property'. Similarly, Aboriginal people could hunt on the land but only outside the fenced-off areas where they did not disturb the stock.[76] The impracticality of these suggestions can be put in perspective by noting that Lukin's property was over a million acres in size, traversing the Lennard River as well as several Aboriginal language groups including the Bunuba, Unggumi and Warwa.

Table 5.1: Kimberley Police at 19 August 1887

District	Officers	Constables	Native Ass.	Horses
Derby	1 Sub Inspector, 1 Sergeant	8	4	20
Goldfields	1	8	4	33
Wyndham	1	7	4	18
Total	4	23	12	71

Broome's opinion was that, while he understood the 'anxieties' of the pastoralists who 'undertook pioneer colonisation', he had a duty to the 'wild race' whose hunting grounds had been appropriated by 'the white men'.[77] The clauses in the pastoral leases would not be changed nor would enactment of new laws to punish the 'ignorant natives' be enacted. A stockowner, he went on to say, already had 'much law to protect him. Beyond this much must be trusted to a vigilant care of his property and much to the increasing docility and civilisation of the natives of this district.'[78] The government's position, to protect the rights of Aboriginal people of the Kimberley, was reassuring to the British government and the concerned people in faraway Perth. However, there was a disconnection between official rhetoric and the reality on the Kimberley frontier. While Broome was insisting pastoralists adhere to the law regarding the rights of Aboriginal people, there was far more political support for pastoralists' interests from members of the Western Australian government.

Despite the government residents of Wyndham and Derby explicitly rejecting the reduction of police numbers in late 1887, Fraser ordered a further reduction in the police force to reduce expenditure in early 1888.[79] Phillips requested more police; however, financial limitations precluded this.[80] Phillips' response was to change the rules and regulations regarding the use of firearms. These new rules were questioned by Broome, and then by the newly arrived English emigrant Attorney General Charles Warton, particularly Phillips' pronouncement 'that a person committing a felony' may 'be lawfully killed providing he cannot be otherwise apprehended'.[81] Broome asked if 'the word "kill" [is] not used with undue prominence and emphasis?'[82] Phillips then changed the wording to read, 'be lawfully "fired upon" providing he cannot be otherwise apprehended'.[83]

Under official police rules, firearms could be used if no other means of preventing the escape of the person being pursued by police was available. In reality the line for bush police between legal and illegal use was often indistinguishable. The ambiguity around what was the legal use of firearms would remain another defining feature of the period. The likelihood of this happening was not lost on Warton, who stated with concern that:

> There is a great danger of the police forgetting that they are essentially a civil not a military body...It is not right to form rules as if it was a natural or constitutional or normal condition of a policeman to be armed to the teeth.[84]

This tension, exacerbated by imperatives of economic development taking precedence over Aboriginal rights and protections under law, would see rules changed to accommodate the needs of police. The impetus for these changes came not from the judiciary but from debates in the Western Australian parliament.

The Western Australian Parliament: 'The Last Straw'

In the early years of pastoral expansion there was little debate in the Western Australian parliament about the effectiveness of the police in the Kimberley. Police had arrested the killer of Anthony Cornish (he was consequently executed at Rottnest Island) and they continued patrols and investigations into the pearling industry and stock theft.[85] In the process, many Aboriginal people were arrested or killed. This did not prevent what pastoralists said were not only significant stock losses but also threats to the European presence in the Kimberley.[86] During late 1888 the debates in parliament on problems in the Kimberley increased in regularity. They concerned not just the numbers of the police in the Kimberley but also their efficacy. The crucial question was exactly what type of force were the police? Were they a native police force? In what situation could they use firearms on Aboriginal people? How could they protect pastoralists while respecting the rights of Aboriginal people? And did they need to respect these rights?

Many, if not all, of the parliamentarians who voiced their opinions were those with pastoral leases in the Kimberley. One of the main protagonists was Alexander Forrest. In November 1888 Forrest in the Legislative Council moved that: 'Protection must be taken to protect the settlers in the Kimberley from the treacherous hostility of the Aborigines' and that the 'most humane' way to deal with the Aboriginal groups was to engage groups of special constables to assist the police to use force 'and leave a lasting impression upon the minds of these aborigines…to make it plain to them that an attitude of hostility towards the settlers will not be permitted'.[87] He read a colonist's letter to the House that said that if he continued to come under attack from 'hordes of savages' then he 'did not know what he would do'.[88] Forrest's resolution was greeted with considerable concern and several members asked him to withdraw it. He refused, stating that while he was 'not in favour of shooting these natives', if the government didn't help the pastoralists then who would? They would simply act with impunity.[89] Forrest, while seemingly not officially endorsing and recommending shooting, was certainly implying that pastoralists be allowed to take the law into their own hands.

Other parliamentarians supported him. One was Robert Sholl, who had pearling interests in the Kimberley, another was Alexander Richardson, founder of Murray Squatting Company and of Yeeda Station. Richardson supported the resolution, with amendments, so as to prevent a state of 'guerilla warfare and regrettable reprisals'.[90] Richardson went on to add that the government should pay more attention to the pastoralists in the Kimberley, 'men of practical experience and trustworthy character', and less to the 'utterance of Exeter Hall' types.[91] Another prominent pastoralist from the North West and owner of *The West Australian* newspaper, Charles Harper, described the approach by the government as one of 'masterly inactivity' which had in fact contributed to the current state of affairs.[92] In 1887 Reverend Gribble had sued Harper for libel after attacking him in *The West Australian* for making claims of abuse and mistreatment in the North West (see chapter 3).[93]

Fraser assured the House that the government's sympathies were with these members (Forrest and Richardson), although he 'regretted the resolution'.[94] Declaring the government could only do so much, Fraser pointed out that police numbers were reduced in late 1887 and early 1888 due to budgetary constraints, but in any case it was 'impossible' to give the colonists the amount of protection they asked for.[95]

Fraser took strong offence to the wording of the resolution put forward by Forrest, suggesting instead that the wording 'an attitude of hostility towards the settlers will not be *permitted*' be changed to 'will be *prevented*'.[97] How this was to be achieved was unclear, though Fraser appeared to be putting the onus back on the colonists. John Forrest, who was soon to become the first premier of Western Australia, voiced disdain that no one in government had shown any 'sympathy with the blacks'.[98] He endorsed the view held by the police that much of the alleged conflict and depredations was misrepresented by pastoralists and he did not endorse 'dispersing' the Aboriginal people.[99] John Forrest's suggestion was to increase the number of small police camps at places that were acknowledged to be 'troublesome', that is at Poulton Station, Grant Ranges and the Lennard River. This, he suggested, would be a far better way of dealing with the troubles than the one suggested by his brother Alexander. Perhaps with a view to securing his stewardship as premier, Forrest asserted that if this approach were to be adopted and pastoralists 'took practical precautions' then the 'whole matter would be satisfactorily settled within twelve months'.[100]

These discussions in late 1888 in the Western Australian parliament had an immediate effect and a formal discussion paper, *The Necessity of Increased Protection for the Settlers in the Kimberley District from the Aboriginal Natives No. 27*, was tabled in the Legislative Assembly. As a result the strength of the police force was increased to forty-eight.[101] In the West Kimberley new police were positioned at Derby headquarters where the inspector resided, on the Fitzroy, Lennard and Robinson rivers, and in the goldfields. In the East Kimberley they were positioned midway between Wyndham and the goldfields. These places were Fletcher Creek Station, Denham Station, and Parry's Lagoon.

As far as pastoralists were concerned, while a small increase in numbers of police was an improvement, they doubted it would provide a solution. As we have seen, early police reports stating that Aboriginal people were not responsible for all stock losses went only to the commissioner of police and some newspapers. However, by early 1888 police reports were tabled in the Western Australian parliament. Sub Inspector Troy's report on 'the native depredations' were published in *The West Australian* on 18 February 1888, starting what would be a stream of claims and counter-claims between pastoralists and police about what was occurring and who was responsible. It was apparent that pastoralists blamed Aboriginal people for all manner of losses: drought, wild dog attacks and, most damningly, mismanagement, a point not lost on some police. It seems here that Commissioner Phillips believed police accounts above those of the pastoralists. Phillips himself wrote that stock depredations were 'the result of the perfunctory system of management observed on some of the principal stock stations' rather than caused by Aboriginal people.[102]

To add insult to injury Sergeant Sherry observed that since the stations did not provide enough rations to Aboriginal groups on *country*, they had to kill the sheep to prevent starvation.[103] To say Sherry's reports caused indignation among Kimberley pastoralists was an understatement. In January 1889 Lukin (who by now seems to have lost his sympathy for Aboriginal people), as representative of the Kimberley Pastoral Association, wrote to both *The West Australian* and *Western Mail* newspapers expressing outrage at Sherry's account, denouncing police as unable to police Aboriginal people effectively and calling for colonists to have the same powers as police. Lukin claimed Sherry had told him it was useless to try and arrest Aboriginal people in the Napier Range and 'the only possible way of dealing with them would be to shoot them'.[104] In other letters to the newspapers, Lukin laid out his complaints in far more detail, accusing Sherry and the police in general of writing the original reports in 'order to shift the blame from the shoulders of the police to those of the settlers'.[105] He went on to write that the police were responsible for the current predicament as they gave 'special protection of the blacks only' and not the colonists, to the point where 'both blacks and whites have thorough contempt for them'.[106]

It is evident that there were significant political issues around stock losses and the reasons why pastoralists would inflate the figures. Pastoralists only counted stock once every six months or at certain times during a year. Aboriginal people clearly took stock but nowhere near the number claimed. Cattle duffers would steal large amounts of cattle though typically this was not reported. But this did not stop pastoralists beginning an informal campaign to get government support in the form of more police and government services.

In 1884 a notice had been placed in the *Government Gazette* outlining new regulations that attempted to compensate for the problem of the small number of police.[107] It stated that a pastoralist could detain Aboriginal offenders 'whom he finds committing or attempting to commit a felony'. However, they had no powers other than preventing the alleged offenders escaping and had to 'at once or as soon as possible hand the offender over to some legal authority'. The question raised by those in the pastoral industry was why the onus was on them and what could they do if Aboriginal people resisted? Pastoralists were already aggrieved that they had to issue rations to Aboriginal groups, an increasingly onerous obligation as more Aboriginal people came and *sat down* on stations.

The issues with policing were practical in nature, particularly on more remote stations. If owners found that their stock was being killed, then by law the onus was on them to find out the names of those doing the killing, go into the nearest town, report the crime and get warrants for arrests so that, with these, police would act. However, it might be anywhere from three months to a year before the police could come out. If the individual was actually identified and caught, the colonist then had to make another trip into town to act as a witness to enable a prosecution, at great cost to themselves.[108]

Pastoralists expected police to be arresting people and providing rations. The police and the government thought differently. Pastoralists were the ones who had colonised the land and the onus, according to the government, was on them to both look after their stock and 'civilise the blacks'. A representative of the Kimberley pastoral industry, writing to *The West Australian* newspaper in February 1889, stated:

> Your contemporary [Sergeant Sherry] states that the natives are being dispossessed of their hunting grounds. We would ask who is responsible for the despoliation [sic] of the natives: the Government who receive rents for the land, or the lessee who occupies the country with the full consent of the Government?[109]

One final, ironic insult that pastoralists felt deeply was that Aboriginal people were ordering pastoralists off *their country*.

Jackson Poulton ordered a group off his station and was astonished when they 'ordered me off' their land. He wrote, 'It is a hard case when a pioneer has spent his capital and years of his life in opening new country for which he pays a heavy rental to the State, to be talked to in this fashion by a horde of roving insolent savages.' He, too, thought shooting Aboriginal people was a way to solve the problem.[110]

Poulton had good cause to be scared as killings of Europeans were taking place nearby in the coastal areas of the Kimberley. In early 1885 Captain Rickinson and shipmate Shenton of the schooner *Pearl* had been speared and killed and their cook Ah Sing wounded by Warwa people at Swan Point in King Sound.[111] Another European was killed on the coast in November 1886. Captain John George Piton, a sailor and perhaps a trader of about seventy years of age, was killed, possibly by Unggarangi people.[112] Piton was bringing goods from Derby by boat on the Robinson River to Grant, Edgar and Anderson's stations.[113] In December 1888, in a possible payback killing, stockman Alex Rummer and a Chinese cook by the name of Ah Hee were killed by what were likely Warwa people on the Robinson River on Poulton's station.[114] Their bodies 'were frightfully mangled', the local paper wrote, possibly by the 'same tribe' which had killed Shenton and Rickinson.[115]

'They are Generally All Implicated More or Less'

The response from Commissioner Phillips to the killings was to encourage more aggressive policing in the Kimberley. The moderate Inspector Patrick Troy was transferred to Bunbury in March 1888 and replaced by Inspector Francis Wheatley Lodge, previously stationed in the British colony of the South African Natal Police Force.[116] It is unclear whether Troy left willingly or was moved, as he did not fit the criteria required for his new position. Lodge favoured a punitive approach to Aboriginal policing as he saw all Aboriginal people implicated in crime at some level. The profound difference one officer could make was revealed in Lodge's disconcerting advice to Commissioner Phillips:

> I am not in favour of the natives being shot down without provocation but I do maintain that in cases of murder by uncivilised natives who cannot be arrested, the only way and the kindest, to the natives themselves, is to send a strong party with fuller powers than they have at present as to the use of firearms and should the natives be punished in this way, *they are generally all implicated more or less,* even should some be killed who had not actually committed the murder it would be the best and only way they the natives understand and would probably be the means of saving other white men's lives in the future.[117]

The increase in police numbers ameliorated one issue in as much as police did not have to travel from Derby to respond to pastoralists' complaints. But the increase also created new problems, principally the adequate supervision of officers in bush camps. This point was not lost on Governor Broome, who insisted:

> the operation of the police against the natives must be confined to the most strict and absolute necessary protective work, and the greatest care must be taken to impress any excess of zeal or anything like entering upon a campaign against the natives of the hills.[118]

In any case the matter remained unresolved for a couple of months as the officer who was to man one of the camps, LC Wall, was suspended for being drunk and Lance Corporal Farrell had to attend court in Perth as a witness in a murder case.[119] Lodge ended up sending the much-criticised PC Ritchie.

Regulations regarding the lawful 'firing against natives' were published in the *Police Gazette* on 10 October 1888 and distributed to all police in the Kimberley.[120] Phillips' directives to Inspector Lodge regarding the West Kimberley laid out the plans. 'Experienced bush police', as Phillips called them – constables Joseph Thomson, Pollard, Waldock, Baldery, Adams and Edward Jennings – were to proceed to Derby to take up office.[121] Sergeant Kennedy was instructed 'to select and forward five good Roebourne native assistants at the usual rates'. Together they would form the new squads to patrol the Fitzroy, Lennard and Robinson rivers:

> These patrol parties are to be actively and constantly employed visiting the various stations and they are to take prompt and vigorous measures to protect the settlers and their stock against the depredations of the natives which are reported to be both serious and alarmingly frequent. If the natives continue to give trouble and of this there is little doubt a severe example must be made of some of them and in such a manner as to have a lasting and salutary effect upon them...Diaries of the proceedings of the respective parties of police are to be kept and sent in for the information of the Governor and in all cases the police must be careful to state the precise nature of the depredation committed,

the number of natives concerned or seen, the number arrested, wounded or killed, by whom shot and the circumstances under which resort was had to the use of firearms. These reports are to be regarded as confidential and the proceedings of the police are not to be made generally known. The patrol and other parties should receive frequent visits at irregular intervals from yourself or the Sergt and whenever practicable it is desirable that you should accompany the police on their forays against the natives.[122]

Inspector Lodge did not share Phillips' good opinion of some of the officers sent to the Kimberley. He asked the commissioner to 'send four good bush Constables to replace Jennings, Waldock, Adams and Pollard[;] these men are perfectly useless here'.[123] Lodge found Waldock 'a steady, willing young man but totally unfitted for the duties of a police officer in this district'.[124] He added PC Frover to the list of incompetent officers, which meant that five of the seven officers sent were considered unsuited and thus totally ineffective.

They are none of them bushmen which is absolutely necessary, even if they are out with a good man they handicap him as it takes all his time to look after them. I have no fault to find with any of them except that they are unfitted for the work required.[125]

In 1889 William Lukin brought in three prisoners from Lennard River Station amid further reports of sheep killing at Lillamaloora.[126] As a result Lodge sent Sergeant Sherry out with PC William Armitage and PC Watts to pursue offenders. On this patrol an incident ensued which set off significant changes in policing in the Kimberley. On 18 August 1889 PC Armitage shot and killed a sixteen-year-old Aboriginal boy. Government Resident Lovegrove, on hearing of the matter, considered this an unlawful killing and had Armitage and Watts arrested for wilful murder.[127] Commissioner Phillips ordered police patrols to cease at once and that 'no wild natives are to be arrested'.[128] Armitage's native assistant, Jerry, indicated in a witness statement that it was an unlawful killing.[129]

In October 1889, shortly after the arrest of Armitage, thirty-nine West Kimberley colonists from all backgrounds, including pastoralists, blacksmiths and station workers, petitioned Governor Broome that all Aboriginal people in proximity to Lukin and Monger's Lennard River Station and Munro's Lillamaloora Station be 'outlawed'.[130] The petitioners claimed that it was 'impossible for the police to carry out their duties properly, as it is perfect madness to think of sending small parties (say two or three) police amongst a tribe of infuriated savages unless invested with most ample powers'.[131] They went on to claim that Lukin had lost 2000 sheep in the last twelve months to Aboriginal depredations and Munro had lost 4000 during the same period.[132] They asserted that should this state of affairs continue then they should have to 'throw up their leases and abandon the country'. They then claimed that 'in addition to the reasons given above, the well-known fact that the natives have for some time been planning a descent upon the two stations mentioned, with the object of killing all the Europeans on them.'[133]

In Perth, Alexander Forrest led a deputation to Governor Broome and a letter from Lukin protesting the arrest of Armitage was read out.[134] Forrest's demands were bleak and assertive. The party stated that if the arrest was legal then 'steps should be taken to alter the law' so that police could not be charged with murder. They repeated the demand that in certain parts of the Kimberley 'the wild natives should be declared outlaws' and demanded that police be allowed to shoot absconders and outlaws.[135] Broome explained that the petition was no longer relevant as no charges would be laid against Armitage. Broome went on to remind the deputation that they were bound 'by the legal means at our command. Nothing like the indiscriminate slaughter of natives, as some settlers seem to propose...will be permitted.'[136] Natives would, however, be prosecuted within the law, and the use of firearms was clearly laid out in regulations. While reiterating that the government had a duty to protect the Aboriginal people of the Kimberley, the governor made a critical statement:

> Settlers in a wild district are justified in employing firearms against natives who actually attack them or who are in the act of plundering their flocks, and cannot otherwise be arrested. The Government will be always ready to place a fair interpretation on the acts of settlers engaged in protecting their flocks, provided both acts are within proper limits and are lawful.[137]

Importantly at this point, police reports, which were what the government used to justify its decisions, once again contradicted pastoralists' accounts. Inspector Lodge, in furnishing his annual reports for 1889, made clear that the petitioners' claims of 'wholesale destruction' were gross exaggerations. Far from facing ruin, Lodge claimed that the previous year had 'been an exceptionally good one for the settlers' and that good rain brought 'plenty of good feed and water'.[138] More telling was his assertion that 'there has been a considerable increase both in sheep and

214

cattle', particularly those situated on the Fitzroy River; a 15% rise in sheep numbers and a 46% rise in cattle numbers.[139] In reference to the claims of pastoralists, Lodge explained that the Poulton and Nichols station had been sold to Mr Marmion of the Meda Company for cattle only. Sheep numbers had decreased from 2300 to 1880 when taken over by Meda. 'This decrease is in no way attributable to the natives as there have been no wild natives in the paddock since December 1888 when A. Rummer and a chinaman were murdered.'[140] Lodge noted that he was on that particular station in June of 1889 and that eagle hawks were killing all the newborn lambs.[141]

At Lillamaloora, far from falling, sheep numbers had actually increased.[142] Aboriginal people had been killing sheep on this station 'but not nearly so great as represented; bad country, scarcity of water in the dry season and mismanagement' were Lodge's findings.[143] PC Armitage had informed Lodge that 'Mr Martin the manager of the cattle on the station for the last 18 months had never mustered the cattle or even been round these cattle and it is not to be wondered at if the natives killed some of them, in fact it would be surprising if they did not do so.'[144] Armitage also pointed out that he and PC Watts had assisted the station hands in getting sheep across a rapidly rising river, as they were outside their stock run. The upshot was that they saved 1000, 15,000 were stuck on the wrong side of the river and 200 were lost, drowned in the river flood and washed away.[145] More sheep, 500 in total, had been killed by being over-driven to fresh feed. Native dogs killed large numbers too.

Lodge finalised his report on Martin and denounced Munro's accusation tabled in the petition by claiming that on one occasion Martin, when mustering one of the paddocks, 'expected to find 1000 sheep short, but found there were actually 1000 more than he knew anything about'.[146] Lodge reported a similar story on Lukin and Monger's station. Sheep had increased from 9000 to 10,800. Lodge noted only two cases of sheep stealing or loss: sixteen on one occasion and five on another, whereas Lukin had claimed 2000 sheep had been taken.[147] Geoffrey Bolton has documented this period and noted that while there was a massive fall in wool prices in 1886, sheep numbers more than doubled, from 46,839 in 1884 to 107,852 in 1890, while cattle increased from a mere 960 to 17,937.[148]

This evidence challenges some contemporary historiography of this period. Pedersen and Woorunmurra have suggested that the Bunuba people at the time were 'outlawed'.[149] Ironically the reason that Aboriginal people or the 'wild natives' in 'certain districts' were not outlawed at this point was due to these police reports that disputed the allegations of the colonists. At this point in the history of the Kimberley, while still involved in some killings, police were responsible for preventing large-scale shootings from taking place.

In late 1889 the issue of what was the cause of stock depredation was still unresolved and the antagonism between the police, pastoralists and various government residents reached its peak. The pressure mounted by Alexander Forrest and others forced critical changes at the government level. Governor Broome made changes to the makeup of the Kimberley police.[150] Broome thought Lovegrove should have contacted them in Perth before laying the charge against Armitage and he thought Inspector Lodge's reports were 'unhelpful'. In October 1889 he directed the colonial secretary:

My intention is, should the administration of the West Kimberley District be impeded by any more of these departmental difficulties, to transfer Dr. Lovegrove to Wyndham and to remove Inspt. Lodge, and these officers should each receive a copy of this Minute.[151]

It is clear that, while Governor Broome spoke in parliament of the rights of Aboriginal people to be protected and for police to be engaged 'in absolute necessary protective work', he removed those who were monitoring and upholding these standards, and, ironically, assisted the pastoral groups in gaining what they had asked for. The end result was that Dr Lovegrove and Inspector Lodge were removed, while PC Armitage was reinstated and lauded as a 'good bushman' (Armitage went on to stay in the Kimberley).[152] Inspector Overend Drewry took over from Lodge, who became acting government resident until 1890 and then returned to being a police inspector working out of Derby. After several years of relative peace, the way had been opened for an upsurge in violence in the West Kimberley and this is precisely what happened, as we will see in subsequent chapters.

Chapter 6

'A MORE POWERFUL AND WARLIKE RACE'

Early East Kimberley Policing 1882–1890

While Michael 'M.P.' Durack established the East Kimberley pastoral industry in 1882, the antecedents to conflict in the district originated in areas outside the fledgling pastoral and pearling industries.[1] Early policing in the East Kimberley, administered through the Derby and Wyndham police stations, focused on the mining industry during the 1886 Halls Creek goldrush and issues around police protection of the new telegraph line from Wyndham to Halls Creek.[2] It was not until the early 1890s that the focus of conflict shifted to the pastoral industry. That more attention was paid to pastoral interests than to mining may be due to the fact that Western Australians with political interests and influence dominated the pastoral industry.

In this chapter the focus shifts to the East Kimberley. It will demonstrate that in the 1880s policing in this district was intertwined with the West Kimberley. It will describe the similarities between the two regions in terms of police administration and practice, while highlighting significant differences in the social context with regard to both the colonists and the Aboriginal people. Little has been written about the history of the East and largely unarticulated aspects of East Kimberley policing are revealed. During the period under review the East Kimberley was a far more violent place than the West Kimberley and the

Europeans lived in great fear of Aboriginal violence, particularly from those groups from the northeast of the district, such as the Miriuwung, Doolboong and Gajirrawoong people. They were 'said to be a more powerful and warlike race, very much superior physically to the aboriginals of the West Kimberley'.[3] Sergeant Thomas Wheatley wrote of the 'King River natives' south of Wyndham as 'without doubt in my opinion the fiercest and most daring natives I have met since I have been in the Kimberley district'.[4] Similarly, as we will see, Aboriginal people also lived in increasing fear of European violence.

Many more European colonists were speared and killed or wounded in the East Kimberley over a longer period of time than in the West. Those speared included members of the Durack pastoral family, John Durack in 1886 and later Jeremiah Durack in 1901. Correspondingly there is evidence that many more Aboriginal people were shot and killed by colonists and police in the East Kimberley and their bodies were burnt to hide the evidence. The district is home to some of the most notorious massacres of Aboriginal people in Western Australian history. Other evidence of poisoning Aboriginal people exists with one unnamed observer stating:

> The lot of the native in East Kimberley is not a happy one. One settler told me that it was quite common to get rid of superfluous niggers with strychnine – so much easier, don't you know! This is a new experience. A beast is killed, portions well poisoned and handed to the blacks. Then there is a hell of a corroboree for a day, and that is all. The nigger quickly leave that district, and no one is any the wiser.[5]

This killing of Aboriginal people occurred on a far greater scale than is generally acknowledged in the historical record.[6] East Kimberley colonists came from New South Wales and Queensland where native police forces, without the pretence of the rule of law, dealt with Aboriginal people through extreme violence; moreover they often dealt with 'native issues' themselves. Gadjerong man and stockman on Durack stations Jack Banggaiyerri Sullivan talks of the time when 'they [pastoralists] got a bit of ground, quietened the blackfellers, tamed them down and worked them'.[7] Those 'bush blacks', he continued, known as 'myalls' by many in the East Kimberley, who 'would not come in' and settle down on bush camps on the station, the pastoralists 'put a bullet in them'.[8]

It has been shown in earlier chapters how West Kimberley colonists spoke of 'taking the law into their own hands' with regard to Aboriginal people. For the most part these utterances were exasperation-fuelled rhetoric. Evidence shows that in the East Kimberley this attitude was not only far more prevalent but was often acted upon. In the written record there are 'silences' around such events.[9] In exploring these it will be seen how those living in the district, the 'northerners' of the Kimberley, showed solidarity with their 'mates' and justified their actions.

'Natives Were Plentiful...'

Early editorials in *The West Australian* newspaper celebrating the arrival of Michael Durack from Queensland to establish the East Kimberley pastoral industry at Ord River Station noted that the 'natives were plentiful' but posed no threat.[10] However, there was considerably more conflict in the early stages of East Kimberley colonisation during 1886 than in the West Kimberley due to the large numbers of men on the Kimberley goldfields. Additionally, East Kimberley colonists appeared far more antagonistic to the

Aboriginal locals and showed little of the curiosity towards them displayed by their West Kimberley counterparts. An unnamed correspondent reported in *The Queenslander* newspaper of December 1886 the extraordinary first contact of explorer and prospector William Henry James Carr-Boyd's with, probably, Jaru people from Prospect Creek, 16 kilometres northeast of Halls Creek. He apparently used dance to overcome the suspicions of three Aboriginal men and they parted on good terms. It seems that he had considerable experience already in dealing with Aboriginal people.[11]

Police in the East Kimberley experienced the same physical and operational challenges as police in the West Kimberley. These included the oppressive environmental conditions and wet and dry seasons that restricted travel. The terrain was harsh and police stations in the early years were tents or hessian huts. The hardship was palpable. There was also deep confusion about how to police the numerous Aboriginal populations. Aboriginal groups of 100 to 200 people were reported in the 1880s in the East Kimberley.[12] These groups resisted the incursions of pastoralists, attacked them and their stock and, like their West Kimberley counterparts, sought refuge in the ranges and hills of the district: the Carr Boyd and Durack ranges just south of Wyndham and the multitude of smaller ranges such as the Osmand and Hardman, midway between Wyndham and Halls Creek.

It appears that police in the East Kimberley were worse than those in the West, with regard to numbers and quality. They were often poorly trained and equipped and suffered from low morale. Significantly, up to late 1889 at least, the police in the East Kimberley admitted that they did not interfere with the relationship between pastoralists, colonists (including packers and teamsters) and Aboriginal people, preferring them to sort out problems amongst themselves.[13] 'Turning a blind eye' not only had disastrous effects on Aboriginal people, who were often killed by colonists, but also severely undermined police authority in the early 1890s. To fully understand this period we must examine the origins and developments of East Kimberley policing.

The Early Years

On 16 April 1886 Wyndham Police Station, located on top of a vast expanse of country at Cambridge Gulf, was established to monitor harbour shipping and movements of boats and also to patrol and police the new town and associated pastoral and mining districts.[14] From Cambridge Gulf, Wyndham police could look over the King, Pentecost, Durack, Forrest and Ord rivers. Sergeant Trusclove was in charge with six constables, four native assistants and twenty horses.[15] Patrick Troy, who was by then a sub inspector in charge of the East Kimberley, took over the supervision of Wyndham police. A year later Wyndham consisted of 'a couple of public houses 3 miles [5 kilometres] out' and 'one public house 20 miles [32 kilometres] away' situated on the road to the goldfields.[16]

The establishment of a police presence in other locations in the East Kimberley came about as required. The Kimberley goldrush at Elvire Valley that had commenced in 1884 saw thousands of men flocking to the area to find their fortune, despite there being, in one observer's view, 'scarcely a spot on the wide Australian continent more totally cut off from the headquarters of civilisation'.[17] At the end of July 1886 the first government resident at Wyndham, Charles Danvers Price, took over as warden overseeing the police.[18] On 21 September that year a police camp was finally established at Elvire Creek with Sergeant Richard Troy in charge of eight troopers, namely PCs Keen, Sherry, Cornish,

Mallard, Brophy, Buckley and Forbes with farrier Sweeny, three teamsters, four native assistants and twenty-seven saddle and pack horses.[19] One of Sub Inspector Patrick Troy's earliest reports from these goldfields painted a stark picture, reporting that the men on the diggings appeared 'as a rule very much depressed' and were not even finding enough gold to exchange for food.[20]

Just over a year later, on 20 October 1887, the police camp moved to Halls Creek.[21] The principal responsibilities were patrolling the goldfields and carrying mail. As with the West Kimberley, under instruction from Commissioner Phillips, there were strict financial limitations precluding expenditure on many basic police items such as good horses and saddlery. This policy was not followed when James Sherry authorised and paid John Bayes to work as special constable delivering mail from 1 June 1888 until the arrival of Trooper Austin from Wyndham, a task made necessary by the extraordinarily difficult conditions under which the police worked.[22]

Police duties included reporting to the government on general conditions and checking miners' legal documents such as licences. Most miners, however, did not have licences as they couldn't afford them.[23] Beyond Elvire Valley there were smaller diggings on the fields, such as the 'two-mile camp' and the 'four-mile camp', known by 'the dismal and uninviting appellations of Poverty Creek and Starvation Gully'.[24] Sub Inspector Troy reported in August 1887 that there were three main camps at Halls Creek (Brockmans, MacPhee's Gully and Mt Dockrell) and he estimated that there were moving parties of around 500 'diggers scattered' over about 200 square miles (518 square kilometres).[25] Warden Price estimated that the population on the goldfields by mid-1887 was between 1500 and 2000 men with the bulk of them on the Elvire River and MacPhee's Gully.[26] Other accounts suggest there were as many as 10,000 men on the fields at the peak.[27] The mining population, Sergeant James Farley added, gave little trouble to the police 'considering the class of men they were'.[28] One of the most renowned miners was Ivan Fredericks, aka 'Russian Jack', who became celebrated for pushing a sick mate 300 kilometres from Fitzroy Crossing to Halls Creek on his wheelbarrow.[29]

Warden Price's 1887 report is a revealing document of the state of affairs during this goldrush period. There was an unusually high number of men to police. Due to the transient nature of mining few, if any, permanent buildings or shops were established.[30] Food, if available, was prohibitively expensive. Mid-1887 was particularly bad: cattle could not be shipped to any market and were being given away 'as it has no value'; sickness was plaguing the miners – 'fever and ague, dysentery, and scurvy being the most prevalent'.[31] Illness and death were common: 'great numbers were stricken down, in dying condition, helpless, destitute of either money, food or covering, and without mates or friends simply lying down to die, assistance had to be rendered these.'[32] The historical records for this period contain a number of similar accounts.[33]

In the early period men on the mining frontiers looked on the presence of Aboriginal people with general indifference. While there appeared no concerted effort by Aboriginal people to repel the miners as they arrived in greater numbers, this soon changed to a point where it is clear that colonists were intimidated if not outright frightened. Accounts from Elvire police camp from November 1886 detail Aboriginal people throwing spears, 'with about 100 natives on the cliffs yelling and shouting at the time'.[34] Colonists, government representatives and police called for reinforcements. Inspector Finnerty suggested the establishment of a police station at Parry's Lagoon.[35] He also recommended that police camps be established at points midway between Derby and the goldfields and between Roebourne and Derby, 27 kilometres out of Wyndham, and that a mail service linking Wyndham, the Kimberley goldfields (Halls Creek) and Derby be established, with a possible extension to Roebourne. This, he argued, would provide some police protection for travellers to the Kimberley goldfields in addition to the safe delivery of mail.[36] At the same time Sub Inspector Troy, at Wyndham Station, was contemplating a written request from Commissioner Phillips on the state of colonisation and ways of saving money. The mail service was duly reviewed in 1888 due to its high cost.[37]

Policing the goldfields districts, whilst difficult, was possible; policing the emerging pastoral industry was another matter. By August 1887 there were only five working pastoral stations in the entire district, separated by enormous distances and obstacles.[38] Three of them were on the Ord River, between 160 kilometres and 320 kilometres from Wyndham. The other two – Stockdale and Wilkes on the Forrest River, and the Victoria Squatting Company – were on the west side of the Cambridge Gulf and could only be visited by boat. Sub Inspector Troy reported, 'How it is supposed to be visited by police I do not know.'[39]

Exacting 'Dire Vengeance' and the Problem with the Historical Record

Despite police presence by the end of 1886 several Europeans had been speared and killed in the East Kimberley. In February, on Jaru *country*, men named Donohue and McKenzie were speared and killed on the Brockman Creek site on the goldfields; Fred Marriot was killed in June at the Halls Creek site and Sam Johnson and Billy Keelan were speared;[40] and John Durack was speared and killed in November east of the Ord River pastoral station.[41]

These killings would provoke punitive expeditions. In the East Kimberley sometimes twenty men or more participated in expeditions with the sole aim of shooting any Aboriginal person they came across. On the Halls Creek goldfields word that a colonist had been injured or killed by Aboriginal people would lead to a call to arms through a 'rattlin' of the tin' – a billycan used as a bell.[42] Men would organise into groups to track and punish those they believed to be involved.

This was the case with the killing of Fred Marriot.[43] Typically reports would attribute the killing to Aboriginal aggression although the reason for this attack was said to be the miner's abduction of an Aboriginal woman and keeping of her for sexual purposes.[44] Other oral history accounts state that the miner gave Aboriginal people poisoned flour.[45] Johnson and Keelan were wounded and Marriot was killed outright with a spear through the heart.[46] A group of Halls Creek prospectors organised a punitive expedition and as Robert Tennant Stow Wolfe, a member of the party, stated: 'We all went out and dispersed those niggers.'[47] Wolfe was the man the colonists would recommend to head the proposed East Kimberley native police force. The police records for this incident state that of the Aboriginal party pursued, 'one of them were killed and several others supposed to have been wounded'.[48] In pioneer colonist G.H. Lamond's account of this incident, he states 'four blacks were shot and several wounded'.[49] Mary Durack reported that Lamond, a friend of Marriot:

> followed the murderers and in a dawn raid on their camp killed four and wounded as many more as they could hit, then silenced police enquiries by signing a statement that the blacks had shown fight and they fired in self defence. That satisfied everyone especially

Lamond who had felt he had struck a blow for justice in avenging a good mate.[50]

The differing accounts of the actual numbers of people shot, killed and wounded are characteristic of written evidence of these events. Aboriginal oral history accounts and private accounts of this incident differ from the official statistics in the numbers of Aboriginal people shot. In *Moola Bulla: in the shadow of the mountain,* the authors draw from oral accounts and suggest 'as many as 100 Jaru or Kija killed in reprisal for the killing of Merriott [sic] a miner'.[51] Written testimony from different European colonists exists to substantiate this claim. William Routledge states that 'after the killing of Fred Marrott [sic] in spear gully, the Queenslanders went after the murderers, overtook them near Mt Dockrell and exacted dire vengeance'.[52] What exactly 'dire vengeance' meant can be seen explicitly in the private correspondence of a young prospector, George Hale, who wrote that:

> A number of diggers went out to take revenge. Having bailed up a large number of blacks in a gully who showed fight, they proceeded to slaughter them with repeating rifles. It is certain that a great many were killed, some say at least a hundred.[53]

In another letter, Hale wrote of the conspiracy to understate the 'true' numbers of Aboriginal people shot.

> That story was true, except that at least forty blacks were killed and the diggers thought it wise to understate the number. The blacks were bailed up in a gully and then fired upon at long range with repeating rifles. The

diggers afterwards piled up the bodies and burnt them
to prevent them being counted.[54]

The Killing of 'Big' John Durack

John Durack and his cousin John Wallace Durack of the Ord
River Station were ambushed by a group of Aboriginal men
about 97 kilometres from their camp. John Durack was fatally
speared.[55] According to Mary Durack's account, John Wallace
Durack rode to Wyndham and returned to the scene two days
later with Michael Durack to find the body of John Durack
'frightfully mangled by the natives with spears and other weapons'.[56] According to Jack Sullivan:

> When they started forming the stations, Johnnie Durack
> would ride around from the old station with a pack,
> round and round to find the good places. One day he
> was in the lead while another fella drove his pack, and he
> putdown to where he was going to cross a creek. That
> was where he ran into the blackfellers. Instead of fright-
> ening them away he straightaway pulled out a gun –
> bang bang bang bang – and chased one feller down to
> the creek. The blackfeller ducked around and as Johnnie
> passed him, looking out for him, of course he let drive
> from the side and got him. When his mate found out
> he was speared he just galloped away leaving the pack
> horses there. If he had let the blackfellers go it would not
> have happened, but they all had the bloody wind up.[57]

A group of police and Aboriginal assistants left Wyndham
in order to 'try and arrest the natives for the murder', despite
apparently not having any information as to who or where the

murderers were.[58] The police party was eventually joined by a party of men from the Duracks' stations, making a group of twenty men in total. They tracked a group of Aboriginal people and after three days attacked a camp they estimated to include 100 people. The Aboriginal men retaliated by throwing their spears and, according to one police report, two men 'who appeared to be the ringleaders' were shot and killed. The rest escaped into the nearby mountains and because the terrain was too rough the police party did not follow.[59]

Archival records suggest that colonists from across the Kimberley joined forces to form a punitive expedition to track down the offenders and that the conflict was far more serious than the fight described above. Author and solicitor Richard Septimus Haynes described, in a letter to *The West Australian*:

> when 100 or 150 natives were slaughtered in cold blood, happened within the last six years, some little distance inland from Derby, and was related to me by an eye-witness. So far as I know it never formed the subject of an inquiry of any kind. Nor was this an isolated case.[60]

An undated note on the police file in 1892 relating the death of John Durack referred to this letter:

> I have to report to Inspector Back relative to this letter appearing in yesterdays morning paper signed RS Haynes. The eye witness referred to is W (William) Collins a squatter of West Kimberley who informed Mr Haynes that he with others about the time J. Durack was murdered, rounded about 120 natives up and shot a large number consisting of men, women and children.[61]

On the other hand Mary Durack, who blithely acknowledged that a punitive expedition was referred to as a 'nigger hunt',[62] stated that it was impossible to know how many Aboriginal people were killed as 'the conspiracy of silence that sealed the lips of the pioneers added colour to the rumours that spread abroad'.[63] G.H. Lamond, one of the special constables on the expedition, wrote of this incident in his memoir, *Tales of the Overland*, but included no record of interaction at all.[64] The diary entry of Robert Tennant Stow Wolfe makes no mention of contact with the group.[65] However, P.M. Durack, writing in 1933, recalled the incident for the Royal Western Australian Historical Society: 'Later on a punitive force of police and volunteers were sent out by the government and a lot of the blacks were shot.'[66]

As was the case in the West Kimberley the few dissenting public voices about violence were often clergy who saw pastoral expansion on Aboriginal land in humanitarian terms. Aboriginal people were disappearing, the Catholic bishop said, but it was for reasons other than social Darwinism. Aboriginal people stood in the way of pastoral development and the 'whiteman, practically beyond the cognisance of law, shoots straight and shoots often'.[67]

Other less-planned killings involved both police and civilian Europeans in spontaneous massacres in which the victims might be shot and their bodies burnt.[68] The burning of bodies developed as a means of hiding evidence as bodies were easily found in open plains. It is possible to speculate that for police the burden of taking prisoners on foot over areas of several hundred kilometres was a contributing factor to this practice. One account by Hector Chunda, a Kija and Miriuwung man whose father and grandfather were killed by colonists in the 1890s, tells of a massacre north of Turkey Creek, called the Jail Creek massacre:

Some Kartiya bin round em up all the blackfella longa bush, put em chains around their necks. They used to bring em, camp along the road, footwalk, drive em like a mob of cattle. They took em to the right place, Jail Creek. They went up to the rockhole there, having the camp dinner. Then they were carting wood, take them back to the place where they were camping, then tie them up, like a dog. Right, all the kartiya get their guns, line em up, every girl and boy, and shoot em down got a rifle. Whang em all the children on the rocks. [Swung the children by the legs to bash their heads against the rocks.] Chuck em kerosene, put em on the firewood and chuck em all them dead bodies in the firewood place, put em kerosene and chuck em matches. Burn em up them, finished, they all there. That's the way bin call em Jail Creek.[69]

These killings created a serious escalation in conflict between colonists and Aboriginal people. In early 1887 *The Western Mail* reported, 'Great trouble may be anticipated from the natives shortly.'[70] Indeed the killings of Europeans spread throughout the East Kimberley. In January 1888 Thomas Cadley was speared, although he survived, and William Scott was speared and decapitated at Fletcher Creek. In July 1888 George Barnett was speared and killed while travelling between Fletcher Creek and Halls Creek.[71] In September that year Trooper Buckley and stockman E.B. Lockett were speared and killed at the 25 Mile cattle camp near Halls Creek.[72] In almost every case these killings were met with a concerted punitive expedition involving police and colonists, where more Aboriginal people were killed in response.

The punitive expedition that followed Barnett's death is particularly notorious.[73] The death became widely publicised throughout the district with the editor of *Northern Territory Times* (voicing public opinion) writing that the police should disregard any laws, and 'simply admonish them and disperse them in the Queensland fashion';[74] that is, shoot them all. A report in *The Eastern Districts Chronicle* posited that a punitive expedition: 'travelled over 700 miles [1127 kilometres]. The party found and dispersed over 600 adult male natives and a number of females and children.'[75]

The 1929 memoirs of August Lucanus, a special constable on the punitive expedition, stated only that '[t]here must have been at least 200 blacks, and they had not even tried to obliterate their tracks, we soon overtook them and they put up a fight, the women howling and sooling the men on to us. We dispersed them at last, and returned to Wyndham.'[76] In 1946 Mary Durack wrote about this incident with a little more detail than had been offered previously. She claimed that after the spearing of Barnett: 'They [the colonist community] turned out almost to a man to participate in a massacre that is regarded as one of the most sweeping in local history. Barnet's [sic] brother cut a triangular notch in the stock of his rifle for every native he shot with it…and the notches numbered thirty-five!'[77] Colonel Angelo, the government resident of Roebourne at the time, later wrote of this incident:

> accounts differ as to what actually happened but it is almost certain that from sixty to seventy natives there and then paid the extreme penalty. When I visited the scene a couple of years ago human bones were still to be found although over fifty years had elapsed since the massacre…The terrible vengeance meted out by the

enraged diggers on that occasion has indeed proved a salutary lesson to the East Kimberley Blacks.[78]

In addition to the spearings during 1887 through 1888 Aboriginal people of the East Kimberley were recorded as being involved in periodic thefts of items, including food, tools, guns and clothes, when their owners were away from their camps.[79] They also interfered with and often destroyed property such as fences, to use the wire to make spears.[80] They killed pastoral stock for food and used horsehair for ceremonial purposes.[81] Another practice that would infuriate pastoralists was when Aboriginal people would kill cattle and only take the tail off to use as fly or mosquito swats.[82] During 1889 'teamsters and packers', who trucked in food and equipment via horse and cart, reported continuing thefts.[83] The difficulty, if not impossibility, of replacing many essential mining tools in such an isolated district no doubt added to the sense of outrage at the thefts. Wyndham police issued rations such as flour to Aboriginal people in the vicinity in an attempt to assist them and to prevent them raiding camps for food, but this was more symbolic than effective in addressing what was a much larger issue.[84]

In the West Kimberley Aboriginal people could find work on pastoral stations but on the goldfields there was no need for their labour. Police evidence suggests that East Kimberley pastoralists, in the early period at least, had an informal policy of not employing Aboriginal people, indeed of not allowing Aboriginal people anywhere near 'settled districts' or stations for fear of 'them taking advantage of the friendship shown them'.[85] The East Kimberley pastoralists were also sceptical and not as trusting as their West Kimberley counterparts and it meant that few Aboriginal people came onto the station and 'sat down' on *country*.

Sergeant Richard Troy observed this and reported that pastoral stations in the East Kimberley were 'worked by the owners, one or two Europeans, and two or three natives from South Australia. No natives belonging to the country or bush natives about are allowed to come anywhere near the stations.' In 1891 there were only twenty-seven East Kimberley Aboriginal people 'employed by Europeans or living in close proximity to European settlement' and thirty-eight on the goldfields, in contrast to some 145 in the West Kimberley. By 1901 the figure had risen to only forty-eight on stations and ninety-seven on the goldfields in the east and 346 in the West Kimberley.[86]

Sergeant Farley, from Halls Creek Station, observed, 'The natives are very treacherous and will kill a man or steal his rations if they can but by what I saw of them they have a respect for those that keep them at a distance.'[87] If the Aboriginal groups left the pastoralists alone a state of détente ensued. However, if pastoralists interfered with Aboriginal people, particularly Aboriginal women, then this affected relationships. Overall it is clear that pastoralists tolerated Aboriginal people as long as they served a function, such as assisting pastoralists develop the land; if they did not they were branded a nuisance. As the miners and many other working men on pastoral stations came to the vast district without wives or families, they often sought out Aboriginal women. This was to be one of the catalysts for the start of the killings. While the spearing of police (such as Buckley and Lockett in 1888) can be explained as Aboriginal people defending themselves against police, the killings of pastoralists and miners are less explicable. Why, for example, would a group of Aboriginal people risk death to spear solitary men? The case of Marriott reveals one answer: it was because he had taken an Aboriginal woman.

'Brave and Warlike Behaviour'

As with the West Kimberley, local colonists and pastoralists, enraged by the killings of Marriot and Durack, raised the idea of creating a 'Queensland style' native police force. In early 1887 citizens of Wyndham, including P. Durack, A. Buchanan and Francis Connor (part owner of Connor and Doherty pastoral station of Newry), petitioned Governor Broome to establish a native police force in the region because 'it [was] much feared [the blacks would] prove very troublesome and white police [were] not capable of coping with them in their haunts'.[88] Government Resident and future commissioner of police Frederick Hare of Wyndham endorsed this idea, observing that 'the natives here have I believe a strain of Malay blood in them, judging from their appearance and the style of weapons and their brave and warlike behaviour. I find that Europeans are not the slightest use in this country.'[89]

The proposed model would have native police under the control of a non-policeman, the South African-born Robert Tennant Stowe Wolfe.[90] Clearly with an eye on the wide-scale shootings seen under the Queensland model, Commissioner of Police M.S. Smith refused, writing 'protection should be afforded to the aboriginal also'.[91] Smith had made this point when the police were established in the Kimberley in 1882.[92] Governor Broome also did not publicly endorse the plan although the discussion caused the issue to be raised in parliament.[93] Alexander Forrest, as inaugural member for the West Kimberley, raised the need for more police following the killings of Marriot and Durack in the East Kimberley.[94]

The Goose Hill Killings

East Kimberley police were involved in some particularly notorious killings in the 1880s. In September 1888 on a routine police patrol to investigate horse spearing, PC Graham and others, including his native assistant Banjo, shot and killed Aboriginal people at Goose Hill. This was not at first recorded by Graham but was discovered by Sergeant Richard Troy in conversation with him. Police Constable Graham told Sergeant Richard Troy that colonists and police shot and killed Aboriginal people and it was never reported. When PC Graham told Sergeant Payne, he was told to keep it 'quiet' as 'there would only be a row about it if it was known'. The only record in the police occurrence book is the following:

> PC Graham and native assistant Banjo returned to station
> at 7pm from Goose Hill. Report leaving Goose Hill, re.
> Horses being speared by native, with a party of six men
> and three native trackers. About three miles from Goose
> Hill saw about twenty (20) natives. Followed them to
> the Ord River but were unable to arrest any of them,
> they making into the hills.[95]

Upon investigation the story unfolded. In a statement made by Graham with Troy's encouragement, Graham named five colonists who had volunteered to accompany him and Banjo. They had been sent by Sergeant Payne to search for those who had speared two horses belonging to George Howard, who was himself on the party. The party saw three Aboriginal people running away: two were shot as they were running and the third as he climbed a tree to escape his pursuers. Graham reported, 'I requested the party not to fire at the native that I would arrest him, but before I could do anything he was fired at by the party. I reported the whole matter to Sergeant Payne on my return to the station.' Later, when Troy and Banjo returned to the spot where this shooting occurred, they found the remains of a young boy aged about fourteen or fifteen, in a fork of a tree 3 metres high. They found the bleached bones of the first two victims while those of two more victims were found 450–550 metres further away on an open flat.[96]

The witness statement by Native Assistant Banjo, taken 5 September 1888, gives a rare and chilling perspective on the workings of a punitive expedition. Banjo made no distinction between police and colonists. All are called 'whitemen', each carried a revolver and a pistol and each had primed themselves with a lot of 'drink' at the Gordon Hotel, taking more 'grog' with them as they tracked and killed four and attempted to shoot anyone they came across:

I am a police assistant at Wyndham. I remember last summer time soon after Mr Payne came up in the steamer[,] PC Graham told me that the natives had killed a horse of Howard's and that he and I would go tomorrow and catch the natives the next day. PC Graham and I left the station together[,] we went to Goose Hill and slept there that night. Had breakfast and dinner there the next day. After dinner PC Graham[,] five whitemen[,] two blackmen and me started from Goose Hill in search of natives: two of the whitemen names were Howard and Liddelton. I do not know the other man's names: the natives names were Moody and Pompy[,] the former a Roebourne native and the other a Queensland native. PC Graham and all the whitemen had a rifle and revolver each: one native had a rifle and revolver and the other native had a shotgun and revolver each: they all had a lot of drink before we left Gordons Hotel at Goose hill and took grog with them. After travelling a little way we saw the tracks of a lot of natives w[h]ere they had crossed the road, we followed up the tracks and after a while saw the smoke of a fire[. W]e went towards the fire[,] when close we saw the natives running away from the fire; they had no spears with them they left them at the fire; we galloped after them[,] they run into some trees and bushes that were close by[,] we soon over took them and stopped them there, when close up to them the whitefellows and blackfellas all fired on two of the natives and shot them dead[,] the other native who was a very young boy had climbed up a tree; After shooting the two men the party then all fired at the boy in the tree and shot him dead, he fell into the fork of the tree and lay there. Howard went close up to the tree[,] got off his horse and fired at this boy[,] the other whitefellows stood a little further back and fired at him[,] some were on their horses and some were on the ground; After those tree natives were shot the whitefellows stopped there a little while and all had more drink (grog)[. W]e then followed on some native tracks that were leading from the place, we followed them to a place where a lot of natives had been camped, it was not far from where the three natives had been shot, we saw from the tracks that a lot of natives had runaway[. W]e followed up their tracks to the Ord River[,] they had gone through the mangroves;

we then started back to camp near w[h]ere we had
shot the natives[. W]hen close there I saw two natives
coming in a crossing direction from the way we were
travelling, they were going towards where the large
camp of natives had run away from. We all galloped
after those two natives they ran into the water of a creek
or swamp[,] the whitefellows fired on one first and shot
him dead in the water. These two natives had a lot of
spears when I first seen them but as they were running
away they dropped them. We all camped that night
close to where we shot the natives. During the night we
heard the natives shouting and women crying all night
at a distance. The next morning we all went in the
direction we heard the natives, close to the Ord River[,]
we saw a lot of natives running away. We galloped after
them but they got into the mangroves and swam across
the river. One of the whitemen fired at them but they
were too far off. I have since accompanied Sergt Troy to
the place where the natives were shot and showed him
the remains of them.[97]

Sergeant Troy arrested and laid charges against PC Graham
and others who shot the five at Goose Hill. In December that
year Troy reported to the commissioner of police that these arrests
'caused the greatest sensation and indignation in Wyndham'.[98]
Apparently the entire town was incensed at the arrests and at
the house of the editor of *The Nor-West Times* a committee was
formed to procure their release.[99] Troy and the government resident were even concerned that the public might attempt to 'rescue
the prisoners' by breaking them out of gaol.[100] When confronted

with the charge of 'murdering five natives', Howard told police that he thought the killings might have 'blown over', remarking that 'I cannot see that I have done much wrong'.[101]

PC Graham was discharged from the police force in October 1888 for this incident. Banjo was charged with the murder of five Aboriginal people and committed for trial at the Supreme Court in Perth.[102] Other members of the party, John Liddelow and Henry Lewis, were discharged at a lower court. John George Graham, George Howard and his 'boy' Moody, William Hill, and the Queensland Aboriginal man Pompey were committed for trial at the Supreme Court. Despite damning findings from the judge, whose summing up of the case lasted one hour and twenty minutes, the jury took just fifteen minutes to find Graham and Howard 'not guilty'. Given this result and unlikelihood of a successful prosecution, all the other accused were released.[103] To exacerbate this miscarriage of justice it is possible that over sixteen times more Aboriginal people (including women and children) were killed than the ones mentioned. A later newspaper report from 1908 that corroborates much of the detail suggested that 'as many as eighty natives may have been butchered'.[104]

The killings at Goose Hill and Halls Creek reveal the nature of silences in the police records. Self-appointed colonists and special constables not only went on these expeditions with police but also actively encouraged and participated in attacks. They reveal the fact that such men would not speak or write of an event that would incriminate them and others, and that certain police colluded with them to hide the killings from the authorities in Perth. Sergeant Payne, who as a police constable in 1883 had been one of the most ardent supporters of Aboriginal rights against blackbirders and pearlers, had changed his attitude.

After the Goose Hill killings were publicised in Perth newspapers, Attorney General Charles Warton expressed alarm and sought to assert his authority. He wrote to Colonial Secretary Malcolm Fraser in correspondence marked 'secret'.[105] Writing with 'anxiety for the future' and with 'a deep sense of responsibility', he stated that on two previous occasions he had drawn attention to police activities in the Kimberley and that his advice had been disregarded. 'On both those occasions', Warton wrote, 'the police acted unjustly to the natives and on one of those the Commissioner of Police considered their actions "beneficial" and his view was adopted.'[106] Warton then posed a series of questions to the colonial secretary:

This is a question far wider, far more important, far more dangerous than any mere question of obtaining legal 'advice'. It is a question not chiefly of law but of policy, of government, of statesmanship. Are we resolved in maintaining Wyndham *coute qui coute* [at any cost]? Have we the means, have we the men to do so without cruelty and injustice to the natives? Can we indoctrinate either the police there or the adventurers there with an idea of justice to or consideration of the natives? Are we prepared to support the present mode of action of the police and the wishes of the adventurers? Can we hold Wyndham if we do not? Before condemning this way of putting the question I humbly beg leave to call his Excellency's attention to the proved facts.[107]

Having access to Richard Troy's police record of this incident and other witness testimony, Warton detailed what he saw as outrageous and illegal behaviour, writing:

241

that natives have been shot dead before [this occurrence] by persons who were not with the police and nothing was said about it. That such proceeding when reported by a policeman to his sergeant, the sergeant says they had better keep it quiet there would only be a row about it if it were known.[108]

He went on, 'One can hear from general conversation that the natives are seen and shot at immediately with little or no provocation' and 'It is now next to impossible for the police to bring to justice these persons who commit attacks and assaults on the natives.' The constables at the East Kimberley police stations, Warton noted, 'are not men who are adapted for this work, they have no idea how to manage or deal with the natives'.[109]

Warton believed that the situation in the East Kimberley was critical and begged the colonial secretary to suggest changes to the way Aboriginal people were policed.[110] Indeed his question 'Can we hold Wyndham?' emphasised the urgency of the issue.'[111] There is no evidence found that the colonial secretary acted on the request at all. In fact, as we shall see in the next chapter, Fraser would state publicly that the Aboriginal people in the Kimberley were protected.

'A Severe Example Must be Made of Them'

As we have seen in chapter 5, in late 1888 and early 1889, police numbers were increased in the Kimberley and soon after Commissioner Phillips issued a new set of directives. Attention was now to be directed to the areas of most conflict: the goldfields and the telegraph line.[112] Police numbers in the goldfields were to be increased. There would now be one sergeant, four troopers and three mounted constables inclusive of a mail constable plus four native assistants and twenty horses.[113] Inspector Lodge set out new rules relating to shooting Aboriginal people. While he endorsed 'a severe example being made of some of them', he warned that 'this service must be performed by the *Police alone* and they must be careful not to abuse the power entrusted to them', and 'The men must be cautioned against the unnecessary use of firearms and any acts of cruelty or shooting natives without sufficient cause will lead to severe punishment.'[114] Phillips in turn instructed Lodge as follows:

> It is desirable that you should take an opportunity to visit the goldfields and endeavour to place the police force on a more satisfactory footing in regard to the discipline, economy, general conduct, systematic performance of their duties and dealing with the natives. On this matter there should be clear and precise instructions and they must be cautioned not to unnecessarily use firearms but rather by firmness, tempered with kindness and judicious treatment to endeavour to bring about a better state of affairs with the natives.[115]

The Trouble on the Telegraph Line

These directives related to policing the goldfields, the emerging pastoral stations and to protecting a critical piece of East Kimberley infrastructure: the telegraph line. The erection of the line had begun at Wyndham in August 1888 and reached Halls Creek in July 1890 but it was continually damaged by Aboriginal people who had found that the glass and porcelain insulators made extremely effective spearheads.[116] Glass was also exchanged in the regular trade meetings held by the East Kimberley Aboriginal groups.[117]

The telegraph, however, was more important to the colonists. It provided relatively fast communication between the Kimberley and Perth. Police relied on the telegraph line to receive and send instructions. If the line was broken communication was impossible and this, in part, led to the organisational confusion of East Kimberley policing during this period. One imaginative warden suggested police leave piles of broken glass at the foot of many telegraph poles as an alternative glass source for Aboriginal people's spears to preserve the telegraph line, though it is unclear if this ever eventuated.[118]

Local residents were greatly concerned about damage to the telegraph line and police were ordered to make regular patrols. This was not an official police duty, however, and it created considerable resentment given their already stretched resources. Constables were ordered to do 'perpetual' patrols up and down the line from Wyndham to Halls Creek – a distance of some 380 kilometres – and even to repair it when it was damaged. On one patrol in July 1890 of over 193 kilometres, police counted every insulator and examined the state of the wire over the whole length and reported on the results.[119]

Police were also instructed to arrest Aboriginal men found with material from the line. Those convicted of wilful damage were sentenced to periods of imprisonment in the Wyndham gaol of anywhere from three to nine months. This proved ineffective and the rugged East Kimberley ranges, particularly the Carr Boyd and O'Donnell ranges that ran parallel to the telegraph line, made arrests difficult. As well as causing damage by removing or breaking the insulators, Aboriginal people were accused of breaking the wire and damaging poles.[120] By 29 November 1892 the police reported that out of 250 miles (402 kilometres) of telegraph line, 190 miles had been destroyed by Aboriginal people.[121]

But were Aboriginal people to blame? As Sub Inspector Troy had noted pastoralists in the West Kimberley during the same period always blamed stock losses on Aboriginal people. It seemed that the same thing happened on the telegraph line. He wrote in mid-1889 that destruction of 'the bush telegraph' was 'always blamed on the natives but often it was teamsters who knocked it down to take the wire to sell'.[122] And in mid-1890 the government resident wrote that damage to the telegraph line was due to the climatic conditions and the fact that the contractor did such a poor job putting it up in the first place that it simply fell over.[123] Other accounts reveal that the wrong wire was ordered from England and it was constantly breaking.[124] These observations had no effect on policing as police, often armed with firearms, continued to prosecute all Aboriginal people they saw in the vicinity of the line.

Birth of the 'Outcamps'

Policing from small, undeveloped towns such as at Wyndham and Halls Creek was always difficult due to the enormous distances police had to travel. The extra police funding granted through the Western Australian parliament went towards the creation of what were called 'midway camps', 'bush camps' or 'outcamps' at Denham (or Dunham) River and Fletcher Creek. These were created to 'maintain a patrol of the telegraph line to prevent damage by the Aborigines and arrest natives who offend by damaging the line'.[125] This reduced the need for these extensive (and expensive) bush patrols of hundreds of kilometres. The first camp, at Denham River, was officially established on 1 November 1889. It was 74 kilometres from Wyndham, and remained until 27 April 1895 with constables McCann, Gee and Rhatigan as officers in charge. Fletcher Creek camp, established in November 1890, was 235 kilometres from Wyndham and remained until 3 December

1895. Troopers Austin and Kingston were in charge with PCs Inglis and Gordon.[126]

Fletcher Creek and Denham River outcamps were not places policemen generally chose to go. Police, and their native assistants and horses, were solely dedicated to dealing with the 'native question' and preventing Aboriginal people from interfering with the telegraph line. Whilst the infrastructure of the main towns was rudimentary enough, police lived in nothing more than tents at these camps; the first solid timber police station was not built at Fletcher Creek camp until October 1893.[127] Very few records of Fletcher Creek appear to have survived and the physical state of the surviving records at Denham Creek speaks volumes about the physical environment: the occurrence books, for example, have been eaten through by white ants and are mud splattered and water stained.

Records relating to the actual telegraph line patrols from Denham Station are available and reveal that police prosecuted any and every Aboriginal person they found in the vicinity of the line. One example was a bush patrol from Denham Station down Sandy Creek on 28 May 1889 with PCs Fields, Connor, Pollard and Tuke and native assistants Mingo and Johnny.[128] A patrol with four constables was in itself a rare event and would indicate a large-scale operation. Mingo tracked an Aboriginal group until they saw smoke in the bed of the river; the party went to investigate. Tuke's stark account of the event shows little in the way of formal police procedure, as no warnings seem to have been given.

> One native threw a spear at native assistant Mingo. The native took to a big pool of water about 70 yards wide. About 15 natives went into the water. The banks of the river were very steep. Each of the natives had a

large bundle of spears and a lot was floating about on the water. They tried to throw the spears. The party opened fire upon them[,] a lot of shots were fired. PC Field shot one native dead while endeavouring to escape. One of the natives shipped his spear at PC Pollard and PC Tuke. PC Fields fired at him from the opposite side of the pool wounding him in the head but did not kill him he remained clinging on to a tree that had fell into the water. One native and a boy were captured by PC Fields. Another by native Mingo and a boy by Nat Assist Johnny. PC Fields went around to the other side of the pool where the wounded native was and endeavored [sic] to get him out of the water[,] but he would not come [and] at the same time grasping a spear that lay near him in the water and tried to get into a position to throw it. PC Fields fired at him with rifle wounding him in the arm. PC Fields with Native Assistant Mingo went into the water and brought the native out and on examining him found the leg was broken under the knee[,] he being unable to travel we left him on the side of the river. Tuke recorded that this mob had about fifty spears with them.[129]

In these police reports there seems to have been similar confusion to that experienced in the West Kimberley about the legal use of firearms and the use of lethal force. While Constable Armitage from Derby Station had been charged with murder for shooting an Aboriginal boy named Jenella in October 1889, there was a similar case in the East Kimberley at around the same time.

In December 1889 PC Kingston wrote a report from the Halls Creek Station describing a patrol of the telegraph line. When he came across groups that 'were all well-armed with spears some of which *appeared to be made of insulators*' they:

> shewed [sic] a very determined effort to fight, kept constantly shipping their spears at us dodging from boulder to boulder until finally they made their escape into a rocky mountain where it would be impossible to take them alive; as a last resort we fired a few shots upon them but without effect.[130]

The reply of Commissioner Phillips to this testimony was as scathing as it was no doubt perplexing to police. Appearances of insulators 'do not justify the police in resorting to the use of firearms', he wrote.[131] He warned Kingston that he was fortunate he did not hit anyone, as had he done so he would have been charged with 'wilful murder'.[132] It was only 'when the natives are caught in the act of damaging the line…and resist arrest that the police would be justified in using their firearms'.[133] Inspector Lodge later reinforced this by adding that a 'severe lesson' should only be given under the circumstances described by the commissioner and he reiterated that 'prevention of crime, protection of persons and property and preservation of public are the principal duties of the police'.[134] Kingston's superior, Sergeant Farley, replied to Commissioner Phillips pointing out the difficulty in following such instructions. What, Farley wondered, were the police to do, when, if Aboriginal people were caught, they immediately resisted, usually throwing spears?[135]

It was a good question. As we saw in May 1889, PC Fields from Denham River camp shot and killed several Aboriginal people in similar circumstances without comment from the commissioner of police. Yet just over six months later other police such as Kingston were called to account. The meaning of implementing a 'severe lesson' was marked by confusion; indeed it appeared to be something that only the commissioner could define. And, as these two examples show, official action on any given police report seemed to be arbitrary. On the other hand, perhaps the unwanted publicity from the 'Jenella case' in the West Kimberley forced Commissioner Phillips to try to control police behaviour.[136]

When police were not on patrol there were often only single policemen at these stations. This was always a worrying time for such men. Records reveal that rather than police controlling Aboriginal people through intimidation, arrest and punishment, it was sometimes the police who were intimidated.[137] Police records document groups of well over 100 Aboriginal people gathered at times and at night they would often hear corroborees.[138] Other Aboriginal people were avoiding conflict in a variety of ways. On 7 July PC Tuke wrote that 'the natives around here are very numerous[,] fear they will be doing some mischief unless very decisive steps are taken to drive them away…we saw where they had been jumping across the road to avoid leaving tracks'.[139]

However, other groups appeared to be becoming defiant. On one patrol in early December 1890 PC Tuke (riding Cataract), PC McCann (riding Planet) and Native Assistant Tim (on Apollo) found a camp of people stealing from the telegraph.

On approaching the camp they swarmed out in one waving mass, there being sixty or seventy in number of all ages and sexes. The men armed with their spears soon got in the lead[,] I had small hopes of rounding them up the police party being too small so we each singled out a man and we gave chase[.] PC McCann and myself suc-ceeded in capturing two and hearing the report of Tim's revolver I left McCann with the two men and went to Tim's assistance and found him gamely sticking to his man. The native had thrown several spears at him[,] one having struck Apollo in the shoulder in front of the knee pad making a nasty gash. I rode up to within ten yards of him and[,] as he was throwing his spear at me[,] I shot him with a bullet through the centre of the head which killed him dead on the spot. We then attempted to pursue the rest of the mob but found they had made good their escape into the ranges.[140]

This chapter has demonstrated how, during the 1880s, very small numbers of police attempted to police very large groups of Aboriginal people in the East Kimberley and that this policing was characterised by considerable violence. It has shown how attempts to moderate police behaviour in relation to protocols for shooting at Aboriginal people were fraught with difficulty and confusion. Police were caught between attempting to enforce the law and a colonist community that clearly took the law into its own hands and expected that police would protect white lives and property. The 'conspiracy of silence' amongst colonists enabled the killings to be kept 'underground', making the gathering of evidence difficult in the extreme. In any case it is clear that the Western Australian government was aware that killings of Aboriginal people by both police and colonists were occurring but expediency prevailed over the rule of law. With Western Australia entering a period of responsible government from 1890, the situation for the Aboriginal people in the East and West Kimberley would become dire. This is the subject of the following chapter.

Chapter 7

'IN THE HANDS OF A SMALL OLIGARCHY'

Responsible Government in Western Australia

This chapter shifts the focus from the Kimberley to the parliament in Perth. It will examine the significant changes to Western Australian politics and policing during the late 1880s and early 1890s when Western Australia, the last colony of Australia to be granted self-rule, finally attained 'responsible government'. This change meant the creation of a bicameral legislature, with the lower house (the newly created Legislative Assembly) elected on universal male suffrage and the upper house (the Legislative Council) elected on a male-only property franchise. The ministry was elected from the Legislative Assembly and the premier came from the dominant party in the Assembly. The sidelining of the governors and their ministries, who had had control over Western Australia since the establishment of the Swan River Colony in 1829, had significant ramifications for the period in question. This chapter explores how these political changes affected the legal position of Aboriginal people in the Kimberley and so laid the groundwork for changes to policing.

When John Forrest returned from his exploration of the Kimberley in late 1883 he became commissioner of Crown lands as well as surveyor general. He advised that due to the environmental conditions and hardships that 'the easiest terms and conditions' should be given to the colonists there.[1] In 1884, as commissioner for Crown lands and chairman of the commission into the treatment of Aboriginal prisoners, he noted that European colonists had arrived on 'native land' and were 'accelerating their speedy removal from the earth'.[2] He stated that:

> Large revenues, nearly £100,000 a year are now raised from the sale and lease of lands which were originally possessed by its native inhabitants; and therefore it seems reasonable that some portion of this revenue should be devoted to the amelioration of their condition.[3]

By the time Forrest became the first premier of Western Australia on 22 December 1890 it is clear that he no longer held this position. Rhetorically Forrest would continue to assert that he wished to protect Aboriginal people from the ill effects of colonisation, but his actions tell a different story. The reasons for his change of attitude can be found in the changing economic fortunes of Western Australia.

During late 1888 and 1889 pastoral stations in the West and East Kimberley struggled for viability as the price for sheep and wool had dropped. The King Sound Pastoral Company was liquidated and sold to James Munro and others, and the stations that survived this period worked with reduced staff.[4] Critically, rentals for Crown lands diminished.[5] The cattle industry, established on Alexander Forrest's grand promises, was stagnant, commercial failings being exacerbated by the rudimentary transport, marketing and sale facilities.[6] Due to the rugged topography of the Kimberley, not to mention the distances involved, many sheep and cattle producers simply could not get sufficient numbers of quality stock to market. The early prosperity of the Kimberley pastoral industry could not be sustained.

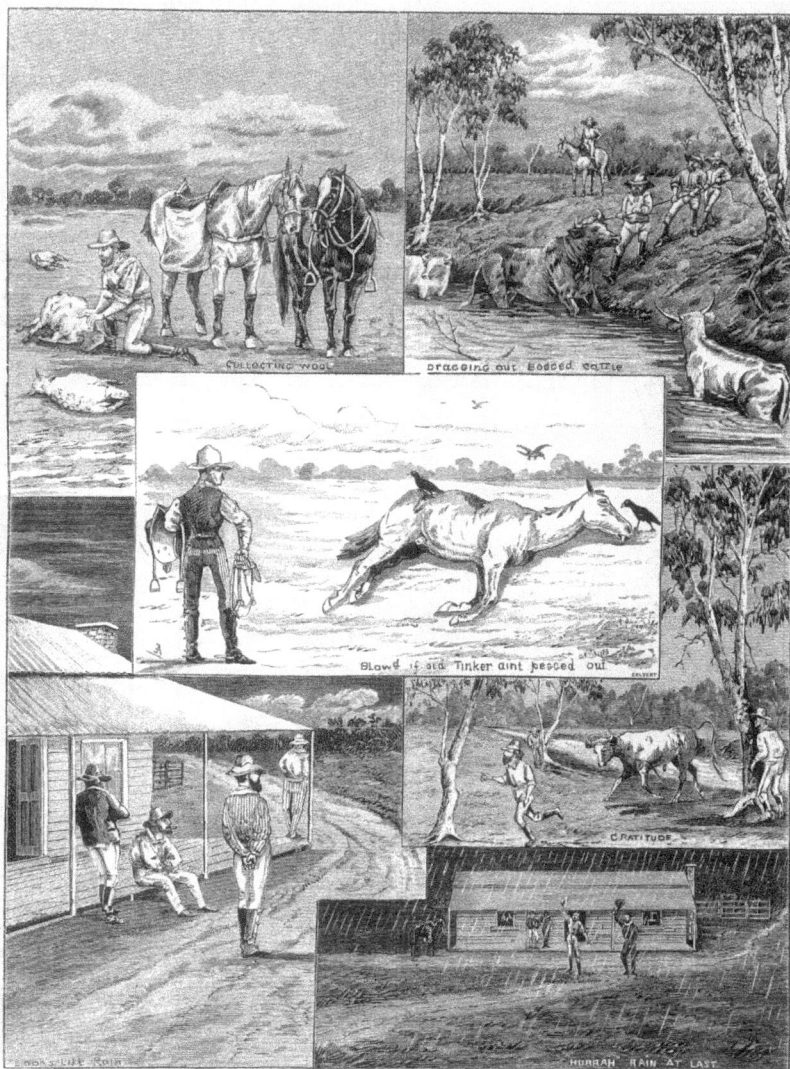

Figure 7.1. Samuel Calvert, The Drought in the Kimberley District, W.A., 1 July 1891, Melbourne: David Syme and Co. Courtesy of the State Library of Victoria, Cons. IAN01/07/91/13.

By the turn of the decade there was an economic depression in Western Australia that affected markets for stock and, at the same time, the Kimberley was hit by drought.[7] Many stations were financially ruined and many thousands of stock perished.[8] There was inadequate rainfall during the wet seasons of 1891, 1892 and 1893.[9] This meant not only less feed for stock but also that the already diminishing natural animal and vegetable food sources for the Aboriginal groups were 'either parched or killed'.[10] This problem was exacerbated by colonists killing great numbers of what was a staple Aboriginal food source, the kangaroo, both for the price they could get for the skins and because kangaroos were considered pests who ate a lot of the same grasses as sheep and cattle.[11] The inevitable result was that Aboriginal people took to killing more stock than ever, although how many animals they killed remained in dispute.

The West Kimberley, already affected by drought and Aboriginal attacks on property, suffered further catastrophic environmental events. By the time stock numbers and prices had improved and the drought had broken, in February 1894 there was what one police officer called 'the greatest flood known in the West Kimberley' which came 'without a moment[']s warning'.[12] The Lennard and Fitzroy rivers flood plains, home of pastoral stations from Yeeda and Oobagooma on the coast to Lillamaloora, Lennard River Station and Liveringa inland, were inundated. The stock losses and associated commercial losses on all stations as reported by police were enormous.[13] Total accounts put the figure at some 30,000 stock lost.[14] Such was the volume of water that Sub Inspector Drewry reported '17 feet [5.18 metres] of water at the Devil's Pass' (Windjana Gorge) and that the Lennard River police camp had been 'washed away'.[15]

In the 1890s the policy confusion that existed around who was responsible for the welfare of Aboriginal people – the government or the colonists – remained unresolved; indeed it became more acute as time went on.[16] Colonists in the North West and

Kimberley pleaded for government assistance and more police to counter what they claimed as potentially catastrophic stock losses through Aboriginal attacks. Police reports in the early 1890s continued to completely contradict colonist accounts blaming Aboriginal people for stock losses and challenged the extent of those losses.

It is clear that pastoralists exaggerated stock losses to gain attention from the government and demand more resources in the districts. That police so often contradicted them added to existing antagonism. For example, police at the Lennard River camp furnished a report on the stations in the subdistrict of West Kimberley to Inspector Lodge in mid-1891.[17] At Lillamaloora, run by William Forrester and owned by the then Premier of Victoria James Munro, PC Armitage observed that there had been no complaints of depredations since the beginning of the year. Less than two years earlier the pastoralists had claimed they had lost 4000 sheep to Aboriginal attacks.[18] PC Armitage, reporting on the state of Lillamaloora Station, ascribed losses to causes other than Aboriginal people.

> everything in connection with the management of the station is carried on in a very loose and unsystematic manner, the paddock fences being in such a bad case of repair that the sheep and cattle have no trouble getting out. And little or no effort is made to recover them again, the consequence are that when they come to muster the sheep they find they are considerable [sic] below the estimated numbers and for the want of a better excuse the losses are put down [to] the natives by the manager.[19]

He continued that losses were so 'heavy' because of 'starvation and want of proper attention', and the presence of native dogs which 'make great havoc amongst the sheep'.[20] These factors, he noted, were not acknowledged by the manager nor was the fact that the Aboriginal workforce on this station was treated poorly, given insufficient food and were placed 'at the mercy of every white man employed there'.[21] Armitage noted that the police had called the manager's attention to this matter several times.[22] The situation on Lillamaloora became so bad that Munro abandoned the station in November 1892 due to chronic financial difficulties and it was taken over by Lukin and Monger. The stock was sold to Emanuel Bros at Gogo Station (Margaret Downs).[23] Lillamaloora Station house became Lillamaloora Police Station. The station's troubles were ironic because Lillamaloora was the station from which thirty-nine West Kimberley pastoralists (including Alexander Forrest) had petitioned the government of Western Australia that 'wild natives be declared outlaws'.

A similar situation existed at William Lukin's neighbouring Lennard River Station. In October 1889 Lukin led the deputation to the Western Australian government claiming he had lost 2000 sheep to Aboriginal attacks.[24] In July 1891 PC Armitage reported that at Lennard River Station no complaints to the police had been made since the beginning of the year. Armitage stated that the reasons for stock losses in 1891 were threefold: native dogs killed a lot of the sheep, other sheep died from starvation, and the station simply 'lost' a lot more.[25] Armitage did observe that the Aboriginal workers seemed to be treated very well and Lukin had something of a reputation with the bush blacks for miles around as a 'good fellow'.[26] Lukin's main problem was that his workforce left at the critical shearing time – for what the pastoralists termed 'pinkeye', or Aboriginal ceremonial business – and when they came back to the station he didn't need them anymore. But now that he didn't want them anymore, Armitage observed, he 'cannot get them to leave'.[27]

There is another important implication to Armitage's reports. Pastoralists – Lukin, Munro and Monger – had unreservedly supported PC Armitage in October 1889 when he was charged with the murder of the Aboriginal boy Jenella, a charge that was subsequently dropped. The fact that Armitage continued to act independently of pastoralist wishes, and indeed to criticise them, is revealing and indicates that police were not completely beholden to pastoralists, at least at this stage in the history of the area, as is suggested in some historical accounts.[28]

Coupled with poor pastoral seasons there was a significant demographic change occurring. The population of Western Australia had increased slowly from some 25,084 in 1870 to 29,019 in 1880, and at a staggering rate during the late 1880s and early 1890s due to the discovery of gold and subsequent gold-rushes. Frank Crowley described how the Forrest government was 'extraordinarily lucky' that so much gold had been found and enormous flows of investment capital in Western Australia commenced.[29] Beginning at Halls Creek in early 1886, other gold-rushes occurred at Yilarn (October 1888), Ashburton (December 1890), and the especially significant finds at Coolgardie (1892), Kalgoorlie (June 1893) and the Murchison District (1899). These discoveries brought enormous population increases to Western Australia mostly from the eastern colonies: 53,285 people in 1891 and around 100,235 in 1895.[30] By 1901 the total population had more than tripled from its 1891 figure to some 184,124 people.[31] With this enormous population increase the market for beef and sheep increased exponentially.[32] This population upheaval would also profoundly affect the composition of Western Australian politics. The survival of the Kimberley pastoral industry became more important than ever before and was facilitated by critical changes at a government level, that being the establishment of responsible government in Western Australia.

Western Australia: 'In the Hands of a Small Oligarchy'

Concerns had been raised in debates in the British House of Commons around granting responsible government. The Member for Kirkcaldy Burghs, Sir George Campbell, raised concerns around the treatment of Aboriginal people. In February 1890 he proclaimed that Western Australia was 'in the hands of a small oligarchy, and that this [Western Australian Constitution] Bill is drawn in anything but a popular manner. It is proposed to exclude all the poorer colonists and all the natives.'[33] In June of the same year he confessed to the house that 'I have some apprehension that, when home control is removed, the scenes in Queensland may be repeated in West Australia'; that is, the notorious widespread shooting of Aboriginal people. He contended 'there are considerable reasons why we should hesitate in handing over control of enormous territory to a small number of people'.[34]

Despite these concerns *The Constitution Act 1889* that established responsible government in Western Australia was given royal assent by Queen Victoria on 15 August 1890 and took effect on 21 October that year with a proclamation by the new governor, Sir William Robinson, who took over from Broome. This was his third appointment as governor, having served from 1875 to 1877 and 1880 to 1883.[35] Under responsible government the Executive Council was dissolved, and the office of colonial secretary (held by Malcolm Fraser) became a ministerial portfolio. Fraser retired on 28 December 1890 rather than contest a parliamentary seat.[36]

After responsible government was implemented John Forrest formed the first government and introduced a 'very bold and extensive' public works policy to develop the state, borrowing some £1,336,000 which would leave even fewer funds for government services than before.[37] Changes in political institutions and subsequent legislation aided and assisted the Kimberley pastoral industry. By early 1891 Forrest's ministry consisted of four cabinet ministers – Colonial Secretary George Shenton, Attorney General Septimus Burt, Commissioner for Crown Lands George Marmion and Commissioner for Railways Harry Whittall Venn – all of whom owned stations in the North West and Kimberley and, as was shown in chapter 2, had earlier experience in dealing with Aboriginal people. Venn (who as noted in chapter 3 had branded one of his workers) would design the facilities for shipping stock at Wyndham and Derby. As W.B. Kimberly noted in his 1897 *History of West Australia* each one had pursued successful and active careers in colonial industry: Forrest as an explorer and land administrator; Shenton as a merchant and property holder; Burt as a prominent lawyer; Marmion as a merchant and investor; and Venn as a pastoralist on a large scale.[38] It was a parochial group; all were Western Australian born or had lived for twenty-five years in the West. Incongruously perhaps, Shenton was a member of the Aborigines Protection Board.[39]

Tom Stannage has referred to Forrest's ministry as a 'quasi-aristocracy', reinforcing Campbell's claim that the ministry was an oligarchy backed by most of the northern pastoralists.[40] He has shown how insular the Western Australian parliament was at this time with twenty-six of the thirty members of the Legislative Assembly being what he terms 'ancient colonists': members of families who had been in the colony a long time with half of them actually born in the colony.[41] This group would steadfastly support land-owning interests. Geoffrey Bolton shows how grossly undemocratic the Legislative Assembly franchise was and how the distribution of seats was skewed towards pastoral interests: just eight seats out of a total of thirty represented electorates north of the Murchison district. North West and Kimberley pastoralists were able to wield influence well out of proportion to the number of people in their electorates. In both Kimberley seats members were elected to represent areas where their commercial interests lay. After the Kimberley was split into East and West, Alexander Forrest sat as parliamentary member for the West Kimberley from 1890 to 1901.[42] The East Kimberley (which existed from 1890 to 1904) became another electoral district of the Legislative Assembly and was represented by independent member Francis Connor, who held the seat from 1893 to 1904.

The role of the governor during this period also changed considerably.[43] Governor Broome was an active participant in Western Australian politics and, as we have seen in previous chapters, often entered debates around Aboriginal policy. He had been one of the key figures in the formation of responsible government, having been asked by the Legislative Council in July 1887 to investigate the proposal.[44] In his capacity as governor he acted as intermediary between the Legislative Council and the secretary of state in England. Broome supported the proposal for responsible government but with several caveats, two of which were that appropriate protection be given to the Aboriginal populations and that the British government might at any time create a separate colony in the north of Western Australia. The secretary of state approved, in principle, the Council's request for responsible government but insisted that permanent protection be given to Aboriginal people by the creation of the Aborigines Protection Board, responsible not to the local legislature but to the British government. This was achieved through the passage of the *Aborigines Protection Act 1886* through Parliament.[45]

Figure 7.2. 'The Last Executive Council before Responsible Government in Western Australia'. Left to right standing: the Hon. Josceline Amherst (Secretary), the Hon. Anthony O'Grady Lefroy (Colonial Treasurer), the Hon. Sir John Forrest (Commissioner for Crown Lands and Surveyor General), the Hon. J. Arthur Wright (Director of Public Works and Commissioner for Railways and Engineer in Chief), the Hon. Sir J.G. Lee Steere (Speaker of the Legislative Council); Sitting: the Hon. Sir Malcolm Fraser (Colonial Secretary), the Hon. Sir Frederick Napier Broome (Governor), the Hon. Charles Nicholas Warton (Attorney General). Courtesy State Library of Western Australia, 032657PD. Photographer unknown.

Broome, who was Canadian born, had worked in the British colony of Natal in 1854, then became lieutenant governor of Mauritius before becoming governor of Western Australia in 1883.[46] Neville Green suggests that Broome insisted on the exclusion of Aboriginal people from the purview of the Western Australian parliament because of his history as colonial secretary in Natal and his involvement in the Natal Charter, which, as would later happen in Western Australia, guaranteed £5000 for black African interests and reserved lands free from the Natal government. The Natal Charter contained a list of requirements that the Natal government could not amend.[47] Responsible government also meant the mediating influence of the government resident was removed from the regions. This office, as the representative of British law, was the 'eyes and ears' of the colonial state in the regions and maintained oversight of police activities. There were, however, clauses in the Act granting responsible government that radically affected the administration of Aboriginal affairs.

Section 70 of *The Constitution Act 1889* provided that £5000, or 1% of annual revenue, be dedicated to the welfare of Aboriginal people in Western Australia. The constitution also provided that the Aborigines Protection Board, rather than a minister of the Crown within a department, should remain responsible for the care of Aboriginal people.[48] Members of the Western Australian parliament objected strenuously to section 70 on two grounds: that it was interference in colonial affairs and that the imperial government thought the parliament of Western Australia could not be trusted to deal fairly with Aboriginal people.[49] Both were true. Remarks in the House of Lords in 1905 by Viscount Knutsford following the release of the Roth Report confirmed that the Act would never have been passed by the imperial parliament without the acceptance of section 70.[50]

These requirements resulted in considerable tension between the British Colonial Office and the Western Australian government.[51] In the first place, the 1% revenue figure rapidly exceeded £5000 due to the revenues generated by the 1890s goldrushes and escalated exponentially. John Forrest, as we have seen earlier, supported the idea of a board overseeing Aboriginal matters but now fiercely rejected the idea. He objected not only on financial grounds but on the grounds that section 70 reeked of paternalism and was an insult, a denial of complete self-government.[52]

Additionally whilst the Aborigines Protection Board was funded by government revenues – independent of parliamentary appropriation – the actual work in distributing relief was done by police and other already over-stretched public service employees.

At a practical level, the travelling inspectors from the Board compiled detailed reports of conditions of Aboriginal people in remote pastoral regions; at the political level the Board wielded significant clout. Its secretary, Charles D'Oyle Forbes, would criticise Forrest and his supporters as being motivated not by a desire for independence from Britain, but by private commercial interests, because the 'members of the present ministry are to a man directly or indirectly connected with sheep farming'.[53] Forbes continued that the colonists did not 'as a rule, recognise the original title of the Aborigines to the land, and whose desire, in all, and is, for cheap land, or labour, or both, as the case may be'.[54] Governor Broome's support of the Aborigines Protection Board put him in conflict with John Forrest and they were so often involved in major disputes that his tenure as governor was not renewed. He left office on 19 October 1890 and was replaced by William Robinson.

Robinson's task was to oversee the introduction of parliamentary government in the colony. Whilst in London he helped the colonial office and delegates from Western Australia pass the Constitutional Bill through the imperial parliament. Back in Perth he arranged for the first elections for the Legislative Assembly; chose the first premier, John Forrest (who would receive a knighthood for 'services to the colony' just one year later); and nominated the members of the Legislative Council.[55] However, he too soon found himself at odds with the new Forrest administration. Robinson did not endorse harsh punitive measures against Aboriginal people and defended the Aborigines Protection

Board, suggesting that Forrest's hostile attitude towards it was 'not in good faith towards her Majesty's government'.[56] Robinson even rebuked Forrest, censuring him for speaking disparagingly of the Board.[57] To the Secretary of State for the Colonies, Lord Ripon, he remarked that 'personally we are excellent friends, but as Premier he is now a difficult, indeed unpleasant man to deal with'.[58] Regarding Aboriginal people Robinson wrote that under the present form of self-government, he as governor could not insist 'upon the clemency of the crown', that responsible government meant that Aboriginal people no longer had protection under British law.[59] Meanwhile reports of abuse of Aboriginal people and allegations of 'slavery' in Western Australia were being received in London and reported in local newspapers. Damning reports of ill-treatment of Aboriginal people in the North West and Kimberley – described as a 'mal-administration of justice' that was 'squatocratic' and a 'horrible farce' – would also appear in journals such as the *Westminster Review.*[60]

In September 1892 Malcolm Fraser, now agent general for Western Australia, wrote a 'lengthy and forcible' letter to the London *Daily Chronicle* denying allegations of slavery in the north of Western Australia and claiming that 'the interests of the natives are well guarded by the government'.[61] Premier John Forrest also wrote to London 'emphatically denying the charges of ill-treatment and slavery'.[62] Forrest clearly resented official advice or reprimands from Robinson, especially over the issues of the Aborigines Protection Board and the treatment and control of Aboriginal people.[63] The practical role of the Western Australian governor in politics diminished partly because of the new constitution and partly because Forrest established his personal dominance over both cabinet and parliament.

Debates in the New Parliament

In the Western Australian political realm, another significant debate on Aboriginal policy began on 14 January 1892 when Robert Sholl, Member for the Gascoyne, put forward a proposal for the 'protection of northern settlers against hostile natives'.[64] In the new parliament, clearly pastoral interests felt free to assert themselves much more forcefully than before. There were two main thrusts to the debate: who was responsible for the protection of pastoralists and stock, and what powers could be utilised to control Aboriginal people? Concern about the welfare of Aboriginal people and what should be done to address their plight seems almost to have fallen off the political agenda.[65] Sholl argued that colonists 'who open up settlement' should not necessarily receive government protection and that beyond a certain latitude and longitude they should be allowed to take the law into their own hands.[66] He complained of too few police for such a vast region and alleged that inexperienced police or 'new chums' were no good in the frontier districts. Member for Toodyay Bernard Clarkson agreed, proposing that 'the idea of sending a new chum to catch a nigger is simply absurd'. Clarkson blamed police for the trouble because they protected Aboriginal rights.[67] He also believed that the solution to Aboriginal violence lay in altering punishment, arguing that Rottnest prison should be abolished as all it did was feed and educate Aboriginal prisoners and was 'a pleasant sort of holiday'.[68]

Everard Darlot, Member for the Murchison, raised questions around the rising number of 'outlaw natives' and the number of police, although he recognised that even doubling the number of police horses in 1888 did not solve the issue as there was still not enough to feed them. William Traylen, Member for Greenough, declared 'police protection expensive but necessary',[69] and went on to make the extraordinary suggestion that Aboriginal people were not unhappy about executions: 'as far as hanging the natives goes, I do not think they care very much about it'.[70] Timothy Quinlan, Member for West Perth, suggested that rather than prisoners being forwarded to Perth for trial and punishment, punishment should be punitive and instant and 'if [offenders are] to hang for an offence they should hang where the crime was committed rather than coming to Perth'.[71]

Others, such as Frederick Piesse, Member for Williams in the south of the state, were less extreme and sought to protect the rights of Aboriginal people. Piesse suggested that the answer was more police, 'though that is very expensive'.[72] Alexander Richardson, Member for De Grey (and Kimberley pastoral station owner), responded bluntly that pastoralists were to blame for 'an excess of humanity' and 'treating the natives too kindly'.[73] This rampant hostility to Aboriginal people reached its pinnacle when the Member for Geraldton, George Simpson, suggested that native troubles were reaching 'ugly proportions' and there was a 'stream of blood gurgling away from the Kimberley to the Irwin'. He added 'all these pioneer settlers may be done to death at any minute by these absolutely useless niggers'.[74] As did other supporters of the motion, he believed that pastoralists should be allowed to take the law into their own hands, saying 'I think it will be a happy day for Western Australia and Australia at large when the natives and the kangaroo disappear.'[75] The Forrest brothers appeared in the debate as voices of reason and moderation. Alexander Forrest, Member for the West Kimberley, accused Simpson of being too radical and suggested that more police and better-equipped protection was required. Premier John Forrest said that pastoralists were exaggerating their problems.[76] At the end of this extraordinary debate, Sholl's motion was passed.

Outside parliament, apart from members of the Aborigines Protection Board, few voices were heard in support of Aboriginal people; one was the Bishop Mathew Gibney. In September 1892 Gibney started a public furore when he proclaimed that in the North West 'for every sheep killed by the blacks, and for which they were most cruelly treated, and in some cases killed, god had punished the settlers by taking away 100 or more sheep in the drought'.[77] A year later many of the same parliamentarians would attack the Aborigines Protection Board in parliament in similar terms to those used a year earlier. Simpson referred to the Board as 'useless old men'.[78] Monger regarded the Board as 'one of the greatest slurs which any country had cast upon it'.[79] Quinlan hoped 'the obnoxious Board will be wiped out'.[80] His hopes were soon realised: John Forrest had consistently lobbied for the abolition of the Board, tabling a bill every year from 1892.[81] In 1898 complete control of Aboriginal affairs was passed to the government of Western Australia.[82] The Board was replaced by the Aborigines Department, which was even smaller than its predecessor.[83]

One of Forrest's first actions after the Aborigines Protection Board was abolished was to reduce expenditure on Aboriginal affairs back to the pre–responsible government figure some ten years earlier, fixed at £5000 per annum.[84] *The Aborigines Act 1897* that abolished the Aborigines Protection Board also removed the requirement that 1% of gross revenue of the colony go towards the welfare of Aboriginal people, which in 1897 was some £30,000.[85] By way of comparison, the state of New South Wales, with an Aboriginal population of an estimated 6800 people and a land mass a quarter the size of Western Australia, expended some £17,000.[86] In April 1896 Forrest had informed the then governor, Gerard Smith, that the parliament of Western Australia was more capable and willing to protect the interests of Aboriginal people than the

Aborigines Protection Board, and yet, at the same time and despite the extraordinary wealth created by the goldrushes of the 1890s, Forrest claimed that the government had no surplus funds to assist Aboriginal people.[87] Indeed in March 1897 Forrest himself, celebrating the success of responsible government, commented on the 'immense revenue' of Western Australia: 'It has been a great change from little things to big things.' He continued, 'six years ago the population was 50,000, and the revenue £400,000. Now the population is 140,000, and the revenue £2,500,000' and the 'trials and struggles of the early settlers have passed away, and we are enjoying to a large extent the fruits of their labours'.[88]

Prior to responsible government the governor had considerable executive and administrative power that he could exert in Western Australian politics. With responsible government the role of the governor became more symbolic. Forrest marginalised Robinson and he retired in March 1895.[89] In October that year Forrest brought in Lieutenant-Colonel Sir Gerard Smith as governor. Smith was the first non-professional governor appointed to Western Australia and, as Frank Crowley has noted, he was not expected to play any part in politics. His duties 'were mainly social and ceremonial'.[90] Political power was now vested even more with Premier John Forrest.

There were other significant changes in government during this period. Prior to responsible government, Charles Warton as attorney general had insisted on the enforcement of procedural rules and, as we have seen, often queried the activities of police.[91] Following responsible government, Warton was replaced with Forrest's choice, Septimus Burt, a much less-sympathetic attorney general. Another significant change was in the position of colonial secretary that, as we have seen, became a ministerial portfolio.[92] In October 1892 Shenton resigned as colonial secretary; the position was taken up by S.H. Parker though he resigned from cabinet in December 1894 after disagreements with the increasingly autocratic Forrest.[93] Then the position of colonial secretary was taken up by none other than John Forrest himself until April 1898.[94] This effectively meant that Forrest, who was also colonial treasurer, had control of the Western Australian police department through the period of the greatest conflict in the Kimberley.

Legalising Ill-treatment

The new independence gained through these administrative changes unshackled many colonists from what they saw as the surveillance of the imperial office and the imposition of unreasonable demands with regard to Aboriginal people who, many argued, were threatening colonisation of the North West and Kimberley districts.[95] The British government's concern that pastoralists influenced the Western Australian government was justified. The government, free of Governor Broome's mediating influence in promoting respect for the laws that protected Aboriginal rights, introduced a range of punitive legislation at the behest of the pastoral industry.[96] Between 1890 and 1897 it passed various Acts that gave pastoralists a decisive say in matters concerning employment and treatment of Aboriginal people.

The *Aboriginal Offenders Act 1883*, which governed the trial of Aboriginal people caught for killing cattle, was amended in 1892.[97] In the same year the criminal offence of cattle spearing was created and whipping, which had been abolished as punishment in 1883, was reintroduced in lieu of imprisonment.[98] Kimberley pastoralists drove this change with many pushing for the greater use of flogging as instant retribution. They believed that prison was a 'holiday' for Aboriginal people where they received food and shelter and then returned to their *country* to continue killing stock.[99] Flogging was better they thought: as pastoralist Frank Wittenoon put it, 'they had all flogged the natives, and though legally wrong they were morally right'.[100]

More punitive changes were introduced in the *Aboriginal Offenders Act Amendment 1893*.[101] Gaol terms for cattle killing were increased from two to three years with or without hard labour, and whipping for a first offence to five years for any subsequent offence. Another amendment to the *Aboriginal Offenders Act 1892* removed the restriction on justices of the peace adjudicating on their own cases. Pastoralists, as justices of the peace, could thereafter adjudicate and prosecute Aboriginal people caught eating beef on their own properties.[102] The Act retained optional work contracts but excluded Aboriginal workers from the *Masters and Servants Act*.[103] Furthermore the clause in pastoral leases granting Aboriginal people permission to 'fire the grass', so intensely protected by Broome under imperial legislation, was finally extinguished in 1897 under new Western Australian Land Regulations after some fifteen years of agitation from Kimberley pastoralists.[104]

Legislative changes by no means emerged just from one side of politics. Members of the opposition often supported legislative changes made by the Western Australian government enacting harsher penalties for Aboriginal people. In January 1893 members from both sides of politics, who were exasperated with the productivity of their North West and Kimberley businesses, joined forces. Led by opposition members R.E. Bush MLC and Robert Sholl, they joined Alexander Forrest, Alexander Richardson and Edward Wittenoon (brother of Frank) to form a political pressure group called the Northerners Association; their slogan was 'A United North!'[105] This group sought to promote the interests of those in the North West and Kimberley by lobbying for infrastructure such as water supply and rail networks. They also called for the abolition of the 'ridiculous' Aborigines Protection Board and for a royal commission into the 'native question' seeking to absolve themselves of imputations of brutality to the Aboriginal people of the district.[106] They felt that they had good reason to complain. By 1892 the Kimberley stocked more cattle than the entire southwest of Western Australia and would soon overtake it in terms of sheep numbers, yet but a fraction of government funding was directed their way.[107]

If Aboriginal people once had a supporter in John Forrest, by the mid-1890s they no longer did. While earlier Forrest had acknowledged Aboriginal people in the development of the Western Australian colony, by the mid-1890s he was no longer prepared to do so.[108] Like many others he now believed that Aboriginal people were dying out and that government should do just enough to ease their passing.[109]

There is probably no race of people which has done so little to leave behind it a record of its existence as the Australian Aboriginal race, and no race has been so little able to cope with civilisation. After existing in their own savage state for an immense time, an intercourse of about half a century with a civilized race has been sufficient to almost remove them from the face of the earth.[110]

In the late 1890s Forrest resisted calls for yet another royal commission into the treatment of Aboriginal people and allegations of cruelty and torture, and refused to agree that Aboriginal station workers be paid in cash.[111] More tellingly, whilst admitting police had shot Aboriginal people 'in the course of their duties', he would assert over and over again that overall Aboriginal people were treated well.[112] Indeed members of Forrest's government, such as Colonial Secretary S.H. Parker, would boldly state that what separated Western Australia from 'other colonies' was that it was 'freer of injustices' where native police forces had elsewhere been sent out 'with almost licenses to shoot natives down'.[113] In September 1894 Parker made the absurd claim that Aboriginal people from the 'northern portions' of the state, including the Kimberley, were 'equally well protected by the police as the whites were'.[114] But then, after all, who could possibly check this claim? The vastness of the colony meant it was exceedingly difficult to investigate anything. And who were the disinterested observers in the Kimberley?[115]

By the mid-1890s the pastoral lobby had achieved unparalleled influence in Western Australian politics. Legislation giving them greater powers over Aboriginal people had been passed through parliament. By the late 1890s, the government had defeated attempts by the British government to retain control over Aboriginal people. John Forrest now refused to use his dominant position in parliament to protect them. Indeed responsible government looked ominous for them. The next chapter shows that changes to policing paved the way for the introduction of ever more punitive forms of control. The Kimberley was headed towards something more akin to warfare than civilian policing.

Chapter 8

'THE SQUATTERS HAVE THEM ALL'

Aboriginal 'Outlaws' and a New Police Force

The effect of the increasingly punitive policies towards Aboriginal people of the Kimberley was profound, coming as it did on the top of the social changes that colonisation had imposed on Aboriginal communities. The arrival of the pastoral economy had affected almost all aspects of Aboriginal life. By the early 1890s many Aboriginal people had experienced ten years of European colonisation. Many Aboriginal children had grown up in the 'two worlds' of their own Aboriginal way and also the colonist economy where they were utilised for whatever services they could provide. Kinship and social hierarchies had altered as younger Aboriginal men and women willingly or unwillingly adapted to European ways as they worked on pastoral stations. Many Aboriginal men from different language groups were arrested for killing stock and sent to prison or shot.

Prison prevented those men from engaging in their communal seasonal and traditional practices, and families had little idea when, or if, they would return. When a man was released from prison and returned to his *country* 'tribal quarrels', as one police officer called them, would arise, as his partner had gone off with another man.[1] Many other, though not all, traditions passed down from Elders were ignored. Young Aboriginal men may have found a sense of power and freedom from traditional Aboriginal cultural hierarchies, such as having previously to wait until they were older to obtain a wife. Traditional marriage patterns were violated as the younger men took to marrying or mixing outside of Aboriginal kin groups. Aboriginal women had often mixed with or been forcibly taken by European men and were used for domestic duties.[2] Aboriginal men could not just move to another part of *country* to get another wife as they would be breaking their own law and would significantly rupture the connection to their own *country*. Inter-group trade and interactions changed as groups were forced into the *country* of other groups. Those Aboriginal people who left their *country* and gravitated towards town centres often found there were few rations supplied to sustain them. In any case police would often be called to drive out of town areas increasingly belligerent and aggrieved Aboriginal populations, who were now exhibiting resistance behaviours to aspects of European expectations.

This chapter looks at these social changes during the early 1890s and at the concurrent changes in policing as police attempted to deal with them. Critically, for the history of policing in the Kimberley, from the commencement of the pastoral industry, pastoralists had taken young Aboriginal boys from the group whose *country* they were on to train them as 'horse boys' and stockmen.[3] The removal of the young men profoundly affected traditional social structures. In the Roth Report one police officer stated that there were no young Aboriginal men left on *country* to act as witnesses to cattle killing because 'There are no young boys in the tribes. The squatters have them all.'[4] Evidence from this period suggests that many of the older men had either been shot, removed or gaoled, leaving a younger generation who were brought up not 'coming in' to station life but rather were born into working on stations under the tutorship of their boss.[5]

Jandamarra may have been typical. He was of the first generation of Kimberley Aboriginal men who were socialised during
colonisation to live across both his own and European culture.
He was born around 1873, before European colonisation of the
Kimberley.[6] He grew up working on William Lukin's Lennard
River Station and during his teenage years saw the establishment
of the pastoral industry. Here he acquired the name Pigeon, given
to him by Lukin, allegedly because of his relative smallness and
his swiftness.[7] Other accounts say a man named Henry Bostock
gave him the name when he was working on Lillamaloora pastoral station.[8] Working with colonists he built up close friendships,
could speak English and was trained in rifle use and stock work.
Jandamarra could live in two cultures, readily negotiating the
colonists' culture but also able to slip back into the world of his
own Bunuba people.

Pastoralists came to believe that Jandamarra had 'turned' from
being a loyal and efficient station worker and later police assistant
into someone who actively opposed them. He had spent time in
prison for stock killing, but had gained skills through working
with the police. He won his 'outlaw' status with these skills, using
stolen firearms to dazzling effect while other Aboriginal groups
used spears and other traditional weapons. The first-hand accounts
describing Jandamarra's exploits show he was indeed remarkable
and it is not surprising that he became a figure in both Aboriginal
and European folklore. Aboriginal people believed he possessed
special powers that helped him evade, overcome and defeat his
attackers. Police recorded Aboriginal witnesses stating 'whites
cannot shoot him because his devil catches the bullets'.[9] Utilising
the natural environment of the Napier Range, Windjana Gorge
and Tunnel Creek, Jandamarra could hide away and evade police

patrols. He also utilised his kinship and family to advantage. In one first-hand account he directed Bunuba women to start smoke signals in one direction, forcing police to investigate, then he raided their camp and stores for weapons and ammunition.[10] As well as those stolen from the police, he made his own bullets with a stolen bullet mould and thus had hundreds of bullets at his disposal;[11] he was also an extremely good shot. There is a documented incident in which he shot a gun out of Joe Blythe's hand.[12] Jandamarra understood the tactics police used in pursuit of Aboriginal people and used this knowledge to evade capture. Police, pastoralists and the government of the day regarded his killing of police and others as exceptional in its treachery and betrayal. But there were many others like him. For example, other less well-known Aboriginal men from the West Kimberley, such as Yardicarinna, Coolaja and later Challaday, took to using guns against the colonisers. In the East Kimberley there was Nalmurchie from the Forrest River area, a man called 'Knight' from Wyndham who police attempted to arrest for several years, and many others.[13]

Many Aboriginal men went through a cycle of arrest, trial, imprisonment and release. Police and pastoralists believed that imprisonment was one of the main causes of resistance by Aboriginal people like Jandamarra. Complaints abounded that sending Aboriginal men (often boys) to prison only 'schooled them in crime' and 'inspired the bush natives' to resist arrest and to try to escape.[14] However, pastoralists were also worried about the wider problem of 'bush blacks' who came to work on the stations, learnt English, acquired knowledge of European customs, then came to resent the position that they and their people were put in. European stockmen were paid wages but Aboriginal workers were paid with rations and they were at the whim of their employers in ways that white stockmen were not. They soon learnt how to extract what they saw was rightfully theirs from their bosses. This point was emphasised by a police officer by the name of Edwin Overend Drewry who, as detailed later, would become one of the most influential figures in Kimberley policing. In July 1893 when complaining about the rise of what he termed 'the Native Outlaw' he wrote of:

> Natives that have been in the service of the settlers but who are so badly disposed that they have to be turned off their runs, who have learned a great deal more than is good for them and who will fire the country wilfully and maliciously if they don't get food and tobacco when they ask for it, but who will not work and are consequently a perpetual menace to the settlers.[15]

While the police, pastoralists and government defined Aboriginal resistance in criminal terms, the reality was that Aboriginal men such as Jandamarra were created by the social conditions imposed on them. Increasingly punitive police actions were altering behaviours in whole Aboriginal groups and families on *country*. Because of the economic depression in the early 1890s many Aboriginal workers were released from their station work and had little to subsist on but station cattle.[16] By the year 1892 it is clear the interrelationships between the pastoralists and local Aboriginal people had broken down. Aboriginal people lived by the principle of reciprocity and expected goods in exchange for services. After being in a colonial capitalist economy for some years, an increasing number of Aboriginal people were demanding fair trade but finding that an increasing number of pastoralists simply could not or would not comply.

The relationships between Aboriginal women and white colonists were also causing problems. In most areas of the Kimberley there were few, if any, European females. Most men came to the Kimberley alone, without wives and family, to make money. Certainly there were limited opportunities for European women if they did come to the district. The lack of white female company over the entire district meant that white men, including police and pastoral station owners, sought out Aboriginal women.[17] It is clear that the taking of Aboriginal women for sexual and domestic purposes was one of the main reasons for Aboriginal attacks on people and property. As one north Kimberley Aboriginal man said in a recorded oral history: 'If they challenged them when taking the young woman away, shoot the man and take the woman.'[18] In other cases if a particular Aboriginal woman was taken, Aboriginal men retaliated by spearing the perpetrator. In the Fairbairn Commission report of 1882 Fairbairn observed that conflict between pastoralists and Aboriginal people was due to 'men keeping aboriginal women'.[19] In late 1889, in the lead up to the Jandamarra conflict, Government Resident Thomas Lovegrove claimed that the unusual level of hostility around Lillamaloora Station was because seven or eight women were kept on the station for 'immoral purposes'.[20] Even in 1905, at Walter Roth's Royal Commission, PC Inglis identified the cause of Aboriginal thefts and attacks on property thus: 'in nine cases out of ten it is because his woman has been taken by the white man'.[21]

Typically this issue was difficult to police and, in any case, police would be socially castigated for attempting to, sometimes because colonists in positions of authority were involved. In early 1898 a drover by the name of John James Butler reported seeing a young Aboriginal girl of about twelve years of age detained, or as Butler described it, 'a gin chained to a tent', for sexual purposes in Wyndham. Butler reported this to Attorney General Septimus Burt, and to *The Sunday Times*, where his letter was published.[22] The attorney general referred it to the resident magistrate but because, Butler asserted, the magistrate was a friend of the accused, the 'matter lapsed'. The accused man was Henry Mckenzie Skinner who was the clerk of courts for Wyndham and a local justice of the peace.[23] It also appears that pastoralists and police would reward their station workers and native assistants by giving them Aboriginal women taken from *country*.[24] One critic stated: 'From Hall's Creek to Wyndham you encounter "Komboism" in every form. Everyone has an ebony consort.'[25]

In October 1896, George Marsden, an inspector from the Aborigines Protection Board reporting on the state of affairs in the Kimberley, wrote that there were already offspring of European and Aboriginal liaisons living in the Fitzroy district who were ten years old.[26] The district had only been colonised eleven years earlier so this interaction had started immediately after Europeans came to the district. Marsden detailed accounts of rape of Aboriginal women by white men, reporting it as a frequent occurrence, although the evidence suggests that some women also willingly cohabitated with white men.[27] Certainly the attitude of many white men in the district was that Aboriginal women were theirs for the taking. East Kimberley station owner Fred Booty was asked how he got his labour force for Lamboo Station, as he was the only white man on the station, to which he replied, 'breed it meself [sic]'.[28] Whether or not these alliances were undertaken willingly, the effect on the social structure of Aboriginal groups was significant.

But there were other implications from this contact. In the years after European colonisation the devastating effect of introduced sexually transmitted diseases became more evident. The

Aborigines Protection Board wrote in 1895: 'Entire population infected with syphilis in some areas with horrendous results limbs falling off parts of face missing.'[29] As a consequence police, in addition to rounding up and arresting cattle killers and other suspects, also sought out the sick, particularly those who were suspected as suffering from syphilis and other venereal diseases.[30] General health services for Aboriginal people in the Kimberley remained poor at best. An epidemic of leprosy (introduced by indentured Asian labourers) would later spread throughout the district.

Labour in the 1890s

As Aboriginal labour had become enmeshed in the pastoral industry, the numbers of workers and their roles on the stations expanded. By late 1895 on Lukin and Monger's stations (the latter managed by Joe Blythe) there were around nineteen workers: eight 'boys' employed shepherding, horse hunting, team-driving and doing general station work, and eleven women who acted as shepherds, water-carriers, wood cutters and general workers. Typically the workers would be fed in the morning at the station kitchen 'on meat, flour, and tea' which would last them until night-time.[31] Withholding these rations, including tobacco, was also a standard form of punishment for workers who broke the rules of their employment, as the pastoralists saw them.[32]

The way in which Kimberley stations acquired their Aboriginal labour force during the 1890s reflected the quasi-feudal position of pastoral station owners and the social position of Aboriginal people. Supported by government legislation Aboriginal people as young as six could be indentured to stations. When a pastoralist required labour he would apply to another pastoralist who was a justice of the peace to sign on to him as many Aboriginal people on *country* in the vicinity of his homestead as he needed. Once employed Aboriginal workers could be (and were) threatened with gaol should they disobey 'their master's lawful commands' or abscond from his service.[33] If they did abscond then police had the power to arrest and prosecute them or hand them back to the pastoralist. It was this issue of labour conditions that would generate claims of slavery.

Figure 8.1. 'Aboriginal Women Sorting Fleece in the Shearing Shed', Upper Liveringa pastoral station, early 1900s. Courtesy State Library of Western Australia, 001350D. A.O. Neville.

Aboriginal people absconded from stations for a variety of reasons, primarily ill-treatment. But even those who were well looked after absconded. While Aboriginal people could move in and out of pastoral work depending on the season, some pastoral stations prevented Aboriginal people from engaging in specific traditional activities and trade; this removed them from their kin groups, families and relatives.

Despite legal requirements to comply with the labour conditions established in the mid-1880s, it appears that, a decade later, only a minority of Aboriginal people living on stations were actually contracted as workers. George Marsden noted in October 1896, for example, that at Yeeda Station none of the workers were signed on under agreement with owner Angus Rose.[34]

Social networks and kin grouping links between 'station blacks' and 'bush blacks' were maintained. That Aboriginal people learnt to navigate between the 'two worlds' would have been lost to most pastoralists. The pastoralists disliked their 'station blacks' interacting with the 'bush blacks' as they believed the latter corrupted the former. To the station owners, those who sat down to work on the stations had been rescued from a life of barbarism and any return to the 'bush' represented a step backwards. Of course protecting their labour source was their primary concern but they also believed that 'station blacks' would work against them if they came into contact with 'bush blacks'. By the 1890s the 'bush blacks', who were at first regarded with indifference and later as a nuisance to the fledgling pastoral industry, had become a major problem for the pastoralists. Besides their simple presence scaring stock, they were also becoming increasingly militant in opposing European colonisation.

With the burgeoning of pastoralism in the 1890s, and increasing stock numbers coupled with the claim that pastoralists often could not afford to pay white stockmen, the free labour of Aboriginal people was more critical than ever. Many white stockmen had also left the district to try and find their fortunes on the Kimberley and Kalgoorlie goldfields. The government attempted to regulate the remaining Aboriginal workers through increasingly punitive use of the *Masters and Servants* legislation. This involved police issuing warrants and arresting Aboriginal people for breach of contract, an offence for which they were often arrested. In Perth this practice had not gone unnoticed. Bishop Riley condemned:

the cruelty of the system by which natives are indentured by the settlers. This is only a form of slavery, as the natives for the most part do not know what it means or further do not dare to refuse to sign the agreement. As soon as a man is indentured he is absolutely under the power of his master, and just as some masters treat their animals well and others treat them badly and so is the treatment of the natives.[35]

Bishop Riley caused considerable offence to some by describing this practice. Because his comments were reported overseas, his allegations were fiercely rejected in the Western Australian parliament as 'vile', 'erroneous' and 'crude, misleading, and unreliable'.[36] John Forrest replied by stating that Aboriginal people were 'simply employed for a specific time'.[37]

It is clear that this system of indenturing Aboriginal workers to pastoral stations under contract was a key cause of increasing unrest and discontentment among Aboriginal groups. One observer in 1902 described the 'farcical signing-on system' that operated in the Kimberley as a significant contributing factor to Aboriginal resistance, showing how little the system had changed over the years. Another cause for resistance was the fact that if an Aboriginal person left the employment of the pastoralist, the police arrested and gaoled them before forcefully returning them to the station they wanted to leave.[38] Indeed, Aboriginal people often did not sign the indenture that bound them to the station but were still liable to be imprisoned should they disobey the pastoralist's orders or abscond from service.

The Role of Alexander Forrest

The significance of Alexander Forrest's role in resurrecting the Kimberley pastoral industry during the early 1890s cannot be overstated. Alexander Forrest owned or part-owned many of the stations in the Kimberley and further south.[39] In the Kimberley, with J.H. Monger, he held Oscar Range Station and in mid-1891 acquired Oobagooma Station. This was one of the first stations near Derby to complain of significant troubles with Aboriginal people and one that was first acted upon by the police.[40] Purchasing Oobagooma, along with others such as Gilgully Station, was a bold move as the local paper had regarded pastoral stations in such a poor financial state as 'unsaleable'.[41] By 1892 Forrest was acting as the agent for other West Kimberley interests and the district was shipping 11,240 head of cattle to Perth annually.[42] Forrest took it upon himself to rectify the unresolved issues of rudimentary shipping facilities and how best to ship cattle to market, and went into the cattle shipping industry. In 1893 he contracted with the Adelaide Steamship Company to serve the North West ports and formed a partnership with Isadore and Sydney Emanuel for the shipment of Kimberley cattle to the Perth and goldfields markets.[43] By 1893 nearly 2000 cattle were leaving Derby annually under his direction.[44]

Through retail contacts, Forrest, Emanuel & Company also came to dominate the livestock trade especially after their main rival, the Wyndham firm of Connor, Doherty & Durack, was disadvantaged by quarantine regulations against tick-infested East Kimberley cattle in 1897.[45] Forrest even had an interest in the abattoir business and the meat wholesale and retailing arms of Holmes Bros and Carmihal and Company.[46] In June 1890, in conjunction with G.C. Rose from Yeeda Station, he experimented by sending fifteen bulls by boat from Derby to Perth.[47] Perth had traditionally had a shortage of meat during the winter months and this new venture was a success. It was aided by a protective stock tax introduced in 1887 to the Western Australian parliament by none other than Alexander Forrest, as the inaugural member for the Kimberley district in the Western Australian Legislative Council, and imposed by the Western Australian government on imported beef from other colonies. Geoffrey Bolton shows that between the depression years of 1887 and 1894 this stock tax played a large role in keeping the Kimberley pastoral industry solvent.[48]

Alexander Forrest came under intense criticism as the creator of what critics called the 'meat ring'. This was an amalgamation of local suppliers exploiting what was a booming Perth and gold-fields market.[49] The 'meat ring coalition' sold cheap meat from the Kimberley to Perth butchers at a very high price. According to Bolton, the person 'chiefly responsible for the maintenance of the tariff and the chief beneficiary of the meat ring was Alexander Forrest'.[50] Between 1893 and 1898 he was a persistent defender of the protective stock tax despite repeated pressure by consumers for its reduction or abolition.

Alexander Forrest showed little subtlety in combining his business activities and his duties as a government minister from 1887. In 1890 Forrest was elected to the Legislative Assembly as member for West Kimberley. In early 1892 opposition member Robert Sholl claimed in parliament that Forrest was 'not only financing the government' through his businesses by generating taxation but 'also driving them'.[51] Others sarcastically suggested that whenever Alexander Forrest obtained land, soon after rail-ways, platforms and amenities would follow.[52] While his brother, the premier, could defend Alexander Forrest's business interests in the South West as they supported the common good of the majority of the population, it was harder to deny the conflict of interest when it occurred in the sparsely populated Kimberley.[53] In one case the government funded the building of anchorage and shipping facilities at Owens Anchorage, just south of Fremantle port, for the unloading of Kimberley cattle boats. This was on land that had just been purchased by Alexander Forrest.[54] The matter was raised but nothing came of it in parliament or elsewhere, and his brother John quickly diffused the matter.[55] Political matters aside, commercially, Forrest, Emanuel & Company did exceptionally well as they had an effective monopoly over cattle export from Derby, shipping 'virtually every one' of over 7000 cattle through their agency to Fremantle port for the Perth market from the period 1894 to 1901.[56]

While Forrest had mostly resolved the issue of the shipment of cattle, there was still the problem of an increasingly belligerent Aboriginal presence in the Kimberley. Indeed Forrest claimed that Aboriginal people not only interfered with and killed cattle on the stations but also interfered with the shipment of those cattle.[57] When he first began to represent his Kimberley constituents in parliament, his major aim was to strengthen police numbers and provide greater protection for Kimberley pastoralists.[58] To understand how numbers were strengthened it is necessary to return to examining the changes in the Western Australian police force under the command of Alexander Forrest's colleague George Phillips.

Police in the 1890s

In April 1887 George Braithwaite Phillips, who had never been a policeman nor visited the Kimberley, was appointed to the position of commissioner of police.[59] Phillips was well connected socially to the Perth and Western Australian colonial elite and was a close friend of Alexander Forrest and, to a lesser extent, John Forrest. He was born in Perth in 1836, the son of John Randell

Phillips, an early Swan River colonist who arrived in 1831 and was resident magistrate at Albany.[60] Phillips was a member of the Weld Club, an exclusive club of 'old families', legislators and business people.[61] Phillips' second wife was the sister of his successor Frederick Hare and thus Phillips was the son-in-law of former Police Superintendent Edward Gustavus Hare.[62] Phillips' third wife was the sister to Mr R.G. Burges, MLC for York from 1894 until 1903.[63] Frederick Hare's appointment was criticised for, like Phillips, he had no practical police experience but was friends with John Forrest. Hare's wife was the cousin of John Forrest's wife, Lady Margaret.[64] Phillips possessed the honorific title of lieutenant colonel, which he acquired as head of the Western Australian volunteer militia.[65] While Phillips had no policing experience he had extensive public service experience as registrar general, acting colonial treasurer, acting postmaster general and acting colonial secretary as well as being a justice of the peace and a member of the governor's Executive Council.

As seen in chapter 3 his predecessor, M.S. Smith, had demonstrated interest in and had taken steps to investigate exploitation of Aboriginal people in the Kimberley. Smith also resisted government interference in police matters.[66] Phillips was less attentive to the rights of Aboriginal people though he dealt with a completely different situation in the 1890s, with widespread and alarming Aboriginal resistance occurring. And, as shall be shown, Phillips accepted government interference in police operations.

Once appointed, Phillips appointed both friends and outsiders into senior positions within the Western Australian police force, working in concert with Sub Inspector Drewry to get the most suitable, qualified men. In his search he looked to imperial outposts such as Singapore, New Zealand and South Africa and for men with military backgrounds. Peter Conole has observed that of the eighteen commissioned appointments made by Phillips, at least two-thirds of them were men born overseas.[67] One key appointment as inspector was Francis Wheatley Lodge from the Natal police force in August 1887.[68] Lodge had been in Western Australia little more than a year, having previously been part of the British Prince Alfred's Guard, an infantry regiment of the South African army. There he was involved in the Basutoland campaign of 1880 and 1881 and was a training officer in the Bechuanaland field artillery.[69] New Zealanders Michael Harvey Brophy and Richard Pilmer were two more important appointments. Pilmer's father, Captain A.A. Pilmer, served in the Maori wars of the mid-1850s.[70]

Pilmer was not a policeman but a surveyor who only came to Western Australia in 1891. A year later on 16 July 1892, after meeting Inspector McKenna, he was convinced to become a police officer in the Western Australian police force.[71] By June 1894 he was stationed in the Kimberley.[72] Michael Brophy had served in the New Zealand Armed Constabulary since he was nineteen years old. This frontier police force was formed to protect the New Zealand colonists from the indigenous Maori who resented the encroachment of Europeans into their territory.[73] As one newspaper reported, Brophy was a member of the force that 'made history in the early eighties [1880s] by the storming of the Parihaka and the capturing of the Maoris, Te Whiti and Tonu, who were posing as prophets and leading their tribes into rebellion'.[74] Commencing in 1886 as a constable, Brophy served in the Kimberley for over sixteen years, ultimately being rewarded and promoted to sub inspector in charge of the East Kimberley in early 1898.[75] State librarian and historian J.S. Battye described him as an officer who 'gathered more information in regards to the natives than any other member of the force'. He was far from illiterate. Battye also noted that Brophy was an educated man, 'keen on outdoors sport, employed many leisure hours in reading historical works, is a student of Shakespeare, and conversant with Australian literature in its various forms'.[76] To a lesser extent than Pilmer, Brophy is synonymous with the East Kimberley and many of the Aboriginal oral histories that associated Pilmer with the area could possibly be referring to Brophy rather than Pilmer.

Arthur Harold Buckland was a former bank teller from Rockhampton, Queensland, who had served with the native police there. PC Buckland was involved in the conflicts in the West Kimberley and was recruited by Inspector Drewry who described him as 'a strongly built man, is acclimatised, a good horseman, suitable for work in this district and is well educated'.[77] Another important appointment, Sub Inspector Orme, had 'military experience' in Victoria.[78] Orme's appointment was criticised as being based on his social connections and the fact that he had met Commissioner Phillips. Phillips had apparently learnt that Orme had put in an application to become a mounted trooper and two weeks later, without 'one day's experience', he was appointed sub inspector of police.[79] Phillips also appointed Weld Club friend John Finnerty as inspector of police at Roebourne, although Finnerty resigned shortly after to become resident magistrate and warden of the Kimberley goldfields.[80]

Phillips appointed Sub Inspector Craven (Henry) Harry Ord as a sergeant in 1893.[81] Ord was born in Aden, Yemen in 1856, while his father was stationed there with the British army. Ord was also a nephew of Sir Harry Ord, a former governor of Western Australia.[82] According to a report in *The Western Mail* Ord gained experience and a reputation as a strong, authoritarian figure for his role suppressing piracy in the Malaccan straits where he worked for his father, who was Lieutenant Governor of Malacca.[83] At the age of twenty-eight he was appointed officer in charge of the Sikh police in Singapore.[84] After serving for two years in Mount Gould, west of Shark Bay, Ord was promoted to sub inspector and sent to Derby in the Kimberley district. Ord was in that role from 1895 to 1899, where he led the two-year hunt for Jandamarra.[85] *The Western Mail* described Ord as having 'taken an active part in the extirpation of the formidable gang'.[86]

One of the most significant changes Commissioner Phillips made to the makeup and administration of the Kimberley police was to employ Edwin Overend Drewry. One of Western Australia's longest serving police officers, Drewry was born in London in 1866 but left and spent four years with the Canadian Mounted Police before coming to Western Australia, joining the force on 16 February 1891 and serving for over twenty-five years.[87] Four months later on 1 June 1891 he was sent to the Kimberley as acting sergeant in charge of the Kimberley gold-fields.[88] By 1 September 1892 he was promoted to sub inspector in charge of the Kimberley district.[89] Having served with the Canadian Mounted Police he possessed considerable experience in dealing with indigenous populations. He was a sober, literate and intelligent man and his appointment would have significant ramifications for both East and West Aboriginal groups of the Kimberley. Drewry gained a reputation in the East Kimberley for his efficient and authoritative style and for the way he went about reshaping a police force that was plagued by poor equipment and incompetence. One of his key strategies was to require each police patrol to obtain information on 'the tribes and runs of the natives' so he could map the *country* of the Kimberley Aboriginal people and thus make it easier to police them.[90]

August Lucanus, who held a particularly malevolent attitude to Aboriginal people, referring to them as 'the niggers', was active as a special constable in punitive expeditions. His memoirs, which were serialised in *The Daily News* newspaper, show he killed very large numbers of Aboriginal people in different locations and periods.[91] His background, however, and where he gained his sought-after experience was firstly as a soldier in the German army then as a well-regarded 'ex-Territory' (Northern Territory) trooper of the South Australian mounted native police force.[92] He officially joined the Western Australian police force in April 1893 after an invitation from Inspector Drewry.[93]

This evidence shows that certain police were progressively removed or left the district to be replaced by police who were clearly sent and employed to do a specific job. Their military or native police background indicates that their job was to 'pacify' and control Aboriginal resistance to colonisation.

Training and Regulations

Recruits started as probationary constables. If their superiors considered them satisfactory they became second-class constables. However, clauses in the *Police Act 1892* allowed for rapid promotion based on merit. Reginald Nash Spong joined the Kimberley police force (with William C. Richardson) on 9 May 1894 and was promoted to second-class constable less than a month later.[94] Personal recommendations from the commissioner of police also allowed for promotion. Commissioner Phillips acknowledged this when he stated in police circular orders of 1886 that:

All vacancies will be filled up from the next inferior grade. At the same time it must be clearly understood that seniority, length of service and good conduct are not the only recommendations for promotion. They

291

will always have due weight but efficiency, sobriety and
adaptation for vacancy will count. [95]

The 'adaptation for vacancy' referred to an officer's potential
suitability for the particular situation. This was explained under
section 7 of the *Police Act*. Some of the most valuable Western
Australian police officers who served in the Kimberley had gained
experience or had served their 'bush apprenticeship' in the earlier
colonised Murchison and Gascoyne districts. Patrick Troy, for
example, worked in the Gascoyne and Murchison districts, and
PCs Armitage, Lemon, Houlihan and Payne worked in Cossack
in the Murchison.[96]

Changes in the *Police Act* facilitated the commissioner hand-
picking officers. Under section 7 the commissioner could promote
police simply for serving three years in the Kimberley district.
He also had the power to hire non-commissioned officers at
his discretion.[97] Other changes due to the local conditions were
introduced. In 1892, in order to reduce the workloads of police
who worked under difficult conditions and under the *Aborigines
Protection Act (Amendment) 1892*, police were no longer obliged to
serve summonses or execute an arrest more than 80 kilometres
from the place of issue unless officially directed to do so by the
resident magistrate.[98] Also in 1892, because there was a marked
increase in resignations by police trying their luck on the newly
established goldfields, the police commissioner authorised regulations that:

> no non-commissioned officer or constable will be at
> liberty to resign his office or withdraw himself from
> the duties thereof…unless authorised in writing to do
> so by the commissioner of police or unless giving three

months notice, *if stationed beyond two miles from Perth*, or one calendar month if stationed within that distance.[99]

Clearly this regulation was designed to target police serving in the north.

Such were the numbers of police leaving the district during the late 1880s and early 1890s that, despite Phillip's selection of particular officers for the Kimberley, it was difficult to get good and appropriate police. The outcome was that 'bush police' evolved as an efficient force for the district and also as a combination of 'characters' known for their individuality. Many not only tolerated but also embraced the harsh conditions they lived in and even the increasingly hostile Aboriginal response to their presence. Indeed they learned from each other and evolved intimate understandings of Aboriginal laws and customs that assisted in their policing. Richard Pilmer described the tutelage he received from Patrick Troy as a 'baptism in bushcraft and native lore'.[100] Pilmer appears to have been one of the most knowledgeable police in the Kimberley and the most thorough and accurate recorder of Aboriginal names. Interestingly, he also gained a reputation for being harsh on colonists who mistreated Aboriginal people and was also regarded as highly dictatorial and difficult to work with.[101]

By the mid-1890s the Kimberley force comprised experienced bushmen and their native assistants, experienced with firearms, horses and 'bush work'. In the West Kimberley police such as William Armitage, Arthur Buckland, Reginald Nash Spong and Pilmer were employed to deal with the ongoing conflict, specifically with the 'native outlaw' Jandamarra. In the East Kimberley Mick Rhatigan, Michael Brophy, Thomas Wheatley, Arthur Freeman and August Lucanus were similarly positioned.

Rhatigan and Brophy, for example, stayed in the East Kimberley for over fifteen and sixteen years respectively.[102] PC Rhatigan in particular had a very brutal reputation. Turkey Creek stockman Doug Moore blithely referred to him as 'one of the best shots in the country and he missed very few blacks if after them, especially on the Osmond River where they were pretty well cleaned up', that is, killed.[103]

As this chapter has shown, pastoralism caused great changes in Aboriginal culture in the Kimberley. Communities were disrupted as Aboriginal people became trespassers on their own land, found they needed to kill cattle to survive, saw their social hierarchies change as young men increasingly worked on pastoral stations, older men were gaoled for a range of offences and young women entered either willingly or unwillingly into relationships with white men. Increasingly pastoralism and policing were leading Aboriginal people to resist, hence the considerable changes to policing in the 1890s. A distinction arose between junior police officers who achieved promotion by joining as probationary constables and by 'serving their time' in the Kimberley, and between 'bushmen' police who were recruited almost solely to treat the emerging conflict. The men in the latter category, recruited to deal with the 'native question', did not adhere to police regulations: most were over thirty and were 't'othersiders', not West Australian. Critically, many were men with broad and extensive military and policing backgrounds whose experience, as we shall see in the next chapter, would be utilised to devastating effect on the Aboriginal people of the Kimberley.

Chapter 9

'WILL YOU AT ONCE TAKE ACTION'

The West Kimberley Police 1890–1898

The previous chapter outlined both the changing position of Aboriginal people in the Kimberley and the changing political context of policing as it affected the Kimberley police. European and Aboriginal conflict, which had been building since the mid-1880s, was exacerbated by the 1889 petition to the Western Australian government tabled by Alexander Forrest which demanded that in certain areas of the Kimberley 'the wild natives should be declared outlaws', a warning of things to come.[1] Changes in legislation, the removal or sidelining of sympathetic government residents and resident magistrates, and the introduction of specialist police with military and frontier policing experience all showed that police were a civil force in official rhetoric only and, as we shall see, operated more as a quasi-military force. Police took vigorous actions to protect the pastoral industry, to stop stock killing and to isolate Aboriginal pastoral workers from the 'bush blacks'. Punitive measures began at Oobagooma on the coast and spread along the Fitzroy River Valley. By the end of the 1880s earlier opinions of Aboriginal people of the Kimberley as 'unlikely to provide a source of any annoyance to future colonists' were quickly changing.[2] A December 1889 editorial in *The West Australian* described the Aboriginal population in the Kimberley as 'numerous, bold and war-like'.[3] With a force intent on suppression and an Aboriginal people building resistance, a war seems to have been inevitable.

Indeed, as the new decade began, more killings of colonists would occur but not on pastoral lands. On 22 December 1891 on the northwest coast in the Prince Frederick Harbour a killing related to pearling and fishing interests occurred. Martin Lilycroth and an Aboriginal 'boy' worker named Henry from Roebuck Bay were attacked 'by a group of thirty blacks', possibly Wunambul people. Henry and Lilycroth were killed by a combination of spears and *nullahs* (throwing clubs) thrown at them.[4] The group stole Lilycroth's dingy and when associates of Lilycroth pursued them they abandoned the dingy and went to the top of the hills overlooking the bay. The pursuers reported that 'about sixty in number, showed themselves on the top of the cliffs, six hundred yards [549 metres] distant, yelling and dancing, and shaking spears and nullahs in defiance'.[5]

This defiance would spread along the Fitzroy Valley when on 8 June 1892 three prospectors, Robert Allen, Thomas Henry and Robert Henry, were camped on the Barker River north of the King Leopold Ranges. They were attacked by a group of Aboriginal men at midnight and all three men were speared.[6] Thomas Henry died within fifteen minutes and Robert Allen, with a spear wound in the stomach, died three hours later.[7] Robert Henry, although speared three times, survived. Henry's account of what occurred and why is valuable as it reveals the changes in social behaviours amongst Aboriginal people. The suspects were Kerralin, Meralmaddie, Merrigal, Yemin, Jinkymarra and a man named Packer, an ex–station hand from Lillamaloora Station.[8] Packer and others were the guides who had helped the three prospectors through the King Leopold Ranges. Henry reported that Packer was unhappy with the compensation he received for assisting the three and thus speared them in retaliation.[9] Aboriginal people, it seems, no longer feared colonists and had learnt to fight for what they believed was theirs. The police party that was sent to arrest Packer consisted of four constables and four native assistants. Led by PC Armitage the patrol took over a month to find Packer and shoot him. They then shot another seven men and arrested one more. PC Armitage, no doubt learning from his arrest in late 1889 for unlawful killing, pointedly stated 'the natives were camped in a very rough place and it was a matter of impossibility to effect the arrest of them alive'.[10]

On 28 September 1892 Commissioner of Police George Phillips made a significant change to the Kimberley police. He replaced Inspector Lodge and commissioned Edwin Overend Drewry, who had been serving as a sub inspector of the East Kimberley since June 1891, to become sub inspector in a new position 'in charge of the Kimberley district'. His salary was £250 per annum and he was moved from Halls Creek to Derby.[11] Because of the unusually close relationship he had with the commissioner of police, Drewry was given considerable latitude to change the nature of policing in the entire Kimberley district. Drewry was far from lawless and not without a keen sense of the importance of following rules and regulations, but it was how he interpreted and reported them that was important. Beginning with his first reports from Wyndham in June 1891 and then from Derby Police Station in early 1892, he commenced a frank dialogue with the commissioner of police about the state of affairs regarding Aboriginal people, consistently asking for more police powers. His views were stark: police, he wrote, had not used their powers sufficiently prior to 1892 and 'there had been very little work done amongst the natives'.[12] 'Little work' here was a euphemism for shooting.

In late 1892 Drewry summarised what he saw as the reasons for the escalating tensions in both Kimberley districts.[13] It was, he wrote, the Western Australian government's policy to not interfere with the relationship between Aboriginal people and colonists that was to blame for the current state of affairs. Police, he suggested, had not acted in a sufficiently punitive manner. He considered that the continuing and unresolved problem of damage to the East Kimberley telegraph line was unacceptable. Referring to reports of damage to 190 miles (305 kilometres) out of a total of 250 miles of line, which he blamed on Aboriginal people, he dismissed the current police practice of arrests and cautioning as ineffective.[14] Continuing, he argued that both gaoling and whipping of Aboriginal people was a 'farce'.[15] He observed, on the problem of firing of grass, that legislation should be passed penalising perpetrators with a fine of £50 or twelve months' hard labour.[16] He was unimpressed by native assistants, or 'black trackers' as he called them, and wanted more 'latitude' and more 'decisive orders' to be given to the police.[17] His rationale: the police would carry out 'their duty' in a 'more responsible way' and 'with more discretion' than black trackers.[18]

In an attempt to justify increased police powers, Drewry quoted from *The Digest of Criminal Law* by Sir James Fitzjames Stephenson who wrote: 'The intentional infliction of death or bodily harm is not a crime, when it is done by any person to arrest a traitor, felon or pirate, altho [sic] such traitor, felon or pirate, offers no violence to any person.'[19] He argued that this approach could be utilised in the East Kimberley to protect the telegraph line. '[I]f there is no chance to arrest the natives [because of the nature of the countryside] the police should be allowed to make use of their rifles in a judicious manner. I think you would find in a very few months the natives would leave the insulators alone.'[20]

Drewry's frequent reports to the commissioner of police were frank and forthright and many were published in local and Perth newspapers.[21]

In early December 1892 Drewry gave instructions to his officers in the Kimberley regarding the interpretation of the police Circular Order No. 6/972 that dealt with the use of firearms against Aboriginal people. He wrote: 'A constable in the execution of his duty can fire upon a person who assaults or resists him, that he may repel by force and if the person is unavoidably killed in a struggle, the constable is justified.' In relation to Aboriginal people on the telegraph line, he made his point even clearer: the 'larceny of insulators and telegraph wire constitutes a felony...the natives along the telegraph line are to be dispersed and their camps broken up.'[22]

Here Drewry was not just justifying shooting Aboriginal people on the telegraph line but all over the Kimberley as a means of compelling Aboriginal people to observe the law. Police now had orders to pursue a more aggressive and ultimately punitive approach. These instructions, some three years before Jandamarra killed Constable Richardson at Lillamaloora, would be the impetus for much Aboriginal resistance across the Kimberley.

Drewry's suggestions were accepted when, in early 1893, Commissioner Phillips replied, giving tacit but guarded approval, stating that 'if the natives show fight police must resort to the use of his firearms to protect themselves and drive the natives from the line'.[23] He continued: 'At the same time it must be clearly understood that anything approaching indiscriminate slaughter of natives will subject the constables to severe punishment.'[24] He reiterated that police alone must use firearms and they must not allow colonists the same privilege.[25] Phillips would repeat this in later instructions, too.[26]

The tension between Drewry's requests to use firearms more liberally, veiled as they were in terms like 'judicious use', and Commissioner Phillips' directive that 'indiscriminate slaughter of natives was not allowed' was one of the defining exchanges of the period. It allowed police to interpret the authority of the commissioner how they saw fit. The line between a legal and an illegal shooting was further blurred and any restraint demanded by the commissioner was ignored.

The Implementation

By June 1893 Sub Inspector Drewry was implementing the changes he had suggested. One officer he took to singling out for praise was Constable Armitage, who had formerly been charged with the murder of the Aboriginal boy Jenella. Alluding to his policing style as 'steady work', he noted how Armitage would go on patrol and slowly make his way across the country, 'making his presence felt'. This type of police patrol if undertaken for 'over a year or more', he observed, would see that 'the native will soon be taught to leave the persons and property of colonists alone'.[27] There were some police who could not perform to Drewry's expectations. He admonished Constable Clifton for his policing style after he brought in some 'decrepit natives', most likely Elders. Drewry had heard 'that the natives up the Fitzroy are bragging that the police can only catch men who are very old, blind or deaf'.[28]

Drewry particularly wanted police to initially arrest not the 'bush blacks', but those 'that have been in the employ of the whites' and had gone back to the bush.[29] Some police, such as PC Armitage, had observed that ex–pastoral workers were disgruntled with their treatment (whipping had been re-legislated the year before), did not receive enough food and were prevented from leaving the station for ceremonial business.[30] They had obviously learnt they were being exploited and protested their treatment. However, while Drewry ordered his police to target the 'outlaw' rather than the 'bush black', dispersals targeting the latter would continue.

Drewry felt enormous personal pressure to sort out the problems in the Kimberley and was extremely sensitive to criticism in newspapers in Perth about police actions. In May 1893 he wrote to the commissioner of police to defend himself and his officers, claiming that he had 'the whole of the North at my back' over the 'native issue'.[31] Much like letters and articles disputing pastoralists' claims of stock losses, newspapers published letters and articles that fiercely criticised police and made allegations of police brutality. Drewry was outraged at a letter to *The West Australian* newspaper on 9 August 1894 by 'Blind Paddy', who criticised police for allowing prisoners to get sick.[32] Drewry wrote indignantly to the commissioner that the weather was cold, they were well fed but all had influenza.[33]

Drewry continued to seek the recruitment of yet more specialist police with the aid of Commissioner Phillips' discretionary recruitment powers. This yielded immediate results. On 1 October 1894 Richard Henry Pilmer arrived in the Kimberley to take up duties as a first-class constable.[34] Pilmer's arrival coincided with significant changes in the judicial process. With some exceptions, by the early 1890s police procedures in the Kimberley and the associated judicial process for arrest, charge and prosecution had been corrupted to the point of travesty. Often it was hopelessly unclear exactly who police had arrested and who was prosecuted. One critic of police practices suggested that the 'usual custom' was for police to go 'out to the ranges' on bush patrol and indiscriminately arrest any Aboriginal person they came across. They were then convicted on police evidence as Aboriginal people could not speak English, let alone defend themselves in the court.[35]

Richard Pilmer's memoirs provide a revealing insight into how indifferent some police were to suspects' guilt or innocence. On his first patrol in the West Kimberley Pilmer described how his duty was to 'arrest natives caught in the act of killing and consuming stock'.[36] On 'his round' he 'collected 25 offenders' and took them to Mt Abbott for trial. No mention is made of their culpability for this offence. Isadore Emanuel, pastoralist and owner of Liveringa Station (and friend and business partner of Alexander Forrest), acted as the local magistrate in the court, which was a small 3 metre by 3.7 metre police hut, and quickly found them guilty. Pilmer wrote that 'after having been duly found guilty and condemned to imprisonment in Derby gaol, the natives were chained in a circle round [a] tree' then walked 'on the chain' on a trip taking three weeks to Derby gaol where they were imprisoned.[37]

It is clear that certain police such as Pilmer were brutal. When George Marsden from the Aborigines Protection Board was inspecting Fitzroy Police Station he found that the whip made by Constable Pilmer to use on prisoners was a 'cat-o'-nine-tails': 'It consisted of nine lashes, each lash was plaited green-hide and the handle of the same material. The person who first spoke to me about it told me that when it was used, it carried away skin and flesh at every stroke.'[38] Pilmer was later accused of 'butchering cruelty to the natives' after flogging thirty Aboriginal people at a time on a triangle rack for ten shillings per head where 'he boasted that he worked so hard that he had to rub himself with eucalyptus after-wards, he was so stiff'.[39] Marsden did not, however, have the power to stop such practices. In any case whipping was not a police duty at all. Commissioner Phillips reminded his officers in a circular order in mid-1892 that they were not legally bound to carry out whipping but rather were to assist and each policeman should 'do his best to obtain the services of some other person to do it'.[40]

Whilst Drewry was happy with an officer of Pilmer's style, he still found the police under his command a mixed lot. He forced PC Clifton to resign for incompetence.[41] Writing to Phillips he suggested that PC Wisbey should be 'dismissed from the force' as 'he never so far as my knowledge goes made a single arrest or endeavoured to do anything more useful than ride up and down the goldfields main road'.[42] He put a trained police officer, PC McGillivray, whom he had 'serious doubts about', in charge of Robinson River camp to give 'him a chance to prove himself'.[43] But two months later Drewry claimed he was 'riding around anywhere but where the natives are'.[44] PC Childs could not get on with McGillivray at Robinson River camp. He advised Childs that 'if I have any more nonsense from him I shall advise his dismissal at once' and 'he can't get on with Clifton or cannot get on with anyone'. PC Goodridge, too, Drewry claimed was 'also in a discontented state and is always wanting to be transferred or shifted to any camp but the one he is on'.[45]

With Commissioner Phillips' approval he commenced hiring his own officers. He was keen to employ men who were not policemen at all but who lived and worked in the Kimberley and thus had 'bush' experience, but the only person he could find was 'ex–territory trooper' August Lucanus.[46] After hearing that another man named William Turner wished to join the force, Drewry advised him to 'send in an application (a letter just stating you wish to join, that you are a good bushman, rider etc.)' and told him he would promote his interests.[47] Similarly he recommended another bushman by the name of David Brice. Both these 'good bushmen' were from Queensland.[48]

It was clear that the change in policing style had only exacerbated an increasingly difficult local situation, having the opposite effect on Aboriginal groups than was intended. Rather than pacifying the people and bringing them under British law, the changes instilled fear into most Aboriginal groups, encouraged resistance and created a war.[49] Aboriginal people made overt and covert payback attacks on police and pastoralists, many of whom reportedly lived in fear for their lives and of being driven off their stations. Pastoralists persistently complained that their stock was killed 'wantonly and maliciously'.[50]

In November 1892 Drewry sent PCs Armitage and Goodridge to quell 'native troubles' at Secure Bay near Collier Bay in Warwa *country*. The police had gone to arrest a man called Coolaja, the alleged ringleader of the murderers of Peyton [Piton], killed in 1886, and Rummer and Ah Hee, killed in 1888.[51] Following information that a corroborree was to take place the police followed a group to Mt Nellie:

> As the natives made no attempt to get away, we thought we were going to make an easy capture as they were answering me as I was talking to them in their native tongue. But just as we got about 25 yards away from them there was a shower of spears thrown, two of which passed through my shirt on the left front across the abdomen just over the skin and another on the 4th finger of the left hand taking the flesh with it, whilst PC Goodridge had one pass through the right leg of his trousers. I at once saw it was an ambush for us, so shouted to PC Goodridge to make use of his rifle...[52]

Figure 9.1. 'Derby Police about to Mount Up, Police Horse Isadore on Left, 1898'.
Courtesy State Library of Western Australia, 026298PD. D. Falconer.

Following this fight the police found four dead Aboriginal people including Coolaja and a woman who was acting as a spear carrier for the others. There were forty-one spears thrown at the police party.[53] Armitage reported that he had learnt through a female informant that 'the natives were collecting at that place for the purpose of arranging for a raid to be made on Messrs Forrest and Co's Station to kill those that were there and to rob the place'.[54]

By this point Armitage had considerable experience in the West Kimberley and considered the coastal Warwa people 'the most desperate natives in the Kimberley[,] they are all belonging to the sea coast, and object to the whites settling on the country'.[55] Although police shot and killed four people, Drewry remarked that 'the lesson they received does not seem to have done much good'.[56]

Oobagooma

The information Armitage received seemed to be verified as escalating reports of conflict appeared about the Warwa people on Alexander Forrest's Oobagooma Station near Derby and close by the Robinson River police camp. In March 1893 Sub Inspector Drewry received a report from the manager, Mr Perry, that the 'blacks were being very bad' and had attacked the station on at least ten separate occasions.[57] Perry reported that it was 'imperatively necessary that something be done' regarding Aboriginal people on the station. He pointed out that Alexander Forrest 'has been at great expense in introducing the best strains of blood into the herd' to build the quality of cattle and that the worry was not the numbers of cattle speared but 'the presence of the natives on the line of country in which the cattle pasture' and that cattle should not be 'interfered with' during the wet season fattening-up process.[58] He claimed he would 'have to resort to extreme measures' to protect himself and his stock and property if nothing were done. A simple response to this report came from Alexander Forrest himself who wrote to Commissioner Phillips requesting assistance:

> My dear sir,
>   Will you at once take action to protect property and lives on the station.
>   Alex Forrest[59]

Forrest's directive to Commissioner Phillips is remarkable given that not only was he the member for the West Kimberley in the Western Australian parliament but he also owned the station.

Phillips instructed Drewry to act. First Drewry ordered his officers to identify individual 'outlaws'. He put PC Handley in charge of Robinson River camp and instructed him to compile a list of all warrants extant 'for murders committed by natives in that district'.[60] He told Handley that his Native Assistant Peter could 'identify all the natives in that part'. He then instructed police that their duty was to protect the station residents from Aboriginal attacks. He identified leaders who were armed with guns and not spears, these included Yardicarinna and Coolaja, though Drewry did not realise the latter had already been killed by PC Armitage in November of the previous year. These men, he claimed, were 'men of the worst character and will not hesitate to take your lives if you give them a chance and [you] must act accordingly'.[61] Having already 'withstood the police by force of arms in numbers', Drewry stated that 'if they attempt this with you, you are justified in using your firearms with or to compel the proper observance of the law'.[62]

Drewry issued a further series of directives to counter the growing threat especially on the Robinson River.[63] Because escaping prisoners had used spears on police, all Aboriginal weapons were to be collected and kept at police camps. Police were to ensure handcuffs and chains worked correctly. Attempting to get police horses 'up to condition' was a priority. He informed Commissioner Phillips in his early reports from Derby Station in June 1893 that 'due to the extraordinary hilly nature of the country it is almost impossible to arrest natives alive'.[64] He advised his officers on stealth protocols for bush patrols: 'When in pursuit of the natives in the ranges of this country no loud talking, singing or firing at game should be allowed, no large fires should be kept at night.'[65]

One outcome of the increasing conflict was that men who might otherwise have become native assistants refused to join up. On 1 June 1894 PC Handley complained that he could not carry out patrols as he could not procure any native assistants.[66] There were two reasons for this: the first was that they often suffered bad treatment from the police but the second was a fear that they would be targeted and speared by the local groups.[67] In desperation, in June 1894 Drewry applied to the resident magistrate of the West Kimberley 'to use two imprisoned natives as native assistants with the police'.[68]

By early 1894 another problem had arisen: Drewry's patience with many of his officers had waned. He reported that McGillivray, who had actually arrested some Aboriginal men, took the prisoners to Lillamaloora Station (instead of Derby prison) where Native Assistant Barney 'let them go'.[69] Later that same month he complained that PC Handley made 'such a mess' of his last report that Drewry had him 'make a fair copy of the whole'.[70] The conduct of PCs Handley, Childs and McGillivray was such that 'at present on the three important bush camps I have not a single native assistant', and of Childs he wrote, 'I cannot get natives to stay with him. It is simply a waste of money to keep men of this sort in the police.'[71] It seems that Drewry regarded the native assistants as more important than his own officers. Childs was subsequently sacked in May 1894.[72] Handley was considered a good officer and stayed, whilst Chilcott was considered 'no bushman at all'[73] and McGillivray resigned one month later.[74]

'Native Affairs are Assuming a Serious Complexion All Over the Kimberley'

By April 1894 Drewry's tone in his correspondence with the commissioner of police became more urgent. He suggested that if police 'called on the natives to stop and lay down their arms' and they didn't, the police should fire on the ringleaders under 'wider discretion'.[75] He also continued to try to find better officers.

Police regulations regarding training and experience before promotion continued to be bent or disregarded. He recommended
to the commissioner that another police officer, Arthur Harold
Buckland, whom he described as 'a strongly built man, is acclimatized, a good horseman, suitable for work in this district and
is well educated', be employed.[76] On 9 May 1894 Reginald Nash
Spong, who was to become almost as notorious as PC Pilmer,
joined the police force. Less than a month later he was promoted
to second-class constable.[77] Drewry's directions to Spong reveal a
great deal about the interpretation of police rules and regulations.
Spong was told 'you must read up on your police regulations',[78]
and that he was 'allowed two native assistants': 'If you treat the
boys properly I think you will have no trouble getting good
ones…it has been bad treatment and starving them that has in my
opinion caused them to run away.'[79] He then added what would
exemplify the web of interdependence between some police and
the colonist population:

> I have no doubt that a constable who does his duty in
> a straightforward manner and minds his own business
> will be supported by the owners and manager of the
> station on the river. Lately the people [pastoralists] have
> been afraid to give information to the police especially
> in cases concerning white people on account of the
> police not keeping the information to themselves.[80]

This seems to indicate that some police behaved in clear violation
of police rules and regulations. Pastoralists would help police
with food rations and horses if the police helped them. If police
reported on them they could expect no favours in return.

The police were also affected by the informal relationships between Western Australian government ministers, the police hierarchy and those with vested interests in the Kimberley. *The West Australian* reported that in July 1894, Alexander Forrest met 'prominent pastoralists' of the West Kimberley at Derby for a luncheon put on 'for his behalf'.[81] At the luncheon Forrest listened to a range of issues, the most prominent being 'the native question'. He responded by saying that 'he would do all in his power on our behalf' to assist the pastoralists.[82] It was Isadore Emanuel, owner of Liveringa Station and business partner in Forrest, Emanuel & Co., who raised this issue and proposed that 'the evils of the present way of coping' with this 'required altering'. Emanuel praised Sub Inspector Drewry as a competent man but considered that 'his hands were so tied that he was unable to do anything without special permission from the authorities in Perth'.[83] Forrest was reported as replying that:

> he quite understood before coming here that Mr Drewry had great latitude, and was able to act at his own discretion. He promised to see the members for the different north districts, and to get this state of affairs altered if possible, as he considered that when a man who was supposed to be a competent man was appointed as police inspector to a district, he should have large discretionary powers.[84]

This comment was greeted with applause. That Forrest, parliamentarian, could know that an inspector of the Kimberley police force 'was able to act at his own discretion' and that, at the same time, he sought to have police powers and practices changed is probably not surprising. As a leading pastoralist his actions speak volumes on the relationships between politics and pastoralism.

In June 1894 Drewry believed that the state of affairs in the Kimberley was close to crisis point. Aboriginal people in both districts could not be controlled by conventional policing and were threatening to drive the police and pastoralists out of the district. Drewry wrote that Aboriginal people:

> often kill three, four or five sheep at the one time and the damage done to the stock does not actually stop at those actually killed, the natives often drive a mob into marsh country in the wet season[. T]his causes overhot joints and cause[s] abortions and ruptures to the cows in calf and often drowns many young calves besides those actually killed or wounded by spears. I consider it my duty to disabuse your mind as to this being the only part of the Kimberley that cattle spearing is going on[, it is going on] in the East Kimberley and the goldfields just as much as it is at the Fitzroy Crossing country…stock owners have to ride 150 miles [241 kilometres] to lay charges against 20. I have reported to you several times that native affairs are assuming a serious complexion all over the Kimberley and that prompt measures will have to be taken in the end[. T]here are over 60 escaped prisoners that have escaped from Wyndham goal since November last[,] some of whom speared a Denham police assistant…[I] am concluding that the whole of the stock country in the Kimberley will work under one set of orders and not four…the management of police should be left to the police officers in charge of

the district (rather than the Resident Magistrate)[,] they received far more information than them...[85]

By November 1894 the crisis point appeared to have been reached.[86] PC Spong had told Drewry that 'the gins [females] told them the natives spear all the horses and the white men'.[87] In early November 1894 Spong reported that he had run out of usable horses as 'so many of the station horses have died of poisoning or been speared by the natives that the manager cannot now assist the policeman in horses'. Aboriginal groups knew that without horses police could not patrol. They were effectively hobbling the police force of the Kimberley.[88]

The 'Pigeon Affair' Begins

This account of the 'Pigeon affair' is based on numerous accounts of the episode.[89] In late 1894 the focus of conflict shifted from the Robinson River Station to Lillamaloora. On 3 November Jandamarra (aka Pigeon), who was PC Richardson's informal native assistant, in concert with another Aboriginal man called Captain, who came from Esperance on the southwest of Western Australia and was sent to Derby on parole after being imprisoned for murder, shot PC Richardson dead at Lillamaloora police station.[90] Captain was regarded as being as good with guns as Jandamarra. The two then released the thirteen prisoners that Richardson had just arrested, including Pyaberra (aka Toby), Jewarrna (aka Bool), Ellemarra, Mullabuddin, Larawa and Lillimarra (aka Jacky), and, armed with rifles, fled to Windjana Gorge.[91] On 7 November they ambushed and killed two stockmen, Frank Burke and jackeroo 'Bill' Oswald Cuthburt Gibbs, who were attempting to push cattle into Plum Plain Station in Bunuba *country*.[92] The cattle belonged to Emanuel and Alexander Forrest from Meda Station.

Commissioner Phillips, prompted by the latest events, took Drewry's advice and split control of the Kimberley police into two districts. West Kimberley remained under Drewry's command so that he could focus on catching Jandamarra. Frederick John Orme was appointed sub inspector of police in charge of the East Kimberley.[93]

At the same time there were significant administrative changes involving the Western Australian police force. On the 4 December 1894 Colonial Secretary Stephen Parker retired from the position at the age of forty-eight after 'disagreements' with Premier John Forrest.[94] Forrest himself took the position up the very next day. Forrest now administered the police force. After Richardson, Burke and Gibbs were killed, a clearly panicked Drewry telegrammed Commissioner Phillips five times.[95] He also took the unusual step of notifying the resident magistrate in Derby, Charles Warton, and Premier Forrest, requesting special constables and more resources.[96] Kimberley pastoralists, including his brother Alexander, then actively lobbied the premier.[97] John Forrest wrote to Warton stating: 'Hope you will use every means to deal with the murderers – expense must not be considered – it is the desire of this government to act with promptness and decision.'[98]

That Warton and Drewry had telegraphed the premier irritated Phillips as they had bypassed the official chain of command. Drewry received a stern rebuke; it was, Phillips wrote, 'quite unnecessary to trouble the Premier' and accused Drewry of being 'incoherent...your telegram appears worded under a feeling of intense excitement instead of with that coolness which is essential in cases of emergency'.[99] Phillips told Drewry 'to take such steps as you deem necessary to deal with the natives and settlers from further molestation...and that you will accomplish

313

this by bold[,] vigorous and energetic measures which are not to be abandoned until the wet season compels you to do so – keep me informed of your doings'. He also instructed Drewry to 'swear in as many special constables as is needed'.[100] Drewry regarded what was occurring as a war and he then ordered an additional ten Winchester rifles, ten Snider rifles, extra revolvers and an extraordinary 4000 rounds of ammunition for the rifles.[101]

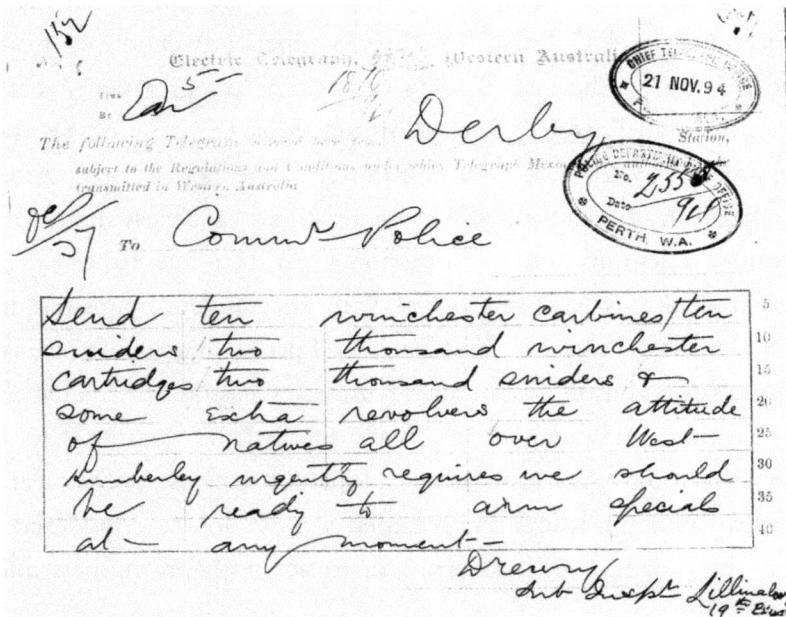

Figure 9.2. Telegram from Drewry to Commissioner of Police, 21 November 1894, in WAPD, 'Capture of Wild Natives in the Oscar and Barrier Ranges', 10 November 1894, SROWA, Cons. 430, File 3548/1897.

The Western Australian government was clearly alarmed with what it saw as resistance spreading from 'bush blacks' to 'station blacks'. The reports of 'natives in the West Kimberley having broken into open hostility towards the whites' caused Commissioner Phillips to bring in reinforcements, led by Inspector William Lawrence from Roebourne, to take charge of the pursuit

of Jandamarra. Lawrence was given two constables, special constables if required, and six native assistants to head the pursuit.[102]

Jandamarra was now to be pursued from three police camps:
the Fitzroy, Lennard and Robinson camps. Drewry made several
requests for 'Queensland boys' or non-local native assistants to
work with the police.[103] He apparently suspected that local native
assistants could turn against the police as Jandamarra had done.[104]
He organised an usually large punitive expedition that consisted
of PCs David Brice and Clarke, native assistants Hector, Friday,
Banjo, Charlie, Paddy and five 'Queensland boys' whom he had
acquired from Derby (three of whom were hired from colonist
Thomas Daly at '30 shillings a week'). In addition several colonists
from the district, Felix Edgar and Francis Hamilton, and stockmen
Magee, Turner, Dean and Jimmy Black, were sworn in as special
constables. Drewry then acquired six more 'Queensland boys'
from owner Alf Barnett of Balmaningara Station. By this time the
party had grown to thirty men.[105]

Drewry's first tactic was to send 'the six Queensland boys'
from Barnett's station into Windjana Gorge to pretend they
had killed Barnett and wanted to join Jandamarra and Captain's
group. This apparently failed and they returned to the police
party, at which point Drewry's party launched an 'all out' attack
on the caves and gorge area. This involved extensive shooting by
police, which was met by shooting in return.[106] The party arrested
seven Aboriginal women and suspected that they had wounded
Jandamarra. Drewry noted that without 'the Queensland boys'
and the other native assistants they would not even have seen
him.[107] He estimated that the actual number of outlaws was 'not
more than nine men and their gins in the gorge'.[108]

Following the failure of this raid, Drewry split the police
party into two groups: he led one group and Corporal Cadden

led the other. Both parties were to patrol the Leopold and Napier ranges. Drewry's party came across Jandamarra's group several times although they were unable to arrest or shoot any of them. He did, however, report that they were terrified as 'they run like dogs[,] the excrement dropping from them whenever my party surprises them'.[109] On one patrol he was able to surprise an Aboriginal camp in the Leopold Ranges, killing nine men and capturing several Aboriginal women. One captive named Terrawarra said that Jandamarra had died of wounds received in a previous affray.[110] Believing that police had killed Jandamarra the party returned to Derby Station.

While the police focus was on Jandamarra there was conflict in other areas of the West Kimberley. On 19 November 1894 PC McDermott and Joseph Blythe (the owner of Brooking Gorge Station who was acting as a special constable) pursued a group of Aboriginal people into the Geikie Gorge. Blythe was injured in a fight where seven Aboriginal people were shot. McDermott's report, reflecting Drewry's instructions no doubt, stated that those killed were 'killing cattle in a wholesale way' and that the shooting was necessary as the rock formations made it 'very difficult to arrest them'.[111] Blythe reported to Inspector Lawrence that the natives 'had killed over 100 head of sheep', were armed and were threatening them 'every night'.[112]

In another patrol PC Pilmer, with 'a party of ten', had gone on patrol to Geikie Gorge on 13 December and, according to his record of events, by 26 December had killed anywhere between seven and twenty people.[113] According to Drewry two of those killed 'were associated' with the murder of Richardson.[114] He believed that the others who were killed were 'more or less' involved in the fight with McDermott and Blythe on 19 November. Lawrence's telegram to Phillips recorded a death toll of seventeen, four being prisoners who had escaped when PC Richardson was murdered.[115]

Much of the significant conflict at the turn of the year in January 1895 centred on the coastal Warwa people. At Robinson River Station PCs Spong and Chisholm with native assistants Peter and Billy commenced patrols.[116] Spong's reports are terse and functional, recording very little other than finding the carcasses of cattle that had been eaten and tracking 'Natives all day'.[117] In one instance Chisholm recorded 'that 5 natives swam Robinson River last night and came up close to [the] house[,] went through [the] garden [and] speared two station horses killing them as well spearing the police horse in the shoulder'.[118] Clearly Aboriginal people were still intent on hobbling police movement.

Meanwhile, whilst Drewry's police party, with special constables and five native assistants, chased suspects on the Barrier Range, Lawrence's party left on 15 December 1894 'to disperse natives on the Fitzroy River'.[119] In Lawrence's first action he reported that his party came across 'about thirty natives in the bed of the Margaret River'.[120] Lawrence sent Special Constable Blythe down with five native assistants whilst the remainder of the police party took up hidden positions.[121] Upon seeing the rushing police, some went for their spears whilst others ran. Lawrence reported that 'the police fired on them killing eleven'.[122] At this camp the police found the remains of two bullocks that Lawrence presumed to be from MacDonald's stock and wrote that the party they dispersed 'was a bad hostile lot' who could have defeated 'a lesser police party'.[123]

Lawrence's three-month campaign ran from November 1894 to January 1895 and only once did his men engage and kill an individual for whom there was a police warrant. This was ex–station hand Long Frankey, who had allegedly murdered three

Aboriginal station hands and threatened to burn down the Fitzroy Crossing telegraph station;[124] he was killed on 7 January 1895. Every other shooting in this period was of 'bush blacks'. There is little record of who they were or what they had done.

Lawrence's party then headed towards the Oscar and Leopold ranges and came across a 'camp of about seventeen natives'.[125] 'Three of the mob mounted the hills with their spears', Lawrence wrote, where 'police were compelled to fire on them', killing them, 'as they would not leave the hills'. Lawrence wrote that the remainder of the Aboriginal party 'were dispersed to the Leopold ranges and told not to return', adding the caveat that 'those killed were notorious cattle killers'. He considered that police work was now complete in the lower area of the Leopold and Oscar ranges, that they were 'free from natives except those working for the settlers'.[126] He then split the police party up with Blythe on one side of the Fitzroy and the rest of the party on the other. The patrols of Blythe's party are not documented; however, Lawrence's reports show that Blythe's party headed down the Fitzroy through to Jurgurra Creek Station, dispersing groups and killing several people.[127]

Meanwhile, Lawrence's party had followed a request from Edwin Rose, the manager of Quanbun Station, and killed one man in the process of forcing the removal of all the others from the station, including old men and women.[128] The following day he found the same group that he had banished from the area, among them were some blind and disease-affected men, women and children who were 'quite unable to get their own living'. Lawrence's party 'dispersed them from the paddock'.[129] Isadore Emanuel's wishes for more punitive police action were granted when Lawrence's party travelled further onto Emanuel's Noonkanbah Station where they found a large group of up to twenty young men 'hunting on the river in Emanuel's sheep paddocks'. Sending his native assistants to meet them they reported that the men would not put down their spears, so the police fired on them, killing one man who 'had given all sorts of impertinence'.[130] Lawrence's party then went to Liveringa Station, where an undetermined number of people were killed.[131]

Lawrence's reports during this period show that his party attacked the Aboriginal people before any attack was made on them. His intention appears to have been to rid the district of 'bush blacks' by either killing them or driving them from the district. Correspondence between Lawrence and Commissioner Phillips may have endorsed this approach, although Phillips suggested that Lawrence should 'continue operations against natives but endeavour to disperse them with as little bloodshed as possible'.[132] How Lawrence was to interpret directions to 'disperse them' but 'with as little bloodshed as possible' was unclear, although clearly Phillips wanted to be seen to be acting within the law.

Police believed that they had 'cleared the area of blacks' but on 15 March 1895 another European colonist, prospector William Phillips, was speared, although not killed, while camped at 92 Mile Range near the Oscar Range.[133] Police were acutely aware that this was retaliation against dispersals. Overall, however, the police actions had for the most part the desired, albeit temporary, effect of reducing attacks by Aboriginal men. Local pastoralists of the district were happy with the results.[134] The *Northern Public Opinion* newspaper regarded them as essential in making Aboriginal people see 'the mosaic law of life for a life'.[135]

However, it is clear the police actions had not succeeded completely. On 21 April 1895 Drewry wrote to Phillips stating that the situation was again 'very serious' and that unless the police made 'themselves felt during the next twelve months there will be further troubles'.[136] Drewry outlined his case by sending a list of unexecuted warrants that had been issued but for which no arrests had been made. Phillips responded with trenchant advice:

> If, as you report there are still forty-four natives still at
> large who are implicated in the recent murders, why are
> you not in hot pursuit of them? They must be hunted
> down and shot if they will not surrender, every round
> being made to tell. Random firing at rocks and mouths
> of caves etc upon chance of hitting natives is as useless as
> it is wasteful. These instructions apply to the murderers
> only.[137]

Yet, his orders and opinions were often confusing and contradictory. In May 1895, for example, Constable Brice from Lennard River Police Station reported on policing near the Napier Ranges, 'the natives tried to get away and we started firing on them…we shot four altogether namely Chungara, Tamadee and two others, name unknown'. Brice justified these shootings by claiming, 'Chungara was supposed to be in the Wingenah [sic] Gorge when Burke and Gibbs were murdered'.[138] Phillips was unimpressed, calling it an 'unproved and illegal attack'.[139] He wrote:

> the circumstances herein reported did not justify the
> police in firing upon the natives. There is nothing to
> show that they were committing an offence or that they
> had been implicated in any depredations. The mere
> fact of Chungara being supposed to have been in the
> gorge on the occasion of Burke and Gibbs murder was
> no excuse for the extreme measures resorted to by the

police, more especially as it was not known that he was one of the mob until he was killed. PC Bryce [sic] reports that it was quite unnecessary to fire upon them with a view to their dispersion…PC Brice may be an expert bushman and an excellent hand at running down the natives, but it is evident he is entirely ignorant of his powers as a police constable or of the regulations regarding the use of arms, and if he continues to make unjustifiable use of arms against the natives he will get into serious trouble.[140]

In March 1895 Sub Inspector Drewry taught his officers how to write out reports so police were seen to be resisting attack and were justified in shooting offenders dead. He wrote, 'Write down the left hand side then turn the page over and right [sic] on the other side. In the shooting of the native at Wambarrilla and in your special report *you do not say whether the native resisted you* or not. It is advisable to do this.'[141] PC Brice must not have received this directive.

It is clear that Commissioner Phillips knew police were engaged in unlawful killings for at times he directly criticised certain killings. It is also quite clear that he did not have control of his police force. Practically, for many police, interpreting the instructions that came from the commissioner to sub inspectors to their constables would have been difficult. On the one hand, following the shooting of PC Richardson by Jandamarra, Commissioner Phillips could instruct police 'to take such steps as you deem necessary to deal with the natives'.[142] On the other, only four months later, he could threaten an officer with prosecution for murder following another shooting of Aboriginal people.[143] But if the messages from Perth were confusing there is no doubt that local police took advantage of them to police essentially as they saw fit.

Craven Henry (Harry) Ord Arrives

In July 1895 it was reported that Jandamarra was very much alive and hiding out in the Napier and Leopold ranges.[144] A month later Commissioner Phillips commissioned Craven Henry (Harry) Ord and he joined in the pursuit of Jandamarra in August.[145] Ord, as we have seen, had considerable international experience and was regarded as a strong, authoritarian figure. He built on Drewry's policing style and using his experience brought more discipline and military style to policing.

Figure 9.3. 'Police Officer Craven Harry Ord on Police Horse Isadore with Aboriginal Nugget, Police Horses, Horror and Chancelor, and Sgt. Pearson in Buggy, Derby', 1898. Courtesy State Library of Western Australia, 026295PD. D. Falconer.

The attacks on Aboriginal groups showing any sort of belligerence continued but widened to include Aboriginal groups in areas that had not hitherto been policed, and a new forcefulness came to characterise them. On 8 April 1895 PCs Chisholm and Spong reported that the Robinson River Police Station was 'visited by natives at midnight', as the dogs they used to guard the homestead started 'barking furiously'.[146] The PCs fired into the night but hit nothing, not being able to see much. At daylight two native tracks were seen in the garden.[147]

In late September the police at Robinson River Station noted that Aboriginal people from the Stewart River 'had burned all the country for miles'. PC Spong's reports gave little evidence of police procedure being adhered to as he went in pursuit.

saw four natives on side off range[,] called upon them several times in the usual way to stop but they would not. Myself and party fired on them[,] a native woman got a Winchester bullet through the thigh. Natives being two or three yards off[,] could not tell men from women[,] took wounded woman to Oobagooma station[,] the rest of the natives escaping through the ranges.[148]

In mid-1895 there were many more shootings. PC Pilmer and his native assistants were sent to MacDonald's station following reports of 'wholesale killing of cattle in the Margaret River area'.[149] Pilmer reported coming across a group, who were likely Gooniyandi people, of about thirty, twenty of which were males. They immediately fled after the police raid and the group started making use of their 'spears, dowirks and quondis to such an extent that we were compelled to fire upon them...' He reported killing nine men whose names were Murjarri, Widali, Wonboni, Coolya, Mulabia, Mungar, Calapi, Mulyalli and Culcul, who were in possession of 'between 12 and 13 Cwt [centum weight] of beef'.[150] The unofficial number killed was likely far higher.

Then on 31 January 1896 Jandamarra along with Mullabuddin and Lillimarra struck again in a raid on Lillamaloora Station, where they stole all the beef rations and retreated to Windjana Gorge after threatening the lone police officer, James Price, with spears.[151] Price was the new chum who was there with Fred Edgar and his station boy Peter Skene. Ord suggested Price was a 'delicate man unused to bush life'.[152] Price followed and shot one and wounded another. In May 1896 police reported that groups of Aboriginal people, possibly the Unggarangi people on the flat Fitzroy River floodplains, attacked the manager of Noonkanbah Station, William Cox, and stole firearms, and that native 'Albert' (aka Noormandie) and Darbelin speared a boundary rider named Duncan. Ord had described how Duncan had 'got to his gun' with a spear hanging out of him and that his police group had tracked the culprits for some 40 kilometres before giving up the chase in the mountains.[153] Ord explained that:

> Albert has been persuading blacks that they can stand against police and burn out the whites[. C]onsiderable damage has been done by fires all up the river[,] have strong party[,] hope to report all things settled in a few weeks[,] only difficulty being as usual horses[,] six police horses knocked out by carrying ballot papers to Halls creek from Derby in six days...[154]

Police reported that Albert, Darbelin and another Aboriginal man named Frankey were 'station natives' who had 'stirred up the bush natives' in an attempt to drive the colonists from the district.[155] Ord, along with native assistants and PC Phillips, went after the offenders on 27 July 1896. PCs Pilmer and Nicholson from Fitzroy Crossing joined up later.[156] After tracking them for over ten days they came upon the group and killed three unnamed individuals, the rest escaping into the 'almost inaccessible stronghold in the St George Range'. They continued tracking the group until 14 August when they surprised them in a dawn raid and 'dispersed the mob', killing six and wounding two although the alleged ringleaders escaped punishment.[157] Albert was not arrested until over a year later when it was reported in the *Northern Public Opinion* that PC Nicholson had arrested him.[158] Police activity escalated again, probably in August 1896, when more Aboriginal attacks occurred and several thousand acres along the Fitzroy River 257 kilometres from Derby were set on fire.

The problem of police reports appearing in local and national newspapers was that the police perspective was often highly exaggerated, bringing unwanted attention to the events. PC Pilmer's reports in particular were ridiculed for their perceived embellishment. The *T'Othersider* newspaper carried an article mercilessly mocking Pilmer's 'riotous imagination'. Quoting Pilmer's telegrams the writer stated:

When Pilmer had surrounded the natives, one of the latter Pigeon, delivered a 'shower of well directed rifle shots' none of which hit Pilmer. Pilmer acknowledged the ovation with a 'storm of bullets' which apparently did contradictory quantities of damage to the beleaguered hosts...a native boy was wounded owing to the 'dense smoke during the rapid firing.'[159]

Hyperbole aside it was clear that large numbers of Aboriginal people were being killed through police shootings. It was during this period and after many media reports that Travelling Inspector

George Marsden, under instruction from the Aborigines Protection Board, demanded details of the shootings of Aboriginal people.[160] He reported 'that beyond the returns made by police it is impossible to ascertain the number of natives that have been shot by police' and 'from what I can gather by inquiries amongst the constables of Kimberley District no shooting is ever done unless the natives resist and then only as much as is absolutely needful.'[161] Yet he had not been deceived completely. He had been informed by Edwin Rose of Oobagooma Station that Aboriginal men had killed two men on the outstation at Mundooma and had been killing cattle at the rate of 200 to 300 each year. It had been impossible to prevent this, Marsden observed, since they only kill stock in the wet season, when pursuit on horse back is impossible and, when the local groups 'drive the cattle till they bog and then kill them at their leisure'.[162] Ominously, he heard that a conspiracy was afoot as on 'one occasion the natives sent in word by gins that they were going to rush the whole station and drive the cattle off and join the barrier range natives and expel the white men from the district'.[163]

He reported that PC Spong and his native assistants 'struck a camp of eighty buck natives, in full war paint with cow tails hanging all over them. These natives, each of which had one or two gins with him carrying spears, commenced throwing their spears.'[164] The police dispersed them, Marsden wrote, with 'the loss of some twenty bucks. Since then they have never attempted to rush the station, but have kept well back in the hills.'[165]

Marsden's reports must have been read by Bishop Riley in Perth because he wrote to Governor Smith in July 1896, suggesting that the 'expression "dispersing the natives," should be clearly defined so that they [police] may understand what it means'. He was also concerned police had 'too much power placed in their hands' and should not be able to shoot at Aboriginal people unless they were actually under attack.[166] These reports made little headway in Perth as the government was set on the wholesale pacification of the West Kimberley.

Since the beginning of 'operations' against Jandamarra in November 1894 the police parties had recorded killing at least eighty Aboriginal people (with an unknown and possibly larger number killed in 'dispersals') and an undisclosed number had been killed at Oobagooma and Liveringa. A survey of the police bush patrol diaries of Inspector Lawrence, Sub Inspector Ord and PCs Pilmer, Nicholson, Chisholm, Spong and Freeman show an almost complete breakdown of proper police process. The diaries of Spong and Chisholm, both of whom pursued Jandamarra, contain almost no information but in most of the other diaries, police report the party shooting at any Aboriginal people they came across, with their native assistants doing much of the shooting. The whole exercise appears much more like a military operation than policing.

Meanwhile, Jandamarra and his followers had remained quiet throughout late 1896 and did not strike again until 16 March 1897, when Lillimarra, aka 'Jacky', killed stockman Tom Jasper as he slept near the Oscar Range Station.[167] Commissioner Phillips had clearly had enough of Jandamarra and telegrammed Ord demanding that 'Pigeon and others implicated in the murder of Jasper are to be captured dead or alive. Pursuit is not to be relinquished until the band is accounted for.'[168] PC Pilmer and Nicholson and four native assistants went in pursuit of the group in the Oscar Ranges on 18 March 1897. Finding them, they killed two men, Rowally, aka Demon, and Murramin, aka Jimmy, as well as wounding three others, and collected an amount of ammunition and guns. Concurrently Ord issued instructions:

PCs Chisholm, Buckland and Special Constable Joseph Blythe were to approach the group from the northern end of the Oscar Range while PCs Anderson and Spong were to approach the Napier Range along the telegraph line. Another Aboriginal native assistant from Roebourne called Mingo Mick was contracted to assist.[169]

On 27 March 1897, whilst on patrol near Tunnel Creek with prisoners 'on the chain', PC Chisholm and his Native Assistant Mick with Special Constable Blythe and his Native Assistant Wisego Billy came across Jandamarra. The reports of this encounter, which has contributed much to the Jandamarra legend, described a fire fight in which Jandamarra was seemingly felled by a gunshot from Mick. Blythe galloped up to the prone and wounded figure of Jandamarra with a pistol in his hand but Jandamarra rolled over unleashing a rifle and shot the revolver from Blythe's hand shattering two fingers in the process.[170] He was then able to escape.[171] The next morning when the native assistants were collecting the police horses Jandamarra shot and killed Wisego Billy, likely to prevent him tracking him.[172]

On 31 March 1897 the same group finally cornered an injured Jandamarra. PC Anderson came upon him, fired and wounded him again. It was Native Assistant Mick who delivered the *coup de grace*. He wounded him again then took aim and shot him in the head, killing him outright.[173] Commissioner Phillips was delighted, telegraphing his officers congratulating them for 'having disposed of Pigeon' and destroyed 'his gang of murderers' but he added, significantly, that 'police operations were to be continued until natives throughout the district are brought under subjection'.[174] Ord replied saying the district 'may be said to be in as quiet a state as it is possible to be' and that he was 'not relaxing vigour of police actions'.[175]

Killing Jandamarra did not end the conflict in the West Kimberley and localised 'flare-ups' would continue. These were minimal until August 1897 when West Kimberley countrymen Lillimarra (aka Jacky), Pyaberra (aka Toby), Warrinmarrah (aka Dickey), Jewarrna (aka Bool) and Merrima (aka Jimmy) escaped from Derby Gaol.[176] This was despite being restrained with riveted-on, double-leg irons (weighing 6.3 kilograms) and with neck chains and padlock.[177] In December 1897 there were still reports of 'marauding' Aboriginal people on stations such as Liveringa and Myroodah who had 'frequently robbed camps, broken into houses…taken part in cattle and sheep stealing'.[178] And in March 1899 at Mt Broome, Mullabuddin and Woonmillina killed prospector John Dobbie.[179] They were captured in early 1900 and hanged for their part in this murder and Jandamarra's resistance, as was Lillimarra when he was captured again.[180]

By 1898 the last of the unstocked land on the southern part of the King Leopold Ranges was taken up for pastoralism when Leopold Downs and Fairfield Stations took over what was Lillamaloora. In that same year pastoral expansion north of the ranges was finally established when Queenslander Frank Hann explored the district.[181] In 1899 Joseph Blythe and his sons founded Mount House Station in the area north of the ranges. By 1900 it seemed that the military style police operations had succeeded in breaking Aboriginal resistance in the West Kimberley.

However, the events outlined in this chapter were not the end of the conflict during the period under study but they did represent the most sustained conflict where most Aboriginal people were either killed or arrested. Reports of cattle killing at Oobagooma, Yeeda and Fossil Downs continued until well into the twentieth century, though the attacks were more sporadic than previously. If, however, the violence gradually diminished, popular memory of the conflict grew among Aboriginal people and Jandamarra came to represent both the violence of the district and the resistance of Aboriginal people.

Chapter 10

'THEY SHOW FIGHT ON THE APPROACH OF ANY WHITE MAN'

'The Killing Times' in the East Kimberley 1890–1898

While the East Kimberley pastoral industry had been established in 1882 its development was slow, as the environment was harsh and infrastructure non-existent. When the 1886 Halls Creek goldrush ended in 1889 only a small local market remained and prices for stock were depressed.[1] Droughts across the Kimberley from 1890 to 1892 further stalled pastoral expansion.[2] Pastoralists found it difficult to dispose of their stock because it had to be driven overland to the port at Derby, 480 kilometres away, or at times driven even further overland across the border to Port Darwin.[3] However, in the 1890s several factors contributed to a resurgence in prospects.

The discovery of gold at Coolgardie in 1892 and Kalgoorlie in 1893 greatly increased the population of Western Australia, and provided a massive boost in the market for beef.[4] The improvement of Wyndham port, first used in April 1894 for live cattle export, made exporting more economical and pastoral expansion more attractive as the port could ship nearly twice as many cattle to Perth than Derby port.[5] The drought had broken and beef production had become a viable concern. On the Ord River Station, for example, cattle numbers increased from 4000 in 1885 to an estimated 35,000 in 1896.[6] The number of cattle on other East Kimberley stations by mid-1896 was enormous. Hill and Durack's station had 15,000 head; Argyle 9000 head; Newry 3000 head;

Rosewood 4000 head; Carlton 1000 head; Flora Valley 2000 head; and Sturt Creek 4000 head.[7] The effect of this prosperity was that stations were packed to capacity with stock, and that of the fourteen stations that had been under mortgage in 1893 only two still were by 1896.[8] The pastoral industry had begun to thrive but the future of the numerous Aboriginal people of the East Kimberley would become clouded as stock destroyed and displaced food resources. This chapter examines the history of policing in the East Kimberley during the mid- to late 1890s in the context of economic growth and social and political change in both Perth and the East Kimberley itself.

As with the West Kimberley a process of attrition and amalgamation occurred amongst leaseholders and the number of stations reduced considerably as firms joined up to form single companies.[9] As Bolton noted, the pastoral stations that managed to survive the early years were either those of pastoralists with extensive drive, experience and resources behind them or companies of squatters that amalgamated to become one, large firm.[10] The Duracks, Emanuels and Alexander Forrest, along with Tom Kilfoyle, rationalised their holdings and established pastoral stations. They reserved eight abutting 202 square kilometre blocks along the banks of the Ord, 607 square kilometres near Negri Junction, and blocks on the Nicholson Plans, Margaret River and both sides of the Fitzroy, with some of these blocks abutting the King Sound Pastoral Company holdings.[11] Most of the pastoral expansion occurred along the lower Ord and Dunham rivers and a number of smaller stations were established in more remote country on the Bow, Panton and Margaret rivers. Carlton Station (stocked by Hart Bros) built up stock between 1893 and 1898 and the Durack brothers stocked numerous other leases on the Dunham River. They, along with W.H. Osmand, consolidated

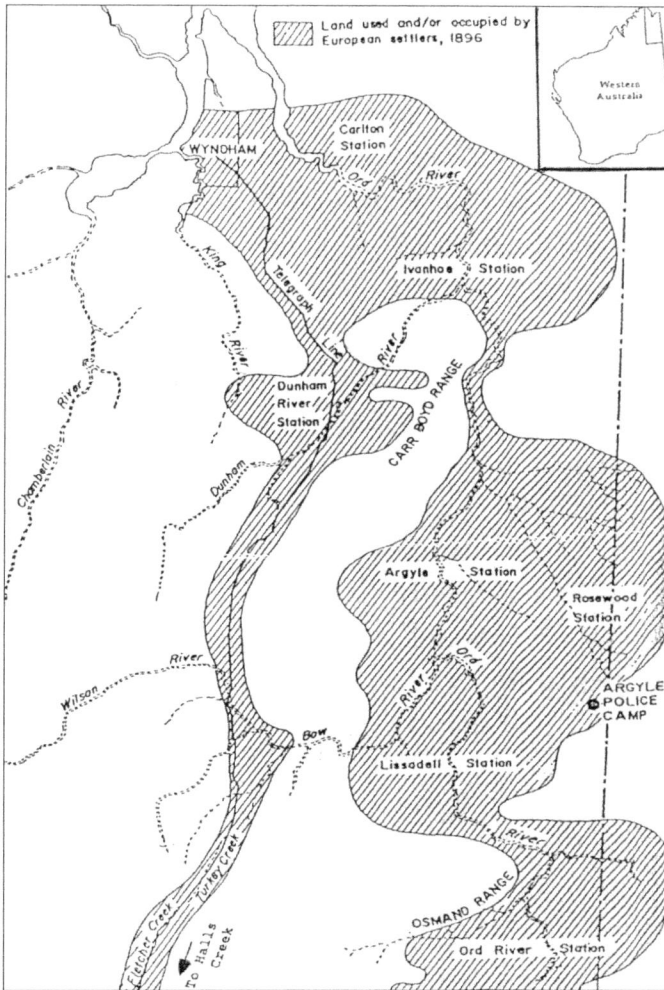

Figure 10.1. The East Kimberley, 1896. Courtesy Cathie Clement and the Royal Western Australian Historical Society.

their holdings on the Ord River.[12] Jack Kelly, an ex-stockman from the Ord River Station, formed Texas Downs in late 1897.[13] Also in 1897 Connor and Doherty amalgamated with the Durack Bros to form Connor, Doherty and Durack, the major pastoral company and beef producer in the East Kimberley district. Their pastoral empire covered 'roughly ten thousand square miles' (25,900 square kilometres). This and the company of Alexander Forrest and Isadore Emanuel in the West Kimberley became the two pillars of a Western Australian beef-producing empire.

As in the West Kimberley, little thought was given to what Aboriginal people on *country* were to do other than simply accept colonisation. And despite a police presence Aboriginal people of the East Kimberley continued to kill stock (including prize stock and horses), destroy property and harass and intimidate colonists, often in covert hit-and-run attacks.[14] By the early 1890s the flood of men to the Halls Creek goldrush had dwindled and as colonists were less numerous Aboriginal groups were less fearful of them. In the country where the pastoral stations were situated and on the East Kimberley goldfields there were significantly higher numbers of Aboriginal people than in the West Kimberley. Police records reveal accounts of pitched battles with fifty to one hundred East Kimberley Aboriginal men and women throwing spears at police.[15]

Police actions in patrolling the telegraph line, where extensive shooting and numerous arrests occurred, antagonised and terrified the East Kimberley groups. The punitive expeditions following the killings of Durack and Barnett exacerbated a fragile situation and by 1890 many Aboriginal people, clearly in fear of their lives, would 'fly at the sight of the white man'.[16] More killings of colonists occurred: on 27 June 1890 William Miller (who was speared through the stomach) and Joseph Webb (speared under the shoulder) were both killed at Mt Dockerell in the Kimberley goldfields;[17] on 17 November 1890 Tudor Shadforth was speared at the Osmand Creek near the Ord River Station.[18] Written records reveal palpable fear, particularly in the case of the more isolated colonists in the East Kimberley, especially in the early

1890s when further pastoral expansion encroached on Aboriginal land. Jack Sullivan, a Gadjerong man and stock worker employed by the Durack family, talks of the 'killing times' around Patsy Durack's Newry Station:

> I lived on the Keep river, which goes right from the coast to Newry Station. There were all Gadjerong people along the coast until the white men shot them. Half of them died and some of the young men were brought into the stations to quieten them and to learn the horses, like me. All the Gadjerong people were taken out of their country or were put on the stations or were killed. There are no people left there now.[19]

Sub Inspector Drewry in the East Kimberley

The isolation, environment and conflict with Aboriginal people no doubt led to high levels of stress for police in these camps and clearly there were the same significant problems with police discipline and organisational structure as there had been in the late 1880s. Attempts by senior police to instil a sense of order and decorum amongst junior police were met with resentment in many East Kimberley police stations. In May 1889 Sergeant Richard Troy reprimanded police at these stations for not filling out reports properly.[20] In November he reported PC Connor to the commissioner for not reporting that the telegraph line was down at Bow River and Fletcher Creek.[21] Alcohol was the cause of other problems; in May 1890 Troy requested Commissioner Phillips to:

> appoint a man of temperate habits as great temptation exists in the goldfields[,] road grog being carried by all

the packers and disposed of to travellers. I am aware that a great deal of drinking is carried on by the police at the Denham [River police camp] and on patrol duty especially at watering places where they meet pastures, but it is very difficult to sheet it home to them as they shield each other and the civilians are very reticent about giving information on such matters. Such men as Tuke and Archdeacon are not to be trusted as they cannot resist drink whenever its obtainable if they are out of sight of an officer.[22]

In fact PC Tuke had pleaded with the commissioner to transfer him south as he feared the climate was 'permanently injuring his health' and resigned when the commissioner ignored him.[23] PC Archdeacon resigned after becoming dangerously ill with fever and dysentery, possibly exacerbated by drinking.[24] Sergeant Houlihan reported PC Gee for being so drunk that he had fallen off his horse. He also reported instances of Gee's 'sly drinking'.[25] A new officer, Constable Oakes, arrived in Wyndham but was assessed by a superior officer as 'no horseman, no knowledge of horses, unacquainted with firearms, no experience of bush life and has not the least inclination to do anything about it…he is simply useless at cleaning saddles even'. He was too 'fond of playing for card money', feigned illness to avoid bush patrol and was generally so incompetent 'he will endanger the men'.[26]

Houlihan's assessment was borne out when Oakes was caught drinking at the Custom House Hotel where he refused Houlihan's orders to leave the hotel and return to his quarters.[27] In 28 November 1890 Sergeant Houlihan inspected Denham River police camp to find that white ants had eaten through the occurrence, horse return and letter books. He was annoyed that

PC Tuke had made no mention of it. He also reported that police gazettes, important documents from the central office conveying news about changing regulations and circular orders were also left carelessly out in an open box available for anyone to look at.[28] He further found that PC Tuke had falsely claimed that a tent was blown down. Many of these complaints made their way to Perth, but there was little that could be done. Commissioner Phillips' response was: 'There are no experienced men available to send to Wyndham' and that it was the duty of senior officers to train the junior officers in bush work.[29]

There is also ample evidence of hostility between police. PC Pollard reported Tuke to Sergeant Troy for swearing at him, drunkenness and neglect of duty. Then in May 1890 Pollard and Tuke reported Gee and McCann to Troy for using offensive language.[30] In June 1890 Sergeant Troy was shot in the back whilst on bush patrol 217 kilometres from Wyndham, which resulted in his death three days later.[31] The *Eastern Districts Chronicle* of 5 July 1890 reported that 'murderous blacks' had shot Troy, but he was actually accidentally shot by PC Pollard while police were ambushing an Aboriginal camp near Sandy Bow River.[32]

Tension between individual police officers sometimes resulted in violence. At Halls Creek in March 1891 Trooper Kingston fought with Trooper Austin, assaulted him and then shot at him (but missed) over a dispute about a piece of damper under a bunk in their tent.[33] PC Guilfoyle did not get along with his colleagues and was accused of stealing rations.[34] Guilfoyle seems to have been a troubled man, one of the unfortunate new chums in the Kimberley who could not cope with the physical and the social environment. In July 1891 Guilfoyle was staffing the Denham River police camp; his writing in the occurrence book reveals an air of panic and desperation as each page gets progressively harder to read. He pleaded for more support and reported being terrorised nightly by Aboriginal people massing near and around the police tent. On 9 July he complained 'that the camp is not safe at this present time…natives are burning the land'.[35] He could not understand 'why Sergeant Lavery did not pay any attention to reports'.[36] This was the last report Guilfoyle made as Sergeant Lavery handed over the charge of the camp to PC Pollard. With native assistants Mickey, Rocket and Willie they cleaned up the camp, which had been 'neglected for some considerable time by my predecessor. Everything is in a dilapidated condition.'[37] PC Guilfoyle was relieved of his duty though he may not have been exaggerating the extent of Aboriginal encroachment on the station's camp. Sergeant Lavery reported in late September: 'Observes Abo nat tracks in the Denham River just opposite the tents, we found the tracks of three natives where they had crawled within 6 yards [5 metres] of the store tents on their knees.'[38]

There were also conflicts of interest between colonists and police. In February 1892 Sergeant Houlihan reported that PC Kingston was engaged in corrupt behaviour while at Fletcher Creek camp. He allegedly had set up an arrangement with the Wyndham gaoler to purchase police prisoners to work (essentially as slaves) on his own property. Kingston would deliver them for £1 per head. Drewry reported Kingston to both Inspector Ord and the commissioner. Kingston denied the accusation while his colleague, PC Rhatigan, testified that no such arrangement existed.[39] Clearly, finding corroborating witnesses was difficult.

The chaotic behaviour and reporting from the Kimberley police stations forced change in the organisational structure of the force. Edwin Overend Drewry was promoted to head the force in the whole Kimberley district.[40] He began his work quickly – as he had done in the West Kimberley, he commenced an aggressive and frank assessment and communicated his opinions to the commissioner on the situation in the East Kimberley.[41] On 22 September 1892 he visited Denham camp and made a damning assessment of both the quality of officers and the nature and use of their work.[42] In the previous ten-month period he had written regarding Denham camp, 'the Fletcher Creek police with one constable less had arrested over 90 more natives'.[43] Drewry arrived back in Wyndham on Christmas Day 1892 to 'find that the work has been carried out in a very inefficient manner'.[44] He was fiercely critical of the police stationed there, particularly Sergeant Lavery. Despite a spate of robberies the police had 'not a native arrested'. There had been no 'energetic' work done and 'the idea seems too prevalent with some officers that when anything happens they are alright if they do nothing but report at length about the matter'.[45] Clearly Lavery was the wrong type of officer for the times. In Wyndham in February 1893, he was disciplined for not shooting Aboriginal people. The title of the police report that prompted the disciplinary action spoke volumes itself: 'Expedition to Disperse Natives on King River – December 1892. Failure from Serg Lavery to Shoot Natives Defeated the Purpose of the Trip.[46] Lavery claimed that he 'could not shoot a nigger in cold blood' in spite of orders to do so.[47]

With regard to the pastoral station patrols it seems that they were all but non-existent. Drewry found that despite complaints by pastoralists about cattle and valuable imported bulls being speared, 'I cannot find any record of a police party having left Wyndham during the last two years to arrest the depredators.'[48] He was, nevertheless, glowing in appreciation of the work of those police regarded as uncompromising, such as PCs Rhatigan and Kingston, and he recommended Trooper Brophy for a promotion, which was duly received. He was scathing about town constables;

they were 'of comparatively little use in Kimberley. I find their experience usually teaches them to take too much care of themselves[,] the consequence of which is they let the native question severely alone.'[49]

Drewry wanted 'more stringent measures' to be used to defend the telegraph line.[50] His directives, conveyed to both West and East Kimberley police, were blunt. Police were to leave Halls Creek on the 1st and 17th of each month to travel to Fletcher Creek and Denham stations:

> Constables are to remember that is their duty to prevent the natives from breaking the line; any natives camped near the line and found prowling around it, are to be driven from it and kept from it. Constables are not to go long distances from the line looking for natives but are to go as far as may be necessary for protection of the line. Prisoners shall not be taken; unless absolutely necessary; as for instance, as the police shall come upon them breaking the line; or natives that have just done it; under these circumstances as many as possible are to be arrested; if the natives show fight or violently resist the police in the execution of their duty, constables will use their firearms to protect themselves with, but that indiscriminate slaughter of natives will not be allowed. Every collision with natives is to be reported to the commissioner.[51]

Clearly with this new approach both the commissioner of police and Drewry wanted exemplary punishment imposed on Aboriginal lawbreakers.

One particularly odious example reveals the vagaries of police authority and the ad hoc judicial system at this time. In late December 1891 Commissioner Phillips advised Inspector Lodge at Derby headquarters that the Aboriginal men caught and convicted in Roebourne Court of the murders of William Miller and Joseph Webb, at Mt Dockerell on 27 June 1890, were to be executed at the scene of the murder. This was in keeping with a policy of local hangings instigated in 1875 that was an attempt to show Aboriginal people what would happen to them if they committed serious crimes.[52] John Forrest had raised this in the Western Australian parliament as a solution to the problem of Aboriginal crime earlier in the year.[53]

The prisoners – Coorandine (aka Mr Dicky), Teuibi (aka Tomahawk) and Tehawada (aka Jumbo) – were transferred from Roebourne gaol by police escort back to Wyndham and then to Halls Creek, where they were to meet Sub Inspector Drewry who had been sworn in as sheriff's deputy.[54] Drewry led the police party and chose the route to the murder site to avoid the 'more populous nigger country' with the police party consisting of himself, troopers Brophy, Fenton, Court and Wisbey, and native assistants Charlie and Rocky. Also on the trip was the unnamed official 'executioner' from Perth.[55] Sergeant Houlihan remained behind to bring the coroner out when the deed was done.

Arriving at the location in the heart of Kija *country* on 18 February 1892, Drewry sent troopers Brophy and Fenton out to 'collect natives' to witness the event and, presumably, to learn a lesson. The officers came back with some 'sixty seven able bodied natives' and 'also a lot of children and the wives of two of the murderers'.[56] As the executioner had been 'ill with dysentery for over a week' Drewry took an active role in the execution. The men, who were chained with some 28 pounds (13 kilograms) of pig iron, 'made a show to bite and fight but that was soon put a stop to by securing them properly'. Drewry described the execution:

> As two feet was all the drop I could give them off the dray I took up the slack of the irons and strapped it and then tied together the dray was then backed up to the hole dug under the branch from which they hanged. Whilst the executioner placed the ropes around their necks I was up the tree allowing the drop and making it all fast. As soon as I came down I asked if Wisby and Executioner (who were in the dray holding the prisoners up) were right, they jumped out, I shot the bolt, the dray tilled and was drawn forward[,] at same time the three hanged at once. 20 minutes from time handcuffed their hands behind their backs to the time they dropped they hanged for an hour and ten minutes. The abo. Natives were arranged in a semi-circle fronting the scene. Brophy and the police natives being mounted behind them to prevent their running away. The hole for the drop served afterwards for a grave. I had a good interpreter there and whilst prisoners where hanging told the natives why they were hanged and that if they did the same thing they too would surely hang. I did not say too much[,] what I said was to the point and couched in language that could be well interpreted to them.[57]

Drewry considered the execution a 'most successful one' and it 'produced an impression amongst the blacks that witnessed it that will not be forgotten in a day'. Newspapers of the time reported on this significant event. The *Northern Territory Times and Gazette* quoted Brophy as saying that: 'the natives have taken it very much to heart, and have resolved to become more friendly and less troublesome to the whites. The natives' version of the hanging has been spread from camp to camp, and has reached tribes who were hundreds of miles from Mt. Dockerell at the time.'[58]

Other newspaper reports added far more detail than Drewry and Brophy had provided. One account suggested they waited for the crowd of witnesses, who had been attracted by 'provisions and presents', to be large enough.[59] The *Northern Territory Times and Gazette* wrote that the police party was joined by 'numerous white settlers from the fields and district generally' who were friends and associates of those murdered, who assisted in gathering together any Aboriginal people with the lure of flour and 'tucker'.[60] And rather than there being sixty or seventy witnesses there were up to 500, although this figure was unsubstantiated. It noted that the hanging provoked terror in those witnesses.[61]

Indicative of the ongoing administrative confusion in the Kimberley about who had authority over the police was the decision by Resident Magistrate E.P. Dowley not to pay for rations for the sixty-seven Aboriginal witnesses to the execution. Drewry had bought up hundreds of pounds of flour, beef, a little tea and tobacco, and had given them 'clay pipes and present of matches at leaving'. Drewry complained to the commissioner that 'the magistrate here has a great personal dislike to me because the police are now the police and not his general utility men, all civility has always been paid to him by members of the force here'.[62] The antagonism was exacerbated by Dowley making complaints against Drewry and his troopers for ill-treatment of Aboriginal prisoners and Drewry complaining about Dowley using his horse.

Dowley's antagonism towards Drewry extended beyond the issue of payment for rations; he prompted a formal inquest with a jury into the legality of the hanging itself. Correspondence between Drewry and J.B. Roe, the sheriff and inspector of prisons, revealed that Roe had not issued formal warrants of execution. After the inquest Drewry wrote to Roe: 'at the inquest there was a row about the document you sent me, which merely states the law was to be carried out on [these men]…anyway I hanged them first and faced the music afterward.'[63] The coroner advised an open verdict but the jury thought otherwise, finding that the men were lawfully hanged. It did recommend, though, that if anything of the sort occurs red here again it 'would be as well to send a copy of the warrant of execution'.[64] The fact that Drewry would effectively ignore legal process, face no recriminations and then be promoted speaks volumes about the tenor of the times.

As in the West Kimberley, Phillips' and Drewry's actions had the opposite effect to that intended. In late 1892 a Wyndham correspondent of *The West Australian* wrote: 'The white population of this district are unanimous in the opinion that warrants for the arrest of natives should be done away with, and that cartridges should be supplied instead.'[65] The historical record for this period is replete with instances of Aboriginal attacks. For their part Aboriginal groups became more strategic and daring, even entering the town of Wyndham and attacking police.[66] In December 1892 carriers of supplies to Fletcher Creek were held up and essential items, including 273 kilograms of flour and 22 kilograms of sugar, were taken.[67] In January 1893 a teamster on the way to the goldfields had his Winchester rifle and ammunition stolen along with his rations, and narrowly escaped being speared.[68] Six months later Fletcher Creek station was burnt down and the police horses were speared.[69]

Initially, Aboriginal people killed stock for food but later, in what must have been acts of resistance, stock were disturbed or killed without the meat being used. Patrick Durack reported in 1893 that the cattle on his station were being killed and 'they must be doing it for fun clearly as none of the meat is taken'.[70] By early 1893 *The West Australian* reported that Aboriginal aggression had 'assumed a most alarming aspect' and people on stations 'are held in the most imminent danger, and anxious men and women keep watch by day and night with Colts revolvers and Winchester rifles, dreading a premeditated attack'.[71] Other reports stated that Wyndham was being subjected to a 'reign of terror' by local Aboriginal people who were 'threatening Wyndham with absolute annihilation'.[72] Locals corroborated many of these reports. Mr Booty, manager of the Ord River Station, reported to police in October 1893 that the 'Osmand blacks' had got so daring that it is 'not safe to send the stockman on that part of the run unless the party is a large one'.[73] Station workers lived in a heightened state of fear during this period. In one instance a boundary rider by the name of Napier, working on one of the Durack properties, shot and killed his own 'boy' station worker at night thinking his camp was under attack.[74]

Events at Wyndham gaol, in which Aboriginal prisoners were kept, only worsened the situation. Sick prisoners were given food 'unfit for human consumption' then released to walk 260 kilometres back to their *country* on the Fletcher River. It was reported they were so weak they were 'dying on the road' with the resident magistrate, who was a doctor, failing to treat them.[75] Additionally, two autopsies of dead inmates had taken place just outside the building and:

> the mutilation of the [Aboriginal] bodies by cutting off
> a portion to keep as a curio was seen by the natives and
> the inhabitants. There is direct evidence of this, and the

matter is currently being discussed in town. If things like these continue the inhabitants may expect great trouble with the natives in the district.[76]

There was already chronic overcrowding: Wyndham gaol was 'too small for thirty prisoners' yet frequently held over sixty.[77] Under such conditions it is unsurprising that there were several mass escapes of prisoners, often using keys stolen from the gaolers: on 9 December 1893 thirty-three prisoners escaped;[78] two days later another twenty-five escaped;[79] on 15 May 1894 seventeen prisoners escaped;[80] on 8 August 1894 'all' of the prisoners, presumably over sixty in number, escaped.[81] Re-imprisonment was made more difficult when it was discovered that, when the prisoners were eventually caught back on *country* and chained up again, they used the very same keys the previous escapees had stolen and passed around to countrymen to release themselves.[82] Aboriginal men would attempt to rescue their countrymen from Wyndham gaol and, as in the case of Jimbony in early 1896, were charged with 'attempting to rescue prisoners'.[83] The overcrowding of the local gaols during this period was exacerbated by what Colonial Secretary S.H. Parker said was the new 'policy of the government, where practicable, to keep the natives in their own country'.[84] Even though Parker regarded the Kimberley groups as 'wild and uncontrollable' they were not sent to Rottnest Island Prison unless for serious crimes such as murder.[85]

During this time more attacks were made on trackers and native assistants and fencing was destroyed.[86] Aboriginal women were observed to be 'in the habit of going in and out of the station and acting as spies to the bush natives'.[87] One resident of the district later wrote of houses fortified against attack: 'stone building walls 2'6" thick, no windows, verandah, only doors. Built for safety when blacks bad.'[88] He also spoke of how 'the majority of stockmen carried revolvers on their belts, but when boundary riding and doing slow work where blacks were bad, always carried their .32 rifles under the saddle'.[89]

The Spearing of Trooper Collins

From late 1892 through 1893, Drewry's work focused on the West Kimberley, although the aggressive approach to the policing of Aboriginal people in the East stayed in place. As we have seen Commissioner Phillips, alarmed by the escalation of conflict in the West Kimberley, separated the East from the West, leaving Drewry to command the West and appointing Frederick Orme to command the East Kimberley.[90] A significant impetus for further aggressive police actions occurred when, in a police raid on an Aboriginal camp along the Behn River near Rosewood Station in July 1893, Trooper Joe Collins was speared. Twenty-three Mirriwong people were recorded as killed in this ambush although the actual figure may have been higher.[91] The publicised killing of this many Aboriginal people sparked an outcry in Perth in which the Catholic Bishop of Perth publicly denounced the killing of Aboriginal people in the Kimberley:

In the affair on Behn River, therefore, the troopers had the game in their own hands. And on their own showing, brutally did they use their advantage. It is not credible that the natives obstinately stood their ground and threw futile spears until the whole twenty-three had fallen.[92] It is perfectly clear that in this case no choice of surrender was given to them. Some were slain fighting and some as they ran and how many of these deliberately followed up and shot down as they made off? This was

no 'fight'. It was a massacre…The story of their accusers
we have heard but their defence we shall never hear.[93]

Again there seemed to have been little support for his protest.
Indeed after Collins' death a large-scale punitive expedition was
sent out to catch Collins' killers. Phillips had directed that the
'party not to be accompanied by settlers'.[94] It comprised Sergeant
Brophy, PCs Rhatigan, McCarthy and Lucanus, and native assistants Rocket, Willie, Mickey and Dickey.[95] Over nearly two
months from 1 October to 24 November 1893 they travelled 1091
kilometres and, as their reports indicate, shot thirty Aboriginal
people.[96] Sergeant Brophy's record of the event shows little
adherence to police rules and regulations and he often appeared
surprised that the Aboriginal groups would throw spears when
chased by police on horseback. On 14 October he reported killing
four men and catching 'a few old men and women who could not
run away'. He instructed his native assistant to tell them that if
they kept killing cattle or breaking insulators on the telegraph line
'all the natives would either be shot or put in gaol'.[97] The following
day the police party came across another group along the Ord
River and because he 'could plainly see that the natives intend to
fight it out', six more who he wrote were 'notorious cattle killers'
were killed.[98] On 19 October four more were killed. On 23
October the party discovered a group camped who he described
as 'the most treacherous in the district'. Each officer took thirty
rounds of ammunition and they waited until daybreak to raid the
camp. In the dawn raid the 'women and children ran away' but
all the men took to the rock hideaway with spears. Brophy wrote,
'It was not until 10 were shot dead that they made any attempt to
run away. In all my experience with natives I have never known
them to make such plucky and determined fight as those blacks.'[99]

Between 31 October and 3 November Brophy split the police party up on either side of the Osmand River with himself and PC Lucanus and one tracker taking one side and PCs Rhatigan and McCarthy and the other tracker taking the other. More Aboriginal people were shot dead by different police parties.[100] Brophy's report to Commissioner Phillips stated that:

> The natives we had to deal with are no doubt the worst in Western Australia and had the party not been a good strong one[,] all with a good knowledge of the bush and natives[,] the result of the expedition may not have ended up so successful[,] the punishment given to these natives will I am certain have a good effect as to arrest them in the high ranges is simply impossible for they show 'fight' on the approach of any white man.[101]

Drewry justified the deaths to Commissioner Phillips in similar terms to Brophy. As the Aboriginal people in Ord country 'were simply living on beef' it was necessary that the lesson they had been given 'be applied annually for the next three years'. Finally he wrote that 'I feel certain that no unnecessary shot was fired'.[102] From the aforementioned summary from July to November 1893 police recorded shooting and killing at least eighty-one Aboriginal people, but the unrecorded number, again, was likely much higher.

Perhaps the most profound and influential change following responsible government was in the parliamentary representation of the East Kimberley. The inaugural member of the Legislative Assembly for the East Kimberley was Francis Connor. He was an active partner in the Connor and Doherty Company and a representative of the pastoral industry. Debates about what many pastoralists saw as a crisis in the East Kimberley – and the threat of being driven from the land – took place in parliament just as they had a year earlier. In October 1893 Connor declared:

> No doubt there will be a lot of sentiment spoken about putting these blacks off their own country, and no doubt exception will be taken to the idea of dispersing them. But I hold that it is simply a question of whether the natives are to have this country or the whites?[103]

Connor's speech, seconded by Alexander Forrest, was in reaction to the spearing of police officer Joe Collins. Both men put forward a motion for the establishment of a 'native police force' and hence more aggressive policing. Forrest's concerns were the 'hill tribes' who killed stock and threatened West Kimberley settlements. He asked whether 'the life of one European is not worth a thousand natives, as far as settlement of this country is concerned'.[104] The motion was withdrawn after pressure from Premier John Forrest, who said he did not wish to sanction the 'indiscriminate slaughter of blackfellows'.[105] Despite these claims police actions in the East Kimberley would tell a different story and involve extensive killings. In late September 1894, on the King River just out of Wyndham, Aboriginal people raided and took 'possession of' a colonist's hut. When police were alerted Sergeant Wheatley, PC Cadden and two native assistants tracked the group of what they described as 'fifty blacks', likely Mirriwong people, and they 'dispersed the mob' though ominously said the people of the area were 'dangerous and getting bolder'.[106]

Claims and Counterclaims on the New Pastoral Frontiers

Policing the telegraph line continued in the fashion ordered by Drewry. In early 1895 police reported that 'Native depredation from the telegraph line seem to have been stopped'.[107] On 2 April 1895 it was decided that Denham River police camp be closed and in December the Fletcher Creek camp was closed as well. The closing dates of these camps are significant. They show that police believed the telegraph line needed less protection but they also signify a fundamental shift in the focus of East Kimberley policing, from the telegraph line to the pastoral stations. By 1898 the police were no longer patrolling the telegraph line and linesmen were employed to inspect and maintain it.

It is likely that increased policing of the East Kimberley accompanied the growing prosperity of the beef industry for which the condition of stock was crucial. Bolton notes that the two leading companies, Forrest, Emanuel and Company and Connor, Doherty and Durack, stipulated a minimum weight of 700 pounds (318 kilograms) for each animal, allowing for a loss of 100 pounds (45 kilograms) on the journey to Fremantle. Clearly Aboriginal people distressing the stock would cause loss of condition, as well as time spent rounding up dispersed stock – both would result in financial losses.[108]

By 1895 the complaints by colonists would become increasingly personal and desperate. In May 1895 the Ord River pastoralist William H. Osmand, increasingly anxious about his stock, wrote to Francis Connor, proclaiming: 'The police appear to be a useless lot up there.'[109] Connor in turn forwarded this letter to Attorney General Septimus Burt, suggesting the necessity for 'some stringent measures to be taken'.[110]

Figure 10.2. 'Connor and Durack's Stores Loaded on Wagons', Wyndham, 1894. Courtesy State Library of Western Australia, 001282D. Photographer unknown.

In response to a demand from Nathaniel Buchanan, the new manager of Osmand's station, Commissioner Phillips instructed the new Sub Inspector Orme, who was stationed in Wyndham, to establish the extent of stock depredations in the Argyle area and surrounds. Orme did not have the same relationship with Commissioner Phillips that Drewry had. He also was, initially at least, less aggressive in his attitude to Aboriginal people and his support for East Kimberley pastoralists was weaker. This would affect how police would respond. On 19 February 1895 Buchanan had written that 'Blacks have been very troublesome and were killing in all directions...they seem to be getting more daring every day'. Buchanan demanded police protection, pointing out that the nearest police were either 210 miles (338 kilometres) north in Wyndham or 130 miles south in Halls Creek, and claiming that he had lost 7000 cattle to depredations since the station was first stocked.[111]

Orme, in reply, expressed incredulity at Buchanan's inflated allegations and claimed that Buchanan was exaggerating losses because he had little idea of how many cattle were on the run. He then expressed concern that the 'strain of Mr Buchanan's letter means the extermination of the Aboriginals, which I am not in favour of, as I am sure they can be made quiet if the station owners will only work with the police'.[112] A month later Orme wrote to Phillips again, this time emphasising more reasons for Buchanan's accusations. He stated 'with confidence' that the claims made by Buchanan were false, indeed the 'natives on Ord River Station were not troublesome' and that mismanagement and incompetence of the new owner, Mr Osmand, were to blame. Of his stockmen, Orme wrote, 'it is a fact that not one of them yet know on what part of the run the majority of cattle are on' and 'cannot go out without being lost and it is always necessary to send a blackboy with them'. Besides he had only four men to look after 20,000 cattle over 150 square miles (338 square kilometres). And, he added, they were scared of the 'Ord River natives'. Orme concluded, 'I think that Buchanan wrote the letter in order to save himself, as they have no idea how the mustering will turn out.'[113] Mary Durack substantiates much of what Orme wrote. She stated that after Osmand had bought out his partner, J.A. Panton, in 1894, he had directed 'a succession of discouraged managers' from Melbourne via 'enigmatic telegrams and autocratic letters'. Osmand, she believed, was using the business as an investment and had planned to sell when he had built up enough stock. He 'clearly had no interest in improving the property' or responding to requests from workers for improved amenities.[114]

Osmand continued his campaign for help in more letters to the government.

The losses in cattle speared by the blacks is about £28,000 and now after eleven years of this sort of thing a daily brutal killing of cows calving and heavy in calf still goes on. I think the government must admit that this is not the sort of treatment English settlers expect (after having risked their capital) from the government of a British Colony...The premier was interviewed some time about November last by Mssrs Durack[,] who was then in Perth, and Mr. Frank Connor[,] MLA Parliamentary Representative for East Kimberley[,] representing complaints then made by Kimberley settlers of the wholesale cattle slaughtering that was going on at that time. Promises were made that the police should put a stop to it and there it ended. Things are now worse than ever.[115]

It appears that Osmand's letters had an effect, as a telegram from the office of the premier advising him that police would 'visit the stations regularly' was sent to Osmand in Victoria.[116] Demands for more protection also came from pastoral stations further north, particularly those owned by the Durack family. However, Orme also disputed these on similar grounds. He reported that Mantinea Station was leased by Pat Durack, who at the time was actually managing Lissadell Station over 160 kilometres away, and the cattle had no overseer. 'No wonder they are disturbed', he said, 'yet the police have to bear the abuse and the complaints which are made. They will not look after their own cattle, and yet expect the police to stop the cattle killing.' At Lissadell, when the manager complained of stock losses, Orme forthrightly stated to Phillips that 'Lissadell report natives very troublesome but I am not prepared to believe this. This station is continually making reports of cattle killing, but they are too frightened to go out and see for themselves.'[117] Sergeant Wheatley, who visited Lissadell Station in May 1895, substantiated this after being informed by a stockman that 'no one had been around the run or amongst the cattle for over eight months and they know of no cattle being killed'.[118] Orme reported that all the stations in the East Kimberley would 'kill beasts at regular intervals for the natives, all Durack stations being exceptions'. Sergeant Wheatley had, however, observed Durack killing stock for the 'bush blacks' on 9 May 1895.[119] Orme went on to state: 'All stations, bar Duracks, wish me to bring in the natives in to the homestead when, with the help of the police, they will civilise them.'[120] Disputed and exaggerated claims abounded. Some of the Duracks expected police to be their personal boundary patrol. Wheatley told Durack at Ivanhoe Station that 'he must not expect police to be stockmen for him'.[121]

George Marsden, the travelling inspector of the Aborigines Protection Board, documented a valuable insight into the nature of the deteriorating relationship between pastoralists and Aboriginal people in the East Kimberley.[122] In 1896 he reported of Michael and Ambrose Durack that:

> Mr Durack was the first settler in the Kimberley and he says at first he was never troubled by the natives at all as they seemed to fear the 'white man', but as soon as the police came to Kimberley and blacks got into trouble and were arrested and then escaped or returned after their time[,] then the trouble with the cattle began. Mr Durack spoke very warmly as to the utter ruin and eventual disaster which will arise from the blacks escap- ing[,] apparently whenever they like[,] from Wyndham

gaol. As most of these natives who have escaped belong to the Denham, Lizerdell [sic] and Argyle countries, all of which join one another, they have returned with utter contempt for the 'white man', except that when he is around and awake. They prowl around at night now…a thing which in former years has never happened, and if they find the camp asleep they throw spears into it. This shows pretty plainly that they are becoming bolder and this can only arise from the fact that they know the white men at Wyndham cannot hold them… Mr Durack spoke rather significantly as to his present treatment of bush natives. He says: – 'In former years I used to treat them kindly, I killed bullocks and fed them: they returned my kindness by driving my bullocks over the ranges, and scattering them on the runs and I have turned "dog" on them now.'[123]

The animosity between police and pastoralists was based on the belief that the other party had created the situation. Pastoralists, police claimed, were undermanned, incompetent, untruthful and too afraid to patrol their runs because Aboriginal resistance was so fierce. Police, pastoralists claimed, were incompetent, too far away, or too slow to arrest any 'ringleaders', indeed were to blame for the entire state of affairs.[124] Mary Durack describes her family's hostility to the police in her books, quoting M.P. Durack who claimed: 'Ye're all useless anyway without the blacks to help you with the dirty work.'[125] When police arrested some cattle killers within their leases, the Duracks claimed they were not doing enough and were only arresting 'old men, women and children'.[126] Osmand asserted that an unnamed Durack had told him that escapes from Wyndham gaol were 'understood and arranged' by the police so they could re-arrest the same offenders. Thefts of cattle were not reported, he claimed, as they only resulted in the Aboriginal people being imprisoned and returned to their *country* more able to avoid police. They were critical of Commissioner Phillips and suggested that 'a more active and smarter man of more modern ideas is required for the position'.[127]

Figure 10.3. 'Aboriginal Prisoners in Chains, Posed with a Policeman and Aboriginal Trackers', East Kimberley, circa 1890. Courtesy State Library of Western Australia, 003168D. Photographer unknown.

Pastoralists wanted more decisive and effective police action. Mostly they wanted Aboriginal people off the land and the police to do the job. They saw this as their right as they paid their taxes to the government. By exaggerating stock losses and creating a sense of urgency they hoped to bring more police to the district. Furthermore, blaming Aboriginal people for all losses would defuse issues relating to mismanagement. By 1896 official stock losses attributed to Aboriginal people were being recorded and reveal they were a fraction of what was being claimed.[128] Other accounts by an industry newspaper suggested that Connor, Doherty and Durack Limited had a 'growing surplus of cattle' that they could not sell if new markets were not opened up.[129]

One thing they did not mention was 'cattle duffing' or stealing by whites. In his memoirs one stockman, Doug Moore, asserted that 'in fact no less than 6 stations were made around the Ord River by shaking [stealing] Ord River cattle'. This included Texas Downs Station, stocked by 'a confirmed cattle thief', Jack Kelly.[130] Moore stated that cattle duffing by white men was 'thought nothing of in those days'. Stockmen were employed to take stock off another's land and were 'receiving wages with one hand and robbing with the other'.[131] This easygoing attitude was in stark contrast to the outrage expressed when Aboriginal people took cattle.

'A War of Extermination'

Police responded to the pastoralists' allegations by sending out a party from Wyndham on 22 April 1895.[132] Sergeant Thomas Wheatley, PC Mick Rhatigan and Native Assistant Dicky visited Hart Bros' Carlton Station, where 'Mr Hart kindly lent me his native boy Pompy and a horse saddle', and Ivanhoe Stud Station, where they registered stock numbers but reported no problems. On 4 May they arrived at Argyle Downs Station, where Pat Durack reported 'no natives had killed cattle of late'. On 5 May, however, they went to Prospect Creek where, Sergeant Wheatley stated, they 'saw cattle running and natives chasing them'. PC Rhatigan fired on them, 'killing four men'.[133] Orme reported to Phillips that the shooting 'gave some natives whom they found in the act a lesson that they will remember'.[134]

Here police had begun systematically eradicating Aboriginal people from pastoral land and it is quite evident the government of Western Australia was aware of what was occurring. Octavius Burt, the undersecretary to Premier John Forrest and brother of Septimus Burt, was sympathetic to the rights of Aboriginal people and wrote to Forrest plaintively stating:

> There can be no doubt that from these frequent reports that a war of extermination is being waged on these unfortunate blacks in the Kimberley district and the owners and managers are tacitly if not deliberately encouraging such a state of things by not making any attempt to protect their herds, which are left to these untutored savages to attack as they please, and then the police are called in to kill and slay. How often do we read that the police 'fell in' or 'came up' with a party of natives and then there follows a record of the slain or the statement that 'they were taught a severe lesson' – and in many cases there is nothing whatever to show that it was the guilty that suffered. Surely this is a thing that should not be.[135]

There is no indication that either John Forrest or the commissioner of police took any action on this letter.[136] It is clear that Forrest knew about these claims as Octavius Burt, who regarded police reports as 'very instructive', would inform him of events.[137] That said it is clear that the police actions, as far as the pastoralists were concerned, were having the desired effect. During this time 'record numbers' of cattle were being shipped from Wyndham port. In early September 1895, nearing the end of the dry season, some 308 cattle in 'the largest shipment yet made' were sent from Wyndham port via the SS *Tagliaferro*. At the same time there seemed to be significant trouble between pastoralists and Aboriginal people on *country*.[138]

Despite visits from police Osmand continued to send telegrams to Connor and Forrest demanding action against cattle killing.[139] With police reports disputing most of these claims Phillips wrote to Octavius Burt endorsing the police: 'It is very certain that Mr Osmond is wilfully misinformed by his representatives in the East Kimberley. Sergeant Brophy at Halls Creek reports that the natives are very quiet and have expressed a desire to be on friendly terms with the whites.'[140] However, on other stations such as Newry, allegations of cattle killing continued. Denis Doherty sent a letter from Fremantle to Phillips:

> Blacks are worse now than ever they were known to be. Michael (MP) [Durack] can tell you what he saw at Newry[:] reports this morning a wholesale slaughter of imported stock and horses at stud station[. W]e see by paper reports to Commissioner are at variance[,] let commissioner know this. Mr MP Durack will be here tomorrow[,] he anxious to have a chat with you. Kindly let me know when it would be convenient for you to see him. I have taken the duty of writing to you as F. Connor is in the Eastern Colonies.[141]

Personal visits by M.P. Durack and Osmand, Connor and Doherty's correspondence clearly put pressure on Phillips who wired Orme disputing his claims and ordered, without any ambiguity, that Sergeant Wheatley and his party were 'to remain on stations and disperse all natives'.[142]

Curiously, when *The West Australian* interviewed Doherty just months later, he claimed that the natives were 'not troublesome' and that 'now and then cattle were speared by the natives'. He thought this was only a natural thing for hungry men to do and he was personally 'favourable to the squatters making allowance of as many head to the natives each year'.[143] Certainly, in the context of a rapidly growing and lucrative cattle trade (cattle numbers shipped to Perth increased from some 4000 in 1895 to over 6000 in 1896), it appears, publicly at least, that some pastoralists wanted events in the Kimberley to be kept as low-key as possible.

The 'Dispersal' in Action

Commissioner Phillips' attitude to the East Kimberley troubles was profoundly influenced by the earlier West Kimberley campaign against Jandamarra. Fear of more outbreaks of 'outlaw behaviour' was the impetus to carry out further dispersals. Certainly none of the past uncertainty about police practices was evident. The telegraph line was by now fully functional and was used to full effect by authorities in Perth to issue immediate instructions to East Kimberley police, who would now operate in the manner of a de facto native police force.

The occurrence book for Wyndham Station states that in November 1895 a large police party had been ordered to undertake a bush patrol and for several days PC Rhatigan had been busy shoeing a large number of horses for the long trip.[144] The police party consisted of Rhatigan, Sergeant Wheatley, four native assistants (Mickey, Willy, Joe and Bubby) and thirteen horses.[145] Sergeant Wheatley's private notebook, curiously the only surviving record of this event, describes how the police party left Wyndham on 6 November, arrived at Ivanhoe Stud Station on 9 November and, after tracking until 11 November, found a group deemed responsible for cattle killing. Sergeant Wheatley described the scene:

> Left camp at 6.30am and followed the tracks and came upon the natives in a large lagoon, the assistants told them to come out of the water and reeds, two of them came which we arrested[. T]he rest of them tried to escape but in doing so we fired on them killing twenty men[,] the women and children making good their escape. The two we arrested shewed [sic] us where they killed the cattle and told us they had killed plenty[;] the following are the names of the two we arrested[:] Ginnare, Cunbiliger.[146]

This shooting was one of the single largest killings recorded by police in the Kimberley district. For the next two weeks the police party travelled along the Ord River and around Ivanhoe Stud Station looking for Aboriginal people. On 22 November the police found an Aboriginal camp where there were twenty-five women and thirty children, and twelve men whom they arrested.[147] The party, with their prisoners chained by the neck, then went to Lissadell where they picked up rations and supplies from the homestead and Michael Durack reported that they had seen 'the remains of 18 head of cattle killed by natives'. They proceeded to Rosewood Station where Tom Kilfoyle said that 'the natives had not interfered with his cattle since last wet season', and then to Connor and Doherty's Newry station, where the manager said 'the natives had killed cattle two months ago on the Keep River'. They then returned to Ivanhoe Stud Station, where Wheatley observed that 'natives had not interfered with the stock since we dispersed them on our way up'. Wheatley and party stopped for a day on 16 December, as three of the prisoners were too exhausted to walk any further.[148]

The patrol returned to Wyndham over six weeks later with fourteen prisoners 'on the chain' and two witnesses.[149] Since the prisoners' arrest they had walked, chained together and chained to trees at night, over 260 miles (400 kilometres).[150] In Wyndham court, on 23 December, before F. Pearse and J.W. Durack JP, thirteen prisoners were charged with 'being in the unlawful possession of beef' and sentenced to two years with hard labour and fifteen lashes of the cat-o'-nine-tails. One Aboriginal boy was remanded for eight days, pending the arrival of Michael Durack to charge him.[151]

After this police activity a telegram from a more compliant Orme to the commissioner of police revealed a little more than the usual police reports, indicating the patrol shot the entire group of Aboriginal people they came across:

> Returned today[,] met police party about eighty miles from here[,] they have had most successful trip[. T]ribe recently killing at Durack Bros Ivanhoe Stud Station thoroughly dispersed *not one escaping*. Durack Bros reports no killing on Argyle Downs station[.] Sergt Wheatley met Halls Creek police party at Lissadell station where both parties dispersed several tribes.[152]

By 7 February 1896 Sub Inspector Orme declared to the commissioner: 'settlers throughout district express great pleasure at actions of police latterly and also express opinion that there is little doubt but that cattle killing will cease for a while'.[153]

Consolidation of Forces and the Opening of Argyle Police Camp

Under Commissioner Phillips' instructions a new camp at Argyle Downs was established as a more cost-effective way to police the new pastoral districts. Rather than police travelling from Wyndham or Halls Creek, which was often extremely difficult in the wet season, the new station would be more central to the areas requiring police attention. The Argyle camp was actually situated at Wild Dog Springs (hence the general name), a spot situated on the mail route from Wyndham down to the goldfields and Halls Creek.[154] The main role of the new camp was to patrol Lissadell, Argyle, Ivanhoe Stud, Carlton, Mantinea and Ord River stations.[155]

Officially established on 23 April 1896 'Wild Dog' originally consisted of three seasoned bush constables, four native assistants and sixteen horses, under the command of Fred Orme.[156] Complementing this force were the constables from Fletcher Creek and Denham River camps, who had been withdrawn in December 1895.[157] Police observed very large Aboriginal groups on *country*. On one occasion PC Freeman observed fifty males gathering in one place that he surmised was a meeting place for 'tribal groups' from the north of South Australia and a group from the Ord River.[158] In another case shortly after a police raid near Spring Creek, PC Rhatigan gathered together ninety-six women telling them 'they should not tuch [sic] cattle and the white men would not interfere with them'.[159]

The available records from this camp are testimony to the actions of bush police engaged in a process of 'pacification' through ambush, arrest and shootings. Inspector Orme and Commissioner Phillips endorsed what they called an informal 'system' of patrols to pacify and control the Aboriginal populations.[160] The details of the 'system' shall be revealed later. From 22 September 1896 until January 1897 PCs Rhatigan and Freeman and four native assistants (Pluto, Corriway, Paddy and Wallily) patrolled Rosewood, Ord River and Lissadell runs on several different patrols. Their diaries describe deaths under the guise of 'skirmishes' and 'resisting arrest' or 'escaping'.[161] Legal use of firearms was unchecked, there were never attempts to arrest 'ringleaders', and many people were shot only for 'being in possession of beef', with the evidence often found after people had been killed. Others were killed simply because they were there. On every patrol a fight ensued with an unspecified number of Aboriginal people shot − often referred to in the record as 'several'.[162] Police did, however, record expending several hundred rounds of ammunition in what would have been recurrent shooting.[163]

In another case Orme reported to Phillips of one of PC Rhatigan's late January 1897 patrols when he arrested a total of seven people but expended sixty rounds of ammunition in doing so.[164] Rhatigan covered in this patrol the Lissadell, Argyle and Ord River runs and noted his surprise 'as I never travelled over such a lot of country and saw the natives so scarce. All the cattle I saw were very quite [sic].'[165] It is curious and revealing that PC Rhatigan resigned very shortly after these episodes on 19 March 1897 and became a telegraph linesman operating out of Turkey Creek.[166]

By January 1898 police parties patrolled the Osmond River, with PC Freeman recording that there was 'only a comparatively small group of blacks now living in the vicinity of Osmond'.[167] With pastoralist consent and indeed assistance, police had actively cleared pastoral runs of Aboriginal people by killing. The number of Aboriginal people shot, likely being in the hundreds, is not possible to calculate from the written record, but Mary Durack later reflected on policing at Argyle writing: 'The methods used would seem to have been effective, as the estimated number of cattle speared fell abruptly in the following year, to considerably less than half.'[168] Official records of stock losses show the reduction was even more marked at some 70%.[169]

As Cathie Clement has noted, many pastoral stations in the East Kimberley owed their survival largely to the actions of police.[170] These actions involved some of the most widespread 'dispersals' of Aboriginal people in Western Australian history with little public comment from police authorities. The 1897 Police Annual Report, tabled in parliament, made reference to the continued hostility towards pastoralists by 'West Kimberley Natives' and Jandamarra, but made no mention of the East Kimberley other than reporting that 'in other districts the natives have been fairly quiet'.[171] In the 1898 Report, however, it states that the East Kimberley 'police have been fully occupied in looking after the natives',[172] and by 1899, as reported by Acting Commissioner William Chipper Lawrence, the man who had pursued Jandamarra: 'The natives generally have been kept well under control during the year.'[173] Paying less attention to the East Kimberley in police reports during the 1890s was a strategy by the Western Australian government to minimise any controversy both locally and overseas about continuing violence in the newly colonised parts of the colony.

In the 1890s police, under instruction from the highest levels of the government, contained and controlled Aboriginal people not only by arrests and prosecutions but also by extensive killings so that the Kimberley pastoral industry could develop free from Aboriginal interference. This brings us to the question: were police engaged in a war with Aboriginal people in the 1890s? Many colonists and government officials including the then premier, John Forrest, did indeed describe conflict in the Kimberley as war. As we saw, policing in the Kimberley did not begin as a form of warfare but became so later, when Aboriginal people undertook a more concerted resistance against the pastoral industry, responding in kind to punitive actions against them. However, this was a local, guerilla, undefined and largely unspoken kind of war, described largely by the use of euphemisms like 'depredations' to describe cattle killing and 'dispersal' to explain organised military-style attacks on Aboriginal groups. Indeed 'dispersals' were ordered by telegrams from the commissioner of police in Perth.[174]

To finalise this chapter we must revisit the 'system' of policing referred to earlier because the reasons for its establishment and the subsequent government endorsement of it would set the tone for policing up to the time of the Roth Report in 1905. In late 1897 disagreements between the Wyndham resident magistrate, the police and the government around the legality and manner of Aboriginal arrests had risen again. Resident Magistrate in Wyndham Fred Pearse raised his concerns in a letter to the government undersecretary seeking advice on what he called 'the much vexed native question'.[175] Pearse suggested that insufficient effort had been made in establishing 'friendly relations' with the local Aboriginal people. He had serious reservations regarding due legal process and the mass arrest and gaoling of Aboriginal people with inadequate or no evidence.[176] In addition Pearse stated there was no interpreter available at the trials to explain to prisoners what was occurring and, as such, they would invariably plead guilty and be convicted on their own evidence. Legally, Pearse stated, pastoralists were required to give evidence of cattle killing before a magistrate, and police were only to arrest Aboriginal people lawfully, that is with a warrant or if they were caught 'red handed'. In the ensuing correspondence it is clear Pearse's comments are seen as impudent, what Phillips labelled 'an uncalled for and injudicious interference with the police'.[177]

The letter started a chain of correspondence from now ex–East Kimberley Inspector Orme to Commissioner Phillips to Premier John Forrest. Orme stated that he himself had designed the police 'system' involving tracking, mass arrests and gaoling and it worked well, though undoubtedly the 'system' was more a continuation of what Sub Inspector Drewry had started many years before. Orme stated that having pastoralists lay testimony in front of a magistrate was more expense than it was worth, as well as intensely annoying to them by taking up their time. Orme suggested it was hopelessly impractical for the effort involved and that the 'system' they had started should be followed. Orme also instructed police never to arrest Aboriginal women.[178] Phillips then wrote to Pearse to say there was to be no change to policing and that they were to continue with the 'system' designed by Orme. In early 1898 a telegram from the undersecretary puts forward John Forrest's views, stating 'the system hitherto has worked well without pressing any undo severity upon the natives'.[179]

Forrest continued to support and defend the actions of police. This was despite the fact that during the 'killing times' of the 1890s police killed more Aboriginal people in the Kimberley than in the previous sixty years in the whole of Western Australia.[180] Displaying astonishing hypocrisy, during the same period his government appealed to Britain to repeal section 70 of *The Constitution Act 1889* guaranteeing funds for the welfare of Aboriginal people, claiming that it 'incurs the undeserved opinion of being incapable of dealing in a just and humane manner with the Aboriginal natives of Western Australia'.[181]

The matter of 'dispersals' or extensive killing was not even raised by Pearse, possibly because he was not aware they were occurring. In the same correspondence Orme stated that 'extreme measures' were only ever resorted to when 'natives were caught in the act of killing' and 'on their endeavouring to escape'.[182] The preceding evidence of extensive killing does not support Orme's assertion. Expediency would prevail: there would be no new policing processes with rules of evidence and due process. This would be the same policing system that Walter Roth uncovered some seven years later.

Chapter 11

'NECESSITY REQUIRES NO PRECEDENTS'
New Methods of Control 1897–1905

We have seen how, before Western Australia joined the Australian Commonwealth in 1901, John Forrest claimed his government was looking after the welfare and interests of Aboriginal people. Shortly after Federation and as Australian Minister for Defence, Forrest defended his home state's reputation from increasing criticism of mistreatment of Aboriginal people by declaring that they were 'really well treated' state-wide.[1] But were they? This chapter looks at the changes to policing in the Kimberley up to and after Western Australia joined the Australian Commonwealth to the time of the Roth Report in 1905. It also examines the changing nature of Western Australian and Aboriginal society and the divide between political rhetoric like Forrest's and the reality of the new policies towards Aboriginal people.

Beginning in February 1897, in attempts to avert public criticism of the quality of police recruits, Commissioner Phillips established the first official training school for applicants to the police force, incorporating drill instruction and police duties.[2] Now, rather than the ad hoc informal training police received, the new recruits were required to undergo training under a drill instructor that would last up to six months. Then, in 1898, new regulations were introduced that sought to remedy the laxness of police procedures. Strict rules on reporting were introduced

which officers were expected to follow. Police were given registra-
tion numbers (usually kept on a badge on their caps) to assist in
identification but these numbers seldom appear in police records.[3]
Critically the new rules toughened the practices around the use of
native assistants, the key rule being: 'when engaged in pursuing
offending aborigines, members of the force must not under any
circumstances, send out native assistants alone to capture or disperse them while the police remain in camp'.[4]

Yet there are reports that police in the East Kimberley stayed
at their station and sent their native assistants out armed for 'nigger
hunting' to 'wipe out many an inoffensive black' in direct contra-
vention of their 1898 regulations.[5] This was the case after Forrest
River 'outlaw' Nalmurchie killed the 'Chinese gardener' Ah Sing
on the King River near Wyndham on 1 November 1898. In several different patrols police sent their native assistants out armed
and alone and they were responsible for a large number of deaths.
These police were heavily criticised by Commissioner Phillips
and Inspector Brophy for poor and misleading reporting.[6] It is
clear that this mode of policing – sending out armed native assistants who would engage in unrecorded killings – replaced many
'official' police shootings.[7] Despite regulations the native assistants
remained, as they did in the 1880s and 1890s, in a situation where
no laws applied or could be applied to them. They were used to
devastating effect as they carried out their police officers' bidding,
effectively absolving the officers of any responsibility.

After the mid-1890s 'dispersals', many of the more prominent
police who were involved left the police force or were removed
from the district. Senior Constable August Lucanus transferred
to Perth.[8] Inspector William Lawrence was promoted to superintendent and returned to Perth as did Sub Inspector Ord.[9] The
influential Sub Inspector Drewry, with his work in setting up

new police practices done, left for medical treatment and became an inspector at Cue and Roebourne.[10] In late 1897 PC Pilmer, regarding his work as complete and now claiming that the district was 'reasonably safe from the ravages of wandering law breakers', was transferred south to Onslow.[11] In 1900 Pilmer and Michael Harvey Brophy along with Inspector Ord went to South Africa where they were part of the Western Australian Bushmen's Contingent fighting in the Boer War.[12] On Brophy's return in 1901 he was transferred to Kalgoorlie, returning to the East Kimberley in 1905. Sergeant Richard Pilmer returned to police service at the southwest town of Collie where it is clear he had trouble adapting to a more sedate policing environment. From 1901 to 1904 he was so unpopular that he was subjected to sustained attack by *The Sunday Times* newspaper:

> Pilmer the cruel flagellator of natives; Pilmer, the horse racing cheat, Pilmer the assaulter of a helpless man; Pilmer the one time pimp for the Nor'-West squatters – and we are expected to look up to him?[13]

In late 1893 PC William Armitage left the police force and opened a hotel in Bunbury. PC Rhatigan, as we have seen, after the dispersal period resigned in early 1897. PC Spong, whose poor reporting was tolerated in the hunt for Jandamarra, was sacked in 1901 for his 'very unsatisfactory' reporting.[14] In early 1898 Sub Inspector Orme also returned to Perth having done his three years' duty and was later replaced by Sub Inspector James Duncan, followed by Sub Inspector McCarthy.[15] Other experienced police, such as PC Ritchie (who by 1898 had resigned and been readmitted as a police officer four times) and PC Bertram Forbes, remained.[16] New recruits posted to the Kimberley to patrol pastoral stations included PCs William Caldow, J.H. Hill, M. O'Brien, T.P. Napier and James Campbell Thomson. This last officer along with PC Ritchie displayed considerable bravery and they were not afraid to upset the status quo of the Kimberley, as we will see, putting themselves at significant risk in doing so.

In 1898, after noted explorer Frank Hann explored the uncolonised North Kimberley over the Leopold Ranges, home of the Worla and Ngarinyin people, cattle were introduced and former stockmen turned police constables John Wilson and Bertram Forbes manned the newly established Isdell Police Station with native assistants Onearra, Bobby, Toby and Charlie.[17] Wilson had extensive experience of the Kimberley having undertaken multitudes of bush patrols between 1898 and 1905, riding out from stations all over the Kimberley. Senior police regarded him (much like PC Inglis who worked around the same time in different locations) as very efficient although he was also very ruthless. PCs Wilson and Inglis were also to be key witnesses in the Roth Report investigations.

Some police stations, such as at Lennard River, closed in 1901 but new stations were established on the Dampier Peninsula at Beagle Bay (1898), home of Bardi, Jawi and Nyul Nyul people, and further south at La Grange Bay (1901), home of the Karajarri, staffed by PCs John Zum Felde and Bertram Henry Fletcher. These changes reflected changing needs and reveal what would become a growing cause of public concern and thus police attention: the coastal pearling areas of the West Kimberley on the Dampier Peninsula. The population of Aboriginal people here, typically living in smaller groups than in inland areas, was large and estimated at 1500 before European contact.[18] Before these issues are explored, however, it is necessary to look in detail at the significant changes in government policy relating to Aboriginal people in Western Australia as Federation approached.

In April 1898, after the Aborigines Protection Board was dissolved and replaced by a new Aborigines Department under the *Aborigines Act 1897*, a new position was established wherein the chief protector of Aborigines headed the department under the watch of Premier and Treasurer John Forrest. In May 1898 Henry Prinsep, who was a friend of Forrest and a previous undersecretary for mines but who had no experience in Aboriginal affairs, was appointed. Forrest argued the new arrangements ushered in a new approach to Aboriginal policy. However, the reality was that Prinsep was appointed to do Forrest's bidding. As Malcolm Allbrook in his biography of Prinsep shows, Forrest 'wanted the job done as he determined'.[19] During these years Forrest was determined to avoid the debates and criticism that had occurred around the Aborigines Protection Board. Forrest positioned the Aborigines Department so it would not become a social and political embarrassment for the government. Additionally he could contain threats to the government's reputation and authority from public outbursts by people like Reverend John Gribble, whose allegations about Aboriginal matters in the late 1880s had shocked many people.[20]

On 1 May 1898 John Forrest issued a government circular published in the police and government gazettes which declared that the 'care and protection' of Aboriginal people was now 'devolved upon the government'.[21] As a consequence the respon-sibility for Aboriginal welfare fell onto regional resident medical officers, resident magistrates and police. These positions were ex-officio and imposed on them as an extension of their existing jobs. In conjunction with the chief protector, Forrest asserted that resident magistrates and police would now 'assist in every way in promoting the welfare of the natives' and providing relief to elderly Aboriginal people. Needless to say this was the subject of much annoyance to the already overstretched public servants.

In the West Kimberley ration or relief stations were established at available locations such as pastoral stations, police stations and private residences. These were at Derby, Broome, Fitzroy telegraph station, Oobagooma, Sunday Island and La Grange Bay. In the East Kimberley relief stations were situated at Wyndham, Halls Creek, Flora Valley, Argyle and Turkey Creek, and public officers compiled a list of Aboriginal people who received relief there.[22] The relief system profoundly affected Aboriginal society. For example, at Fitzroy telegraph station, while there were only around twenty-five Aboriginal people receiving relief there were up to 200 'bush blacks' camping around the station, many of whom shared the available rations.[23] However, the system also benefited local pastoralists as it meant either that they did not have to feed the local Elders on their *country* or that they would be reimbursed if they did. That said, many pastoralists on older stations already looked after older and 'infirm' Aboriginal people on *country*.[24] For example, M.P. Durack killed 'twenty bullocks' in 1898, as described in a Northern Territory newspaper, to 'feed the niggers'.[25]

Overall, government policy demanded that Aboriginal people should cost the government as little as possible.[26] The position of travelling inspector – which included the detailed reporting by inspectors such as George Marsden – was abolished. Mission subsidies were reduced and the distribution and amount of rations consisting of 2 pounds (907 grams) of damper and 1 pound (450 grams) of meat daily for adults (and half that amount for children) were halved.[27] Forrest's attitude near the turn of the century was that too much money had been spent on Aboriginal people and since he still believed they were dying out, they had no place in the future state. He thought they should obtain work on farms or pastoral stations where the owner of the station would be responsible for feeding them and, if they didn't, Aboriginal people should sustain themselves in their 'traditional way'. What Aboriginal people were to do where colonisation had destroyed traditional food resources or where there were no farms or pastoral stations to work on or supply food was not explained. And by the late 1890s food shortages were a serious problem. Aboriginal people coming into Wyndham in late 1898 told police that 'they do not want to kill cattle if they can get work and food'.[28] Moreover in the burgeoning coastal pearl diving industry, which had been one of the areas where Aboriginal people had once found work, Aboriginal divers had all but disappeared by 1900. Japanese, Malays and Filipinos (known colloquially as 'Manilamen') had taken over, utilising the new deep-water diving equipment that enabled them to breathe underwater.

But this was just one of many changes. By the end of the nineteenth century significant demographic changes had irrevocably altered Aboriginal society and culture in the Kimberley. By the early 1900s, of the estimated 5000 Aboriginal people who remained in the Kimberley, 1500 worked on pastoral stations.[29] Large numbers of Aboriginal people had died through introduced diseases or had been killed, so now a smaller proportion was still living a traditional life on *country*. Acts of resistance still occurred but many Aboriginal people, though not all, were now acculturated to the reality of colonisation. Indeed, after the earlier 'dispersal' period Aboriginal people may have looked upon the pastoral industry as a safe haven from killing. In addition, younger Aboriginal people were becoming socialised in European ways and saw themselves as having freedoms from the strict kinship obligations and hierarchies of Aboriginal society.

From the late nineteenth century racial difference arose as a major factor in the shaping of Australian society. And as Federation approached what place did Aboriginal people have in the new nation?[30] They were neither allowed to maintain autonomous societies nor were they permitted to become equal citizens of their own *country*. This effectively guaranteed that they would live on the periphery of white society. The non-Aboriginal population of the Kimberley had increased significantly to some 2237 people (primarily men), although the majority were not associated with the pastoral industry but rather were pearling on coastal areas of the West Kimberley. Of this population, 1620 were classified as 'Asian aliens' in 1901. By late 1904 the non-Aboriginal population was 4400.[31]

In pearling locations such as at Broome and LaGrange Bay (193 kilometres south of Broome), a troubling issue with significant ramifications was developing largely unchecked by authorities. In a practice known among the white population as 'komboism', Aboriginal women and often girls as young as ten were taken or traded by Aboriginal men and prostituted to pearlers.[32] *The Sunday Times* alleged in 1905 that girls were exchanged for 'gin, tobacco, flour and rice'.[33] European men also engaged in this practice although typically they were less policed than non-Europeans.[34]

In the years around the turn of the century there were a growing number of children born to Aboriginal women and non-Aboriginal (white and Asian) men. These 'mixed race' liaisons created what the government and white colonists termed the 'half-caste problem'. Children of mixed parentage were an affront to prevailing modes of racial thinking as they were considered to not have a racial allegiance to either parent.[35] They were considered neither Aboriginal nor 'white' and were thought to be genetically inferior to both parents; indeed, influenced by the then popular pseudoscience of eugenics, many thought that they would inherit their parents' 'criminality'.[36] PC Zum Felde claimed that children who were the offspring of liaisons between Aboriginal women and Asian men would have 'all the vice of the Asiatic mixed with the black blood of the mother and will prove a nuisance, if not criminals, to the country'.[37] Henry Prinsep was also concerned about the emerging 'half-caste problem' and prostitution and the reports of the enormous rise of venereal disease.

In the early period of the Aborigines Department, Prinsep aligned himself with Forrest's views in declaring that the previous Aborigines Protection Board had 'taken a decidedly generous view' of the colony's obligations to 'its Aboriginal population'.[38] Even though there were few reporting procedures instituted on what was actually being spent, Prinsep sought to curtail what he called the 'unduly lavish methods' of supplying relief. With a 75% reduction in budget in its first year the Aborigines Department was allocated just £5000, which immediately crippled it. Prinsep led a very small department that initially had only two staff (and one after 1899). After Prinsep's salary (£550 per annum) and that of his staff were deducted, along with two grants to 'native missions' in the southwest totalling £1200, there was only a small amount of money left to cater for the entire Aboriginal population of the state. The statutory figure of £5000 proved so desperately inadequate that by 1900 Prinsep had to request an additional £5000 from the Western Australian government.[39]

More critically still, the chief protector had no statutory powers. Local honorary officers and justices of the peace had more powers and could override any decision of the chief protector.[40] With no power over them Prinsep had to rely on their goodwill to answer to him. Given the resentment already felt by these officers over their additional work, this was a difficult proposition. In short Prinsep had a department with no legal powers, little money, few resources and a pitifully small number of staff, especially considering the size of Western Australia – indeed, his office was located in Perth and he had never been to the Kimberley. It is not difficult to conclude that the lack of funding and limits on his statutory powers were designed to curtail the department's activity. The small amount of relief that the Aborigines Department could provide to Aboriginal people was the only support the Western Australian government offered. Vastly more money was spent on the judicial apparatus and associated policing than on their welfare.

And what of government support for Aboriginal missions? By 1900 Bishop Mathew Gibney's mission at Beagle Bay, which was operating on government land, was struggling to survive. The reasons for this were primarily financial. Gibney had been granted 10,000 acres (40 square kilometres) of freehold land, on condition that £5000 worth of improvements be made. However, after spending several thousand pounds of his own money and receiving annual grants as low as £250 from the government, Gibney was heavily in debt and was forced to abandon the mission. The Pallotines took over the mission in 1901.[41]

As noted earlier, the government refused to supply rations to all Aboriginal people, and instead pastoralists were encouraged to provide rations themselves and then claim reimbursement by the government. In June 1898 Prinsep issued a circular stating that those seeking reimbursement had to have the document signed and certified by a resident magistrate, government medical officer or police officer. And all Aboriginal people who were sick and unable to work, with the exception of 'old, blind and infirm', had to produce a medical certificate to get on the permanent rations list.[42] Where Aboriginal people of the Kimberley were to get medical certificates was not explained. The new system proved so ineffectual that police began giving returning prisoners rations out of their own expenses.[43] And later, in the East Kimberley especially, large numbers of Aboriginal children required permanent rations. Why so? All their fathers were in prison for cattle killing.[44] Given this background it is no surprise that the new policy approach of the Aborigines Department was an abject failure. The savings expected by abolishing Aboriginal inspectors turned out to be unrealised and in 1899 the government had to employ G.S. Olivey as a 'travelling inspector of Aborigines' who, travelling vast distances on a bicycle, had to monitor the new ration and relief system as there was simply no reporting system.[45] Finally, illustrating the complete lack of communication between government, department and local officers, in 1905 the Resident Magistrate and District Medical Officer in Wyndham Dr Dodwell Brown admitted that more than six years after Forrest's 1898 government circular was issued, he did not know of its existence or the directive that he was responsible for the welfare of Aboriginal people.[46]

'Necessity Requires No Precedents'

Despite the limitations on his power and work, Prinsep did seek to alleviate much of the criticism the government received from imperial quarters regarding the lack of attention to Aboriginal people. He sought to improve labour conditions on stations by strengthening labour contracts between employers and Aboriginal labourers (the existing *Masters and Servant* legislation had legally bound Aboriginal people to their 'white bosses'). This, Allbrook suggests, would have the effect of protecting the Aboriginal 'family from the ravages of colonisation'.[47] Prinsep also sought money for schooling and training for Aboriginal children. In 1900 he told Forrest that the inaction of the government, and not the forces of evolution, would be blamed by future generations for the loss of

Aboriginal people.[48] He believed that removing Aboriginal people from 'corrupting influences' by establishing Aboriginal reserves and passing regulations to control Aboriginal people was the way forward.[49] These were not radical ideas and, in 1902, the idea of Aboriginal reserves was debated in the Legislative Assembly.[50]

Prinsep's position stood in direct contrast to Forrest's formal (and personal) policy of non-interference, except in the case of providing aid to those who could not fend for themselves. The result was that Prinsep became a source of great irritation to Forrest and his suggestions, which made their way into early Aborigines Department annual reports, were so offensive to Forrest that he refused to print the reports.[51] In addition, in late 1900, Prinsep created and submitted a draft bill to the premier, which he called the Aborigines Act 1900, that outlined new protective legislation that would amend the *Aborigines Act 1897*. The Bill proposed the total separation of Aboriginal people from 'other inhabitants' by the creation of autonomous Aboriginal-only reserves with severe penalties for non-Aboriginal people who went onto the reserve. In proposing penalties for 'interfering' with underage Aboriginal women, the Bill was designed to halt the problem of 'komboism'.[52] But Forrest, who would soon leave for federal politics, took deep offence at the opening paragraph in the Bill, which sought to set up legislative protection of what Prinsep called Aboriginal 'health and morals'.[53] In his initial response, which he wrote on his printed version of the Bill, Forrest underlined 'morals' and wrote 'They have none, try well-being'. In fact Forrest objected to almost the entire Bill, heavily annotating almost every page with criticisms using words such as 'too absurd' and 'unworkable'.[54]

Just as Forrest was leaving for federal politics Prinsep was still trying to persuade him to introduce the Bill, writing:

381

on the eve of your departure from your very honourable and responsible position you may consider what a
great thing it will be for you in future days to look back
and point to such a monument to your memory as the
initiation of laws that which will do much to preserve
the health and morality of the coming race and prevent
that ancient and interesting Aboriginal race from sink-
ing into a degraded grave and an infamous memory.
Necessity requires no precedents.[55]

Prinsep's words fell on deaf ears and the proposed Bill progressed
no further. In February 1901 Forrest left Western Australia to
become the federal minister for defence.

If Prinsep never visited the Kimberley, who was sending him
the reports that described what was occurring there? As was the
case nearly twenty years earlier when government officials had
relied on police with the reports on blackbirding, again it was
reports from the police. PC Zum Felde was one policeman who
provided detailed written reports to Prinsep and the Aborigines
Department. Zum Felde, who policed coastal areas of the West
Kimberley, sought to discharge his duties with fairness. He, like
Travelling Inspector Olivey, noted the disastrous effects of colonisation on Aboriginal society and that far from disappearing or
dying out, Aboriginal people were surviving. He also attempted
to police the abuse of women.[56] He believed that young women,
who had traditionally assisted the Elders in day-to-day activities
such as food gathering, had now become a commodity to be
traded for goods such as food and alcohol.[57] He found, he wrote,
that these young women were 'stolen' not just by pearlers but
also by young Aboriginal men who, now spurning tradition,
traded and prostituted the women to the pearlers. This was not a

minor issue. In the larger Broome area Zum Felde estimated that over 1100 of the Aboriginal population in various coastal areas were living on the profits of prostitution.[58] And venereal diseases were rife. In mid-1901 Zum Felde had reported to Olivey that women were dying 'miserable and slow deaths'.[59] He also claimed that older Aboriginal women sometimes killed children born of prostituted women, because a mother with child was a liability and could not be traded with 'Malays'. Without a child she would, he asserted, 'flourish' as a trading item.[60]

Zum Felde became exasperated at the government's lack of attention to this issue and his inability to do much more than report what was occurring. His attempts to police it were hampered by the fact that he did not have a boat (the police department claimed they could not afford one) to enable him to visit the schooners moored off-shore.[61] In confidential correspondence to the Aborigines Department he wrote:

> I have seen many parts of Australia but never anything like this district for disgraceful crime permitted by the authority and I shall do all in my power to have now existing carry-on amended at all cost.[62]

In 1902 Zum Felde resigned from the police force, calling it 'scandalous' and 'shameful' that pearlers exploited Aboriginal women on the coast and the authorities did nothing about it.[63] However, Prinsep reported Zum Felde's observations to the government and printed them in Aborigines Department annual reports, after which a 'special police unit' of two men was set up in 1903 around Beagle Bay to help police 'komboism'.

Zum Felde's replacement at La Grange Bay was PC Bertram Henry Fletcher, also known as Kuhlman. Kuhlman received no directions from either the Aborigines Department or the police department but described his duties as 'protecting the natives and keeping immorality down'. His reports indicated that he, too, worked extremely hard to end komboism by visiting Aboriginal camps in inaccessible mangrove swamps, often at midnight, trying to catch 'Malay's [sic] with Aboriginal women'.[64] However, he faced the same issues as Zum Felde. He had requested a boat from the police department to visit the pearling boats and get evidence to sustain a conviction 'several times' but was told he 'didn't need one'.[65] When he reported that, based on observation 'from a distance', Aboriginal women were being forced to go on a boat with pearlers, he received a 'rap on the knuckles' from his superior officer in Broome for reporting the issue 'without clear proof'.[66] All he could do, he lamented, 'was report what was going on'.[67] As it stood there was no legislation whatsoever to stop pastoralists, pearlers, teamsters, indeed any colonist, from taking Aboriginal women and children away from their *country* and not returning them.[68]

It was not compulsory or socially acceptable amongst white people at the time for non-Aboriginal fathers to support their 'half-caste' offspring.[69] Prinsep's approach to this issue foreshadowed the later removals of children of 'mixed parentage'. He sought to remove them to institutions for education and he requested legal powers to enable him to compel parents to submit. However, lacking the necessary authority, which would not appear until the *Aborigines Act 1905,* he could only ask parents to voluntarily surrender their children. Some parents did consent, but more did not. The department reported 'parents will not give them up' and 'mothers refuse to give them up'.[70]

As Western Australia was now part of the Commonwealth, allegations of colonist and police brutality towards Aboriginal people in the Kimberley resonated through the new nation. Now on the national stage, Forrest continued to defend the treatment of Aboriginal people in Western Australia despite the fact that there was still conflict in the Kimberley. Forrest denied any brutality whilst simultaneously asserting that Aboriginal people were fully protected. In 1901 he said:

> With regard to the general treatment of our West Australian natives, the general opinion of those who visit the country districts – officially or otherwise – is that the natives are really well treated. The Government has a special department, with special inspectors, while all JPs and resident magistrates are official...protectors of the aborigines, and, more, the police are specially charged with reporting and repressing any cruelties that come under their notice. The relations between the natives and the settlers are good.[71]

But while Forrest's denials served his political purpose it did not silence critics of Western Australia's treatment of Aboriginal people who added to a growing clamour of calls for a royal commission into Aboriginal affairs. The commission was finally set up but not until after another four years of tumultuous administrative and political change in Western Australia.

The Death of Commissioner Phillips

One of the critical administrative issues occurred on 26 March 1900 when Police Commissioner Phillips died after a short illness. John Forrest posted a eulogy in the *Police Gazette* expressing 'his profound sorrow at the lamented death' of his commissioner.[72] Phillips was clearly held in great respect by the Perth establishment.

His funeral, with 'full military honours', was attended by most of the colonial elite of Perth, including pallbearers Alexander Forrest, Septimus and Octavius Burt, Charles Yelverton, 'C.Y.' O'Connor, John Forrest and George Shenton.[73] Superintendent Lawrence, whose record of ruthlessness in the Kimberley has already been described, temporarily acted as commissioner until, in May 1900, Frederick Hare was appointed to the role.[74]

Despite the fact that Hare was an inspector of police and resident magistrate in the 1880s he was not highly regarded and was subject to intense criticism by the press.[75] He had little of Phillips' diplomatic restraint and frequently embarrassed the government with public outbursts. Whereas Phillips had been fortunate that his administration coincided with substantial support from the formidable John Forrest, Hare did not have such a luxury and faced a general public whose attitudes to frontier violence had changed considerably. He also inherited a culture of policing resistant to change and a government unwilling to spend the money required for equipment for adequate policing. Under Hare the police, once again, had to buy their own guns and horses as they believed that what was supplied to them was inadequate.[76]

Between 1901, when John Forrest left, and 1904 Western Australian politics was unstable. The death of Forrest's brother Alexander on 20 June 1901, aged just fifty-one, further weakened the existing political hierarchy. Forrest's successor and his supporter George Throssell could not form a ministry and in that first year there were four different ministries, George Leake forming two of them with the support of the new party in parliament, the Australian Labor Party.[77] Indeed between Forrest leaving office on 15 February 1901 and 25 August 1905 there were five different premiers.

Prinsep suffered considerably under the volatility of this new world. He now faced great uncertainty with his department being administered first by Forrest, then Throssell, then three colonial secretaries, none of whom showed any interest in Aboriginal issues. He also had to contend with the unresolved 'native question' in the Kimberley pearling industry and with new problems in the burgeoning pastoral industry and it is to these we now return.

On Pastoral Country

Claims of stock losses throughout 1900 at Leopold Downs, Oobagooma and Fossil Downs were by now typically linked both to acts of resistance by Kimberley Aboriginal groups and increased fear on the colonists' part. These claims continued as pastoralism continued to consolidate its hold on the region. In 1901 the West Kimberley Leopold Downs Station was raided.[78] In the East Kimberley reports of outlaw behaviour and stock depredations continued, particularly in the Halls Creek, Alice Downs and Sturt Creek area, although these kinds of activity were less policed than in previous years.[79] One particularly emotive report in late May 1901 came from Member of the Legislative Assembly Francis Connor, who declared via telegram to Premier Throssell that the 'blacks of the district have practically taken charge of all the stations on the goldfields road', the main road between Halls Creek and Wyndham, 'including Mabel Downs, Frog Hollow, and Fletcher's Stations killing the cattle indiscriminately'.[80] In a concurrent newspaper story Connor called for a police presence and station near Turkey Creek and added, predictably enough, that if they did not receive protection they 'must abandon their holdings and stock'.[81] In the same edition, however, noted explorer and pastoralist Frank Hann ridiculed the claim.[82]

A resident partner of Sturt Creek and Margaret River Pastoral Company known as 'Stretch' endorsed Connor's summary of events but revealed that the 'indiscriminate slaughter' of cattle was in fact nothing more than the discovery of the remains of eight cattle. But there were other, greater losses. At Sam Muggleton's Frog Hollow Station thirteen (of twenty-five) 'milkers' were allegedly taken. And at Joseph Bridge's Mabel Downs Station, thirty of 300 cattle were killed. Even with these losses the figures pale into insignificance when one looks at the total stock figures for the district supplied by W.H. Stretch: Ord River 50,000 head; Victoria River 30,000; Argyle Newry and Auvergne 45,000; Wave Hill 20,000; Lissadell 15,000.[83] Stretch thought that the problem might be solved by increasing rations to older Aboriginal people, a system, he argued, that was 'badly in need of extension', but existing government policy precluded it. In 1902 Edwin Rose of Leopold Downs made the extraordinary allegation that not only were Aboriginal people killing cattle on his run but they 'have gone into the business systematically, by erecting two slaughter yards'.[84] Behind this hyperbole we see a recurring theme. As was the case in the 1890s, it was not so much the killing of stock but more the presence of Aboriginal people around stock that disturbed the cattle, made them 'wild' and caused them to lose condition and often not breed. In any case cattle stations were saleable and very profitable. In 1902 Sam Copley purchased Ord River Station for the large figure of £47,000 and, starting Copley Bros, entered into trade and shipping competition against Connor, Doherty and Durack, and Forrest and Emanuel.[85]

Stock-loss claims aside, broadly speaking, after 1900 official records indicated that the practice of cattle killing was falling both in number and in all areas with the exception of Sturt Creek.[86] By late 1902, despite continuing claims of stock losses, the pastoral industry was regarded as prosperous as the number of cattle was approaching 200,000.[87] By the end of 1903 police were asserting that cattle spearing had reduced significantly and the 'depredators were well in hand'.[88] Later, however, the Margaret River, Christmas Creek and Brooking stations and north of the Leopold Ranges reported stock losses.[89] One result of this was the opening of the Turkey Creek Police Station in 1904. As stock losses generally continued to fall, police also reported that Aboriginal workers were 'well treated' and looked 'happy and contented'.[90] Unpaid Aboriginal labour remained essential during the early 1900s, although by 1905 some workers were being paid wages.[91]

New Modes of Control

Under Hare's watch there were some alterations to policing Aboriginal people. One example was that police attempted to enforce the law regarding *inter se* Aboriginal killings, albeit with limited success.[92] Generally, official police reporting on pastoral country after 1900 was briefer than hitherto and there were fewer references to dispersals. While shootings still occurred the dominant method of controlling Aboriginal people was through wholesale arrest and the removal of large groups off pastoral country.[93] If shootings in the Kimberley were diminishing overall, the evidence for mass arrests is substantial, particularly in the East Kimberley.[94] The number of arrests and convictions for 'cattle killing and taking the flesh' in the 1900 to 1901 period was forty-eight; in 1901/02 it was 111;[95] and in 1902/03 there were 162 arrests. In 1904, 144 Aboriginal people were arrested with seventy-two from Halls Creek and twelve from the Leopold Ranges.[96] It should be noted that the official conviction records vary depending on the sources. Aborigines Department figures vary (often with two different figures in the same report) from police reports.[97]

One cause of the increasing number of arrests was the lack of regulation regarding arrests and the lack of discrimination police showed in whom they arrested. Senior police such as Sub Inspector Duncan openly admitted that 'only a small percentage of cattle killing was actually reported' by pastoralists and police on patrol arrested most people on evidence they themselves found.[98] Police also detained entire family groups, at times in very large numbers, as there was no limit placed on how many witnesses they were allowed to bring in. Given that police received 2 shillings and 5 pence per day per head (or what they called 'per knob') for the maintenance of prisoners, they certainly had an inducement to arrest, rather than shoot, as many people as possible. Some police may also have seen this as a form of compensation for, as we saw in the introduction, having to pay for the chains themselves. The lack of clear policy opened up avenues for other even more dubious processes. One allegation suggested that a pastoralist offered beef to a 'troublesome' mob on *country*. The group then came in to the station to eat at which point they were arrested for cattle killing and gaoled.[99] Mary Anne Jebb, in documenting Isdell Station records from 1904 to 1908, recorded 283 arrests, which would explain the extraordinary amount PC Wilson earned (£462). As Jebb also observed, police were more able to identify the males who were regarded as troublesome or a threat to the pastoral industry, and to arrest and remove them. This would have the effect of dismembering the men's families and making the women more dependent on white men.[100]

Reflecting both a need to reduce expenditure (as prisoner transport was considered very expensive) and a new but informal policy of imprisoning Aboriginal people in their own *country*, in June 1902 the government closed Rottnest Island prison to Aboriginal prisoners.[101] Kimberley prisoners were still sent to Derby gaol up until 1902 when it was also closed, and then prisoners were sent to either the expanded Broome or Roebourne gaol.[102] Roebourne gaol seems to have been an appalling place, similar to the gaol in Wyndham. Perth newspaper *The Daily News* claimed it was a 'crime against humanity' with fifty or sixty men enclosed in a ramshackle hut.[103] Escapes from gaol were still an enormous problem, as they had been in the 1890s: there were eighty-two escapes in 1902.[104] This brings us back to the issue of unrecorded killings.

Conspiracy of Silence: 'Twenty Bastards Will Not Take Me'

'Troublesome' Aboriginal people, such as those who escaped from gaol many times, were sometimes killed in clandestine ways. By the early twentieth century, police (and colonists) in general knew of the ramifications of illegal killing and went to greater lengths to hide bodies, often by burning the remains. Burning Aboriginal bodies to hide evidence appeared to escalate in the 1900s as more public attention was given to the Kimberley.[105] The practice continued into the 1920s and 1930s at least and was aided and abetted by the pervasive conspiracy of silence that, nearly twenty years after the establishment of the Kimberley force, remained stronger than any belief in the rule of law.[106]

Reports of killings were often ventilated in Western Australian newspapers, however. In July 1901 an article in *The Kalgoorlie Miner* by an 'ex Kimberley police constable', which outlined scathing accounts of the treatment of Aboriginal workers on stations, asserted that Aborigines 'have in places been shot by scores, put in heaps and burnt, both men and women'.[107] While stories such as these were invariably anonymous and so were easy to dismiss as slander and gossip, there is a body of first-hand evidence in police reports of police documenting the practices described. Aboriginal people at this time were killed by colonists directly or by colonists instructing their 'stock boys' to do it. Pastoralists Sam Muggleton and Joe Bridge of Turkey Creek reportedly told police that 'they did not want the police[,] they could keep the blacks out of their cattle themselves'.[108] And this is what they did.

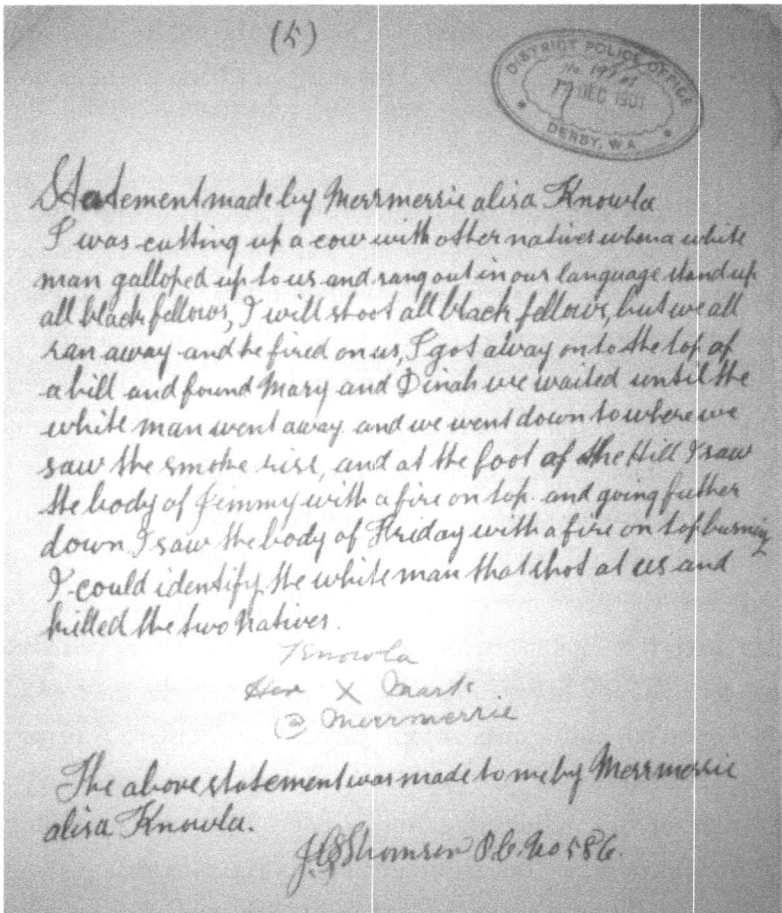

Figure 11.1. Witness statement of Merrmerrie alias Knowla, 'Alleged Murder of Two Natives by Thomas McLoughlin [sic]', SROWA, AN 5/2, Cons. 430, Item 1382/1905, Courtesy SROWA.

In late October 1901 PC James Campbell Thomson from Argyle police camp investigated allegations of the murder of two Aboriginal men on Texas Downs Station and the burning of their bodies. In the course of his investigations he visited the site where the bodies were burnt and found the remains of both visible.[109] He gathered five independent Aboriginal witnesses who could corroborate the fact that Texas Downs stockman Thomas McLaughlin shot and killed two Aboriginal men and burnt their bodies at a spot 48 kilometres east of Turkey Creek telegraph station (see figure 11.1).[110] Thomson's extraordinary record of attempting to arrest McLaughlin under warrant speaks volumes of the culture of the Kimberley frontier:

When I got within about twenty feet of the house I saw McLaughlin sitting down on the verandah. I got off the horse in doing so I asked native witness Charly if that was the man individual McLaughlin that shot the natives and he said yes. I walked towards McLaughlin and he said good day but only got within 15 foot of him when he said what's your game Thomson I said I arrest you under the Kings name[,] with that he jumped up and took a Mauser Rifle from behind his back and covered me[,] he then said take me now[,] I said it was not safe. [H]e said that twenty bastards would not take him and that I was trumping up a charge against them[,] he said you have not told me what charge you have against me[. I] said for shooting two natives[,] he said I thought so then he said that I better get onto the plain if I meant business with him[. I] said it was not safe as he had the drop on me[,] he then laughed[. H]e said he would let me off this time but if he saw me again I can

393

say good bye[,] he then said get off the station and leave me that nigger, I will fix him up[. I] said no he was my prisoner[,] then he said get off and look out[. W]ith that I went to my horse and told native witness Charly to walk in front of me[. M]y rifle was in the off side of the saddle[,] he said that he was watching me[,] I led my horse away to where I left natives[. I]t was getting dark. Mr Durack stopped behind as McLaughlin sang out get off your horse. Durack came after me to get his horse[,] I asked him what was McLaughlin up to[,] he said you'd better be careful as he means to do you in.[111]

Thomson felt that he could not leave his witnesses in this area for fear that 'some of the other white men might shoot them' so he returned with them to Argyle camp.[112] East Kimberley colonists rallied behind McLaughlin and collected £300 enabling him to escape to South Australia; as a consequence charges were never brought against him.[113] Later Thomson recorded in his journal that the manager of the Ord River Station, Fred Booty, refused to sell rations to him and his police assistants because of this investigation. Thomson, it seems, was 'blackballed' by the pastoralist community; P.B. Durack even told him it 'served him right'.[114] Durack then reminded him 'that it was an understood thing that the commissioner had not to take notice of such cases'.[115]

Another police officer also alleged that Commissioner Phillips had entered into a 'gentlemen's agreement' in which Europeans would not be investigated or prosecuted for murdering Aboriginal people. While on patrol PC Hill met Durack who informed him that Thomson 'had done a dirty trick for trying to hang his fellow man for shooting savages at the Texas Downs Station', again alleging that 'the late commissioner [Phillips] did not want it done'.[116] Hill had earlier recorded:

> Mr P Durack informs me that people seem to have a down on Const. Thomson now for doing what he has[,] putting away McLaughlin shooting blacks. Mr Durack also remarked that he thought Constable Ritchie bad enough in trying to hang [arrest] his uncle [J Durack]. He said that any of the police who put away a man for doing in the blacks always got the chuck out of the police.[117]

This case referred to occurred in November 1897 at a place Aboriginal people called Char-rang-goana and the 'whites' called Wheelbarrow Creek.[118] PC Ritchie was investigating reports that Jeremiah 'Jerry' Durack, after he had confronted two 'troublesome' men named Mannawary alias 'young Jacky' and Monday and broken their spears, had incited his Aboriginal stockman, Nipper, to shoot them.[119] Jacky was killed and Monday was wounded. Nipper told PC Ritchie: 'Jerry came up give me revolver told me go shootem on hill I go shoot Jacky first Monday ran away.'[120] Charges were laid against Durack but after another senior officer, Sergeant Evans, took over the case, Evans reported to Commissioner Phillips that Durack was not implicated.[121]

A month later in December 1897, on a trip to the Carr Boyd Ranges, PC Ritchie received information from an Aboriginal prisoner, Lucaranus, and a man named Stewert who showed him the sites on McPhee's Creek, 48 kilometres south of Denham Station, where Charles Lincan, Mick Cassidy, 'Jack' and one of Jerry Durack's stockmen, 'Pompey', shot three women and one man and burnt their bodies.[122] 'The camp was quite visible', Ritchie wrote, and he noted that there were rumours circulating about this incident. 'Saw the place where the bodies were burnt. Saw one skull and lower jaw in the sand and ashes also some smaller bones much burnt.'[123] Despite the evidence of murder no prosecution was even attempted. Shortly after this episode Ritchie was transferred out of the Kimberley to Perth then, in November 1898, to Mt Gould Police Station in the Gascoyne Junction.

After his transfer to Mt Gould he was soon involved in more controversy.[124] Here Ritchie was suspended after he claimed Magistrate Henry Walsh (who owned Mileura Station) and other station workers at Berringarra Station (owned by Everard Darlot, member of parliament for the Murchison) were mistreating Aboriginal workers, which he called 'disgraceful and brutal in the extreme'.[125] Ritchie alleged that Aboriginal people were being flogged with a whip that was 22 ounces (nearly three quarters of a kilogram) in weight and nearly five times more in weight than officially permitted. The whip consisted of 'the butt end of a billiard cue and nine thongs of leather each thong half an inch thick.'[126] Ritchie claimed Walsh, with other station owners, colluded 'to have him removed from the district' for reporting these activities. His allegations instigated a police inquiry though it was Ritchie who was found to be at fault by being what was termed 'obnoxious' over reporting to the local magistrate.[127] In August 1899 Ritchie was forced to resign from the police force with all those accused exonerated. He died the following year.[128] While Ritchie was an experienced and valuable 'bushman' clearly there were informal limits to police authority which he frequently overstepped. In attempting to prosecute colonists and protecting the rights of Aboriginal people Ritchie made many enemies.

This indicates, once again, the close links to those with pastoral interests and police authorities.

On 23 February 1901, back in the Kimberley, Jeremiah Durack was shot dead as he slept on his Denham River Station homestead verandah. His son, Patsy, was wounded in the head.[129] Jeremiah and Patsy Durack ran the station with five young Aboriginal station workers. This killing highlighted the continuing conflict between the Duracks and local Aboriginal people given that it occurred over fifteen years after 'Big Johnnie' Durack was speared in 1886.[130] Before anyone was arrested for killing Durack, twenty special constables were sworn in at Wyndham to assist in apprehending the alleged murderers. Henry Prinsep wrote to the premier expressing concern that 'I have heard a remark that possibly it may resolve itself in a retaliatory raid by which natives may be shot down wholesale.'[131] Two Aboriginal boys, fifteen-year-old Amaranga, alias Banjo, and sixteen-year-old Rochie, alias Roger, were arrested and charged over Durack's death.[132] The trial was held in Perth so that the accused would have a better chance of receiving a fair hearing.[133] Evidence from the trial suggested that Durack 'was killed in revenge for some shooting affairs in earlier days'.[134] In his evidence Patsy Durack referred to the aforementioned 'Wheelbarrow Creek' episode and under cross-examination from Richard Septimus Haynes agreed that 'Winchester rifles were used for shooting natives'.[135] During the trial, defence counsel Haynes argued that, 'When a white man was murdered, all blacks knew to make themselves scarce because Heaven help the black found within shooting distance of the avenging party.'[136] Banjo was acquitted and Rochie was found on the lesser charge of feloniously wounding and sentenced to a long term of imprisonment.[137] Notably in mid-1887 Haynes had made a name for himself in Perth legal circles in his role in the Gribble libel case referred to in chapter 3. And in 1892 Haynes made public allegations of large-scale massacres of Aboriginal people.[138]

Allegations of mistreatment continued. In 1903 Dr Richard Henry Wace, the resident magistrate and district medical officer at Derby, expressed his outrage that white employers who had infected Aboriginal women workers with venereal disease were sending them to him for treatment.[139] And later in 1904 he raised allegations to Prinsep about brutality on stations and suggested certain people should not be able to sign on Aboriginal people as employees as they were mistreating them.[140] The lack of clarity regarding roles and responsibilities described earlier meant individuals such as Wace, who was not officially gazetted as a protector of Aborigines, would 'sit on the bench' but at the same time act as defence for accused Aboriginal prisoners.[141] Wace recognised fully what the issues were: the Aboriginal people of the West Kimberley 'had his country taken from him, his game destroyed, his dogs killed, his methods of hunting limited', yet received almost nothing in compensation. Wace recommended the creation of large reserves where 'several tribes' could meet and carry on traditional activities.

Another who voiced concerns to Prinsep was Wyndham Resident Magistrate Dr Belgrave who, Prinsep stated, in 1904 proposed the creation of more reserves and camping areas for Aboriginal people released from gaol. These plans were thwarted through 'want of means and no legal authority'.[142] His successor, Dr Dodwell Brown, raised concerns in August 1904 imploring Prinsep to do something about cohabitation and the taking of Aboriginal women by teamsters who would infect them with 'advanced stages of venereal disease' and leave them unsupported.[143] Clearly Prinsep used magistrates Belgrave and Brown in his department's annual reports to emphasise the need for reform.[144] By 1904 he was clearly exasperated by the absence of progress on his concerns. He reported that the government was still not taking note of his suggestions to change existing laws and implement his Aborigines Act 1900.[145]

Resident magistrates such as Wace and Brown had a pivotal role in alerting authorities to what was occurring in the Kimberley. They also exposed the critical legal issue that was raised in the East Kimberley in 1897. This was when Resident Magistrate Fred Pearse sought to have the court follow proper judicial process and apply rules of evidence. We have seen that Aboriginal people were charged with various offences under the *Aborigines Offenders Act 1883* (amended in 1892) and dealt with summarily. In response to growing public concerns about judicial practices and confused (indeed what one legal critic said was the 'patchwork') legislation in the old statutes, the Act was replaced in 1902 by a new *Criminal Code*.[146] This removed all discriminatory legislation towards Aboriginal people. It also provided that a magistrate could now deal with charges of cattle killing just four times a year at quarter sessions.[147] This had an enormous effect on the police and judicial system and was greeted with howls of outrage by the pastoralist community.

Police Inspector Duncan echoed these grievances and complained of the enormous increase in police work required in obtaining and keeping witnesses on hand, and the consequent 'enormous expense to the state' since the repeal of the *Aboriginal Offenders Act 1883*.[148] Commissioner Hare endorsed Duncan's view of the increased expense, and as a result amendments were drafted to the *Criminal Code 1902* reversing many of the reforms in the very same year they were implemented. Section 5 of the amendments re-established extraordinary powers to magistrates and justices of the peace to impose summary punishment if a prisoner pleaded guilty to cattle killing, although the sentence 'could not exceed three years gaol'.[149] Given that almost every prisoner pleaded guilty this amendment simply re-guaranteed a conviction and therefore the removal of Aboriginal people to prison.

While these changes restored the status quo in the Kimberley for pastoralists and police they did not stop the steady stream of reports of slavery and brutality in the North West and Kimberley.[150] Reports in Britain had already given Western Australia a bad name for abuse but in the late 1890s they went well beyond newspaper articles. The Aboriginal Protection Society of London and other antislavery groups took up more claims.[151] In 1899 reports on the situation in Western Australia appeared in the London *St James's Gazette* which alleged that there was a conspiracy of newspaper 'silence' on allegations of cruelty and abuse towards Aboriginal people and that there was 'much hushing-up and smoothing-over' going on.[152] In April 1899, in response to more reports of the recent ill-treatment of Aboriginal people, Secretary of State for the Colonies Joseph Chamberlain asked the Governor, Colonel Sir Gerard Smith, to report to him upon the matter.[153] And while there had been calls for a royal commission into affairs in the north of the state since at least 1886,[154] it is against the background of a late-nineteenth-century upsurge of global antislavery agitation that campaigning for a royal commission into Aboriginal affairs in Western Australia began in earnest. It would not come about until significant changes occurred in Western Australian politics following Federation. These changes and the history of the Roth Royal Commission are described in the next chapter.

Chapter 12

'THEY MUST BE ALLOWED THE WHEREWITHAL TO LIVE'

The Roth Report

By 1900 the political and social environment of Western Australia had changed significantly. The population more than tripled during the 1890s due to the influx of non-Western Australians who flocked to the Eastern goldfields during the goldrushes. Those newly arriving in the colony found its political makeup parochial, conservative and dominated by what were called 'the six hungry families'.[1] A consequence of this massive demographic change and a newly arrived political radicalism was a fundamental realignment in the state's politics. John Forrest's government had been weakened in the 1897 election with the loss of the dominant Western Australian members who had supported him in the past. Of the twenty new members of the parliament no less than nine were hostile to his government.[2] Then on 31 July 1900 Western Australia became the final colony in the country to vote for Federation and the following year became part of the Commonwealth of Australia. The new constitution, however, left authority over Aboriginal people in the hands of the states and Western Australia, both by commission and omission, continued to act against the Aboriginal people of the Kimberley. Some Western Australian ministers used Federation to absolve themselves of responsibility for Aboriginal affairs. Just six months after the Commonwealth was formed Member for the East Kimberley Francis Connor inaccurately declared that 'the native question was largely under the control of the Federal government'.[3]

The 'ancient colonists' of Western Australia who had dominated the old Legislative Assembly lost control of their own government at the turn of the century to the new arrivals from other colonies who brought with them reformist, sometimes radical, politics.[4] And a new political force appeared: the 't'othersiders' in new towns like Kalgoorlie and Coolgardie built on the growth in trade unions in Perth, combining with them to form the new Labor Party.[5] In the election of April 1901 a majority of members voted into parliament were not part of the landed 'ancient colonist' groups. George Leake and especially Walter James, both premiers after Federation, believed that Western Australia's land, wealth and power was concentrated in too few hands. James was a radical liberal, interested in social reform with cautious rural development.[6] They headed governments much more likely to respond to the allegations of abuse coming from the Kimberley.

In response to these continuing reports, critics of the pastoral industry now included the Labor Party and associated trade unions, the clergy and the more sympathetic and liberal newspapers in Perth, which all criticised the oppressive conditions of Aboriginal workers in the North West and the Kimberley. The advent of photographs in newspapers added to the outrage, as photos of chained prisoners were now being published to shocked readers across the world. Worried locals continued to raise concerns about abuse and 'slavery' in the north and these allegations were publicised in the wider Australian and British press. Two Melbourne newspapers, *The Age* and *The Argus,* were outspoken in calling for Commonwealth intervention in Western Australia. During this period there were repeated calls from a variety of quarters, including members of the new Commonwealth parliament, for the establishment of royal commissions to inquire into Aboriginal affairs.

In August 1901 Labor Member for Coolgardie Hugh Mahon put forward a motion in the federal parliament for a national inquiry into the 'WA system of slavery'.[7] The *Northern Advertiser* newspaper made demands for an inquiry as did Member for Roebourne Dr J.T. Hicks.[8] Irishman Walter Malcolmson, a prominent critic who had spent some time working in the North West, described a 'brutal slavery in full swing in this part of the Empire' in the pastoral north and claimed in *The London Times* that any inquiry would 'end the cheap labour that the pastoral industry so depended upon and thus could never occur'.[9]

In 1902 more reports followed and several Western Australian parliamentarians called for a royal commission.[10] Following the call of William Butcher, the member for the Gascoyne, editorials in the *Morning Herald* newspaper turned attention to who might head it, calling for an 'independent expert' as commissioner. In this connection the name of noted Assistant Protector of Aborigines in Queensland, London-born and Oxford-educated surgeon and ethnographer Dr Walter Edmund Roth was prominent.[11]

Malcolmson continued to attack the Western Australian government and the pastoral industry. He described Western Australia as the 'slave state of the Australian commonwealth' and that Aboriginal people of the 'north west and Kimberley were worse off than the Negro in the American slave days'.[12] Malcolmson was widely derided in Western Australia but he was also supported by local Aboriginal men such as William Harris, who was described by *The Sunday Times* as an 'educated half-caste' who had worked in the North West. Harris, as we will see, became one of the most vocal critics of government policy and sought equality for Aboriginal people. Harris witnessed mistreatment and starvation of Aboriginal people and made detailed and serious charges against the colonists and government of Western Australia who, he suggested, supported the 'legalised slavery' of the North West.[13] Malcolmson's statements, Harris said, were 'utterly justified: 'If they have any fault it is that they do not go far enough.'[14] Prominent Presbyterian clergyman and Professor of Theology at Ormond College Dr John Laurence Rentoul spread concerns regarding 'the slave state' of Western Australia in newspaper articles Australia-wide.[15] In May 1904 Malcolmson had another scathing letter with a litany of cases of abuse in the North West region published in *The Times*.[16]

Figure 12.1. Dr Walter E. Roth, John Oxley Library, Courtesy State Library of Queensland, 117810. Photographer unknown.

Henry Prinsep took Malcolmson's concerns sufficiently seriously that he instructed Sub Inspector Lappin of Roebourne to
investigate the allegations. Lappin largely rejected the claims as
'ancient' and said he could not comment as he had only been in
the district for the last two years. Prinsep reported this response
in the 1904 Aborigines Department annual report.[17] The public
debate about a royal commission had continued through five
different premiers until a new government led by Walter James,
which had amongst other reforms legalised trade unions and
introduced workers' compensation, acted. In mid-1904 James,
under direction from Governor Frederick Bedford, appointed Dr
Roth to head a royal commission.[18]

The Royal Commission

The Royal Commission's terms of reference required it to report
upon seven issues, all of which involved the police directly or
indirectly:

> The Administration of the Aborigines Department; The
> employment of Aboriginal natives under contracts of
> service and indentures of apprenticeship; Employment
> of Aboriginal natives in the pearlshell fishery and
> otherwise of boats; The native police system; The treat-
> ment of Aboriginal prisoners; The distribution of relief;
> and, Generally into the treatment of the half caste and
> Aboriginal inhabitants of the state.[19]

The terms of reference, which dictated what Roth could examine,
were not particularly restrictive. What did restrict the inquiry was
what appears to be the time available, and so Roth chose only to
accept evidence from the years 1901 to 1904, effectively ignoring

the long history of violence in the north.[20] Roth also based his findings on a very limited survey of particular areas, areas that he described as 'portions of the state along which his investigations lead him'.[21] He took evidence from forty-two witnesses, the majority being from the East Kimberley. Out of all this evidence only two short paragraphs of testimony from two Aboriginal people – about whom the Royal Commission was purportedly concerned – were included.[22] Some of the most damning and revealing testimony regarding police actions came from these two witnesses. It also came from people with no vested social or commercial interests in the district.

What the Evidence Revealed

Over a period of five months Roth examined witnesses on a range of issues, revealing many disturbing practices as well as serious flaws in legal processes. In the pearling areas Roth interviewed Broome Trappist priest 'Father Nicholas', who ran a small 'orphan school' and church in Broome with his own personal funds and public charity. Father Nicholas confirmed that there were many sexual encounters between pearlers and Aboriginal women just as PCs Zum Felde and Fletcher had reported years earlier. He alleged that of these liaisons, forty-four children had been killed by their mothers, and even made the astounding claim that one child of four years of age had been killed and eaten by its mother.[23] Witnesses reported and confirmed what Prinsep had repeatedly reported over the years, that venereal disease had stayed at high levels and many women were dying.[24] Prinsep's claims were supported at the Royal Commission by PC Fletcher, who alleged that at La Grange Bay a quarter of the Aboriginal population, estimated to be 400, were infected with venereal disease and many women as young as sixteen had died of the disease.[25]

On keeping Aboriginal prisoners neck chained in gaol it was revealed that there existed no legal authority, regulation or rule to allow it and that the safety of prisoners was consistently disregarded.[26] However, Octavius Burt, sheriff and controller general of prisons, claimed that neck chaining was simply informally accepted as 'one of those things so universally adopted that it is never questioned. The practice has been in vogue for about thirty years'.[27] The reality, as Roth observed, was that chains were left on prisoners in gaols in the North West and Kimberley because the prisons were so decrepit and inadequate that prisoners could easily escape unless chained to each other.[28]

In the East Kimberley Alfred Woodroffe of Wyndham accused Justice of the Peace and Acting Resident Magistrate Henry McKenzie Skinner from Wyndham of extreme bias in sentencing Aboriginal people, adding: 'I have walked out of the court disgusted at what is called British justice.'[29] Skinner's replacement, Dr Dodwell Brown, displayed no such bias. He was critical of flaws in the judicial process and the difficulties Aboriginal suspects faced, often, according to Brown, not even being aware what they were arrested for or why they were being charged and imprisoned. Brown also criticised police. When he queried why children of fourteen were being charged with cattle killing, he was told 'They are able to chuck a spear as well as any older man.'[30] Brown implicated PC Thomson and Corporal Goodridge in exploiting the rationing system (where police were paid per day allowances for prisoner upkeep) by keeping prisoners for far longer than was required. Brown accused them of making considerable sums of money in what he called the 'needless expenditure of state money grabbed by police'.[31]

One account reveals that a police party out for over three months brought in thirty-three men and women 'on the chain' as well as seven more witnesses.[32] In 1894 one police officer had earned over £80 through exploiting the 'per knob' prisoners' ration allowance.[33] A decade later PC Wilson had received over £462 for the same practice – well over twice his annual salary and near to what senior government officials were earning.[34] Goodridge admitted police 'rorted' the allowance system by arresting as many people as possible and made 'considerable' profits but claimed he had not reported it for fear of being seen as a 'black sheep' of the police force.[35] Later when asked to explain this remark he stated that police boasted of 'shouting' others drinks on what he called 'nigger money'.[36] Constables John (Jack) Inglis and John Wilson's testimonies were terse and minimal. Clearly police were concerned about implicating themselves.[37]

The evidence also indicated that many witnesses, including senior police, did not know their legal obligations or their obligations to the Aborigines Department regarding the treatment of Aboriginal people.[38] For example, in a revealing admission, Sub Inspector Lappin described the way police returned absconding station workers to their employer as analogous to police ordering a drunken person from a town within twenty-four hours, despite there being no legal requirement to do it and despite the fact that no magistrate could order it.[39]

The evidence also showed that the distribution of rations to Aboriginal people through the Aborigines Department was dysfunctional and haphazard because no one person seemed to be responsible for it. There was no systematic inspection of relief by field officers, nor was the departmental budget sufficient to provide for destitute Aboriginal people. Police and other government officials such as postmasters and even publicans and private citizens dispersed rations. Many witnesses suggested that relief frequently did not get to the people it was intended for. Indeed police were often unaware of who was distributing the relief in their districts.[40] Other evidence indicated that Aboriginal people did not receive the blankets intended for them. At Turkey Creek telegraph station 'government blankets were used…to keep the sun off the veranda'.[41] Police at Argyle (Wild Dog) Station used their blankets for the same purpose.[42]

The evidence also showed that the investigative methods often employed by police went far beyond regulations, including terrorising prisoners into making self-incriminating admissions. This was evident in the testimony of a fourteen-year-old boy named Boodungarry who was serving two years' hard labour for cattle killing. His witness statement – one of the two from Aboriginal people – is quoted in full:

I was caught by Jack Inglis and Wilson. Some others, named Manulla and Goominyah, were with me and the other men. We were caught on the camp at Mt Barrett. I had been working for a white man but left and went to the bush. Wilson asked if I killed cattle. I said 'no'. Wilson and Inglis then talked together and they said they would shoot me. Inglis put a cartridge in his rifle, pointed it at me, and said he would burn me at a rock. It frightened me, and then I said I did kill a bullock. The first time I said I did not kill any cattle, but this time I was frightened when he said he would shoot, and I said I did kill cattle. He took me and some other blackfellows who were also frightened. They all said they had killed a bullock because they were frightened. The policeman put handcuffs on our legs and hands. Two of us were chained by the legs. They then caught some more blackfellows – a big mob and some gins and took us away. Wilson got a gin and took her into a gully. I have seen Policeman Wilson 'marry' plenty of gins. We were taken to Halls Creek. At the courthouse I said nothing because Inglis told me not to talk. Wilson hammered plenty of blackfellows with Nulla Nulla [throwing club]. I do not know why he 'Wommered' [beat] them but he frightened me and I did not talk in the courthouse. The gins did all the talking. The magistrate only spoke to them. He did not ask me if I killed a bullock.[43]

The other Aboriginal witness, a man named Garngulling, corroborated many of these claims. He alleged that PC Inglis caught him and used him to track and find alleged cattle killers. Identifying a suspect named 'Larry', Inglis asked him if he had killed cattle belonging to Ben Cranwell. When Larry said 'no' Inglis said, 'Now tell the truth, if you don't I will burn you in the fire', then said 'he will shoot him'. Garngulling then implicated other police named Wilson, Callow and O'Brien in the rape of Aboriginal women.[44]

Leaving aside the litany of allegations in this short testimony – intimidation, coercion, rape, fraud, evidence obtained under duress – the evidence given to the Royal Commission supports Paul Hasluck's observation, made in his book in 1942, that there was a routine relationship between arrest, conviction and gaoling of an Aboriginal offender and the courts were simply the means by which Aboriginal people were sent to gaol. They had failed in their duty to provide defendants with a fair, open and transparent trial.[45]

Roth's Findings

Commissioner Roth made several findings, criticisms and recommendations. In relation to government policy generally he made two major criticisms. The first was that the administration of the Aborigines Department was chaotic and the protection that the *Aborigines Act 1897* provided for Aboriginal people was dismal. Roth confirmed Prinsep's admission that the chief protector of Aborigines had neither legal powers nor status to enforce the provisions of or to compel any government official under the Act.[46] The British undersecretary of state for the colonies (the Duke of Marlborough) was correct when he stated in 1905 that there was 'very little doubt that the machinery for carrying into effect the wishes and desires of the Government has entirely broken down'.[47]

In a second criticism Roth damned the Western Australian government for failing in its 'grave responsibility' of providing for Aboriginal people by 'pursuing a policy of allowing large areas of country to be taken up and occupied without the slightest provision being made for the natives who are thus dispossessed of their hunting grounds'.[48] As he recognised, by 1905 the ongoing movement of Aboriginal people who lived a 'bush life' to a 'station life' was being consolidated but with this came the loss of their rights to land and opportunity to hunt in their traditional ways. Roth recommended that Aboriginal reserves be established, not only on humanitarian grounds, but also on the grounds of 'practical policy' much like the reservations that had been established in Canada and the United States for Native Americans. The alternative, he argued, was to continue the present disastrous system whereby landowners leased what was once Aboriginal land, which would inevitably lead to the following:

bloodshed and retribution will be certain to ensue, and the Executive, in its efforts to restore law and order, and in the costs of rations to make up deficiencies in the natural food supplies, will be ultimately put to an expenditure considerably in excess of the total rents received. Carrying the present practice of Might against Right to a logical conclusion, it would simply mean that, were all the land in the northern areas of the state to be thus leased, all the blacks would be hunted into the sea.[49]

Roth simply demanded that Aboriginal people 'must be allowed the wherewithal to live'.[50] He found, too, that some pastoralists did not believe it was their responsibility to support the elderly Aboriginal people who had worked on their stations, sometimes for a generation, insisting instead that the government should foot the bill through spending more money on rationing.

Roth then moved on to Aboriginal labour. He found that fewer than one in twelve workers in the Kimberley worked under contract despite the law requiring that they be contracted. He found that there was no penalty in the legislation for failing to use a contract despite Aboriginal workers, including young children, being forced to work on stations and being illegally returned by police if they absconded.[51] Roth also found that in the pearling industry most Aboriginal workers were not employed under enforceable contracts and, for the most part, the few actual contracts that existed were ignored.

Roth's second major area of concern was the administration and running of the Western Australian police department. He described the way in which Aboriginal people were arrested, charged, convicted and imprisoned for cattle killing, which was described in the introduction to this book as 'a most brutal and outrageous condition of affairs'.[52] To secure a conviction, Roth stated, the accused were 'made to plead guilty – at the muzzle of a gun if needs be'.[53] The legislation in the form of the *Criminal Code Amendment Act 1902*, which enabled a magistrate to deal with the matter summarily, was what Roth called 'a suitable weapon' for police as it guaranteed their conviction. Curiously Roth appears to have based his opinion of the number of Aboriginal arrests on conviction statistics supplied by Chief Protector Prinsep when he was questioned. These were probably understated. Conviction figures for 1904, revealed in the previous chapter and drawn from official police annual reports, are nearly four times more than the figures Prinsep had supplied.[54]

Roth recommended the abolition of neck chains for prisoners and the introduction of 'wrist-cuffs', a recommendation that all the officers in charge of the North West gaols supported.[55] He dedicated less than a page to the use of Aboriginal trackers in the police force, calling it 'The Native Police system'. He did not address the killing of Aboriginal people by police, possibly being unaware of its extent, although he observed that on 'at least two occasions' armed native assistants had shot prisoners and recommended they not be allowed to carry firearms.[56] But then how could Roth possibly know what was occurring with native assistants? They lived and worked in a 'grey' legal world where they were almost bureaucratically invisible.

Roth was also fiercely critical of the judicial system, in particular of the disproportionate sentences given to Aboriginal prisoners, the way they were convicted on their own evidence, the harsh treatment of Aboriginal prisoners and the imprisonment of Aboriginal children[57] – and many of those arrested were children. In Halls Creek Aboriginal children as young as ten were arrested, charged and imprisoned for periods of up to six months with hard labour.[58] One fifteen-year-old boy was sentenced to nine months for killing a goat and another eight children between fourteen and sixteen years received two years' gaol with hard labour for cattle killing.[59]

Reactions to the Report

Roth's report was immediately enormously controversial.[60] A barrage of newspaper articles reporting on Roth's findings appeared locally and Australia wide.[61] Opinion in Perth on the Roth Report was divided. Generally those with commercial interests in the North West and Kimberley, such as Robert Frederick Sholl, were dismissive of Roth and dismissed the reports of abuse by police.[62] Others such as respected prospector William Carr-Boyd said the Roth Report was 'mild in the extreme' and the condition of Aboriginal people in the Kimberley was far worse: they were 'disgusting, filthy, deplorable and miserable' and were 'starving, ragged and rotten' with the 'most disgusting diseases' acquired from the 'whites'.[63]

Well-attended public meetings were held in town halls in Perth on 24 February 1905 and in Fremantle on 9 March to discuss the report.[64] *The West Australian* reported on a rowdy Perth meeting with over fifteen speakers, among them Bishop Gibney and other religious leaders, Lord Mayor of Perth Harry Brown, MLA for the Murchison John Nanson and other members of parliament. Feelings were so high that some speakers had trouble being heard between 'uproar', 'disorder' and interjection.[65] Several resolutions were passed including one that called for the 'immediate repudiation of concurrence in the shocking violations of justice, humanity, law and honour' disclosed in the Roth Report. To widespread applause Bishop Gibney stated the Roth

Report was 'substantially true'. Others suggested the establishment of 'vigilance committees' to 'protect the natives'. Mayor Brown called for more money to be spent on Aboriginal people.[66]

However, not all speakers were outraged at the findings in the report. One uninvited guest made his way to the podium and took to the stage. In a sign he was a 'bushman' he was holding his large felt hat. To a cry from the audience of 'Who are you?' the man replied 'Bill Armitage is my name if you're so anxious to know', and he proceeded to utter a spirited defence of the North West squatters, telling the crowd stories of 'murders by blacks', while wagging his finger at an increasingly hostile crowd yelling at him to 'sit down'.[67] This was, of course, ex-police constable William Armitage who, as we saw in chapter 5, was a lauded police 'bushman' who undertook many bush patrols involving heavy shooting. In 1889 he was arrested for murder for killing the Aboriginal boy Jenella, a charge that was subsequently dropped. Armitage clearly thought the Perth audience had little idea of what the Kimberley squatter had to endure. To cheers from the audience he was ejected from the stage.[68]

In Britain the Archbishop of Canterbury, Lord Tennyson, raised the report in the House of Lords stating that 'a great wave of indignation had swept over the whole of Australia due to the report's revelations'.[69] Other members of the Lords hoped that Western Australian statesmen would display 'energy' in reinforcing regulations to vindicate the state from claims that they were not progressive and humane towards Aboriginal people. John Forrest, now ensconced in the federal parliament and soon to become treasurer in Alfred Deakin's government, criticised the report and what he called its 'sensational character'. He voiced his now familiar arguments, dismissing the findings and 'the foolish action' in having t'othersiders commenting on his state's affairs.[70] He continued to support and defend the actions of police. In February 1905, he told *The West Australian*:

> My own opinion is, and I have had a large experience of the police throughout the whole of Western Australia that, taking them as a body, they have always been an exemplary class of men. I have always found them mindful of the interests of the aborigines, and, it is recognised by the aborigines and by all other persons, including station-owners, that the police are the protectors of the natives. That the police do their duty well may be gathered from the fact that persons in prominent positions have occasionally felt aggrieved at the action of the police in being too indulgent in their treatment of aborigines.[71]

Back in Perth, senior Western Australian government officials, including Sheriff and Controller General of Prisons Octavius Burt and Commissioner of Police Captain Frederick Hare (both of whom provided testimony to Roth), publicly criticised the report. Hare described the evidence as coming from the 'scum and the riffraff of the north' and not from 'respectable members' of the district.[72] The foolishness of this statement was revealed publicly when *The Daily News* reported that the vast majority of the witness testimony came from state government employees working in the Kimberley.[73] Hare's statement earned him temporary suspension for breaching the *Public Service Act* and he later apologised claiming that he had not read the report.[74]

Not to be deterred, Hare continued to campaign against the report. In June 1905 he undertook his own inquiry in the North

West and Kimberley and published his findings. He claimed that the 'state of Western Australia has been maligned and a stigma placed upon its inhabitants' and then attempted to repudiate many of Roth's allegations. He claimed the Aboriginal witness to the Royal Commission, Boodungarry, made 'a wild statement' in his allegations that police abused prisoners and Aboriginal women. He gave an 'emphatic denial' to these charges.[75] On allegations that police murdered Aboriginal people and raped Aboriginal women, Hare stated: 'It is hardly worthwhile my comment upon this. The evidence (page 16 of report) is of such a trivial nature that no one can believe that there is any truth in it.'[76]

Hare justified the practice of police obtaining 'blood money' or making a profit from arresting large numbers of prisoners by suggesting that it was also done in the Northern Territory. Yet, he went on, the practice in the Kimberley made it cheaper than in the Northern Territory and, in any case, Roth had been unfair because he had not taken into account the cost of rations supplied to prisoners, which police often had to pay out of their own pockets. On the manner of arresting Aboriginal people he again claimed that the practice was the same as that in the Northern Territory and was therefore appropriate in Western Australia. He also defended the use of neck chains and concluded by saying that he 'had nothing but good accounts of the police in all of the districts'.[77] *The Sunday Times* was scathing, describing him as a 'maladroit' and a 'veneered and illogical barbarian'.[78]

Indeed, Hare's view of the situation stands in stark contrast to others. Renowned German doctor and Professor of Physical Anthropology Hermann Klaatsch undertook a tour of northern Australia from 1904 to 1906 that included a period in Wyndham. Here, he noted, he could only 'sustain the correctness' of Roth's findings. Klaatsch likened the Kimberley to Van Diemen's Land (later renamed Tasmania) during 1820 to 1830 in what was known as the 'Black War', where the near total destruction of local Aboriginal populations occurred.[79] Around Wyndham he found it impossible to get in friendly contact with the 'wild tribes' because the relationships between the 'whites and the blacks' was so bad. Every white person, Klaatsch noted, was regarded 'with the dread that the natives attached to police officers, who in their mind, were likened to dangerous animals'.[80]

Boodungarry's claims of rape at Isdell Station raised concern within the state government so it appointed Patrick Troy, who was by then resident magistrate and warden at Cue in the midwest region of Western Australia, to inquire into the allegations. Troy was by now fifty-four years old and a very experienced senior police official. His account, whilst not displaying the innocence found in his descriptions of his experiences over twenty years previously, showed the same earnest professionalism and evocative descriptions of events and people. Troy interviewed the woman named Nimbandi, one of the women Isdell police officer Wilson had allegedly raped, and her husband Yarreh, alias Paddy.[81] Then on a four-month investigation, which ran from late February to late May 1905, Troy travelled with Nimbandi, PC Hamilton and their tracker Tommy to the Leopold Ranges to gather evidence of sites where the murders and rapes were said to have occurred. However, he could not get any information from 'bush natives' because his party could not understand their language.[82] He was unable to corroborate many of Nimbandi's allegations, could not find the site of any of the alleged killings and deduced that the allegations of rape were 'unworthy of credit'.[83] On his return to Derby he concluded that Nimbandi's and therefore Boodungarry's allegations were unfounded.[84] He did, however, endorse Roth's findings that police at Isdell had 'badly and carelessly kept records', were destroying Aboriginal property after arrests were made, and were arresting Aboriginal people without reasonable evidence that they were the offenders.[85]

As historian Peter Biskup has noted, the outrage in Western Australia over the Roth Report was disproportionate to the findings, particularly as Roth was largely dismissive of accusations of cruelty and maltreatment by pastoralists. He took no evidence regarding the events in the East Kimberley from police or pastoralists in the pre-1901 period despite official police records documenting evidence of cruelty and maltreatment. However, the inquiry did provide evidence that police practices introduced in the early days of policing were very much still in operation.

'It Will Take Years to Again Get the Natives Under'

Roth, no doubt, was optimistic that his report would lead to changes. In the British House of Lords, Lord Tennyson reported to members that the government of Western Australia had 'pledged themselves' to make significant changes to the treatment of Aboriginal people. In the Lords debate Earl Spencer finalised the British perspective on this matter by stating: 'I trust that the instances of grievous wrong-doing to the natives of Western Australia will now cease, and that the aborigines in that region will be governed in a humane, just, and generous way.'[86]

Roth's report did prompt immediate changes in the form of a directive from Commissioner Hare: children were to be released from gaols; police were directed to be more specific in their charges; rather than charging Aboriginal people with 'cattle killing', the offence was now to be 'in the unlawful possession of beef'; police were to limit the number of witnesses to two; and they were to certify on oath that they distributed rations appropriately.[87] At the government level significant recommendations made by Roth were acted upon. The response of the Labor government, led by Henry Daglish, which came to office in August 1904 and replaced Walter James, was swift and contained wide-ranging reforms. The new colonial secretary issued a raft of strict new regulations that he hoped would remedy the criticisms found in the report. Police now had to confirm that Aboriginal people were employed under contract; those employed without contract were to be reported; police, as they had been doing for decades, were now forbidden from returning Aboriginal people to employers without evidence of contracts; police were to be diligent against cases of 'komboism'; police were only to arrest Aboriginal people on direct evidence, that is possession of beef, and no more witnesses than necessary were to be brought in; no more female witnesses were to be brought in; and rations supplied by police were to be paid for by vouchers. In addition the use of chains on prisoners in gaol was to cease and 'the use of neck chains on Aboriginal prisoners was to be prohibited'.[88] Chief Protector of Aborigines Prinsep was directed to move north to Derby or Broome. However, none of these regulations were enforced and Prinsep stayed in Perth. The Daglish government was a victim of the tumultuous Western Australian politics of the early twentieth century and lost office in August 1905, and in the Kimberley the status quo of these issues remained.[89]

Subsequent governments refused to abolish the use of neck chains, recommending instead that chains of a lighter gauge be used. Roth suggested that native assistants should be employed under contract and that they 'should not be allowed to carry firearms' but this was also ignored.[90] He recommended the introduction of a minimum wage for Aboriginal workers as well as a centralised rationing station that would end the apparent 'rorting' and waste of departmental money. It is clear that subsequent governments were reluctant to introduce any measures that would loosen the controls over Aboriginal people, even when the report had shown them to be illegal.

Yet, while governments before and immediately after the Roth Report did very little to advance the welfare and protection of Aboriginal people, on both sides of the Kimberley magistrates were introducing change. In the West Kimberley Richard Wace, the Derby resident magistrate, ceased sentencing Aboriginal offenders summarily (after being abolished in the 1902 Criminal Code, summary hearings of Aboriginal offenders had been reintroduced with the *Amendment to the Criminal Code 1902)* and demanded procedural fairness and justice for Aboriginal people accused of a crime. One consequence of this was that, because of the expense of keeping witnesses for later trials, police withdrew their cases.[91]

This, as it had done in the 1880s and 1890s, prompted intense criticism from northern pastoralists who complained that the standards of justice expected by magistrates such as Wace were unrealistic. In July 1905 a deputation visited Commissioner Hare to argue that the new approach to sentencing had done 'incalculable damage' to the task of controlling Aboriginal people. In a now predicable refrain, indeed they had used it when the Criminal Code was introduced in 1902, they again insisted that they would be forced to take the law into their own hands or abandon their holdings if the new practices were continued.[92] In the East Kimberley Dr Dodwell Brown had also criticised summary prosecutions and released Aboriginal children with a caution. With cattle killing in Halls Creek and Wyndham still prevalent, Acting Sub Inspector McCarthy declared that the leniency of magistrates like Brown and the fact that he demanded concrete evidence for a conviction was the reason. To support his case he pointed out that Aboriginal people who had previously received longer sentences of three years were now receiving sentences as short as one month.[93]

Charles Annear, the telegraph operator and provider of relief in the upper Fitzroy River area, wrote to Chief Protector Prinsep supporting these arguments; indeed Prinsep thought that his claims were serious enough to be published in the 1906 Aborigines Department annual report. Annear complained that the 'leniency' Wace displayed was not helping the local situation; quite the contrary, his judgments had serious and possibly disastrous ramifications. He had allowed an 'alarming rise in cattle killing' and created an impression that police had no authority over Aboriginal people, with the result that the 'blacks were becoming saucy' and 'useless'.[94] He claimed 'it will take years to again get the natives under'.[95] Prinsep offered tacit endorsement to Annear, observing that the Kimberley required a 'firm hand' and a 'great disaster' would occur if Aboriginal people, who he described as 'unreasoning creatures', thought they could 'overpower their employers'.[96]

Prinsep did concede that imprisoning Aboriginal people was expensive and observed that 'we have been in the game for many years now, and surely it is time to try some other measures'.[97] However, the main complaint of pastoralists in the Kimberley was what they alleged were the consequences of applying rules of evidence and adhering to proper procedural fairness in sentencing Aboriginal people. As ever, even if the processes were illegal and unjust towards Aboriginal people, they believed that the most practical, expedient and invariably punitive practices should prevail as they kept 'the natives under'.

While some relatively minor recommendations of the Roth Report were introduced in Western Australia and many more were not, the major result of Roth's Royal Commission was the *Aborigines Act 1905*. This Act, based to some extent on Prinsep's largely ignored Aborigines Act 1900, was in part intended to bring the affairs of the North West and Kimberley under the ambit of Western Australian law, to stop the frontier violence and to increase the powers of the chief protector of Aborigines. However, the focus of Prinsep's thinking had changed in the intervening years, from preservation of Aboriginal people and their culture on dedicated reserves to the administration and control of Aboriginal people. The 1905 Act sought to provide a solution to what was considered by white Western Australians the growing problem of 'half-caste' children and it gave the chief protector the legal guardianship of 'every aboriginal and half-caste child' up to the age of sixteen years. The result of these changes was to establish the early administrative structure for the surveillance and control of all Aboriginal people, and give legal authority to the removal of children from their parents that would have devastating out-comes for Aboriginal people not only in the Kimberley but also throughout Western Australia for the rest of the twentieth century.

★

This has been the history of policing Aboriginal people in the Kimberley from 1882 to 1905. By undertaking a wide-ranging historical survey it has reassessed the history of policing in the Kimberley district of Western Australia as a whole, showing there were more similarities than differences between the West and East Kimberley. It has exposed the complex web of social relations around police work and argued against the reduction-ism that characterises much writing about conflict between Kimberley colonists and Aboriginal people. It reveals that after the establishment of responsible government in Western Australia, political machinations in far-away Perth, driven by economic and commercial imperatives, changed police practices. It shows that the development and success of the Kimberley pastoral industry in the twentieth century could not have occurred without police in the period under study controlling and removing Aboriginal people, who threatened the industry, from their land. It shows that policing changed significantly over the course of the period under study, from a situation where police would often seek to protect Aboriginal people from colonist violence to one of apparent warfare against Aboriginal resistance. The formation of the Commonwealth of Australia did not mean an end to the dispossession. The new constitution left authority over Aboriginal people in the hands of the states and the state of Western Australia, both by commission and omission, continued to act against the Aboriginal people of the Kimberley.

Policing was exceptionally difficult in the Kimberley. The financial restrictions imposed on the police force limited numbers and, coupled with their limited authority and the vast area of country they had to cover, had a profound effect on policing. The physical and social environment, too, created and necessitated a unique form of policing and required, and attracted, a unique form of officer. In the early to mid-1880s, policing involved a great deal of surveillance and reporting on social and economic development and on the nature of Aboriginal culture. Conflict between Aboriginal people and colonists was not pervasive and the relationship for the most part was more one of mutual curiosity than hostility. Police seemed to embrace a protective role or at least a general suspicion that pastoralists' claims about Aboriginal 'depredations' were spurious. However, they also sought to impose British law on a people who did not understand it. It is clear that in this period, police actively prevented colonists from killing Aboriginal people. This was certainly a factor in colonists concealing violence. Yet, this changed as economic imperatives and political changes influenced and altered police practices. The arrival of responsible government and the organisation of pastoralists in parliament into a powerful, self-interested lobby, supported by the government and the premier, led to radical changes in the laws affecting Aboriginal people and the practice of policing itself.

Although the Kimberley police were always legally a civil and never a military force, native assistants effectively doubled police numbers, which were further extended at times by special constables. This was not through official policy (unlike the model of the Queensland Native Police for example) but developed organically. Police rules and regulations were flexible and often of questionable legality. The result was a uniquely evolved and operational mobile police force that used extreme violence in its campaigns. The welfare of Aboriginal people was secondary and certainly there was little incentive in the police culture to enhance it.

How many Aboriginal people died as a result of police actions, including shootings and forced marches 'on the chain', during this period? Given the uncertainty about pre-contact population numbers and population estimates in general it is very difficult to ascertain. It is also impossible to know how many Aboriginal people were killed because police and others had a vested interest in under-reporting the numbers. Pre-contact population figures, as articulated in the introduction, were estimated at around 10,000 (and possibly more). Post-1900s figures were estimated at 'approximately' 5000 with 1500 of those employed in the pastoral industry.[98] Disease was doubtless the major factor in the population decline but even so the numbers killed by police would be significant. A minimum number drawn from the surveyed police records of the West and East Kimberley, leaving aside the number killed in events described as 'operations' and 'dispersals', would be in the several hundreds of people. Those who died while on forced marches on the chain cannot be known, and the numbers wounded, while likely to be substantially higher than those killed, can only be imagined. Similarly, the numbers killed by colonists in massacres and other killings is almost impossible to ascertain given collusion and the hiding of evidence, but they would be significant.

Many of the 'silences' around issues to do with Aboriginal people that underpin many colonial accounts have been revealed. We have seen how this colonial expansion that established commercial dynasties came at enormous cost to Aboriginal people. And ironically perhaps, it is clear Aboriginal people with their unpaid labour were significant component, if not the key component, in the success of the Kimberley pastoral industry. We have seen how colonists and government refuted allegations of mistreatment of Aboriginal people: by denial. Where were the disinterested individuals in the Kimberley and who could investigate this? That isolation was an important factor in Kimberley policing almost goes without saying. It enabled local police to police without central oversight. It enabled pastoralists to engage in violence against Aboriginal people with relative impunity. It made it extremely difficult to investigate claims of mistreatment and encouraged collusion amongst colonists: the 'freemasonry of silence' made information gathering practically impossible. And it may have encouraged pastoralists to pressure and limit the authority of police whenever they, the pastoralists, felt that police were not acting in their interests. Such police could be 'black-balled', marginalised and threatened.

With the exception of the underfunded Aborigines Protection Board and its section 70 legislated provisions and the successor Aborigines Department with funding even lower, there is a recurrent theme throughout this period of confusion about who exactly was responsible for the welfare of Aboriginal people and a corresponding reluctance by anybody to take responsibility. The legal status of Aboriginal people sat in a grey area as neither protected citizens nor adversaries who could be conquered by force. This legal status only enforced their social marginalisation. The *Roth Royal Commission on the Condition of the Natives* – commissioned only after years of allegations and great reluctance from defensive and parochial locals – and the *Aborigines Act 1905* designed to protect Aboriginal people, should have brought the frontier violence to a close, exposing as they did some of the brutality with which Kimberley Aboriginal people were treated. This was not to be.

POSTSCRIPT

*'In No Other Country are the Aborigines
Better Looked after than in West Australia'*

In the years after the Roth Report, many issues remained unresolved in regard to policy, treatment and especially the policing of Aboriginal people in the Kimberley. Attention to these fluctuated according to which political party was governing Western Australia and which of the many government departments were overseeing Aboriginal affairs. It also fluctuated according to the continuing influence of humanitarian bodies, the influence of the Commonwealth government, the broader Australian sentiment about the treatment of Aboriginal people and the actions of Kimberley Aboriginal people themselves.

In the 1905 state election Francis Connor lost his seat for the new electorate of the Kimberley, the result of the amalgamation of the East and West Kimberley the year before.[1] Henry Prinsep used the 1905 annual report of the Aborigines Department to launch a spirited defence of his own position as chief protector and a thinly veiled attack on those who had prevented him from acting on the Aboriginal welfare issues he had been reporting on 'for years past'.[2] Prinsep left the position in 1907 and was replaced in 1908 by the chief inspector for fisheries, Charles Frederick Gale, who would hold the two positions. The vocal resident Kimberley magistrates were removed from the district: Dr Dodwell Brown was transferred to Port Hedland, Dr Belgrave was moved to Sharks Bay,[3] and by 1906 Richard Wace had moved to Esperance.[4] Federal minister John Forrest continued to defend Western Australia from allegations of cruelty, after William Redmond in the British House of Commons in mid-1907, criticised the continuing practice of neck chaining of detained Aboriginal people. Forrest, in his now familiar rhetoric, boldly asserted:

> There is no inhumanity. I will undertake to say that in no other country are the Aborigines better looked after than in West Australia. Every policeman, and every justice is a protector of aborigines. I would be the last to sanction anything in the nature of cruelty, but as one who understands the circumstances I have no hesitation in saying a great fuss is being made about a very little.[5]

Policing could still be dangerous. In mid-1906 Constable Forbes was speared twice but survived when his police party was arresting an Aboriginal offender on the Charnley River in the West Kimberley.[6] Episodes of Aboriginal people showing concerted resistance to Europeans and avoiding arrest for extended periods still occurred. Major from the East Kimberley was outlawed in 1908 and Challaday was outlawed at Broome in 1910.[7] Violence between competing interests on pastoral stations continued. Police were still involved in shootings and 'bush blacks' were still killing 'station blacks' well into the twentieth century.[8]

What of the commercial status of the Kimberley cattle industry? We have seen how pastoralists and politicians often alleged that the industry was close to collapse due to Aboriginal depredations, but by 1905 cattle numbers had nearly doubled from their 1902 figure of close to 200,000 to 380,994, with 20,000 leaving the Kimberley ports (which were running at full capacity) of Derby and Wyndham for sale each year, and by 1910 cattle numbers in the West Kimberley alone were 300,000.[9] The success of the cattle industry is also shown by the massive reduction in pastoral stations' debts to banks.[10] Three companies (Connor, Doherty and Durack; Forrest and Emanuel and Co; and Copley Bros) dominated the industry, which by 1910 had spread to overseas markets such as the Philippines.

However, the market to Perth for south East Kimberley pastoralists was restricted as cattle were affected by tick infestation and the pastoralists were prevented from driving their cattle through the West Kimberley in case they spread the infestation.[11] The solution was an exploration by surveyor Alfred Canning and party in 1906 over what would become the Canning Stock Route. The plan was that cattle could be transferred over a distance of 1150 miles (1850 kilometres) from Halls Creek to Wiluna in the Midwest region. This stock route, over extraordinarily harsh and often drought-ravaged country, traversed at least nine different Aboriginal language groups.

After the expedition (led by Aboriginal guides), allegations surfaced that the exploration party had caught local Martu men along the route and forced them to drink salty water or eat salty meat until they were so dehydrated they would reveal water sources.[12] In addition there were charges that the party had chained and abused the Aboriginal guides and forced them to find water. They also were charged with destroying Aboriginal water sources, stealing Aboriginal weapons and possessions and abusing Aboriginal women.[13] These allegations led to the *Royal Commission to inquire into the Treatment of Natives by the Canning Exploration Party 15 January – 5 February 1908*.[14] Of the three commissioners two were familiar names, Chief Inspector for Aborigines and Fisheries C.F. Gale and Warden John Finnerty. The third was Labor party parliamentarian George Taylor MLA.[15] The Royal Commission which, unlike the Roth Report, was not tabled in parliament, found the detaining of Aboriginal guides 'reasonable', and exonerated Canning and his party of all charges and then approved the construction of the route.[16]

The role of Kimberley police changed many times over the years, and took on activities such as reporting the numbers of children of mixed descent and people with venereal disease (largely described as 'syphilis'), smallpox, and later leprosy which spread throughout the Kimberley. From 1908 those infected, or thought to be infected according to police assessment, would subsequently be removed and segregated on 'Lock Hospitals' at the male-only Bernier Island and female-only Dorre Island.[17] Amateur ethnographer Daisy Bates, who spent some time on the islands doing research, described them bleakly:

> There is not, in all my sad sojourn among the last sad people of the primitive Australian race, a memory one-half so tragic or so harrowing, or a name that conjures up such a deplorable picture of misery and horror unalleviated, as these two grim and barren islands of the West Australian coast that for a period, mercifully brief, were the tombs of the living dead.[18]

The Derby Leprosarium opened in 1936.[19]

There were substantial changes in the practice of imprisoning Aboriginal people. James Isdell, who became the travelling protector of Aborigines in 1907, suggested in 1909 that the imprisonment of Aboriginal people for cattle killing was 'doing more harm than good'.[20] In 1909 police were issued with directives to only arrest 'ringleaders' for cattle killing and not whole groups. This resulted in an enormous drop in imprisonment. In 1910 only ten Aboriginal people were imprisoned in Derby and twelve in Wyndham, compared to 197 for the previous year.[21]

The Aborigines Department continued until 1909 when it was amalgamated with the Fisheries Department to form the Aborigines and Fisheries department. In 1910 reserve and feeding stations, as recommended by Roth and supported by Chief Protector Gale, were established at Greenvale, Mt Barrett and Nicholson Plains (later renamed Moola Bulla Station) on some 1,123,000 acres of land. In 1911 the 1,000,000 acre Marndoc and Violet Valley stations were established the year after. Moola Bulla also became a place where children of mixed descent were sent for schooling. After initial financial losses Moola Bulla Station not only became successful and profitable for the government as a cattle station, but also, as it was designed to do, successfully reduced cattle killing and so kept Aboriginal people out of gaol. Housing, schooling and work opportunities were provided at Moola Bulla and by the 1950s some 260 people lived there.[22]

In 1911 the 'per head' ration allowance for prisoners that had been so misused by police was changed to a system of prepaid payment for stores, thus removing the potential for exploitation.[23] In the same year the *Aborigines Act Amendment Act* was passed ordaining that Aboriginal people could no longer be convicted of a crime on their own evidence and that the same rules of evidence would now apply to Aboriginal offenders as they did to 'any other race'.[24] By 1913, this alteration to the law, together with the establishment of Moola Bulla, resulted in further drops in imprisonment. Prison costs for the Aboriginal population, which had been between £7000 and £9000 per year, dropped to just £330 per year.[25] And in 1913 Gale concluded in the *Aborigines and Fisheries Department Annual Report* that the gaoling of Aboriginal people for cattle killing in the Kimberley had 'proved a failure' and an expensive one at that as it was shown to be no deterrent to crime.[26] Importantly, he went further, arguing that the money spent on policing and court proceedings over the years were 'uselessly spent' and should be directed to other areas.[27] Gale also reported that other introduced diseases continued to wreak havoc on local Aboriginal populations. In 1914 he reported an epidemic of measles, which started in Wyndham, had swept through the entire Kimberley district killing large numbers of people of all ages.[28]

After a new minority Labor government was formed in late 1914 the minister responsible for Aboriginal affairs, Rufus Henry Underwood, forcefully retired Gale from office. Gale's replacement was Auber Octavius Neville, a man who saw himself as a personal guardian for all Aboriginal people in Western Australia.[29] Underwood carried out severe cost cutting across the Aboriginal affairs areas. In conjunction with Neville they rejected funding for religious missions for Aboriginal people arguing they could not control what occurred there, such as marriages between Aboriginal people. Neville advocated strict implementation of the *Aborigines Act 1905* including segregation of children of mixed descent in state institutions such as Moore River Native Settlement and the separation of Aboriginal people on reserves.[30]

Despite Neville's objections missionaries continued their work in the Kimberley. Ernest Gribble (John Gribble's son) took up the Forrest River Mission at Oombulgurri in late 1913, and would make himself as controversial and unpopular in Western Australia as his father. In 1926 he exposed what became known as the Forrest River massacre (described later) and in 1928 proclaimed that 'no country in the world has done so little for its Aborigines as has Australia'.[31] He was removed from his post the same year.

The antagonism between the pastoralists and police over who was responsible for protection of cattle continued for decades. In 1907 Francis Connor, J. Blythe and other pastoralists made representations to the Western Australian government, complaining about stock losses due to Aboriginal 'depredations'.[32] In 1908 Connor was a witness in an all-party royal commission, which was appointed to inquire into and report upon the allegations of monopoly control (the 'meat ring') of the meat supply in Western Australia, its findings reported in the *Report of the Royal Commission to Inquire into and Report upon the Meat Supply*.[33] In the mid–1890s he was adamant that stock losses caused by Aboriginal people were crippling the cattle industry. By 1908 he had changed his tone, now saying, 'It's not so much the number they kill as the way they interfere with the cattle…nothing keeps cattle back more than to get them wild and nothing gets them wilder than the way they are raced by the natives'.[34] Overstating cattle losses due to Aboriginal people was still common but understating (or more accurately not mentioning) losses due to cattle duffing still occurred.[35] When asked at the Royal Commission, Connor refused to say where the 'small men', that is, small pastoralists, got their stock.[36] While Connor had lost his Kimberley electoral seat in 1905 it would not be long until another familiar Kimberley name took it over. In 1917, Michael 'M.P.' Durack, one of the pioneer pastoralists of the early 1880s, and significant figure through the 1890s, entered the Western Australian Legislative Assembly as the Nationalist Party member for the Kimberley.[37]

In early 1910 over 100 'warlike natives' were reported to have taken over Mt Hart Station, the station manager claiming that they would be forced to abandon it unless better police protection was sent. Police investigated, reporting that the allegation was 'greatly exaggerated', indeed that there was nothing unusual occurring there at all.[38] In 1925, in response to claims of 'native troubles' at the Secure Downs Station at Walcot Inlet, District Inspector Douglas reported to Police Commissioner Connell that he had instructed his police not to investigate because:

> Cattle killing attributable to not enough white labour employed. At Walcot [Sale and Secure Downs] about 4000 head roaming about a million acres. They can afford to lose 30 head a year, but they cry for help at one loss by natives. Natives do nearly all the work.[39]

And what of the police whose names appear most often in this story? After the political furore caused by the Roth Report had abated, PC Jack Inglis was transferred to Carnarvon and PC John Wilson resigned, though he stayed in the Kimberley district. Inglis resigned shortly afterwards, returned to the Kimberley and started up a store in Halls Creek and died in 1917.[40] Wilson married an Aboriginal woman from Mt Barrett, and became a stockman and station boss in various Kimberley locations until his death in 1939.[41] Reginald Spong, who employed Wilson at times, took up the Glenroy pastoral lease in the north Kimberley and died in 1916.[42]

One of the witnesses to the 1908 Royal Commission was Thomas McLaughlin who, as we have seen, was wanted for killing (and burning) Aboriginal men and police had a warrant for murder issued against him. However, despite the overwhelming witness testimony (and attempts at arrest by PC James Campbell Thomson) by 1908 the charges against him were withdrawn, as no witnesses could be located.[43] McLaughlin returned to the East Kimberley in 1906 and took up cattle farming with, as he said, a small herd he had brought back. He sold his herd to the Forrest and Emanuel Company.[44]

August Lucanus left the police force and opened a hotel in Wiluna.[45] James Campbell Thomson also left the police force in 1907 and became part owner of Billiluna Station near Halls Creek. In April 1911 whilst driving cattle down the newly opened Canning Stock Route, Thomson and two others were killed by being bludgeoned by local Aboriginal people north of Wiluna.[46] In 1911 Commissioner of Police Fred Hare selected Sergeant Pilmer, whose skills as a bushman the police continued to utilise, to go on a patrol to track down the alleged Aboriginal killers of the three men (one of whom was Thomson). *The Southern Cross Times* reported 'Pilmer's Pilgrimage' asserting he was the right man for the job because he had undertaken 'more nigger hunts than any person in Australasia'.[47] The patrol, which was openly known and reported on as a successful 'punitive expedition' on which seven Aboriginal people were shot dead, included two future police commissioners, David Hunter and William Douglas.[48] Aboriginal testimony recorded in Pilmer's diary during the trip suggests drovers using the Canning Stock Route were shooting a lot of Aboriginal people which may have been the reason for Thomson's reprisal death.[49] Pilmer resigned from the force in October 1919 and died in 1952.[50]

Despite intense criticism, Frederick Hare remained commissioner of police until 1912, even surviving an attempt on his life in April 1907, when a disgruntled ex-police officer entered his office and shot him twice.[51] In 1912, a year after a Labor government led by John Scaddan won power in the Western Australian parliament, Hare, along with Inspector Lawrence, was forcibly retired.[52] Robert Connell, who was well regarded in government, replaced him and remained commissioner for the next twenty years.[53] Patrick Troy also continued to be held in high regard and reached the rank of chief inspector before becoming a warden and resident magistrate at Coolgardie and Kalgoorlie; he died in July 1916.[54] Sub Inspector Michael Brophy, also highly regarded for his policing, died on 5 February 1923 having served thirty-six years in the Western Australian police force.[55] Craven Ord was a lieutenant of the Western Australian mounted infantry in the Boer War but returned to Western Australia in 1902. He earned two campaign medals in South Africa and was made an honorary major in the Australian army. He died in Perth in November 1923.[56]

Other police returned to the Kimberley. Inspector Edwin Overend Drewry was stationed at Northam in 1913 and a year later was at Broome Station. In correspondence to Commissioner Connell in 1915 it is clear he had not moderated his approach to policing. He suggested to Connell that Kimberley Aboriginal people still on *country* should be forcibly moved and that the current policing approach, mercifully now free of systematic police 'dispersals', should return to being more punitive.[57] Sadly for Drewry, these sentiments, which were enthusiastically endorsed and adopted by the commissioner of police twenty years previously, were now considered grossly inappropriate and Commissioner Connell told him so:

> It is just as well for you to very clearly understand that the old system of dealing with natives will not again be resorted to. This is a point upon which politicians of all shades are fully agreed upon.[58]

Overend Drewry died in 1920 whilst on long service leave.[59]

Neville Green and later Mary Anne Jebb have described a process of pacification of Aboriginal people on pastoral country during the twentieth century, showing that violence against Aboriginal people continued and was used as a means by which pastoralists and police maintained authority.[60] Massacres of Aboriginal people and the burning of their bodies to hide the evidence continued in the Kimberley. These incidents were consistent with earlier massacres: a general policy of pacification; payback for stock or horse loss; killing or threatening to kill a colonist; and access to Aboriginal women.

In 1915 Mick Rhatigan, who had stayed in the Kimberley and continued to work as a telegraph linesman working out of Turkey Creek station, was implicated in a massacre at Mistake Creek near Turkey Creek.[61] Constable John Franklin Flinders reported that Rhatigan and his two native workers, Nipper and Wyne, 'shot and burned five or six Aborigines'. The 'charred remains' of two bodies were found at Mistake Creek and the bodies of five others named 'Hopples, Nellie, Mona, Gypsy and Nittie' were found some distance away.[62] This was supposedly in reprisal for allegedly killing Rhatigan's cow.[63] Rhatigan died in 1920 and entered Kimberley frontier folklore. He became one of many characters in Keith Willey's 1971 book, *Boss Drover,* a biography of a Kimberley drover named Matt Savage.[64] The Mistake Creek massacre is retold in the book and refers to an unnamed 'cold heartless bloke' who killed 'plenty' of Aboriginal people.[65] This was clearly a reference to Rhatigan.[66] There were others like him. Jebb, utilising oral history from her informants who worked on the Kimberley stations, describes a notoriously cruel stockman named Jack Carey who, between 1919 and 1924, 'threatened most Aboriginal people he met' and shot and burnt large numbers of men, women and even children.[67] Carey once shot a man so he could take his Aboriginal wife, Mary Karraworla. There appeared no limit to his pettiness. Carey shot three stockmen dead because they had left the goat yard gate open.[68]

There was another massacre at Geegully Creek, Mowla Bluff, in 1916. This, Nyikina Elder John Watson said, was a punitive expedition by police and other colonists that took place after a station manager, Georgie 'George' Why, was assaulted by some Mangala people over a small dispute.[69] Instead of just arresting those involved the punitive expedition wreaked havoc on men, women and children from the Nyikina Mangala people. They were rounded up, ordered to collect firewood, and then shot and their remains burnt.[70] Watson says he was told that three or four hundred were killed and only three escaped.[71]

Despite Walter Roth's recommendations, Aboriginal trackers and native assistants continued to be armed, and remained so not just for months or years after 1905 but for decades. In 1921, stockman Harry Annear was speared on Bedford Downs Station, the reason, an Aboriginal witness said, was that he was stealing young women.[72] The police responded when one policeman, a 'volunteer', the aforementioned John Wilson and five native assistants, proceeded to shoot and terrorise Aboriginal people at Mt Barnett to such an extent that they sought sanctuary in the Forrest River mission. This episode prompted Ernest Gribble to write the first of many letters to Chief Protector of Aborigines A.O. Neville alerting authorities to what was happening.

> the native trackers [pursuing Annear's killers]…after making themselves friendly to a large camp of natives, had suddenly shot them all in a ravine difficult to escape from. They further state no white police were there only 'police boys' [native assistants]…[73]

In 1924 Constable Flinders, who worked out of Broome, Halls Creek and Turkey Creek, was investigated after reports that his native assistants had shot Aboriginal people on a two-month bush patrol (over 740 miles; 1191 kilometres) to capture and kill outlaw 'Willie'.[74] Flinders had such a fearsome reputation that Aboriginal people had 'an absolute terror' of him.[75]

Figure 13.1. Constable John Flinders with police trackers Moses, Dilli, Paddy and Brophy at Halls Creek, circa 1925. Battye Library, 012443D. Charles Edward Flinders collection of Kimberley photographs. Courtesy State Library of Western Australia.

That same year another notorious massacre occurred at Bedford Downs Station. Aboriginal oral history remembers the violence. Kija Elder Dottie Watby describes how, in response to the killing of a valuable bullock, Kija and Worla people were forced to cut wood. They were then given damper (bread) that was poisoned. After they were poisoned (as Dottie stated, they 'drop down') managers and stockmen from adjacent stations, including

Jack Carey, started shooting everyone.[76] She remembered that they 'Killem all dem blackfellas, family for us mob.' Then:

> Right, dem bin gettem dat wagon, gettam dat donkey and pullem la fire. They loadem in big pile like dat and chuckem allawood, chuckem, chuckem, chuckem, kerosene, chuckem kerosene, Dey bin light dat fire – terrible.[77]

In 1926 Ernest Gribble exposed the infamous Forrest River massacre at Oombulgurri, prompting such national and international media attention that it generated yet another royal commission, the *Royal Commission of Inquiry into Alleged Killing and Burning of Bodies of Aborigines in East Kimberley and into Police Methods when Effecting Arrests* chaired by George Tuthill Wood.[78] The 'Forrest River massacre', in reality a series of massacres, shows how police and pastoralist violence continued.[79] In May 1926 Lumbia speared a stockman of Nulla Nulla Station, Fred Hay, allegedly because Hay had raped one of Lumbia's wives.[80] In mid-1926, in the wake of the killing, two police parties consisting of thirteen men – Leopold Rupert Overheu (part-owner of Nulla Nulla Station with Hay), Daniel Murnane (a vet), two special constables (Bernard Patrick O'Leary, a pastoralist from Gallway Valley Station, and Richard John Jolly), seven armed native assistants and forty-two horses led by PCs Dennis Regan and James St Jack – went on a six-week pursuit of Lumbia. The party had between 400 and 500 rounds of ammunition and each man carried a .44 Winchester rifle.[81]

Before the expedition Leopold Overheu wrote a letter to his father reporting the murder, which was published in the Perth *Daily News*. Overheu wrote of the 'treacherous mobs' on his run that were killing his cattle and had killed other pastoralists. Included were two sentences with ominous undertones:

> I'm going to pilot the police out and give them any assistance possible, so as to make the place safe for myself in the future. In officially reporting the matter to police, I've asked for a strong force to go out, and also that the natives be dealt with drastically.[82]

During the expedition through late June and early July Aboriginal people were shot and burned. Estimates of the number killed vary widely. In 1968 the brother of Overheu told historian Neville Green that his brother had admitted to killing 300 people though this figure is unlikely and is in dispute.[83] In the subsequent Royal Commission Inspector Douglas gave evidence that 'sixteen natives were burned in three lots: one, six and nine'.[84] Commissioner Wood reduced this figure and found that eleven people had been murdered and their remains burnt.[85]

What became apparent at the Royal Commission was that threats to witnesses were real and collusion amongst colonists, many of whom had funded the police defence, continued to conceal the killing of Aboriginal people in the Kimberley. After the expedition on 7 July 1926 Bernard Patrick O'Leary confronted Gribble in Wyndham saying: 'If ever I catch you on my tracks in any nigger business I will put a bullet in you.'[86] Much to the exasperation of Commissioner Wood, three key eyewitnesses, the native assistants on the patrol, 'escaped to the bush' just days before they were due to testify despite being under police watch (or perhaps because they were under police watch). Their witness statements contradicted police evidence.[87] Other eyewitnesses now claimed they saw 'nothing'.[88] The defence lawyer coached one eyewitness, Wood implied.[89]

Inspector Douglas was not hopeful of finding the truth, telling the commissioner of police that it would be 'extremely difficult to prove anything' with 'everyone in the district except Rev. Gribble up against me'.[90] Wood noted that the 'conspiracy of silence' around the massacre was so extensive that it included 'the entire European community of Wyndham and all associated pastoral holdings in the district'.[91] He also found that evidence from the 'whites' and police suggested collusion, was full of discrepancies and generally defended the police. He regarded Sergeant Buckland's evidence as particularly 'unreliable and unsatisfactory'.[92]

PCs Regan and St Jack were the only members of the expedition charged with murder, though with the absence of eyewitness testimony, a magistrate found the evidence insufficient to go to trial.[93] The two constables were subsequently transferred out of the Kimberley.[94] Buckland served in the Kimberley for over thirty years. Shortly after the Royal Commission he too was transferred to Roebourne;[95] like the police of the 1880s and 1890s he was moved when the spotlight shone on his actions. And what of the native assistants? As almost nothing they did was recorded and their stories were never told, we will never know.

However, this Royal Commission reaffirmed that native assistants (now also at times called 'black trackers') were still armed and shooting Aboriginal people without police supervision, although the commissioner of police denied that they were even armed.[96] Sergeant Buckland openly admitted to the commissioner that they were indeed sent out armed and that there had never been any regulation allowing it.[97] In 1927 A.O. Neville reported that he had written to the minister for the North West 'many times' between 1922 and 1924 alerting him to the fact that native assistants were still armed, were often sent out without police supervision and were involved in 'promiscuous shooting' of other Aboriginal people.[98]

William Harris, who as we saw in chapter 12 made allegations of cruelty by colonists and the Western Australian government, continued to agitate for the rights of Aboriginal people. Harris, legally classed a 'half-caste', fell under the oppressive regime of the *Aborigines Act 1905*. In March 1913 he protested the proposed segregation of Aboriginal people on reserves and their forced removal to institutions such as Moore River Native Settlement.[99] While Harris farmed in the Morawa district and paid rates and taxes, he was prohibited from voting and entering hotels thereby denying him one of the few social interactions available in rural areas.[100]

Following the reporting of the Forrest River massacres in November 1926 Harris wrote to *The Sunday Times* stating that since the inauguration of responsible government in Western Australia the situation for Aboriginal people had gone from 'bad to worse' and was now 'intolerable'.[101] Aboriginal people, Harris wrote, were tired of being 'robbed, and shot down, or run into miserable compounds' and there were 'heaps of human bones mixed with cartridge shells' in different parts of Western Australia that confirmed the massacres. Harris asserted that when people hear of the 'dispersion of natives' they think a 'few shots are fired over their heads to scatter them. This dispersion takes a different form altogether.'[102]

On 9 March 1928 Harris along with six other Western Australian Aboriginal men formed the 'Native Union', the first Aboriginal deputation to march on the Western Australian parliament. The group met with Premier Philip Collier to voice their concerns and demand exemption from the *Aborigines Act 1905* and gain what Harris said was the freedom to 'live our lives our own way'.[103] Despite the premier promising to look into their complaints the deputation achieved very little. Indeed, conditions for Aboriginal people, especially those considered 'part-Aborigines', became more oppressive, not less, and more Aboriginal people became subject to a new Act.[104]

Influenced by international trends in eugenics in the USA and Germany, Neville became a strong advocate for 'breeding out the colour' across generations, through intermarriage with lighter castes and eventually with whites.[105] Neville claimed the natural outcome was for 'black to go white' and eventually, after generations, all distinguishing Aboriginal features would disappear. Perversely, the problems perceived to be created through intermarriage between Aboriginal people and non-Aboriginal people would be solved by more aggressive legislatively controlled intermarriage.[106] This way, through 'assimilation', Aboriginal people would effectively become white Australians.[107] The legislative tools to enable this plan were created with the introduction of the *Native Administration Act 1936*, which amended the 1905 Act. This Act gave the government unprecedented powers over Aboriginal people regarding their movement and lifestyle options.[108] Now, all marriages between Aboriginal people had to be approved by the commissioner of native affairs. No Aboriginal parent had the guardianship of his or her children or 'half-caste' children.[109] Commissioner of Native Affairs A.O. Neville had complete control over children until they were 21 years old and children continued to be removed from their parents. Furthermore, Aboriginal people could be ordered onto reserves and confined there; they could be ordered out of towns and other prohibited areas.[110] Typically this role fell on the police.

This legislation with its associated regulations only guaranteed further repression of Aboriginal people's legal status and thus their civil rights. In fact, Aboriginal people had more equal rights over a hundred years earlier when Governor Stirling claimed the Swan River Colony in 1829. How this new legislation was to aid in the original legislative goal of 'protection' and 'civilising' of Aboriginal people was unclear. Indeed, as Paul Hasluck remarked, it is difficult to see what other possible outcome could be achieved when Aboriginal people were confined 'within a legal status that has more in common with that of a born idiot than that of any other class of British subject'.[111]

In 1934 allegations of 'slavery in the north' appeared again in the *Anti-Slavery Reporter* in London and Melbourne leading to a further royal commission: *The Report of the Royal Commissioner Appointed to Investigate, Report, and Advise upon Matters in Relation to the Condition and Treatment of Aborigines* conducted by H.D. Moseley.[112] The commission focused on the fate of mixed-race children and reinforced segregation and institutionalisation.[113] Moseley visited Moola Bulla and Violet Valley stations and recommended developing Moola Bulla so that more Aboriginal people could be employed and that children of mixed descent could undergo vocational training.[114] Moseley noted that in comparison to other states, Western Australia, with the largest Aboriginal population, continued to be one of the lowest funding states. For example, in 1934 Western Australia with an Aboriginal population of 29,021 expended £28,340; Queensland with a population of 16,956 spent £41,128.[115]

Moola Bulla Station continued in operation for many years, until in 1955 the then Commissioner for Native Welfare, Stanley Middelton, recommended to the government that it be sold. He had come to regard it as an 'administrative bugbear' that was 'crushing' his department.[116] The new owners gave the Aboriginal tenants and workers at Moola Bulla verbal and written assurances that they would all be kept on or allowed to stay, but immediately after the sale the entire population of over 250 Aboriginal people, including eighty children attending school, was evicted and forced into Halls Creek, camping on the town racecourse.[117] Others found their way to the United Aborigines Mission in Fitzroy Crossing.[118]

In 1938 there was yet another investigation into the legality of allowing native assistants to carry firearms. Police correspondence indicates that the issue remained as legally doubtful as it had been in the 1890s. The *Aborigines Act 1905,* section 47, required all Aboriginal people to have a licence to use a gun, but in Wyndham in 1938 the resident magistrate found that, despite native assistants working closely with police, they were not members of the police force so he refused to grant licences to them. The fact that they still routinely carried firearms made them in breach of the *Aborigines Act* and also the *Gun Licensing Act*.[119] As ever, these Acts were simply ignored.[120] As late as 1944, the Department of Native Affairs was still investigating native assistants shooting Aboriginal people.[121] The legal status of native assistants was only clarified in 1975 with an amendment to the *Police Act 1892*. Aboriginal assistants were granted the title Police or Aboriginal Aides, updated to, Aboriginal Police Liaison Officers in the mid-1990s. Section 38A of the amendment gave police aides the same powers as their officer.[122]

Treatment of prisoners on the way to court also remained a contentious issue. As late as 1927 it was reported that an Aboriginal prisoner by the name of 'Billy Joe' was forcibly marched 'on the chain' over sand that was so hot that it caused 'the soles of his feet from toes to heel to come off' leaving him permanently crippled.[123] By 1934 neck chains had been banned in the Northern Territory under Commonwealth government orders yet they continued to be used in Western Australia for many years.[124] In 1949 photographs of chained Aboriginal prisoners at Fitzroy Crossing appeared in overseas periodicals and the British Anti-Slavery Society took the issue up with Western Australian Premier Ross McLarty and even with the Soviet Union's foreign minister at the United Nations.[125] Western Australian authorities attempted to defuse the allegations by saying the photograph was 'old' and taken before 1939, but this was discredited by a Kimberley local who confirmed the photo was recent.[126]

Police finally ceased using neck chains in 1956, but this was not a sign that they had chosen to adopt more humane methods of prisoner transfer.[127] Rather, the numbers of 'bush blacks' had reduced significantly, and police motor vehicles had largely replaced horses so the chaining and walking of prisoners behind mounted police was redundant.[128] As ever expedience and practicality was the reason for change.

Allegations of slavery continued to be made. A year after Aboriginal people became Australian citizens under the 1948 Commonwealth *Nationality and Citizenship Act*, the owner of Corunna Downs pastoral station admitted that there was what he called 'a mild form of slavery' in the North and that pastoralists could not work the stations profitably without Aboriginal 'slave labour'.[129] Part payments to stockmen expanded in the 1950s although the system was chiefly a fixed wage 'pocket money' payment administered by the station owner that coincided with the commencement of some welfare payments which gave Aboriginal people some freedoms to move.[130]

Other changes were afoot. In late 1953 the new state Labor Minister for Native Welfare William Hegney described the provision of the *Native Administration Act 1936* as a failure and 'punitive, outmoded and reprehensible' to the Aboriginal community.[131] Under Commissioner of Native Affairs Stanley Middleton (1948-1962) many of the more repressive elements of state legislation were dismantled and Aboriginal people had some civil rights restored. In 1954 The *Native Welfare Act* repealed the *Native Administration Act* and removed many of the specific clauses relating to the employment of Aboriginal people.[132] The duty of police as honorary Aboriginal protectors ended and police were replaced with paid native welfare officers. One of their duties was to check that station owners were fulfilling their responsibilities to Aboriginal workers to provide minimum living and working conditions. On many stations native welfare officers considered the living conditions for workers as squalid, lacking the most basic items of sanitation and water, suggesting the profits of the station, as ever, took precedence over Aboriginal welfare.[133]

The *Native Welfare Act 1963* finally repealed the *Aborigines Act 1905* and removed what was now called the commissioner of native welfare's powers to remove children from their parents. During the 1960s many racially discriminatory clauses in Commonwealth legislation governing the payment of old-age pensions and maternity allowances to Aboriginal people were removed. However, Aboriginal people were still being gaoled for cattle killing.[134] And, as the 1960s passed, equal wages arrived, welfare payments expanded and technological changes made many workers redundant, leading to widespread eviction of Aboriginal people from pastoral stations all over the Kimberley and, hence, from their very *country.*

The 1967 referendum removed two discriminatory amendments to the Australian Constitution. For the first time Aboriginal people were to be counted in the national census and the Commonwealth government could now make national laws for Aboriginal people.[135] Following the referendum new policies of self-determination facilitated the 'homelands movement' where Aboriginal people, the funding for which was split between the Commonwealth and state governments, were encouraged to return to *country* significant to them. In Western Australia hundreds of discrete communities were established, the majority of them being in the Kimberley.

In 1972 the *Native Welfare Act* was replaced with the *Aboriginal Affairs Planning Authority Act (AAPA Act)*. This Act officially removed government intervention into the lives of Aboriginal people and stipulated that an Aboriginal Affairs Advisory Council would be established to consult with Aboriginal people, for their 'economic, social and cultural advancement'.[136] This department, which was not well funded relative to other government agencies, would later become the current Department of Aboriginal Affairs. But if a new world was on the horizon for Aboriginal people, freedom from repressive legislation and its associated overt racism, emerging rights and formal legal land rights were more difficult to achieve. In the mid-1970s, as Aboriginal sites of significance and spiritual beliefs were being recognised and acknowledged in the wider non-Aboriginal community, Commonwealth land rights legislation was being discussed and Aboriginal people were now being called the Traditional Owners. The Commonwealth government introduced the *Aboriginal Land Rights (Northern Territory) Act 1976* allowing freehold title, that is, Aboriginal ownership of the land and the ability to manage the resources of the land.[137]

In Western Australia rights to land were more tenuous, as was revealed in the disputes over Noonkanbah Station on the Fitzroy River on Nyikina and Walmajarri *country*.[138] The Emanuel brothers had established this station in 1885 and Aboriginal labour had worked it for generations. In 1976, in an initiative begun by the Labor government of Gough Whitlam, the Noonkanbah pastoral lease was purchased by the Aboriginal Land Fund to be developed by the Yungngora people.[139] This group had previously worked on the station but in 1971 had 'walked off' due to disputes over pay, conditions and ill-treatment.[140]

The mid-1970s coincided with a mining boom in the North West and Kimberley and by 1978, despite Aboriginal ownership of the Noonkanbah pastoral lease, nearly 500 claims for oil and mineral rights had been pegged on the land. Traditional Owners were not consulted and, under Western Australian law, had no right of veto.[141] Western Australian government reports, written under the aegis of the *Aboriginal Heritage Act 1972*, showed the areas in the vicinity of Pea Hill or Umpampurru were considered significant and sacred sites.[142] Despite this, Liberal Premier Charles Court, who was hostile to the notion of Aboriginal land rights, was determined that the exploration should go ahead and, backed by a forceful police presence, drilling commenced. This episode sparked national and international concern about rights of Aboriginal people in Western Australia.[143] In 1980 Aboriginal leaders took the Noonkanbah case to the Subcommittee on the Prevention of Discrimination and Protection of Minorities in the United Nations Commission on Human Rights.[144]

Meanwhile the changing social status of Aboriginal people was reflected in political representation. Some 90 years after Alexander Forrest had first held the seat of the West Kimberley, Halls Creek local Ernest 'Ernie' Bridge, representing the Labor Party, was voted into the seat of the Kimberley. Bridge became the first Aboriginal person in the Western Australian parliament and, in 1986, the first to be a cabinet minister in an Australian government.[145] In other significant 'firsts', Carol Martin became the first Aboriginal woman to be elected to any Australian federal, state or territory parliament and succeeded Bridge in 2001. And in 2013 Kija Elder Josephine 'Josie' Farrer succeeded Martin.

The 1980s land rights debates remained contentious. In March 1983 the newly elected federal Labor Party led by Bob Hawke promised national legislation in which were proposals to give Aboriginal people freehold title, the power to veto mining, the protection of Aboriginal sites on country and shares in mining royalties.[146] In May 1983 the new Western Australian Labor government led by Brian Burke announced an inquiry, headed by lawyer Paul Seaman, QC, into the implementation of land rights in the state. Burke had promised this as one of his government's pre-election policies.[147] Seaman had interviewed and accepted submissions from hundreds of Aboriginal people across Western Australia.[148] Amongst Seaman's proposals was to give Aboriginal people freehold title to land and the power to veto mining developments.[149]

In early 1985 the Western Australian Aboriginal Land Bill 1985 was passed in the Legislative Assembly but was defeated in the Legislative Council by the Liberal and Country parties.[150] In 1985 the Australian Labor Party adopted national land rights as policy, though in a heavily modified form reducing powers of veto. Following heavy pressure and racially based media campaigning from the mining and pastoral industry, which speciously suggested private property was under threat, the policy stalled and Premier Burke rejected it.[151] The following year the national land rights policy was abandoned.[152]

Following the failure of both the Western Australian Aboriginal Land Bill 1985 and Commonwealth land rights legislation the Commonwealth and state governments agreed to a form of compensation by jointly funding new programs such as the Aboriginal Land Agreement and the Aboriginal Communities Development

Program. The Western Australian government supplied land for Aboriginal residential needs in areas of traditional significance that were often in remote areas. The Commonwealth would fund essential and municipal services.[153]

In the 1992 Mabo Decision, the assumption that Australia was unoccupied when Europeans arrived, *terra nullius*, was finally overturned by the High Court leading to the legislative provision of the Commonwealth *Native Title Act 1993*. The native title era promised much to Aboriginal people and while some significant agreements have been finalised many of the social and economic benefits are yet to be realised. Under the *Native Title Act* Aboriginal people were required, despite the destructive effect of European colonisation on people and culture, including policies to remove, if not eradicate, the people themselves, to demonstrate that they had maintained a traditional connection to their land and waters since sovereignty, where acts of government had not extinguished it.

Significantly, native title does not provide Aboriginal people with ownership of the land (freehold) nor the ability to stop development, as land rights promised to, but rather generates a limited number of rights, held under pre-sovereignty laws and customs. And, while native title is symbolically important in recognising some Traditional Owners, the process has created calamitous intra-Aboriginal conflict over whom in each claim, possibly among hundreds of people, holds the native title. Despite the high burden of proof on Aboriginal claimants, in August 2001 the Tjurabalan native title claim, south of Halls Creek into the Great Sandy and Tanami deserts, was the first Kimberley claim to be determined, and native title, generating limited rights, was recognised in other parts of the Kimberley. In April 2007 the Yungngora people had their native title recognised over Noonkanbah.[154]

While the Commonwealth government could make laws for Aboriginal people since the 1967 referendum, legacy issues led to an ongoing battle with the states about responsibility over who funded what and what programs were delivered. The frequently fractious relationships, particularly when opposing political parties at the Commonwealth/state level were in government, have often led to incoherent and conflicting policies. One of these issues is what is called 'remote communities'. The Commonwealth government had indicated, since 2006, that funding for Aboriginal communities should be a matter for the states and in September 2014 the Commonwealth government announced that it would no longer fund essential and municipal services to remote communities. Concerned, in part, about the ability to service many of the smaller communities, the Western Australian government signalled the possible closure of many. While at the time of writing this has not yet occurred, in the Kimberley the result would be the movement of hundreds of Aboriginal people back into major towns, which could exacerbate existing social problems, problems that self-determination, the homelands movement and reconnecting Aboriginal people to their traditional *country* were designed to forestall.

While Aboriginal culture, traditions and connection to *country* are now being recognised and respected more widely and 'reconciliation' is the approach of non-Aboriginal Australians, many legacies of colonisation remain unaddressed and largely unacknowledged.[155] The current joint Commonwealth and state government policy response called 'Closing the Gap' aims to equalise Aboriginal and non-Aboriginal life experiences. Evidence suggests the gap is not closing.[156] Intergenerational trauma from the many decades of oppression, historical neglect and marginalisation has occurred. The separation of Aboriginal children from their families and their *country* (the 'Stolen Generations') created intractable mistrust between Aboriginal people and agents of government. Exclusion from mainstream education and economies has resulted in unemployment. For the majority, an inability to secure freehold land tenure or rights to resources in their *country* that would generate incomes and equity has resulted in enduring intergenerational poverty. Confusion around Aboriginal policy and program delivery and the funding responsibilities between the state and Commonwealth has meant great uncertainty for Aboriginal communities.

Aboriginal people, especially the young, are still chronically over-represented in the criminal justice system with over-policing resulting in over-imprisonment. Today many Aboriginal children see being chased by police and being sent to a detention centre as a 'rite of passage' to adulthood, according to Western Australia's chief justice.[157] These same children are often imprisoned as a result of the culmination of a series of minor offences. Incarceration rates for Aboriginal children are 24 times higher than for non-Aboriginal children across Australia, and 52 times higher in Western Australia.[158] Statistics show, as of June 2015, the rate of imprisonment of Aboriginal children in Australia is not only the highest in Western Australia but also one of the highest rates in the world.[159] These issues are often described as the enduring 'Aboriginal problem'. As we have seen, in the 1880s and 1890s, imprisonment was the fate of many Aboriginal people, especially from the pastoral regions of the North. Much has changed since 1905, but some things may not have changed at all.

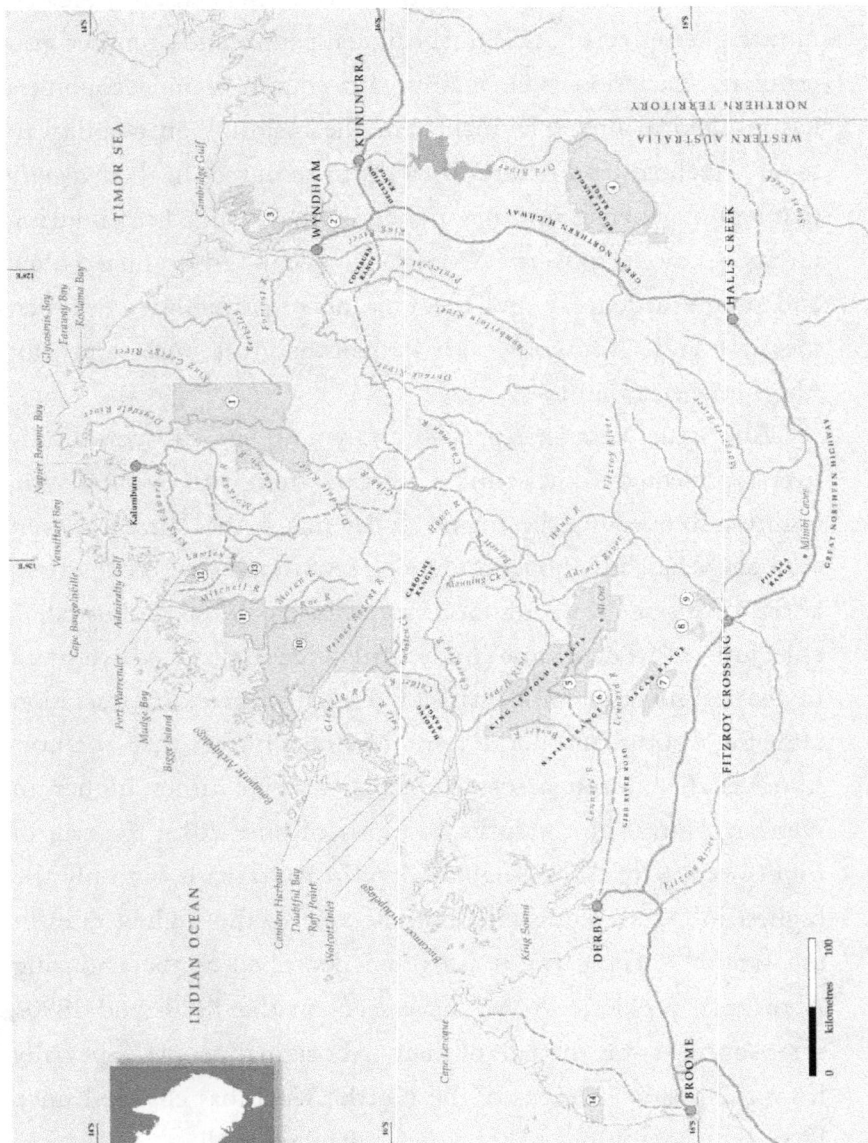

APPENDIX 1

Map of the Kimberley. Courtesy Mike Donaldson.

Major parks and reserves (in shaded areas) are:

Drysdale River National Park
Parry Lagoons Nature Reserve
Ord River Nature Reserve
Purnululu National Park and Conservation
King Leopold Ranges Conservation Park
Windjana Gorge National Park
Devonian Reef Conservation Park
Brooking Gorge Conservation Park
Prince Regent National Park
Geike Gorge National Park
Mitchell River National Park
Lawley River National Park
Laterite Conservation Park
Coloumb Point Nature Reserve

APPENDIX 2

Total losses of horses, cattle and sheep directly attributed to Aboriginal people in the Kimberley District 1896–1902.[1]

Year	Losses directly attributed to Aboriginal people	Total stock losses in the Kimberley (East and West combined)
Horses		
1896	14	1300
1897	15	1263
1898	61	787
1899	1	736
1900	1	741
1901	1	667
1902	10	870
Total	103	6364
Cattle		
1896	1507	4774
1897	1522	6279
1898	1927	9890
1899	574	6881
1900	506	7575
1901	312	9130
1902	162	8366
Total	6510	52,895
Sheep		
1896	50	100,178
1897	270	133,672
1898	100	68,638
1899	100	95,398
1900	100	58,325
1901	NA	40,233
1902	NA	78,659
Total	620	575,103

---

1   WA Statistical Register 1896–1902. After 1902 no differentiation was made between the cause of stock losses. Quoted In A. Gill, 'Aborigines, Settlers and Police in the Kimberleys 1887–1905', *Studies in Western Australian History*, no. 1, 1977, p.22.

NOTES

List of Abbreviations
AIATSIS – Australian Institute of Aboriginal and Torres Strait Islander Studies
CSO – Colonial Secretary's Office
HRO – Historical Records of Australia
RWAH – Royal Western Australia Historical Society
SROWA – State Records Office of Western Australia
UWA – University of Western Australia
WAPD – Western Australian Police Department

Introduction
1   *Western Mail*, Saturday 18 February 1905, p.24; J. Lydon, *The Flash of Recognition: photography and the emergence of Indigenous rights*, Sydney, NewSouth Publishing, 2012.
2   For a detailed description of Wyndham gaol see 'The Ways of Wyndham, Native Gaol Life, How the Blacks are Treated', *The Daily News*, 21 October 1903, p.8; H. Klaatsch, 'Some Notes on Scientific Travel Amongst the Black Population of Tropical Australia in 1904, 1905, 1906', *Australasian Association for the Advancement of Science*, Adelaide, 1907, p.583.
3   W.E. Roth, *Royal Commission on the Condition of the Natives, Presented to Both Houses of Parliament by His Excellency's Command*, (hereafter Roth Report), Perth, Government Printer, 1905, 2nd Session, no.5. <http://www.parliament.wa.gov.au/intranet/libpages.nsf/WebFiles/Royal+Commissions++Report+of+the+Royal+Commission+on+the+condition+of+the+natives/$FILE/Report+of+the+Royal+Commission+on+the+condition+of+the+natives.pdf>
4   See witness statement by PC Inglis, ibid., pp.92–5.
5   See for example 'The Aborigines Question, The Investigations by Dr Roth', *Western Mail*, 4 February 1905, p.14.
6   'Blacks Brutally Treated. Western Australian Sensation. Report of a Commissioner. Horrible Cases of Cruelty. Blacks Half-Starved. And Terrorised Over', *The Sydney Morning Herald*, 1 February 1905, p.6; 'Dr Roth's Disclosures. Council of Churches. Horror-Stricken and Sorrowful', *The Daily News*, 15 February 1905, p.5; 'The Aborigines of West Australia, Dr Roth's Report, A Shocking State of Affairs', *The W.A. Record*, 4 February

1905, p.4; 'Congo Cruelties Paralleled. Dr Roth Demolishes the System. The "Sunday Times" Strictures Authoritatively Endorsed. "The Slave State" – Isn't it Justified?' *The Sunday Times*, 5 February 1905, p.5.

7 For English and Scottish reports see 'Black Man's Burden', *Manchester Courier and Lancashire General,* 2 February 1905, p.8; 'Australian Scandal', *Dundee Courier,* 2 February 1905, p.5; 'Australian Race Problem', *Manchester Courier and Lancashire General Advertiser,* 11 January 1907, p.7.

8 See witness statement by PC Inglis, Roth Report, 1905, pp.92-5.

9 'The Aborigines Question, Testimony by P.C. Fletcher to Walter Roth', *The West Australian*, 15 February 1905, p.2. See also testimony by PC Inglis, Roth Report, Pt. 1352, p.88.

10 Roth Report, p.13.

11 Witness statement by George Scott, gaoler, Wyndham, Roth Report, 1905, op.cit., Pt. 1752, p.103.

12 *Rules and Regulations for the Government and Guidance of the Police Force of Western Australia as Approved by John Forrest*, Perth, Sands and McDougall 1898, Pt. 647, p.123.

13 Witness statement by William Paterson, gaoler, Broome, Roth Report, Pt. 498, p.54.

14 See witness statement by PC Inglis, Roth Report Pt. 1562, p.94.

15 'The Black Slaves of West Australia,' *Truth,* 6 March 1904, p.8

16 Witness statement by Octavius Burt, Sheriff and Controller General of Prisons, Roth Report, Pt. 241, p.44.

17 Witness statement by George Scott, gaoler, Wyndham, Roth Report, Pt. 1747, p.103.

18 Witness statement by PC Inglis, Roth Report, Pt. 1487, p.92.

19 Witness statement by James John Pond, gaoler, Roebourne, Roth Report, Pt. 1068, p.77.

20 Witness statement by Octavius Burt, Roth Report, Pt. 246, p.44.

21 Witness statement by Dodwell Brown, Resident Magistrate and District Medical Officer, Wyndham, Roth Report, Pt. 1667, p.99.

22 Witness statement by William Paterson, gaoler, Broome, Roth Report, Pt. 513, p.54.

23 Witness statement by George Scott, gaoler, Wyndham, Roth Report, Pt. 1765, p.104.

24 Roth Report, p.20.

25 Witness statement by Mr Alfred Earnest Victor Woodroffe, Roth Report, p.84.

26 Witness statement by Constable John Inglis, Halls Creek Police Station, Roth Report, p.94.

27 Roth Report, p.18.

28 S.J. Hallam, 'The First Western Australians', in C.T. Stannage (ed.), *A New History of Western Australia,* Perth, UWA Press, 1981, p.35.

29 Exact Aboriginal population figures for the pre-European colonisation period are difficult to calculate; however, early studies suggested a figure

of 10,000. See A.P. Elkin, 'Social Organisation in the Kimberley Division of North Western Australia', *Oceania*, vol. 2, no. 3, March 1932, p.297. Peter Biskup later put the figure at an estimated 30,000, in P. Biskup, *Not Slaves, Not Citizens: the Aboriginal problem in Western Australia 1898–1954*, St Lucia, Queensland, University of Queensland Press, 1973, p.20. More recent studies by White and Mulvaney, quoting economic historian Noel Butlin, also suggest a figure of 30,000. See J.P. White and D.J. Mulvaney, 'How Many People?' in D.J. Mulvaney and J.P. White (eds.), *Australians to 1788*, New South Wales, Fairfax, Syme and Weldon, 2007, pp.115–17. See also G. Bolton, 'Black and White After 1897', in T. Stannage (ed.), *A New History of Western Australia*, Perth, UWA Press, 1981, p.124.

30 'The Kimberley Police District', *The West Australian,* 12 September 1902, p.6.

31 G. Bolton, *A Survey of the Kimberley Pastoral Industry from 1885 to the Present*, Master's thesis, University of Western Australia, 1953, p.133.

32 A detailed newspaper report can be found at 'Pastoral Settlement in Western Australia', *The West Australian*, 29 August 1885, p.7. This editorial regarded the Kimberley as the 'only remaining portion of the large continent of Australia hitherto unoccupied'.

33 *The Perth Gazette and Western Australian Journal*, 10 September 1836, p.760.

34 Roth Report, p.3.

35 See for example J. Bohemia and B. McGregor, *Nyibayarri: Kimberley tracker*, Canberra, Aboriginal Studies Press, 1995; B. Shaw, *My Country of the Pelican Dreaming: the life of an Australian Aborigine of the Gadjerrong, Grant Ngabidj, 1904–1977,* Canberra, Aboriginal Studies Press, 1981; *Banggaiyerri: the story of Jack Sullivan as told to Bruce Shaw*, Canberra, Australian Institute of Aboriginal Studies, 1983; *When the Dust Come in Between: Aboriginal viewpoints in the East Kimberley prior to 1892, as told to Bruce Shaw*, Canberra, Aboriginal Studies Press, 1992; S. Hawke and M. Gallagher, *Noonkanbah: whose land, whose law,* Fremantle, Fremantle Arts Centre Press, 1989; M. Munro and M.A. Jebb (ed.), *Emerarra: a Man of Merarra*, Broome, Magabala Books, 1996; V. Ryan (ed.), *From Digging Sticks to Writing Sticks: stories of Kija women*, Perth, Catholic Education Office, 2001; C. Clement, *Historical Notes Relevant to Impact Stories of the East Kimberley*, East Kimberley Working Paper, East Kimberley Impact Assessment Project, Canberra, 1989, no. 29; H. Ross (ed.) and E. Bray (translator), *Impact Stories of the East Kimberley*, East Kimberley Working Paper no. 28, East Kimberley Impact Assessment Project, Canberra, 1989; S. Kinnane, *Shadowlines*, Fremantle, Fremantle Press, 2003, p.17.

36 See for example C. Johnson, 'Long Live Pigeon!' in *Meanjin* (Aboriginal Issue), vol. 36, no. 4, December 1977; H. Pedersen, *Pigeon: an Aboriginal rebel, a study of Aboriginal European conflict in the West Kimberley, North Western Australia during the 1890s,* Honours thesis, Murdoch University, 1980; C. Johnson, *Long Live Sandawarra*, Melbourne, Hyland House, 1987; H. Pedersen and B. Woorunmurra, *Jandamarra and the Bunuba Resistance*, Broome, Magabala Books, 1995; J. Nicholson, *Kimberley Warrior: the story of Jandamarra,* Sydney, New South Wales, Allen & Unwin, 1997; K. Moran, *Pigeon,* Carlisle,

Hesperian Press, 2011.

37 A. Gill, 'Aborigines, Settlers and Police in the Kimberleys 1887–1905', *Studies in Western Australian History,* no. 1, 1977, pp. 1–28; C. Clement, 'Monotony, Manhunts and Malice: East Kimberley law enforcement, 1896–1908', *Early Days,* vol. 10, part 1, 1989, pp. 85–96; N. Green, *The Forrest River Massacres,* Fremantle, Fremantle Arts Centre Press, 1995; K. Moran, *Sand and Stone Foreign Footprints: police in the Kimberley 1880–1890s,* Carlisle, Hesperian Press, 2009.

38 J. Milroy, 'Aboriginal Culture and Society', in J. Gregory and J. Gothard (eds.), *Historical Encyclopedia of Western Australia,* Nedlands, UWA Press, 2009, p.11.

39 WAPD, 'Detailed Police Reports from Police in the Kimberley, Letter from LC P. Troy to M.S. Smith', 3 October 1883, SROWA, AN 5/6, Cons. 129, File 856/1883.

40 *Police Gazette,* 19 November 1884, no. 47, p.191.

41 WAPD, Halls Creek Police Station, Occurrence Book, SROWA, AN 5/1, Cons. 1422, File 1585/1888.

42 WAPD, Halls Creek Police Station, Occurrence Book, SROWA, AN 5/1, Cons. 1422, File 208/91.

43 WAPD, 'PC Lee Submits Resignation', SROWA, Cons. 430, File 1077/1883. He would later rejoin.

44 CSO, 'Sergeant Troy, Derby – Shooting of Aboriginal Native Julemar alias Dan by George Riley', SROWA, AN 24, Cons. 527, File 1977/1884.

45 CSO, 'Sub Inspector Troy, Derby – Native "Charcoal" Kicked to Death by ex PC John Eatch', SROWA, AN 24, Cons. 527, File 4947/1886.

46 See also WAPD, 'Derby – Journal of PC Sherry During Visit to Lennard River Enquiring into Report of Chaining of Natives at Clune and Butters Station', SROWA, Cons. 430, File 917/1884.

47 'News and Notes', *The Inquirer and Commercial News,* 14 April 1893, p.29.

48 John Forrest speech, *Western Australian Parliamentary Debates,* 1894, p.925, quoted in F. Crowley, *Big John Forrest 1847–1918,* Nedlands, UWA Press, 2000, p.141.

49 'Wyndham News, Trouble with the Natives, A Black Tracker Killed', *The West Australian,* 26 March 1895, p.3.

50 Roth Report, p.13.

51 In 1870 Governor Frederick Weld oversaw the establishment of representative government in Western Australia, which was largely symbolic as the governor still retained executive control of the colony and only men who owned property of a certain value were allowed to vote. B.K. De Garis, 'Political Tutelage 1829–1890', in C.T. Stannage (ed.), *A New History of Western Australia,* Perth, UWA Press, 1981, pp.325–6.

52 *Country* is the term for different language group areas of Aboriginal land and custodianship but can also include areas of the sea along the coast.

53 For a detailed discussion of the etymology of the term 'myall' see E.E. Morris, *Austral English: a dictionary of Australasian words, phrases and usages,*

Cambridge, Cambridge University Press, 2011 (first published 1898), p.311.

54 See T. Roberts, *Frontier Justice: a history of the Gulf Country to 1900*, Brisbane, University of Queensland Press, 2005.

55 *Police Act 1892:* an act to consolidate and amend the law relating to the police in Western Australia, <http://www.austlii.edu.au/au/legis/wa/consol_act/pa189275/>.

56 'The Police Report', *The West Australian*, 11 October 1907, p.4.

57 'The Police: the Commissioner Report 1897–98', *The West Australian*, 14 July 1898, p.3.

58 Police constable breakdown was Derby eight; Wyndham seven; Goldfields eight: WAPD, Derby Police Station, Letterbook entry by Sub Inspector Troy, 'Being the Letter book for the Derby Police Station from 2.8.1886–16.4.1892', 19 August 1887, SROWA, AN 5, Cons. 241/1.

59 Police records are now heavily relied upon in Native Title cases as they show Aboriginal *country* and boundaries in great detail.

60 WAPD, 'PC. Sherry, Kimberley District – Application for Some Remuneration for Learning the Native Language of the District', SROWA, AN 24, Cons. 527, File 2907/1884.

61 WAPD, 'Derby Police Station, Sub Inspect, Report by Sub Inspector Troy to Commissioner Phillips', 2 August 1887, SROWA, AN 5, Cons. 241/1.

62 I. Idriess, *Outlaw of the Leopolds,* Sydney, Angus and Robertson, 1952.

63 WAPD, 'Capture of Wild Natives in the Oscar and Barrier Ranges', 10 November 1894, SROWA, Cons. 430, File 3548/97.

64 Online versions can be found at State Library of Western Australia, The Police Gazette of Western Australia, <http://www.slwa.wa.gov.au/find/eresources/police_gazettes>.

65 CSO, 'A.B. Wright – Hostility of Natives and Protection for Telegraph Construction Party, as to', Letter from George Phillips to Inspector Lodge, Derby, 5 December 1888, SROWA, AN 24, Cons. 527, File 3258/1888. Other police records such as Duty books, Forage books and Ration books are not included as they generally do not contain detailed written information. See also Inspector Lodge's statement regarding confidentiality, WAPD, Halls Creek Police Station, Letterbook, 21 December 1888, SROWA, Cons. 1422.

66 'Commissioner Phillips to Police, Circular Order 6/6657', *The Police Gazette*, August 1895, No 32, 1895, p.141.

67 ibid.

68 See L. Marsh and S. Kinnane, 'Ghost Files: the missing files of the Department of Indigenous Affairs archives', in C. Choo and S. Hollbach (eds), *Studies in Western Australian History: History and Native Title*, no. 23, 2003, pp. 111–27.

69 WAPD, See report by Sergt R. Troy delivering mail across the flooded Ord River, 'East Kimberley District, Wyndham Station. Report on Goldfields Mail; also Daily Diary of Trip made by Sgt. Troy, P.C. Pollard and Native Assistant Johnny, via Stations to Goldfields during May 1889', 28 May 1889, SROWA, AN 5/1, Cons. 430, File 939/1889. Troy had to 'break the mail open and dry it out'.

70   The main files on the 'Hall's Creek Post Office, File 2969/1888 – Telegraph Office at Hall's Creek – Advise Erection of, and File 1718/1889 – Erection of Post and Telegraph Office at Hall's Creek', have been destroyed.

71   See for example 'News from Wyndham. Further Native Depredations', *The Inquirer and Commercial News*, 28 September 1894, p.8.

72   'Private Diary of Sergeant Thomas Wheatley During Police Patrols from Wyndham from 6 November to 23 December 1895', 11 November 1895, Battye Library, Cons.1266A.

73   Argyle Police Station, Uncatalogued Police File, Western Australian Police Service, 'Journal of PC Thomson and Barney, Bow and Joe from 12 January 1902 to 10 February 1902', 30 January 1902; Argyle Police Station, Uncatalogued Police File, Western Australian Police Service, 'Journal of PC Thomson whilst on Shooting Case of Two Aborigines Named Friday and Jimmy from 15 November 1901 to 23 December 1901', 16 December 1901; Argyle Police Station, Uncatalogued Police File, Western Australian Police Service, 'Journal of PC Hill and Police Assistant Barney from 23 November 1901 to 6 December 1901', 27 November 1901; Argyle Police Station, Uncatalogued Police File, Western Australian Police Service, 'Journal of PC Hill from 4 December 1901 to the 21 December 1901 whilst Distributing Statistics', 16 December 1901.

74   This file was discovered when the SROWA archive files were put online at http://aeon.sro.wa.gov.au/investigator/investigator.htm. See WAPD, 'Alleged Murder of Two Natives by Thomas McLoughlin [sic]', AN 5/2, Cons. 430, File 1382/1905.

75   Also known as Accession 430.

76   WAPD Records are housed under: AN 5 for the year 1885, AN 5/1 for the years 1886–1904; 5/2 1904–1919; 5/3 1920–1959. With the exception of 'Early Police Dept Records', which are housed at AN 5/6, Cons. 129, 1878–1879.

77   A point made by R. Foster, '"Don't mention the war": frontier violence and the language of concealment', *History Australia*, vol. 6, no. 3, 2009, p.68.

78   H.G.B. Mason, *Darkest Western Australia: A Treatise Bearing on the Habits and Customs of the Aborigines and the Solution of 'The Native Question', 1909*, facsimile edition, Perth, Hesperian Press, 1980, p.1.

79   ibid., p.1.

80   ibid., p.3.

81   ibid.

82   ibid. See also: 'The more one fraternises with him the more insolent he becomes. The white man who allows a nigger to sit at the table, or plays cards, boxes, or skylarks with him is much to be deplored', p.40.

83   ibid., p.56.

84   G.H. Broughton, *Turn Against Home,* Brisbane, Jacaranda Press, 1965.

85   K. Willey, *Boss Drover,* Adelaide, Rigby Books, 1971. Savage stated 'shooting Aborigines was fairly common in the bush', p.12.

86   A. Forrest, *North West Exploration; journal of expedition from DeGrey River to*

Port Darwin, Perth, Government Printer, 1880; M. Donaldson and I. Elliot (eds.), F.H. Hann, *Do Not Yield to Despair: Frank Hugh Hann's exploration diaries in the arid interior of Australia 1895–1908*, Perth, Hesperian Press, 1998; D.W. Carnegie, *Spinifex and Sand*, facsimile edition, Perth, Hesperian Press, 1982 (first published 1898); T. Willing and K. Kenneally (eds.), *Under a Regent Moon: a historical account of pioneer pastoralists Joseph Bradshaw and Aeneas Gunn at Marigui Settlement, Prince Margaret River, Kimberley, Western Australia, 1891–1892*, Perth, Department of Conservation and Land Management, 2002; G. Buchanan, *Packhorse and Waterhole: with the first overlanders to the Kimberley*, facsimile edition, Carlisle, Western Australia, Hesperian Press, 1984 (first published 1933); G.H. Lamond, *Tales of the Overland: Queensland to Kimberley in 1885*, Perth, Hesperian Press, 1986. For a comprehensive listing of references see C. Clement, *A Guide to Printed Sources for the History of the Kimberley Region of Western Australia*, Perth, Centre for Western Australian History, University of Western Australia and UWA Press, 1996, especially Section C: 'Exploration and Later Expeditions'.

87 Carnegie, *Spinifex and Sand*, p.189.

88 ibid., pp.339–50.

89 C. Clement and P. Bridge (eds.), R.H. Pilmer, *Northern Patrol: an Australian saga,* Perth, Hesperian Press, 1996, p.14. The original manuscript of this account is available at the Battye Library.

90 See for example George Nunkiarry 'no bell ringin no bell ringin' talking about police in 1886 in Kimberley Language Resource Centre, *Moola Bulla: in the shadow of the mountain*, Magabala Books, 1996, p.37, and Ben Duncan, 'A Story from Old Times', p.54.

91 C. Clement and P. Bridge (eds.), *Kimberley Scenes: sagas of Australia's last frontier,* Perth, Hesperian Press, 1991. Memoirs of Western Australian police officers in the North West and other works in the life-writing genre vary from the sympathetic works of E. Morrow (The Law Provides, London, Herbert Jenkins, 1937) to the caustic chronicle of G.J.C. McDonald's *Beyond Boundary Fences*, (Perth Hesperian Press, 1986).

92 M. Durack, *Kings in Grass Castles,* Australia, Corgi Books, 1990 (first published Constable, 1959); M. Durack, *Sons in the Saddle*, London, Bantam Australia, 1983; see also M.P. Durack, 'Pioneering in the East Kimberley', *Western Australia Historical Society Journal and Proceedings*, vol. II, part XIV, 1933, pp.1–46. There is a strong tradition in Australian literature of romanticising pastoral station and remote settlement. See Jeannie Gunn's *We of the Never Never*, being Elsey Station on the Roper River in the Northern Territory. J. Gunn, We of the Never Never; and, The Little Black Princess, Sydney, Angus & Robertson, 1982.

93 J.S. Battye (ed.), *The History of the North West of Australia: embracing Kimberley, Gascoyne and Murchison districts. With descriptive and biographical information compiled by Matt. J. Fox,* Perth, Hesperian Press, 1985 (first published 1915), pp.118–19.

94 M.P. Durack, 'Pioneering in the East Kimberley', p.19.

95   ibid, p.43. This paper was read at the Western Australia Historical Society in August 1932 where, after the killing of John Durack by Aboriginal people, 'a punitive expedition consisting of police and volunteers was sent out against the natives, a lot of whom were killed'. 'Historical Society. Early Days in the Kimberley', *The West Australian*, 1 August 1932, p.10.

96   M. Durack, *Kings in Grass Castles,* p.336. For Lucanus reference see A. Lucanus, 'Goldfields of the North', in Clement and Bridge (eds), *Kimberley Scenes*, pp.2–57. See also B. Wilson, *A Force Apart: a history of the Northern Territory police force 1870–1926*, Hong Kong, Peacock Academic Press, 2001, p. xix.

97   B. Niall, *True North: the story of Mary and Elizabeth Durack*, Melbourne, Text Publishing, 2012, p.26.

98   Ross (ed.) and Bray (translator), *Impact Stories of the East Kimberley*. Also known as Gardiya, Guddeeyu.

99   ibid. See the accounts by Frank Budbaria at Turkey Creek, p.2: 'They used to do em down here, they shot big mob just down the bottom camp here (Turkey Creek) that side of the flat rock there. Just past the bottom camp, they shot big mob there. Burn em up on the flat rock on top;' account by Biddy Malingal of massacres at Lightman Creek, Violet Valley and Panton River, p.6: 'They [*kartiya*] went back and shot all the babies, kids and teenage girls and all the old ladies, their mothers and grandmothers, and all the old men. They had all climbed up trees, poor things. They shot them like birds and they fell down like birds. Finished. They got all the wood, and piled it up. They pulled all the people and put them on top of the wood, put kerosene on it and lit the fire;' account by Kenny Bray, p.9; account by Bob Nylcas, p.12.

100 Clement, *Historical Notes Relevant to Impact Stories of the East Kimberley*. See also P. Smith, *Mistake Creek Massacre Site,* Flinders University, https://www.flinders.edu.au/ehl/archaeology/research-profile/current-projects/kimberley-frontier-archaeology-project/mistake-creek-massacre-site.cfm

101 Bohemia and McGregor, *Nyibayarri.*

102 Shaw, *My Country of the Pelican Dreaming*; *Banggaiyerri, The Story of Jack Sullivan, as told to Bruce Shaw*; *When the Dust Come in Between*; and Munro and. Jebb (ed.), *Emerarra*.

103 M.A. Jebb, *Blood, Sweat and Welfare: a history of white bosses and Aboriginal pastoral workers*, Perth, UWA Press, 2002.

104 Ryan (ed.), *From Digging Sticks to Writing Sticks.*

105 A.M. Chalarimeri, *The Man from the Sunrise Side*, Broome, Magabala Books, 2001; Munro and Jebb (ed.), *Emerarra*; E.J. Hudson and P. Lowe (eds), *Out of the Desert: stories from the Walmajarri Exodus*, Broome, Magabala Books, 2002.

106 P. Marshall (ed.), *Raparapa Kularr Martuwarra: stories from the Fitzroy River drovers*, Broome, Magabala Books, 1988, pp.226–7.

107 Hawke and Gallagher, *Noonkanbah*, pp.50-57.

108 ibid.

109 D.B. Rose, *Hidden Histories: black stories from Victoria River Downs, Humbert River and Wave Hill Stations*, Canberra, Aboriginal Studies Press, 1991.

110 ibid., p.111.

111 ibid., p.29.

112 T. Roberts, *Frontier Justice: a history of the Gulf Country to 1900*, St Lucia, University of Queensland Press, 2005.

113 A.P. Elkin. 'Social Organisation in the Kimberley Division of North Western Australia', *Oceania*, vol. 2, no. 3, March 1932, p.297.

Chapter 1: 'Schooling the Unruly Aboriginal into Obedience'

1   A.L. Haydon, *The Trooper Police of Australia: a record of mounted police work in the Commonwealth from the earliest days of settlement to the present time*, London, A. Melrose, 1911.

2   ibid.

3   ibid., p.329.

4   ibid.

5   J.S. Battye, *The Cyclopedia of Western Australia: an historical and commercial review: descriptive and biographical facts, figures and illustrations: an epitome of progress*, Adelaide, Hussey & Gillingham, 1912, p.528.

6   G.M. O'Brien, *The Australian Police Forces*, Oxford, Oxford University Press, 1960.

7   More recent histories of police forces which include backgrounds to Australian policing and a more thorough, though not necessarily complete, social context, include K. Milte, *Police in Australia: development, functions, procedures*, Sydney, Butterworths, 1977.

8   The first detailed study of an Australian police force only appeared in 1986 with Robert Haldane's social history of the Victorian police: R. Haldane, *The People's Force: a history of the Victorian Police*, Melbourne, Melbourne University Press, 1986. This was followed by R. Clyne, *Colonial Blue: a history of the South Australia police force*, Netley, South Australia, Wakefield Press, 1987, then William Ross Johnstone's history of the Queensland police, W.R. Johnstone, *The Long Blue Line: a history of the Queensland police*, Boolarong, Brisbane, 1992.

9   For a useful summary of these changes see H. Reynolds, 'The Breaking of the Great Australian Silence: Aborigines in Australian historiography 1955–1983', The Trevor Reese Memorial Lecture 1984, University of London, Institute of Commonwealth Studies, Australian Studies Centre, 30 January 1984, http://www.kcl.ac.uk/artshums/ahri/centres/menzies/research/Publications/1984ReeseLecture.pdf, accessed 30 June 2008.

10 A centralised police force had seventeen divisions, each with four inspectors and 144 constables.

11 A.A. Ramsay, *Sir Robert Peel*, Freeport, New York, Books for Libraries Press, 1969. They were also known as 'Peelers'.

12 See C. Emsley, *Policing and its Context 1750–1850*, London, Macmillan, 1983; S. Palmer, *Police and Protest in England and Ireland, 1780–1850*, Cambridge, Cambridge University Press, 1990; D. Taylor, *The New Police in Nineteenth-century England*, Manchester, Manchester University Press, 1997; D. Taylor,

Crime, Policing and Punishment in England, 1750–1914, London, Macmillan, 1998. For Scottish policing see D.G. Barrie, *Police in the Age of Improvement: police development and the civic tradition in Scotland 1775–1865*, Devon, Willan Publishing, 2008; K. Carson and H. Idzikowska, 'The Social Production of Scottish Policing 1795–1900', in D. Hay and F. Snyder (eds), *Policing and Prosecution in Britain 1750–1850*, New York, Clarendon Press, 1989; B. Godfrey and G. Dunstall, *Crime and Empire 1840–1940: criminal justice in local and global context,* Cullompton, Willan Publishing, 2005. For revisionist accounts of this view see B. Dodsworth, '"Civic" Police and the Condition of Liberty: the rationality of governance in eighteenth century England', *Social History,* 2004, vol. 2, no. 29, pp.199–216; A.T. Harris, *Policing the City: Crime and Legal Authority in London, 1780–1840.* Columbus, Ohio State University Press, 2004; E.A. Reynolds, *Before the Bobbies: the night watch and police reform in metropolitan London, 1729–1830,* London, Macmillan, 1998; R. Paley, '"An imperfect, inadequate and wretched system"? Policing London before Peel', *Criminal Justice History,* vol. 10, 1989.

13   J. McGowan, *Policing the Metropolis of Scotland: a history of the police and systems of police in Edinburgh and Edinburghshire, 1770–1833*, Mussleburgh, Turlough, 2010, p.296.

14   ibid., p.294.

15   R. Storch, 'The Plague of the Blue Locusts', *International Journal of Social History,* vol. 20, 1975, pp.60–90.

16   C. Edwards, 'Democratic Control of Police: how 19th century political systems determine modern policing structures', in M. Enders and B. Dupont (eds.), *Policing the Lucky Country,* Sydney, Hawkins Press, 2001, p.15.

17   ibid. Edwards shows that the modern police took on the role of conspicuous patrolling – asserting a police presence – through deployment of uniformed though unarmed police officers.

18   R. Storch, 'The Plague of the Blue Locusts', p.64.

19   See D. Philips, *Crime and Authority in Victorian England,* London, Croom Helm, 1977; D. Philips and R.D. Storch, *Policing Provincial England 1829–1856: the politics of reform,* London, Leicester University Press, 1999; W. Miller, *Cops and Bobbies: police authority in New York and London, 1830–1870,* Chicago, University of Chicago Press, 1973.

20   H.S. Cooper, 'The Evolution of Canadian Police', in W.T. McGrath and M.P. Mitchell (eds.), *The Police Function in Canada,* Toronto, Methuen Publications, 1981.

21   C. Emsley, *Gendarmes and the State in Nineteenth-century Europe,* Oxford, Oxford University Press, 1999. The term *maréchaussée* (or *marshalcy*) can also be used.

22   ibid.

23   C. Emsley, Gendarmes and the State in Nineteenth-Century Europe, Oxford, Oxford University Press, 1999, p.22.

24   D.M. Anderson and D. Killingray, 'Consent, Coercion and Colonial Control: policing the empire 1830–1940', in D.M. Anderson and D. Killingray,

Policing the Empire: government, authority and control, 1830–1940, Manchester, Manchester University Press, 1991, p.3.

25 See M. Finnane, 'The Varieties of Policing: colonial Queensland, 1860–1900', in Anderson and Killingray (eds), *Policing the Empire*, p.49.

26 Anderson and Killingray, *Policing the Empire*, p.5.

27 For studies of the 'Irish Model' in colonial settings see R. Hawkins, 'The "Irish model" and the Empire: a case for reassessment', in Anderson and Killingray (eds), *Policing the Empire*; G. Marquis, 'The "Irish Model" and Nineteenth-century Canadian Policing', *The Journal of Imperial and Commonwealth History*, vol. 2, no. 25, 1997; D. O'Sullivan, *The Irish Constabularies 1822–1922*, Dingle, Brandon, 1999.

28 For more on what is termed 'Irish' policing see S. Breathnach, *The Irish Police*, Dublin, Anvil Books, 1974; J. Herlihy, *The Royal Irish Constabulary*, Dublin, Four Courts Press, 1997; S.H. Palmer, *Police and Protest in England and Ireland, 1780–1850*, Cambridge, Cambridge University Press, 1990.

29 Anderson, and Killingray, *Policing the Empire 1830–1940*, p.3.

30 M. Finnane, 'Police and Politics in Australia – The Case for Historical Revision', *Australian and New Zealand Journal of Criminology*, vol. 23, 1990, p.218.

31 Michael Sturma's *Vice in a Vicious Society* and examples from Britain, particularly David Philips in *Crime and Authority in Victorian England*, reveal the changes in crime and the associated changes in policing patterns. The topic of crime in these histories is placed within the broader social context of industrialisation and urbanisation, unrest in the emerging labour market, fears about a 'criminal class' and the rise of organised crime. M. Sturma, *Vice in a Vicious Society: crime and convicts in mid-nineteenth century New South Wales*, St Lucia, University of Queensland Press, 1983; D. Philips, *Crime and Authority in Victorian England: the black country 1835–1860*, London, Croom Helm, 1977; see also T.A. Critchley, *A History of Police in England and Wales 1900–1966*, London, Constable, 1966; Phillips and Storch, *Policing Provincial England 1829–1856*; Palmer, *Police and Protest in England and Ireland 1780–1850*; Taylor, *The New Police in Nineteenth century England*.

32 M. Finnane (ed.), *Policing in Australia: historical perspectives*, Sydney, New South Wales University Press, 1987; J. Richards, *The Secret War: a true history of the Queensland native police*, St Lucia, University of Queensland Press, 2008, which is based on J. Richards, *A Question of Necessity: the native police in Queensland*, PhD thesis, Griffith University, 2005.

33 Finnane (ed.), *Policing in Australia: historical perspectives*; M. Finnane, *Police and Government: histories of policing in Australia*, Melbourne, Oxford University Press, 1994; M. Finnane, *Colonization and Incarceration: the criminal justice system and Aboriginal Australians*, London, 1997; M. Finnane, *Punishment in Australian Society*, Melbourne, Oxford University Press, 1997; M. Finnane and H. Douglas, *Indigenous Crime and Settler Law: white sovereignty after empire*, Basingstoke, Palgrave Macmillan, 2010.

34 Finnane, 'Police and Politics in Australia', p.218.

35 Taylor, *The New Police in Nineteenth century England*, p.2.
36 Finnane (ed.), *Policing in Australia*, p.10.
37 ibid., p.219.
38 R.W. Connell and T.H. Irving, *Class Structure in Australian History*, Melbourne, Longman House, 1992, p.93.
39 Making the very same point is D. Taylor, *The New Police in Nineteenth Century England: crime, conflict and control*, 1997, op.cit., p.3.
40 M. Finnane and S. Garton, 'The Work of Policing: social relations and the criminal justice system in Queensland 1880–1914', Part I, *Labour History*, no. 62, May 1992, p.54.
41 ibid.
42 ibid.
43 Finnane and Garton, 'The Work of Policing', p. 54.
44 ibid.
45 ibid.
46 Haldane noted 'Police drunkenness was a perennial problem' in Haldane, *The People's Force*, p.20; Sturma noted that 'Drunkenness amongst constables was apparently a universal problem' in M. Sturma, 'Policing the Criminal Frontier in Mid-nineteenth-century Australia, Britain and America', in M. Finnane (ed.), *Policing in Australia*, p.20.
47 C. McConville, '1888 – A Policeman's Lot', in A. Mcleary (ed.), *Australia 1888: a bicentennial history bulletin for the study of Australian history centred on the year 1888*, Bulletin no. 11, May 1983.
48 ibid., p.66.
49 R. Ward, *The Australian Legend*, Oxford, Oxford University Press, 1960, p.149.
50 ibid., p.144.
51 ibid., p.145.
52 M. Finnane, 'Police Rules and the Organisation of Policing in Queensland, 1905–1916', *Australian and New Zealand Journal of Criminology*, vol. 22, 1989, p.96; P. Robb, 'The Ordering of Rural India: the policing of nineteenth century Bengal and Bihar', in Anderson and Killingray, *Policing the Empire*, pp.127–8; J. Richards, *The Secret War: a true history of the Queensland native police*, 2008, op.cit.
53 See for example R.S. Hill, *Policing the Colonial Frontier: the theory and practice of coercive social and racial control in New Zealand 1767–1867*, Wellington, NZ Government Printer, 1986.
54 J. Richards, 'Moreton Telegraph Station 1902: the native police on Cape York Peninsula', proceedings of the History Of Crime, Policing and Punishment conference, Canberra, December 1999, p.5, quoted in B. Wilson, *A Force Apart: a history of the Northern Territory police force 1870–1926*, Hong Kong, Peacock Academic Press, 2001, pp.48–9.
55 N. Loos, *Invasion and Resistance: Aboriginal–European relations on the North Queensland frontier 1861–1897*, Canberra, Australian National University Press, 1982, p.23; see also A. Vogan, *The Black Police: a story of modern*

Australia, London, Hutchinson & Co., 1890; E. Kennedy, *The Black Police of Queensland*, London, Murray, 1902; R. Evans, K. Saunders and K. Cronin, *Race Relations in Colonial Queensland: a history of exclusion, exploitation, and extermination*, St Lucia, University of Queensland Press, 1975.

56 M.H. Fels, *Good Men and True: the Aboriginal police of the Port Phillip district 1837–1853*, Melbourne, Melbourne University Press, 1988.

57 ibid., p.87.

58 G.T. Wood, *Royal Commission of Inquiry into Alleged Killing and Burning of Bodies of Aborigines in East Kimberley and into Police Methods when Effecting Arrests*, Perth, Government Printer, 1927, p.72.

59 P. Marshall (ed.), *Raparapa Kularr Martuwarra: stories from the Fitzroy River drovers*, Broome, Magabala Books, 1988, p.223.

60 L. Skinner, *Police of the Pastoral Frontier: native police 1849–1859*, St. Lucia, University of Queensland Press, 1975, p.13.

61 ibid.

62 Richards, *The Secret War*.

63 ibid., p.208.

64 ibid., p.200.

65 South Australia administered the Northern Territory from 1863. G. Reid, *A Picnic With the Natives: Aboriginal–European relations in the Northern Territory to 1910*, Melbourne, Melbourne University Press, 1990; B. Wilson, *Sillitoe's Tartan in Northern Australia: a view of black and white policing in the Northern Territory, 1884 to 1935*, Honours thesis, Northern Territory University, 1996; Wilson, *A Force Apart*; R. Foster, R. Hosking and A. Nettelbeck, *Fatal Collisions: the South Australian frontier and the violence of memory*, Adelaide, Wakefield Press, 2001; A. Nettelbeck, 'Writing and Remembering Frontier Conflict: the rule of law in 1880s central Australia', *Aboriginal History*, vol. 28, 2004, pp.190–206; A. Nettelbeck and R. Foster, *In the Name of the Law: William Willshire and the policing of the Australian frontier*, Adelaide, Wakefield Press, 2007; R. Foster and A. Nettelbeck, *Out of the Silence: the history and memory of South Australia's frontier wars*, Adelaide, Wakefield Press, 2012.

66 The Northern Territory was part of colonial New South Wales from 1825 to 1863, excluding a brief time between February and December 1846 when it was part of the colony of North Australia.

67 Wilson, *A Force Apart*, pp.206, 322.

68 Nettelbeck, 'Writing and Remembering Frontier Conflict. p.191; see also Nettelbeck and Foster, *In the Name of the Law*, p.179.

69 Nettelbeck and Foster, *In the Name of the Law*, pp.2–3.

70 H. Pilmer, *Northern Patrol: an Australian saga*, C. Clement and P. Bridge (eds), Hesperian Press, 1998, p.110.

71 Noongar men Tommy Dower and Tommy Pierre were guides on Alexander Forrest's 1879 expedition to the Kimberley: *Northern Territory Times and Gazette*, Saturday 18 October 1879, p.3. See also M. Allbrook, 'Imperial Family': the Prinseps, empire and colonial government in India and Australia*, PhD thesis, Griffith University, 2009; T.R. Moreman, *The Army in India and the*

Development of Frontier Warfare, 1849–1947, London, Macmillan, 1998.

72 P. Curtin, *Disease and Empire: the health of European troops in the conquest of Africa,* Cambridge, Cambridge University Press, 1998, pp.16–18, quoted in J. Richards, *The Secret War,* p.10.

73 See K. Hopkins, *Conquerors and Slaves,* Cambridge, Cambridge University Press, 1978; V. Hanson, *The Western Way of War,* Oxford, Oxford University Press, 1989; J. Richards, *The Secret War,* p10.

74 Richards, *The Secret War,* p.185.

75 F. Smitha, 'India's Sepoy Mutiny', *Macrohistory and World Timeline* 2015, <http://www.fsmitha.com/h3/h38sep.htm>, accessed 29 June 2016. See also J. Richards, *The Secret War,* p.186.

76 D. Killingray, 'Colonial Warfare in West Africa 1870–1914', in J.A. De Moor and H.L. Wesseling (eds), *Imperialism and War: essays on colonial wars in Asia and Africa,* Leiden, EJ Brill / Universitaire Pers Leiden, 1989, p.146.

77 M. Echenberg, *Colonial Conscripts: the tirailleurs Sénégalais in French West Africa, 1857–1960,* Portsmouth, Heinemann, 1991. See also J. Lunn, '"Les Races Guerrieres"': racial preconceptions in the French military about West African soldiers during the First World War', *Journal of Contemporary History,* vol. 34, no. 4, 1999, pp.517–36.

78 ibid., p.209; see also A. R. Graybill, *Policing the Great Plains: rangers, mounties, and the North American frontier, 1875–1910,* Lincoln, University of Nebraska Press, 2007, p.13.

79 ibid.

80 Sturma, 'Policing the Criminal Frontier in Mid-nineteenth-century Australia, Britain and America'.

81 ibid.

82 For a history of the water police see M. McKeough, *Rescues, Rogues and Rough Seas: 150 years of water police in Western Australia,* Fremantle, Western Australian Water Police and Police Historical Society, 2001.

83 Convicts were not an issue for the Kimberley police as they were not allowed north of the Murchison district.

84 C. Rowley, *The Destruction of Aboriginal Society,* Canberra, Australian National University Press, 1970, p.123.

85 ibid. See also C. Rowley, *Recovery: the politics of Aboriginal reform,* Melbourne, Penguin, 1986.

86 H. Reynolds, 'Violence, the Aboriginals, and the Australian Historian', *Meanjin,* vol. 31, no. 4, 1972; H. Reynolds (ed.), *Aborigines and Settlers: the Australian experience, 1788–1939,* Melbourne, Cassell Australia, 1972; H. Reynolds, 'Racial Violence in North Queensland', in B.J. Dalton (ed.), *Lectures on North Queensland History, Second Series,* Townsville, James Cook University, 1975; H. Reynolds, *The Other Side of the Frontier,* Melbourne, Penguin Books, 1982; H. Reynolds, *Frontier: Aborigines, settlers and land,* Sydney, Allen & Unwin, 1987; H. Reynolds, *With the White People: the crucial role of Aborigines in the exploration and development of Australia,* Melbourne, Penguin, 1990; H. Reynolds, 'Violence in Australian History', in D. Chappell,

P. Garbosky and H. Strang (eds.), *Australian Violence: contemporary perspectives*, Canberra, Australian Institute of Criminology, 1991; H. Reynolds, 'The Unrecorded Battlefields of Queensland', in Reynolds (ed.), *Race Relations in North Queensland*, Townsville, James Cook University, 1993; H. Reynolds, *This Whispering in Our Hearts*, Sydney, Allen & Unwin, 1998; H. Reynolds, *An Indelible Stain: the question of genocide in Australia's history*, Melbourne, Viking, 2001; R. Broome, 'The Struggle for Australia: Aboriginal-European warfare, 1770–1930', in Michael McKernan and Margaret Browne (eds), *Australia: two centuries of war and peace*, Canberra, Australian War Memorial, 1988; R. Broome, *Aboriginal Australians: black responses to white dominance, 1788–2001*, Sydney, Allen & Unwin, 2001; R. Broome, *Aboriginal Australians: a history since 1788*, Sydney, Allen & Unwin, 2010. See also Loos, *Invasion and Resistance*; Evans, Saunders and Cronin, *Race Relations in Colonial Queensland*; L. Ryan, *The Aboriginal Tasmanians,* St Lucia, University of Queensland Press, 1981; G. Reid, *A Nest of Hornets*, Melbourne, Oxford University Press, 1982; J. Connor, *The Australian Frontier Wars 1788–1838*, Sydney, New South Wales University Press, 2002; T. Roberts, *Frontier Justice: a history of the Gulf Country to 1900*, Brisbane, University of Queensland Press, 2005; B. Attwood and S.G. Foster (eds), *Frontier Conflict: the Australian experience*, Canberra, National Museum of Australia, 2003; Foster and Nettelbeck, *Out of the Silence*. See also T. Bottoms, *The Conspiracy of Silence: Queensland's frontier killing times*, Sydney, Allen & Unwin, 2013; H. Reynolds, *The Forgotten Wars*, Sydney, NewSouth Publishing, 2013.

87 Reynolds, *The Other Side of the Frontier*, p.158.
88 H. Reynolds, *Aboriginal Sovereignty: reflections on race, state, and nation*, Sydney, Allen & Unwin, 1996, p.96.
89 This view has been disputed by Keith Windschuttle, who views Aboriginal actions purely in terms of criminal behaviour. See K. Windschuttle, 'The Myths of Frontier Massacres in Australian History Part II: The Fabrication of the Aboriginal Death Toll', *Quadrant,* vol. 44, no. 11, 2000; K. Windschuttle, *The Fabrication of Aboriginal History: Volume One, Van Diemen's Land 1803–1947*, Sydney, Macleay Press, 2002. For a rejoinder to this account see R. Manne (ed.), *Whitewash: on Keith Windschuttle's fabrication of Aboriginal history*, Melbourne, Black Inc. Agenda, 2003.
90 See B. Attwood, 'Historiography on the Australian Frontier', in B. Attwood and Foster (eds), *Frontier Conflict*, p.171.
91 B. Reece, 'Inventing Aborigines', *Aboriginal History,* vol. 11, no. 1, 1987.
92 D.J. Mulvaney, *Encounters in Place: outsiders and Aboriginal Australians 1606–1985*, Brisbane, University of Queensland Press, 1989; Ann McGrath, *'Born in the Cattle': Aborigines in cattle country*, Sydney, Allen & Unwin, 1987.
93 McGrath, *'Born in the Cattle'*, p.21, quoted in Attwood, 'Historiography on the Australian Frontier', p.172.
94 See J. Hirst, *Sense and Nonsense in Australian History*, Melbourne, Black Inc. Agenda, 2005, pp.86–7.
95 For a summary of recent literature see A. Atkinson, *The Europeans in Australia:*

a history. Volume Two: Democracy, Melbourne, Oxford University Press, 2004; M. Finnane and J. Richards, "'You'll get nothing out of it"?: the inquest, police and Aboriginal deaths in colonial Queensland', *Australian Historical Studies,* vol. 123, 2004, pp.84–105; Reid, *A Picnic with the Natives;* Nettelbeck, 'Writing and Remembering Frontier Conflict; Nettelbeck and Foster, *In the Name of the Law;* C. Owen, '"The Police Appear to Be a Useless Lot Up There": law and order in the East Kimberley 1884–1905', *Aboriginal History,* vol. 27, 2003, pp.105–130; A. Nettelbeck, 'Practices of Violence/Myths of Creation: Mounted Constable Willshire and the cultural logic of settler nationalism', *Journal of Australian Studies,* vol. 32, no. 1, 2008, pp.5–17; D.J. Mulvaney (ed.), *From the Frontier: outback letters to Baldwin Spencer,* Sydney, Allen & Unwin, 2000; M. Finnanen and F. Paisley, 'Police Violence and the Limits of Law on a Late Colonial Frontier: the "Borroloola Case" in 1930s Australia', *Law and History Review,* vol. 28, no.1, 2010, pp.141–71; P. Vallee, *God, Guns and Government on the Central Australian Frontier,* Canberra, Restoration, 2006; A. Nettelbeck and R. Foster, 'Colonial Judiciaries, Aboriginal Protection and South Australia's Policy of Punishing "with Exemplary Severity"', *Australian Historical Studies,* vol. 41, no. 3, 2010, pp.319–36.

96 Foster and Nettelbeck, *Out of the Silence,* pp. 106-114.

97 ibid., p.106.

98 ibid., p.81. See 'The Culture of the Settler Frontier', pp.78–86. See also Foster, Hosking, and Nettelbeck, *Fatal Collisions,* p.7; R. Foster, '"Don't Mention the War": frontier violence and the language of concealment', *History Australia,* vol. 6, no. 3, 2009, pp.68.1–68.15.

99 J.A. Allen, *Sex and Secrets: crimes involving Australian women since 1880,* Melbourne, Oxford University Press, 1990, p.3.

100 ibid., p.4.

101 ibid.

102 McGrath, *'Born in the Cattle',* Sydney, Allen & Unwin, 1987, pp.68–94.

103 K. Windschuttle, 'The Myths of Frontier Massacres in Australian History', *Quadrant,* Vol. 44, No. 10, October 2000. Part II: 'The Fabrication of the Aboriginal Death Toll', *Quadrant,* Vol. 44, No. 11. November 2000. Part III: 'Massacre Stories and the Policy of Separatism', *Quadrant,* Vol. 44, No. 12, December 2000.

104 ibid.; N. Green, *The Forrest River Massacres,* Western Australia, Fremantle Arts Centre Press, 1995; R. Moran, *Massacre Myth: an investigation into allegations concerning the mass murder of Aborigines at Forrest River,* Perth, Access Press, 1999. For other examples see R. Moran, 'Was There a Massacre at Bedford Downs?' *Quadrant,* Vol. 46, No. 11, November 2002, pp.48–51; Clement has refuted this article in C. Clement, 'National Museum of Australia Review of Exhibitions and Public Programs Submissions', *National Museum of Australia,* 2003 <http://www.nma.gov.au/__data/assets/pdf_file/0015/2409/Dr_Clement.pdf>, accessed 29 June 2016.

105 See N. Green, 'Windschuttle's Debut' in R. Manne (ed.), *Whitewash,* pp.187–98.

106 K. Windschuttle, 'The Myths of Frontier Massacres in Australian History', *Quadrant*, Vol. 44, No. 10, October 2000, p.20.

107 Wood, *Royal Commission of Inquiry into Alleged Killing and Burning of Bodies of Aborigines in East Kimberley*.

108 K. Windschuttle, 'Doctored Evidence and Invented Incidents', in Attwood and Foster (eds), *Frontier Conflict*, pp.99–112; for Clement's response see C. Clement, 'Mistake Creek' in Manne (ed.), *Whitewash*, pp.199-217 in R. Manne, 'Whitewash', see Statement of Peggy Patrick, pp.215–17; C. Clement, 'National Museum of Australia Review of Exhibitions and Public Programs Submissions'; C. Clement, 'The impact of denial: an interrogation of evidence relevant to massacres at Mistake Creek', *Australian Historical Association Bulletin*, no. 96, June 2003, pp.66–77; P. Smith, *Mistake Creek Massacre Site*, Flinders University, <https://www.flinders.edu.au/ehl/archaeology/research-profile/current-projects/kimberley-frontier-archaeology-project/mistake-creek-massacre-site.cfm>, accessed 29 June 2016.

109 K. Windschuttle, 'The Myths of Frontier Massacres in Australian History', *Quadrant*, Vol. 44, No. 10, October 2000, p.13.

110 Windschuttle, *The Fabrication of Aboriginal History: Volume One*, pp.65–77, 95–103. Windschuttle was to develop his themes in a projected three-volume series on Australian frontiers, to be entitled *The Fabrication of Aboriginal History*. *Volume One, Van Diemen's Land 1803–1847* was published in 2002; Volume Two, which was due in 2003, would purportedly refute Henry Reynolds' claims about violence on the Queensland frontier; whilst Volume Three, promised for 2004, was to be on Western Australian frontiers. Volume Three appeared in 2009, however, the topic had changed significantly to 'the Stolen Generations': K. Windschuttle, *The Fabrication of Aboriginal History: Volume Three, The Stolen Generations 1881–2008*, Sydney, Macleay Press, 2009. Volumes Two and Four are to be published 'later' <http://www.macleaypress.com/index.php?page=shop.product_details&flypage=vmj_genx_img1.tpl&product_id=16&category_id=8&option=com_virtuemart&Itemid=4&vmcchk=1&Itemid=4 >, accessed 29 June 2016.

111 Windschuttle, *Volume One*, pp.387–97.

112 ibid., p.402.

113 These included Henry Reynolds, Lyndall Ryan, Derek Mulvaney and even an earlier generation of conservative historians such as Brian Plomley and Lloyd Robson. S. Macintyre, 'Reviewing the History Wars', *Labour History*, no. 85, November 2003, p.213.

114 ibid., pp.213–15.

115 Attwood, 'Historiography on the Australian Frontier', in pp.99–112.

116 See Manne, *Whitewash*; Attwood, 'Historiography on the Australian Frontier'; G.D.B. Smithers, 'Reassuring "White Australia": a review of *The Fabrication of Aboriginal History: Volume One*', *Journal of Social History*, vol. 37, no. 2, Winter 2003, pp.493–505; S.G. Foster, 'Contra Windschuttle', *Quadrant*, vol. 47, no. 3, March 2003.

117 Windschuttle, *The Fabrication of Aboriginal History: Volume One*, pp.387–97.

118 Quoted in Attwood and Foster (eds), *Frontier Conflict*, p.180.

119 See for example extensive references in H. Reynolds, 'The Written Record', pp.79–87, R. Broome, 'The Statistics of Frontier Conflict', pp.88–98, and R. Evans, 'Across the Queensland Frontier', pp.63–75, in Attwood and Foster (eds), *Frontier Conflict*; and R. Foster, "'Don't mention the war".

120 Broome, 'The Statistics of Frontier Conflict', p.96.

121 R. Evans and R. Ørsted–Jensen, "'I cannot say the numbers that were killed": assessing violent mortality on the Queensland frontier', presented at Conflict in History, Australian Historical Association, 33rd Annual Conference, University of Queensland, 7–11 July 2014.

122 Evans, 'Across the Queensland Frontier', in Attwood and Foster (eds), *Frontier Conflict*, p.73.

123 P.W. Nichols, *Police Powers in Western Australia 1829–1970*, Master's thesis, University of Western Australia, 1975; J. McArthur, *Policing the Colony of Western Australia 1829–1850,* Honours dissertation, University of Western Australia, 1995; A. Gill, *The WA Police Force, 1880–1910,* Honours dissertation, University of Western Australia, 1973; A. Gill, *Aspects of the Western Australian Police Force, 1887–1905*, unpublished, 1974.

124 Nichols, *Police Powers in Western Australia 1829–1970*, p.41.

125 McArthur, *Policing the Colony of Western Australia 1829–1850*, p.272.

126 M. Bentley, *Grandfather was a Policeman: the Western Australian police force 1829–1889*, Perth, Hesperian Press, 1993; see also K. Moran, *Sand and Stone: a social history of Western Australia as recorded by police of the eastern frontier,* London, Frickers International Publishing, 2000.

127 A.R. Pashley, *Policing Our State: a history of police stations and police officers in Western Australia 1829–1945,* Perth, Educant, 2000.

128 P. Conole, *Protect and Serve: a history of the Western Australian police service*, Perth, Access Press, 2002.

129 ibid., see for example pp.xiii–xiv, 181–7.

130 ibid., p.7.

131 ibid., p.129.

132 ibid. pp.181–7. Conole states it is 'disturbing to note that the manufacture of massacre myths has, in certain quarters, become almost a cottage industry'. See C. Clement, 'The Impact of Denial', pp.66–77.

133 A. Gill, 'Aborigines, Settlers and Police in the Kimberleys 1887–1905', *Studies in Western Australian History*, no. 1, 1977, pp. 1–28.

134 ibid., p.1.

135 ibid., p.2.

136 See Loos, *Invasion and Resistance*, pp.33–44.

137 R.E. McGregor, *'Answering the Native Question': the dispossession of the Aborigines of the Fitzroy District, West Kimberley, 1880–1905*, Honours thesis, James Cook University, 1985.

138 ibid., p.161.

139 R. McGregor, 'Law Enforcement or Just Force? Police Action in Two Frontier Districts', in Reynolds (ed.), *Race Relations in North Queensland*, p.63.

140 Clement, 'Monotony, Manhunts and Malice', p.94.

141 Green, *The Forrest River Massacres.*

142 ibid., p.19.

143 ibid., p.34.

144 K. Moran, *Sand and Stone – Cattle & Conflict, Volume One and Two,* Perth, Hesperian Press, 2009; K. Moran, *Sand and Stone-Foreign Footprints: police in the Kimberley 1880–1890s,* Perth, Hesperian Press, 2009; K. Moran, *Pigeon,* Perth, Hesperian Press, 2011.

145 Moran claims 'Academia no longer embraces difference and any who have proffered a different viewpoint to the ordained perspectives by the influential group-think historians has seen unfettered and malicious attacks upon both the person, his capacity and his work as a historian.' Moran, *Sand and Stone-Foreign Footprints,* p.vii. In a similar vein in the volume *Pigeon* Moran's narrative includes material that is clearly drawn from a combination of the work of Ion Idriess and Howard Pedersen and Banjo Woorunmurra's oral history, which is at odds with Moran's claim that Aboriginal oral history is an 'invented oral tradition'. Moran also takes exception to the authenticity of the film version of the Jandamarra story; see K. Moran, 'ABC – Questions as to the Truth – Pigeon – Jandamarra's War', *The Morant,* 20 January 2013, <http://themorant.wordpress.com/2013/01/20/abc-questions-as-to-the-truth-pigeon-jandamarras-war/>, accessed 29 June 2016.

146 See for example 'The Native Question', *The West Australian,* 22 March 1897, p.5.

147 'When Pigeon Roamed the Kimberley', *Western Mail,* 19 October 1939, p.10.

148 H. Pedersen, 'Jandamarra (1870–1897)', *Australian Dictionary of Biography,* National Centre of Biography, Australian National University, 1990. <http://adbonline.anu.edu.au/biogs/A120263b.htm>, accessed 29 June 2016

149 For a first-hand report see 'The Murder by Natives', *The West Australian,* 13 November 1894, p.5.

150 See *Golden Age Newspaper,* 22 March 1897, p.3; *The West Australian,* 6 December 1894, p.5; *The West Australian,* 18 December 1894, p.5; *The West Australian,* 20 March 1897, p.5; *The West Australian,* 22 March 1897, p.5.

151 For other Australian reports see, for example, *The Brisbane Courier,* Wednesday 14 November 1894, p.5; 'The Kimberley Murder. Bushranging Feared', *South Australian Register,* Wednesday 14 November 1894; 'The Outrage By Blacks. Desertion Of Native Police. Great Alarm Felt. Government Action. Perth', *The Argus,* Wednesday 14 November 1894, p.5; 'An Aboriginal Raid. Fight with the Police. Three White Men Shot', *Barrier Miner,* Tuesday 13 November 1894, p.3; 'Outrage by Blacks in West Australia. Mutiny and Desertion of Native Troopers. A Constable and Two Stockmen Murdered. Outlawry of the Lennard Tribes Demanded. Perth', *Launceston Examiner,* Thursday 15 November 1894, p.3; 'Murder By Natives in Western Australia. Fighting and Cannibalism', *The Argus,* Thursday 20 December 1894, p.5.

152 'The Niggers of the North; A Massacre Feared', Interview with R.H. Pilmer, *The Sunday Times,* Sunday 17 March, 1912, p.20.

153 I. Idriess, *Outlaw of the Leopolds,* Sydney, Angus and Robertson, 1952.

154 'Policeman's Patrol', *The West Australian,* 16 June 1934, p.19.

155 WAPD, 'Proposed book to be written by I. Idriess dealing with work of Mounted Police in Northern Australia. Request for assistance in obtaining information for', 20 July 1932, AN5/2, Cons. 430, File 4751/1932. The police named were Inspector W. Douglas, G. Johnstone, D. Hunter, Sergeant Flinders, G.H. Hulme, J. McKenna, Constable S. Dewar, W.J. Mcguigan, E.J. Pollet, W.H.L. Walter, W. Fanning and A. Buckland. Idriess told the commissioner that he was looking for more than police records and that he wanted 'balance' such as 'white men's stories'. WAPD, 'Letter from Ion Idriess to Commissioner of Police', 1 December 1932, SROWA, AN5/2, Cons. 430, File 4751/1932.

156 See for example I. Idriess, *Man Tracks: the mounted police in Australia's wilds,* Sydney, Angus and Robertson, 1935; *Over the Range: sunshine and shadows in the West Kimberley,* Sydney, Angus and Robertson, 1937.

157 I. Idriess, 'The Battle of Wingina [sic] Gorge, Outlaw of the Leopolds', *The Sunday Herald,* 28 December 1952, p.7; Idriess, *Outlaw of the Leopolds.*

158 *The Countryman,* 13 September 1956, p.25; see first-hand account 'J. Blythe, Why Pigeon Roamed the Kimberley', *Western Mail,* 18 January 1940, p.8; C.E. Flinders, 'Trouble in the Nineties when Armed Natives Attacked the Whites, North-West Memories, Manhunt in the Oscar Range', *Western Mail,* 9 January 1947, p.5. For a detailed account of the multitude of different interpretations see editorial comments by Clement in Pilmer, *Northern Patrol.* In Pilmer's account he conflates entire years, at times melding two years into one, see p.47.

159 Clement in Pilmer, *Northern Patrol.*

160 Jandamarra is noted in the current *Australian Dictionary of Biography* as an 'Indigenous Resistance Fighter', Pedersen, 'Jandamarra (1870–1897)'. The most recent publication following this theme is an illustrated children's book, M. Greenwood and T. Denton, *Jandamarra,* Sydney, Allen & Unwin, 2013. Jandamarra is described as something of a 'black Ned Kelly', a man who overcame injustice for his people. For 'black Ned Kelly' references see V. Mills, 'Jandamarra: a black Ned Kelly', *ABC Kimberley,* 17 March 2008, <http://www.abc.net.au/local/stories/2008/02/07/2156878.htm>.

161 H. Pedersen and B. Woorunmurra, *Jandamarra and the Bunuba Resistance,* Broome, Magabala Books, 1995. This book is based on Pedersen's Honours dissertation, which was also the basis for a 1984 article, H. Pedersen, 'Pigeon: an Australian Aboriginal rebel', *Studies in Western Australian History,* no. 8 December 1984, pp.7–15; H. Pedersen, *Pigeon, an Aboriginal Rebel: a study of Aboriginal-European conflict in the West Kimberley, north western Australia during the 1890s,* Honours dissertation, Murdoch University, 1980. In 2011 a full film version was released: *Jandamarra's War,* dir. M. Torres, ABC, 12 May 2011, <http://www.abc.net.au/tv/programs/jandamarraswar.htm> (television program). See also F. Prior, 'Film Project Brings History to Life', *The West Australian,* 7 August 2010, <http://au.news.yahoo.com/thewest/a/-/

mp/7724764/film-project-brings-history-to-life/>.

162 After Banjo Woorunmurra died George Brooking took the role of custodian of the story.

163 Idriess had described how the colonists of the West Kimberley were 'backed by a pitifully small police force' in 'Battle of Wingina [sic] Gorge', *The Sunday Herald*. Pedersen describes them as 'the most powerful police regiment in the colony'.

164 In many accounts an absence of references and conflating of chronology around certain events make it impossible to verify the way events are linked.

165 For example, on p.40 of *Jandamarra and the Bunuba Resistance*, Pedersen and Woorunmurra have Inspector Francis Wheatley Lodge leading a punitive expedition after the spearing of a sailor named Captain John George Piton in August 1886. For an account of this see 'The Kimberley Murders', *Western Mail*, 18 December 1886, p.28. Lodge was not active in the Kimberley in 1886 (being in Natal, South Africa, at the time) and commenced duty in the Kimberley nearly two years later in mid-1888. 'Death of Chief Inspector Lodge', *The West Australian,* 31 July 1899, p.3.

166 See for example C. Johnson, *Long Live Sandawarra,* Melbourne, Hyland House, 1987, based on 'Long Live Pigeon!' in *Meanjin* (Aboriginal Issue), vol. 36, no. 4, December 1977, pp.494–507; *Pigeon,* dir. J. Noble, Filmwest, c1975 (video recording); S. Muecke, A. Rumsey and B. Wirrunmarra [sic], 'Pigeon the Outlaw: history as texts', *Aboriginal History,* vol. 9, no.1–2, 1985, pp.81–100. Problematically, earlier oral history accounts, such as those recorded in the early 1980s by Russell McGregor and later by Alan Rumsey, are not included. Here Woorunmurra described Jandamarra as a solitary figure who was as much an outlaw against his own Bunuba people as against the colonial powers. Someone who, Woorunmurra states, was 'not a friend of anybody now, he was on his own, an outlaw' for transgressing Bunuba law by having sexual relations with people outside his own kin groups; see Muecke, Rumsey and Wirrunmarra [sic], 'Pigeon the Outlaw', p.89. Additionally, the reason Jandamarra killed PC Richardson is disputed and possibly will never be known. In Pedersen's 1980 account he attributes it to the fact that Jandamarra had arrested his own *countrymen* for stock killing and they, led by Ellemarra, convinced him to rebel, shoot Richardson and let them go; Pedersen, 'Pigeon, An Aboriginal Rebel', p.11. This position is expanded upon in *Jandamarra and the Bunuba Resistance* where Pedersen and Woorunmurra assert Jandamarra falls under Ellemarra's 'spellbinding influence' and, to make amends for his sins, such as violating Bunuba law by sleeping with many of the Bunuba men's wives, he had to make reparations; Pedersen and Woorunmurra, *Jandamarra and the Bunuba Resistance,* p.118. Ellemarra, Pedersen writes, 'beckoned the young man home to his people and the law'. Pedersen adds other reasons, such as suggestions of sexual jealously and that Richardson was taking advantage of Bunuba women; ibid., p.116. Puzzlingly the introduction to this book contains an oral history extract from co-author Woorunmurra which states that the motive for the killing was

due to the fact that the prisoners were hungry and wanted some kangaroo and, instead of shooting the kangaroo, Jandamarra shot Richardson; ibid., p.1. This position is also supported in Pilmer's memoirs: *Northern Patrol*, p.50.

167 Green, *The Forrest River Massacres*, p.49.

168 N.B. Tindale, *Aboriginal Tribes of Australia: their terrain, environmental controls, distribution, limits, and proper names, with an appendix on Tasmanian tribes by Rhys Jones*, Berkeley, University of California Press, 1974, p.256. Tindale writes 'in the pre contact period the Njikena [Nyikina] were known to be hostile. Tradition in the tribe [Bunuba] says they were driven south out of the Leopold Ranges by the Ngarinjin [Ngaringin] before the coming of the white man', p.256.

169 See for example Finnane (ed.), *Policing in Australia*; Finnane, *Police and Government*; Finnane, *Colonization and Incarceration*.

170 Foster and Nettelbeck, *Out of the Silence*, pp.5–7.

Chapter 2: 'The Only Remaining Portion of the Large Continent of Australia Hitherto Unoccupied'

1 The chapter title is drawn from 'Pastoral Settlement in Western Australia', *The West Australian*, 29 August 1885, p.7.

2 CSO, 'Conditions for Land Grants at Swan River', Colonial Office, 5 December 1828, SROWA, HRA Series 3, vol. 6, pp.594–5.

3 This annual grant-in-aid from the British parliament would cover the difference between revenue and expenditure of the colony. Governors were instructed to minimise expenditure until the need for the grant was eliminated, which did not occur until 1856. See B.K. De Garis, 'Political Tutelage 1829–1890', in C.T. Stannage (ed.), *A New History of Western Australia*, Perth, UWA Press, 1981, p.303. For a general history of the Swan River Colony see R.T. Appleyard and T. Manford, *The Beginning: European discovery and early settlement of Swan River Western Australia*, Perth, UWA Press, 1979; P.S. Drew, *James Stirling: admiral and founding governor of Western Australia*, Perth, UWA Press, 2003, p.261; J. McArthur, *Policing the Colony of Western Australia 1829–1850*, unpublished thesis, University of Western Australia, 1995, pp.85–90. For a more recent account see J. Host with C. Owen, *'It's Still in My Heart, this is My Country': the single Noongar claim history*, Perth, UWA Publishing, 2009.

4 For an early account of the Swan River Colony see W.B. Kimberly, 'Chapter VIII, Exploration; Social condition; Abolition of Land Grant System, 1831', in W.B. Kimberly, (ed.), *History of West Australia, A Narrative of her Past, Together With Biographies of Her Leading Men*, Melbourne, F.W. Niven, 1897, <http://en.wikisource.org/wiki/History_of_West_Australia/Chapter_8>.

5 Historical Records of Australia (HRA) Series 111, vol. 6, SROWA, p.616. See also P. Conole, *Protect and Serve: a history of the Western Australian police service*, Perth, Access Press, 2002.

6 E. Russell, *A History of the Law in Western Australia and its Development from 1829 to 1979*, Perth, UWA Press, 1980, p.186.

7   M. Bentley, *Grandfather was a Policeman: the Western Australian police force 1829–1889*, Perth, Hesperian Press, 1993, p.5.

8   A. Hunter, *'A Different Kind of Subject': colonial law in Aboriginal–European relationships in nineteenth century Western Australia 1829–1861*, Canberra, Australian Scholarly Publishing, 2012, p.6.

9   For a useful summary of this issue see ibid.

10 ibid.

11 G.F. Moore, 'Brief Chronicle of the Principal Events which have Occurred, Connected With the Colony of Western Australia, Since First Settlement within its Limits in the Year 1826', *The Inquirer,* 27 September 1843, p.2.

12 ibid., Noongar is also spelt as Nyungar, Nyungah, Nungar, Yungar.

13 N. Ogle, *The Colony of Western Australia: a manual for emigrants,* London, James Fraser, 1839, p.54.

14 Drew, *James Stirling*, 2003, p.261. Moore, whilst he made it clear that he could not understand what Yagan was saying to him, interpreted one statement as 'You came to our country; you have driven us from our haunts; and disturbed us in our occupations; as we walk in our own country; we are fired upon by the white man; why should the white man treat us so?' G.F. Moore, *Diary of Ten Years Eventful Life of an Early Settler in Western Australia and also a Descriptive Vocabulary of the Language of the Aborigines*, London, 1884, facsimile edition, Perth, UWA Press, 1978, p.191.

15 CSO, J. Stirling, Proclamation, *Swan River Papers*, 3 October 1831, SROWA, Cons. 58, col. 12, pp.16–18.

16 Moore, 'Brief Chronicle of the Principal Events which have Occurred, p.2.

17 Petition from the Swan River Settlers, SRP, vol. 10, 1832, p.25.

18 Moore, 'Brief Chronicle of the Principal Events which have Occurred, p.2.

19 ibid.

20 G.F. Moore, 'Letters Illustrative of the Early Years of the Colony', *The West Australian,* Tuesday 25 January 1881, p.3. Moore's letters would be published in 1884 as Moore, *Diary of Ten Years Eventful Life of an Early Settler in Western Australia*, p.120.

21 McArthur, *Policing the Colony of Western Australia*, pp.85–90.

22 'Murder of Thomas and John Velvick by a Party of Natives', *The Perth Gazette and Western Australian Journal*, 4 May 1833, p.71.

23 'A Native Shot', *The Perth Gazette and Western Australian Journal*, 4 May 1833, p.71; for explicit detail of 'payback' see 'From a Correspondent', *The Perth Gazette and Western Australian Journal*, 1 June 1833, p.87.

24 'Execution', *The Perth Gazette and Western Australian Journal*, 25 May, 1833, p.83.

25 'Yagan and Heegan, Two Natives Shot', *The Perth Gazette and Western Australian Journal,* 13 July 1833, p.110.

26 Nesbitt had over '30 jagged wounds over his body and his head was mangled and crushed by heavy blows. His tongue was cut out and his fingers chopped over and inserted in his mouth.' Another soldier, Private Barron, in the Murray district south of Perth, was wounded. Drew, *James Stirling*, pp.260,

280–1.

27 Russell, *A History of the Law in Western Australia*, p.37.

28 B. De Garis, 'The First Legislative Council, 1832–1870', in D. Black (ed.), *The House on the Hill: a history of the Parliament of Western Australia*, Perth, Parliament of Western Australia, 1991, p.28.

29 See for example 'The Natives Again!', *The Perth Gazette and Western Australian Journal*, 27 April 1833, p.67; 'The Natives!' *The Perth Gazette and Western Australian Journal*, 15 June 1833, p.94; 'The Natives', *The Perth Gazette and Western Australian Journal*, 22 June 1833, p.98; 'The Natives', *The Perth Gazette and Western Australian Journal*, 20 July 1833, p.114; 'The Natives Again!', *The Perth Gazette and Western Australian Journal*, 17 August 1833, p.130; 'The Natives Again!', *The Perth Gazette and Western Australian Journal*, 10 May 1834, p.282; 'The Natives', *The Perth Gazette and Western Australian Journal*, 14 March 1840, p.27.

30 R. Lyon, 'A Glance at the Manners, and Language of the Aboriginal Inhabitants of Western Australia; With a Short Vocabulary', *The Perth Gazette and Western Australian Journal*, 30 March, 1833, pp.51–2. B. Devenish, 'A Most Maligned Man', *Early Days: Journal of the Royal Western Australian Historical Society*, vol. 13, no. 2, 2008, pp.157–72.

31 J. Backhouse, *Extracts from the Letters of James Backhouse, Vol. 2*, London, Harvey and Darton, 1838, p.55. Lyon's real name was Robert Lyon Milne.

32 'Mounted Police', *The Perth Gazette and Western Australian Journal*, 18 October 1834, p.374. 'This corps promises, according to the arrangements laid down by His Excellency Sir James Stirling, to afford a most substantial protection of the Colonists against the natives...'

33 ibid.

34 ibid.

35 For an account of Stirling's goals see Drew, *James Stirling*.

36 CSO, J. Stirling No. 14 to Stanley, 1 November 1834, CO 18/14 f134. Quoted in Drew, *James Stirling*, p.261.

37 N. Green, 'Aborigines and White Settlers', in C.T. Stannage (ed.), *A New History of Western Australia*, Perth, UWA Press, 1981, pp.84–5. For an account describing this event as a justifiable battle see Drew, *James Stirling*. For an account describing it in terms of massacre see *The Pinjarra Massacre Site Research & Development Project*, Pinjarra, Murray Districts Aboriginal Association, 1998.

38 Stirling to Stanley, Secretary of State for Colonies, 1 November 1834, CO. 18.14, Australian Joint Copying Project: 299–300. See also Lord Glenelg to Stirling, and John S Roe, Registered Field Book, 3, 1834–1838, Department of Land Management, Perth, quoted in J. Harris, 'Hiding the Bodies: the myth of the humane colonisation of Aboriginal Australia', *Aboriginal History*, 2003. Keith Windschuttle has argued: 'The name by which this incident has long been known, the Battle of Pinjarra, remains an accurate one. Even though the British had overwhelming superiority in firepower, it was a real battle between warring parties, with casualties on both sides, rather than a

massacre of innocents. It was not an ambush, since the Aborigines were well aware of the troopers' presence beforehand. It was not a punitive expedition either.' K. Windschuttle, 'The Myths of Frontier Massacres in Australian History', *Quadrant*, Vol. 44, No. 10, p.8.

39 Quoted in P. Hasluck, *Black Australians: a survey of native policy in Western Australia, 1829–1897,* Melbourne, Melbourne University Press, 1942, pp.48–9.

40 *The Perth Gazette and Western Australian Journal*, 1 November 1834, p.383.

41 Glenelg to Stirling, 23 July 1835, CO 397/2, Reel 304, pp.181–4, quoted in Hunter, *'A Different Kind of Subject'*, pp.51–2.

42 'Memorial of the Colonists to His Majesty's Principal Secretary of State for the Colonies', *The Perth Gazette and Western Australian Journal*, 4 April 1835, p.472.

43 See Drew, *James Stirling*, pp.280–1. For an account of the parlous state of the Swan River Colony see I. Berryman (ed.), *Swan River Letters*, Glengarry, Swan River Press, 2002.

44 'Report of Legislative Council Proceedings', *The Perth Gazette and Western Australian Journal*, 4 April 1835, quoted in Drew, *James Stirling*, pp.280–1.

45 Ogle, *The Colony of Western Australia*, p.54.

46 *The Perth Gazette and Western Australian Journal*, 29 October 1836, p.790; see also 'The Native Language. Francis Armstrong's work', *The West Australian*, 25 April 1936, p.5.

47 Hunter, *'A Different Kind of Subject'*, pp.167–8.

48 ibid.

49 'The opinion of the home government, we have heard it stated, is in favor of a purchase being made from the natives of the land we occupy in this territory. The deed of transfer would be a curious document, but not a very difficult one to obtain; neither would the bargain or sale be effected at a very ruinous rate to His Majesty's treasury. Mr. Munday, a seemly looking personage, claims the land between Perth and the Peninsula Farm, which, he distinctly gives us to understand, belongs to him, but that the houses are the property of the white mew, and he will make it over to us for a modicum of flour. The experiment may not be undeserving a trial. Mr. Shenton bought, the other day, 7 acres for as many shillings, and the bargain was sealed by a solemn assurance, on the part of the vendors, to protect him from any intrusion on the part of their sable friends.' *The Perth Gazette and Western Australian Journal*, 10 September 1836, p.760. See also J.S. Turner, 'George Shenton, The Elder, 1811–1867', *Early Days: Journal of the Royal Western Australian Historical Society*, vol. 11, no. 3, 1997, pp.379–93.

50 *The Perth Gazette and Western Australian Journal*, 10 September 1836, p.760.

51 Minutes of the Executive Council, 13 September 1836, CO 20/1, Reel 1118, p.152, quoted in Hunter, *'A Different Kind of Subject'*, p.166.

52 N. Green and S. Moon, *Far From Home: Aboriginal prisoners of Rottnest Island, 1838–1931,* Perth, UWA Press, 1997.

53 A.R. Pashley, *Policing Our State: a history of police stations and police officers in Western Australia 1829–1945,* Perth, Educant, 2000, p.5.

54 C. Owen, 'Native Police', entry in J. Gregory and J. Gothard (eds), *Historical Encyclopedia of Western Australia,* Perth, UWA Press, 2009, p.624.

55 The language recording, which drew on George Grey's earlier work, was serialised in *The Perth Gazette* and published as an addendum to Moore, *Diary of Ten Years Eventful Life of an Early Settler in Western Australia.* Other measures Hutt introduced were monetary land bounties offered to colonists who trained Aboriginal people to apprentice standards, though by 1848 this was abolished.

56 A. Hunter, 'John Hutt: the inconspicuous governor', *Early Days: Journal of the Royal Western Australian Historical Society,* vol. 13, no. 3, 2009, pp.309–22.

57 Two protectors were appointed by the Colonial Office in England: Charles Symmons was stationed in Perth and patrolled the area from Perth down the coast to Augusta; Peter Barrow was stationed at York and patrolled the area around York inland down to Albany. The protector's role was to 'protect and civilise' and mediate between Aboriginal people and the government. In 1849 the title of protector of Aborigines was changed to guardian of Aborigines and protector of settlers.

58 Hunter, 'John Hutt'.

59 *An Ordinance to Provide for the Summary Trial and Punishment of Aboriginal Native Offenders and to Summarily Try Aboriginal People in Certain Cases* (12th Vic. No. 18).

60 ibid. Hunter.

61 N. Green, *Broken Spears: Aboriginals and Europeans in the Southwest of Australia,* Perth, Focus Education Services, 1984, pp.226–31.

62 See Hasluck, *Black Australians,* pp.129–30.

63 Russell, *A History of the Law in Western Australia,* p.188.

64 ibid.

65 Superintendents of police to follow were William Hogan (1854), Alexander Cockburn-Cambell (1858), William Hogan (1861), Robert Henry Crampton (1863), G.E.C. Hare (1867), William Henry Timperley (Acting Superintendent 24 April to 9 May 1871), Matthew Skinner Smith (Superintendent 9 May 1871, Commissioner 13 January to 18 April 1887), George Braithwaite Phillips (Acting Superintendent 9 December 1885 to 13 January 1887, Commissioner April 1887 to 26 March, 1900), William Chipper Lawrence (Acting Commissioner 26 March to 18 April 1900 and 22 to 28 February 1905), Frederick Arthur Hare (Commissioner 18 April 1900 to 31 March 1912). Western Australia Police, 'WA Police Commissioners 1867–1958', 2015, <https://www.police.wa.gov.au/About-Us/Our-history/Episodes-in-our-policing-history/WA-Police-Commissioners-1867-to-1958#RC>

66 *Rules and Regulations for the Government and Guidance of the Police Force of Western Australia as Approved by Governor Hampton,* Perth, 1863, p.2.

67 ibid.

68 De Garis, 'Political Tutelage 1829–1890', pp.325–6.

69 In 1884 Superintendent of Police, Smith, advocated what he called a 'bit of well-timed severity' to teach Aboriginal people the concept of private

property and to 'break him into the ways of civilisation'. M.S. Smith, 'Criminal Statistics and Report of the Superintendent of Police for the Year 1884', Paper No.4, WAPP, 1885.

70 Hunter, *'A Different Kind of Subject'*.

71 'The Case of Mr Lockler Clere Burges to the Public of Western Australia', *The Inquirer & Commercial*, 11 December 1872, p.2.

72 The case, including a comprehensive list of petitioners, is found in detail at, 'Government Despatch', *The Perth Gazette and West Australian Times,* 21 February 1873, p.3. For another account of this episode see K. Forrest, *The Challenge and the Chance: the colonisation and settlement of North West Australia 1861–1914*, Perth, Hesperian Press, 1996, pp.82–6.

73 See for example 'A Voice from the Gascoyne', *The West Australian*, 30 May 1882, p.3; 'The Native Difficulty', *The West Australian*, 26 May 1882, p.2; 'The Native Question', *The West Australian*, 30 May 1882, p.3; 'Black v. White', *The West Australian,* 20 June 1882, p.3; 'Public Meeting at the Gascoyne', *The West Australian*, 20 June 1882, p.3; 'The Suggested Native Police Force', *The West Australian*, 25 July 1882, p.3; 'The West Australian', *The West Australian*, 1 August 1882, p.2; 'Legislative Council', *The West Australian*, 1 August 1882, p.3; 'Mr. Burt and the Kimberley District', *The West Australian*, 15 August 1882, p.3; 'Mr. Fairbairn's Report', *The West Australian*, 18 August 1882; 'Debate of the Native Question, Legislative Council', *The West Australian*, 29 September 1882, p.1; 'The Natives on the Murchison', *The West Australian*, 3 October 1882; 'Native Affairs in the Gascoyne', 'Correspondence', *The West Australian*, 6 October 1882, p.3; 'Mr. Bush in Reply', *The West Australian*, 31 October 1882, p.1; 'Mr. Fairbairn's Report', *The West Australian*, 31 October 1882, p.1; 'Police at Port Gascoyne', *The West Australian*, 14 November 1882, p.3.

74 'Deputation to His Excellency the Governor', *The West Australian*, 23 May 1882, p.3. The Aboriginal people were 'a most defiant, insolent, and audacious set, and, from all reports, were clearly masters of the situation'.

75 ibid.

76 Green and Moon, *Far From Home*, p.26.

77 *Instructions to and Reports from the Resident Magistrate Despatched by Direction of His Excellency on Special Duty to the Murchison and Gascoyne Districts,* WA Parliament, LCVP, 1882, p.10. For a summary of Fairbairn's report see J.T. Reilly, *Reminiscences of Fifty Years in Western Australia,* Perth, Sands and McDougall, 1903, p.685. For an explicit account of this practice see the letter by Ernest Lee Steere, 'The Native Question', *The West Australian*, 22 June 1892, p.3.

78 *Instructions to and Reports from the Resident Magistrate Despatched by Direction of His Excellency on Special Duty to the Murchison and Gascoyne Districts*, p.13.

79 ibid.

80 Hasluck, *Black Australians*, p.181.

81 L. Ford, *Settler Sovereignty: jurisdiction and indigenous people in America and Australia 1788–1836,* Cambridge, MA, Harvard University Press, 2010, p.100.

82 For detailed cases in Western Australia see A. Nettelbeck, '"Equals of the White Man": prosecution of settlers for violence against Aboriginal subjects of the Crown, colonial Western Australia', *Law and History Review*, vol. 31, no. 2, 2013, pp.355–90.

83 The Fitzroy River, rises in the King Leopold Ranges and flows some 622 kilometres into King Sound south of Derby. The Fitzroy River has twenty tributaries including Margaret River, Christmas Creek, Hann River, Sandy Creek, Geegully Creek, Little Fitzroy River, Collis Creek, Adcock River, Cunninghame River, Yeeda River, Mudjalla Gully and Minnie River. The combined length of the Fitzroy and its major tributary, the Hann, is 733 kilometres. The river was named by Lt J.L. Stokes after Vice-Admiral Robert FitzRoy, captain of Charles Darwin's boat, the HMS *Beagle*, on 26 February 1838. See R. FitzRoy, *Narrative of the Surveying Voyages of His Majesty's Ships Adventure and Beagle between the years 1826 and 1836, Describing their Examination of the Southern Shores of South America, and the Beagle's Circumnavigation of the Globe. Proceedings of the Second Expedition, 1831–36, under the Command of Captain Robert Fitz-Roy, R.N.,* Henry Colbourn, London, 1839, <http://darwin-online.org.uk/content/frameset?itemID=F10.2&viewtype=text&pageseq=1>.

84 The Ord River was named after Harry Ord, governor of Western Australia from 1877 to 1880.

85 The five longest of the Ord tributaries are the Bow River, Nicholson River, Dunham River, Panton River and Negri River. Where the Lennard River splits into two channels just north of Mount Marmion near the Kimberley Downs homestead, the two arms are the Meda and May rivers. The Meda River was named by the Kimberley pioneer G. Julius Brockman, during a private expedition in search of grazing land north of the Fitzroy River in 1881, after the Admiralty surveying vessel HMS *Meda*, which was engaged in hydrographic surveys in the vicinity under Staff Commander W.E. Archdeacon RN, and who located the mouth of this river in 1880. The May River flows for about 69 kilometres into Stokes Bay northeast of Derby. The May was also named by Brockman in 1881 during the same expedition. He named it after Mary Matilda Lucille (May) Thomson (1858–1946) of Brookhampton (near Bridgetown), a granddaughter of Western Australia's first Surveyor General, John Septimus Roe.

86 The ranges are part of a Devonian reef complex that extends for around 350 kilometres along the northern margin of the Canning Basin. The ranges are 350 million years old. See D.C. Edinger, 'Windjana Gorge: geology, history and anthropology', Kimberley Society, <http://www.kimberleysociety.org/oldfiles/1996/WINDJANA%20GORGE%20September.pdf>

87 WAPD, Lennard River Police Camp, 'Journal of Patrol by PC Armitage and PCs Goodridge, Yates and Handly and 4 Native Assistants to Affect the Arrest of the Murderers of Thomas Harry and Robert Allen', 12 July 1892, SROWA, AN 5/1, Cons. 430, File 1465/1892.

88 Tracking along the coast are the Jukin (Broome area), Yawuru (south of Jukin),

Ngumbarl (northwest of Jukun), Jabirrjabirr (Cape Baskerville area), Nyul Nyul (north of Jabirrjabirr), Bardi (Lombardina, Cape Leveque area), Djawi (islands in King Sound), Nimanburu (King Sound area), Nyikina (Derby, Looma, Noonkanbah, Fitzroy Crossing area), Warwa (King Sound area), Unggarangi (northwest of Warwa), Umida (Koolan Island area), Unggumi (area east of Warwa), Punuba/Bunuba (Fitzroy River area), Gooniyandi (southeast of Punuba/Bunuba), Worla (King Leopold Ranges, Durack Range area), Ngarinyin (Drysdale River area), Worora (Augustus Island, Collier Bay, Prince Regent River area), Wunambul (Bonaparte Archipelago, Bigge Island area), Gamberre (Cape Bougainville, Kalumburu area), Miwa (Cape Londonderry area), Kwini (southeast of Miwa), Yiiji (southeast of Kwini), Doolboong (Wyndham, Ord river area), Kadjerong (area east of Doolboong), Miriwoong (Kununurra, Lake Argyle area), Kija (Lake Argyle, Turkey Creek area). Spellings may vary. These names are drawn from a map of the language groups: D. Horton, *Indigenous Language Map*, Aboriginal Studies Press, AIATSIS and Auslig/Sinclair, Knight, Merz, 1996 <http://www.ourlanguages.net.au/languages/language-maps.html>. 'This map indicates only the general location of larger groupings of people which may include smaller groups such as clans, dialects or individual languages in a group. Boundaries are not intended to be exact.' For an earlier seminal study see N.B. Tindale, *Aboriginal Tribes of Australia: their terrain, environmental controls, distribution, limits, and proper names by Norman B. Tindale; with an appendix on Tasmanian tribes by Rhys Jones*, Berkeley, University of California Press, 1974.

89 'Halls Creek tools 50,000 years old', *The West Australian*, 9 December 2009, p.28.

90 There are an estimated 100,000 of these paintings spread across 50,000 square kilometres of country in the Kimberley. See I.M. Crawford, *The Art of the Wandjina: Aboriginal cave paintings in Kimberley, Western Australia*, London, Oxford University Press, 1968; Bradshaw Foundation, 'The Australian Rock Art Archive: the ancient rock paintings of the Kimberley', 2011, <http://www.bradshawfoundation.com/bradshaws/index.php>; Ngarjno, Ungudman, Banggal and Nyawarra with J. Doring (ed.), *Gwion Gwion: secret and sacred pathways of the Ngarinyin Aboriginal people of Australia*, Köln, Könemann, 2000; M. Donaldson, *Kimberley Rock Art, Volume 1: Mitchell Plateau Area*, Perth, Wildrocks Publications, 2012; M. Donaldson, *Kimberley Rock Art, Volume 2: North Kimberley*, Perth, Wildrocks Publications, 2012; M. Donaldson, *Kimberley Rock Art, Volume 3: Rivers and Ranges*, Perth, Wildrocks Publications, 2013.

91 A. Redmond and F. Skyring, 'Exchange and Appropriation: the Wurnan economy and Aboriginal land and labour at Karunjie station, North-Western Australia', in I. Keen (ed.), *Indigenous Participation in Australian Economies: historical and anthropological perspectives*, Canberra, ANU E Press, 2010. <http://epress.anu.edu.au/apps/bookworm/view/Indigenous+Participation+in+Australian+Economies/5161/upfront.xhtml>.

92 K. Akerman, 'Material Culture and Trade in the Kimberley Today', in R.M.

Berndt and C.H. Berndt (eds), *Aborigines of the West: their past and present*, Perth, UWA Press, 1979, p.247.

93 V. Blundell, *Ethnohistory*, vol. 27, no. 103, 1980, pp.111–12; V. Blundell and R. Layton, 'Marriage, Myth and Models of Exchange in the West Kimberleys', *Mankind*, vol. 11, no. 3, 1978, pp.231–45.

94 M. Jebb, *Gardia Coming: collecting and interpreting Aboriginal oral sources*, unpublished, 1991; B. Shaw, *Is the Pen Mightier than the Word? a comparison between oral and written sources on the East Kimberley*, Canberra, Aboriginal Studies Press, 1998; Kimberley Language Resource Centre, *Moola Bulla: in the shadow of the mountain*, Broome, Magabala Books, 1996; H. Ross (ed.) and E. Bray (trans.), *Impact Stories of the East Kimberley*, East Kimberley Working Paper No. 28, Canberra, East Kimberley Impact Assessment Project 1989; C. Clement, *Historical Notes Relevant to Impact Stories of the East Kimberley*, Canberra, East Kimberley Impact Assessment Project, 1989.

95 Cited in Clement, '17th Century Visitors to the Kimberley Coast', Kimberley Society talk, June 2006, <http://kimberleysociety.org/oldfiles/2006/17TH%20CENTURY%20VISITORS%20TO%20THE%20KIMBERLEY%20COAST%20Jun%2006.pdf>.

96 Leslie Marchant concludes that this activity took place at Karrakatta Bay, west of Sunday Island in King Sound. W. Dampier, *A New Voyage Round the World*, London, 1699, chapter XVI, quoted in L.R. Marchant, *An Island unto Himself: William Dampier and New Holland*, Perth, Hesperian Press, 1988, p.108–9.

97 ibid., p.155.

98 ibid., p.156.

99 ibid., p.176.

100 ibid., p.155. Typically, Dampier's description of Aboriginal customs of the Kimberley in the same manuscript is often ignored when the above is quoted.

101 M.A. Clark and S.K. May (eds), *Macassan History and Heritage: journeys, encounters and influences*, Canberra, ANU E Press, 2013, pp.1, 58, <http://epress.anu.edu.au/wp-content/uploads/2013/06/whole.pdf>.

102 I.M. Crawford, *We Won the Victory: Aborigines and outsiders on the north-west coast of the Kimberley*, Fremantle, Fremantle Arts Centre Press, 2001.

103 J.S. Battye, *The Cyclopedia of Western Australia, an historical and commercial review, descriptive and biographical facts, figures and illustrations, an epitome of progress*, Adelaide, Hussey & Gillingham, 1912, p.180.

104 P.P. King, *Narrative of a Survey of the Intertropical and Western Coasts of Australia: performed between the years 1818 and 1822, Volumes One and Two*, London, John Murray, 1826.

105 King's mission was to find a river passage into the interior of Western Australia. He sailed up one of the rivers, which he named the King River after himself. His account of the countryside was less than favourable. King made four earlier voyages between December 1817 and April 1822 and was assigned to survey the parts of the Australian coast not already examined by Matthew Flinders.

106 G. Grey, *Journals of Two Expeditions of Discovery in North-West and Western*

Australia, During the Years 1837, 38, and 39, vol. 1, 1841, facsimile edition, Perth, Hesperian Press, 1983, p.1. Grey later became the Governor of South Australia, New Zealand and the Cape Province.

107 Grey's vivid description of Kimberley flies is at ibid., p.81.

108 ibid., p.149.

109 ibid., p.147; for Wandjina art see pp.202–3.

110 ibid.

111 K. Palmer, *Noongar people, Noongar land: the resilience of Aboriginal culture in the south west of Western Australia,* Canberra, Aboriginal Studies Press, 2016, p.8.

112 A. Forrest, *North-West Exploration: journal of expedition from DeGrey to Port Darwin,* Perth, Government Printer, 1880, preface. See also Western Australia, Parliamentary paper, No. 3, 1880. The Legislative Council agreed to fund the trip which consisted of a party of twenty-six horses, rations for six months and the following men: Fenton Hill (geologist and second in command), James Carey, John Campbell, Mathew Forrest (brother of Alexander), Arthur Hicks and two Noongar men who would act as trackers and guides from Bunbury and Pinjarra respectively, Tommy Pierre and Tommy Dower, known as 'Pierre' and 'Dower'.

113 Forrest, *North-West Exploration,* p.21.

114 ibid., pp.3 and 40.

115 ibid., p.40.

116 ibid., see 26 April on pp.5 and 10.

117 ibid., see 10 May on p.13.

118 Forrest's record of first-contact meetings are worth quoting. On 11 March 1879 Forrest came across what were likely Bardi people who 'appeared excessively frightened, and apparently had never seen white men before', ibid., p.5. Over the next few days his party near La Grange Bay noted groups spying on them from a distance yet making no contact, see 17 March entry, p.5. The group of up to thirty had been following the party on their trek through their *country* for over two weeks. Forrest attempted to induce them into their camp to no avail. By 10 April something of a level of mutual trust had been established. Forrest's men supplied one Aboriginal man near Beagle Bay with some damper, a pipe and some tobacco 'which he greatly seemed to relish', p.9. The next day a Bardi man approached and showed them the way to water where both parties shared some tea. Trust had been established as on 11 April thirty Bardi people joined them at Beagle Bay, staying all day and presenting them with fish to eat, p.9. At Beagle Bay the principle of Aboriginal reciprocity was evident; Forrest became aware that an exchange of goods was expected. 'The natives have supplied us constantly during our stay with fish and crabs, for which, however, they want double value', p.9. He did, however, give them some flour. The Bardi people indicated to Forrest a corroboree would be performed 'in our honor'. That night Forrest observed forty people performing this dance. On 14 May, travelling onto the Fitzroy River, Forrest remarked that the 'Fitzroy natives were a fine race of men'. He described them as 'perfectly naked' with markings and their front teeth

removed which he took to mean a certain tribal affiliation, p.14. Here Forrest had travelled into Nyikina, Bunuba, Unggumi and Warwa and Ngariyin *country*. This is a particularly rocky and treacherous countryside alongside the King Leopold Ranges where Forrest had great difficulty in keeping his horses (and men) alive. On 20 June a pivotal encounter ensued: just after camping Forrest heard 'the shouts of a large party of natives' he estimated at fifty who approached the party each 'carrying a large bundle of spears', p.21. Ordering his party 'to arm and be prepared for the worst', the party, possibly Warwa or Nyikina, then deliberately put their spears down and approached Forrest 'and began to talk vociferously in their (to us) unintelligible jargon' indicating Forrest should leave, p.21. On 20 June an Elder, or an 'old man' as Forrest described him, left the group and approached him indicating they should leave. Forrest gave him some damper and sugar after which the party left. However, they returned to Forrest's party, this time too close for what Forrest considered comfortable, and Forrest decided that the best course of action was to 'show them the use to which firearms could be put' and with that fired a round into a nearby tree, p.21. The effect was to frighten 'them so effectually' that they cleared out at once. By late July 1879 the party was on the border of Kija *country* and what would become the Western Australian and Northern Territory border. The party encountered three women 'whose terror deprived them of their speech' upon seeing Forrest's men, p.25. Later a group 'set the country alight all around them', 14 August, p.30, although in the entire trip of over nine months through numerous different language groups the party was never involved in any conflict or was attacked.

119 The Calvert Scientific Exploring Expedition in 1896 and 1897 included Larry Wells (leader), Charles Wells (his cousin and the second in command), George Jones (mineralogist and photographer), George Keartland (naturalist) and James Trainor, with Dervish Bejah and Said Ameer (camel drivers) and twenty camels. The camels could not cope with the poisonous plants of the Kimberley and Charles Wells and Jones died of dehydration in attempting to find a forward campsite and water.

120 Forrest named the Margaret and Ord rivers, the King Leopold Ranges (after King Leopold II of Belgium), and a vast tract of well-watered pastoral country on the Fitzroy and Ord rivers.

121 For a newspaper report of this trip see 'Early Kimberleys, Forrest's expedition, An Adventurous Trip', *Western Mail,* 15 April 1937, p.5.

122 Votes and Proceedings, 1880, Paper no. 3, quoted in G. Bolton, 'The Kimberley Pastoral Industry', *University Studies in History and Economics,* vol. 11, no. 2, 1954, p.10.

123 A detailed newspaper report can be found at 'Pastoral Settlement in Western Australia', *The West Australian,* 29 August 1885, p.7.

124 G. Bolton, 'The Kimberley Pastoral Industry', p.10.

125 See M. Durack, *Kings in Grass Castles,* London, Constable, 1959, pp.188–94; G. Bolton, *Alexander Forrest: his life and times,* Melbourne, Melbourne University Press with UWA Press, 1958, p.28.

126 Bolton, *Alexander Forrest*, p.44.

127 J.S. Battye, *The History of the North West of Australia Embracing Kimberley, Gascoyne and Murchison Districts*, Perth, VK Jones, 1915, p.36; C. Clement, 'Early Pastoral Leases in the Kimberley', Kimberley Society talks, February 1998, <http://kimberleysociety.org/oldfiles/1998/EARLY%20PASTORAL%20 LEASES%20IN%20THE%20KIMBERLEY%20Feb%2098.pdf>; Bolton, *Alexander Forrest*, pp.27–34; G. Bolton and H. Pedersen, 'The Emanuels of Noonkanbah and GoGo', *Early Days: Journal of the Royal Western Australian Historical Society*, vol. 8, part 4, 1980, pp.5-21; C. Clement, *Australia's North-West: a study of exploration, land policy and land acquisition, 1644–1884*, PhD thesis, Murdoch University, 1991; C. Clement, *Kimberley District Pastoral Leasing Directory, 1881–1900*, Perth, National Heritage, for the Kimberley Historical Sources Project, 1993.

128 Clement, 'Early Pastoral Leases in the Kimberley'.

129 Bolton, 'The Kimberley Pastoral Industry', p.10.

130 Bolton, *Alexander Forrest*, p.29.

131 ibid., pp.29–30.

132 'Land Regulations for the Kimberley District', *The Inquirer and Commercial News,* 29 December 1880, p.5.

133 Clement, 'Early Pastoral Leases in the Kimberley'.

134 ibid.

135 Bolton, *Alexander Forrest*, p.29.

136 Clement, 'Early Pastoral Leases in the Kimberley'.

137 See 'Kimberley Land Grab', *Sunday Times*, 16 August 1908, p.3; Bolton, *Alexander Forrest*, p.32.

138 Clement, 'Early Pastoral Leases in the Kimberley'.

139 Battye, *The History of the North West of Australia Embracing Kimberley, Gascoyne and Murchison Districts*, p.119.

140 Clement, 'Early Pastoral Leases in the Kimberley'.

141 Bolton, *Alexander Forrest*, p.29; Bolton, 'The Kimberley Pastoral Industry', De Launey Edgar and Co acquired 5,500,000 acres, A.R. Wallis 2,270,000 acres, J.A. Game 2,224,080 acres, Durack and Associates 2,150,000 acres, Kimberley Pastoral Association 2,000,000 acres and King Sound Pastoral Company (from Melbourne) 1,350,000 acres.

142 For biographical information see W.B. Kimberly, *History of West Australia*, Melbourne, FW Niven, 1897; Reilly, *Reminiscences of Fifty Years Residence in Western Australia*; R. Erickson, *Dictionary of Western Australians, Volume 3, Free 1850–1868*, Perth, UWA Press, 1979.

143 Battye, *The History of the North West of Australia Embracing Kimberley, Gascoyne and Murchison Districts*, p.38.

144 In March 1869 Forrest searched for the explorer Ludwig Leichhardt through Leonora and Laverton over some 3600 kilometres. In March 1870 Forrest with Alexander, second in charge, Police Constable Hector McLarty, farrier William Osborn, and Noongar trackers Windich and Billy Noongale tracked from Western Australia to South Australia. In April 1874 he embarked on an

expedition to find new pastoral land from Geraldton to the Murchison River, and then east through the unexplored centre of Western Australia to the overland telegraph line from Darwin to Adelaide. See J. Forrest, *Explorations in Australia, Explorations in search of Dr. Leichardt and Party. 2. From Perth to Adelaide, Around the Great Australian Bight. 3. From Champion Bay, Across the Desert to the Telegraph and to Adelaide. With an Appendix on the Condition of Western Australia. Illus.* by G.F. Angas, London, Sampson Low, Marston, Low and Searle, 1875; 'Explorer – Surveyor. Famous Amongst Pathfinders', *The West Australian*, 9 August 1947, p.5; 'Builders of the State. The Forrest Brothers. Explorers', *The West Australian*, 19 June 1937, p.4. An electronic edition of Forrest's *Explorations in Australia* can be found at <http://www.gutenberg.org/files/9958/9958-h/9958-h.htm>.

145 Forrest, *Explorations in Australia*, see 13 June 1874.

146 J. Forrest, *Report on the Kimberley District, North-western Australia by John Forrest, Surveyor General and Commissioner of Crown Lands*, Perth, Government Printer, 1883. pp.31–2.

147 Forrest compiled a list of the afflictions and ailments one could experience in the Kimberley: festered fingers, boils, prickly heat, constant vomiting, sore lips, sore eyes, mosquito and flies, boiling heat, water in rivers too hot to drink, bad diet, grass seeds. ibid., p.130.

148 F.K. Crowley, *Forrest 1847–1918: apprenticeship to premiership,* Brisbane, University of Queensland Press, 1971, pp.129–30.

149 Brockman was possibly unaware of the new 'ballot' regulations that had superseded the existing land regulations of the North West. As a consequence his claim was disallowed although he was later compensated and allocated a block of land near G.J. Poulton's property on the Meda River on Warwa country. J.G. Brockman, *Journal of an Exploring Trip from Beagle Bay to the Fitzroy River and Back Again, December 4 1879 to January 10 1880*, Battye Library, No. 384A; Battye, *The History of the North West of Australia Embracing Kimberley, Gascoyne and Murchison Districts*, p.118.

150 Battye, *The History of the North West of Australia Embracing Kimberley, Gascoyne and Murchison Districts*, p.210; A.R. Richardson, *Early Memories of the Great Nor' West*, Perth, E.S. Wigg, 1914, p.61. Richardson had been a pioneer pastoralist of the North West Pilbara district. In 1864 he established the Portland Squatting Company and the Pyramid station on the Grey River. He had properties in Serpentine near Perth and by 1879 held prime runs round the Yule, De Grey and Oakover rivers in the northwest. N.E. Withnell-Taylor, *Yeera-Muk-A-Doo, A Social History of the Settlement of the North West Australia Told Through the Withnell and Hancock Families 1861 to 1890*, Fremantle, Fremantle Arts Centre Press, 1980, p.193.

151 In 1885 George leased Mount Anderson, 96 kilometres east along the Fitzroy, where he was joined by his elder brother John Charles. George would lease the adjoining Lower Liveringa of 1214 square kilometres. When Edwin arrived that year he and Charles selected Kimberley Downs on the Lennard River and Cherrabun to the southeast. When his half-brother Augustus Frederick

(Gus) arrived in 1891 he joined Edwin on a new station, Quanbun Downs. A.C. Staples, 'Edwin Rose and George Canlar Rose', *Australian Dictionary of Biography* <http://adb.anu.edu.au/biography/rose-edwin-8520>.

152 'The Far North Stock Industry', *The West Australian*, 7 February 1907, p.2.

153 Also known as Lillamaloola.

154 See police account of Forrester, along with Victorian owners F.E. Beaver, J. Munro, J. Fergusson, K. Gunn WAPD, 'Kimberley District, Derby Station. Visiting Settlers on Roberson and Lennard Rivers, and Arrest Native Offenders', 27 April 1886, SROWA, AN 5/1, Cons. 430, File 1013/1886.

155 Kimberly (ed.), *History of West Australia, A Narrative of her Past, Together With Biographies of Her Leading Men*, p.269.

156 Battye, *The History of the North West of Australia Embracing Kimberley, Gascoyne and Murchison Districts*, p.32. For the police report of Lukin's sheep losses see Kimberley District 'Report by Lance Corporal Payne', 6 June 1883, SROWA, Cons. 856, File 1545/75.

157 Bolton, 'The Kimberley Pastoral Industry'.

158 Bolton and Pedersen, 'The Emanuels of Noonkanbah and GoGo', pp.5–21.

159 G. MacKenzie, *Fossil Downs: a saga of the Kimberleys, Australia's longest droving trip*, Yeppoon, Queensland, Gordon Mackenzie, 1995. Also on the original trek were Peter Thomson, James McGeorge and Jasper Pickles although they left before the trek finished.

160 F. Crowley, *Big John Forrest 1847–1918, A Founding Father of the Commonwealth*, Perth, UWA Press, 2000, p.58.

161 See debate in 'Legislative Council', *The West Australian*, 25 June 1886, p.3; Battye, *The History of the North West of Australia Embracing Kimberley, Gascoyne and Murchison Districts*, p.33.

162 Bolton, *Alexander Forrest*, p.14.

163 Bolton, 'The Kimberley Pastoral Industry', p.18.

164 ibid., p.21.

165 Hann's previous station in the Gulf Country had become unviable in 1894 after a series of poor seasons and low prices for cattle. He had set out for the north of Western Australia in search of new opportunities. See M. Donaldson and I. Elliot (eds), F.H. Hann, *Do Not Yield to Despair; Frank Hugh Hann's Exploration Diaries in the Arid Interior of Australia 1895–1908*, Perth, Hesperian Press, 1998; G.C. Bolton, 'Frank Hugh Hann (1846–1921)', *Australian Dictionary of Biography*, 1972, <http://adb.anu.edu.au/biography/hann-frank-hugh-3906>. Hann named the Charnley and Isdell rivers and identified some areas he considered to be promising pastoral country. 'Death of Frank Hann', *The Daily News*, 23 August 1921, p.7. Hann himself took up a lease of over 2590 square kilometres, but because of his poor finances he was not able to stock it. The area he had identified and made accessible was then taken over by already established Kimberley pastoral families.

166 The party followed the Pentecost River south from Wyndham, and then northwest through the King Leopold Ranges to Walcott Inlet and returned along the Drysdale River, reaching their depot on 26 November

1901. W. Bermin, 'Frederick Slade Drake-Brockman (1857–1917)', *Australian Dictionary of Biography*, 1981, <http://adb.anu.edu.au/biography/drake-brockman-frederick-slade-6015>

167 Bolton, 'The Kimberley Pastoral Industry', p.13.

168 See P.M. Durack, 'Pioneering in the East Kimberleys', *Early Days: Journal of the Royal Western Australian Historical Society,* vol. 2, pt.14, 1933, pp.1–46.

169 There are notable Kimberley ranges named after these two men south of Wyndham.

170 Bolton, 'The Kimberley Pastoral Industry', p.30. Bob Button was the manager.

171 ibid., p.75.

172 Bolton, *Alexander Forrest*, p.34.

173 ibid., p.15. Three geographical features in the Kimberley bear Edward Hardman's name: Hardman Point, Hardman Range and Mount Hardman.

174 C. Clement, *Old Halls Creek: A Town Remembered*, Perth, National Heritage, 2000.

175 For an account of this meeting see Durack, *Kings in Grass Castles,* p.190.

176 Bolton, *Alexander Forrest*, p.45.

177 Crowley, *Forrest 1847–1918:* pp.129–30.

178 Bolton, 'The Kimberley Pastoral Industry', p.28.

179 Bolton, *Alexander Forrest*, p.28.

180 ibid.

181 *The Inquirer,* 6 May 1882. See also Bolton, *Alexander Forrest*, pp.46–7.

182 M. Durack, *Kings in Grass Castles,* 1959, op.cit., p.192.

183 Bolton, *Alexander Forrest*, p.48.

184 ibid., p.30.

185 ibid.

186 Bolton suggests Forrest sought to promote other diverse industries in the Kimberley such as sugar plantations and coal mining; ibid., p.30.

187 ibid., p.48.

188 ibid., p.17.

189 *Government Gazette*, 2 March 1887, quoted in Bolton, *Alexander Forrest*, p.34; 'Election Notice, A. Forrest', *The Inquirer and Commercial News*, 4 January 1889, p.6.

190 Bolton, *Alexander Forrest*, pp.30–2.

191 See 'Kimberley Land Grab, Nearly Forty Million Acres Monopolised; a Hundred People in Possession of an Area as Large as Four European States; Together Belgium, Holland, Servia and Denmark; Parliament in a Pliant Mood the Scandal of the Far North; How Long Will the People Stand It?' *The Sunday Times,* 16 August 1908, p.3.

192 ibid.

Chapter 3: 'Weather Hot, Flies Troublesome...'

1 CSO, 'Letter to Colonial Secretary from M.S. Smith', 18 November 1881, SROWA, AN 24, Cons. 527, File 1437, no. 86. For popular opinion on the need for a police force in the Kimberley, see 'Police Protection in the

Kimberley District', *The West Australian*, 27 February 1883, p.3.

2   WAPD, 'Reports on Establishment and Supplies Required for Kimberley Stations, Letter from Superintendent M.S. Smith to LC Troy', 31 October 1882, SROWA, AN 5/6, Cons. 129, File 20/1883. The sergeant was to be paid £185 and the constables £135 per annum.

3   ibid.

4   WAPD, 'Reports on Establishment and Supplies Required for Kimberley Stations, Letter from LC Troy to M.S. Smith', 6 December 1882, SROWA, AN 5/6, Cons. 129, File 20/1883.

5   WAPD, 'Reports on Establishment and Supplies Required for Kimberley Stations, Letter to LC Payne from M.S. Smith Chief Office', 30 July 1883, SROWA, AN 5/6, Cons. 129, File 20/1883.

6   WAPD, 'Detailed Police Reports from Police in the Kimberley, Letter from LC Troy to M.S. Smith', 2 July 1883, SROWA, AN 5/6, Cons. 129, File 856/1883.

7   WAPD, 'Reports on Establishment and Supplies Required for Kimberley Stations', forage list from the boat *Amur*, SROWA, AN 5/6, Cons. 129, File 20/1883.

8   WAPD, 'Journal Corporal Payne on Sea Trip from Fremantle to Roebuck Bay, Report from LC Payne to Supt Police, King Sound Station Kimberley', SROWA, AN 5/6, Cons. 129, File 395/1883.

9   ibid.

10   WAPD, 'Detailed Police Reports from Police in the Kimberley, Report from LC Payne, King Sound Station', 2 June 1883, SROWA, AN 5/6, Cons. 129, File 856/1883.

11   ibid.

12   ibid.

13   ibid., 3 June 1883: 'Mr Coucher, Manager, Alfred Barnett, Mr Lavender, Chas Farmer, Jos. Alwell, William Allcock, Alfred Green, Geo. Stevens and H. Porter'.

14   ibid.

15   ibid.

16   ibid.

17   On 4 June he reported visiting Morgan and McDermott's station; there were five white workers and 16,000 sheep at this station. John Riley represented 'Morgan', Jas McDermott, G.J. Poulton, George Riley and Alec Slater. Poulton informed Payne that he thought there was some kind of poison near the riverbank as they had lost several sheep that showed symptoms of poisoning. These men had only seen '7 natives since their arrival there and they appeared very friendly and told them they must not go up the river as the natives higher up were no good'. On 6 June 1883 Payne crossed the junction of the Meda River and May River and visited Lukin and Monger's station. There were, he said, '7 white persons and one Gascoyne Native on this station': Mr Lukin, F.H. Monger, Peter Brown, Henry Bostock, Theo Lowe, Mr Burrows, an expiree John Cronin and native Bobby of Gascoyne.

They had 1900 sheep and about 400 lambs with a prospect of a good lambing. They had scab slightly having been in Coucher's camps. They were using every available means to keep it down and did not believe scab could live there unless they got rain. They said they had seen seven natives since their arrival there about four weeks since. They appeared friendly, had some food, went up the river and promised to return but they had not seen them since. Payne noted that this company had had very bad luck in getting to the Kimberley, having lost 2300 sheep chiefly on board ship. They gave the country a very bad name for mosquitoes in summer but others said Mr Lukin 'very much exaggerates it'. WAPD, 'Detailed Police Reports from Police in the Kimberley, Report from LC Payne, King Sound Station', SROWA, AN 5/6, Cons. 129, File 856/1883.

18 ibid. Payne returned to camp on 10 June having seen 'only one native and very few traces of natives'. He surmised he could not 'conceive they are plentiful for fifty miles up the Meda River otherwise there would be more traces of them.' He did add that he stayed one night with Mr Johnson, surveyor, on 7 June on the Meda and he informed him he 'had not seen any natives in all his rounds and only a few odd traces'.

19 ibid.

20 The Minnie River is a 33 kilometre long branch of the Fitzroy located close to the mouth of the river, south of Derby. The name was first recorded by Hamlet Cornish and George Paterson of the Murray River Squatting Company in 1881. Between 14 and 19 June Payne visited stations to ascertain their status and condition, first travelling on the 'Yeda' [sic], Fitzroy and Minnie rivers. He travelled to Mr Gaines, station (formerly the Murray Squatting Company) known as the 'Yeda' [sic] station. Here he recorded 'one Nichol Bay Native, two Fremantle Natives and two Roebuck Bay Natives' employed on this station. Mr Rose informed LC Payne he had a number of 'Fitzroy Natives' signed on as general servants who were not yet at work for him and had to come in at stated times. 'There are 11 persons': G.C. Rose, F. Loard, Joseph Larmer, Mr Jones, Robert Norton, Geo. Eagan, Robert Mcattee, Theo Larkin, Hamlet Cornish and Ephrain Brown and one Chinamen Ah Leck. WAPD, 'Detailed Police Reports from Police in the Kimberley, Report from LC Payne, King Sound Station', SROWA, AN 5/6, Cons. 129, File 856/1883.

21 ibid.

22 ibid.

23 ibid.

24 There were 8000 sheep (scab slightly), thirty-four head of cattle and fifty-three horses on Yeeda Station and were doing exceedingly well. On 16 June Payne crossed the Fitzroy River, which was running strong with splendid fresh water, and visited the Kimberley Pastoral Company's station on the Fitzroy and Minnie rivers. Manager John McLarty was absent in Perth. There were at present six white persons: William McLarty, Charles Warbuton, Charles Elliot, expiree Felix Cogan, Arthur Manning and expiree William Norman,

one mission native and two Fitzroy natives employed on this station. They have 6000 sheep and twelve horses, all doing well; they had scab slightly. On 19 June he visited J.H. Daly's station on the Minnie River. There were only two people on this station: the owner Daly and Henry Hickey, his expiree. They have only 300 sheep that were doing remarkably well and had no scab. Mr Daly was 'highly pleased with the country' and was about to visit Cossack immediately after shearing four more sheep. He stated that he has seen no natives since he had been at this station. WAPD, 'Detailed Police Reports from Police in the Kimberley, Report from LC Payne, King Sound Station', SROWA, AN 5/6, Cons. 129, File 856/1883.

25 ibid. Payne recorded that the whole of the country travelled over, from the Yeeda to about 64 kilometres up the Fitzroy and Minnie rivers was 'magnificent country, good feeding grasses for sheep and water in abundance. All of the sheep, cattle and horses were all looking remarkably well.' He considered that part of the country 'far superior for both sheep and cattle to any country' travelled on the Meda or May rivers; the grasses were thicker and finer and water more plentiful. McLarty informed Payne that for 96 kilometres further up the Fitzroy the country 'was splendid'.

26 For a summary of Fairbairn's report see J.T. Reilly, *Reminiscences of Fifty Years in Western Australia*, Sands and McDougall, 1903, pp.670–95. For Fairbairn's report see *Western Australian Legislative Council Votes and Proceedings* 1882, vol. 33, pp.3–14. For the colonists' letters and Fairbairn's reply to them see the *West Australian Government Gazette*, 5 December 1882, No. 53, pp.519–22.

27 *Report of a Commission Appointed by his Excellency the Governor to Inquire into the Treatment of the Aboriginal Native Prisoners of the Crown in the Colony; and also into Certain Other Matters Relative to Aboriginal Affairs*, paper no. 32, 2 October 1884, p.5, report published in *Government Gazette*, SROWA, Cons. 495, File 71.

28 CSO, 'Sub Inspector Troy – Treatment of Natives in the Ashburton, Gascoyne and Murchison Districts', 11 February 1889, SROWA, AN 24, Cons. 527, File 0827/1889.

29 'Sergeant Troy's Report, 3 July 1886', *The West Australian*, 13 August 1886, p.3.

30 See for example 'Report from the Government Resident Derby', *The West Australian*, 3 August 1886, p.3; 'The Kimberley Goldfields: Sub Inspector Troy's latest Report', *The West Australian*, 5 January 1887, p.3; 'Kimberley Police Expedition', *The Inquirer and Commercial News*, 6 July 1888, p.3.

31 'The Kimberley Goldfields Sergeant Troy's Report', *The West Australian*, 10 August 1886, p.3.

32 See for example 'The Aboriginal Protection Board', *The West Australian*, 19 March 1888, p.3.

33 WAPD, 'Detailed Police Reports from Police in the Kimberley, Letter from LC P. Troy to M.S. Smith', 3 October 1883, SROWA, AN 5/6, Cons. 129, File 856/1883. He was also expected to inspect water wells being sunk by Elliot and Cornish.

34 ibid.

35 ibid.

36 ibid.

37 ibid.

38 ibid.

39 ibid.

40 WAPD, 'Sgt Troy Report on Employment of Aborigines by Settlers', 21 August 1884, SROWA, AN 5/6, Cons. 129, File 1468.

41 ibid.

42 See WAPD, Derby Police Station, 'Report by Sub Inspector Troy to Commissioner Phillips', SROWA, AN 5, Cons. 241/1.

43 See for example WAPD, 'Ethnological Report by E. Curr to the Colonial Secretary', 21 April 1879, SROWA, AN 5/6, Cons. 129.

44 'The Mission of the Trappists to the Aborigines of the West Kimberley', *The West Australian,* 19 October 1892, p.6.

45 C. Choo, 'Mixed Blessings: establishment of Christian Missions in the Kimberley' in C. Clement, J. Gresham and H. McGlashan (eds), *Kimberley History: people, exploration and development,* Perth, Kimberley Society, 2012, p.196.

46 Small reserves of some 12 hectares were created in 1874 at New Norcia and, later, reserves that could be turned into mission schools of between 4 hectares and 40 hectares were created in Roebourne, Carnarvon and Bridgetown. P. Biskup, *Not Slaves, Not Citizens: the Aboriginal problem in Western Australia 1898–1954,* Brisbane, University of Queensland Press, 1973, p.101.

47 Department of Indigenous Affairs, 'Lost Lands Report', Perth, Government of Western Australia, 2004, p.11. In 1878, 202 square kilometres were granted in the Murchison, and in 1883 a 4046 square kilometre reserve near Mt Dalgety on the Gascoyne River was set aside. In 1884, 2428 square kilometres was reserved on the Fraser River on the western side of King Sound so that Aboriginal people 'could continue to have access to traditional means of subsistence'. This Kimberley reserve was cancelled in 1891 to be replaced by an even larger 2832 square kilometres reserve on the Dampier Peninsula which would later become the site for the Beagle Bay mission.

48 Aborigines Protection Board, 'General Report of the Kimberley District, Report of the Aborigines Protection Board', 12 March 1897, SROWA, Cons. 495, File 12.

49 See M.A. Jebb, *Blood, Sweat and Welfare: a history of white bosses and Aboriginal pastoral workers,* Perth, UWA Press, 2002. For a perspective on Aboriginal labour in the southwest of Western Australia see S. Hodson, 'Nyungars and Work: Aboriginal experiences in the rural economy of the Great Southern region of Western Australia', *Aboriginal History,* vol. 17, nos. 1–2, 1993, pp.73–92; S. Hodson, 'Making a Rural Labour Force: the intervention of the state in the working lives of Nyungars in the Great Southern, 1936–1948', in C. Fox (ed.), *Historical Refractions: studies in Western Australian history,* no. 14, 1993, pp.26–41.

50 Biskup, *Not Slaves, Not Citizens*, p.18.

51 Quoted in S. J. Hunt, *Spinifex and Hessian: women's lives in north-west Australia, 1860–1900*, Perth, UWA Press, 1986, p.149.

52 'Pink eye' designates a period of leave undertaken by Aboriginal people who feel the need the leave the place where they are in contact with white society and return to their traditional way of life.

53 'Instructions to and Reports from the Resident Magistrate Despatched by Direction of his Excellency on Special Duty to the Murchison and Gascoyne Districts, WA Parliament', LCVP, 1882, p.11. For witness testimony supporting this claim see CSO, 'Sub Inspector Troy – Treatment of Natives in the Ashburton, Gascoyne and Murchison Districts', 11 February 1889, SROWA, AN 24, Cons. 527, File 0827/1889.

54 'Kimberley and the Natives', *The Western Mail*, Saturday 18 August 1888, p.36.

55 A. Redmond, 'Strange relatives: mutualities and dependencies between Aborigines and pastoralists in the Northern Kimberley', *Oceania*, vol. 75, no. 3, 2005, p.235.

56 C. Owen and C. Choo, 'Deafening Silences: understanding frontier relations and the discourse of police files through Kimberley police records', in C. Choo and S. Hollbach (eds), *Studies in Western Australian History: History and Native Title*, no. 23, 2003, pp.135–6.

57 P. Marshall (ed.), *Raparapa: stories from the Fitzroy River drovers*, Broome, Magabala Books, 1988; A.M. Chalarimeri, *The Man from the Sunrise Side*, Broome, Magabala Books, 2001; Jebb, *Blood, Sweat and Welfare*; M. Munro and M.A. Jebb, *Emerarra: a man of Merarra*, Broome, Magabala Books, 1996; E. Richards, J. Hudson and P. Lowe (eds), *Out of the Desert: stories from the Walmajarri exodus*, Broome, Magabala Books, 2002.

58 H. Cornish, *The Call of the Kimberleys: pioneering in 1880*, BL No. 312A, pp.29–31. See also I. Shackcloth, *The Call of the Kimberleys*, Melbourne, Hallcraft Publishing, 1950, p.219; see report in *The West Australian*, 3 March 1883, p.3. In Shackcloth's novel, Cornish's brother attributed it to the 'murderous instinct of the blacks'. Sergeant O'Connell was sent on patrol to arrest the murderer of Anthony Cornish at the Fitzroy. 'Reports on establishment and supplies required for Kimberley Stations', Letter from Superintendent of Police to Resident Office Roebourne, 8 January 1883, SROWA, AN 5/6, Cons. 129, File 20/1883. Guerilla was executed at Rottnest on 18 June 1883.

59 WAPD, 'Detailed Police Reports from Police in the Kimberley', Report from LC Payne, King Sound Station, June 1883, SROWA, AN 5/6, Cons. 129, File 856/1883.

60 W. Lambden Owen, *Cossack Gold: the chronicles of an early goldfields warden*, Sydney, Angus and Robertson, 1933, p.149. See also M. Durack, *Kings in Grass Castles*, Melbourne, Lloyd O'Neil, 1974 [1959], pp.326–31.

61 See testimony of PC Goodridge to Walter Roth, 'The Aborigines Question, Dr Roth's Investigations, Prosecution of Aborigines, Female Witnesses, Child Prisoners, The Food Question', *The West Australian*, Thursday 16

February 1905, p.2.

62 See 'The "Native" Blue Book', *The West Australian*, 2 November 1886, p.3.

63 CSO, 'Letter from John Cowan to Right Honourable Secretary of State for the Colonies', London, 21 October 1886, SROWA, Cons. 856, File 1545/75.

64 'The West Australian Blacks, How They Are Treated', *Port Pirie Recorder and North Western Mail*, 16 April 1904, p.3.

65 Western Australian Parliamentary Debates, vol. xi, p.458, quoted in P. Hasluck, *Black Australians: a survey of native policy in Western Australia, 1829–1897*, Melbourne, Melbourne University Press, 1942, p.223.

66 *Masters and Servants Amendment Act 1882* (46 Vict., No. 11).

67 See *Roth Royal Commission on the Condition of the Natives. Presented to Both Houses of Parliament by His Excellency's Command*, Roth Report, WAPP, 1905: interview with Corporal William Goodridge, Question No. 1685, p.100. This condition was still being written about by police in 1933 in correspondence regarding police duties. See Circular Order 6059/27, Derby Police Files, Property of Western Australian Police Service.

68 See G.W. Broughton, *Turn Again Home*, Brisbane, Jacaranda Press, 1965. Stanley (stockman) came back to the station to kill his assistant 'Charcoal' for having deserted him, p.71.

69 See G. Bolton, 'Black and White After 1897', in C.T. Stannage (ed.), *A New History of Western Australia*, Perth, UWA Press, 1981, p.127.

70 L.R. Marchant, *Aboriginal Administration in Western Australia, 1886–1905*, Canberra, Australian Institute of Aboriginal Studies, 1981, p.11.

71 CSO, 'Sub Inspector Troy – Treatment of Natives in the Ashburton, Gascoyne and Murchison Districts', 11 February 1889, SROWA, AN 24, Cons. 527, File 0827/1889.

72 Aboriginal Protection Board, 'General Report of the Kimberley District, Report of the Aborigines Protection Board', 12 March 1897, SROWA, Cons. 495, Item 12. This report was published verbatim in *The West Australian*: George Marsden, Annual Report, 'Aborigines Protection Board', *The West Australian*, 29 May 1897, p.9.

73 K. Akerman and J. Stanton, 'Riji and Jakuli: Kimberley pearl shell in Aboriginal Australia', *NT Museum of Arts and Sciences*, no. 4, 1994, p.19.

74 Hunt, *Spinifex and Hessian*, p.148. See also CSO, 'Register of Native Agreements for the Quarter Ending 31 December 81', SROWA, AN 24, Cons. 527, Subject 1444, Letter 77; WAPD, 'Return of Natives Engaged in Pearl Shell Diving to 30 June 1882', SROWA, AN 5/6, Cons. 129, File 32/916; CSO, Copy of the 'Register of Natives' Agreements for 3/4 of the Year Ended 31 December 1883', SROWA, AN 24, Cons. 527, File 1409/1884.

75 ibid., Graham Blick, District Medical Officer and Acting Resident Magistrate Broome, October 1904, Roth Report, 1905, Pt 750, pp.64–6.

76 Aborigines Protection Board, 'Government Resident Kimberley Kidnapping is carried on from La Grange Bay mouth of the Fitzroy (Part 1) (28/09/1883). Correspondence - re pearling (Part 2) (1582/83)', SROWA, Cons. 388, File

3; 'The West Australian: the new regulations under the new Pearl Shell Fishery Act', *The West Australian*, 14 December 1880, p.2.

77 See J.B. Gribble, *Dark Deeds in a Sunny Land or Blacks and Whites in North-West Australia*, Perth, UWA Press, 1987 [1886].

78 For a history of this period see M.A. Bain, *Full Fathom Five*, Perth, Artlook Books, 1982, pp.15–33; K. De La Rue, *Pearl Shell and Pastures: the story of Cossack and Roebourne, and their place in the history of the North-West, from the earliest explorations to 1910*, Cossack, Cossack Project Committee, 1979.

79 CSO, 'Governor's Confidential Despatches, Governor Weld to Secretary of State Colonial Office, London, March, entry 1, 1873', SROWA, Cons. 390, WAS 1174, Item 47, vol. 1, 1869–85.

80 ibid.

81 CSO, 'Report By Sub Inspector Piesse, Governor's Confidential Despatches, Governor Weld to Secretary of State Colonial Office, London, March, entry 1, 1873', SROWA, Cons. 390, WAS 1174, Item 47, vol. 1, 1869–85.

82 ibid.

83 An 1873 Act required Aboriginal divers to enter into an agreement authorised by a justice of the peace or police officer to ensure the diver was acting of his own free will. In 1875 the *Pearl Shell Fisheries Regulation Act* further sought to regulate Aboriginal labour conditions. In 1880 a government commission to investigate conditions in the pearl-shell industry was undertaken and tabled in parliament: Legislative Council of Western Australia, 1880, Paper A16.

84 De La Rue, *Pearl Shell and Pastures*, p.79; Bain, *Full Fathom Five*, p.22.

85 'The West Australian Blacks, How They Are Treated', *Port Pirie Recorder and North Western Mail*, 16 April 1904, p.3. The anonymous 'M' referred to in this articles Thomas Mountain. See also Statement from Resident Magistrate Angelo, quoted in Hunt, *Spinifex and Hessian*, p.24; evidence at Aborigines Department, 'Mrs Eliza Tracey (to Dr Roth) Re: Ill Treatment of Natives in the North West', SROWA, Cons. 255, File 0006/1905. Tracey wrote 'the Lockyer Brothers sold natives to Pearlers for £8 a head. The two men who were employed to round them up like cattle were Mountain and Topin. The Lockyer Brothers burnt their feet to prevent them returning to their own country. Also detained young native girls as slaves for their own use and purposes. These men – Lockyer Brothers - also tied natives up to trees and murdered them.'

86 WAPD, 'Detailed Police Reports from Police in the Kimberley, Report from LC Payne, King Sound Station, 25 June 1883', SROWA, AN 5/6, Cons. 129, File 856/1883.

87 ibid.

88 ibid.

89 ibid.

90 On 28 August 1883 with a temporary police camp established at King Sound Station, LC Payne instructed constables Lemon and Buckley to proceed to Beagle Bay to 'make careful enquiry relative to pearlers engaged in Native Hunting': WAPD, 'Report from LC Payne to PC Buckley and PC Lee, 28

August 1883', SROWA, AN 5/6, Cons. 129, File 856/1883. They were instructed not to arrest anyone unless people were being taken by force but to report in full to Superintendent of Police M.S. Smith in Perth. Lemon recorded that an Aboriginal man by the name of Jabenabal, alias 'Charley', was caught near the Yeda River the year before last by Mr Bryan, E. Wilson, H. Hunter and A. Mayall and chained by the neck with 'other natives' Yannyre, Cockey and Jackey, who were all taken against their will. WAPD, 'Report from LC Payne to Superintendent of Police, Derby Station, 31 August 1883', SROWA, AN 5/6, Cons. 129, File 856/1883. Jabenabal joined the police service as a native assistant. Lemon also said 'last year Henry Hunter beat an Aboriginal man named Pennian with a rope while in the water and he drowned. Later on that year Jabenabal was caught by the same men on the west side of King Sound and chained up with another Aboriginal man named Liangmorra, alias 'Lumpy'. Both times they were taken to Beagle Bay to the Lacepede Islands then taken to Cossack. Jabenabal stated that there were a great number of Aboriginal people on the Lacepede Islands. Other Aboriginal witnesses, Shaoboth and Duncan, who were now employed by George C. Rose on Yeeda Station, stated that last year they were caught on the Fitzroy by Mr Bryan and Mr Wilson and chained together by the neck and taken to Beagle Bay and from there to Cossack. Another witness, 'Legs', who was also employed on Yeeda Station, stated that last year he was going to Beagle Bay and when at Bungarra he saw Mr Bryan, E. Wilson and 'other whites' with five Aboriginal men chained together; they were Yeedabuckee, Dubberdabs, Weerdajerabel, Maanbol and Jerambing. They were taken to Beagle Bay and from there to the Lacepede Islands. He reported that they had 'still not returned to their *country*'. 'Liangmoora', who LC Payne knew from their Police Camp, corroborated this evidence and stated it was Alf Mayall, the owner of pearling company Mayall and Wilson, who chained him up last year. CSO, 'Copy of the Register of Natives' Agreements for 3/4 of the Year Ended 31.12.83', SROWA, AN 24, Cons. 527, File 1409/1884. They stated that when diving they get 'nothing to eat but damper and water to drink (no tea or sugar) except when they stop at any island they then catch some turtle'. LC Payne's report was furnished to the superintendent of police on the 15 of September 1883 'but noted that since the pearling season starts on October 1 very little could be done this season'. Report from LC Payne to Superintendent of Police, SROWA, AN 5/6 Cons. 129, File 856/1883. PC Lemon reported that his witnesses said 'a great many strange natives', or Aboriginal people from different areas or different *country*, were taken from the peninsula and in many instances were in chains. There was a man named Kelly in charge of the Lacepede Islands who was aiding the pearlers in their kidnapping by not making the fact of the natives being on the islands public. Charles Clifford, whom PC Lemon saw at Beagle Bay, said in course of ordinary conversation: 'Oh, he gets some good presents from the pearlers.' The implication was that he was paid for his services. WAPD, 'Report from PC Lemon Lee, 11 September 1883', SROWA, AN 5/6, Cons. 129, File

856/1883.

91   ibid., WAPD, 'Report from PC Lemon Lee, 11 September 1883', SROWA, AN 5/6, Cons.129, File 856/1883.

92   See Gribble, *Dark Deeds in a Sunny Land*, pp.38–44. Lemon's police party met other European men who were blackbirding. On 2 September 1883 he met C.W. Paterson and Sydney Hadley and one Aboriginal man from Cossack. Lemon stated that: 'an old native here who states that he has seen Bryan, Wilson, Hunter, and two other white men with a great many natives chained up a short time ago and that the natives had been taken to the Pearling Vessels at Beagle Bay and from thence to the Lacepede Islands.' Payne describes how he let an Aboriginal man give evidence and gave him a 'native chain' (the police chains used for prisoners) to describe the manner in which he had seen the natives chained by putting a part of it around PC Buckley's neck and part around his own. WAPD, 'Report from PC Lemon, 2 September, 1883', SROWA, AN 5/6, Cons. 129, File 856/1883. He informed the police that the boats had all checked out a day or two before. The schooners *Water Lily* and *Kate* 'are lying some miles off and there is no communication with them what ever'. 'This place' [Brockman's old house], from what Lemon could glean from Charles Clifford, seemed to be 'a general resort for the whites when they are getting natives'. Lemon recorded the names of various parties who came from Roebourne overland with horses to Beagle Bay for the purpose of 'procuring natives for diving' vis: W.M. Bryan and D. Thomas of the schooner *Katy* and E. Wilson and A. Mayall of the schooner *Water Lily* with ten horses; H. Hadley, Hunter and C. Clifford of the cutter *Rover* with six horses; C.W. Paterson and C. Doust of the schooner *Swan* with six horses. WAPD, 'Report from PC Lemon, 10 September 1883', SROWA, AN 5/6, Cons. 129, File 856/1883. On 5 September 1883, the police party noticed a party of horsemen led by 'Lumpy' (from Bungarra). PC Lemon recorded: 'the native was greatly agitated and stated that the party had caught him that day and that they were driving him from his country against his wish to make him go diving.' This party consisted of Alfred Mayall (the man Lumpy alleged had chained him up the previous year), David Thomas, James McAtlee, and one other Aboriginal man. Lemon told Mayall 'what the native said' and asked him whether he had an agreement of any sort with him. Mayall replied that he 'did not know he was doing any harm, and also that he, himself had no agreement with the native but he believed that William Bryan had.' Lemon informed Mayall that 'he had no right to force the native from his country. I also asked the native whether he had an agreement with Bryan for Pearling and he said "No" and that he would not go pearling any more, as he did not like it and the whites ill-treated him.' WAPD, 'Report from PC Lemon, 5 September 1883', SROWA, AN 5/6, Cons. 129, File 856/1883.

93   Aborigines Protection Board, 'Report from Sergeant Troy to Superintendent of Police, Kimberley District, Derby Station, Correspondence from His Excellency the Governor to Superintendent of Police, Re Kidnapping of 20 natives on the Fitzroy River, 2 November 1883', SROWA, Cons. 388, File

3686/86, Item 19. He wrote that 'Capt. Tuckey has been in King Sound since the 1st of September. Their principal object in coming here was to get natives for the pearl shell fishing.' On the first trip they procured '14 natives which were put on board Argo', then McLarty and Tuckey 'went out on a second hunt' at which time 'they went 70 or 80 miles up the Fitzroy and got 19 natives in the neighbourhood of Mt Abbott, six of these made their escape and the remaining 13 (who are said to be boys from 10 to 18 years old) were bought into Mr McLarty's station and are to be put on board the Argo next Monday.' Sergeant Troy was unable to determine how they were secured though they were put on the *Argo* under armed watch.

94 'Edward McLarty, J.P., M.L.C.', in W.B. Kimberly (ed.), *History of West Australia, A Narrative of her Past, Together With Biographies of Her Leading Men,* Melbourne, F.W. Niven, 1897, available at <http://en.wikisource.org/wiki/History_of_West_Australia/Edward_McLarty>.

95 Patrol to 'visit settlers, arrest native offenders, deliver letters, and also to enquire from natives into the manner in which Mr McLarty and his party have been obtaining natives for diving purposes'. WAPD, 'Report of PC Lemon, 8 November 1884', SROWA, AN 5, Cons. 2229.

96 ibid.

97 ibid. On 16 November PC Lemon reported that they could not find any young natives around as they had 'run away afraid of the white men'. 'Report of PC Lemon, 16 November 1884', SROWA, AN 5, Cons. 2229. On 17 November he reported: 'There were other young natives here who state that they have been hunted from one place to another by John McLarty and his party for the purpose of taking them to go pearling.' WAPD, 'Report of PC Lemon with PC Buckley and Native Assistant Mickey, 17 November 1884', SROWA, AN 5, Cons. 2229.

98 WAPD, 'Journal of PC Sherry, PC Adlam, PC Wilson and Native Assistant George on Patrol from Derby to Lennard River, 27 December 1884', SROWA, Cons. 430, File 532/1885.

99 'Derby Correspondent 27 July 1885', *The West Australian,* 15 August 1885, p.7.

100 See for example Aborigines Protection Board, 'The Governor - Statements of D Carley (vi) re: murder of two natives at Roebourne (with butt-end of gun) (3683/86), SROWA, Cons. 388, File 17; 'The Governor - statements of D Carley (x) re: sale of 10 kidnapped natives at Cossack (3657/86),' SROWA, Cons. 388, File 08; 'The Governor - Statements of D Carley (v) re: branding of natives (3682/86)', SROWA, Cons. 388, File 16; 'The Governor – Statement of D Carley (ii) re: slaughter of natives at "Flying Foam" passage (3679/86)', SROWA, Cons. 388, File 13; 'The Governor - Statements of D Carley (iv) re: Native girl, Fanny, dragged to lock up for carnal purposes (3681/86)', SROWA, Cons. 388, File 15; 'The Governor - Statements of D Carley (vii) re: murder of native at Roebourne - 78 (struck on head with paddle) (3684/86)', SROWA, Cons. 388, File 18; 'The Governor - Statements of D Carley (ix) re: kidnapping of 20 natives on the Fitzroy (3686/86)', SROWA,

Cons. 388, File 19. See also Gribble, *Dark Deeds in a Sunny Land,* pp.30–1.

101 Tom Gara, *The Flying Foam Massacre: an incident on the northwest frontier,* in M. Smith (ed.), *Archaeology ANZAAS,* Perth, Western Australian Museum, Anthropology Department, 1983, p.91.

102 A summary of Carley's allegations can be found at 'The "Native" Blue Book', *The West Australian,* 2 November 1886, p.3.

103 'The Native Question, Letter by David Carley, *The Daily News,* 22 June 1886, p.3.

104 'The "Native" Blue Book', *The West Australian,* 2 November 1886, p.3. For debates about Carley, see 'Legislative Council, David Carley and the Rev. J.B. Gribble', *The West Australian,* 12 July 1886, p.3.

105 'The Native Question, Letter By David Carley', *The Daily News,* 22 June 1886, p.3.

106 'Mr. David Carley Retorts', *The Daily News,* 16 July 1886, p.3; 'David Carley and the Legislature', *The Inquirer & Commercial News,* 21 July 1866, p.5; Legislative Council, 'David Carley and the Rev J. B. Gribble', *The West Australian,* 12 July 1886, p.3; see also *Papers Respecting the Treatment of Aboriginal Prisoners in Western Australia, presented to the Legislative Council,* Perth, Government Printer, 1886, SROWA, Cons. 993, File 344/1933.

107 'Bengallee', 'A trip overland from Roebourne', The *West Australian,* 4 May 1886, p.3.

108 ibid.

109 WAPD, 'Report to Superintendent of Police re investigation of Ab Native Charlie being killed by John Wells', 29 November 1886, SROWA, Cons. 430, File 26/1887.

110 ibid.

111 ibid.

112 ibid. In other cases Payne attempted to prosecute it is clear that Aboriginal witnesses would be manipulated to contradict themselves. 'The natives in their examination in chief strictly adhered to their first and the case appeared clear against Mugford [the accused], but in their cross examination they were so baffled by extraordinary questions from counsel that they certainly contradicted themselves very materially and they stated they never made a complaint.'

113 'Colonel Angelo', *Western Mail,* 27 November 1886, p.29.

114 CSO, 'Government Resident Wyndham – Natives (5) Shot by PC. Graham & Others in April 88. Report, File Note, G.B. Phillips, Commissioner of Police to Hon. Colonial Secretary, Enclosing Reports from Sergeant Troy and Statements from PC Graham and Native Assistant Banjo, 2 October 1888', SROWA, AN 24, Cons. 527, File 2776/1888; CSO, 'File Note, A.N. Warton, Attorney General to Hon. Colonial Secretary, 6 October 1888', SROWA, AN 24, Cons. 527, File 2776/1888.

115 See S.J. Hunt, *'The Gribble Affair': A Study of Aboriginal European Labour Relations in the North-West Australia during the 1880s,* Honours thesis, University of Western Australia, 1978.

116 Article 6 went on to state: 'They shall, without distinction of creed or nation, protect and favour all religious, scientific or charitable institutions and undertakings created and organized for the above ends, or which aim at instructing the natives and bringing home to them the blessings of civilization. Christian missionaries, scientists and explorers, with their followers, property and collections, shall likewise be the objects of especial protection. Freedom of conscience and religious toleration are expressly guaranteed to the natives, no less than to subjects and to foreigners. The free and public exercise of all forms of divine worship, and the right to build edifices for religious purposes, and to organize religious missions belonging to all creeds, shall not be limited or fettered in any way whatsoever.' 'Provisions relative to protection of the natives, of missionaries and travellers, as well as relative to religious liberty', *General Act of the Berlin Conference on West Africa,* 26 February 1885.

117 Marchant, *Aboriginal Administration in Western Australia,* p.20.

118 S.J. Hunt, 'The Gribble Affair: a Study in Colonial Politics', in Gribble, *Dark Deeds in a Sunny Land,* p.67. For a contemporary report of Gribble's allegations see 'Gribble V. *The West Australian,' Western Mail,* 21 May 1887, pp.9–15.

119 Gribble, *Dark Deeds in a Sunny Land,* p.29.

120 'Supreme Court – Civil Side', *Western Mail,* 2 July 1887, p.12; Kimberly (ed.), *History of West Australia,* p.19.

121 'Supreme Court – Civil Side', *Western Mail,* 2 July 1887, p.12.

122 Gribble, *Dark Deeds in a Sunny Land,* p.29.

123 Correspondence 'Bishop Gibney and the Nor' West Settlers, *The West Australian,* 14 November 1892, p.3.

124 'The North West Natives, Vindication of Mr. Gribble.' *The Daily News,* 1 April 1905, p.3.

125 Under *An Act to Provide for the Better Protection and Management of the Aboriginal Natives of Western Australia, and to Amend the Law Relating to Certain Contracts with such Aboriginal Natives* (statute 25/1886). *An Act to Provide Certain Matters Connected With the Aborigines* (statute 24/1889); See N. Green, 'Aborigines and White Settlers', in C.T. Stannage (ed.), *A New History of Western Australia,* Perth, UWA Press, 1981, pp.109–10; Marchant, *Aboriginal Administration in Western Australia,* 1981.

126 *British Parliamentary Papers,* vol. 31, pp.380–2. In 1996 'Snowy Judamia, Crow Yougarla, Paddy Yarbarla, Billy Thomas and Leslie Ankie on behalf of themselves and all other Aboriginal inhabitants of Western Australia, brought an action against the State of Western Australia claiming that the two legislative attempts to repeal s70 in 1897 and 1905 were flawed, and that, as a result, s70 is still a validly enacted law. If that is the case, they contended further that the terms of s70 suggest that the State of Western Australia voluntarily accepted a fiduciary obligation to pay money for the welfare of the Aboriginal inhabitants of Western Australia, and that, as s70 is still valid, the fiduciary obligation continues to the present day. Further, the State of Western Australia has failed to pay money, in accordance with its obligation under s70, since 1897 (when the first attempt at repealing s70 occurred), and it

is thus in breach of its fiduciary obligation.' E. Cowdery, 'Aboriginal Citizens and the Western Australian Constitution: Judamia & Ors v State of Western Australia' [1996], *Aboriginal Law Bulletin*, vol. 3, no. 83, 1996, pp.12–15. They we not successful, with the case going to the High Court which found Section 70 had been repealed in the 1905 Act if not the 1897 Act. 'Yougarla v Western Australia – Case Summary' [2001], *Australian Indigenous Law Reporter*, vol. 6, no. 4, 2001, p. 38. For a summary of the history of this case see S. Churches, 'Put Not your Faith in Princes (or Courts) – Agreements Made from Asymmetrical Power Bases: the story of a promise made to Western Australia's Aboriginal people', in P. Read, G. Meyers and B. Reece (eds), *What Good Condition? Reflections on an Australian Aboriginal Treaty 1986–2006*, Canberra, ANU Epress, 2006, pp.1–14, < http://press.anu.edu.au?p=15621>.

127 N. Green, 'From Princes to Paupers: The Struggle for Control of Aborigines in Western Australia 1887–1898', *Early Days: Journal of the Western Australian Historical Society*, vol. 2, no. 4, 1998, p.453.

128 The board members after 1889 (and at different periods) were George Leake (member of the Legislative Council), Charles D'Oyle Forbes (secretary of the Colonial Board of Health), Dr A.R. Waylen (Colonial Surgeon), Rev. C.G. Nicolay (chaplain to Fremantle prison), Mr S.H. Parker (former member of the Legislative Council), E.T. Hooley (Pilbara pastoralist and member of the Legislative Council), and later Mr Sewell and Mr Moorhead (Attorney General) and Rev. David Garland (chaplain to the Anglican Bishop).

129 Green, 'From Princes to Paupers', p.452.

130 *The Aborigines Protection Act*, No 25 of 1886, assented to 2 September 1886, see Parts III and IV.

131 Biskup, *Not Slaves, Not Citizens*, p.24.

132 George Marsden observed one protector, a man by the name of Wheelock, had been charged with such offences. Aborigines Protection Board, 'Correspondence, October 1896', SROWA, Cons. 495, Item 12.

133 'The Aborigines Protection Board', *The West Australian*, 19 March 1888, p.3.

134 Aborigines Protection Board, 'G. Marsden, General Report of the Kimberley District, Report of the Aborigines Protection Board, 12 March 1897', SROWA, Cons. 495, Item 12. This report was published verbatim in *The West Australian*: George Marsden, 'Annual Report, Aborigines Protection Board', *The West Australian*, 29 May 1897, p.9.

135 WAPD, 'Witness Statement from Corporal W. Goodridge (No. 112.) Regarding Allegations he Made in Roth Commission Report, Wyndham, East Kimberley, 24 May 1905', SROWA, Cons. 430, File 540/1905.

136 For an explicit account of this attitude and frontier shootings in the Kimberley see K. Willey, *Boss Drover*, Sydney, Rigby Books, 1971, p.60. See for example the Mistake Creek massacre of 1915 and the Bedford Downs massacre of 1924 in C. Clement, *Historical Notes Relevant to Impact Stories of the East Kimberley*, Canberra, East Kimberley Impact Assessment Project, 1989; the Mowla Bluff massacre of 1916, *Whispering in Our Hearts: the Mowla Bluff massacre*, dir. G. Isaac, Australian Film Finance Corporation, 2002 [videorecording]; the 1926

Forrest River massacre as detailed in N. Green, *The Forrest River Massacres*, Fremantle, Fremantle Arts Centre Press, 1995. For examples from the Northern Territory see D.R. Rose, *Hidden Histories: black stories from Victoria River Downs, Humbert River and Wave Hill Stations*, Canberra, Aboriginal Studies Press, 1991, pp.20–4. For examples from the Gulf Country of the Northern Territory and Queensland see T. Roberts, *Frontier Justice: a history of the Gulf Country to 1900*, Brisbane, University of Queensland Press, 2005. For Queensland references see T. Bottoms, *The Conspiracy of Silence: Queensland's frontier killing times*, Sydney, Allen & Unwin, 2013.

137 In 1865 near La Grange Bay in the Kimberley punitive killings occurred following the spearing death of three explorers, Frederick Panter, James Harding and William Goldwyer. The expedition to find the men responsible was led by Maitland Brown and was described by Brown as an 'exploration'. However, on 6 April 1865 Brown's party engaged in a battle with a large group of Aboriginal people. Most accounts state that the party walked into an ambush, but at least one account asserts that they attacked a native camp. The official death toll was twenty although personal accounts written years later put the toll much higher. E.S. Ilbery, 'The battle of Pinjarra: the Passing of the Bibbulmun', *Early Days*, vol. 1, 1927, p.18. *The Inquirer*, 31 May, 1865, quoted in K. Forrest, *The Challenge and the Chance*, Perth, Hesperian Press, 1996, pp.16–19; Forrest has the date as 31 May 1865. M. Brown, 'Journal of an Expedition in the Roebuck Bay District, under the Command of Maitland Brown, Esq., in Search of Messrs. Panter, Harding, and Goldwyer, Reprinted from the *'Perth Gazette and W. A. Times'*, of 19 and 26 May, 1865'. In 1865 the Camden Harbour settlement had been abandoned due to Aboriginal attacks; for an account of this incident see De La Rue, *Pearl Shell and Pastures*, pp.27–30; see also B. Scates, 'A Monument to Murder: celebrating the conquest of Aboriginal Australia', in L. Layman and T. Stannage (eds), 'Celebrations in Western Australian History', *Studies in Western Australian History*, no. 10, 1989, pp.21–31. Up to 150 people were alleged to have been killed over several months. Prominent colonist Alex McRae led one party in the punitive expedition and John Withnell led the other party. The actual number of Aboriginal people killed was erased from a letter from McRae to his sister. K. Forrest wrote that their report of this expedition seemed 'intentionally ambiguous': *The Inquirer*, 1 April 1868, quoted in Forrest, *The Challenge and the Chance*, pp.59–61. See also Gara, *The Flying Foam Massacre*, pp.86–93; M.R. Dyson, *Flying Foam Massacre: a grey era in the history of the Burrup Peninsular* [sic], *British justice or downright vengeful bloody murder*, Karratha, CAD Centre, 2002. Other less well-known examples from Beagle Bay in 1883 exist, including a letter simply stating 'John McAtee in charge of stores at Brockman[']s old camp belonging to George Rose sent a note to me by a native stating a white man belonging to Alexander Forrest's party had been murdered on the Fitzroy and the whites had turned out and killed about twenty natives'. Written archival records such as this are the only testaments to the events occurring. CSO, 'Letter signed by Edgar (Master) to Colonial

Sec. M Fraser, 12 June, 1883', SROWA, AN 24, Cons. 527, File 1530/71.

138 J. S. Durlacher, (with an introduction by Peter Gifford), *Landlords of the Iron Shore*, Perth, Hesperian Press, 2013 [1900], p.xii.

139 A. Nettelbeck, '"Equals of the White Man": prosecution of settlers for violence against Aboriginal subjects of the Crown, colonial Western Australia', *Law and History Review*, vol. 31, no. 2, 2013, pp.355–90.

140 R. Allen, 'Reminiscences', manuscript at 448A, Battye Library, p.15.

141 'Minnie-Pool Charley, A few remarks about the customs, &c., of the natives of West Kimberley', *Eastern Districts Chronicle*, 18 November 1893, p.2.

142 'The Buck North', *Sunday Times*, 30 March 1902, p.3.

143 Willey, *Boss Drover*, p.60.

144 Aborigines Protection Board, 'Correspondence, 21 August 1896', SROWA, 'Private' Item 58, Cons. 495.

145 Broughton, *Turn Again Home*, p.35.

146 ibid., p.53.

147 ibid., p.37.

148 ibid., p.53.

149 D. Swan, 'Rough Justice' Memoirs published in *The Western Mail* 1929, in C. Clement and P. Bridge (eds), *Kimberley Scenes: sagas of Australia's last frontier*, Perth, Hesperian Press, 1991, p.104.

150 Many other examples of these 'northern' agreements in the literature exist. W.L. Owen wrote of the understanding in the north that: 'One would not employ another man's natives', meaning that on a patch of land worked, the local Aboriginal groups came with it. Owen, *Cossack Gold*, p.149. Mary Durack refers to the 'unwritten etiquette of the country that one did not question a man about his background'. M. Durack, *Sons in the Saddle*, London, Constable, 1983, p.13. Certainly, there was nothing to gain by alienating one of the few compatriots of the district by enquiring about his possibly dubious past.

151 T. Willing and K. Kenneally (eds), *Under a Regent Moon: a historical account of pioneer pastoralists Joseph Bradshaw and Aeneas Gunn at Marigui Settlement*, Perth, Department of Conservation and Land Management, 2002, p.47.

152 A.R. Richardson, quoted in Reilly, *Reminiscences of Fifty Years Residence in Western Australia*, p.355; see also A.R. Richardson, 'Correspondence, The Native Question', *The West Australian*, 7 November 1892, p. 3.

153 G. Buchanan, *Packhorse and Waterhole: with the first overlanders to the Kimberley*, facsimile edition, Perth, Hesperian Press, 1984 [1933], p.59.

154 ibid., p.117.

155 ibid.

156 You who tread safe the city's beaten tracks,

May well believe in kindness of the blacks

Would you still hold your dusky friend so dear

If he was dodging you around with a spear

Suppose yourself by great and wondrous change

Camped in the heart of some mountain range....

Would not a deadly rage upon you creep
When tired distressed and much in need of sleep,
You dare not close your over-wary eye
Because you know to do so were to die?
Young man, before you judge another's case
In fancy put yourself in that man's place....
How else than cold the lonely stockman's heart
Who sees his horse lay slain by savage dart?
Picture the frenzy on the squatter's brain
When speared bullocks dot the spreading plain,
Or how the solitary traveller feels
When round his camp the sneaking nigger steals....
No suppliants they save who would disguise
Their bloody purpose from their victim's eyes....
Thoughtless he turns towards the waiting hack,
Too late-Too late! The spear is in his back....
Ah who shall judge the bushman's hasty crime?
Righteous the hate with which the soul is filled
When man must slaughter or himself be killed....
In Durack, *Kings in Grass Castles*, pp.303–4.

157 G.C. Bolton, 'The Kimberley Pastoral Industry', *University Studies in History and Economics*, vol. 11, no. 2, 1954, p.23.

158 'Sketcher,' *The Queenslander*, 20 January 1906, p.7; 'In Northern Seas', *The Register*, 6 December 1904, p.6.

159 See 'No Intention of Legitimate Stocking', 'The Northern Territory, Neglected Australia, Commercial and Political Aspects', *Western Mail*, 16 March 1907, p.19; 'Alleged Duffing', *Northern Times*, 21 April 1906. p.2.

160 'These men muster clean-skins [unbranded] on their runs, and they use the permit as a blind for cattle-duffing. There is an instance of a man selling several hundred beasts, and he never bought a hoof. This is not an isolated case, and it is not confined to the Territory, 'Alleged Duffing', *Northern Times*, 21 April 1906, p.2.

161 ibid.

162 'Doug Moore's Memoirs', Private Manuscript, (nd.), MS, Battye Library, Cons. 3829A, MN 1237, p.1.

163 ibid.

164 ibid.

165 'A Prison Escapee, Captured in the Kimberley District, A Notorious Horse Thief', *The Daily News*, 30 December 1899, p.4.

166 'Alleged Duffing', *Northern Times*, 21 April 1906, p.2.

167 Rose, *Hidden Histories*, p.67.

168 'Kimberley Scenes', *Western Mail*, 7 November 1929, p.9.

Chapter 4: 'Show Civility and a Readiness to Assist'

1   M. Finnane and S. Garton, 'The Work of Policing: social relations and the criminal justice system in Queensland 1880–1914: Part I', *Labour History*, no. 62, 1992, p.59.

2   M. Finnane, *Police and Government: histories of policing in Australia*, Melbourne, Oxford University Press, 1994, p.9.

3   ibid.

4   For the Tasmanian example, see S. Petrow, 'Economy, Efficiency and Impartiality: police centralisation in nineteenth century Tasmania', *Australia & New Zealand', Journal of Criminology*, vol. 31, no. 3, August 1998, pp.243–66.

5   Finnane, *Police and Government*, p.9.

6   C. Edwards, 'Democratic Control of Police: how 19th century political systems determine modern policing structures', in M. Enders and B. Dupont (eds), *Policing the Lucky Country*, Sydney, Hawkins Press, 2001, p.16.

7   Finnane, *Police and Government*, pp.23–30.

8   R. Haldane, *The People's Force: a history of the Victorian police*, Melbourne, Melbourne University Press, 1986, pp.2–3; Finnane and Garton, 'The Work of Policing: social relations and the criminal justice system in Queensland 1880–1914', p.59.

9   Finnane, *Police and Government*, p.16.

10 E. Russell, *A History of the Law in Western Australia and its Development from 1829 to 1979*, Perth, UWA Press, 1980, p.18.

11 WAPD, 'Journal Corporal Payne on Sea Trip from Fremantle to Roebuck Bay, Report from LC Payne to Supt Police, King Sound Station Kimberley', SROWA, AN 5/6, Cons. 129, File 395/1883. For a report of Fairbairn's instruction in the Kimberley see 'Magisterial Duty at Kimberley', *The Inquirer and Commercial News*, 21 March 1883, p.3.

12 W.B. Kimberly (ed.), *History of West Australia: a narrative of her past, together with biographies of her leading men*, Melbourne, FW Niven, 1897, p.87. Lovegrove was born in Sussex, South England, in 1845.

13 ibid.

14 For the period of this study the government residents were Robert Fairbairn (March 1883–5), Thomas Lovegrove (November 1885–7), John Finnerty (August 1887–9) and E.P. Dowley (1889). 'The word "Magistrate" shall mean a Government Resident, or a Resident Magistrate, or a Police Magistrate, and shall not be taken to mean any other Justice of the Peace.' *Aboriginal Offenders Act*, 47 Vic. 8, 1883.

15 Russell, *A History of the Law in Western Australia and its Development from 1829 to 1979*, p.18.

16 ibid.

17 WAPD, 'Kimberley District. Derby Station. Altercation between Sergeant P. Troy and Government Resident, 11 March 1885', SROWA, AN 5, Cons. 430, File 584/1885.

18 ibid.

19 Russell, *A History of the Law in Western Australia and its Development from 1829*

to 1979, p.187.

20 Police Regulations 1898, quoted in P. Conole, *Protect and Serve: a history of the Western Australian police service*, Perth, Access Press, 2002, p.111.

21 Introduction to Police Regulations 1898, quoted in ibid., p.111.

22 *Rules and Regulations for the Government and Guidance of the Police Force of Western Australia as Approved by John Forrest*, Perth, Sands and McDougall, 1898.

23 ibid., p.63.

24 ibid.

25 P. O'Farrell, 'Success and Defeat in Western Australia 1891–1907', *Letters from Irish Australia 1825–1929*, Sydney, New South Wales University Press, 1984, p.88.

26 ibid.

27 Inspector P. Troy services and promotions: 1 July 1873, duty at Fremantle Station; 1 January 1874, transferred to in charge of Harvey Station; 1 April 1875, transferred to Victoria Plains; 1 November 1876, lance corporal; 15 September 1879, first-class constable; 16 February 1880, in charge of Mt Wittenoom Station; 1 March 1883, sergeant Kimberley District; 14 June 1886, sub inspector, West Kimberley, in charge of Gulf Force; 1 July 1887, to take charge of the police in the Kimberley Districts, with headquarters in Derby; 1 March 1888, transferred to Bunbury to take charge of the Southern District (Inspector Lodge took over in the Kimberley); 1 July 1888, transferred to in charge of Northern District; 1 December 1889, inspector (junior); 13 December 1894, travelling inspector, with headquarters in Perth; 1896, inspector of the police force; 1 June 1896, resigned as inspector of the police force. Rewards and favourable records: 6 April 1875, arresting an absconder 21/964; 14 June 1877, obtaining conviction against sly grog sellers 24/828; 9 July 1877, obtaining conviction against sly grog sellers 24/909; 31 December 1878, general activity, zeal in performing duties during year 1878; December 1886, energy, tact and ability in arresting Frank Hornrig for murder, on the Kimberley Goldfields. WAPD, 'General Functional Police Files', report on the career of Patrick Troy 1915 (nd.), SROWA, AN 5, Cons. 430, File 3974/1915.

28 R. Erickson (ed.), *The Bicentennial Dictionary of Western Australians pre-1829–1888*, Perth, UWA Press, 1988, p.3111. See also 'Death of Warden P. Troy. Long and Honorable Public Career', *Western Mail*, 21 July 1916, p.2.

29 The title would later change to chief inspector again (1913), deputy commissioner (1953), senior assistant commissioner (1974) and deputy commissioner (1986).

30 WAPD, 'General Functional Police Files, Report on the Career of Patrick Troy 1915', SROWA, Cons. 430, No. 3974 (nd.).

31 WAPD, 'Report to the Colonial Secretary by P. Troy, Warden, Murchison Goldfield Following his Trip to the West Kimberley District to Investigate Charges of Rape and Murder of Aborigines Against Local Police, 30 May 1905', SROWA, Cons. 481, File 1243.

32 R. Ward, *The Australian Legend*, Oxford, Oxford University Press, 1960,

p.149.

33 WAPD, 'Perth, Instructions Re Rates of Pay of Police in the Kimberley District, 17 November 1884', SROWA, Cons. 430, File 1958/1884.

34 *The Daily News*, 27 November 1882, p.3.

35 O'Farrell, *Letters from Irish Australia 1825–1929*, p.133.

36 A. Gill, 'Social Conflict and Police Loyalty in Western Australia in the Late 19th Century', unpublished paper, University of Western Australia, 1981, p.5.

37 *Annual Report of the Commissioner of Police for Year Ending 30th June 1902*, WALCVP Paper no. 15, p.3.

38 ibid.

39 Gill, 'Social Conflict and Police Loyalty in Western Australia in the Late 19th Century', p.5.

40 ibid.

41 WAPD, Wyndham Police Station, Letterbook, 1 November 1890, SROWA, AN 5, Cons. 741.

42 WAPD, Wyndham Police Station, Letterbook, 10 May 1890, SROWA, AN 5, Cons. 741.

43 Testimony of Octavius Burt, *Roth Royal Commission on the Condition of the Natives. Presented to Both Houses of Parliament by His Excellency's Command*, Roth Report, WAPP, 1905, Pt. 246, p.44.

44 *Rules and Regulations for the Government and Guidance of the Police Force of Western Australia as Approved by John Forrest*, Pt 647, p.123.

45 ibid., Pt 648.

46 ibid., Pt 654.

47 'Kimberley Notes', *The Inquirer and Commercial News*, 3 August 1894, p.8.

48 'Native Murderers in the North. A Desperate Gang Still at Large', *Western Mail*, 8 October 1897, p.9.

49 'The Aborigines Question. The Riff Raff Witnesses', *The Daily News,* 9 February 1905, p.9.

50 'The North-West Natives and their Treatment', *The West Australian,* 29 June 1904, p.10.

51 'The Ways of Wyndham, Native Gaol Life, How the Blacks are Treated', *The Daily News*, 21 October 1903, p.8.

52 'How We Civilize – Or White On Black', *The Daily News*, 10 May 1889, p.3. 'How We Civilize – Or White On Black', *The Inquirer & Commercial News*, 10 May 1889, p.5.

53 N. Green and S. Moon, *Far From Home: Aboriginal Prisoners of Rottnest Island 1838–1931,* Perth, UWA Press, 1997, p.28.

54 'Is there Slavery in Australia? Treatment of Blacks in Western Australia', *Kalgoorlie Miner*, 3 April 1903, p.6.

55 WAPD, 'Derby Police Station, Letterbook 30 May 1893–13 May 1895, Sub Inspector Drewry to Commissioner of Police, circa April 1892', SROWA, AN 5, Cons. 738/22.

56 ibid.

57 *Police Act 1892*, An Act to consolidate and amend the law relating to the police

in Western Australia. <http://www.austlii.edu.au/au/legis/wa/consol_act/pa189275/>.

58 *Rules and Regulations for the Government and Guidance of the Police Force of Western Australia as Approved by John Forrest,* Pt 460, p.90.

59 ibid., Pt. 471, p.90. Italics in original.

60 ibid., Pt. 472, p.92.

61 ibid., Pt. 474.

62 *Rules and Regulations for the Government and Guidance of the Police Force of Western Australia as Approved by Governor Hampton,* Perth, 1863, p.2; *Rules and Regulations for the Government and Guidance of the Police Force of Western Australia as Approved by John Forrest.*

63 R. McGregor, 'Law Enforcement or Just Force? Police Action in Two Frontier Districts', in H. Reynolds (ed.), *Race Relations in North Queensland,* Townsville, James Cook University, 1993, p.63.

64 See for example WAPD, 'Letter from Sub Inspector O. Drewry to Commissioner of Police Phillips', Derby, 13 October 1892, SROWA, Cons. 2276/92.

65 See Inspector Drewry's instructions to Constable Handly taking charge of Robinson Rover Camp. WAPD, Derby Police Station, Letterbook 30 May 1893–13 May 1895, 4 August 1893, SROWA, AN 5, Cons. 738/22. A particular example occurred at Oobagooma Station when conflict was escalating and attacks on homesteads were increasing: a native assistant identified a man named Mungo from his footprints. WAPD, Robinson River Station, Occurrence Book 1893–1898, 8 April 1895, SROWA, AN 5, Cons. 737, Item 1.

66 WAPD, Derby Police Station, Letterbook, 'Sub Inspector O. Drewry to Commissioner of Police, 31 March 1894', SROWA, AN 5 Cons. 738/22, see also 29 June 1894. According to Keith Willey they were essential and 'In fact even the best policeman would scarcely have been able to find their horses in the morning without a tracker along.' K. Willey, *Boss Drover,* Sydney, Rigby Books, 1971, p.79.

67 CSO, 'Encounter with Native Offenders in East Kimberley District H. Collins Killed in. Reporting – Sub Inspector Drewry, Journal of a Trip by Sergt Brophy and Party in Pursuit of Natives who are Killing Cattle on the Ord Osmand and Other Rivers, 24 October 1893', SROWA, AN 24, Cons. 527, File 90/1894.

68 WAPD, 'Salaries of the Native Assistants at Derby and Goldfields', Cons. 430, File 955/1888; see testimony of PC Goodridge to Walter Roth, 'The Aborigines Question, Dr. Roth's Investigations – Prosecution Of Aborigines, Female Witnesses, Child Prisoners, The Food Question', *The West Australian,* 16 February 1905, p.2.

69 WAPD, Derby Police Station, Letterbook, 'Report by Sub Inspector Drewry, 2 May 1894', SROWA, AN 5, Cons. 738/22. Many native assistants absconded because their police officer was not providing them with enough food.

70 *Police Gazette,* Circular Order, 6/784 no. 47, 24 November 1886, p.191.

71 See also Roth Report, 1905, op.cit., p.12.
72 WAPD, 'Telegram from LC P. Troy, Geraldton to Supt. of Police Requesting Assistants for the Kimberley District, 5 March 1883', SROWA, AN 5/6, Cons. 129, File 20/1883.
73 WAPD, Derby Police Station, Letterbook, 'Sub Inspector Drewry, 23 March 1895', SROWA, AN 5, Cons. 738/22.
74 On 22 March 1895, Native Assistant Rocket was killed in pursuit of 'bush blacks' by the Ord River near Ivanhoe Station in the East Kimberley. WAPD, 'Reports Re. Native Assistant "Rocket" Killed whilst in Pursuit of Other Natives', 26 March 1895', SROWA, AN 5/1, Cons. 430, File 747/1895. See also 'Wyndham News, Trouble with the Natives, A Black Tracker Killed', *The West Australian*, 26 March 1895, p.3. Rocket and another native assistant, Jackey, had attacked a large number of people suspected of killing Ivanhoe Station cattle. On this occasion, two women and two children were also shot. See also C. Owen and C. Choo, 'Deafening Silences: understanding frontier relations and the discourse of police files through Kimberley police records', in C. Choo, and S. Hollbach (eds), *Studies in Western Australian History: History and Native Title,* no. 23, 2003, p.141; 'Derby – Murder of Native Tracker "Joe" by Natives on Barker River 14.11.1904', SROWA, AN 5/2, Cons. 430, File 4337/1904.
75 WAPD, 'Native Assistant Willy Speared Dead while in Pursuit of Native Offenders', 3 July 1896, SROWA, AN 5/1, Cons. 430, File 2029/1896.
76 WAPD, 'Police Constable Farley (305) and Others Report of the Murder of Aboriginal Assistant, Dicky, Speared by Hostile Natives at Durack River While Trying to Apprehend Murderers of Ah Sing', East Kimberley District, Wyndham Station, July 1899, SROWA, AN 5/1, Cons. 430, File 2873/1899.
77 'Derby – Journal of Constable Turner (526) 19 July to 23 September 1902; Six Natives Arrested for Cattle Killing; "Murperadoo" Arrested for Escaping from Wyndham Gaol; Murder of Native Tracker "Wallaby" by Prisoners who Escaped', SROWA, AN 5/2, Cons. 430, File 5051/1902.
78 CSO, 'Government Resident Derby – Native "Jeneella" Shot by PCs. Armitage & Watts', SROWA, AN 24, Cons. 527, File 2627/1889.
79 See for example 'More of the Black Nor-West', *Sunday Times,* 30 July 1905, p.7.
80 Willey, *Boss Drover,* p.79.
81 WAPD, 'Under-Secretary, Premier's Department – Halls Creek District – Reporting that Blacks have Become Troublesome – Police Protection Requested. Natives Killing Cattle at Halls Creek; Police Station Required at Turkey Creek; Horses & Gear at Wyndham Reported to be in Unserviceable Condition', SROWA, AN 5/1, Cons. 430, File 2157/1901.
82 Section 5, *Police Ordinance 1861* (25 Vict. No. 15).
83 Section 36, *Police Act 1892,* op.cit.
84 'Letter from Sub Inspector Drewry to Commissioner of Police Phillips Derby, 13 October 1892', SROWA, Cons. 2276/92.
85 See for example 'Report by Sub Inspector Drewry, Wyndham Letterbook, 11

November 1891', SROWA, AN 5, Cons. 741 /11.

86   WAPD, Derby Police Station, Letterbook, 'Report to Constable Mitchell, Sub Inspector O. Drewry, 21 September 1893', SROWA, AN 5, Cons. 738/22.

87   WAPD, 'Report from LC Payne to PC Buckley and PC Lee, 28 August 1883', SROWA, AN 5/6, Cons. 129, File 856/1883. PC Lemon's horse Stanhope nearly died from dehydration. The quality and numbers of horses were debated in the Western Australian parliament in January 1892. For debates about the importance and quality of police horses in the North West and Kimberley see 'Protection of Northern Settlers against Hostile Natives', *Parliamentary Debates Legislative Council, vol. II (7 December 1891 to 8 March 1892)*, 14 January 1892, Perth, pp.245–61.

88   *Rules and Regulations for the Government and Guidance of the Police Force of Western Australia as Approved by Governor Hampton*, pp.28–31, 52, 53.

89   *Rules and Regulations for the Government and Guidance of the Police Force of Western Australia as Approved by John Forrest*, p.93.

90   Denham Police Station, Occurrence Book 2, 'Report by Sergt Lavery, 21 December 1892', SROWA, AN 5, Cons. 739.

91   WAPD, Derby Police Station, 'Report by Constable Spong, 1 November 1894', SROWA, AN 5, Cons. 738/22.

92   WAPD, 'Letter from Sub Inspector O. Drewry to Commissioner of Police Phillips Derby, 13 October 1892', SROWA, Cons. 2276/92.

93   ibid. Commissioners Phillips replied to the 'jest' comment by saying 'Police officers should avoid the use of expressions not consistent with a calm temper, and with an absence of personal feeling.' See also report of police horses as 'a miserable rag-tag', 'Native Crime in the Nor'-West', *Western Mail*, 30 December 1899, p.11.

94   *Western Australian Parliamentary Debates 1891–1892*, vol.2, p.531.

95   See for example a speech by Mr Steere, M.L.C., *The West Australian*, 4 July 1882, p.3. 'Therefore, I say, there is no necessity to call upon the Legislature for a larger police vote, to enable the Government to afford increased protection to the settlers in the disturbed districts. It is not an additional vote that is wanted, but a reorganization of the force, by reducing the staff employed in the more settled districts, and correspondingly increasing it in those districts where the natives have made themselves masters of the situation. That is what is wanted, and if I had the management of the force, I would soon send some of them up there. (Hear, hear.) I think if the two Inspectors of Police now stationed at Bunbury and at Geraldton, where, in my opinion, they are not required were seated to the North, with a posse of policemen, who could also be well spared, from this part of the colony, without involving any increased expenditure, the native difficulty might, to a very great extent, be met. I do not think the Legislature ought to be called upon to provide for any additional expenditure in connection with the redistribution of the force. The men could easily be spared from the settled parts of colony, and transferred to the disturbed districts, without any increased demand upon the

public funds. Of course, I cannot say what the Legislature may do when the question comes before it again. We may be told by the Government that they cannot spare any police constables from this part of the colony to go to the North, and that if we want any increased police protection for the settlers up there, we must find the money to pay for it. If the Executive say that, I don't know what the Legislature is to do. Increased protection must undoubtedly be provided but I certainly think it might be provided, without any increase of expenditure.'

96 'Witness Statement by Constable John Inglis, Halls Creek Police Station', Roth Report, Pt. 1488, p.94 also Sergeant Farley had to pay for his own cartage, quoted in K. Moran, *Sand and Stone: foreign footprints: police in the Kimberley 1880–1890s*, Perth, Hesperian Press, 2009, pp.160–1.

97 In 'Mr F. Connor', M.L.A. *The Inquirer & Commercial News*, 28 June 1901, p.15.

98 Halls Creek Station, Letterbook, vol. 2 1887–1893, AN 5, 15–19 August 1889, SROWA, Cons. 1422.

99 ibid.

100 'The Police: the commissioner report 1897–98', *The West Australian*, 14 July 1898, p.3. See 'Journal of Constable Hill (517) Escorting Native Prisoners and Ballot Boxes to Wyndham', AN 5/1, 26 March to 6 April 1901, SROWA, Cons. 430, File 3291/1901.

101 I. Coates, *The Social Construction of the John Forrest Australian Aboriginal Collection: past and present,* unpublished Honours thesis, Australian National University, 1989, p.9.

102 See A. Hunter, *A Different Kind of 'Subject': colonial law in Aboriginal European relations in 19th century Western Australia, 1829–61*, Canberra, Australian Scholarly Publishing, 2012.

103 P. Hasluck, *Black Australians: a survey of native policy in Western Australia, 1829–1897*, Melbourne, Melbourne University Press, 1942, p.133.

104 For summary of this see Hasluck, ibid., pp.129–34.

105 'Western Australia, Sir F. Napier Broome', *The West Australian*, 28 April 1885, p.3.

106 Western Australian Legislative Council, 1886, part 2, 'Papers Respecting the Treatment of Aboriginal Natives', p.3, quoted in Hasluck, *Black Australians,* p.134.

107 *Western Australian Government Gazette*, 1887, p.337, quoted in P. Hasluck, *Black Australians,* 1942, op.cit., p.134.

108 WAPD, Derby Police Station, Letterbook, Sub Inspector Drewry, 8 November 1894, SROWA, AN 5, Cons. 738/22.

109 WAPD, Denham River Police Station, Occurrence Book 2, 'Report by Sergt. Wheatley, 17 December 1894', SROWA, AN 5, Cons. 739.

110 WAPD, Wyndham Police Station, Letterbook, 10 January 1891, SROWA, AN 5, Cons. 741/11. A description of Wyndham circa 1890.

111 C. McIntyre, *Suicides and Settlers: Their Place in 19th Century West Australian Social History*, Perth, Hesperian Press, 2008, p.182.

112 Willey, *Boss Drover*, p.73. For malaria references see 'Report on the West Kimberley District for the Half Year Ending 30th June, 1896 by the Resident Magistrate, Derby, W.A.', *Minutes and Proceedings of Parliament 1896*, vol. 1, Paper No. 15.

113 WAPD, Halls Creek Police Station, Letterbook, 'Report by H. Bosville, 18 March 1889', SROWA, Cons. 1422. Apparently he left the station in 'terrible confusion'.

114 WAPD, Wyndham Police Station, Letterbook, 4 November 1891, SROWA, AN 5, Cons. 741/11. Sergeant Cadden's resignation letter after obtaining medical advice to 'eat more vegetables' and 'move to a better climate'.

115 WAPD, Letterbook, 'Description of Halls Creek Police Station 1889 by Sergeant Farley, Halls Creek Police Station, 17 August 1889', SROWA, Cons. 1422/2.

116 During the year 1889 the criminal record consisted of fifty-eight cases as against twenty-eight cases in 1888. Of the fifty-eight cases, thirty were drunkenness, obscene language and other minor offences, twenty-seven larceny and possessing of stolen property and one of murder. WAPD, Halls Creek Police Station, Sergeant Farley, Annual Report Halls Creek Letterbook, vol. 2, SROWA, Cons. 1422.

117 WAPD, Wyndham Police Station, Letterbook, 10 May 1890, SROWA, AN 5, Cons. 741/11.

118 Derby Police Station, Letterbook 30 May 1893–13 May 1895, Sub Inspector Drewry, 27 April 1893, SROWA, AN 5, Cons. 738/22.

119 On Sunday 7 July 1889 PC Tuke arrested 'Monkey', a native assistant, for absconding from service. PC Tuke came across Mr Brockman's survey party, which as travelling from Wyndham to the goldfields. Brockman demanded to see the arrest warrant for Monkey, as he 'belonged to him'. PC Tuke not having a warrant 'very reluctantly gave him up not knowing whether it was doing right or wrong'. Brockman further berated Tuke and instructed him 'that I should have consulted him' before exerting police authority. WAPD, 'Report by PC Tuke, Denham River Police, Occurrence Book 1, 7 July 1889', SROWA, AN 5, Cons. 739.

120 WAPD, Wyndham Police Station, Letterbook, 'Description of LC Cadden by Sergeant Houlihan, 10 November 1890', SROWA, AN 5, Cons. 741/11.

121 WAPD, 'Derby Police Station, West Kimberley District, Report on LC Wall being drunk whilst on duty, 28 July 1888', SROWA, AN 5, Cons. 430, File 1125/1888.

122 WAPD, Wyndham Police Station, Letterbook, 'Description of PC Oakes by Sergeant Houlihan, 11 October 1891', SROWA, AN 5, Cons. 741/11.

123 WAPD, Wyndham Police Station, Letterbook, 'PC Troy's Description of PC Archdeacon, (circa April 1890)', SROWA, AN 5, Cons. 741/11.

124 'Native Crime in The Nor'-West, the Influence of Escapees. (from a Correspondent.) No. II', *The West Australian*, 16 December 1899, p.3.

125 *Western Australian Government Gazette*, 17 October 1888, no. 50, p.652.

126 ibid.

127 WAPD, Wyndham Police Station, Letterbook, 'Correspondence from Commissioner of Police George Phillips, 27 July 1891', SROWA, AN 5, Cons. 741/11.

128 See for examples WAPD, Wyndham Police Station, Letterbooks 1889–1891, SROWA, AN 5, Cons. 741/11.

129 WAPD, Derby Police Station, Letterbook, 'Letter from Superintendent of Police Perth to Kimberley Police, 4 April 1883', SROWA, AN 5, Cons. 241.

130 WAPD, Derby Police Station, Letterbook, Sub Inspector O Drewry Report, 8 April 1894, SROWA, AN 5, Cons. 738/22.

131 WAPD, Halls Creek Letterbook, 'Sergeant Farley at Halls Creek Police Station, 21 May 1890', SROWA, Cons. 1422/2.

132 WAPD, Derby Police Station, Occurrence Book, PC Scott responding to claims he was 'very intockised [sic] on duty', 5 March 1886, SROWA, AN 5, Cons. 738/2.

133 See for example 'Cattle-Spearing: how natives are captured', *The Sydney Morning Herald,* 12 February 1927, p. 11. 'Tracking a Killer Across the Leopold Ranges', *The West Australian,* 1 October 1936, p. 13.

134 'Plant' refers to equipment and horses used by the police on patrol.

135 CSO, 'Sergeant of Police at Derby – Shooting of Aboriginal "Nuglay" by PC Ritchie in the Ranges Near Mess. Poultin & Nichols Station on the Robinson, Letter from Inspector Finnerty to superintendent of police, 3 September 1886', SROWA, AN 24, Cons. 527, File 3922 /1886.

136 WAPD, 'Expedition to Disperse Natives on King River – December 1892. Failure from Serg Lavery to Shoot Natives Defeated the Purpose of the Trip', 7 February 1893, SROWA, AN 5, Cons. 430, File 0264/1893. It was apparently practice in Queensland for the police to cry out 'Surrender in the Queen's name', see E. Kennedy, *The Black Police of Queensland,* London, Murray, 1902, p.119; G. Buchanan, *Packhorse and Waterhole: with the first overlanders to the Kimberley,* facsimile edition, Perth, Hesperian Press, 1984 [1933], p.11.

137 CSO, 'Sergeant of Police at Derby – Shooting of Aboriginal "Nuglay" by P.C. Ritchie in the Ranges near Mess. Poultin & Nichols Station on the Robinson, Finnerty to Inspector of Police, Derby Police Station, 12 September 1886', SROWA, AN 24, Cons. 527, File 3922 /1886.

138 Business is an Aboriginal English term that refers to Aboriginal Law activities. Owen, and Choo, 'Deafening Silences: understanding frontier relations and the discourse of police files through Kimberley Police Records,' p.143.

139 Section 5 of the 49th Victoria no 10: an Act to amend the Dog Act 1883.

140 CSO, 'A.B. Wright – Hostility of Natives and Protection for Telegraph Construction Party, as to, Letter from Geo Phillips to Inspector Lodge, 5 December 1888', Derby, SROWA, AN 24, Cons. 527, File 3258/1888.

141 R. Evans, 'Across the Queensland Frontier', in B. Attwood and S.G. Foster (eds), *Frontier Conflict: the Australian experience,* Canberra, National Museum of Australia, 2003, p.73.

142 CSO, *Police Gazette No. 29,* Wednesday 16 July 1884, File 939/1892.

143 'Fremantle to Darwin', *The West Australian*, 28 June 1938, p.17; 'Giant Bottle Trees', *The Queenslander*, 26 February 1931, p.54.

144 For a history of Rottnest Prison see Green and Moon, *Far From Home: Aboriginal prisoners of Rottnest Island, 1838–1931*.

145 See for example private diary of Sergt. Thomas Wheatley detailing police patrols from Wyndham from 6 November to 23 December 1895. Wheatley and party had twelve Aboriginal prisoners on the chain for over four weeks and 418 kilometres. Three became 'too weak to travel'. Private Manuscript, Battye Library, Cons. 1266A.

146 A. Gill, 'Aborigines, Settlers and Police in the Kimberleys 1887–1905', *Studies in Western Australian History*, no. 1, 1977, p.21.

Chapter 5: 'These Puerile Attempts at Arrest'

1   'The Kimberley Pastoral Association', *The West Australian*, 24 April 1885, p.3. It also included the men named as Thomas Lavender, Conway, Malet, V.T. Palmer, E.F. Palmer and Nichol.

2   'Kimberley Pastoral Association', *The West Australian*, 25 April 1885, p.3.

3   See for example 'A Kimberley Grievance', *The West Australian*, 11 July 1885, p.6.

4   'Murders by the Kimberley Natives', Letter by Robert Wolfe, *The West Australian*, 13 November 1888, p.3.

5   G. Bolton, *Alexander Forrest: his life and times*, Melbourne, Melbourne University Press in association with UWA Press, 1958, p.34.

6   J.S. Battye, *The History of the North West of Australia Embracing Kimberley, Gascoyne and Murchison Districts*, Perth, VK Jones, 1915, p.32.

7   Bolton, *Alexander Forrest*, pp.17–18.

8   See B. Gammage, *The Biggest Estate on Earth: how Aborigines made Australia*, Sydney, Allen & Unwin, 2011, p.176. See also L.M. Head, 'Landscapes Socialised by Fire: post-contact changes in Aboriginal fire use in northern Australia, and implications for prehistory', *Archaeology in Oceania*, vol. 29, no. 3, 1994, pp.172–81. For the southwest region see S.J. Hallam, *Fire and Hearth: a study of Aboriginal usage & European usurpation in south-western Australia*, Canberra, Australian Institute of Aboriginal Studies, 1975.

9   'Arrival of Governor Hutt', *The Perth Gazette and Western Australian Journal*, 5 January 1839, p.3.

10   CSO, 'Report Respecting Settlers Residing on Lennard & Meda Rivers, Visits by Police, Government Resident Kimberley, 20–21 January 1884', SROWA, AN 24, Cons. 527, File 2037/1884. See also report of Sergt Troy, 25 January 1884.

11   CSO, 'Sergt Troy to Col Secretary, 25 August 1884', SROWA, AN 24, Cons. 527, File 1175/85.

12   CSO, 'Letter from J.P. McLarty, Kimberley Road Board to Government Resident, 7 May 1885', SROWA, AN 24, Cons. 527, File 1175/85.

13   In the 1887 regulations the governor was empowered to grant lease of land to Aboriginal people of not more than 200 acres (81 hectares). F.M. Robinson

and P.W. Nichols, (eds) E. Russell, *A History of the Law in Western Australia and its Development from 1829 to 1879*, Perth, UWAP, 1980, p.320.

14 Regulations for the Sale of Waste Lands 1864, Chapter V, no. 19, *Government Gazette*, Perth, 24 August 1864; Regulations for the Disposal of Waste Crown Lands in the Northern Districts of Western Australia, 1865, Regulation 25, *Government Gazette*, Perth, 20 January 1865; Land Regulations 1872, Regulation 69, *Government Gazette*, Perth, 20 March 1872; Land Regulations, 1878, Schedule 10 'Form of Pastoral Leases', *Government Gazette*, 14 September 1878; Land Regulations 1887, as amended to 1893, Schedule 9 'Form of Pastoral Lands' and Land Act, No. 37 of 1898, Schedule 24 'Form of Pastoral Lease'. For later appeals to challenge these regulations see CSO, 'William Lukin – Natives Setting Fire to Grass in Paddocks, Killing Sheep etc., Colonial Secretary to Government Resident Derby, 16 August 1888', SROWA, AN 24, Cons. 527, File 2315/1888.

15 'Kimberley Pastoral Association', *The West Australian*, 25 April 1885, p.3.

16 ibid.

17 ibid.

18 For a summary of Fairbairn's report see J.T. Reilly, *Reminiscences of Fifty Years in Western Australia,* Perth, Sands and McDougall, 1903, pp.670–97.

19 Report from Sergt P. Troy to Supt of Police re flooding on Fitzroy and Lennard Rivers, 24 March 1885, SROWA, AN 5/6, Cons. 129, File 673 /1885.

20 In March 1885 PCs Adlam and Wilson and Native Assistant Charlie visited the settlers on the Lennard to ascertain what losses had been incurred from the heavy floods. On 10 March they met William Buress from Morgan and McDermott who informed them that 'all the sheep belonging to that station were swept away on the night of the 28th of February nearly all of which are the result of three years pioneering in the Kimberley district'. WAPD, 'Journal of PC Adlam with PC Wilson and Native Assist Charlie to Visit Settlers on the Lennard to Ascertain What Losses Incurred from the Heavy Floods Derby Station, 1 March 1885', SROWA, AN 5/6, Cons. 129, File 666/1885. Sergeant Troy recorded a loss of some 908 sheep. WAPD, 'Report from Sergt P. Troy to Supt of Police Re Flooding on Fitzroy and Lennard Rivers, 24 March 1885', SROWA, AN 5/6, Cons. 129, File 673/1885. 'Buress said that he and McDermott were in the water for 36 hours and were without food during that time and were quite exhausted when they reached Mssrs McLean and Davies station. On the 13th March they reported Poulton and Nichols narrowly escaping losing their sheep by the flood they were confined to one small patch of ground. The water running under some of the sheep's bellies before it began to subside. Here they even came across the inspector of sheep Mr Morrison who nearly drowned and lost his packhorse. On the 22nd March they visited Emanuel's camp also and Mr Lavender informs me that he "lost 1360 sheep and two horses".' 'Journal of PC Adlam with PC Wilson and Native Assist Charlie to Visit Settlers on the Lennard to Ascertain what Losses Incurred from the Heavy Floods, Derby Station, 13

March 1885', SROWA, AN 5/6, Cons. 129, File 666/1885.

21 Sergeant Patrick Troy reported these flood details of February 1885 to the superintendent: 'Fitzroy and Lennard flooded all the plains country along their banks to an extent unknown since the settlement of the district.' Troy was informed that 'the Lennard came down with a sudden gush giving no time to do anything on the contrary the Fitzroy was rising slowly for many days and gave timely notice of the danger...it is said that it looked like an inland sea...the whole country was a quagmire...horses bogged everywhere till the bottoms of their pack bags were sunk in the mud. Settlers Rose and McLarty in great danger of starving.' WAPD, 'Report from Sergt P. Troy to Supt of Police Re Flooding on Fitzroy and Lennard Rivers', 24 March 1885, SROWA, AN 5/6, Cons. 129, File 673/1885.

22 WAPD, 'Kimberley District, Derby Station. Journal of P.C. Ritchie, 26 April 1886', SROWA, Cons. 430, File 706/1886.

23 ibid.

24 WAPD, 'Report by Sergt P. Troy, 8 February 1883', SROWA, AN 5/6 Cons. 129, File 33/224.

25 See for example 'Kimberley Police Expedition, Journal of PC Armitage on Patrol from Derby Police Station', *Western Mail*, 7 July 1888, p.43.

26 WAPD, 'Derby Station. P.C. James Adlam's Journal Reporting on the Attempted Arrests of Elamarra, Nooklemarra and Jedburrawilya for Stealing Flour from Lukin and Monger, 27 July 1885', SROWA, Cons. 430, File 1164/1885.

27 On the 22 February 1885 PC McAtlee discovered the effect of the introduction of measles to the West Kimberley district. Mr McLarty informed him that 'three white men and two natives' had died of measles. McAtlee himself contracted the disease and became 'laid up' but did not die. WAPD, 'Journal of PC McAlee on Patrol from Derby Station, 7 March 1885', SROWA, AN 5/6, Cons. 129, File 666/1885, Kimberley district, Derby Station. In early 1885 Sergeant Troy, PC Sherry and their native assistants all contracted the disease. Native Assistant George was the only one who died. Measles had, however, spread through the native population. WAPD, 'Report from Sergt P. Troy to Supt of Police Re Measles Epidemic, 28 March 1885', SROWA, AN 5/6, Cons. 129, File 672/1885.

28 Troy reported that the government resident ordered settlers 'to get the sick natives provided with food and shelters'. WAPD, 'Report from Sergt P. Troy to Supt of Police Re Measles Epidemic. 28 March 1885', SROWA, AN 5/6, Cons. 129, File 672/1885.

29 On 17 March 1885 Sgt Sherry had left Derby Station to visit settlers and give them letters instructing them to 'relieve natives suffering from measles and to supply them with food during their illness at Government expense'. WAPD, 'Journal of PC James Sherry', SROWA, AN 5/6, Cons. 129, File 666/1885, Kimberley district, Derby Station. He visited the Roses at Mt Anderson 'where several natives had measles all recovered except an 8 year old girl'. McLarty at Grant Range informed that Mr Rose 'is very ill with the measles.'

On 24 March 'found native encampment where a number of the natives are suffering from the measles. I informed them that if they visit the station they would be supplied with food during their illness.'

30 WAPD, 'Kimberley District. Derby Station. Journal of P.C. James Sherry 9.12.1884 to 20.12.1884, 12.12.1884 to 6.1.1885', 9 December 1885, SROWA, Cons. 430, File 532/1885.

31 ibid.

32 PC Sherry wrote 'The natives are very numerous amongst the ranges in this locality and no doubt a more regular patrol will be necessary than in any other part of the Kimberley. Little danger may be apprehended from them in their present wild state but as civilisation and cunning spreads amongst them they may be regarded as more formidable opponents in their mountainous resorts. Especially when they discover that their everyday haunts will prove almost a safe retreat for them to evade the vigilance of the Police!' WAPD, 'Kimberley District. Derby Station. Journal of P.C. James Sherry 9.12.1884 to 20.12.1884, 12.12.1884 to 6.1.1885', 18 April 1885, SROWA, Cons. 430, File 532/1885.

33 WAPD, Derby Police Station, 11 February 1886, SROWA, Cons. 738/3.

34 ibid. Derby police recorded station worker Thomas Burns hearing an Aboriginal 'coo-ee' from outside his hut and he had 'his own native employee' answer. On asking the employee what it meant he said 'there was a lot of young natives close by who wanted to kill anybody either blackfellow or whitefellow and they advised him to retire to his hut and get his gun ready'. Referring to a letter from Con Daly regarding employee Thomas Burns, WAPD, Derby Police Station, 6 February 1886, SROWA, Cons. 738/3.

35 See for example 'Pastoral Settlement In Western Australia', *The West Australian*, 29 August 1885, p.7.

36 WAPD, Derby Police Station, 'Visiting Settlers on Roberson and Lennard Rivers, and Arrest Native Offenders, Journal of PC McAtlee, 27 April 1886', SROWA, Cons. 430, File 1013/1886.

37 ibid., 14 May 1886.

38 See H. Pedersen and B. Woorunmurra, *Jandamarra and the Bunuba Resistance*, Broome, Magabala Books, 1995, pp.34–8.

39 ibid., p.118.

40 WAPD, Derby Police Station, 'Visiting Settlers on Roberson and Lennard Rivers, and Arrest Native offenders, 16 May 1886', SROWA, Cons. 430, File 1013/1886.

41 ibid.

42 ibid.

43 ibid., 21 May 1886.

44 CSO, Sergeant of Police at Derby, 'Shooting of Aboriginal "Nuglay" by P.C. Ritchie in the Ranges Near Mess. Poulton & Nichols Station on the Robinson, 28 August 1886', SROWA, AN 24, Cons. 527, File 3922/1886.

45 ibid.

46 ibid.; CSO, 'Letter from Nichols to Allyn, 28 August 1886', SROWA, AN

24, Cons. 527, File 3922/1886.

47 ibid.; CSO, 30 August 1886, SROWA, AN 24, Cons. 527, File 3922 /1886.

48 For a biographical study of Warden John Michael Finnerty see P. Statham, 'The First (W.A.) Finnerty's – Father and Son', *Early Days,* vol. 9, no. 2, 1984, pp.16–26. CSO, 'Letter from Inspector Finnerty to Superintendent of Police Smith', SROWA, AN 24, Cons. 527, File 3922 /1886.

49 ibid., 3 September 1886.

50 CSO, 'Shooting of Aboriginal "Nuglay" by P.C. Ritchie in the Ranges Near Mess. Poultin [sic] & Nichols Station on the Robinson, 24 September 1886', SROWA, AN 24, Cons. 527, File 3922/1886.

51 ibid.; CSO, 'Finnerty to Inspector of Police, Derby Police Station, 12 September 1886', SROWA, AN 24, Cons. 527, File 3922/1886.

52 ibid.

53 ibid.

54 ibid.

55 CSO, 'Visiting Settlers on Roberson and Lennard Rivers, and Arresting Native Offenders, Kimberley District, Derby Station, 3 August 1886', SROWA, AN 24, Cons. 527, File 1013/1886.

56 ibid.

57 ibid. Ritchie wrote 'We went up close to them and asked them to put down their spears but they would not. They shipped them at us[.] [T]he country was very rough and we could not do anything with the horses. After remonstrating with them for about 15 minutes and finding we could do no good I said we had better go down the river about half a mile and camp and then come back and try them on foot and see if they would come. We then went back and camped. About two hours after we returned to where we left the natives and found them in the same place w[h]ere we left them. I then went up close to them and spoke[,] as I did so they got up and shook their spears at me. I then started to go back onto the river where PC Powell and SPC Walker and now Mr Gunn was. As soon as they saw me going back one of the old men came down towards me and threw a spear at me[.] I then fired at him with my rifle and wounded him in the left arm[;] this did not stop him. I then put a cartridge in the rifle again but could not close the block in opening it I had throwing the block back to[o] far and caused the rim to pass through then. I could not close it. The native was still coming towards me I took my revolver and fired four shots at him without effect as I thought for he did not seem to feel it. I then turned to run when I saw PC Walker and Mr Gunn coming up to my assistance. I said shoot him or he will spear me[,] my rifle is no good[.] [A]t the same time they both fired at him and he fell. One shot broke his right arm and the other passed through his body and killed instantly. I also struck him twice with the revolver which was a flesh wound. The other natives as soon as they saw him fall went on top of the ranges and...shaking their spears at us they were then about 300 yards in front of us. We think it is best to leave them today and try again tomorrow and see if they will give in as we do not want to shed unnecessary blood.'

58 ibid., the police record 'Lambnada shot dead by PC Powell. Larrowanda the Other Native Shot Dead by PC Walker and Gunn'.

59 ibid., The police recorded their names viz 'Marlmadda, Wyannie, Larriah Left Handed, Charyou Nugget, Manjeah, Chingermarru, Younarra, Garrlin, Wingandah, Gooyburra King Wattie, Gnoonarpaul, Gnooena, Garralgnoo, Jannibendah shot dead by PC Powell, Larrouwan shot dead by SPC Walker and Mr Gunn.'

60 ibid., 5 October 1886. In July 1886 William Forrester, the manager of the King Sound Pastoral Company died from 'inflammation of the lungs'. A man named Gunn replaced Forrester as Munro's manager. 'News From The Goldfields', *The West Australian*, 3 August 1886, p.3. Police record states when they had 'gone a few hundred yards up we heard stones falling on the side our natives were on[,] one of which very nearly struck our natives in the head it having knocked his hat off. We could not see the natives but the rocks were coming out of the caves and the top of the barrier. We had to turn back as we expected stones to come down on our side every minute. This is the same place where the natives attacked Mr Forrester and party in November last. The natives have been camped on top of the barrier for some time there is no shifting them unless with a rifle and that means a lot of men…we reached Derby at 5pm a native came over into the station and told Mr Gunn that as soon as the police go away they intend to come over into the station and stop there as the Leopold Range natives are coming down to kill them…they also state that when our natives go out for the horses they will come down and spear them. To prevent this one of us will go out with the natives for the horses.'

61 See for example CSO, 'Government Resident Wyndham – Natives (5) shot by PC. Graham & Others in April 88', SROWA, AN 24, Cons. 527, File 2776/1888. Sergeant Sherry found that as soon as they turned up, the groups 'retire to the most secure places for their safety, and return to their old haunts and renew their depredations when the police leave the neighbourhood'. He added that: 'The natives are becoming so cunning and civilised that they don't fail to take advantage of the absence of police, from the neighbourhood of the Lennard River in particular.'

62 *Western Australian Government Gazette*, 11 February 1886, p.89.

63 CSO, 'Sergeant of Police at Derby, Shooting of Aboriginal "Nuglay" by P.C. Ritchie in the Ranges Near Mess. Poultin & Nichols Station on the Robinson, Letter from Thomas Lovegrove to Commissioner of Police, 30 November 1886', SROWA, AN 24, Cons.527, File 3922/1886.

64 ibid.

65 ibid.; CSO, 'Memo from Thomas Lovegrove to Commissioner of Police', SROWA, AN 24, Cons. 527, File 3922/1886.

66 CSO, 'Letter Malcolm Fraser, 27 April 1887', SROWA, File 3053, No. 17, p.75.

67 WAPD, 'Derby Police Station, Letterbook Entry by Sub Inspector Troy, 25 July 1887', SROWA, AN 5, Cons. 241/1. For a report of this see

'Retrenchment in the Police Force', *Western Mail*, 10 March 1888, p.14.

68 ibid., 1 August 1887.

69 'Sub Inspector Troy's Report', *Western Mail,* 18 February 1888, p.10.

70 One particular report is worth quoting in full for its detail: 'I beg to report to the commissioner of police on the aboriginals of the Kimberley District. I must confess that I am unable to furnish anything like full information on this subject. A very small percentage of this country is settled and the great bulk of the natives are in their wild state still. They are nomadic and move about in small families, the old men being acknowledged as, heads or chiefs of each family and exercise complete control over the young men. Polygamy is practised and the old men monopolise all the young women; one man having in one instance as many as seven wives. Young men are prohibited from marrying until grey hairs begin to appear in the beard and moustache, and then some old woman is generally the first bride. The natives are divided into four great classes or families, and a man must not take a wife from his own class or family; chastity is rigidly enforced amongst the women – infidelity being punished with great violence and sometimes death. Physically the men are generally tall[,] well built and very active; their features are very much the same as the other Australian natives; they have very little whiskers but grow a beard on the skin and a moustache. The women as far as I have seen are generally poor miserable looking creatures. Measles carried off large numbers when it was in the district about 2 and half years ago. Chest, skin, and eye diseases are very common. There is nothing that I have noticed that is very peculiar in their manner or customs. They live in a state of nudity and do not build any places to protect themselves against the weather. They subsist on small animals, reptiles of every kind, roots, seeds, fish, muscles [sic] and the bark[,] nut or fruit of the boab tree. They collect together once or twice a year to have a corroboree and they perform the rites of circumcision, knocking out their front teeth, and scarring their bodies. The septum of their nose is also separated and a bone thrust through the hole. On such occasions weapons, feathers and other ornaments are freely exchanged, marriages arranged. Everything usually goes on peacefully till towards the conclusion of then a quarrel generally occurs which sometimes ends in a sort of free fight. These so far as I know, are the only wars that are practised. Their only religion seems to be a belief in evil spirits. They seldom look upon death as a natural result, but generally refer to the cause to the malice of some unfriendly tribe and hence the practise of killing a member of the suspected tribe whenever a death occurs. The weapons comprise shields[,] spears[,] throwing sticks[,] kylies and waddies. The weapons are inferior in make and quality to the natives off the south, but the stone headed spear is a most dangerous implement; it is a shaft about eight feet long, one half bamboo and the other half solid wood, the stone head is made of either white or crystallized quarts. From 1 to 3 or 4 inches long, about 1 and a half inches wide at the base, and worked down to a point as sharp as a needle. This is fixed to the wood of the spear by means of a resinous substance made

from a mixture of spinifex and leaves pounded together. Whenever a wound is inflicted by one of these spears, the stone head breaks off and remains in the hollow of the wound. These natives are not without some degree of ingenuity as evinced by the rafts they construct to cross rivers, and even to pass channels, separating islands in the sea. Neat baskets they make of a species of reedy grass, and strong string or fibre made of grass fibres. They are very fond of iron and will always strip a wreck of all they can. They convert it into tomahawks, chisels and knives. During the mosquito season they construct a place to sleep in without being tormented by that pest. It is a circular hole in the ground 2 feet or 2 feet 6 inches deep, logs or wood are laid across, and bushes and grass placed over them, then a covering of soil completes the structure. A hole large enough to admit the body by crawling is left and a bunch of grass made ready to block up the hole, and exclude the mosquitoes when the natives retire to sleep. It is wonderful how six or seven natives occupy such a place without being suffocated. The coast and hill natives are hostile and treacherous, those inhabiting the "plains" and the "pindan" seem to be the most tractable and of a better disposition altogether. With regard to the number of natives I could not make even a guess. All I can say is that I do not consider them numerous. It is true that about Roebuck, and Beagle Bay, Swan Point and along the courses of the Fitzroy River there a good many natives but you may also ride over hundreds of miles of country and find traces of only a few natives. About Roebuck Bay, Beagle Bay, Langrange bay and the Fitzroy River large numbers of natives are being utilised as pearl shellfishers, shepherds and station hands. On the Lennard at the Goldfields on the Ord River and about Wyndham the natives will not make friends with the white man…There are various dialects spoken by the Kimberley natives and they are so distinct that I have seen natives belonging to different parts of the district quite to exchange a single idea with each other.' WAPD, 'Derby Police Station, Sub Inspect, Report by Sub Inspector Troy to Commissioner Phillips, 2 August 1887', SROWA, AN 5, Cons. 241/1.

71 CSO, 'Phillips to Colonial Secretary, 30 May 1888', SROWA, Cons. 527, AN 24, File 1496/1888.

72 CSO, 'Natives (5) Shot by PC. Graham & Others in April 88', Government Resident Wyndham, SROWA, AN 24, Cons. 527, File 2776/1888.

73 CSO, 'William Lukin – Natives Setting Fire to Grass in Paddocks, Killing Sheep etc. Malcolm Fraser to Lovegrove, 16 August 1888', SROWA, AN 24, Cons. 527, AN 24, 2315/1888. Fraser wrote in August 1888 'that this condition must be upheld or an injustice will be done to the natives. Ever since we have been in the country this condition has been insisted upon in all pastoral leases and I trust will be protected in the interests of the natives.'

74 ibid., 'William Lukin to Govt Resident Derby, 7 July 1888'.

75 ibid.

76 ibid.

77 CSO, 'William Lukin – Natives Setting Fire to Grass in Paddocks, Killing Sheep etc. Governor Broome to Lovegrove, 22 August 1888', SROWA, AN

24, Cons. 527, File 2315/1888.

78 ibid.

79 WAPD, 'From Government Residents, Wyndham & Derby, & Derby Station. Replying to the Suggestion that the Police Force be Reduced in the West Kimberley'. SROWA, AN 5/1, Cons. 430, File 1026/1887. See *Police Gazette*, 25 January 1888, CO 6/840, vol. 4, 1888, p.15.

80 M. Bentley, *Grandfather was a Policeman: the Western Australian police force 1829–1889*, Perth, Hesperian Press, 1993, p.141.

81 CSO, 'Commissioner of Police – Use of Arms by Police', *Draft Rules for the Use of Firearms*, G Phillips, point 3, SROWA, AN 24, Cons. 527, File 2833/1889.

82 ibid.; CSO, 'Correspondence from FN Broome to Commissioner of Police, 3 October 1888', SROWA, AN 24, Cons. 527, File 2833/1888.

83 ibid.; CSO, *Draft Rules for the Use of Firearms*, G Phillips point 3, SROWA, AN 24, Cons. 527, File 2833/1888.

84 ibid.; CSO, 'Correspondence Regarding the Use of Firearms by Police Attorney General Warton, 4 November 1888', SROWA, AN 24, Cons. 527, File 2833/1888.

85 N. Green and S. Moon, *Far From Home: Aboriginal prisoners of Rottnest Island, 1838–1931*, Perth, UWA Press, 1997, p.118. Guerilla was executed at Rottnest on 18 June 1883.

86 WAPD, 'Letter from Superintendent of Police to Resident Office Roebourne', SROWA, AN 5/6, Cons. 129, File 20/1883.

87 'Legislative Council', *The West Australian,* 20 November 1888, p.3.

88 ibid.

89 ibid.

90 ibid.

91 ibid.

92 ibid.; see also 'Correspondence, Kimberley Natives and the Settlers', *The West Australian,* 18 February 1889, p.4.

93 'Gribble V. The West Australian', *Western Mail,* 21 May 1887, pp.9–15.

94 'Legislative Council', *The West Australian*, 20 November 1888, p.3.

95 ibid.

96 ibid.

97 ibid.

98 ibid.

99 ibid.

100 Votes and Proceedings of the Legislative Council, VPLC, no. 27, 1888.

101 Report by Commissioner Phillips to Honourable Colonial Secretary, 'Papers Respecting the Necessity for Increased Police Protection for the Settlers in the Kimberley District form the Aboriginal Natives, 20 November 1888', WALCVP, 1888, p.5. The reports of Constable Ritchie claimed similar reasons for stock losses. Lukin was embarrassed to read that a native told Constable Ritchie that Lukin's sheep were actually on another man's station. *The West Australian,* 28 November 1888, p.3. A week earlier Sergeant Sherry

had made similar observations at other stations and was damning in his report that was not only tabled in the Legislative Council in 1888 but reported in full in *The West Australian*, 21 November 1888, p.3; no doubt this caused indignation and embarrassment. Journal of Sergt Sherry, VPLC, 1888, West Kimberley District, Derby Station, p.8. Sherry wrote, 'With the exception of the Grant, Anderson and Edgar stations the other stations on the Lennard and Robinson Rivers are all worked short handed, the stock are not properly looked after, especially sheep, scores of which are killed by wild dogs, through not having sufficient men and horses employed for boundary riding purposes, and trusting too many half-civilised native shepherds. When the sheep are counted and the losses ascertained by the manager, he attributes all losses to the natives.'

102 ibid., '...they had no flour for over a week previous to my visit; the allowance of flour is only issued for one man (10lbs) and nothing else, which is always consumed in one day.'

103 'Native Depredations in the West Kimberley', *Western Mail*, 23 March 1889, p 4. 'Up to the present time not a single native has been arrested on the Lennard River for sheep stealing by the police unless assisted by settlers. Many of the warrants taken out years ago against the worst of the natives have fallen through by the death of one manager and his successor leaving the district in disgust from the inability of the police to put a stop to the wholesale destruction of sheep that has been carried on for years past on this station. The ringleader causing most of this trouble is an outlaw, and has been so for the last few years. This speaks for itself. If the government would give the settlers the same powers to shoot the natives that the police had, I don't think he would trouble us for long. In conclusion I may state that Sergt Sherry has not visited this river for some years. On that occasion he returned with the impression that it was useless to attempt to arrest natives whilst in the Napier Range and the only possible way of dealing with them would be to shoot them.'

104 *Western Mail*, 2 March 1889, p.7.

105 ibid. Also reported in *The West Australian*, 26 February 1889, p.3. 'The police themselves are largely responsible for the present state of affairs with the natives in the Kimberley. For several years during the early settlement of the district they were looked upon by the settlers as the curse of the country. They appeared to consider their sole duty was to protect the blacks, and were always eager to "work up" the most trivial native cases against the whites. They instilled into the minds of the natives the belief that they could do almost anything they chose without the whiteman touching him and gave them the idea that police were placed there for the special protection of the blacks only. While performing this portion of their duties so zealously they neglected the legitimate interests of the pioneer and in most cases when called upon to perform any service for the settlers benefit they have proved themselves most inefficient and incapable body of men, so much so, that both blacks and whites have thorough contempt for them.'

106 ibid.

107 *Western Australian Government Gazette,* 1884, p.111.

108 For an example of this complaint see *NorWest Times,* 16 January 1892.

109 'Kimberley Natives and the Settlers', *The West Australian,* 18 February 1889, p.4.

110 'Kimberley Natives and Settlers Property', *The West Australian,* 20 April 1888, p.3.

111 For an account of this incident see 'The Northern Territory', *South Australian Register,* 25 December 1885, p.6.

112 For an account of this incident see 'The Kimberley Murders', *Western Mail,* 18 December 1886, p.28. Piton was also known as 'Peyton'.

113 ibid. Six men of West Kimberley named Witowanda, alias Yandigriwell, Congerland alias Cooraunna, Marndinga, Jardarrie alias Cooraunna alias Sambo, Wargue alias Langarimal and Beingarra, were charged with the wilful murder of John George Piton, of Robinson River, on or about 28 November 1886. The jury brought in a verdict of guilty against Witowanda, Congerland, Jardarrie, and Wargue, and the death sentence was passed upon them, while the other two prisoners were found guilty of manslaughter and were each sentenced to fifteen years' in prison. 'Murders at Roebourne', *The Daily News,* 13 June 1896, p.2.

114 CSO, 'Government Resident Derby – Murder of Rummer and Ah Hee by Natives to Arrest of Natives on Robinson and Other Rivers, 27 December 1888', SROWA, AN 24, Cons. 527, File 1889/0078.

115 'Broome News', *The West Australian,* 15 May 1894, p.5.

116 WAPD, 'General Functional Police Files, Report on the Career of Patrick Troy 1915', SROWA, Cons. 430, File 3974/1915 (nd.); *The West Australian,* 31 July 1899, p.4.

117 WAPD, 'Report Insp F.W. Lodge, Derby Station, to Commissioner of Police, 5 February 1892', SROWA, AN 5/1, Cons. 430, File 116/1892. Emphasis added.

118 CSO, 'Governor F.N. Broome to Commissioner of Police, 31 May 1888', SROWA, Cons. 527, AN 24, File 1496/1888.

119 CSO, 'Inspector Lodge to Commissioner of Police, 31 May 1888', SROWA, Cons. 527, AN 24, File 1496/1888.

120 WAPD, 'Derby Police Station, Letterbook, Entry by Sub Inspector Troy', SROWA, AN 5, Cons. 241/1, File 202/89.

121 CSO, 'A.B. Wright – Hostility of Natives and Protection for Telegraph Construction party, as to, Letter from Phillips to Inspector Lodge, 5 December 1888', Derby, SROWA, AN 24, Cons. 527, File 3258/1888.

122 ibid.

123 WAPD, 'Derby Police Station, Letterbook, Entry by Inspector Lodge, 30 June 1889', SROWA, AN 5, Cons. 241/1.

124 ibid., 11 July 1889.

125 ibid.

126 WAPD, 'Derby Police Station, Letterbook, Entry by Inspector Lodge. 30

June 1889', SROWA, AN 5, Cons. 241/1.

127 WAPD, 'Police Constables Armitage and Watts Charged with Wilful Murder of Native at Napier Range, Papers and Telegrams', SROWA, AN 5, Cons. 430, File 1207/1889.

128 ibid., File 195/89.

129 The statement of 'Jerry', gives an account of the event: 'I am a native assistant. I went with Armitage and Watts into the Napier Range. I was with them when a native named Jenella was shot. It was early in the morning before the sun was up. It was one morn ago. It was daylight we could not see very much but it was coming daylight. I saw six natives there. I recognised one "hedger". I only heard one shot. I was positive it was Armitage that shot it. I was only a short distance off. He shot Jenella. Jenella was a young fellow about sixteen[.] (This witness here walked to about distance Armitage was from Jenella when he fired 13 paces[.]) Armitage was as close as I was. I could not tell when he was running whether Jenella was a man or a boy. I was sure he was a male. The body I showed the doctor in the Napier Range was the body of the native shot by Armitage "Jenella"[.] Watts did not fire at Jenella. He did not fire at all in the range[;] his Killaman (gun) was no good. His cartridge would not come out. Prisoners said nothing to me about shooting natives when they went into the range. I had no firearms (Killaman)[. W]hen Armitage fired Watts was in the camp where the natives had been sleeping. Watts was about 80 yards away when Armitage fired. I had my revolver (Killaman) on my strap but never took it out. When I said I had no Killaman (no firearms) I did not understand. I am positive I did not touch my revolver. I was carrying it on my strap. Native assistant Jacky was with us. He was walking along a creek. Jacky did not fire. No other police were there. The bullet struck Jenella in the right side (putting his finger in his stomach about 6 inches to the right of the navel) blood came out left side. Jenella spoke said he was going to die. I did not hear Armitage say anything to Jenella, but he called me to look out for Jenella, Watts was not near, he was at the camp. I have been a policeman for a long time. Forget how long.' By William Armitage: The Native, CSO, 'Government Resident Derby – Native "Jeneella" Shot by PC's Armitage & Watts', SROWA, Cons. 527, File 2627/1889.

130 CSO, 'Settlers West Kimberley – Natives in Barrier Ranges. That Stringent Measures be Adopted', Petition to Sir Frederick Napier Broome Knight Commander of the Most Distinguished Order of Saint Michael and Saint George Governor and Commander in Chief in and over the Territory of Western Australia its Dependencies, Derby, October 1889, SROWA, AN 24, Cons. 527, File 3398/1889. Reported in *The West Australian*, 29 November 1889, p.4.

131 ibid.

132 ibid.

133 ibid.

134 Including 'Mr A. Forrest, M.L.C., Mr McKenzie Grant, M.L.C., and Mr E. T. Hooley', *The West Australian*, 28 November 1889.

135 ibid.

136 ibid.

137 ibid.

138 WAPD, 'Annual Police Report 1889 by Inspector Lodge to Commissioner of Police', SROWA, Cons. 430, File 3573/1903.

139 ibid.; Lodge claimed there were now 95,353 sheep and 15,087 cattle, being an increase of 14,802 sheep and about 7000 cattle.

140 WAPD, 'Stock and Stations, 1889 Annual Report by Inspector Lodge to Commissioner of Police', SROWA, Cons. 430, File 3573/1903.

141 ibid. Lodge claimed that 'Mr Nichol informed me some time later that he had lost all the lambs through the hawks'. At Mr Davis's station 284 sheep had been lost from a total of 1200. The manager informed Lodge that 'he did not know of one single sheep having been killed by natives since he had been on the station (April 1889)'.

142 ibid., Sheep number increased from 14,150 to 14,442.

143 ibid.

144 ibid.

145 ibid.

146 ibid.

147 Lodge refuted Lukin's claim by stating that in personal conversation with Lukin he had told him that the only sheep that he knew of having been killed by natives since the police had been stationed on the river were those he had already referred to viz 21 'and these were killed when PC Waldock was alone'. CSO, 'Settlers West Kimberley – Natives in Barrier Ranges. That Stringent Measures be Adopted, Derby, October 1889', AN 24, Cons. 527, File 3398/1889.

148 Bolton, *Alexander Forrest*, appendix vi.

149 Pedersen and Woorunmurra, *Jandamarra and the Bunuba Resistance*, p.49.

150 CSO, 'Government Resident Derby – Native "Jeneella" Shot by PCs Armitage & Watts, 17 October 1889', SROWA, AN 24, Cons. 527, File 2627/1889.

151 ibid., p.50.

152 Lovegrove went on to become Western Australian Principal Medical Officer (1895) and the foundation member of the Western Australian Medical Association (1898).

Chapter 6: 'A More Powerful and Warlike Race'

1 See P.M. Durack, 'Pioneering in the East Kimberleys', *Early Days: Journal of the Royal Western Australian Historical Society*, vol. 2, pt. 14, 1933, pp.1–46.

2 For a useful summary of the discovery of the Kimberley Goldfields see P.E. Playford and I. Ruddock, 'Discovery of the Kimberley Goldfield', *Early Days*, vol. 9, pt. 3, 1985, pp.76–106.

3 'The Natives in the East Kimberley', *Western Mail*, 6 October 1888, p.30.

4 WAPD, 'Journal of Sergeant Wheatley on Patrol from Wyndham Station, 14 October 1895', SROWA, Cons. 430, File 2951/1895.

5   'More of the Black Nor-West', *Sunday Times,* 30 July 1905, p.7.

6   See for example C. Clement, *Impact Stories of the East Kimberley,* East Kimberley Working Paper no. 29 Canberra, East Kimberley Impact Assessment Project, 1989. Clement details evidence of at least ten massacres.

7   B. Shaw, *Banggaiyerri: the story of Jack Sullivan,* Canberra, Australian Institute of Aboriginal Studies, 1983, p.65.

8   ibid.

9   For an account of this in the Northern Territory see D.R. Rose, *Hidden Histories: black stories from Victoria River Downs, Humbert River and Wave Hill stations,* Canberra, Aboriginal Studies Press, 1991, pp.20–5.

10 See *The West Australian,* 5 January 1883; see also Durack, 'Pioneering in the East Kimberleys'.

11 Sighting some Jaru people Carr-Boyd 'laid down his gun as a sign of our peaceful intentions, and cooeeing held up his hands, at the same time advancing alone in the direction of the blackfellow', to which the Jaru man 'sprang to his feet and commenced flourishing a womerra at us, the while yelling at us in a furious manner'. Carr-Boyd did not retreat but rather continued to pursue the man who ran off. Moments later, however, this man was joined by many other Aboriginal men who had climbed the ridges above and who 'seemed to take fresh outrage, and favored us with what appeared to be a broadside of invectives' suggesting they leave the area. The explorer party adopted a military attitude and looked for higher ground to view 'our probable foes' when all the Aboriginal men came out of their hiding places 'brandishing their weapons in a most menacing manner, at the same time maintaining a furious din'. Their behaviour 'made our blood tingle' although the party resisted the 'inclination to give them a broadside', by which they meant shooting at them, because they would then have to leave the area where they were prospecting at once as reprisal would ensue. A group of three Aboriginal men left the group and started walking towards Carr-Boyd's party, the leading man without weapons but the other two with spears and womerras while the others sang out 'an incessant yell' of support. Carr-Boyd responded by putting his firearm down and engaging with them in dance that put both parties on friendly terms. Carr-Boyd 'started corroborring [sic], clapping his hands, and singing a Queensland aboriginal song to keep time to his movements[.] The blackfellows, one and all, seemed not a little astonished, and well they might, for he danced around with an energy truly wonderful. In a short time the three blacks came a little nearer to him and began beating time with their bands and weapons, giving expression to their admiration by grunts of approval, which broke out into a loud shout whenever Mr Carr-Boyd performed a more than usually extraordinary evolution in his dance. I need not say that we who were on the hill regarded the whole proceedings as something unique in the extreme. At length Mr Carr-Boyd became exhausted, and sat upon the ground, and clearing the stone away on one side of him he invited the leading blackfellow to come and sit beside him. One blackfellow now boldly advanced up to him, his

two comrades remaining some twenty yards off with their spears poised as if ready to cast them at an instant[']s notice. The behaviour of the blacks at this time made us feel that it was a critical moment, and Mr S. Williams, who was lately a member of the Charters Towers Defence Force, and a good shot, covered the nearest armed blackfellow with his rifle; but, fortunately, Mr. Carr-Boyd succeeded in establishing a friendly understanding with the natives. Carr-Boyd's group met the Kija group the next day and conveyed that they were there for prospecting only and meant no harm and exchanged foodstuffs.' Before they left 'they took the liberty to over haul us, feeling our arms, legs, and chests, and seemed not a little astonished to find that we were formed of flesh and blood like themselves'. Carr-Boyd's party stayed in the area for four or five days and, although away from their camp for 6 or 8 kilometres at a time, their camp was not robbed, indicating that trust had been established. One Queensland newspaper report stated: 'Mr. Carr-Boyd says, when the Myalls first see a white man they believe he has come to kill them, and then they cast about for means to compass the white man's death, and hence bloodshed ensues. This might be avoided by conciliatory behaviour on the part of the whites.' 'Kimberley Goldfields Halls Creek', *The Queenslander*, 4 December 1886, p.906.

12 WAPD, Denham River Police Station, Occurrence Book 1, see for example 'Memo, 12 October 1889', SROWA, AN 5, Cons. 739; WAPD, Denham River Police Station, Occurrence Book 1, 'Entry by PC Tuke 1 Dec 1890', SROWA, AN 5, Cons. 739.

13 WAPD, 'Halls Creek Police Station, Letterbook Report by Sergeant Farley to Commissioner of Police, 26 November 1889', SROWA, AN 5, Cons. 1422.

14 John Forrest had chosen the site for the town of Wyndham. 'Hosts and Guests', *Kalgoorlie Western Argus*, 10 September 1896, p.16.

15 The PCs were T. Connor, H.R. Strickland, W.H. Kelly, O. Crowe, W. Johnson and A.S. Forbes.

16 There was one sergeant, seven constables, four native assistants and eighteen horses whose principal duties were town patrol and mail carrying. WAPD, 'Derby Police Station, Letterbook Entry by Sub Inspector Troy, Derby Kimberley Police, 19 August 1887', SROWA, AN 5, Cons. 241/1.

17 'The Kimberley Goldfield', *The Star,* Issue 5630, 28 May 1886, p.3. For an account of this period see W.H. Lamond, 'Five Years in the Kimberley', *Early Days: Journal the Royal Western Australian Historical Society*, vol. 7 pt. 3, 1971, pp.29–49.

18 'Report upon the Kimberley Goldfields, by the Warden, Wardens Camp, Elvire Gorge, Kimberley, 30 June 1887', in WALCVP, 1887, Paper A19.

19 WAPD, 'Derby Police Station, Letterbook Entry by Sub Inspector Troy, 23 July 1887', SROWA, AN 5, Cons. 241/1. For a report of the police party leaving Perth see 'Departure of the Gold Escort for Kimberley', *The West Australian*, 30 June 1886, p.3.

20 'Report by Sub Inspector Patrick Troy, the Kimberley Goldfields', *The West Australian,* 9 November 1886, p.3.

21 The officer in charge was Sergeant Sherry with troopers Keen, Farley and Brophy.

22 Acting Sergeant Keen wrote to the commissioner outlining the arrangements for mail delivery in the goldfields. He wrote stating his reasons for hiring John Bayes as a special police constable (SPC). Bayes was to help Constable James Sweeny until Trooper Austin arrived from Wyndham – a trip of twelve days by horse. Sergeant Keen had the police horses held at Elvire Gorge but, since the horses were constantly straying, he ordered SPC Bayes to look after them until the arrival of troopers Buckley and Brophy who were in Wyndham on duty. Trooper Brophy was to bring back a 'waggonette' to convey ex-police officer J. Lee to Wyndham as he was extremely ill. The wagonette, however, broke down 30 miles (50 kilometres) from Wyndham and was left on the side of the road leaving Lee stranded and ill. Trooper Buckley was otherwise detained with warden Finnerty in Wyndham and furthermore there was a solitary prisoner (held for larceny) at the goldfields camp who required constant supervision as there was no lock-up there. Troopers Austin and Sweeny would be leaving in four days on the next mail run. Clearly, despite orders from Commissioner Phillips in Perth, police on this frontier were extremely limited in many practical senses in what they could do. WAPD, 'Goldfields District Wardens Camp. Re Swearing in of John Bayes as Special Police Constable on 1 July 1888', 30 June 1888, SROWA, Cons. 430, File 963/1888.

23 See 'Report by Sub Inspector Patrick Troy, the Kimberley Goldfields', *The West Australian*, 9 November 1886, p.3.

24 ibid.

25 WAPD, 'Derby Police Station, Letterbook Entry by Sub Inspector Troy, 19 August 1887', SROWA, AN 5, Cons. 241/1.

26 Men were also at Halls Creek, the 12 mile camp, Elvire River, Brockman and Halls Gully. 30 June 1887, Report upon the Kimberley Goldfields, by the Warden, Wardens Camp, Elvire Gorge, Kimberley, in WALCVP, 1887, Paper A19.

27 G. Bolton, *Alexander Forrest: his life and times,* Melbourne, Melbourne University Press in association with UWA Press, 1958, p.15.

28 WAPD, Halls Creek Police Station, Letterbook, 17 August 1889, SROWA, AN 5, Cons. 1422.

29 'The Storied Past, The Kimberley Rush', *The West Australian*, 15 October 1932, p.5. See also P. Bridge, *Russian Jack*, Perth, Hesperian Press, 2002.

30 Even by mid-1889 the services on the goldfields remained rudimentary at best. Sergeant James Farley reported police wore no uniform 'as none had been issued to them' and they and the warden still lived in tents. WAPD, 'Halls Creek Police Station, Letterbook, 17 August 1889', SROWA, AN 5, Cons. 1422. Description of the camp as made by the newly arrived Sergt Farley for report to the head office.

31 'Report upon the Kimberley Goldfields, by the Warden, Wardens Camp, Elvire Gorge, Kimberley, 30 June 1887', in WALCVP, 1887, Paper A19. See

also WAPD, 'Kimberley Goldfields, Halls Creek Station, Report of Death of a Man James Burns, of Liverpool, England, Due to Consumption and Scurvy', SROWA, Cons. 430, File 1890/0144.

32 ibid.

33 See 'Report by Sub Inspector Patrick Troy, The Kimberley Goldfields', *The West Australian*, 9 November 1886, p.3; 'The Kimberley Goldfields, Sub Inspector Troy's Latest Report', *The West Australian*, 5 January 1887, p.3. See for example, 'Report that 2 men, Michael Anderson and Conrad Hobin, entered camp on the Fletcher in an emaciated condition after having become lost while making their way to the Richenda [sic] diggings', WAPD, Kimberley Goldfields, Halls Creek Station, Cons. 430. File 1888/0578. 'Edward or Edwin Williams is reported to have died from sunstroke sometime in December last about 25 miles [40 kilometres] from Wyndham on the road to Halls Creek', WAPD, SROWA, Cons. 430, File 1892/0463. 'Kimberley Goldfield, Halls Creek Station, Reported Death of Joseph Webb, a Miner, from Snake Bite', WAPD, 9 April 1896, SROWA, Cons. 430, File 1896/1048.

34 Quoted in K.J. Moran, *Sand and Stone: a social history of Western Australia as recorded by police of the Eastern frontier,* London, Frickers International Publishing, 2000, p.86.

35 WAPD, 'Report from Government Resident to Colonial Secretary re Police Station at Parry Lagoon, 8 November 1886', SROWA, Cons. 430, File 1899/1996.

36 CSO, 'Government Resident East Kimberley – Police Station at Parry's Lagoon, 17 miles from Wyndham, immediate establishment of, minute paper from Government Resident, East Kimberley, 8 November 1886', SROWA, AN 24, Cons. 527, File 5135/1886.

37 WAPD, 'Derby Police Station, Letterbook Entry by Sub Inspector Troy', SROWA, AN 5, Cons. 241/1; see 'Legislative Council March 20', *The West Australian*, 21 March 1888, p.3.

38 WAPD, 'Derby Police Station, Letterbook Entry by Sub Inspector Troy, 19 August 1887', SROWA, AN 5, Cons. 241/1.

39 ibid.

40 WAPD, 'Report by Sergt Troy Regarding Death of Fred Marriot, Derby Police Station, 3 July 1886', SROWA, AN 5, Cons. 738/3. See also W.H. Lamond, 'Five Years in the Kimberley', *Early Days, Journal and Proceedings of the Royal Western Australian Historical Society*, vol. vii, Pt. 3, 1971, pp.29–-30.

41 WAPD, 'Report from PC Ritchie of the Wilful Shooting of "Young Jacky" and "Monday" by "Nipper". J.J. Durack Implicated. December 28, 1897', SROWA, Cons. 430, File 298/1898.

42 A.C. Angelo, 'Kimberley and North West Goldfields', *Early Days,* WAHS, vol. 3, 1948, p.38.

43 For an account ascribing the killing of Marriot to 'bloodthirsty wretches' see 'News from Derby, Latest from the Goldfields', *The Daily News*, 10 August 1886, p.3.

44 C. Clement, *Old Halls Creek, a Town Remembered*, Mt. Lawley, Western

Australia, National Heritage, 2000. p.6; also C. Clement and P. Bridge (eds), *Kimberley Scenes: sagas of Australia's last frontier,* Hesperian Press, 1991, p xiii.

45 Kimberley Language Resource Centre (eds), *Moola Bulla; In the Shadow of the Mountain,* Kimberley Language Resource Centre, Broome, Magabala Books, 1996, p.37.

46 WAPD, 'Report by Sergt Troy from R. Mcphee Regarding Death of Fred Marriot, Derby Police Station, 3 July 1886', SROWA, AN 5, Cons. 738/3.

47 Robert Tennant Stow Wolfe, one of the men on the punitive expedition, quoted in C. Clement and P. Bridge (eds.) *Kimberley Scenes,* 1991, op.cit., p.160.

48 WAPD, 'Report by Sergt Troy from R. Mcphee regarding death of Fred Marriot, Derby Police Station, 3 July 1886', SROWA, AN 5, Cons.738/3.

49 G.H. Lamond, *Tales of the Overland: Queensland to Kimberley in 1885,* Hesperian Press, 1986, p.51.

50 M. Durack, *Kings in Grass Castles,* London, Constable, 1959, p.278.

51 Kimberley Language Resource Centre, *Moola Bulla; In the Shadow of the Mountain,* 1996, op.cit., p.xv.

52 'William Routledge, Golden Days, A Nor Wester's Memories', *Western Mail,* 24 June 1937 and 1 July 1937, quoted in C. Clement and P. Bridge (eds), *Kimberley Scenes,* 1991, op.cit., p.221.

53 G.B. Hales, 'Letters Written from the Kimberley Goldfields 1886', Cons. 688, quoted in N. Green, *The Forrest River Massacres,* Fremantle, Fremantle Arts Centre Press, 1995, p.59.

54 ibid, also reported in 'The Latest from Kimberley', *Evening News,* 22 November 1886, p.5.

55 The report stated 'I have to report for the information of the Superintendent of police that on the 26th of November[,] East Master John Durack reports that on the 17th November[,] as he and his cousin Mr John Durack of the Ord River station were out cattle hunting about sixty miles from their station[,] they suddenly came across a large number of natives who were lying in the long grass[. T]he natives jumped up and some of them threw spears[,] one of which struck Mr. John Durack (the elder) in the chest and killed him on the spot[,] the other master John Durack then galloped away. Both the Duracks were armed at the time of the murder but the natives attacked them so sudden that they had no time to use them – the names of the natives were not known.' WAPD, East Kimberley Wyndham Police Station, 'Ambush of John Durack and Party by Natives, 17/11/86 to 12/12/86', report 11 January 1887.

56 M. Durack, *Kings in Grass Castles,* p.285.

57 Shaw, *Banggaiyerri: the story of Jack Sullivan,* p.68.

58 WAPD, 'East Kimberley Wyndham Police Station, Ambush of John Durack and Party by Natives, 17/11/86 to 12/12/86, Report 11 January 1887'.

59 The police report stated 'I left Wyndham to go in search of the murderers accompanied by PC Strickland and Kelly and one native assistant. On arrival at the twenty mile camp I got SPC Reen who was camped there and took him with me. I arrived at Mssrs Durack Station on the Ord River on the 3rd

of December and left again on the 6th accompanied by Mr Michael Durack, Master John Durack and a party of seven others [who] made up twenty Men of Mr Durack's Stations[. O]n the 9th the tracks of the natives were picked up near the scene of the murder and were followed up until the twelfth when we came upon about 100 natives[. T]he country was very stoney [sic] and a great many deep creeks[. W]e endeavoured to arrest some of them[;] they threw spears and PC Strickland had a very narrow escape from being speared. I myself had a very narrow escape of being speared by a native who was hiding behind a tree on the bank of the creek. Mr Michael Durack fired just in time to baulk this native as he was in the act of throwing the spear. I then fired and killed him. Several shots were fired by the remainder of the party and another native was killed. After this the other natives made their escapes into the creeks where we were unable to follow them[. A]t first they seemed determined to fight but after the first shots were fired they scattered in all directions, George Trusclove Sergt Police. East Kimberley Police Station', WAPD, 9 January 1887, SROWA, Cons. 430, File 298/1898. See also WAPD, 'East Kimberley Wyndham Police Station, Ambush of John Durack and Party by Natives, 17/11/86 to 12/12/86, Report 11 January 1887'.

60 Correspondence 'Bishop Gibney and the Nor' West Settlers', *The West Australian,* 14 November 1892, p.3.

61 WAPD, 'East Kimberley, Wyndham Station, Death of John Durack by Natives, Undated Note Signed 'Gurney', Det, Received by the Police Dept, 15 November 1892', SROWA, AN 5/1, Cons. 430, File 2108/1892.

62 M. Durack, *Kings in Grass Castles,* p.286.

63 ibid., p.301.

64 Lamond stated 'we picked up the tracks of a big mob of blacks, making away towards the hills from where they had killed Durack...we saw the blacks but could not get near them; so, after a long hunt we had to go back to the Ord River disappointed. The police party went back to Wyndham and we back to Halls Creek.' G.H. Lamond, *Tales of the Overland,* pp.54–5.

65 Stowe wrote '1886. 6 Monday Started out. 4 police and 9 of Duracks party to avenge the death of J. Durack killed by blacks. Camped 20 NE. 7 Tuesday Went to hays new camp on stockyard creek camped for dinner and then east 10 miles [16 kilometres]. 8 Wednesday Travelled NE and E for about 20 miles and camped. A little rain at night. 9 Thursday Looking about for tracks – very hot. 10 Friday Raining part of night. About 12 miles travelling looking for niggars [sic] Party, named a mountain Mt Wolfe.' Robert Tennant Stow Wolfe, quoted in Clement and Bridge (eds), *Kimberley Scenes,* pp.180–1.

66 P.M. Durack, 'Pioneering in the East Kimberleys', p.43.

67 *The WA Record,* 5 October 1893, p.7.

68 See Clement, *Historical Notes Relevant to Impact Stories of the East Kimberley,* pp.1–20; see also P. Marshall (ed.), *Raparapa Kularr Martuwarra: Stories from the Fitzroy River Drovers,* Broome, Magabala Books, 1988, pp.222–6; M.A. Jebb (ed.), *Emerarra; A Man of Merarra,* Broome, Magabala Books, 1996, pp.54–6.

69 H. Ross (ed.) and E. Bray (trans.), *Impact Stories of the East Kimberley,* East

Kimberley Working Paper no. 28, Canberra, East Kimberley Impact Assessment Project, 1989, p.18.

70 'Wyndham Notes', *Western Mail,* 26 February 1887, p.24.

71 WAPD, 'Wyndham Police Station, Occurrence Book, 21 August 1888', SROWA, AN 5, Cons. 741/1.

72 WAPD, 'Goldfields District. Warden's Camp. Report by Lt. Cpt. H. Bosville Re Attack on Trooper Buckley and E.B. Lockett by Natives, 2 September 1888', SROWA, Cons. 430, File 1585/1888.

73 For a fuller account of the punitive expedition in response to the killing of Barnett see C. Owen and C. Choo, 'Deafening Silences: understanding frontier relations and the discourse of police files through Kimberley police records', in C. Choo and S. Hollbach (eds), *Studies in Western Australian History: History and Native Title,* no.23, Press, 2003, pp.128–56.

74 *Northern Territory Times,* 18 August 1888, quoted in G. Davidson, J.W. McCarty and A. McLeary (eds), *Australians, 1888,* Sydney, Fairfax, Syme & Weldon Associates, 1987, p.120.

75 *The Eastern Districts Chronicle,* 13 October 1888, p.2.

76 'Goldfields of the North, Fight with Blacks on Durack's Stations', *The Daily News,* 5 September 1929, p.6. See also A. Lucanus, 'Goldfields of the North. Items from a Police Troopers Log', published in Clement and Bridge (eds), *Kimberley Scenes,* p.46.

77 M. Durack, 'Golden Days of the Kimberley', *Walkabout,* 1 April 1936, pp.35–6, quoted in Clement, *Historical Notes Relevant to Impact Stories of the East Kimberley,* p.8.

78 Angelo, 'Kimberleys and North-West Goldfields', p.38.

79 Wyndham Occurrence Book, 30 November 1887, SROWA, AN 5, Cons. 741/2; 'Report by PC Rhatigan About Complaint from Carrier William Hill, Fletcher Creek Police Station Occurrence Book, 29 Dec 1892', AN 5, Cons. 740.

80 WAPD, Derby Police Station, Letterbook Entry by Sub Inspector Troy who reported 'a number of spears made out of fencing wire', 24 July 1887', SROWA, AN 5, Cons. 241/1.

81 WAPD, 'Report of Sergt Troy to Commissioner of Police Re M. Durack Complaint that Natives had Speared his Horses, 29 July 1888', SROWA, AN 5/1, Cons. 430, File 1188/1888.

82 'Goldfields of the North, Fight with Blacks on Durack's Stations', *The Daily News,* 5 September 1929, p.6.

83 Halls Creek Letterbook, SROWA, 17 August 1889, AN 5, Cons. 1422.

84 WAPD, 'Commissioner of Police – Flour issued to Natives on Wyndham Road', SROWA, AN 5, Cons. 430. File 2492/1890.

85 WAPD, 'Annual Report on East Kimberley District by Sergt R. Troy, 2 January 1890', SROWA, AN 5, Cons. 430, File 3573/1903.

86 ibid., 'Settlers Stations'. See also S. Hunt, *Spinifex and Hessian: Women in North-West Australia 1860–1900,* Perth, UWA Press, 1986, Appendix.

87 WAPD, 'Halls Creek Police Station, Letterbook, 17 August 1889', SROWA,

AN 5, Cons. 1422.

88 CSO, 'Letter, Buchanan, A. Lucanus, H.F. Keep, C.J. Heppperton, Smallpage Bro & Co, F. Connor, P.J. Durack, A.G.D. Beresford, Wyndham to His Excellency, Sir Frederick Napier Broome, Governor of Western Australia, Perth, 11 January 1887', SROWA, AN 24, Cons. 527, File 677/1887.

89 CSO, 'Honorable Government Resident East Kimberley – Establishment of Native Police Force, and Appointment of Officer in Charge, 4 January 1887', SROWA, AN 24, Cons. 527, File 677/1887.

90 ibid.

91 ibid.

92 CSO, 'Letter to Colonial Secretary from M.S. Smith, 18 November 1881', SROWA, AN 24, Cons. 527, File 1437, no. 86. For popular opinion on the need for a police force in the Kimberley see 'Police Protection in the Kimberley District', *The West Australian*, 27 February 1883, p.3.

93 Governor Broome insisted 'the operation of the police against the natives must be confined to the most strict and absolute necessary protective work, and the greatest care must be taken to impress any excess of zeal or anything like entering upon a campaign against the natives of the hills', CSO, 'Governor FN Broome to Commissioner of Police, 31 May 1888', SROWA, Cons. 1496.

94 *Western Australian Government Gazette*, 2 March 1887, quoted in Bolton, *Alexander Forrest*, p.34.

95 CSO, 'Government Resident Wyndham – Natives (5) shot by PC Graham & others in April 88. Report, File Note G.B. Phillips, Commissioner of Police to Hon. Colonial Secretary, enclosing reports from Sergeant Troy and statements from PC Graham and Native Assistant Banjo, 2 October 1888', SROWA, AN 24, Cons. 527, File 2776/1888.

96 ibid.

97 ibid.

98 Troy wrote that the 'whole of the people being much excited and indignant about the matter. A meeting was held that night at the Customhouse Hotel for the purpose of forming a Committee…to see what steps were to be taken to procure counsel for the defence. Afterwards I believe private meetings were held at the residences of Mr F. Smallpage. [After the arrest of George Howard, Liddlow [sic] and native Moody on 7 November] on my arrival in town a few persons who were assembled at the Customshouse Hotel gave three groans of indignation. Prominent among those persons was Mr Ernest Giles (the explorer[,] he had just returned from the fields). Public feeling at that time was in a great state of indignation and excitement, it was thought by the Government Resident and myself that an attempt would be made by the public to rescue the prisoners. Every precaution was taken that was possible with the small staff at hand. All sorts of rumours were afloat as to what the public would do. After a few days the great excitement died away and public feeling subsided on the matter. ibid., 'Report Sergt Troy, Wyndham Station, East Kimberley to Commissioner of Police, 6 Dec 1888'.

99 ibid.

100 ibid.

101 'Supreme Court-Criminal Sittings', *The West Australian,* 31 January 1889, p.3.

102 Banjo's testimony is compelling. 'Banjo, a Gascoyne native, examined by the Crown Solicitor, deposed: I know Howard, Goose Hill, Liddelow, Lewis, Dick, and the blackfellows named Moody and Pompey. Pompey comes from Queensland. I remember going to Goose Hill with them, three months ago. Sergt Connor and Payne were up at that time. We went to Goose Hill to see some horses which had been speared, and to look for the natives who had speared them. I saw the smoke of a fire where three blackfellows were roasting wallabys [sic]. When they saw the horses they ran away. Graham and Howard both had guns. A blackfellow went to hit one of the whitefellows, with a womera, who fired at him. He ran round the tree, and then the whitefellow shot him. He died. He threw his spear at Dickdead Dick. After that the whitefellow fired at him. Graham did not shoot. He must have hit him as, he died. Two blackfellows tumbled down on the grass. A young boy got up in a tree and called out. He was frightened. Neither of the two persons fired. Graham called out, "You want to catch him do not fire." The other one also called out. When the blackfellow was shot the other one got away. He ran away when he heard the shot. I tracked him up to the creek. We wanted to follow the track up the Ord River, but it was too boggy. The whitefellows then waited to go through the mangroves. They came back, and then I saw two blackfellows crossing the plain. The whitefellows galloped after them. After that I might have heard three shots. The one who fired the shots must have been dead Dickie. (Laughter.) I saw one blackfellow dead. The second blackfellow got into the water, and went away in the bush. He had a spear. I did not see the whitefellows fire. I took Sergeant Troy out and showed him the blackfellow's bones, and a dead blackfellow in the tree. [Cross examined.] I remember going out with Payne, Graham, and Butcher to the Ord River after some natives who threw a spear at Liddelow, Sergeant Payne saw the bones and smelt them. I saw them; they lay just alongside the Ord. They were blackfellow's bones; the same I showed Troy. Sergeant Payne said to me, "Blackfellow's?" I said, "Yes." When the party saw the natives at the creek, I saw one spear and, one dowark thrown, and a blackfellow threatening Howard, with a tomahawk.' 'Supreme Court—Criminal Sittings', *The West Australian,* 31 January 1889, p.3.

103 'Supreme Court—Criminal Sittings', *The West Australian,* 1 February, 1889, p.3.

104 'The blacks had been guilty of spearing cattle, and a punitive expedition was sent out to punish them. Constable Graham was the leader, and he had with him three civilians named Hill, Howard and Pompey, besides a number of black trackers. They located a mob of blacks hiding in a scrub, but whether they were the real culprits will never be known for the whole lot were slaughtered. The massacre was carried out in a horribly merciless way. First one end of the scrub was set on fire, and as the niggers were driven out by the flames they were shot down until there was not one of them left alive. It was

a cruel holocaust, men, women and children down to the smallest babe being destroyed. One boy was found in a tree with from 30 to 40 bullets in him or through him. It is said that as many as eighty natives were butchered. When Warden Troy; who was the in charge of the Kimberley district, heard of the massacre, he had the whole of the party arrested and sent down to Perth for trial, which took place on January 30 and 31, 1889. The charges only referred to the killing of the boy in the tree, and evidence was produced which alleged that this boy, if not the whole eighty, had been shot by a man known as "old Dick". Well, old Dick must have been a glutton at murder, and should have been rechristened "old Nick". He was not arraigned at an earthly tribunal, for by a remarkable coincidence he passed in his kit at Derby before the trial came off.' 'An Old-Time Massacre', *The Sunday Times*, 13 September 1908, p.3.

105 CSO, 'Government Resident Wyndham – Natives (5) shot by PC Graham & Others in April 88. Report, Letter from A. Warton to the Colonial Secretary, 6 October 1888', SROWA, AN 24, Cons. 527, File 2776/1888. Warton indicated that this correspondence would be marked 'secret'.

106 ibid.

107 ibid.

108 ibid., quoting Richard Troy's report, dated 3 September 1888.

109 ibid., 2 October 1888.

110 Warton wrote 'The native question here will be a difficult matter to deal with in consequence of this district being settled or travelled over by a class of people who appear to have no desire to civilise or secure the natives viz. packers, carriers[,] prospectors and the stock owners are the same, their sole aim is to keep the people off. The natives in the Kimberley district are courageous and warlike. In 1886 they attacked a party of miners on the goldfields. A white man was killed. Can there be any doubt that, though not perhaps official burden, a wholesale voyage was taken by the miners and that the very few who refused to join in indiscriminate slaughter were looked on as sneaks and cowards? The sober unvarnished truth is that when a handful of white men, of not perhaps the highest character, are, for love of gain, determined to force their way into the territory of a warlike set of natives this kind of thing has been done and is being done (as this occasions shows) and will inevitably be done. I should like his Excellency to consult some experienced settler like Mr Charles Harper and learn from him what occurred between settlers and natives as so warlike as these with particulars of the battle of Pinjarrah [sic]. One can read between the lines of the Resident Magistrates minute of 11.9.88 to see that it does not wish to take any steps to check this "murder of a wholesale and brutal description". The official opinion peeps out in the examination of the difficulties in the way of bringing anybody to justice. I should like to see his comments on those passages from Troy which I have selected above and to have his clear "aye or no" to the statements therein contained. That is the best advice I can offer.' ibid., 'File Note G.B. Phillips, Commissioner of Police to Hon. Colonial Secretary, Enclosing Reports from

Sergeant Troy and Statements from PC Graham and Native Assistant Banjo, 2 October 1888'.

111 CSO, 'Government Resident Wyndham – Natives (5) Shot by PC. Graham & Others in April 88. Report, Letter from Attorney General A. Warton to the Colonial Secretary, 6 October 1888', SROWA, AN 24, Cons. 527, File 2776/1888.

112 *Papers Respecting the Necessity of Increased Police Protection for the Settlers of the Kimberley District from the Aboriginal Natives,* VPLC no. 27, 1888, p.10; CSO, 'A.B. Wright – Hostility of Natives and Protection for Telegraph Construction Party, as to', SROWA, AN 24, Cons. 527, File 3258/1888.

113 WAPD, 'Halls Creek Police Station, Letterbook, Confidential Report by Inspector Lodge to Sergeant Keen, 21 December 1888', SROWA, AN 5, Cons. 1422.

114 ibid., 21 December 1888. Emphasis in original.

115 CSO, 'A.B. Wright – Hostility of Natives and Protection for Telegraph Construction Party, as to, Letter from Geo Phillips to Inspector Lodge, Derby, 5 December 1888', SROWA, AN 24, Cons. 527 File 3258/1888.

116 Clement, *Historical Notes Relevant to Impact Stories of the East Kimberley,* p.8.

117 Police found a glass spearhead in the skull of Pirate, who had been murdered by other Aboriginal people. WAPD, 'Derby – Murder of Aboriginal Native "Pirate" by Aboriginal Natives "Duldulgie" alias "Nipper" and "Boydene" alias "Gillie" at Cragie Gorge about 2.3.1906. Escape of Above Named from Constable Thurlow (854) on 29.4.1906, 7 September 1906', SROWA, AN 5/2, Cons. 430, File 4868/1906.

118 D. W. Carnegie, *Spinifex and Sand,* facsimile edition, Perth, Hesperian Press, 1982, p.340.

119 Police found that there 'were seven more insulators broken at Hells gates and that the wire was down on the ground at the Little rock hole. The cause of the wire being down was that there was some very bad splices at work on the line and that there are 8 more insulators broken close to the Sandy Bow River and several of the stays are pulled out of the ground[,] they not being in the ground far enough[,] and that the wire had come apart about two miles north of Turkey Creek through a bad splice. 2 insulators being broken between Mistake Creek and Turkey Creek. These were erected broken. This amount of damage has been done while we were out in pursuit of the natives on the bow Rivers. This is the correct and full amount of damage done to the telegraph line from the crossing of the Denham river to Turkey creek which the midway police have to patrol. 7 insulators broken[,] wire on the ground close to Mcphee's creek. 40 insulators broken at Hells gates. 17 insulators broken and wire down on the ground at Wild Dog Springs. Wire come unspliced at Little rock hole. 122 Insulators broken from Pompey's Pillow to Big bow River. 33 insulators broken from big bow river to sandy bow river. 73 insulators broken from Sandy Bow rivers to within 2 miles of the Stoney Bow river and that several of the stays are loose and are pulling themselves out of the ground as there is too much strain on them. 2 insulators broken

between Mistake Creek and Turkey creek[,] they were erected broken[,] and wire come unspoiled at Turkey Creek.' WAPD, 'Denham River Police Station, Occurrence Book 1, 11 July 1890', SROWA, AN 5, Cons. 739.

120 In the police records available for the period from 1888, including the areas of Dillon Springs, Denham, Bow River, Turkey Creek, Fletcher's Creek and Ord River Crossing.

121 WAPD, 'Derby Police Station, Occurrence Book, 29 November 1892', SROWA, AN 5, Cons. 738/21.

122 WAPD, 'Derby Police Station, Letterbook Entry by Sub Inspector Troy, (nd.) circa August 1889', SROWA, AN 5, Cons. 241/1, File 203/89.

123 CSO, 'Warden Kimberley – General Report on the Field, See Report by East Kimberley Government Resident "Defects in Telegraph Line as Erected", 26 August 1890', SROWA, AN 24, Cons. 527, File 1757/1890.

124 ibid. Postmaster General's Annual Report, 1889, p.6.

125 WAPD, 'Denham River Police Station, Occurrence Book 1, 18 November 1889', SROWA, AN 5, Cons. 739.

126 WAPD, 'Fletcher Creek Police Station, Report by Austin, 1 November 1890', SROWA, AN 5, Cons. 740. Constable Inglis, James and Wilson left Fletcher Creek to form Argyle police station.

127 Police described it as: 'The walls average in height 7ft nine inches [2.36 metres] and are one foot [30 centimetres] thick. The station consists of one living room 14ft x 14ft [4.26 metres] an office and store room combined 6 x 14 [1.8 metres by 4.26 metres] a saddle room 6 x 7 [1.8 metres by 2.1 metres] a kitchen 8 x 7 [2.4 metres by 2.1 metres] exclusive of the fire place. It will take some considerable time to complete the station as a large amount of timber is yet to be cut and squared. The walls have to be plastered and mud floors will be provided for each room... the police have already moved into the building which is certainly one of the best of the kind in the district and with proper care ought to last for the next twenty years.' WAPD, 'Fletcher Creek Police Station, Report by PC Rhatigan, 3 October 1893', SROWA, AN 5, Cons. 740.

128 WAPD, 'Denham River Police Station, Report by PC Tuke, Occurrence Book 1, 28 May 1889', SROWA, AN 5, Cons. 739.

129 ibid.

130 WAPD, 'Halls Creek Police Station, Report by Trooper Kingston, Letterbook, 10 December 1889', SROWA, AN 5, Cons. 1422. Emphasis added.

131 ibid., 25 January 1890.

132 ibid.

133 ibid.

134 ibid., (nd.), circa 25 January 1890.

135 WAPD, 'Halls Creek Police Station, Report by Sergeant Farley, Occurrence Book', SROWA, AN 5, Cons. 1422.

136 CSO, 'Settlers West Kimberley – Natives in Barrier Ranges. That stringent Measures be Adopted With, Derby, October 1889', SROWA, AN 24, Cons. 527, File 3398/1889; reported in *The West Australian*, 29 November 1889, p.4.

137 PC Tuke was on his own at Denham River camp on 1 May 1889. He reported in his occurrence book: 'Memo: Writing the above half past 9pm nigger fires have started blazing up within less than half a mile of the camp.' WAPD, 'Denham River Police Station, Report by PC Tuke, Occurrence Book 1, 1 May 1889', SROWA, AN 5, Cons. 739.

138 ibid., 'Entry by PC Tuke, 1 December 1890'.

139 ibid.,7 July 1889. The following day he and others left camp at 7am and after travelling about 6 kilometres they saw large bushfires. Tuke reported 'Here we saw a very large mob of natives hunting kangaroos by means of surrounding them with fire. On seeing us they did not seem very much inclined to run away[,] went slowly to the rocky hills and flourished their spears in the air[. T]here being no complaints about them did not molest them in any way.' WAPD, Denham River Police Station, Report by PC Tuke, Occurrence Book 1, 8 July 1889, SROWA, AN 5, Cons. 739. In October 1889, a packer by the name of Mr J. Card from the Halls Creek goldfields reported that when he was camped on Watery Gauge (about 14 kilometres away from Fletcher Creek): 'about 100 natives surrounded his camp with their spears shipped[. H]he fired a shot in the air with a fouling piece the natives cleared to the hills shouting at them[. T]hey never attacked them but followed for two days.' ibid., 12 October 1889.

140 ibid., 2 December 1890.

Chapter 7: In the Hands of a Small Oligarchy

1 F.K. Crowley, *Forrest 1847–1918: apprenticeship to premiership*, Brisbane, University of Queensland Press, 1971, p.130.

2 *Report of a Commission Appointed by His Excellency the Governor to Inquire into the Treatment of the Aboriginal Native Prisoners of the Crown in the Colony; And Also into Certain Others Matters Relative to Aboriginal Affairs Paper No. 32*, 2 October 1884, report published in *Government Gazette*, SROWA, Cons. 495, Item 71.

3 ibid., p.9.

4 'Inter-Colonial', *The West Australian*, 21 July 1888, p.3.

5 W.B. Kimberly (ed.), *History of West Australia, A Narrative of Her Past, Together With Biographies of Her Leading Men,* Melbourne, F.W. Niven, 1897, p.310.

6 G. Bolton, *Alexander Forrest: his life and times,* Melbourne, Melbourne University Press in association with UWA Press, 1958, p.91.

7 G. Bolton, 'The Kimberley Pastoral Industry', *University Studies in History and Economics*, vol. 11, no. 2, 1954, p.17; Bolton, *Alexander Forrest*, p.91. See also Kimberly (ed.), *History of West Australia* p.310, <http://en.wikisource.org/wiki/History_of_West_Australia/Chapter_20>.

8 ibid. Kimberly wrote 'Many squatters in the northern parts of the colony were ruined, while the more stable men found it difficult to tide over the period of distress. Runs were abandoned, the rentals for crown lands diminished, whole flocks were annihilated and the export returns for wool were seriously affected. For all their years of striving in the semi-tropical country, the squatters had nothing to show but dry fields, covered with white bones. In

1891 the horses of settlers were in such an emaciated condition that men had to carry rations to shepherds on remote parts of some of the stations on foot. Thousands of lambs were killed to save the ewes. On two stations alone 10,000 lambs were immolated to this end, and 26,000 sheep died of starvation.'

9   For report of drought and Aboriginal depredations see WAPD, 'Trooper Brophy's Report on the Kimberley Goldfields District, 14 November 1892', SROWA, Cons. 430, File 2293/1892; 'The Drought In the West Kimberley', *The West Australian*, p.3.

10 'Native Crime in the North', *The Nor'West Times*, 30 September 1893.

11 See 'Debate on the Game Bill', *Western Australian Legislative Assembly*, 21 December 1891, p.151, <http://www.parliament.wa.gov.au/Hansard/hansard1870to1995.nsf/vwMainBackground/18911221_Assembly.pdf/$File/18911221_Assembly.pdf>.

12 WAPD, 'Derby Police Station, Sub Inspector O Drewry, 16 February 1894', SROWA, Cons. 738/22; 'Disastrous Floods at Kimberley', *The Inquirer and Commercial News*, 2 March 1894, p.16.

13 Sub Inspector Drewry reported 'At Lillamaloora 2000 sheep, 1500 lambs; Lukin 12,000[;] Barnett's unknown number[;] Edgar on the Meda River 1300 sheep; Oobagooma and Daleys, not heard of yet[;] Emanuel Liveringa 700'. WAPD, 'Derby Police Station, Letterbook, Sub Inspector O Drewry, 16 February 1894', SROWA, Cons. 738/22.

14 Bolton, 'The Kimberley Pastoral Industry', p.17.

15 WAPD, 'Derby Police Station, Letterbook, Sub Inspector Drewry, 16 February 1894', SROWA, Cons. 738/22.

16 See for example 'The Native Question', *The West Australian*, 27 June 1892, p.6; 'Around Australia, the Native Question', *The West Australian*, 3 November 1892, p.3.

17 WAPD, 'West Kimberley District. Lennard Sub-district. Lennard River Police Camp. A Report on the Stations in this Sub-District. 21 July 1891', SROWA, Cons. 430, File 1360/1891.

18 CSO, 'Settlers West Kimberley – Natives in Barrier Ranges. That Stringent Measures be Adopted With, Derby, October 1889', SROWA, AN 24, Cons. 527, File 3398/1889, reported in *The West Australian*, 29 November 1889, p.4.

19 WAPD, 'West Kimberley District. Lennard Sub-district. Lennard River Police Camp. A Report on the Stations in this Sub-district. 21 July 1891', SROWA, Cons. 430, File 1360/1891.

20 ibid.

21 ibid.

22 ibid.

23 R.H. Pilmer, *Northern Patrol: An Australian Saga,* C. Clement and P. Bridge (eds), Perth, Hesperian Press, 1998, p.49.

24 CSO, 'Settlers West Kimberley – Natives in Barrier Ranges. That Stringent Measures be Adopted With, Derby, October 1889', SROWA, AN 24, Cons. 527, File 3398/1889; reported in *The West Australian*, 29 November 1889, p.4.

25 WAPD, 'West Kimberley District. Lennard Sub-district. Lennard River Police Camp. A Report on the Stations in this Sub-district. 21 July 1891', SROWA, Cons. 430, File 1360/1891.

26 ibid.

27 ibid. At Davis and Mclean's station Armitage reported there was no complaints whatsoever, no losses and everything looked well. The Aboriginal workforce was 'well looked after and are well fed'. A similar state of affairs existed at Meda Station. Armitage noted that 'Lukin, Meda and Maclean/Davis would have a decrease in sheep clips but Munro's Barrier Station will have an increase. Given the drought period of 1890–1892 also there will be serious losses.' WAPD, 'West Kimberley District. Lennard Sub-district. Lennard River Police Camp. A Report on the Stations in this Sub-district. 21 July 1891', SROWA, Cons. 430, File 1360/1891.

28 See for example H. Pedersen and B. Woorunmurra, *Jandamarra and the Bunuba Resistance,* Broome, Magabala Books, 1995, p.50. 'The Bunuba were now at the mercy of the police and settlers who wanted all Aboriginal people ruthlessly shackled inside the fences of pastoral settlements.'

29 F.K. Crowley, 'Sir John Forrest (1847-1918)', *Australian Dictionary of Biography,* Australian National University, 1981, <http://adb.anu.edu.au/biography/forrest-sir-john-6211>.

30 N. Jarvis, *Western Australia: an atlas of human endeavour*, Perth, Education Department of Western Australia, 1986, p.121.

31 T. Stannage, 'The Composition of the Western Australian Parliament:1890–1911', *University Studies in History,* vol. 4, no. 4, 1966, p.1.

32 G. Bolton, *A Survey of the Kimberley Pastoral Industry from 1885 to the Present,* Masters, thesis, University of Western Australia, 1953, p.69.

33 Speech by Sir George Campbell, Western Australian Constitution Bill. No. 112, Second Reading, HC, 27 February 1890, vol. 341, cc1353–97, <http://hansard.millbanksystems.com/commons/1890/feb/27/second-reading#column_1366>.

34 Speech by Sir George Campbell, Western Australian Constitution Bill, No. 256, Committee HC debate, 30 June 1890, vol. 346, cc345–413, pt 345, <http://hansard.millbanksystems.com/commons/1890/jun/30/western-australia-constitution-re-co#S3V0346P0_18900630_HOC_332>.

35 Extraordinary Government Gazette per CSO 4374, 2532/90; *Western Australia Government Gazette*, 21 October 1890, Proclamation per CSO 4415; *Western Australia Government Gazette*, 11 September 1890.

36 See Crowley, *Big John Forrest 1847–1918*, p.73. In April 1892 Fraser came out of retirement to accept the position of the first Agent General for Western Australia in London, which he held until 1898.

37 J.T. Reilly, *Reminiscences of Fifty Years in Western Australia,* Perth, Sands and McDougall, 1903, p.310; Kimberly (ed.), *History of West Australia*, p.301.

38 ibid., p.300, <http://en.wikisource.org/wiki/History_of_West_Australia/Chapter_20>.

39 L. Marchant, *Aboriginal Administration in Western Australia, 1886–1905,*

Canberra, Australian Institute of Aboriginal Studies, 1981, p.19.

40 M. Aveling, *Westralian Voices: Documents in West Australian Social History*, Perth, UWA Press, 1979, p.52.

41 Stannage, 'The Composition of the Western Australian Parliament: 1890–1911', p.2. Also sometimes referred to as the 'six hungry families'.

42 Bolton, *Alexander Forrest*, p.93.

43 William Robinson (second time), 10 April 1880–1 June 1883; Sir Frederick Broome, 2 June 1883–19 October 1890; Sir William Robinson (third time), 20 October 1890–22 December 1895.

44 F.K. Crowley, 'Sir Frederick Napier Broome (1842–1896)', *Australian Dictionary of Biography*, Australian National University, 1969, <http://adb.anu.edu.au/biography/broome-sir-frederick-napier-3068>.

45 The British government also supported Broome's proposal for a possible division of Western Australia into two colonies. ibid.

46 See N. Green, 'From Princes to Paupers: the struggle for control of Aborigines in Western Australia 1887–1898', *Early Days: Journal of the Royal Western Australian Historical Society*, vol. 11, no. 4, 1998, p.450.

47 ibid.

48 *The Constitution Act 1889*, an Act to confer a Constitution on Western Australia, and to grant a Civil list to Her Majesty.

49 Western Australian Parliamentary Debates, vol. XV, p.163.

50 Hansard, House of Lords, 'The Natives of Western Australia', vol. 145, cc 1298–321, 9 May 1905, <http://hansard.millbanksystems.com/lords/1905/may/09/the-natives-of-western-australia#column_1309>.

51 S. Churches, 'Put Not Your Faith in Princes (or Courts) – Agreements Made from Asymmetrical Power Bases: the story of a promise made to Western Australia's Aboriginal people', in P. Read, G. Meyers and B. Reece (eds), *What Good Condition? Reflections on an Australian Aboriginal Treaty 1986–2006*, Aboriginal History Monograph 13, Canberra, ANU Epress, 2006, pp. 1–14 <http://press.anu.edu.au?p=15621>.

52 Crowley, *Big John Forrest 1847–1918*, pp.68–9.

53 ibid., p.454.

54 Forbes to Robinson, *British Parliamentary Papers*, pp.88–90, 4 June 1893, quoted in Green, 'From Princes to Paupers: the struggle for control of Aborigines in Western Australia 1887–1898', p.455.

55 F. Crowley, 'Sir William Cleaver Francis Robinson (1834–1897)', *Australian Dictionary of Biography*, Australian National University, 1976, <http://adb.anu.edu.au/biography/robinson-sir-william-cleaver-francis-4494>. He had earlier recommended Forrest to the position of surveyor-general.

56 Governor Robinson to Secretary of State, 1 June 1893, SROWA, CO 18/218.

57 Governor Robinson to John Forrest, 2 October 1893, SROWA, CO 18/219.

58 Crowley, *Big John Forrest 1847–1918*, p.142. Quoting W.C.F. Robinson to Lord Ripon 27 April 1894, GD confidential 390, WAA.

59 Governor Robinson to Secretary of State, 13 July 1893, CO 18/218.

60 C. Slaughter, 'The Aboriginal Natives of North-West Western Australia and

the Administration of Justice', *Westminster Review*, vol. CLVI, no. 6, 1901, p.411.

61 'The Charges Against Western Australia', quoted in *The Daily News*, 16 September, 1892, p.3.

62 'The Alleged System of Slavery in W.A. Statement of the Marquis Ripon', *The Inquirer & Commercial News*, Wednesday 21 September 1892, p.7; for a summary challenging Forrest's humanitarianism see E. Goddard and T. Stannage, 'John Forrest and the Aborigines' in B. Reece & T. Stannage (eds), *Studies in Western Australian History: European-Aboriginal Relations in Western Australia*, no. 8, 1984, pp.42–51.

63 See 'The Treatment Of Aboriginals', *Western Mail*, 16 October 1896.

64 'Protection of Northern Settlers against Hostile Natives', *Parliamentary Debates Legislative Council*, 14 January 1892, vol. II, p.245.

65 See Green, 'From Princes to Paupers: the struggle for control of Aborigines in Western Australia 1887–1898', p.453.

66 'Protection of Northern Settlers against Hostile Natives', pp.245– 61.

67 ibid., p.250.

68 ibid.

69 ibid., p.254.

70 ibid.

71 ibid., p.351.

72 ibid.

73 ibid., Speech by Alexander Richardson, p.253.

74 ibid.

75 ibid., p.256.

76 ibid., Speech by John Forrest, p.261.

77 Reilly, *Reminiscences of Fifty Years in Western Australia*, p.312. A summary of the correspondence can be found at pp.312–68.

78 Quoted in Green, 'From Princes to Paupers: p.454.

79 ibid.

80 ibid.

81 See for example report to Secretary of State calling for the abolition of the Board, 'The Aborigines Protection Board', *Western Mail*, 30 September 1893, p.44; 'Reservation of Royal Assent to the Aborigines Board (Constitution) Bill', Legislative Assembly, *The Inquirer and Commercial News*, 11 October 1895, p.3.

82 See N. Green, 'Aborigines and White Settlers', in C.T. Stannage (ed.), *A New History of Western Australia*, Perth, UWA Press, 1981, pp.109–10. The Aborigines Department was established in 1898 as a consequence of the *Aborigines Act 1897* (which abolished the Aborigines Protection Board) and operated as a sub-department of the Treasury, with a small staff under the Chief Protector of Aborigines.

83 P. Biskup, *Not Slaves, Not Citizens: the Aboriginal problem in Western Australia (1898–1954)*, Brisbane, University of Queensland Press, 1973, p.45

84 ibid., p.45.

85 'Protection of Aborigines', *The Inquirer and Commercial News,* 12 November 1897, p.3.

86 Aborigines Department, *Annual Report of the Aborigines Department ending 30 June 1899,* No.40, p.8, Perth, Government Printer.

87 John Forrest to Gerald Smith, *Western Australian Parliamentary Debates,* 9 April 1896, vol. 5, pp.129–30, quoted in Green, 'From Princes to Paupers', p.457.

88 'Banquet to the Premier', *The Daily News,* 11 March 1897, p.4; see also 'Sir John Forrest at Bunbury', *Kalgoorlie Western Argus,* 18 March 1897, p.11.

89 A. Robb, 'Sir William Cleaver Francis Robinson', *Dictionary of Canadian Biography,* University of Toronto and Université Laval, <http://www.biographi.ca/009004-119.01-e.php?&id_nbr=6401>.

90 F.K. Crowley, 'Sir Gerard Smith (1839–1920)', *Australian Dictionary of Biography,* Australian National University, 1988, <http://adb.anu.edu.au/biography/smith-sir-gerard-8468/text14891>.

91 'The New Attorney General', *The Inquirer & Commercial News,* 6 October 1886, p.5; D. Black and G. Bolton, *Biographical Register of Members of the Parliament of Western Australia, Volume One, 1870–1930* (revised edition), Perth, Western Australian Parliamentary History Project, 2001.

92 'The General Elections', *The West Australian,* 30 June 1894, p.6.

93 'The Resignation of the Colonial Secretary', *Eastern Districts Chronicle,* 8 December 1894, p.6; W. Birman and G. Bolton, 'Sir Stephen Henry Parker (1846–1927)', *Australian Dictionary of Biography,* Australian National University, 1988, <http://adb.anu.edu.au/biography/parker-sir-stephen-henry-7957>.

94 Crowley, 'Sir John Forrest (1847–1918)', <http://adb.anu.edu.au/biography/forrest-sir-john-6211>; 'The General Elections', *The West Australian,* 30 June 1894, p.6.

95 Marchant, *Aboriginal Administration in Western Australia, 1886–1905,* pp.15–30.

96 ibid., p.20.

97 *Aboriginal Offenders Act (1883) 47 Vic. No. 8.* This act repealed the 1874 Act, 'An ordinance to provide for the Summary Trial and Punishment of Aboriginal Native Offenders in certain cases', Vic. 12, No. 18.

98 Marchant, *Aboriginal Administration in Western Australia, 1886–1905,* p.9; *Aboriginal Offenders Act Amendment 1892, 55 Vic. No. 18; Aboriginal Offender Act Amendment 1883,* Statutes of Western Australia, No. 18 1892, Point 3: 'The number of strokes not exceeding twenty five, or in the case of a male offender under the age of sixteen not exceeding twelve.' Point 4: 'No whipping shall be inflicted except in the presence of a Justice of the Peace, Protector of Aborigines or officer of the police not under the rank of Sergeant.'

99 *Nor'West Times and Northern Advocate,* 16 January 1892.

100 Reilly, *Reminiscences of Fifty Years in Western Australia,* p.387. For a particularly brutal example of flogging for station workers who had run away from a Marble Bar station in late 1897 see 'The Flogging of Aboriginals', *Kalgoorlie Miner,* 21 October 1897, p.5. Ernest and Alex Anderson were charged with murder after the flogging of six station workers, which included beatings ('tied up and thrashed with a knotted rope for hours') and strangulation,

resulted in the deaths of three station workers, Biddy, Polly and Spider. Ernest Anderson was sentenced to life in prison. See 'The Flogging of Aboriginals', *Kalgoorlie Miner*, 22 December 1897, p. 5.

101 *Aboriginal Offenders Act Amendment 1893 56 Vic. No. 15.*

102 The original *Aboriginal Offenders Act 1883* stated 'It shall be lawful for a Magistrate, together with one or more Justices of the Peace not interested in the subject matter of the complaint', *Aboriginal Offenders Act 1883, 47 Vic. No. 8,* <http://www.austlii.edu.au/au/other/IndigLRes/1883/1.html>. The 1893 Amendment removed this provision and replaced it with 'any justice of the peace'. *Aboriginal Offenders Act Amendment 1893 56 Vic. 15,* <http://www.austlii.edu.au/au/other/IndigLRes/1893/1.html>.

103 *Masters and Servants Act 1892 55 Vic. No. 28, Section 28.*

104 Marchant, *Aboriginal Administration in Western Australia,* p.9.

105 Bolton, *Alexander Forrest,* p.107.

106 'The Northerners' Meeting', *The Inquirer and Commercial News,* 11 January 1893, p.5.

107 *Nor' West Times,* 19 January 1893, quoted in Bolton, *Alexander Forrest,* p.107.

108 Goddard and Stannage, 'John Forrest and the Aborigines', p.56.

109 ibid., see also 'Hon. John Forrest, Presidential Address Australian Association for the Advancement of Science', January 1890, in M. Aveling, *Westralian Voices, Documents in West Australian Social History,* Perth, UWA Press, 1979, p.50.

110 ibid.

111 Goddard and T. Stannage, 'John Forrest and the Aborigines', p.56.

112 See John Forrest's speeches in *Western Australian Parliamentary Debates,* 1 September 1896, p.547 and 19 October 1896, pp.112–47.

113 Speech by Colonial Secretary S.H. Parker, 'Constitution Act Amendment Bill', *Western Australian Parliamentary Debates,* 19 September 1894, p.659, <http://www.parliament.wa.gov.au/Hansard/hansard1870to1995.nsf/vwMainBackground/18940919_Council.pdf/$File/18940919_Council.pdf>.

114 ibid.

115 'It is old news now that allusion has been made in the Imperial Parliament to it, and that Sir John Forrest has, through the Agent-General, given an official and very flat denial to the Colonial Office that natives and native prisoners are treated cruelly in West Australia', 'Around Australia, the Native Question', *The West Australian,* 3 November 1892, p.3.

Chapter 8: 'The Squatters Have Them All'

1 See for example the Derby Resident Magistrate R. Wace's observation that imprisonment of Aboriginal men 'was one of the most serious things for the native' because 'when taken from his tribe his womenkind go to anyone who can take them, and the man, after herding from twelve months to three years with the scum of the natives in gaol, returns to his country with a feud on his hands', CSO, R. Wace, Resident Magistrate Derby to Under Secretary

Colonial Secretary's Dept., 10 September 1905', SROWA, AN 24, Cons. 527, File 2973/05.

2   See for example 'Native Crime in the North', *The Nor'West Times,* 30 September, 1893.

3   See witness testimony from PC John Inglis, Halls Creek, *Roth Royal Commission on the Condition of the Natives, Presented to both Houses of Parliament by his Excellency's Command,* Roth Report, WAPP, 1905, 2nd Session, no. 5, p.95.

4   ibid., p.94.

5   Other evidence suggested that 'up to until a few years ago the Denham River Station was inhabited by a warlike tribe of Aboriginals' and now there were no men about, only their offspring. 'Denham River Tragedy. The Murder of Mr. J. J. Durack. Trial of Amaranga. Verdict of Not Guilty', *The West Australian,* 10 May 1901, p.2.

6   See *Golden Age Newspaper,* 22 March 1897, p.3; *The West Australian,* 6 December 1894, p.5; *The West Australian,* 18 December 1894, p.5; *The West Australian,* 20 March 1897, p.5; *The West Australian,* 22 March 1897, p.5, Other sources put his birth date as 1870; see H. Pedersen, 'Jandamarra (1870–1897)', *Australian Dictionary of Biography,* Australian National University, 1990, <http://adb. anu.edu.au/biography/tjangamarra-8822>.

7   See first-hand account J. Blythe, 'Why Pigeon Roamed the Kimberley', *Western Mail,* 18 January 1940, p.8; *Golden Age Newspaper,* 22 March 1897, p.3; *The West Australian,* 6 December 1894, p.5; *The West Australian,* 18 December 1894, p.5; *The West Australian,* 20 March 1897, p.5. *The West Australian,* 22 March 1897, p.5.

8   K. Moran, *Pigeon,* Perth, Hesperian Press, 2011, p.15. Lillamaloora pastoral station was abandoned in November 1892 and became Lillamaloora Police Station.

9   WAPD, 'Derby Police Station, Letterbook, Sub Inspector Drewry to Commissioner of Police, 21 April 1895', SROWA, AN 5, Cons. 738/22.

10 Blythe, 'Why Pigeon Roamed the Kimberley', *Western Mail,* 18 January 1940, p.8.

11 ibid.

12 ibid.; 'A Notorious Native', *The Advertiser,* 2 April 1897, p.5; 'News Of The Week', *Western Mail,* 9 April 1897, p.12; 'Western Australia', *The Queenslander,* 10 April 1897, p.782.

13 'North-west News, Reported Arrest of a Native Outlaw', *The West Australian,* 29 January 1895, p.5. For Nalmurchie see N. Green, *The Forrest River Massacres,* Fremantle, Fremantle Arts Centre Press, 1995, p.94. For Challaday see 'Natives Attack Police Party, Notorious Aboriginal Shot', *The West Australian,* 4 October 1910, p.9.

14 See for example 'Native Crime in the Nor'-West, the Influence of Escapees (from a Correspondent) No. II', *The West Australian,* 16 December 1899, p.3.

15 WAPD, 'Derby Police Station, Letterbook, Drewry to R.E. Bush MLC, 29 July 1893', SROWA, Cons. 738/22.

16 G. Bolton, 'The Kimberley Pastoral Industry', *University Studies in History and Economics*, vol. 11, no. 2, 1954, p.18.

17 See S. Hunt, *Spinifex and Hessian; Women in North-West Australia 1860–1900*, Perth, UWA Press, 1986, pp.31–2, 96–117.

18 M. Jebb, *Blood, Sweat and Welfare: a history of white bosses and Aboriginal pastoral workers*, Perth, UWA Press, 2002.

19 Fairbairn Commission, WAPP, 1884, no. 32, pp.10, 13; for Fairbairn's report see *Western Australian Legislative Council Votes and Proceedings 1882*, vol. 33, pp.3–14.

20 CSO, 'Native "Jeneella" Shot by PCs Armitage & Watts, Government Resident Thomas Lovegrove to Colonial Secretary, 20 September 1889', SROWA, AN 24, Cons. 527, File 2627/89.

21 A later account of this incident is referred to here: 'White Savages, Rapes and Murders, Police Intimidated', *Sunday Times*, 20 April 1902, p.4.

22 Witness statement of John James Butler, Roth Report, 1905, p.105.

23 'The Aborigines Question, Testimony by PC Inglis to Walter Roth', *The West Australian*, 15 February 1905, p.2.

24 D.R. Rose, *Hidden Histories: black stories from Victoria River Downs, Humbert River and Wave Hill stations*, Canberra, Aboriginal Studies Press, 1991, p.102.

25 For a detailed account see 'More of the Black Nor-West', *Sunday Times*, 30 July 1905, p.7.

26 Aborigines Protection Board, *Special Report on Half Caste Children by George Marsden*, 24 October 1896, SROWA, Cons. 495, File 2148/96, pp.1–2.

27 ibid. See also R. McGregor, *Answering the Native Question: the dispossession of the Aborigines of the Fitzroy District, West Kimberley, 1880–1905*, Honours dissertation, James Cook University, 1985, p.55.

28 P. Biskup, *Not Slaves, Not Citizens: The Aboriginal Problem in Western Australia 1898–1954*, Brisbane, University of Queensland Press, 1973, p.97; see also 'Kimberley Pioneer Dies', *The Daily News*, 17 May 1944, p.5.

29 Aboriginal Protection Board correspondence, 24 October 1895, SROWA, Cons. 495, Item 35, File 2146/96.

30 *Granuloma inguinale* was a chronic ulceration of the external genitalia that became endemic amongst Aboriginal people of the North West and Kimberley. See Mary Anne Jebb, *Isolating the 'Problem': venereal disease and Aborigines in Western Australia, 1898–1924*, BA (Honours) thesis, Murdoch University, 1987.

31 Aborigines Protection Board, Correspondence, 24 October 1895, Cons. 495, Item 35, File 2146/96.

32 See for example Aborigines Protection Board, *Report on Yeeda Station, G. Marsden*, Correspondence, 29 October 1896, SROWA, Cons. 495, Item 36.

33 'Letter P.J.H., Perth', *The West Australian*, 26 November 1902, p.4.

34 Aborigines Protection Board, *Report on Yeeda Station, G. Marsden*.

35 Aborigines Protection Board Correspondence, 'Jurisdiction of Courts and Protection of Natives', 21 July 1896, SROWA, Cons. 495, Item 58.

36 'Speech by Honourable D. Mckay, Bishop Riley and the Aborigines', *The*

Inquirer & Commercial News, 23 October 1896, p.6.

37 'Employment of Natives, Alleged Form of Slavery', *The Inquirer & Commercial News*, 16 April 1897, p.4.

38 'Letter P.J.H., Perth', *The West Australian*, 26 November 1902, p.4.

39 With J.H. Monger he held Red Hill Station in the Ashburton; with Septimus Burt he held Brick House and Mumgarra in the Gascoyne; and with John and David Forrest he held Mideroo and Hardey Junction in the Ashburton. G. Bolton, *Alexander Forrest: his life and times,* Melbourne, Melbourne University Press in association with UWA Press, 1958, p.91.

40 ibid., p.116.

41 *The Nor'West Times*, 29 August 1891.

42 ibid.

43 G. Bolton and H. Pedersen, 'The Emanuels of Noonkanbah and GoGo', *Early Days: Journal of the Royal Western Australian Historical Society*, vol. 8, part 4, 1980, p.13.

44 Bolton, *Alexander Forrest*, 1958, op.cit., p.92.

45 G. Bolton and Pedersen, 'The Emanuels of Noonkanbah and GoGo', p.13.

46 Bolton, *Alexander Forrest*, p.117.

47 *The Western Mail*, 28 June 1890, p.3.

48 Bolton, *Alexander Forrest,* p.133.

49 ibid.

50 ibid., p.117.

51 ibid., p.100, quoting *The Nor'West Times*, 26 March 1890.

52 ibid.

53 ibid., p.101.

54 Now the Perth suburb of Cockburn, ibid.

55 ibid.

56 Bolton and Pedersen, 'The Emanuels of Noonkanbah and GoGo', p.13.

57 ibid., p.91.

58 See speech by Alexander Forrest, *Western Australian Parliamentary Debates*, 4 October 1893, no.5, p.1052.

59 Letter Malcolm Fraser, 27 April 1887, SROWA, CSO, File 3053, No 17, p.75.

60 'George Braithwaite Phillips', in W.B. Kimberly (ed.), *History of West Australia, a Narrative of Her Past, Together With Biographies of Her Leading Men*, Melbourne, F.W. Niven, 1897, p.121.

61 See for example M. Bentley, *Grandfather was a Policeman: the Western Australian police force 1829–1889,* Perth, Hesperian Press, 1993, p.140; P. Conole, *Protect and Serve: a history of the Western Australian police service,* Perth, Access Press, 2002, p.71; 'Legislative Assembly', *The West Australian*, 23 August 1895, p.3.

62 S.G. Milentis, 'Biographical Sketch of George Braithwaite Phillips' (unpublished manuscript), quoted in Conole, *Protect and Serve*, p.71.

63 'Colonel Phillips', *The Evening Star*, 27 March 1900, p.3.

64 'Commissioner Hare', *West Australian Sunday Times*, 8 April 1900, p.4.

65 *The West Australian*, 27 March 1900, p.7; see also Kimberly, *History of West Australia*, p.121.

66 Conole, *Protect and Serve*, p.75.
67 ibid., p.107.
68 *The West Australian*, 31 July 1899, p.4.
69 *The West Australian*, 27 March 1900, p.7.
70 'Native Murderers, A Policeman's Memories, Early Days in the North', *The West Australian*, 30 June 1936, p.16.
71 ibid. Pilmer claims he was encouraged to join the force after a sergeant 'took special note of my physique and being in need of just such a man...to get outback amongst the natives, they're very troublesome lately'. R.H. Pilmer, *Northern Patrol: an Australian saga*, C. Clement and P. Bridge (eds.), Perth, Hesperian Press, 1998, p.12.
72 ibid., p.168.
73 J.S. Battye, *Encyclopedia of Western Australia*, Perth, VK Jones, vol. 1, 1912, p.528.
74 'Obituary, Inspector M.H. Brophy', *Kalgoorlie Miner*, 6 February 1923, p.5.
75 J.S. Battye, *Encyclopedia of Western Australia*, Perth, VK Jones, vol.1, 1912, p.528.
76 ibid.
77 WAPD, 'Derby Police Station, Letterbook, Drewry to Commissioner of Police, 1 April 1894', Cons. 738/22.
78 *The Sunday Times*, 23 February 1902.
79 ibid.
80 Conole, *Protect and Serve*, p.93, quoting *The Daily News*, August 1887; *The West Australian*, 31 July 1899. For a biographical study of Warden John Michael Finnerty see P. Statham, 'The First (W.A.) Finnerty's – Father and Son', *Early Days*, vol. 9, Pt 2, 1984, pp.16–26.
81 Conole, *Protect and Serve*, p.107.
82 P. Conole, 'A Gentleman Adventurer of the WA Police', *Police Newsbeat*, no.36, 2006, p.16.
83 'Major Craven H. Ord, An Adventurous Career', *Western Mail*, 17 July 1909, p.15.
84 ibid.
85 ibid. Ord collected seventy-nine Aboriginal artefacts during his four years in the West Kimberley. Before he left Derby he donated these to the British Museum. When the museum received the artefacts in July 1899, one of the staff commented Ord was a keen collector, having sent two rare monkeys to the Perth zoological gardens in February 1899. Charles H Read, British Museum, letter to C.H. Ord, 13 November 1899, BM Archives, *Western Mail*, 17 February 1899, p.12. At the age of fifty-nine he married Alice Mohr and they had three children. He died in Perth in 1923.
86 A large hill east of the Edgar Ranges and just south of the Fitzroy River where he operated was named 'Craven Ord Hill' after him, *Western Mail*, 17 July 1909, p.15.
87 'Notes and Comments', *The Sunday Times*, 9 May 1920, p.4.
88 See *Police Gazette*, no 25, 22 June 1892, p.99.

89 Pilmer, *Northern Patrol,* p.35.

90 WAPD, 'Derby Police Station, Letterbook, Sub Inspector Drewry to Commissioner of Police, 16 July 1893', SROWA, AN 5, Cons. 738/22.

91 See for example 'Goldfields of the North', *The Daily News,* 21 August 1929, p.6. 'In the next article Mr. Lucanus declares that Northern Territory blacks were cannibals, and in this respect preferred Chinese'; see also 'Goldfields of the North, Cannibalism in the Gulf Country', *The Daily News,* 22 August 1929, p. 6; 'Goldfields of the North, Fight with Blacks on Durack's Stations', *The Daily News,* 5 September 1929, p.6; for Northern Territory references see T. Roberts, *Frontier Justice: a history of the Gulf Country to 1900,* Brisbane, University of Queensland Press, 2005, pp.145–7; A. Lucanus, 'Goldfields of the North', in C. Clement and P. Bridge (eds), *Kimberley Scenes: sagas of Australia's last frontier,* Perth, Hesperian Press, 1991. pp.2–57.

92 ibid., p.3. See also B. Wilson, *A Force Apart: a history of the Northern Territory Police Force 1870–1926,* Hong Kong, Peacock Academic Press, 2001, p.xix.

93 ibid., p.43.

94 *Police Gazette,* 9 May 1894, CO 6/1040 no.14, p.85; *Police Gazette,* 6 June 1894, CO 6/1042 no 23, 1894, p.103.

95 CO. 6/789, Phillips, 22 December 1886, no.51, p.209.

96 WAPD, Cossack Police Station, Occurrence Book, no. 1, Cons. 366. PCs Armitage and Lemon were working in Cossack on 25 October 1879.

97 *The Police Act 1892,* 55th Vic, no. 27, Section 7. See for example PC Claffey promoted to acting first-class constable while doing duty in the Kimberley, *Police Gazette,* no. 22, 2 June 1886, p.91.

98 *Aborigines Protection Act (Amendment) 1892,* no. 25, Pt. 4. Western Australian Laws, Acts of Parliament, Perth.

99 See *Police Gazette,* Circular Order 6/966 no. 12, 23 March 1892, p.47.

100 Pilmer, *Northern Patrol,* p.63.

101 Of Pilmer Drewry wrote, 'When Pilmer has another man under him I shall be able to better judge the matter but I think Pilmer is inclined to be too dictatorial to the other constables[. W]hen there are only two constables on a camp the less there is of this spirit the better and if the seniors use a little commonsense in his management very little is necessary'. WAPD, 'Derby Police Station, Letterbook, Sub Inspector Drewry to Commissioner of Police, 25 September 1894', SROWA, AN 5, Cons. 738/22.

102 Battye, *Encyclopedia of Western Australia,* p.528.

103 D. Moore, Memoirs, Private Manuscript, Battye Library, Cons. 3829A, MN 1237, (nd.), p.2.

Chapter 9: 'Will You at Once Take Action'

1 'The Kimberley Natives', *The West Australian,* 28 November 1889, p.3.

2 A. Forrest, *North-West Exploration: journal of expedition from DeGrey to Port Darwin,* Perth, Government Printer, 1880, p.40.

3 'Vigilans Et Audax', *The West Australian,* 2 December 1889, pp.2–3.

4 WAPD, 'Kimberley District. Derby Station. Reports on the Murder of Martin

Liljeroth [sic], Mate of the Schooner "Ivy" and an Aboriginal Native Boy, by the Natives near Admiralty Gulf, 5 February 1892', SROWA, AN 5/1, Cons. 430, File 116/1892. Police recorded the name as 'Martin Lilgeroth'. For a newspaper report see 'North-West News, Double Murder by the Natives, The Mate of a Pearling Schooner Killed', *The West Australian*, 2 February 1892, p.2.

5   ibid.

6   'The Murder by Natives in the West Kimberley District', *Western Mail*, 18 June 1892, p.32.

7   ibid.

8   *Police Gazette*, 13 July 1892, No. 28, p.111.

9   ibid. See also *Nor'West Times*, 9 September 1892; CSO, 'Two Men Murdered and Third Wounded by Natives on the Leopold Ranges – Police Corporal Holmes, Derby, [Thomas Henry; Robert Allen; William Armitage; Robert (?) Goodridge; Thomas Yates; Robert Henry; 'Barrier Station'; Ernest Black]' SROWA, AN 24, Cons. 527, File 939/1892.

10 ibid.

11 See *Police Gazette*, no. 25, 22 June 1892, p.99. See also R.H. Pilmer, *Northern Patrol: an Australian saga*, C. Clement and P. Bridge (ed.), Perth, Hesperian Press, 1998, p.35. Lodge went to Mt Gould as police inspector in June 1892 then went on to become acting government resident.

12 WAPD, 'Derby Police Station Letterbook, Sub Inspector Drewry to Commissioner of Police (nd.), circa April 1892', SROWA, AN 5, Cons. 738/22.

13 WAPD, 'Derby Police Station Letterbook, Annual Report from Sub Inspt. Drewry to Commissioner of Police, 27 December 1892', SROWA, Cons. 738/21. Drewry stated 'What with the insufficient number of police camps on the one hand, and the fear of the settler to protect themselves on account of the police on the other, the only happy person amongst the lot are the abo native offenders or otherwise. I have sent orders to all Kimberley stations, strictly lawful orders, that I hope will in time check the natives. But I beg to point out that affairs have not reached the state they are in, in Kimberley in a day. It is several years of giving the natives their own way that is making them bold now and that this state of things cannot be altered in a day, the police will have to carry out the law in a far more drastic way than heretofore.'

14 WAPD, 'Derby Police Station, Letterbook, Report from Sub Inspector Drewry to Commissioner of Police, 29 November 1892', SROWA, AN 5, Cons. 738/21.

15 ibid.

16 WAPD, 'Derby Police Station, Letterbook, Sub Inspector Drewry to Commissioner of Police, (nd.), circa 10 August 1893', SROWA, AN 5, Cons. 738/22.

17 WAPD, 'Derby Police Station, Occurrence Book, Report from Sub Inspector Drewry to Commissioner of Police, 29 November 1892', SROWA, AN 5, Cons. 738/21.

18 ibid.

19 ibid.

20 ibid. Drewry would go so far as to work out the odds of a successful capture: 'One rifle is sufficient arms for two native assistants with the odds of 5 to 1 against them at a camp of 15 yards [13.7 metres].' WAPD, Derby Police Station, Letterbook, 'Sub Inspector O. Drewry to Commissioner of Police, 29 June 1894', SROWA, AN 5, Cons. 738/22.

21 See for example 'The Murders by the Natives, Sub Inspector Drewry's Story, The Pursuit of the Murderers, The Death of Pidgeon [sic], A fight for a Wife, Cannibalism Amongst the Fugitives, The Last of the Ammunition, The Fate of Captain, Precautionary Measure, Motives for the Murderers', *The West Australian,* 18 December 1894, p.5; 'The Native Murders in this North, The Native Murders in the North, Official Telegram, The Punitive Expedition, Report by Sub Inspector Drewry', *The Inquirer & Commercial News,* 21 December 1894, p.5.

22 WAPD, Derby Police Station, Occurrence Book, 'Sub Inspector Drewry Police, 6 December 1892', SROWA, AN 5, Cons. 738/21.

23 WAPD, Derby Police Station, Occurrence Book, 'Letter from Commissioner of Police to Sub Inspector Drewry, 18 January 1893', SROWA, AN 5, Cons. 738/21.

24 ibid.

25 ibid.

26 WAPD, Derby Police Station, Occurrence Book, 'Report by Sub Inspector Drewry to East Kimberley Police Patrolling the Telegraph Line, Telegraph Line Instructions no. 3, 22 February 1893', SROWA, AN 5, Cons. 738/21.

27 ibid., 16 July 1893.

28 ibid., 23 July 1893, quoted in Pedersen and B. Woorunmurra, *Jandamarra and the Bunuba Resistance,* Broome, Magabala Books, 1995, p.93.

29 ibid.

30 WAPD, 'Kimberley District. Lennard River Station. Report by PC Armitage on the Attempt by Natives to Spear a Police Party Near Secure Bay, 19 November 1892', SROWA, Cons. 430, File 1947/92.

31 WAPD, Derby Police Station, Letterbook, 'Sub Inspector Drewry to Commissioner of Police, 29 July 1893', SROWA, AN 5, Cons. 738/22.

32 'Treatment of Natives at Derby, Blind Paddy', *The West Australian,* 9 August 1894, p.3.

33 WAPD, Derby Police Station, Letterbook 14 August 1894, SROWA, AN 5, Cons. 738/22.

34 For Pilmer's arrival see WAPD, 'Journal of PC Pilmer While Out With Inspector Troy which Left from Carnarvon on July 20, 1892 and arrived at Thomas Station on September 12, 1892', SROWA, Cons. 430, AN 5, File 1892/1863; also Pilmer, *Northern Patrol,* p.12.

35 'The Treatment of Natives at Derby', *The West Australian,* 9 August 1894, p.3.

36 Pilmer, *Northern Patrol,* p.37.

37 ibid.

38 Aborigines Protection Board, Correspondence, G. Marsden, 30 May 1896, Cons. 495, Item 36.

39 'The ordinary cat-o'-nine tails would not satisfy him. He got a broom handle and fastened nine bullock-hide strips with knots in them to both ends. The knots were about six inches apart. With this he flogged the blacks at the triangles, and brought flesh and blood at every blow.' 'Ex-Policemen Pilmer', *The West Australian*, 9 June 1901, p.16.

40 *The Police Gazette*, No 27, 6 July 1892, p.107.

41 WAPD, Derby Police Station, Letterbook, 'Sub Inspector Drewry to Commissioner of Police, 28 July 1893', SROWA, AN 5, Cons. 738/22.

42 ibid., 4 August 1893.

43 ibid.

44 ibid., 10 August 1893.

45 ibid.

46 ibid.

47 WAPD, Derby Police Station, Letterbook, 'Sub Inspector Drewry to Commissioner of Police, 27 July 1893', SROWA, AN 5, Cons. 738/22.

48 ibid., 28 July 1893.

49 WAPD, Derby Police Station, Occurrence book, 'Sub Inspector Drewry, 6 December 1892', SROWA, AN 5. Cons. 738/21.

50 *Nor'West Times*, 30 January 1892, p.4; WALCVP, '1892 Report of the Aboriginal Protection Board for 1891', pp.896–97; *Nor'West Times*, 30 September 1893, p.3.

51 WAPD, 'Kimberley District. Lennard River Station. Report by PC Armitage on the Attempt by Natives to Spear a Police Party Near Secure Bay, 19 November 1892', SROWA, Cons. 430, File 1947/1892; see 'Native Troubles in the Kimberley District', *The West Australian*, 11 November 1892, p.6. Police use the spelling 'Cooledger'.

52 WAPD, 'Kimberley District. Lennard River Station. Report by PC Armitage on the Attempt by Natives to Spear a Police Party near Secure Bay, 19 November 1892', SROWA, Cons. 430, File 1947/1892. See newspaper report 'The Native Question Trouble in the Kimberley District Recent Attack on Police', *The West Australian*, 28 November 1892, p.6.

53 WAPD, 'Kimberley District. Lennard River Station. Report by PC Armitage on the Attempt by Natives to Spear a Police Party near Secure Bay, 19 November 1892', SROWA, Cons. 430, File 1947/1892.

54 ibid.

55 ibid.

56 WAPD, West Kimberley, Derby Station. 'Reporting Spearing of Native Boy by Aborigines at Oobagooma Station, Robinson River, 28 March 1893', SROWA, Cons. 430, File 702/1893.

57 ibid.

58 ibid., 'I would also point out that Mr Forrest has been at great expense in introducing the best strains of blood into the herd with a view to producing cattle of a higher class than hitherto raised, and the loss of valuable bulls and

their progeny is a matter of serious import to the station. The chief injury done to the cattle is not so much the number speared as is the harm inflicted through the presence of the natives on the line of country in which the cattle pasture. The above applies more particularly to the wet season as it is of the highest importance that the cattle should not be interfered with during that period, much injury and loss is occasioned through the cattle stampeding over country sodden by rain thus causing many to bog and inflicting incalculable injury on cows and calf.'

59 ibid.

60 WAPD, Derby Police Station, Letterbook, 'Sub Inspector Drewry to Commissioner of Police, (nd.), circa 10 August 1893', SROWA, AN 5, Cons. 738/22.

61 ibid.

62 ibid.

63 ibid.

64 WAPD, Derby Police Station, Letterbook, 'Sub Inspector Drewry Report to Commissioner of Police, 2 June 1893', SROWA, AN 5, Cons. 738/22.

65 ibid., 4 June 1893.

66 WAPD, Robinson River Police Station, Occurrence Book, 1 June 1894, SROWA, Cons. 737, AN 5, Item 1.

67 ibid., 10 July 1894. Handley did procure some help some six weeks later when on 10 July he gets native assistants Roses Bay and Ritchie.

68 WAPD, Derby Police Station, Letterbook, 'Sub Inspector Drewry to Commissioner of Police, 29 June 1894', SROWA, AN 5, Cons. 738/22.

69 ibid., 4 March 1894.

70 ibid., 28 March 1894.

71 ibid., 31 March 1894.

72 ibid., 2 May 1894.

73 ibid., 4 May 1894.

74 ibid., 19 June 1894.

75 ibid., April 1894.

76 ibid., 1 August 1894 Drewry wrote 'Some years ago he was a teller in the Union Bank at Rock Hampton but left that for station work in the gulf country. He is a strongly built man, is acclimatized, a good horseman, suitable for work in this district and is well educated. He is the nephew I believe of either Henty or Colham of Perth.'

77 *Western Australian Police Gazette*, CO 6/1040, no. 14, 9 May 1894, p.85; see also *Western Australian Police Gazette*, 6 June 1894, CO 6/1042, no. 23, 1894, p.103.

78 WAPD, Derby Police Station, Letterbook, 'Sub Inspector Drewry to Commissioner of Police, 2 May 1894', SROWA, AN 5, Cons. 738/22.

79 ibid.

80 ibid.

81 'Mr A Forrest Visit for a Luncheon and a Dance', *The West Australian*, 27 July 1894, p.5.

82   ibid.

83   ibid.

84   ibid.

85   WAPD, Derby Police Station, Letterbook, 'Sub Inspector Drewry to Commissioner of Police, 29 June 1894', SROWA, AN 5, Cons. 738/22.

86   ibid., 8 November 1894.

87   ibid.

88   See for example 'Telegram from Drewry to Commissioner Phillips, 16 February 1895', in WAPD, 'Capture of Wild Natives in the Oscar and Barrier Ranges', 10 November 1894, SROWA, Cons. 430, File 3548/1897.

89   See H. Pedersen, *Pigeon: an Aboriginal rebel, a study of Aboriginal European conflict in the West Kimberley, North Western Australia during the 1890s,* Honours thesis, Murdoch University, 1980; R. McGregor, *Answering the Native Question: the dispossession of the Aborigines of the Fitzroy District, West Kimberley, 1880–1905,* James Cook University, 1985; C. Johnson, *Long Live Sandawarra,* Melbourne, Hyland House, 1987; based on 'Long Live Pigeon!' in *Meanjin* (Aboriginal Issue), vol.36, no.4, 1977, pp.494–507; Pedersen and Woorunmurra, *Jandamarra and the Bunuba Resistance*; J. Nicholson, *Kimberley Warrior: the story of Jandamarra,* Sydney, Allen & Unwin, 1997; K. Moran, *Sand and Stone – Cattle & Conflict,* Vols. 1 and 2, Perth, Hesperian Press, 2009; K. Moran, *Sand and Stone, Foreign Footprints: police in the Kimberley 1880–1890s,* Perth, Hesperian Press, 2009; K. Moran, *Pigeon,* Perth, Hesperian Press, 2011; Mark Greenwood and Terry Denton, *Jandamarra,* Sydney, Allen & Unwin, 2013.

90   WAPD, 'Capture of Wild Natives in the Oscar and Barrier Ranges', 26 January 1895, SROWA, Cons. 430. File 3548/1897; N. Green and S. Moon, *Far from Home: Aboriginal Prisoners of Rottnest Island 1838–1931,* Dictionary of Western Australians, vol. X, Perth, UWA Press, 1997, p.131; see also Pilmer, *Northern Patrol,* p.50.

91   For name references see N. Green and S. Moon, *Far from Home* pp. 196, 225, 271.

92   'Murder By Natives, Police Constable Richardson, Killed, Two Station Hands Shot', *The West Australian,* 12 November 1894, p.3.

93   *Police Gazette,* 5 December 1894, CO 6/1092.

94   W. Birman and G. Bolton, 'Sir Stephen Henry Parker (1846–1927)', *Australian Dictionary of Biography,* Australian National University, 1988, <http://adb.anu.edu.au/biography/parker-sir-stephen-henry-7957>.

95   WAPD, 'Capture of Wild Natives in the Oscar and Barrier Ranges', 26 January 1895, SROWA, Cons.430, File 3548/1897.

96   ibid.

97   ibid.

98   See 'Telegram from Commissioner Phillips to Drewry' in WAPD, 'Capture of Wild Natives in the Oscar and Barrier Ranges', SROWA, Cons. 430, File 3548/1897; also 'The Official Telegrams', *Western Mail,* 17 November 1894, p.39.

99   ibid.

100 WAPD, 'Commissioner of Police Phillips to Sub Inspector Drewry, Capture of Wild Natives in the Oscar and Barrier Ranges, 10 November 1894', SROWA, Cons. 430, File 3548/1897. Quoted in Pedersen and Woorunmurra, *Jandamarra and the Bunuba Resistance,* p.124.

101 See 'Telegram from Drewry to Commissioner of Police, 21 November 1894' in WAPD, 'Capture of Wild Natives in the Oscar and Barrier Ranges, 10 November 1894', SROWA, Cons. 430, File 3548/1897.

102 ibid., 'Telegram from Commissioner Phillips to Lawrence, 22 November 1894'.

103 See 'Telegram from Drewry to Commissioner Phillips, 10 November 1894' in WAPD, 'Capture of Wild Natives in the Oscar and Barrier Ranges', SROWA, Cons. 430, File 3548/1897.

104 The concern about using local assistants was articulated by a writer in the *Northern Public Opinion* who stated 'nearly all the police assistants are natives of the district, many of them being greater criminals than those they go in search of. The natives, while they are in the police service are trained in the use of firearms, and nothing can prevent them from taking to the bush at any time, carrying off rifles or any other weapons that may be handy, and joining their tribe, as in the case of the natives who shot the men at the Barrier and Oscar Ranges. It is nothing short of suicide for the police to have to travel through the disturbed parts, with native assistants, often members of the tribe of which they are in search.' *Northern Public Opinion,* 22 May 1897, p.4.

105 See 'List of Special Constables', in WAPD, 'Capture of Wild Natives in the Oscar and Barrier Ranges, 10 November 1894', SROWA, Cons. 430, File 3548/1897.

106 ibid.

107 ibid., 21 November 1894, 'Drewry to Commissioner of Police'; see *Western Mail,* 8 December 1894, p.10.

108 WAPD, 'Capture of Wild Natives in the Oscar and Barrier Ranges, 26 January 1895', SROWA, Cons. 430, File 3548/1897.

109 ibid., see 'Telegram from Drewry to Commissioner of Police, 15 December 1894'. Quoted in Pedersen and Woorunmurra, *Jandamarra and the Bunuba Resistance,* p.137.

110 WAPD, 'Capture of Wild Natives in the Oscar and Barrier Ranges, 26 January 1895', SROWA, Cons. 430, File 3548/1897; see also McGregor, *Answering the Native Question,* p.79.

111 ibid., 'PC McDermott to Drewry, 16 January 1895'.

112 ibid., 'Lawrence to Police Commissioner, 2 December 1894'.

113 ibid., see 'Telegram from Inspector Lawrence to Commissioner of Police, 5 January 1895'. For a newspaper report of this incident see 'The Murders by Natives in the Kimberley District, Telegrams to the Commissioner of Police, What the Police are Doing?', *The West Australian,* 8 January 1895, p.2.

114 ibid., 7 January 1895.

115 'The Murders by Natives in the Kimberley District', *Western Mail,* 12 January 1895, p.13.

116 WAPD, Robinson River Police Station, Occurrence Book, 30 January 1895,

SROWA, AN 5, Cons. 737, Item 1.

117 ibid.

118 ibid., from 1 February 1895 to 27 February 1895 PC Chisholm's duty was 'attending to spear wound on horse'.

119 'Operate on' was a term often used on patrol. WAPD, 'Lawrence to Police Commissioner, Capture of Wild Natives in the Oscar and Barrier Ranges, 15 December 1894', SROWA, Cons. 430, File 3548/1897; see also 'The Northern Native Outrage. Police Warfare', *The Inquirer and Commercial News*, 4 January 1895, p.15.

120 ibid., WAPD, 'Lawrence to Police Commissioner, 10 January 1895', SROWA, Cons. 430, File 3548/1897; see also McGregor, *Answering the Native Question*, pp.87–8.

121 ibid.

122 ibid.

123 ibid.

124 ibid., see also R. McGregor, *Answering the Native Question*, pp.88–9.

125 ibid., 22 January 1895.

126 ibid.

127 ibid.

128 ibid., 26 January 1895.

129 ibid.

130 ibid., 29 January 1895.

131 ibid., 'Lawrence to Police Commissioner, 11 February 1895'.

132 ibid., 15 January 1895; quoted in Pedersen and Woorunmurra, *Jandamarra and the Bunuba Resistance*, p.132.

133 'Native Outrages in the North, A White Man Speared, Native Police Deserters', *The Daily News*, 19 March 1895, p.3. Pedersen and Woorunmurra characterise William Phillips as a 'mad hatter' loner who abused Aboriginal women and was speared in retaliation. Pedersen and Woorunmurra, *Jandamarra and the Bunuba Resistance*, pp.142–3.

134 *Northern Public Opinion*, 30 March 1895, p.3.

135 ibid., 'Mr Inspector Lawrence is away with his party at the head of the Fitzroy and Margaret Rivers and it is to be hoped that by the time he has completed his work of punishment the aboriginals will be taught to differentiate between a fat bullock and kangaroo when they go hunting for food.'

136 CSO, 'Capture of Wild Natives in the Oscar and Barrier Ranges, Drewry to Police Commissioner Phillips', SROWA, Cons. 430, File 3548/1897.

137 CSO, 'Capture of Wild Natives in the Oscar and Barrier Ranges, Commissioner of Police Phillips to Sub Inspector Drewry', SROWA, Cons. 430, File 3548/1897.

138 ibid., 'Report of Police Constable Brice to Drewry, 13 March 1895'.

139 ibid.

140 ibid., 'Police Commissioner to Drewry'.

141 WAPD, Derby Police Station, Letterbook, 'Sub Inspector O. Drewry Report to Constable Buckland, 17 March 1895', SROWA, AN 5, Cons. 738/22.

Emphasis in original.

142 WAPD, 'Capture of Wild Natives in the Oscar and Barrier Ranges, Commissioner of Police Phillips to Sub Inspector Drewry, 10 November 1894', SROWA, Cons. 430, File 3548/1897.

143 ibid.

144 WAPD, 'Capture of Wild Natives in the Oscar and Barrier Ranges, PC Brice to Sergeant Cadden, 23 July 1895', SROWA, Cons. 430, File 3548/1897.

145 P. Conole: *a history of the Western Australian police service,* Perth, Access Press, 2002, p.93.

146 WAPD, Robinson River Police Station, Occurrence Book 1893–1898, 8 April 1895, SROWA, AN 5, Cons. 737, Item 1.

147 ibid.

148 WAPD, Robinson River Police Station, Occurrence Book, 'PC Spong and PC Anderson on Duty with Native Assistants Mick and Peter', Item 1, SROWA, AN 5, Cons. 737.

149 WAPD, 'Wholesale Killing of Cattle on Margaret River, 23 July 1895', SROWA, Cons. 430, File 1808/1895.

150 ibid.

151 WAPD, 'Kimberley District. Lennard Police Station. Raid on Lillawalloora [sic] Station by Native "Pigeon" and Party. 1 Native Shot & 1 Wounded, 29 January 1896', SROWA, Cons. 430, File 653/1896.

152 ibid.

153 WAPD, Derby Police Station, 'Natives Giving Trouble in Fitzroy, Sub Inspector Ord Leaving Derby to Make Enquiries, 7 August 1896', SROWA, Cons. 430, File 2301/96; see McGregor, *Answering the Native Question,* pp.115–16.

154 WAPD, 'Derby Police Station. Natives Giving Trouble in Fitzroy. Sub Inspector Ord Leaving Derby to Make Enquiries. July 27, 1896, 7 August 1896', SROWA, Cons. 430, File 2301/1896.

155 ibid., Pedersen links these events by explaining that Albert was stabbed by Duncan and sent to Derby gaol where 'here no doubt, Noormadie learned from the Bunuba prisoners of Jandamarra's wondrous exploits in the Limestone ranges'. Pedersen and Woorunmurra, *Jandamarra and the Bunuba Resistance,* p.159. For a newspaper report of the 'runaway station natives' luring the 'bush natives on', see 'The Natives at Derby, Serious Disturbances. Firing the Country', *The Daily News,* 8 August 1896, p.2.

156 WAPD, 'Telegram to Commissioner of Police from Sub Inspector Ord, 7 August 1896', SROWA, Cons. 430, File 2301/1896.

157 ibid.

158 *Northern Public Opinion,* 2 October 1897, p.2.

159 'Shouldn't the Australian governments mobilise Pilmer and send him home to Britain as an Australian contingent in case of a general flare up of this Cretan business?', *T'Othersider,* quoted in WAPD, 'Capture of Wild Natives in the Oscar and Barrier Ranges, 26 January 1895', SROWA, Cons. 430. File 3548/1897.

160 Aborigines Protection Board, 'Correspondence, G. Marsden, 29 October 1896', SROWA, Item 36 Cons. 495, Report on Yeeda station.

161 ibid.

162 Aborigines Protection Board, 'Correspondence, Report for the Secretary of the Aboriginal Protection Board of Western Australia from Mr George Marsden on Oobagooma Cattle Station, 21 December 1896', SROWA, AN 1, Cons. 495, Item 44.

163 ibid.

164 ibid.

165 ibid.

166 Aborigines Protection Board, 21 August 1896, SROWA, Private Item 58, Cons. 495; see also *British Parliamentary Papers*, vol. 34, p.517.

167 See 'Telegram from PC Pilmer to Commissioner Phillips, 19 March 1897', in WAPD, 'Capture of Wild Natives in the Oscar and Barrier Ranges', SROWA, Cons. 430, File 3548/1897; 'The Re-Capture of an Escaped Murderer', *The West Australian,* 14 September 1899, p.4.

168 WAPD, 'Police Commissioner to Ord, 18 March 1897', SROWA, Cons. 430, File 3548/1897; 'The Native Question, The Murder of Mr Thomas Jasper, Rout of Natives by the Police, Two Killed and Three Wounded', *The West Australian,* 22 March 1897, p.5.

169 ibid.

170 See 'Telegram from Corporal Pearson to Commissioner of Police, 2 April 1897', in WAPD, 'Capture of Wild Natives in the Oscar and Barrier Ranges', 26 January 1895, SROWA, Cons. 430. File 3548/1897.

171 See reports 'A Notorious Native', *The Advertiser,* 2 April 1897, p.5; 'News of the Week', *Western Mail,* 9 April 1897, p.12; 'Western Australia', *The Queenslander,* 10 April 1897, p.782; 'Why Pigeon Roamed Kimberley', *Western Mail*, 18 January 1940, p.8; another account is C.E. Flinders, 'Trouble in the Nineties when Armed Natives Attacked the Whites North-West Memories, Manhunt in the Oscar Range,' *Western Mail,* 9 January 1947, p. 5.

172 N. Green, *The Forrest River Massacres,* Fremantle, Fremantle Arts Centre Press, 1995, p.47; Pedersen and Woorunmurra, *Jandamarra and the Bunuba Resistance*, p.190.

173 WAPD, 'Report of Police Constable Chisholm to Sub Inspector Ord, 6 April 1897', SROWA, Cons. 430, File 3548/1897.

174 ibid., 8 April 1897.

175 ibid., 13 April 1897.

176 WAPD, Fitzroy Station, 'Journal of Patrol to Noonkenbah [Noonkanbah] and the Arrest of "Bool" and "Pyabarra", Escapees Charged with Murder. 10 January 1898', SROWA, Cons. 430, File 686/1898.

177 *Northern Public Opinion,* 22 May 1897, p.2; 'Native Murderers in the North. A Desperate Gang Still at Large', *Western Mail,* 8 October 1897, p.9.

178 *Northern Public Opinion,* 18 December 1897, p.4.

179 'The murder at Mt. Broome', *The West Australian,* 24 February 1900, p.5.

180 WAPD, 'Papers Concerning the Decision to Execute Lillamarra. 27.9.1899',

SROWA, Cons. 430, File 3773/1899; 'Lillimarra, Mullabuddin and Woonmillina, were Hanged, Aboriginal Desperadoes', *The West Australian,* 14 May 1900, p.5.

181 F.H. Hann, *Do Not Yield to Despair; Frank Hugh Hann's Exploration Diaries in the Arid Interior of Australia 1895–1908,* M. Donaldson and I. Elliot (eds), Perth, Hesperian Press, 1998.

Chapter 10: 'They Show Fight on the Approach of any White Man'

1 CSO, 'Warden Kimberley – General Report on the Field', SROWA, AN 24, Cons. 527, File 1757/1890.

2 For report of drought and Aboriginal depredations see WAPD, Trooper Brophy's 'Report on the Kimberley Goldfields District', 14 November 1892, SROWA, Cons. 430, File 2293/1892.

3 J. Holmes, *Australia's Open North: A Study of Northern Australia Bearing on the Urgency of the Times,* Sydney, Angus and Robertson, 1963, p.170; see also G. Bolton, *A Survey of the Kimberley Pastoral Industry from 1885 to the Present,* Master's thesis, University of Western Australia, 1953, p.76. Connor and Doherty had first used Derby as a port shipping cattle for the Duracks; Denis Doherty was the Fremantle link and Francis Connor was in Wyndham. In late 1892 Osmand and Panton's stock went to Port Darwin for shipment. See WAPD, 'Derby. Report on the Police Posts in the Kimberley District 1892', Letter from Trooper Brophy to Commissioner of Police Phillips, 13 October 1892, SROWA, AN 5, Cons. 430, File 2276/1892.

4 Bolton, *A Survey of the Kimberley Pastoral Industry from 1885 to the Present,* p.69.

5 M. Durack, *Sons in the Saddle,* London, Constable, 1983, p.4. Mary Durack attributes this to Francis Connor's influence. In 1893, 2470 cattle were imported from East Kimberley and 1407 from Derby; in 1894, 4743 cattle came from Wyndham and 2673 from Derby; and in 1897, 5441 came from Wyndham and 3453 from Derby. 'Parliament, Legislative Assembly', *The West Australian,* 16 December 1897, p.6.

6 'The Goldfields of the Far North, A Chat with Warden Cummins', *The West Australian,* 25 March 1896, p.6; see also Bolton, *A Survey of the Kimberley Pastoral Industry from 1885 to the Present,* p.77.

7 ibid., p.6.

8 G. Bolton, *Alexander Forrest,* Melbourne, Melbourne University Press in association with UWA Press, 1958, p.24.

9 ibid., p.30.

10 Bolton, *A Survey of the Kimberley Pastoral Industry from 1885 to the Present,* p.70.

11 M. Durack, *Kings in Grass Castles,* Australia, Corgi Books, 1990, pp.192–3.

12 Holmes, *Australia's Open North,* p.171.

13 'Doug Moore's Memoirs' Private Manuscript (nd.), MS, Battye Library, Cons. 3829A, MN 1237, p.1.

14 WAPD, Derby Police Station, Occurrence Book, 29 November 1892, SROWA, AN 5, Cons. 738/21. CSO, 'Defects in Telegraphy Line as Erected', 'Warden Kimberley – General Report on the Field', 26 August

1890, SROWA, AN 24 Cons. 527, File 1757/1890.

15 CSO, 'Encounter with Native Offenders in East Kimberley District H. Collins Killed in. Reporting – Sub Inspector Drewry, Journal of a Trip by Sergt Brophy and Party in Pursuit of Natives who are Killing Cattle on the Ord Osmand and Other Rivers', SROWA, AN 24, Cons. 527, File 90/1894.

16 WAPD, Wyndham Police Station, Letter Book, Report Sergeant Houlihan, 28 May 1890, SROWA, AN 5, Cons. 741/11.

17 WAPD, Wyndham Police Station, Letter Book, June 1890, SROWA, AN 5, Cons. 741/11. See also WAPD, 'Report for the Information of the Commissioner that Two Men Named William Miller and Joseph Webb were Speared by Aborigines, The Natives Responsible were Arrested', Halls Creek Police Camp, SROWA, Cons. 430, File 1891/1037.

18 WAPD, Halls Creek Police Station, Letterbook, 17 November 1890, SROWA, AN 5, Cons. 1422.

19 B. Shaw (ed.), *Banggaiyerri: the story of Jack Sullivan as told to Bruce Shaw,* Canberra, Australian Institute of Aboriginal Studies, 1983, p.35.

20 WAPD, Denham River Police Station, Occurrence Book, Memo from R. Troy to Officers, 25 May 1889, SROWA, AN 5, Cons. 739.

21 ibid., 8 November 1889.

22 WAPD, Wyndham Police Station, Letterbook, 10 May 1890, SROWA, AN 5, Cons. 741/11.

23 ibid., 4 November 1891.

24 ibid., May 1890.

25 ibid., 5 March 1891.

26 ibid, and 22 February 1891.

27 Phillips when hearing of this wrote: 'Constable Oakes may consider himself lucky in not having been heavily fined or imprisoned for his gross subordination[,] notwithstanding he has had every support from head quarters and has been given a fair opportunity to acquire a thorough knowledge of the rough and arduous duties required to be discharged by a constable attached to remote stations in unsettled parts of the colony.' WAPD, Wyndham Police Station, Letterbook, 6 November 1891, SROWA, AN 5, Cons. 741/11.

28 WAPD, Denham River Occurrence Book, 'Report by Sergt Houlihan, 28 November 1890', SROWA, AN 5, Cons. 739.

29 WAPD, Wyndham Police Station, Letterbook, 10 May 1890, SROWA, AN 5, Cons. 741/11.

30 WAPD, Denham River Police Station, Occurrence Book 1, 21 May 1890, SROWA, AN 5, Cons. 739.

31 WAPD, Wyndham Police Station, Occurrence Book, 11 June 1890, SROWA, AN 5, Cons. 741/2.

32 Denham River, Occurrence Book, Report by PC Pollard, 11 June 1890, SROWA, AN 5, Cons. 739.

33 WAPD, Halls Creek Police Station, Letterbook, 'Witness statements from Trooper Frank Austin and Trooper Kingston, 21 Mar 1891', SROWA, AN 5, Cons. 1422.

34 WAPD, Denham River Police Station, Occurrence Book, 9 July 1891, SROWA, Cons. 739.

35 ibid.

36 WAPD, Denham River Police Station, Occurrence Book, 'Report by PC Guilfolye, 11 July 1891', SROWA, AN 5, Cons. 739.

37 WAPD, Denham River Police Station, Occurrence Book, 'Report by Sergt Lavery, 13 September 1891', SROWA, AN 5, Cons. 739.

38 ibid., 17 September 1892.

39 K. Moran, *Sand and Stone – Cattle & Conflict,* vols. 1 and 2, Perth, Hesperian Press, 2009, p.84.

40 See *Police Gazette,* no. 25, 22 June 1892, p.99. See also R.H. Pilmer, *Northern Patrol: an Australian saga,* C. Clement and P. Bridge(ed), Perth, Hesperian Press, 1998, p.35.

41 ibid.

42 WAPD, Denham River Police Station, Occurrence Book, 'Report by Sergt Lavery, 22 September 1892', SROWA, AN 5, Cons. 739.

43 WAPD, 'Letter from Sub Inspector O. Drewry to Commissioner of Police Phillips Derby, 13 October 1892', SROWA, AN 5, Cons. 2276/1892.

44 ibid.

45 ibid.

46 WAPD, 'Expedition to Disperse Natives on King River – December 1892. Failure from Serg Lavery to Shoot Natives Defeated the Purpose of the Trip, 7 February 1893', SROWA, AN 5, Cons. 430, File 264/1893.

47 WAPD, Derby Police Station, Occurrence Book, 'Witness report from August Lucanus, 7 February 1893', SROWA, AN 5, Cons. 738/21.

48 WAPD, 'Letter from Sub Inspector O. Drewry to Commissioner of Police Phillips Derby, 13 October 1892', SROWA, AN 5, Cons. 2276/1892.

49 ibid.

50 ibid.

51 ibid.

52 WAPD, Wyndham Police Station, Letterbook, 27 June 1890, SROWA, AN 5, Cons. 741/11; WAPD, Wyndham Police Station, Letterbook, 'Commissioner Phillips to Derby Police, 21 February 1892', SROWA, AN 5, Cons. 741/11. For an account of this practice in Roebourne see the hanging of Cooperabiddy in 'Roebourne News, Execution of a Native Prisoner', *Western Mail,* 25 March 1893, p.43.

53 Speech by John Forrest, 'Protection of Northern Settlers against Hostile Natives', *Parliamentary Debates Legislative Council,* vol. II, 7 December 1891 to 8 March 1892, Perth, 14 January 1892, p.259.

54 WAPD, Wyndham Police Station, Letterbook, 'Commissioner Phillips to Derby Police, 21 February 1892', SROWA, AN 5, Cons. 741/11.

55 WAPD, Wyndham Police Station, Letterbook, 'Report by Sub Inspector Drewry', (nd.), AN 5, Cons. 741/11. Another newspaper reported on the resentment that a 'Kimberleyite', or an unnamed local of the district, expressed that an official hangman was sent from Perth to oversee the execution. This

he suggested was 'an interference with local enterprise. He would hang all the tribe at a remuneration of £5 per head.' 'Sittings, Local and Otherwise', *Northern Territory Times and Gazette,* Friday 15 January 1892, p.3.

56 WAPD, Wyndham Police Station, Letterbook, 'Report by Sub Inspector Drewry', (nd.), SROWA, AN 5, Cons. 741/11.

57 WAPD, Wyndham Police Station, Letterbook, 'Report by Sub Inspector Drewry', (nd.), SROWA, AN 5, Cons. 741/11.

58 *Northern Territory Times and Gazette,* Friday 23 December 1892, p.2.

59 'Notes of the week', *Northern Territory Times and Gazette,* Friday 15 January 1892, p.2.

60 'Mt Dockerell Murder. Three Aboriginals Hanged', *Northern Territory Times and Gazette,* Friday 25 March 1892, p.3.

61 ibid. The report states 'we have it on the authority of a correspondent that as the day crept towards dark they were overpowered by a superstitious dread connected with the execution, exhibiting the utmost terror, and seeking the protection of the whites against the hanged men, who, they alleged, were chasing them to catch and murder them. Acting upon this dread they accompanied the Government party nearly in to Wyndham on the return journey, and could not be kept out of the white men's camp at night time. If all this be true, we hope that the performance at the mount will have good effects.'

62 WAPD, Wyndham Police Station, Letterbook, 'Report by Sub Inspector Drewry', (nd.), SROWA, AN 5, Cons. 741/11.

63 Quoted in M. Aveling, *Westralian Voices, Documents in West Australian Social History,* Perth, UWA Press, 1979, p.101.

64 ibid.

65 'Troubles in the East Kimberley', *The West Australian,* 22 November 1892, p.6.

66 *The West Australian,* 7 December 1892, p.2. Aboriginal people 'entered the town and stole the police boat one day. They threw a spear at the Sergeant of Police in the town another day...All the guns, rifles and revolvers in Wyndham are kept loaded. When will police be sent to protect the people? An attack on the town is said to be feared some night. About forty armed natives are camped near the town. There are only two policemen at Wyndham. Please do not consider these reports exaggerated.'

67 WAPD, Fletcher Creek Police Station, 'Report by PC Rhatigan about Complaint from Carrier William Hill, 29 December 1892', SROWA, AN 5, Cons. 740. Total items included '600 lbs of flour [272 kilograms], 50 lbs sugar, 1/2 dozen James Jams, 4 tins of pressed fruit, 10/-13 bottles Yorkshire relish[,] 18/-1 gallon whisky bulk 3 pound, 1 parcel of singlets 1/2 doz. 1 Winchester rifle in good order and 40 rounds ammunition. 3 Billy cans, 3 enamel pannikins, 3 enamel dishes one small, 5 knives, 3 forks, 2 spoons, 2 tomahawks and 1 axe new. 1 set of shoeing trots value of all is 35 pounds 8/6.'

68 'The Natives in the East Kimberley District, A Teamster Robbed', *Western Mail,* 28 January 1893, p.23.

69   WAPD, Fletcher Creek Police Station, Occurrence Book, 17 June 1893, SROWA, AN 5, Cons. 740. 'Wingbing' was charged with this offence. For newspaper report see 'The Natives in the East Kimberley. Horse and Cattle Spearing Prevalent', *The West Australian*, 28 June 1893, p.5.

70   WAPD, Derby Police Station, Letterbook, 'Report from Sub Inspector O. Drewry, 4 April 1893', SROWA, Cons. 738/21.

71   'Native Depredations in the East Kimberley District', *The West Australian*, 6 February 1893, p.3.

72   'News and Notes', *The Inquirer and Commercial News*, 14 April 1893, p.29.

73   CSO, 'Encounter with Native Offenders in East Kimberley District H. Collins killed in. Reporting – Sub Inspector Drewry, Journal of a Trip by Sergt Brophy and Party in Pursuit of Natives who are Killing Cattle on the Ord Osmand and Other Rivers', SROWA, AN 24, Cons. 527, File 90/1894.

74   WAPD, 'East Kimberley District. Wyndham Sub-district. Wyndham Station. Journal of PC Ritchie of Arrest of Aborigines Accused of Cattle Killing. December 25, 1897', SROWA, Cons. 430, File 393/1898.

75   'Sickness amongst Native Prisoners', *The W.A. Record*, 19 October 1893, p.8.

76   ibid.

77   'Wyndham News', *The West Australian*, 20 December 1893, p.3.

78   'Wyndham News, Wholesale Escape of Native Prisoners', *The West Australian*, 20 December 1893, p.3.

79   ibid.

80   'Wyndham News. Escape of Natives from the Gaol', *The West Australian*, 15 May 1894, p.5.

81   'Wyndham News, Escape of all the Native Prisoners', *The West Australian*, 8 August 1894, p.5.

82   'News from Wyndham, Capture of 11 of the Escaped Native Prisoners', *The Daily News*, 3 September 1894, p.3.

83   *Police Gazette*, No. 19, 6 May 1896, p.100.

84   Speech by Colonial Secretary S.H. Parker, 'Rottnest Island', *Western Australian Parliamentary Debates*, 19 September 1894, p.659, see Loan Bill 1894, 19 September 1894, <http://www.parliament.wa.gov.au/Hansard/hansard1870to1995.nsf/vwMainBackground/18940919_Council.pdf/$File/18940919_Council.pdf>.

85   ibid.

86   WAPD, 'Journal of PC Ritchie Patrolling Settlers in Wyndham District – March 2 to 10, 1897', in conversation with Mick Cassidy, Wyndham Station East Kimberley District, SROWA, Cons. 430, File 1346/1897; WAPD, East Kimberley District, Wyndham Station, 'Police Constable Farley (305) and Others Report of the Murder of Aboriginal Assistant, Dicky, Speared by Hostile Natives at Durack River while Trying to Apprehend Murderers of Ah Sing', July 1899, SROWA, Cons. 430, File 2873/1899.

87   WAPD, Argyle Police Station, Letterbook, 'Journal of PC Thomson PC 586, from 12th January to 10th February, 10 February 1901', Property of Western Australian Police Service.

88 'Doug Moore's Memoirs', p.2.
89 ibid., p.16.
90 *Police Gazette,* CO 6/1092, SROWA, CSO, 1987/1894, 5 December 1894, p.221.
91 'Native Depredations at Kimberley, A Police Constable Killed, Twenty-Three Natives Shot', *The Daily News,* 27 September 1893, p.2; see also *The Western Australian Record,* 5 October 1893, p.7.
92 Durack, *Kings in Grass Castles,* pp.351–2.
93 Quoted in M. Durack, *Kings in Grass Castles,* 1959, op.cit., p.336.
94 CSO, 'Encounter with Native Offenders in East Kimberley District H. Collins Killed in. Reporting – Sub Inspector Drewry, Journal of a Trip by Sergt Brophy and Party in Pursuit of Natives who are Killing Cattle on the Ord Osmand and Other Rivers', Correspondence from Commissioner Phillips, 28 September 1893, SROWA, AN 24, Cons. 527, File 90/1894.
95 ibid., CSO, 'Report by Sergt Brophy to Commissioner of Police, 30 November 1893', SROWA, AN 24, Cons. 527, File 90/1894.
96 ibid., CSO, 'Journal of a Trip by Sergt Brophy and Party in Pursuit of Natives who are Killing Cattle on the Ord, Osmand and Other Rivers, 1 October 1893–24 November 1893', SROWA, AN 24, Cons. 527, File 90/1894.
97 ibid., 14 October 1893.
98 ibid., 15 October 1893.
99 ibid., 25 October 1893. 'I got native dicky to tell them that if they did not lay down their spears and give themselves up for killing cattle that I would shoot them[. T]hey made no reply but a number of them made an attempt to get behind us[. S]eeing this I tried to cut them off and then we noticed that a number of the natives were crawling under cover of the rocks to get within throwing distance[. O]ne native ran out on the clear ground and threw a spear at Nat Micky but with his native instinct he evaded it[,] had it been one of the whites he would certainly have been speared as matters were now getting serious[.] I gave the order to fire[,] the natives fighting most desperate[,] often rushing within thirty yards of us.'
100 ibid., for the remainder of the trip the police continued in a similar fashion. At one time they encountered a camp at the junction of the Ord and Osmand rivers near Black Butt and Spring Creek where 'about 50 started to throw their spears and to protect ourselves we were compelled to fire and 4 natives were shot dead[,] the rest making good their escape.' The police party visited the Durack stations of Lissadell and Behn River where they reported no further depredations. They arrived back at Wyndham on 24 November 1893.
101 ibid., 30 November 1893.
102 CSO, 'Encounter with Native Offenders in East Kimberley District H. Collins Killed in. Reporting – Sub Inspector Drewry, Report from Overend Drewry to Commissioner of Police, 14 December 1893', SROWA, AN 24, Cons. 527, File 90/1894.
103 Speech by Francis Connor, *Western Australian Parliamentary Debates,* no. 5, 4 October 1893, p.1050.

104 ibid., Speech by Alexander Forrest, p.1052.

105 ibid., Speech by Sir John Forrest, p.1065.

106 'News from Wyndham. Further Native Depredations', *The Inquirer and Commercial News,* 28 September 1894, p.8.

107 WAPD, Denham River Police Station, Occurrence Book, Report by Sub Inspector Orme, (nd.), circa January 1895, SROWA, AN 5, Cons. 739.

108 G. Bolton, 'The Kimberley Pastoral Industry', *University Studies in History and Economics,* vol. 11, no. 2, 1954, p.22.

109 CSO, 'Letter from W.H. Osmand to F. Connor', 4 May 1895, SROWA, AN 24, Cons. 527, File 1868/1895.

110 ibid.

111 CSO, 'Letter to Minister for Lands from Nathaniel Buchanan', Ord River Station, Wyndham, February 1895, SROWA, AN 24, Cons. 527, File 823/1895.

112 CSO, 'Letter from O/C Sub Inspector Orme to Commissioner of Police, Halls Creek Station, 3 March 1895', SROWA, AN 24, Cons. 527, File 823/1895.

113 CSO, 'Correspondence from Sub Inspector Fred Orme to Commissioner of Police, Wyndham Station, 6 April 1895', SROWA, AN 24, Cons. 527, File 823/1895.

114 Durack, *Sons in the Saddle,* p.46.

115 CSO, 'Letter from W.H. Osmand, Stawell, Vic to Minister of Lands, 15 April 1895', SROWA, AN 24, Cons. 527, File 823/1895.

116 CSO, 'Telegram from Office of the Premier and Under Secretary to Osmund [sic] Stawell, Vic, 23 July 1895', SROWA, AN 24, Cons. 527, File 823/1895.

117 CSO, 'Correspondence from Sub Inspector Fred Orme to Commissioner of Police, Wyndham Station, 6 April 1895', SROWA, AN 24, Cons. 527, File 823/1895.

118 CSO, 'Journal of Report of Sergeant Wheatley and PC Rhatigan, 22 April 1895–4 June 1895, Wyndham Station, 9 May 1895', SROWA, AN 24, Cons. 527, 823/1895.

119 CSO, 'Journal of Report of Sergeant Wheatley and PC Rhatigan, East Kimberley District 22 April 1895–4 June 1895, Wyndham Station, 9 May 1895', SROWA, AN 24, Cons. 527, File 823/1895.

120 CSO, 'Correspondence from Sub Inspector Fred Orme to Commissioner of Police, Wyndham Station, 6 April 1895', SROWA, AN 24, Cons.527, File 823/1895.

121 ibid., 27 April 1895.

122 Aborigines Protection Board, G. Marsden's 'General Report of the Kimberley District, 12 Mar 1897', SROWA, AN 1/1, Cons. 495, Item 12.

123 Aborigines Protection Board, Correspondence, 'Report for the Secretary of the Aboriginal Protection Board of Western Australia from Mr George Marsden', 3 September 1896, SROWA, AN 1/1, Cons. 495, Item 49. Emphasis in original.

124 Mary Durack refers to the antagonism in *Kings in Grass Castles,* p.354.

125 Durack, *Sons in the Saddle*, p.326.

126 ibid.

127 CSO, 'Cattle Killing in the East Kimberley, Letter from W.H. Osmand to F. Connor, 4 May 1895', SROWA, AN 24, Cons. 527, File 1868/1895.

128 See Appendix 2.

129 *Pastoral Review,* Obituary, Frank Connor, 16 September 1916, pp.827–8.

130 'Doug Moore's Memoirs' p.1.

131 ibid.

132 CSO, 'Journal of Report of Sergeant Wheatley and PC Rhatigan 22 April–4 June 1895, Wyndham Station, 22 April, 1895', SROWA, AN 24, Cons. 527, File 823/1895.

133 ibid., 5 May 1895. In July 1899 'Dicky' was killed by 'hostile natives' or more likely targeted to cripple the police tracking. WAPD, East Kimberley District, Wyndham Station, Police Constable Farley (305) and others report of the murder of Aboriginal assistant, Dicky, speared by hostile natives at Durack River while trying to apprehend murderers of Ah Sing, July 1899, SROWA, Cons. 430. File 2873/1899.

134 CSO, 'Report by Sub Inspector Fred Orme on Sergeant Wheatley's April May Trip, 14 June 1895', SROWA, AN 24, Cons. 527, File 823/1895.

135 CSO, 'Octavius Burt to Premier, 17 July 1895', AN 24, Cons. 527, File 823/1895; see also B.K. De Garis and T Stannage, 'Octavius Burt (1849–1940)', *Australian Dictionary of Biography,* Australian National University, 1979 <http://adb.anu.edu.au/biography/burt-octavius-5644>.

136 A. Gill, 'Aborigines, Settlers and Police in the Kimberleys 1887–1905', *Studies in Western Australian History,* vol. 1, 1977, p.17.

137 CSO, 'Octavius Burt to Hon Premier, 2 June 1896', AN 24, Cons. 527, File 823/1895.

138 'Wyndham News, Record Shipment of Cattle, Beginning of Warm Weather, Trouble with Blacks', *The West Australian,* 7 September 1895, p.2.

139 CSO, 'Telegram from WH Osmand to Frank Connor, Stawell Vic', 'Telegram from WH Osmond to Premier John Forrest', 28 September 1895, SROWA, AN 24, Cons. 527, File 823/1895.

140 'Letter to Undersecretary from Commissioner of Police, G.B. Phillips, 3 October 1895', SROWA, CSO, AN 24, Cons. 527, File 823/1895.

141 CSO, 'Personal Correspondence, Letter to Commissioner of Police GB Phillips from D. Doherty, 18 November 1895', SROWA, AN 24, Cons. 527, File 823/1895. M. Durack had left the Ivanhoe Station on board the boat *Tagliaferro* to report to G.B. Phillips. See CSO, 'Telegram from Orme to Commissioner of Police, 16 November 1895', SROWA, AN 24, Cons. 527, File 823/1895.

142 CSO, 'Telegram from Commissioner of Police G B Phillips to Sub Inspector Fred Orme, 19 November 1895', SROWA, AN 24, Cons. 527, File 823/1895. Another spearing occurred at this time which may have added influence to the commissioner's orders. On 20 October 1895 miner William Meyerhoff was speared at Mt Dockrell though survived. 'News from Kimberley, A

Miner Speared by Blacks', *The Inquirer and Commercial News*, 1 November 1895, p.4.

143 'The Goldfields of the Far North', *The West Australian,* 25 March 1896, p.6.

144 WAPD, Wyndham Police Station, Occurrence Book, 2–6 November 1895, SROWA, AN 5, Cons. 741/3.

145 ibid., 6 November 1895.

146 'Private Diary of Sergeant Thomas Wheatley During Police Patrols from Wyndham from 6 November to 23 December 1895', [Wheatley Manuscript], 11 November 1895, Battye Library, Cons. 1266A, Manuscript.

147 Wheatley records twelve prisoners but only gives the names of ten. The prisoners, names were Didgebrinng, Giniring, Cullingagin, Wallabaring, Bulanine, Gourge, Coolwaring, Gangauire, Caarabang and Gillbangie. Wheatley Manuscript, ibid., 22 November 1895.

148 ibid., 18 December 1895.

149 Wyndham Police Occurrence book records fourteen prisoners.

150 Wheatley Manuscript, op.cit.

151 WAPD, Wyndham Police Station, Occurrence Book, 23 December 1895, SROWA, AN 5, Cons. 741/3.

152 CSO, 'Telegram from Sub Inspector Orme to Commissioner of Police GB Phillips', Wyndham Station, 15 December 1895, SROWA, AN 24, Cons. 527, File 823/1895. See also telegram dated 27 December 1895. Const. Inglis and party 'dispersed several tribes on Lissadell and Ord River Stations', CSO, AN 24, Cons. 527, File 823/1895. There is no surviving record of these Halls Creek police patrols in the State Archives. Emphasis added.

153 CSO, 'Telegram from Sub Inspector Orme to Commissioner of Police G.B. Phillips, 7 February 1896', SROWA, AN 24, Cons. 527, File 823/1895.

154 The camp was 61 kilometres from Argyle Station, 90 kilometres from Ord River Station, 45 kilometres from Rosewood and 80 kilometres from Newry – it was placed in order to be most central to all stations in the district.

155 CSO, 'Correspondence from Sub Inspector Fred Orme to Commissioner of Police, Wyndham Station, 6 April 1895', SROWA, AN 24, Cons. 527, File 823/1895.

156 CSO, 'Telegram from Commissioner of Police GB Phillips to Sub Inspector Orme, Wyndham Station, 2 December 1895', SROWA, AN 24, Cons. 527, File 823/1895.

157 C. Clement, 'Monotony, Manhunts and Malice: East Kimberley law enforcement, 1896–1908', *Early Days: Journal of the Royal Western Australian Historical Society*, vol. 10, part 1, 1978, p.86.

158 WAPD, 'PC Freeman's Journal whilst Patrolling Ord River and Lissadell Runs – December 25, 1896 to January 8, 1897', 6 January 1897, SROWA, Cons. 430, File 1344/1897.

159 WAPD, 'Journal of PC Rhatigan Patrolling the Argyle, Lissadell and Ord River Stations – January 17 to 22, 1897', Argyle Police Camp, 16 January 1897, SROWA, Cons. 430, File 1345/1897.

160 'Resident Magistrate Wyndham – Native Question East Kimberley – Arrest

of Natives for Cattle Killing – for Instructions with Regards to', Series 575, Cons. 527, File 1897/3931.

161 See for example WAPD, 'PC Freeman's Journal whilst on Patrol on Ord River and Lissadell Runs – December 25, 1896 to January 8, 1897', SROWA, Cons. 430, File 1344/1897.

162 ibid.

163 See WAPD, 'Copy of PC Rhatigan's Journal for September 1896', Argyle Camp, 15 September 1896, SROWA, Cons. 430, File 3689/1896; WAPD, 'Copy of PC Freeman's Journal from Wyndham to Argyle Police Camp, 24 October 1896', SROWA, Cons. 430, File 3688/1896; WAPD, 'Copy of PC Rhatigan's Journal whilst Travelling from Argyle Camp to Wyndham from the 5 October to the 22 October 1896', 5 October 1896, SROWA, Cons. 430, File 3690/1896; WAPD, 'PC Freeman's Journal whilst on Patrol on Ord River and Lissadell Runs', 25 December 1896, SROWA, Cons. 430, File 1344/1897; WAPD, 'PC Freeman's Journal whilst on Patrol on Ord River and Lissadell Runs', 6 January 1897, SROWA, Cons. 430, File 1344/1897; WAPD, 'Journal of P.C. Rhatigan Patrolling the Argyle, Lissadell and Ord River Stations – January 17 to 22, 1897', Argyle Police Camp, 15 January 1897, SROWA, Cons. 430, File 1345/1897.

164 WAPD, Report by Fred Orme on 'Journal of P.C. Rhatigan Patrolling the Argyle, Lissadell and Ord River Stations – January 17 to 22, 1897', forwarded to Police Department Chief Office 12 April 1897, SROWA, Cons. 430, File 1345/1897.

165 WAPD, 'Journal of PC Rhatigan Patrolling the Argyle, Lissadell and Ord River Stations – January 17 to 22, 1897', Argyle Police Camp, 15 January 1897, SROWA, Cons. 430, File 1345/1897.

166 Apparently because he found 'it impossible to keep away from drink knowing so many people'. K. Moran, *Cattle and Conflict*, Perth, Hesperian Press, 2010, p.191.

167 WAPD, 'Argyle Police Camp. Copy of PC Freeman's Journal on Patrol, Searching for Natives who had Killed Cattle. January 10 to February 12, 1898', Argyle Police Camp, 16 January 1898, SROWA, Cons. 430, File 1930/1898.

168 Durack, *Sons in the Saddle*, p.48.

169 See Appendix 2.

170 C. Clement, *Historical Notes Relevant to Impact Stories of the East Kimberley*, East Kimberley Working Paper, Canberra, East Kimberley Impact Assessment Project, 1989, p.92.

171 'Report of the Commissioner of Police for the Year ending 30 June 1897', WAPP, Paper 19, p.4.

172 'Report of the Commissioner of Police for the Year ending 30 June 1898', WAPP, Paper 17, p.7.

173 ibid.

174 See for example, CSO, 'Government Resident Derby – Native "Jeneella" Shot by PCs Armitage & Watts', Memo from Governor F. Napier Broome,

17 October 1890, SROWA, AN 24, Cons. 527, File 2627/1889.

175 CSO, 'The Native Question in the East Kimberley', Cons. 527, Item File 3931/1897.

176 CSO, 'Resident Magistrate Wyndham – Native Question East Kimberley – Arrest of Natives for Cattle Killing – For Instructions with Regards', Cons. 527, File 3931/1897.

177 ibid.

178 Witness testimony from John Inglis, *Roth Royal Commission on the Condition of the Natives. Presented to Both Houses of Parliament by His Excellency's Command*, WAPP, 1905, 2nd Session, No. 5, pt. 1521, p.93.

179 CSO, Telegram to the Resident Magistrate, Wyndham, Cons. 527, File 3931/1897.

180 See N. Green, 'From Princes to Paupers: the struggle for control of Aborigines in Western Australia 1887–1898', *Early Days: Journal of the Royal Western Australian Historical Society*, vol. 11, part 4, 1998, p.459.

181 'The Aborigines Protection Board: the memorial to the secretary of state', *The West Australian*, 7 October 1895, p.6; see also 'The Aborigines Protection Board: the memorial to the secretary of state', *Western Mail*, 11 October 1895, p.31.

182 CSO, 'Resident Magistrate Wyndham – Native Question East Kimberley – Arrest of Natives for Cattle Killing – for instructions with regards', Cons. 527, File 3931/1897.

Chapter 11: 'Necessity Requires No Precedents'

1 'West Australian Blacks', *Evening News*, New South Wales, 22 April 1901, p.7.

2 P. Conole, *Protect and Serve: a history of the Western Australian police service*, Perth, Access Press, 2002, p.105.

3 *Rules and Regulations for the Government and Guidance of the Police Force of Western Australia as Approved by John Forrest*, Perth, Sands and McDougall 1898, p.63.

4 ibid., Point 647 and 660.

5 'More of the Black Nor-West', *Sunday Times*, 30 July 1905, p.7.

6 CSO, 'Clerk of Court, Wyndham – Murder of Ah Sing by Blacks – Reporting Supposed', SROWA, Cons. 527, File 2773/1898; see also N. Green, *The Forrest River Massacres*, Fremantle, Fremantle Arts Centre Press, 1995, pp.94–6.

7 See for example 'Derby – Aboriginal Native Prisoner Jumby Jumby shot dead and Aboriginal Native Prisoner Owlalong Wounded by Trackers "Jacky" while in Charge of Constable O'Neil' (436)', SROWA, Cons. 430, File 2050/1904; 'Derby – Constable A. Schultz (837) and party attacked by Natives 12 miles [19 kilometres] east of Sturt Creek Homestead. One Native tracker and one Native (female) witness speared. 25.4.1906. Authority sought for purchase of four additional remounts for Halls Creek Station, and for the engagement of four additional Native Assistants', SROWA, Cons. 430, File 2432/1906; 'Derby – Constable H.A. Baker (885) attacked by Natives at Reedy Creek 17.11.1907. Two Natives shot by police party. Special trackers engaged at Halls Creek', SROWA, Cons. 430, File 5255/1907; '(1)

Depredations by Wyndham Natives. (2) Difficulty in arresting offenders. (3) Suggested employment of Native Assistants from other districts. (4) Suggested Native prisoners serve sentences in gaols in other locations. (5) Sly grog selling by Afghans. (6) Natives procuring women for Afghans. From Broome.' SROWA, Cons. 430. File 4335/1915.

8   *Police Gazette,* No. 30, 24 July 1895, p.131.

9   Conole, *Protect and Serve,* p.131.

10 'Police Inspector's Death', *The Daily News,* 6 May 1920, p.7.

11 R.H. Pilmer, *Northern Patrol: an Australian saga,* Perth, C. Clement and P. Bridge (eds), Hesperian Press, 1998, p.105.

12 'Native Murderers, A Policeman's Memories', *The West Australian,* 30 June, 1936, p.16.

13 *The Sunday Times,* 16 June 1901, quoted in P. Conole, *Protect and Serve,* p.138.

14 'Derby – Leopold Downs Station Raided by Natives; White Man and Native Boy Supposed Killed', Cons. 430, File 2115/1901.

15 'Interview with Sub Inspector Orme', *Kalgoorlie Miner,* 20 May 1898, p.7.

16 'The Black North, Modes of Nigger Flogging,' *West Australian Sunday Times,* 3 September 1899, p.3.

17 M. Jebb, *Blood, Sweat and Welfare: a history of white bosses and Aboriginal pastoral workers,* Perth, UWA Press, 2002.

18 A.P. Elkin, 'Totemism in North-Western Australia, The Kimberley Division', *Oceania,* vol.3, no.3, 1933, p.435.

19 M. Allbrook, *Henry Prinsep's Empire: framing a distant colony,* Canberra, ANU Press, 2014, ch.8.

20 M. Allbrook, *Imperial Family: the Prinseps, empire and colonial government in India and Australia,* PhD thesis, Griffith University, 2009, p.277.

21 *Police Gazette,* No. 24, 15 June 1898, p.201.

22 Aborigines Department, *Annual Report 1902–03,* SROWA, Cons. 255, File 0148/1903.

23 ibid., p.6.

24 Aborigines Department, Aborigines Report, SROWA, Cons. 255, File 0289/1905.

25 'Wyndham', *Northern Territory Times and Gazette,* 9 December 1898, p.3.

26 Allbrook, *Henry Prinsep's Empire: framing a distant colony,* ch.8.

27 A. Haebich, *For Their Own Good: Aborigines and government in the Southwest of Western Australia, 1900–1940,* Perth, UWA Press, 1988, p.55.

28 'Country, Wyndham', *The West Australian,* 7 November 1898, p.5.

29 'The Kimberley Police District', *The West Australian,* 12 September 1902, p.6.

30 See A. Haebich, *Broken Circles, Fragmenting Indigenous Families 1800–2000,* Fremantle, Fremantle Arts Centre Press, 2000, pp.156–8.

31 'The Police Department', *The West Australian,* 14 September 1904, p.5.

32 For extensive description of this at Lagrange Bay in 1901 see Aborigines Department, G.S. Olivey, Appendix, 'Reports on Stations Visited by the Travelling Inspector of Aborigines from 1st September 1899 to 30 June 1901', in *Annual Report of the Aborigines Department ending 30 June 1901,* No.26, p.50.

33   For an account of this see 'More of the Black Nor-West', *Sunday Times*, 30 July 1905, p.7.

34   See testimony from PC Fletcher, *Roth Royal Commission on the Condition of the Natives, Presented to Both Houses of Parliament by His Excellency's Command*, Roth Report, WAPP, 2nd Session, no. 5, 1905, Pt. 1310, p.87.

35   R. McGregor, *Imagined Destinies: Aboriginal Australians and the doomed race theory 1880–1939*, Melbourne, Melbourne University Press, 1997, p.139.

36   ibid.

37   See report by PC John Zum Felde, La Grange Bay, 14 May 1901, Aborigines Department, G.S. Olivey, Appendix, 'Reports on Stations Visited by the Travelling Inspector of Aborigines from 1st September 1899 to 30 June 1901', *Annual Report of the Aborigines Department ending 30 June 1901*, No.26, pp.50–1.

38   'The Aborigines Department', *Western Mail*, 28 October 1899, p.39.

39   *Annual Report of the Aborigines Department ending 30 June 1900*, No.15, p.3.

40   Roth Report, 1905, p.60.

41   'The Mission of the Trappists to the Aborigines of the West Kimberley', *The West Australian*, 19 October 1892, p.6; Aborigines Department, *Annual Report of the Aborigines Department ending 30 June 1903*, No.32, p.8.

42   Aborigines Department, *Report for the Financial Year Ending 30 June 1899*, No. 40, 1899, p.14.

43   Aborigines Department, *Annual Report 1902–03*, SROWA, Cons. 255, File 0148/1903.

44   Aborigines Department, *Annual Report of the Aborigines Department ending 30 June 1905*, No. 25, 1905, p.7.

45   Aborigines Department, G.S. Olivey, Appendix, 'Reports on Stations Visited by the Travelling Inspector of Aborigines from 1st September 1899 to 30 June 1901', *Annual Report of the Aborigines Department ending 30 June 1901*, No.26, p.50.

46   Roth Report, 1905, Pt. 1666, p.197.

47   Allbrook, *'Imperial Family'* p.307.

48   Quoted in Haebich, *For Their Own Good*, p.55.

49   'Aborigines Department', *Kalgoorlie Miner*, 25 November 1902, p.2.

50   'Legislative Assembly', *The West Australian*, 22 January 1902, p.5.

51   Allbrook, *'Imperial Family'*, p.293.

52   'Aborigines Department, Chief Protector of Aborigines. Proposed Amendments in Aborigines Act', SROWA, Cons. 255, File 830/1900.

53   ibid.

54   ibid.

55   ibid.

56   WAPD, West Kimberley District. 'Journal of PC J. Zum Felde on Patrol to La Grange Bay and Whistlers Creek. November 30, 1897 to February 19, 1898', SROWA, Cons. 430, File 993/1898; WAPD, 'West Kimberley District. Broome Station, Journals from PC Zum Felde (330) on Patrol Looking for Native Offenders and the Arrest of Two Malays for Consorting with

Aboriginal women, May 31, 1898', SROWA, Cons. 430, File 2505/1898; WAPD, 'West Kimberley District Broome Station. Journal of PC Zum Felde (330) Patrolling to Beagle Bay, Cygnet Bay 12.2.1900 – 17.3.1900. Damage Done by Storm on 7 February', SROWA, Cons. 430, File 1498/1900; 'West Kimberley District Broome Station. Journal of PC Zum Felde (330) Patrolling to Beagle Bay, Cygnet Bay 12.2.1900 – 17.3.1900. Damage Done by Storm on 7 February', SROWA, Cons. 430, File 1498/1900.

57 See Aborigines Department report by PC John Zum Felde, La Grange Bay, 14 May 1901, G.S. Olivey, Appendix, 'Reports on Stations Visited by the Travelling Inspector of Aborigines from 1st September 1899 to 30 June 1901', *Annual Report of the Aborigines Department Ending 30 June 1901,* No.26, p.50–1.

58 Whistler's Creek and La Grange 450; Broome 300; Beagle Bay 150; King Sound, Cygnet Bay 200. Of the total 300 were young men and boys, 150 underage and old men, the remainder (550) women and children.

59 Aborigines Department, G.S. Olivey, Appendix, 'Reports on Stations Visited by the Travelling Inspector of Aborigines from 1st September 1899 to 30 June 1901', in *Annual Report of the Aborigines Department ending 30 June 1901,* No.26, p.50.

60 ibid., p.51.

61 Aborigines Department, *Annual Report 1902-03,* SROWA, Cons. 255, File 148/1903.

62 Aborigines Department, 'J Felde, Broome. Report re: Disgraceful State of Native Affairs – in Vicinity of Creeks where the Pearling Fleet Tie Up', Cons. 255. File 0537/1902. Zum Felde went so far as to say he had been approached by English journals to give 'graphic account of the native question' but had declined awaiting assurances the issue would be addressed.

63 ibid.

64 See for example WAPD, 'Derby Police Journal, PC Kuhlmann, La Grange', SROWA, Cons. 430, File An5/1, File 4140/1902.

65 Witness statement from Bertram Henry Fletcher (Kuhlmann), October 1904, Roth Report, Pt. 1312–14, p.86–7.

66 ibid.

67 ibid.

68 Roth Report, p.25.

69 ibid., p.25. See report by PC John Zum Felde, LA Grange Bay, 14 May 1901, Aborigines Department, G.S. Olivey, Appendix, 'Reports on Stations Visited by the Travelling Inspector of Aborigines from 1st September 1899 to 30 June 1901', *Annual Report of the Aborigines Department ending 30 June 1901,* No.26, p.50–1.

70 Aborigines Department, 'Report 1901–02, "H.C. Children for Education"', SROWA, Cons. 255, File 0321/1902, p.37.

71 'West Australian Blacks', *Evening News,* NSW, 22 April 1901, p.7.

72 *Police Gazette,* 28 March 1900, No.13, p.95.

73 'The Death of Colonel Phillips', *The West Australian,* 28 March 1900, p.7.

74 William Chipper Lawrence (1848–1923), Acting Commissioner: 26 March

to 18 April 1900 and 22 to 28 February 1905; Frederick Arthur Hare (1852–1932), Commissioner: 18 April 1900 to 31 March 1912. 'Col. George Braithwaite Phillips', East Perth Cemeteries, Western Australia, <http://members.iinet.net.au/~perthdps/graves/bio-24.htm#d>.

75 'Commissioner Hare, A Disorganised Force', *Sunday Times*, 12 June 1904, p.10; 'Open Letter to Police Commissioner Hare, the man who wasn't sacked', *Sunday Times*, 5 March 1905, p.13; see also Conole, *Protect and Serve*, p.138.

76 'Mr F. Connor, MLA', *The Inquirer and Commercial News*, 28 June 1901, p.15.

77 T. Stannage, 'The Composition of the Western Australian Parliament: 1890–1911', *University Studies in History*, vol. iv, no. 4, 1966, p.13.

78 WAPD, 'Derby – Leopold Downs Station Raided by Natives; White Man and Native Boy Supposed Killed', SROWA, AN 5/2, Cons. 430, File 2115/1901.

79 See for example WAPD, 'Journal of Constable Inglis Patrolling Sturt Creek. 17 Nov 1903 to 7 Dec 1903', SROWA, AN 5/2, Cons. 430, File 613/1904; WAPD, 'Journal of Constable Caldow re Cattle killing on Alice Downs, 9 Dec 1903 to 3 Jan 1904', SROWA, AN 5/2, Cons. 430. File 986/1904; also 'The Kimberley Police District', *The West Australian*, 12 September 1902, p.6.

80 WAPD, 'Under-Secretary, Premier's Department – Halls Creek District – Reporting that Blacks Have Become Troublesome – Police Protection Requested. Natives Killing Cattle at Halls Creek; Police Station Required at Turkey Creek; Horses & Gear at Wyndham Reported to be in Unserviceable Condition', SROWA, Cons. 430, File 2157/1901.

81 'The North-West Blacks', *The West Australian*. 29 May 1901, p.2.

82 ibid.

83 ibid. Also Denham 4000; Carlton 3000; Rosewood 5000; Mable Downs 400; Froghollow 600; Koojuhrin 600; Ruby Plains 700; Mount Barrett 800; Flora Valley 6000; Sturt Creek and Margaret River 8000; Mud Springs 800; King River 1000.

84 Aborigines Department, *Annual Report for the Financial Year Ending 30th June*, 1902, No. 21, p.7.

85 G.C. Bolton, 'The Kimberley Pastoral Industry', *University Studies in History and Economics*, vol. 11, no. 2, 1954, p.24.

86 'The Kimberley Police District', *The West Australian*, 12 September 1902, p.6; WAPP, 1902, vol.21, p.17.

87 'West Kimberley', *The West Australian*, 29 December 1902, p.5.

88 'The Work of the Police Force', *The West Australian*, 17 September 1903, p.5.

89 'Native Outrages in the Nor'-West', *The West Australian*. 14 December 1907, p.12.

90 Aborigines Department, 'Sub-Inspector Duncan, Derby. Aborigines in Kimberley District', Cons. 255, File 534/1902.

91 Roth Report., p.110.

92 See for example WAPD, 'Derby – Alleged Murder of Aboriginal Natives in Margaret River District, East Kimberley; Death of Aboriginal Natives "Belming" alias Charlie, "Cranmere", "Murjurning", "Jungabidgelly" & "Warrerbier", Journal of Constable Caldon (615) 6–23 August 1902',

SROWA, Cons. 430, File 1902/4611.

93 For shooting evidence see for example WAPD, 'Fitzroy Station. West Kimberley District Constable MacKellar (448), and His Party Shoot Aboriginal Natives Munguny and Grumbuny', AN 5/2, Cons. 430, File 2489/1900; WAPD, 'Fitzroy Station. West Kimberley District. Journal of Constable T.A. MacKellar (448), and Party 28.4.1900 to 27.5.1900. Five Natives Arrested and Two Shot', SROWA, AN 5/2, Cons. 430, File 2490/1900.

94 WAPD, SROWA, 'Derby – Journal of Constable MacKellar (448) from 16–24 December 1900, Escorting Native Prisoners to Wyndham', AN 5/2, Cons. 430, File 0807/1900; 'Derby – Journal of Constable Mulkerin 16–25 January 1901; Escorting Native Prisoners Jilgree Alias Charley to Derby', AN 5/2, Cons. 430, File 810/1900; 'Derby – Journal of Constable Hill (517) 15 November 1900 to 20 February 1901 in Search of Native Offenders; 12 Natives Arrested for Cattle Killing; Death of Edward Fitzgerald', AN 5/2, Cons. 430, File 3284/1901; 'Derby – Journal of Constable Hill (517) 7–25 May 1901; Natives "Chuckee" Alias Dicky, "Lusine" Alias Peter & "Billunegie" Alias Toby Arrested for Cattle Killing', AN 5/2, Cons. 430, File 3290/1901; 'Derby – Journal of Constable Mulkerin (141) 21 June to 2 July 1901; Chatoo Alias Jimmie, Tegerowa Alias Joe, Noondae Alias Harry, Lalgoora & Diamy Arrested for Cattle Killing; Arrest of Marringa, Gowarra & Mongunger, Escapees from Derby Gaol', AN 5/2, Cons. 430, File 3374/1901; 'Derby – Journal of Constable Inglis (481) 21 June to 6 July 1901; Patrolling District', AN 5/2, Cons. 430, File 3378/1901; 'Derby – Journal of Constable Hill (517) 4 June to 23 July 1901; While in Charge of Turkey Creek Patrol; Arrest of Natives "Malnilgie" Alias Jacob & "Mallerghin" Alias Barney, Unlawful Possession of Beef; Stock of Rifle Broken through Police Horse "Harlequin" Falling', AN 5/2, Cons. 430, File 3688/1901; 'Derby – Journal of Constable Mulkerin (141) 9 November to 1 December 1901; Patrol Leopold Downs; Several Natives Arrested re Cattle Killing', AN 5/2, Cons. 430, File 0326/1902; 'Derby – Journal of Constables Turner (526) & Caldon (615) 30 October to 20 December 1901; Arrest of Natives for Cattle Killing on Coojibiu & Sturts Creek Stations', AN 5/2, Cons. 430, File 0981/1902; 'Derby – Journal of Constable Wilson (254) 19 July to 29 August 1901; On Patrol to Sturt Creek; Cattle Killing at Sturt Creek', AN 5/2, Cons. 430, File 1543/1902; 'Derby – Journal of Constable Caldon (615) 20 November 1902 to 1 January 1903; Cattle Killing of Sturt's Creek Station; Horses "Nymph" and "Josephus" Knock Up and are Left at Sturt Creek Station, "Mungolinuna", "Lunary", "Ololie", "Moolkoola" and "Gillagarra" Arrested for Cattle Killing', AN 5/2, Cons. 430, File 0987/1903; 'Derby – Journal of Constable Mulkerin (141) 20 June to 10 July 1903 – Patrol of Fossil Downs and Leopold Downs Cattle Stations; D. Oliver, Fossil Downs, Reports Natives Killing Cattle on Margaret; Natives Making for New Leopold Homestead', AN 5/2, Cons. 430, File 3037/1903; 'Derby – Journal of Constable Mulkerin (141) 21 September to 20 October 1903; Arrest of Seventeen Aboriginal Natives on Margaret Downs Station for Cattle Killing',

AN 5/2, Cons. 430, File 4172/1903; 'Derby – Journal of Constable Wilson (254) from 15.11.1904 to 7.12.1904, En Route to Leopold Station', AN 5/2, Cons. 430, File 0234/1904; 'Derby – Halls Creek – Journal of Constable Inglis (481) 17.11.1903 to 7.12.1903 – Patrolling Sturt Creek Station', AN 5/2, Cons. 430, File 0613/1904; 'Derby – Fitzroy – Journal of Constable Mulkerin (141) 7.1.1904 to 13.2.1904. Arrest of 10 Aboriginal Natives for Cattle Killing on Consendine Station Near Leopold Ranges', AN 5/2, Cons. 430, File1367/1904; 'Derby – Journal of Constable O'Neil (436) from 27.4.1904 to 19.5.1904; Arrest of Two Aborigines for Cattle Killing; Native Assistant Jack Shoots Aboriginal Native Prisoner Jumby Jumby, and Wounds Aboriginal Native Prisoner Owalalong who Escapes from Custody', AN 5/2, Cons. 430, File 2163/1904; 'Derby – Halls Creek – Journal of Constable Inglis (481) from 9.8.1904 to 27.8.1904; Arrest and Conviction of 14 Aboriginal Natives for Cattle Killing', AN 5/2, Cons. 430, File 3743/1904; 'Derby – Journal of Constable Wilson (254) and Party while in Pursuit of Native Offenders from 17.9.1904 to 6.10.1904; Arrest of 8 Aboriginal Natives for Cattle Killing', AN 5/2, Cons. 430, File 4144/1904; 'Derby – Journal of Constable Inglis (481) from 7.9.1904 to 9.9.1904, from 17.9.1904 to 20.9.1904 and from 24.9.1904 to 26.9.1904', AN 5/2, Cons. 430, File 4145/1904; 'Derby – Isdell Station – Journal of Constable Wilson (254) and Party while on Return Journey from Derby to Isdell 23.7.1904 to 30.8.1904; Death of Aboriginal Native Looligmurra at Barker Gorge Station from Natural Causes', AN 5/2, Cons. 430, File 4148/1904.

95 Aborigines Department, *Annual Report of the Aborigines Department ending 30 June 1902*, No.21, p.14.

96 'The Police Department', *The West Australian*, 14 September 1904, p.5.

97 For example for the year ending June 1902, eighty-eight Aboriginal men were convicted of cattle killing mostly from the Sturt Creek area. WAPP, 1902, vol.21, p.17; Aborigines Department, *Report of the Aborigines Department for the Period 1902*, appendix no. 3, p.17.

98 Sub-Inspector Duncan, Derby, 'Aborigines in Kimberley District', Cons. 255, File 534/1902

99 'The Nor' West Blacks', *Kalgoorlie Miner*, 31 July 1901, p.2.

100 ibid.

101 'Rottnest Island, Abolition of the Prison', *Western Mail*, 14 June 1902, p. 15.

102 WAPD, 'West Kimberley District. Broome Station. Broome Police Move into New Headquarters', SROWA, Cons. 430, File 395/1897.

103 For a vivid description of Wyndham Gaol see 'The Ways of Wyndham, How the Blacks are Treated', *The Daily News*, 21 October 1903, p.8.

104 Aborigines Department, 'Sub-Inspector Duncan, Derby. Aborigines in Kimberley District', SROWA, Cons. 255, File 534/1902.

105 An account of this practice is referred to here: 'White Savages, Rapes and Murders, Police Intimidated', *Sunday Times*, 20 April 1902, p.4.

106 See for example J. Bohemia and B. McGregor, *Nyibayarri: Kimberley Tracker*, Canberra, Aboriginal Studies Press, 1995; Bruce Shaw, *My Country of the*

Pelican Dreaming: the life of an Australian Aborigine of the Gadjerrong, Grant Ngabidj, 1904–1977, Canberra, Aboriginal Studies Press, 1981; B. Shaw, *Banggaiyerri: The Story of Jack Sullivan,* Canberra, Australian Institute of Aboriginal Studies, 1983; B. Shaw, *When the Dust Come in Between: Aboriginal viewpoints in the East Kimberley prior to 1892,* Canberra, Aboriginal Studies Press, 1992; M.A. Jebb (ed.), *Emerarra: A Man of Merarra,* Broome, Magabala Books, 1996; V. Ryan (ed.), *From Digging Sticks to Writing Sticks: stories of Kija women,* Perth, Catholic Education Office, 2001; C. Clement, *Historical Notes Relevant to Impact Stories of the East Kimberley,* East Kimberley Working Paper no. 29; Canberra, East Kimberley Impact Assessment Project, 1989, H. Ross (ed.) and E. Bray (trans.), *Impact Stories of the East Kimberley,* East Kimberley Working Paper, no. 28, Canberra, East Kimberley Impact Assessment Project 1989.

107 'The Nor' West Blacks', *Kalgoorlie Miner,* 31 July 1901, p.2.

108 Quoted in Clement, *Historical Notes Relevant to Impact Stories of the East Kimberley,* p.26.

109 WAPD, Argyle Police Station, 'Journal of PC Thomson while Investigating Shooting and Burning of Natives', 29 October 1901, SROWA, AN 5, Cons. 241/9. A more detailed account of this incident exists in C. Owen, '"The Police Appear to be a Useless Lot Up There": law and order in the East Kimberley 1884–1905', *Aboriginal History,* vol. 27, 2003, pp.105–30. See also 'Durack's are up in Arms' in 'White Savages, Rapes and Murders, Police Intimidated', *Sunday Times,* 20 April 1902, p.4.

110 WAPD, ibid., 31 October 1901.

111 ibid., 5 Nov 1901; see also WAPD, 'Alleged Murder of Two Natives by Thomas McLoughlin', SROWA, Cons. 430, AN5/2, File 1382/1905.

112 ibid.

113 P. Biskup, *Not Slaves, Not Citizens: The Aboriginal Problem in Western Australia 1898–1954,* Brisbane, University of Queensland Press, 1973, p.31.

114 WAPD, Argyle Police Station, Letterbook, 'Journal of PC Thompson whilst on Shooting Case of Two Aboriginals Named Friday and Jimmy from 15 Nov–23 December 1901', Uncatalogued police file, 16 December 1901; WAPS, Argyle Police Station, 'Journal of PC Thomson and NA Barney, Bow and Joe from 12 January 1902 to 10 February 1902', Uncatalogued police file, 30 January 1902. A later account of this incident is referred to here: 'White Savages, Rapes and Murders, Police Intimidated', *Sunday Times,* 20 April 1902, p.4.

115 WAPD, Argyle Police Station, 'Journal of PC Thomson whilst on Shooting case of Two Aborigines named Friday and Jimmy from 15 November 1901 to 23 December 1901', uncatalogued police file, 16 December 1901.

116 WAPD, Argyle Police Station, 'Journal of PC Hill from 4 December 1901 to the 21 December 1901 whilst Distributing Statistics', uncatalogued police file, 16 December 1901.

117 WAPD, Argyle Police Station, 'Journal of PC Hill and Police Assistant Barney from 23 November 1901 to 6 December 1901', uncatalogued police file, 27 November 1901.

118 WAPD, 'East Kimberley District. Wyndham Sub-district. Wyndham Station. Journal of PC Ritchie of Arrest of Aborigines Accused of Cattle Killing, December 25, 1897', 27 November 1897, Cons. 430, File 393/1898.

119 Aborigines Department, 'The Crown Versus Pompey Alias Nipper. Fee for Defending Prisoner,' SROWA, AN 1/2, Cons. 255, File 118/1898.

120 Aborigines Department, 'Statement by Osborne Ritchie', AN 1/2, Cons. 255, File 118/1898. Monday's witness statement asserted 'Durack said shoot Jacky first and then shoot Monday...I understand what Durack say.' 'I [Durack] told Nipper to tell them [Jacky and Monday] that they had no business there as they were frightening the cattle. I told him to ask if they had killed any cattle, and Nipper told me they said they had not. I got Nipper to speak to the blacks as they could not understand me. They do not understand English, therefore do not know what I told Nipper only from what Nipper said. Nipper told me the blacks said they ate Kangaroo. I told Nipper to tell them not "to come back again or else they would get shot". I told him to make them as frightened as he could, and to take them over the hill [between the homestead and Wheelbarrow Creek] where they were accustomed to be. Nipper said that he was frightened...' Aborigines Department, 'Murder of J. Durack, undated statement by J.J. Durack', SROWA, AN 1/2, Cons. 255, File 137/1901.

121 ibid.

122 WAPD, 'East Kimberley, Wyndham Police Station. "Ambush" of John Durack and Party by Natives', 14 December 1897, SROWA, AN 5, Cons. 430, File 298/1898.

123 ibid., quoted in Green, *The Forrest River Massacres*, Fremantle, p.68.

124 'The Black North, Modes of Nigger Flogging,' *West Australian Sunday Times*, 3 September 1899, p.3

125 'Brutality at Berringarra', *West Australian Sunday Times*, 3 September 1899, p.3.

126 ibid.

127 See 'Justice's Justice', ibid.

128 ibid.

129 See for example 'The Nor'-West Tragedy. The Avenging of Durack. Capital Charge Against a Boy', *The Daily News*, 8 May 1901, p.3.

130 *Western Mail*, 2 March 1901. The *Western Mail* argued 'The civilisation of the Kimberleys is the record of one long struggle between the white race and a native population who are fierce, treacherous, and untamable. The Kimberley pastoralist has veritably carried his life in his hands, and Mr Durack's death adds one more to the long list of victims of the native inhabitants of those vast expanses of territory.'

131 Aborigines Department, 'Murder of J. Durack, Minute Paper Chief Protector of Aborigines, Prinsep to Premier', 27 February 1901, AN 1/2, Cons. 255, File 137/1901.

132 See also M. Finnane, 'A Politics of Prosecution: The Conviction of Wonnerwerry and the Exoneration of Jerry Durack in Western Australia 1898', *Law in Context*, vol. 33, no. 1, 2015, pp.60–73.

133 *Western Mail,* 11 May 1901, p.34. See also Durack, *Sons in the Saddle,* p. 81.

134 *Western Mail,* 11 May 1901, p.34.

135 Aborigines Department, 'Murder of J. Durack', notes and address of trial, Regina V. Amaranga (Banjo). SROWA, AN 1/2, Cons. 255, File 137/1901.

136 'Denham River Tragedy. The Murder of Mr. J. J. Durack. Trial of Amaranga. Verdict of Not Guilty', *The West Australian,* 10 May 1901, p.2.

137 'The Nor'-West Tragedy. A Native Boy on Trial. His Defence Impresses the Jury, Who Acquit Him', *The Daily News,* 9 May 1901, p.3.

138 W.B. Kimberly (ed.), *History of West Australia, A Narrative of Her Past, Together With Biographies of Her Leading Men,* Melbourne, F.W. Niven, 1897, p.19; Correspondence 'Bishop Gibney and the Nor'-West Settlers, *The West Australian,* 14 November 1892, p.3.

139 Aborigines Department, 'RM Derby Native Matters', Cons. 255, File 0205/1903.

140 Aborigines Department, Letter RM Wace to Prinsep, 'RMs Broome and Derby. Re: Employment of Natives', SROWA, Cons. 255, File 1904/0295.

141 Witness statement by Richard Henry Wace, Resident Magistrate and District Medical Officer, Roth Report, Pt.1902. p.110.

142 Aborigines Department, *Annual Report of the Aborigines Department ending 30 June 1904,* No.20, p.5.

143 Aborigines Department, 'RMs Broome and Derby. Re: Employment of Natives', Cons. 255, File 0295/1904.

144 See for example Aborigines Department, *Annual Report of the Aborigines Department ending 30 June 1905,* No. 25, p.8.

145 Aborigines Department, *Annual Report of the Aborigines Department ending 30 June 1904,* No.20, p.3.

146 See for example 'The Criminal Code Act 1902', *Kalgoorlie Miner,* 17 April 1902, p.2.

147 Biskup, p.58.

148 Witness statement by Richard Henry Wace, Resident Magistrate and District Medical Officer, Roth Report, Pt.1936, p.112.

149 *An Act to Amend the Criminal Code 1902,* Edward VII, No. 29, Section 5. Section 32 of the *Justices Act 1902* gave power to JPs to adjudicate in the absence of an honorary magistrate if one was not within 10 miles (16 kilometres).

150 'Black Slavery in West Australia', *Barrier Miner,* 19 April 1899, p.2; 'How We Civilize – Or White On Black', *The Daily News,* 10 May 1889, p.3; 'The Treatment of Natives at the Nor'West', *The West Australian.* 29 August 1889, p.3; 'Aborigines' Protection Society. Westralian Natives', *The Mercury,* 9 April 1897, p.3; 'Treatment of W.A. Natives. Worse than Slavery', *Albany Advertiser,* 1 April 1899, p.3; 'Slavery in the North. London Press Condemnation. Too Much Hushing-Up and Smoothing-Over in W.A.', *Kalgoorlie Western Argus,* 25 May 1899, p.11; 'Slavery In Australia', *Barrier Miner,* 9 April 1904, p.2; 'The Slave State. Dr Rentoul Returns to the Charge. Abundant Proofs. Of the Malcolmson Indictment', *The Daily News,* 15 April 1904, p.7; 'Slavery In

West Australia', *Kalgoorlie Western Argus,* 26 April 1904, p.24.

151 'Aborigines' Protection Society. Westralian Natives', *The Mercury,* 9 April 1897, p.3.

152 'Slavery in the North. London Press Condemnation. Too Much Hushing-Up and Smoothing-Over in W.A.', *Kalgoorlie Western Argus,* 25 May 1899, p.11.

153 'Black Slavery in West Australia', *Barrier Miner,* 19 April 1899, p.2.

154 CSO, 'Revd J.B. Gribble – Treatment of Natives in WA., That Royal Commission be Appointed to Inquire into', 30 November 1886, SROWA, Cons. 527, File 1887/1171; see also correspondence 'Bishop Gibney and the Nor' West Settlers', *The West Australian,* 14 November 1892, p.3.

Chapter 12: 'They Must be Allowed the Wherewithal to Live'

1 T. Stannage, 'The Composition of the Western Australian Parliament: 1890–1911', *University Studies in History,* vol. IV, no. 4, 1966. These were the Leake, Stone, Lee Steere, Shenton, Lefroy and Burt families.

2 ibid., p.7.

3 'Parliament', *The West Australian,* 12 July 1901, p.2.

4 Stannage, 'The Composition of the Western Australian Parliament: 1890–1911', p.1.

5 ibid., p.13.

6 L. Hunt, 'Sir Walter Hartwell James (1863–1943), *Australian Dictionary of Biography,* Australian National University, 1983, <http://adb.anu.edu.au/biography/james-sir-walter-hartwell-6824>.

7 'Discussion in the Federal Parliament, Mr. Mahon's Motion', *Kalgoorlie Miner,* 30 July 1901, p.5.

8 'The Nor' West Blacks', *West Australian Sunday Times,* 22 September 1901, p.4; 'Treatment of Kimberley Natives, An Ex-policemen's Shocking Revelations', *Kalgoorlie Western Argus,* 6 August 1901, p.32.

9 *The Daily News,* [London], 4 December 1901, quoted in Malcolm Allbrook, *Henry Prinsep's Empire: Framing a distant colony,* Canberra, ANU Press, 2014, p.275.

10 'Nigger's of the North, Dusky Gins and Desperate Depravity', *Sunday Times,* 9 November 1902, p.5.

11 For a biography of Roth see R. McDougall and I. Davidson (eds), *The Roth Family, Anthropology, and Colonial Administration,* Publications of the Institute of Archaeology, University College London, Walnut Creek, CA, Left Coast Press, 2008.

12 Quoted in 'Slavery in Australia', *Barrier Miner,* 9 April, 1904, p.2; see also 'The Black Slaves of West Australia,' *Truth,* 6 March 1904, p.8; 'The North-West Natives and Their Treatment', *Western Mail,* 9 July 1904, p.12; 'Dr. Roth's Report. London Criticism. Mr Malcolmson Resumes the Attack', *The Daily News,*' 9 March 1905, p.7.

13 'Nor-West Horrors, A Native on the Natives, Statement by William Harris', *The Sunday Times,* 24 April 1904, p.5; see also first-hand accounts from Dr Rennie 'any amount of petty tyranny and ill-usage are practised upon

the poor-fellows, and it is a common thing for the blacks to be fastened by handcuffs or leg-iron to a chain, and nothing but a little water given to them for a day or two until they are starved into subjection.' 'Is there Slavery in Australia? Treatment of Blacks in Western Australia', *Kalgoorlie Miner*, 3 April 1903, p.6.

14 ibid.

15 'The Slave State, Dr Rentoul Returns to the Charge, Abundant Proofs of the Malcolmsen Indictment', *The Daily News*, 14 April 1904, p.1; 'Treatment of Aborigines' *The West Australian*, 14 April 1904, p.2; see also 'International Cables', *Bendigo Advertiser*, 14 April 1904, p.5; 'West Australian Blacks', *Geelong Advertiser*, 14 April 1904, p.4.

16 'Aborigines of Western Australia', *The Times*, 6 May 1904.

17 Aborigines Department, *Annual Report of the Aborigines Department ending 30 June 1904*, No. 20, pp.26–7.

18 G. Bolton, *Land of Vision and Mirage: Western Australia since 1826*, Perth, UWA Press, 2008, p.85.

19 *Roth Royal Commission on the Condition of the Natives. Presented to Both Houses of Parliament by His Excellency's Command*, Roth Report, WAPP, 1905, 2nd Session, No. 5.

20 ibid., p.5.

21 ibid., p.32.

22 Witness statement by Boondungarry and Garnulling, ibid., Pt. 1766–67, p.104.

23 Witness statement from Father Nicholas Maria Emo, Broome, ibid., Pt. 711, pp.61–3.

24 ibid., p.11. See also witness statement of Graham Blick, District Medical Officer and Acting Resident Magistrate, Broome, Pt. 770. p.64; Witness statement by Richard Henry Wace, Resident Magistrate and District Medical Officer, Pt. 1968, p.114.

25 Witness statement by PC Bertram Kuhlman (Fletcher), ibid., Pt. 1283, p.86.

26 ibid., p.44.

27 Witness statement by Octavius Burt, Sheriff and Controller General of Prisons, ibid., Pt. 241, p.44.

28 ibid., p.21.

29 Witness statement by Alfred Earnest Victor Woodroffe, Branch Manager Adelaide Streamship late of Wyndham, ibid., p.85. Referring to this case 'White Savages, Rapes and Murders. Police Intimidated', *Sunday Times*, 20 April 1902, p.4.

30 Roth Report, Pt. 1657, p.99.

31 ibid., Witness statement by Dodwell Brown, Resident Magistrate and District Medical Officer, Wyndham, Pt. 1667, p.99.

32 'The Aborigines Question, Testimony by PC Fletcher to Walter Roth', *The West Australian*, 15 February 1905, p.2; see also Testimony by PC Inglis, Roth Report, pt. 1352, p.88.

33 'The Treatment Of Natives At Derby', *The West Australian*, 9 August 1894, p.3.

34 Constable Wilson was said to receive this amount between March 1900 and October 1903, Roth Report, p.13.
35 ibid., p.100.
36 WAPD,'Witness Statement from Corporal W. Goodridge (112) Regarding Allegations He Made in Roth Commission Report. Wyndham East Kimberley', 24 May 1905, SROWA, Cons. 430, File 540/1905.
37 Roth Report, pp.88–95.
38 See for example ibid., Witness Statement of Graham Blick, District Medical Officer and Acting Resident Magistrate, Broome, p.64.
39 Witness statement by William Lappin, Sub Inspector Police, Roebourne, ibid., Pt 1092, p.78.
40 See for example witness statement by John Byrne, Sergeant of Police, Broome, ibid., p.59.
41 Witness statement by Mathew John Langtree, ibid., p.81.
42 ibid.
43 ibid., p.104. Evidence was taken by Commission Secretary Mr Hartrick.
44 ibid., p.105.
45 P. Hasluck, *Black Australians: a Survey of Native Policy in Western Australia, 1829–1897*, Melbourne, Melbourne University Press, 1942, p.143.
46 Roth Report, p.60.
47 Hansard, HL Deb, *The Natives of Western Australia*, vol. 145, 9 May 1905, <http://hansard.millbanksystems.com/lords/1905/may/09/the-natives-of-western-australia#column_1315>.
48 Roth Report, p.27.
49 ibid., p.28.
50 ibid.
51 Witness statement by Henry Prinsep, Chief Protector of Aborigines, ibid., p.12.
52 The Treatment of Aboriginal Prisoners, ibid., p.13.
53 ibid., p.16.
54 Witness statement by Henry Charles Prinsep, Chief Protector of Aborigines, ibid., Pt. 177, p.41. Prinsep gave the figures of sixty-one and thirty-four for the years 1903 and 1904 respectively.
55 ibid., p.17.
56 ibid.
57 ibid., pp.13–21.
58 ibid., p.18.
59 ibid.
60 ibid.
61 See for example 'The Aborigines Question. The Investigations by Dr. Roth. A Comprehensive Report. Drunkenness, Disease, and Crime. Important Recommendations', *The West Australian,* 30 January 1905, p.7; 'The Aborigines Question. Evidence Taken by Dr. Roth. Testimony of Three Important Witnesses. The Indenture System. Defects of the Present Law', *The West Australian,* 10 February 1905, p.2; 'The Aborigines Question. Evidence

Taken by Dr. Roth. The Testimony of Important Witnesses. Treatment of the Natives. Police Methods in the Kimberley District. The Commissioner of Police Suspended', *Western Mail*, 25 February 1905, p.12; 'Blacks Brutally Treated. Western Australian Sensation. Report of a Commissioner. Horrible Cases of Cruelty. Blacks Half-Starved. And Terrorised Over', *The Sydney Morning Herald*, 1 February 1905, p.6; 'Western Australian Natives. Report by the Commissioner of Police. Dr Roth Criticized', *The Advertiser*, 12 August 1905, p.8; 'Dr. Roth's Disclosures. Council of Churches. Horror-Stricken and Sorrowful', *The Daily News*, 15 February 1905, p.5; 'Westralian Natives', *Zeehan and Dundas Herald*, Tasmania, 7 February 1905, p.3; 'Western Australia', *The Brisbane Courier*, 27 February 1905, p.4; 'Congo Cruelties Paralleled. Dr. Roth Demolishes the System. The "Sunday Times" Strictures Authoritatively Endorsed. "The slave state" – isn't it justified?' *The Sunday Times*, 5 February 1905, p.5.

62 'The Aborigines Question', *The West Australian*, 7 February 1905, p.6.

63 ibid.

64 'The Native Question, Dr. Roth's Report Discussed at Public Meeting', *The West Australian*, 25 February 1905, p.9; 'Dr. Roth's Report, Public Meeting at Fremantle', *Western Mail*, 18 March 1905, p.12.

65 'The Native Question, Dr. Roth's Report Discussed at Public Meeting', *The West Australian*, 25 February 1905, p.9.

66 ibid.

67 ibid.

68 ibid.

69 'Western Australian Natives. Dr. Roth's Report. Discussed in the House Of Lords', *The Sydney Morning Herald*, 11 May 1905, p.5. See Hansard, HL Deb, *The Natives of Western Australia*, vol. 145, 9 May 1905, <http://hansard.millbanksystems.com/lords/1905/may/09/the-natives-of-western-australia#column_1309>.

70 'The Aborigines Question. Dr. Roth's report. Interview with Sir John Forrest. The Difficulty of the Native Question. The Police Defended,' *West Australian*, 4 February 1905, p.7.

71 ibid., Forrest went on to say 'I have seen the police under all conditions in Western Australia – in the newly-found goldfields, where everything was very unsettled and uncomfortable, and where often there was considerable dissipation. I have seen them in the isolated portions of Western Australia, on the out skirts of civilisation, and I have seen them in the towns and in the more settled districts and I have always found them well-disciplined, obliging, and attentive to their duties, and I think it is to be regretted that Dr. Roth, without any experience really of the police of Western Australia, should say anything to their discredit, unless upon the surest and safest evidence.'

72 'Dr Roth's Condemnation of Police Methods, Reply by the Commissioner of Police', *Western Mail*, 4 February 1905, p.19; 'Western Australian Natives. Report by the Commissioner of Police. Dr Roth Criticized', *The Advertiser*, 12 August 1905, p.8; for opinion of Hare see 'Commissioner Hare', *West*

Australian Sunday Times, 8 April 1900, p.4.

73 'The Aborigines Question. The "Riff Raff" Witnesses', *The Daily News*, 9 February 1905, p.9.

74 See 'Captain Hare Reinstated. He Expresses Sincere Regret and Apologises', *The Daily News*, 28 February 1905, p.2; and 'West Australian Blacks. Dr Roth's Report. Captain Hare's Apology', *The Argus*, 1 March 1905, p.8.

75 'The Native Trouble. Captain Hare's Trip to the North-West. Comments on Dr. Roth's Report. "Unfounded Charges." Some Suggestions', *The West Australian*, 11 August 1905, pp.5–6.

76 ibid.

77 'Aborigines of the Nor'-West,' *The Daily News*, 1 February 1905, p.11.

78 'The Fury of Nigger-chainer Fred', *Sunday Times*, 13 August 1905, p.4.

79 'The Treatment of Natives, Address by Dr Klaatsch', *The West Australian*, 11 January 1907, p.5.

80 H. Klaatsch, *Some Notes on Scientific Travel Amongst the Black Population of Tropical Australia in 1904, 1905, 1906*, Adelaide, Australasian Association for the Advancement of Science, 1907, p.583.

81 'Report to the Colonial Secretary by P. Troy, Warden, Murchison Goldfield Following his Trip to the West Kimberley District to Investigate Charges of Rape and Murder of Aborigines Against Local Police', SROWA, 30 May 1905, Cons. 481, File 1243.

82 ibid., p.6.

83 ibid. p.11.

84 ibid.

85 ibid.

86 Hansard, HL Deb, *The Natives of Western Australia*, vol. 145, 9 May 1905, <http://hansard.millbanksystems.com/lords/1905/may/09/the-natives-of-western-australia#S4V0145P0_19050509_HOL_171>.

87 WAPD, 'Commissioner – Arrest of Native Offenders, Suggested Alteration in Mode of Arrest of – to be Charged with Unlawful Possession of Beef and not with Cattle Killing – Number of Witnesses not to Exceed Two – Constable to Certify on Oath as to Rations Supplied', SROWA, AN 5/2, Cons. 430, File 1012/1905.

88 'The Native Question, New Regulations, Use of Neck Chains Prohibited', *Western Mail*, 20 May 1905, p.71.

89 Hansard, HL Deb, *The Natives of Western Australia*, vol. 145, 9 May 1905, <http://hansard.millbanksystems.com/lords/1905/may/09/the-natives-of-western-australia#column_1311>.

90 Roth Report, p.31.

91 Witness statement by Richard Henry Wace, Resident Magistrate and District Medical Officer, ibid., Pt.1938, p.113.

92 R.E. McGregor, 'Answering the Native Question': the dispossession of the Aborigines of the Fitzroy District, West Kimberley, 1880–1905', Honours thesis, James Cook University, 1985, p.148.

93 Aborigines Department, 'Report by Acting Sub Inspector McCarthy' in

Annual Report of the Aborigines Department Ending 30 June 1906, No.29, p.16.

94 ibid.

95 ibid.

96 ibid.

97 ibid., p.14.

98 'The Kimberley Police District', *The West Australian*. 12 September 1902, p.6.

Postscript

1   'Francis Connor', *Kalgoorlie Western Argus*, 29 August 1916, p.29, <http://oa.anu.edu.au/obituary/connor-francis-frank-240>.

2   Aborigines Department, *Annual Report of the Aborigines Department Ending 30 June 1905*, No. 25, 1905, p.5.

3   ibid., p.11.

4   Aborigines Department, *Annual Report of the Aborigines Department Ending 30 June 1906*, No. 29, p.15.

5   'Our Black Brother, Treatment of Natives in Western Australia, *Northern Times*, 13 July 1907, p.3.

6   'The Wild Nor'West, The Conflict with the Natives, Police Officer Speared', *Western Mail*, 4 August 1906, p.43.

7   B. Shaw, 'Is the Pen Mightier than the Word?: a comparison between oral and written sources on the East Kimberley bushranger Major', Perth, Curtin Indigenous Research Centre, 1998; 'Natives Attack Police Party, Notorious Aboriginal Shot', *The West Australian*, 4 October 1910, p.9.

8   WAPD, 'Aboriginal Native "Billy" Shot by W.M. Skinner 13.3.1915. From Broome', SROWA, Cons. 430, File 1903/1915; WAPD, 'Alleged Shooting of Natives by Police at Wyndham. From Chief Protector Aborigines', SROWA, Cons. 430, File 1819/1917; WAPD, 'Re Alleged Shotting [sic] of Natives by Bert Smith at Derby', SROWA, Cons. 430, File 4533/1929; WAPD, 'Two Natives Employed by E.A. Sherwin at Napier Downs Station Murdered by Bush Natives. From Broome', SROWA, Cons. 430, File 1168/1916.

9   G.C. Bolton, 'The Kimberley Pastoral Industry', *University Studies in History and Economics*, vol. 11, no. 2, 1954, p.27.

10 ibid., p.24.

11 ibid.

12 *Mira Canning Stock Route Project Archive*, 'Royal Commission', 2013, <http://mira.canningstockrouteproject.com/tags/royal-commission>.

13 P. Bianchi, (ed.), *Canning Stock Route Royal Commission: Royal Commission to inquire into the Treatment of Natives by the Canning Exploration Party 15 January – 5 February 1908*, Perth, Hesperian Press, 2010, pp. xiv-xv.

14 'Royal Commission appointed to inquire into certain charges made by one E. J. Blake of ill-treatment of Aboriginal natives by the Canning Exploration Party', WAGG, 13 December 1907, No.64, p.4012.

15 'Treatment of Natives, Charges against the Canning Expedition, Inquiry by Royal Commission', The *West Australian*, 30 January, 1908, p.2.

16 *Canning Stock Route Project*, http://mira.canningstockrouteproject.com/tags/

royal-commission

17   'Native Lock Hospitals', *The West Australian*, 2 July 1910, p.9.

18   D.M. Bates, *My Natives and I: Incorporating the passing of the Aborigines: A lifetime spent among the natives of Australia*, P.J. Bridge (ed.), Perth, Hesperian Press, 2004, p.103.

19   M.A. Jebb, 'The Lock Hospitals Experiment: Europeans, Aborigines and venereal disease', in R. Reece and T. Stannage (eds), *Studies in Western Australian History: European-Aboriginal Relations in Western Australian History*, vol. 8, 1984, pp.68–86.

20   Aborigines Department, *Report of the Chief Protector of Aborigines for Year Ending 30 June 1909*, No. 25, 1909, p.10. Isdell reasoned that once Aboriginal people from different parts of the Kimberley went to gaol they became 'friends' and when they returned to their *country* 'become less inclined to carry on their old time feuds and disputes'. Cattle killing was, Isdell postulated, 'taking the place of tribal fights'.

21   Aborigines Department, *Report of the Chief Protector of Aborigines for Year Ending 30 June 1910*, No. 34, 1911, p.4.

22   H. Rumley and S. Toussaint, 'For Their Own Benefit?': a critical overview of Aboriginal policy and practice at Moola Bulla, East Kimberley, 1910–1955', *Aboriginal History*, vol. 14, No. 1, 1990, pp.80–103.

23   P. Biskup, *Not Slaves, Not Citizens: The Aboriginal Problem in Western Australia 1898–1954*, Brisbane, University of Queensland Press, 1973, p.99.

24   Aborigines Department, 'Extract on the Work of the Report of the Aborigines Department for the Year Ended 30 June, 1911', no. 8, p.7.

25   'Treatment of Aborigines', *The Kalgoorlie Miner*, 12 May 1913, p.4.

26   'North-West Natives, Gaoling of Natives a Failure', *The West Australian*, 5 May 1913, p.5.

27   ibid.

28   Aborigines Department, *Annual reports of the Aborigines Department for years ending 30 June 1914*, SROWA, Cons. 388, File 37, p.6.

29   A. Haebich, *Broken Circles, Fragmenting Indigenous Families 1800–2000*, Fremantle, Fremantle Arts Centre Press, 2000, pp.258–9.

30   ibid.

31   'Four Pence a Year Spent on our Aborigines', *Truth*, 1 April 1928, p.16.

32   'Natives in the North, The Spearing of Cattle, Stringent Measures Urged', *The West Australian*, 29 December 1907, p.3. *The West Australian*, 11 October 1917, p.1.

33   *Report of the Royal Commission to Inquire into and Report upon the Meat Supply*, WAGG No. 45, 21 August 1908.

34   ibid., p.44.

35   See 'No Intention of Legitimate stocking'. 'The Northern Territory, Neglected Australia, Commercial and Political Aspects', *Western Mail*, 16 March 1907, p.19.

36   *Report of the Royal Commission to Inquire into and Report upon the Meat Supply*, WAGG No. 45, 21 August 1908, p.44.

37 G.C. Bolton, 'Michael Patrick Durack', *Australian Dictionary of Biography*, Australian National University, 1981, <http://adb.anu.edu.au/biography/durack-michael-patrick-6062>.

38 'The Warlike Natives near Derby, Report Much Exaggerated', *The West Australian*, 24 February 1910, p.8.

39 WAPD, 'Inspector Douglas to Commissioner of Police', 3 August 1925, SROWA, Cons. 430. Item 1347/1925.

40 *The West Australian*, 11 October 1917, p.1.

41 M. Jebb, *Blood, Sweat and Welfare: a history of white bosses and Aboriginal pastoral workers*, Perth, UWA Press, 2002, p.97.

42 ibid., p.71.

43 C. Clement, *Historical Notes Relevant to Impact Stories of the East Kimberley*, Canberra, East Kimberley Impact Assessment Project, 1989, p.21.

44 'The Meat Commission', *Western Mail*, 3 October 1908. p.14.

45 R.H. Pilmer, *Northern Patrol: an Australian saga*, Perth, C. Clement and P. Bridge (eds), Hesperian Press, 1998, pp.131, 141.

46 Y.E. Coate and K.H. Coate, *Lonely graves of Western Australia & burials at sea*. Perth, Hesperian Press, 1986, p.162.

47 'Pilmers Pilgrimage', *The Southern Cross Times*, 16 September 1911, p.2. See also 'The Nigger hunting Expedition', *Leonora Miner*, 23 September 1911, p.2. The writer went on to say: 'It is almost certain that some of the gasbags who enter politics will make political capital out of anything that Pilmer may do or leave undone. If he comes back and reports having shot a dozen or two blacks, the goody stay at home crowd will be displeased; if he finds that the tribe have got away beyond his reach, or dispersed in such a way as to make suitable punishment impossible, the leader will be censured by those who have never been more than a mile or two from a railway station. But, whatever happens, those bucks will have to be taught a lesson, for the Canning stock route was opened up at great cost, and must be kept free from dangerous blacks.' See also Pilmer, *Northern Patrol*, p.131.

48 'Return of Sergeant Pilmer, Punitive Expedition Successful', *The Southern Cross Times*, 10 February 1912, p.3.

49 Pilmer, *Northern Patrol*, p.150.

50 ibid., p.x.

51 'Police Sensation, Commissioner Hare Shot', *Daily News*, 23 April 1907, p.3.

52 P. Conole, *Protect and Serve: a history of the Western Australian police service*, Perth, Access Press, 2002, pp.149–51.

53 ibid., p.184.

54 'Death of Warden P. Troy. Long and Honorable Public Career', *Western Mail*, 21 July 1916, p.2.

55 Conole, *Protect and Serve*, p.179.

56 ibid., p. 131; 'Major Craven H. Ord, an Adventurous Career', *Western Mail*, 17 July 1909, p.15.

57 WAPD, 'Report of Inspector Drewry to Commissioner of Police', SROWA, Cons. 430, File 4335/1915, quoted in Conole, *Protect and Serve*, p.184.

58   ibid.

59   'Police Inspector's Death', *The Daily News*, 6 May 1920, p.7.

60   N. Green, *The Forrest River Massacres*, Fremantle, Fremantle Arts Centre Press, 1995; Jebb, *Blood, Sweat and Welfare.*

61   For Mistake Creek see WAPD, 'Aboriginal Native Tracker "Nipper". From C. of P.' SROWA, Cons. 430, Item 1854/1915. H. Ross (ed.) and E. Bray (trans.), *Impact Stories of the East Kimberley,* East Kimberley Working Paper no. 28, Canberra, East Kimberley Impact Assessment Project, 1989, pp.73–5; see also 'Sensational Charges, Broome Police Report, Natives Shot and Burnt', *Western Mail*, 2 April 1915, p.18.

62   See also 'Murderous Natives, Victims Shot and Burnt', *The Advertiser*, 2 April 1915, p.8.

63   WAPD, 'Aboriginal Native Tracker "Nipper". From C. of P.' SROWA, AN 5/2, Cons. 430, File 1854/1915.

64   See 'Sensational Charges', *The West Australian,* 1 April 1915, p.7; C. Clement, 'National Museum of Australia Review of Exhibitions and Public Programs Submission', <http://www.nma.gov.au/__data/assets/pdf_file/0015/2409/Dr_Clement.pdf>.

65   Clement, *Historical Notes Relevant to Impact Stories of the East Kimberley*, pp.16–17, citing K. Willey, *Boss Drover*, Adelaide, Rigby Books, 1971, pp.15–16.

66   See also P. Smith, *Mistake Creek Massacre Site,* <https://www.flinders.edu.au/ehl/archaeology/research-profile/current-projects/kimberley-frontier-archaeology-project/mistake-creek-massacre-site.cfm>.

67   Jebb, *Blood, Sweat and Welfare,* pp.121–2.

68   ibid.

69   P. Marshall (ed.), *Raparapa Kularr Martuwarra: Stories from the Fitzroy River Drovers*, Broome, Magabala Books, 1988, p.226.

70   *Whispering in Our Hearts: the Mowla Bluff massacre,* dir. M. Torres, [videorecording] Australian Film Finance Corporation, 2002.

71   Marshall (ed.), *Raparapa Kularr Martuwarra*, p.268.

72   WAPD, 'Statement by Lightberi Alias Kitty', SROWA, Cons. 430, File 7871/1921, quoted in Green, *The Forrest River Massacres,* p.75.

73   WAPD, 'Gribble to Chief Protector of Aborigines', SROWA, Cons. 430, File 7871/1921. See also Department of the North West, 'From Rev. Gribble: Re alleged shooting of natives by Police boys, "Quartpot" and "Long Billy", near Durack River', SROWA, Cons. 653, File 655/1922.

74   'End of Man-Hunt, Wild Native Killed', *Western Argus*, 30 October 1923, p.27; WAPD, 'Shooting of Native "Willie" and other Natives by Police Trackers in Charge of Constable Flinders', SROWA, Cons. 653, File 103/1924; WAPD, 'Alleged Cruelty to Natives by Constable J.F. Flinders, Hall's Creek', SROWA, Cons. 430, File 46/1924.

75   Quoted in Green, *The Forrest River Massacres,* p.81.

76   For Bedford Downs see Clement, *Historical Notes Relevant to Impact Stories of the East Kimberley';* V. Ryan (ed.), *From Digging Sticks to Writing Sicks: Stories of Kija Women*, Perth, Catholic Education Office, 2001, pp.63, 65–8; Kimberley

Language Resource Centre, *Moola Bulla: in the shadow of the mountain,* Broome, Magabala Books, 1996, pp. 101–9. For Carey reference see Clement, 'National Museum of Australia Review of Exhibitions and Public Programs Submission', <http://www.nma.gov.au/__data/assets/pdf_file/0015/2409/Dr_Clement.pdf>, p.8.

77 Ryan (ed.), *From Digging Sticks to Writing Sticks,* p.67.

78 G.T. Wood, *Royal Commission of Inquiry into Alleged Killing and Burning of Bodies of Aborigines in East Kimberley and into Police Methods when Effecting Arrests,* Perth, Government Printer, 1927, <http://nla.gov.au/nla.obj-52781180/view> for examples of national coverage see 'An Astonishing Story of Wholesale Slaughter of Natives', *Sunday Times,* 13 March 1927, p.18; 'Murder of a Native, Forrest River Mission', *The Advertiser,* 16 July 1928, p.13; 'Massacre, Missionaries Allegations', *The Sydney Morning Herald,* 8 March 1927, p.11; 'Starling Charges, Natives Slaughtered', *The Brisbane Courier,* 9 March 1927, p.15.

79 Green, *The Forrest River Massacres.*

80 ibid., p.157.

81 Wood, *Royal Commission of Inquiry into Alleged Killing and Burning of Bodies of Aborigines in East Kimberley and into Police Methods when Effecting Arrests,* p.iv.

82 'Station Tragedy, Murder of Hay', *The Daily News,* 8 July 1926, p.4.

83 ibid., p.203. For a discussion on this figure see G.C. Bolton, 'Reflections on Oombulgurri', in C. Clement (ed.), 'Ethics and the Practice of History', *Studies in Western Australian History,* no. 26, 2010, pp.176–90; see also Green, 'Dilemmas, Dramas and Damnation in Contested History'.

84 Testimony of Inspector Douglas, in Wood, *Royal Commission of Inquiry into Alleged Killing and Burning of Bodies of Aborigines in East Kimberley* p.67.

85 ibid., p.x.

86 ibid., p.5.

87 ibid.

88 ibid., p.vi.

89 ibid.

90 ibid., p.vi; See also 'Startling Revelations in N.W. Enquiry, Inspector Douglas Reports to Police Commissioner', *The Daily News,* 5 May 1927, p.2.

91 Wood, *Royal Commission of Inquiry into Alleged Killing and Burning of Bodies of Aborigines in East Kimberley,* pp.vi–xv; see also 'Startling Revelations in N.W. Inquiry, Am Satisfied that 16 Natives were Burned', *The Daily News,* 5 May 1927, p.2.

92 See Green, *The Forrest River Massacres,* p.197.

93 ibid., p.219.

94 For a forensic examination of the familial links between the Europeans who participated in the punitive expedition and who also served in World War I, see K. Auty, 'Patrick Bernard O'Leary and the Forrest River Massacres, Western Australia: examining "Wodgil" and the significance of 8 June 1926', *Aboriginal History,* vol. 28, 2004, pp.122–55.

95 ibid., p.223.

96 Wood, *Royal Commission of Inquiry into Alleged Killing and Burning of Bodies of Aborigines*, pp.xiv, 71.

97 ibid., p.20.

98 ibid., p.71–3.

99 Biskup, 1973, *Not Slaves, Not Citizens*, p.160.

100 A. Haebich, *For Their Own Good: Aborigines and government in the Southwest of Western Australia, 1900–1940*, Nedlands, UWA Press, 1988, pp.270-1.

101 *Sunday Times*, 14 November, 1926, quoted in Biskup, p. 160.

102 ibid.

103 William Harris, 'Natives' worst enemy, Chief Protector Attacked, Abos. wait on Premier', *The Daily News*, 9 March 1928, p.1. The other members were Edward Harris, Norman Harris, Arthur Kickett, Edward Jacobs, Wilfred Morrison and William Bodney.

104 P. Biskup, *Not Slaves, Not Citizens*, p.160.

105 See Haebich, *For Their Own Good*, pp.278–283.

106 R. McGregor, '"Breed out the colour" or the importance of being white', *Australian Historical Studies*, vol. 33, no. 120, p.286.

107 This policy is explained in A.O. Neville, *Australia's Coloured Minority: Its Place in the Community*, Sydney, Currawong Publishing Co., 1947.

108 *Aborigines Act Amendment Act 1936 ('Native Administration Act 1936')*.

109 ibid., see section 8.

110 ibid., see sections 12, 37–41.

111 P. Hasluck, *Black Australians: a Survey of Native Policy in Western Australia, 1829–1897*, Melbourne, Melbourne University Press, 1942, p.161.

112 H.D. Moseley, *Report of the Royal Commissioner Appointed to Investigate, Report, and Advise upon Matters in Relation to the Condition and Treatment of Aborigines*, Perth, Government Printer, 1934.

113 Jebb, *Blood, Sweat and Welfare*, pp.153–4.

114 ibid., p.23.

115 ibid.

116 Department of Native Welfare, *Annual Report of the Commissioner for Native Welfare for the Year Ended 30 June 1955*, Perth, Government Printer, 1955, p.12.

117 Department of Native Welfare, *Annual Report of the Commissioner for Native Welfare for the Year Ended 30 June 1956*, Perth, Government Printer, 1956, p.51.

118 'Natives Forced to Quit W.A. Station', *The Age*, 4 July 1955, p.3.

119 WAPD, 'Aboriginals – General Permit to Commissioner of Police to Employ Native Assistant. Re Native Trackers Carrying Firearms', SROWA, Cons. 430, File 395/1938.

120 See also 'Rev. E. R. Gribble – Alleged Shooting of Natives by Wyndham Police Trackers when out Effecting Loombier's [sic Lumbia] Arrest', SROWA, Cons. 993, File 437/1926; 'Department of Native Affairs. Native Killing in the Kimberleys and Nullagine. Inquiry', SROWA, Cons. 430, File 1215/1943; 'Department of Native Affairs. Inquiry re Killing of a Native and Wounding of other Natives by Police Trackers in Drysdale River Area', SROWA, Cons. 430, File 3906/1944.

121 In one case Frank and Menmuir were investigated when, after being unsupervised, they killed one young boy named Orongo and broke another boy's arm when they fired at the boys as they fled in a canoe in the Drysdale River. The verdict after the investigation was 'accidental death'. 'Department of Native Affairs. Inquiry re Killing of a Native and Wounding of other Natives by Police Trackers in Drysdale River Area', SROWA, Cons. 430, File 3906/1944.

122 Police, *An Act to amend the Police Act 1892 (No. 18 of 1975)*.

123 'Blacktrackers Should Not be Armed', *The Daily News*, 6 May 1927, p.1.

124 Neck chains were reinstated in the Northern Territory shortly after.

125 'Aborigines "in Chains" in this State', *The West Australian*, 26 October 1949, p.8; 'Natives in Chains, Barbarity in WA', *Kalgoorlie Miner*, 25 October 1949, p.4.

126 'Chaining of WA Natives Confirmed', *Tribune*, 9 November 1949, p.8.

127 S. Hawke and M. Gallagher, *Noonkanbah: whose land, whose law*, Fremantle, Fremantle Arts Centre Press, 1989, p.59.

128 WAPD, 'Kimberley Districts – Replacement of Horse Plants with Motor Vehicles', SROWA, Cons. 430, File 903/1955.

129 'Chaining of WA Natives Confirmed', *Tribune*, 9 November 1949, p.8.

130 S. Hawke, *A Town Is Born: the Fitzroy Crossing story*, Broome, Magabala Books, 2013, p.121.

131 'Native Act Punitive and Outmoded', *The West Australian*, 12 November 1953, p.6.

132 *Native Welfare Act 1954*. (3 Eliz. II No. 64)

133 M.A. Jebb, *Blood, Sweat and Welfare: a history of white bosses and Aboriginal pastoral workers*, Nedlands, UWA Press, 2002, p.242.

134 134 'Native matters - Fitzroy Crossing', Report from H.R. Tilbrook, District Welfare Officer, Northern, Derby to Commissioner of Native Welfare, Perth. 23 March 1961, SROWA, Cons. 993, File 972/1944.

135 *Constitution Alteration (Aboriginals)* (No. 55, 1967).

136 *Aboriginal Affairs Planning Authority Act (AAPA Act)* (024 of 1972), p.1.

137 *Aboriginal Land Rights (Northern Territory) Act 1976*.

138 See Hawke and Gallagher, *Noonkanbah*.

139 ibid.

140 ibid.

141 D. Ritter, 'The Fulcrum of Noonkanbah', *Journal of Australian Studies*, vol. 26, issue 75, 2002, p.52.

142 ibid.

143 'Noonkanbah, Mass arrests likely', *The Canberra Times*, 6 July 1980, p.3; 'Outside Noonkanbah, Convoy arrives to AWU ban on oil-rig work', *The Canberra Times*, 13 August 1980, p.1; 'Dispute over Land Control,' *The Canberra Times*, 17 September 1980, p.3.

144 S. Hawke, 'Bieundurry Jimmy (1938–1985)', *Australian Dictionary of Biography*, Australian National University, < http://ia.anu.edu.au/biography/bieundurry-jimmy-12208>; 'New Era after UN', *The Canberra Times*, 14

November 1980, p.9.

145 T. Stephens, Bridge, Ernest Francis (Ernie) (1936–2013), *Obituaries Australia*, Australian National University, <http://oa.anu.edu.au/obituary/bridge-ernest-francis-ernie-16400>.

146 R.T. Libby, *Hawke's Law: The Politics of Mining and Aboriginal Land Rights in Australia*, Perth, UWAP, 1990, p.10.

147 M.W. Hunt, 'Aboriginal Land Rights in Western Australia', *Australian Mining and Petroleum Law Journal*, vol. 30, 1985, p.456.

148 P. Seaman, *The Aboriginal Land Inquiry*, Perth, Government Printer, 1984.

149 Hunt, 'Aboriginal Land Rights in Western Australia', p.456.

150 ibid., p.459.

151 Libby, *Hawke's Law*, p.85.

152 ibid., p.7.

153 W.S. Arthur, 'Funding allocations to Aboriginal people, the Western Australia case', Canberra, Centre for Aboriginal Economic Policy Research, Australian National University, 1991, p.2.

154 These rights include: the right to enter and remain on the land and water, to camp and erect shelters, take and use natural resources, engage in ritual and ceremony and to access, care for, maintain and protect areas of significance. National Native Title Tribunal, 'Extract from the National Native Title Register: Cox on behalf of the Yungngora People v State of Western Australia', 27 April 2007, <http://www.nntt.gov.au/searchRegApps/NativeTitleRegisters/NNTR%20Extracts/WCD2007_002/NNTR Extract_WCD2007_002.pdf>.

155 Reconciliation Australia, 'About', <https://www.reconciliation.org.au/about/>.

156 P. Karvelas, 'Closing the Gap: how are we getting it so wrong?', *The Drum*, 11 February 2015, <http://www.abc.net.au/news/2015-02-11/karvelas-closing-the-gap-how-are-we-getting-it-so-wrong/6086018>; M. Edwards, 'NATSISS results show Australia long way off closing the gap, Indigenous leader says', *ABC News*, 29 April 2016, <http://www.abc.net.au/news/2016-04-29/indigenous-community-still-faces-racial-discrimination/7369800>.

157 C. Hamlyn, 'Young Aboriginal people consider jail a rite of passage, WA Chief Justice says', *ABC News*, 4 August 2015, <http://www.abc.net.au/news/2015-08-04/aboriginal-kids-see-detention-rite-of-passage-wayne-martin-says/6672462>.

158 ABC, 'Fact Check: Amnesty International claim on "shocking" Indigenous child incarceration rates checks out', <http://www.abc.net.au/news/2015-06-17/fact-check-indigenous-children-incarceration-rates/6511162>.

159 ibid.

BIBLIOGRAPHY

Primary Source Material – State Records Office of Western Australia (SROWA)
Police Records

Western Australian Police Department, 'Early Police Department Files', AN 5/6, 1858–1920, Cons. 129.

Western Australian Police Department, 'General Functional Files 1885–1898' [files in this series extend past 1907], AN 5 [1885], AN 5/1 [1886–1904], AN 5/2 [1904–], Cons. 430.

Western Australian Police Department (WAPD), Police Occurrence Books, Duty Books, Circular Orders and Letterbooks 1880–1905, AN 5.

- Argyle Police Station, Letterbooks [uncatalogued, Property of Western Australian Police Service].
- Cossack Police Station, Letterbooks, Report Books and Journals, Cons. 366.
- Denham River Police Station, Occurrence Books, Cons. 739.
- Derby Police Station, Cons. 738/1–20, Occurrence Books; Cons. 738/21–24, Letterbooks.
- Fletcher Creek Police Station, Occurrence Books, Cons. 740.
- Halls Creek Police Station (including Elvire Station), Occurrence Books, Report Books and Journals, Cons. 1422/1–6.
- Isdell Police Station, Journals, Cons. 1588.
- Kimberley Police Station, Letterbooks, Report Books and Journals, Cons. 241/1–9.
- Lennard River Police Station, Occurrence Books and Letterbooks, Cons. 746.
- Robinson River Police Station, Occurrence Books, Report Books and Journals, Cons. 737.
- Wyndham Police Station, Occurrence Books, Report Books and Journals, Cons. 741/1–27.

Western Australian Police Force Applications 1863–1893, Cons. 949.

Rules and Regulations for the Government and Guidance of the Police Force of Western Australia as Approved by John Forrest, Perth, Sands and McDougall 1898.

Colonial Secretary Records

Files of the Colonial Secretary's Office (CSO), 1883–1900, AN 24: Inward Correspondence, Cons. 527; Outward Correspondence, Cons. 488.

'Conditions for Land Grants at Swan River', *Historical Records of Australia*, Series 111, vol. vi, 5 December 1828, Colonial Office.

'Governor's Confidential Despatches', Governor Weld to Secretary of State Colonial office, London, March, entry 1, 1873, Cons. 390, WAS 1174, Item 47, vol. 1, 1869–1885.

Records Relating to Aboriginal People

Aborigines Protection Board, Correspondence, Reports and Files, 1892–1898, Cons. 495.

Aborigines Department, Files 1898–1905, Cons. 255.

General File Series, Chief Protector of Aborigines, 1898–1908, AN 1.

Aborigines Protection Board, Minutes, Reports and Correspondence, 1887–1897, AN 1.

Rottnest Prison Commitment Book, 1886–1900, AN 358.

Unpublished Private Manuscripts – Battye Library (BL)

R. Allen, 'Reminiscences', manuscript BL no. 448A.

J.G. Brockman, *Journal of an Exploring Trip from Beagle Bay to the Fitzroy River and Back Again, December 4 1879 to January 10 1880*, BL no. 384A.

H. Cornish, *The Call of the Kimberleys, Pioneering in 1880*, BL no. 312A.

G.B. Hales, *Letters Written from the Kimberley Goldfields 1886*, Cons. 688.

O.L. Jones, Papers, 1872–1933, *Details of Service with WA Police Force 1872–1884*, Cons. 2461A.

D. Moore, *Memoirs*, Private Manuscript, BL, Cons. 3829A, MN 1237.

P.C. Phillips, *Notebook*, 1902, kept at Roebourne Police Station, Cons. 861A.

R.H. Pilmer, *Men's Work, an Australian Saga, 1937–1941*, Papers of Richard Henry Pilmer, BL, Cons. 4774A, MN 1509.

J. Sweeny, *Diaries, 1886–1888*, Cons. 3083A.

W. H. Timperley, *Papers, 1867–1966*, Cons. 788A, 2892A, 4959A, 4974A, 4975A.

P.B. Watts, *Notebook, 1896*, Police Constable, Cons. 2023A.

T. Wheatley, *Diary, 1895*, Policeman, kept by Sergeant Wheatley during police patrols from Wyndham, Cons. 1266A.

E. Williams, 1858–1947, *Papers*, 1892–1896, Cons. 2608A.

Newspapers

The Advertiser
The Age
Albany Advertiser
The Argus
Barrier Miner
Bendigo Advertiser

Bibliography

Brisbane Courier
The Canberra Times
Dundee Courier
Eastern Districts Chronicle 1877–1900
Evening News
Geelong Advertiser
The Golden Age
The Inquirer
The Inquirer & Commercial News
Kalgoorlie Miner
Kalgoorlie Western Argus
Launceston Examiner
Leonora Miner
Manchester Courier and Lancashire General
The Mercury
Northern Public Opinion and Mining and Pastoral News
The Northern Territory Times and Gazette
The Northern Times
Nor'West Times and Northern Advocate
The Pastoral Review
The Perth Gazette and Western Australian Journal
Port Pirie Recorder and North Western Mail
The Queenslander
The Register
South Australian Register
The Southern Cross Times
The Star
The Sunday Times
The Times
Tribune
Truth
Warwick Examiner and Times
Western Mail
The West Australian
West Australian Sunday Times
Zeehan and Dundas Herald

Government Legislation

Aborigines Act 1897 (61 Vic, No. 5)
Aborigines Act 1905 (5 Edw VII. No. 14 of 1905)
Aborigines Act Amendment Act 1911 (1 Geo. V No. 53)
Aboriginal Affairs Planning Authority Act (AAPA Act) (024 of 1972)
Aboriginal Land Rights (Northern Territory) Act 1976
Aboriginal Offender Act Amendment 1883, Statutes of Western Australia, No. 18,

1892

Aborigines Protection Act 1886 (No. 25 of 1886)

Aborigines Act Amendment Act 1936 ('Native Administration Act 1936')

Aboriginal Heritage Act 1972 (Act No. 053 of 1972)

Commonwealth of Australia Constitution Act: an Act to constitute the Commonwealth of Australia

Constitution Act 1889 (52 Vict. No. 23)

Constitutional Act Amendment Act 1893 (57 Vict. No. 14)

Constitution Alteration (Aboriginals) 1967 (No. 55, 1967)

Criminal Code Act 1902 (1 & 2 Edw. VII No. 14)

Masters and Servants Act 1892 (55 Vict. No.28)

Masters and Servants Amendment Act 1882 (46 Vict. No. 11)

Nationality and Citizenship Act (Act No. 83 of 1948)

Native Title Act 1993 (Act No. 110 of 1993)

Native Welfare Act 1954. (3 Eliz. II No. 64)

Native Welfare Act 1963 (12 Eliz. II No. 79)

An Ordinance to Provide for the Summary Trial and Punishment of Aboriginal Native Offenders and to Summarily Try Aboriginal People in Certain Cases (12th Vic. No. 18)

Pearl Shell Fishery Act 1886 (50 Vict. No. 7)

Pearl Shell Fishery Regulation Act 1873 (37 Vict. No. 11)

Police Act 1892 (55 Vict. No. 27)

Police Ordinance Act 1849 (12 Vic. No 20)

Police Ordinance Act 1861 (25 Vic. No. 15)

An Act to amend the Police Act 1892 (No. 18 of 1975)

Government Reports and Annual Reports

Aborigines Department, Annual Reports

Aborigines and Fisheries Department, Annual Reports

Aborigines Protection Board, Annual Reports

Department of Indigenous Affairs, *Lost Lands Report*, Perth, Government of Western Australia, 2004.

Department of Native Welfare, Annual Reports

Fairbairn Commission, Western Australian Parliamentary Papers, 1884, no. 32.

Forrest, J. *Report on the Kimberley District, North-Western Australia by John Forrest, Surveyor General and Commissioner of Crown Lands*, Perth, Government Printer, 1883.

Moseley, H.D. *Report of the Royal Commissioner Appointed to Investigate, Report, and Advise upon Matters in Relation to the Condition and Treatment of Aborigines*, Perth, 1935.

Papers Respecting the Necessity of Increased Police Protection for the Settlers of the Kimberley District from the Aboriginal Natives, Votes and Proceedings of the Legislative Council, 1888.

Report of a Commission Appointed by his Excellency the Governor to Inquire into the

Bibliography

Treatment of the Aboriginal Native Prisoners of the Crown in the Colony, Western Australian Government Gazette, Paper no. 32, 2 October 1884, report published in *Government Gazette,* Acc. 495, File 71.

Report of the Royal Commission to Inquire into and Report upon the Meat Supply, WAGG No. 45, 21 August 1908.

W. Roth, *Royal Commission on the Condition of the Natives, Presented to Both Houses of Parliament by His Excellency's Command,* Roth Report, WAPP, 1905, 2nd Session, no. 5.

Royal Commission Appointed to Inquire into Certain Charges Made by one E. J. Blake of Ill-treatment of Aboriginal Natives by the Canning Exploration Party, WAGG, 13 December 1907, No. 64, p.4012.

Rules and Regulations for the Government and Guidance of the Police Force of Western Australia as Approved by Governor Hampton, Perth, 1863

P. Seaman, *The Aboriginal Land Inquiry,* Perth, Government Printer, 1984.

Votes and Proceedings of the Western Australian Legislative Assembly

Western Australian Parliamentary Debates

Western Australian Government Gazette

Western Australian Police Gazette

G.T. Wood, *Royal Commission of Enquiry into Alleged Killing and Burning of Bodies of Aborigines in East Kimberley and into Police Methods when Effecting Arrests,* Perth, Government Printer, 1927.

Websites

Australasian Legal Information Institute, http://www.austlii.edu.au/.

Australian Dictionary of Biography, http://www.adb.online.anu.edu.au/.

Australian Institute of Aboriginal and Torres Strait Islander Studies, *Roth* http://archive.aiatsis.gov.au/removeprotect/93169.pdf.

The Bradshaw Foundation: the ancient rock paintings of the Kimberley, http://www.bradshawfoundation.com/bradshaws/index.php.

Mira, Canning Stock Route Project, *Archive,* http://mira.canningstockrouteproject.com/tags/royal-commission

C. Clement, *National Museum of Australia, Review of Exhibitions and Public Programs,* http://www.nma.gov.au/__data/assets/pdf_file/0015/2409/Dr_Clement.pdf.

'Death of the Commissioner of Police', *The West Australian,* 27 March 1900, p.4, <http://members.iinet.net.au/~perthdps/graves/bio-24.htm#d>.

Department of Regional Development, Government of Western Australia http://www.drd.wa.gov.au/projects/Aboriginal-Initiatives/Regional-Services-Reform/Pages/History-of-Remote-Communities.aspx.

Dictionary of Canadian Biography http://www.biographi.ca/en/.

ABC, 'Fact Check: Amnesty International claim on 'shocking' Indigenous child incarceration rates checks out', <http://www.abc.net.au/news/2015-06-17/fact-check-indigenous-children-incarceration-rates/6511162>

Indigenous Australia, http://ia.anu.edu.au.

Jandamarra's War, dir. M. Torres, ABC, 12 May 2011, http://www.abc.net.au/tv/programs/jandamarraswar.htm.

The Kimberley Society, http://www.kimberleysociety.org.

V. Mills, *Jandamarra; a black Ned Kelly,* ABC Kimberley, 2008, <http://www.abc.net.au/local/stories/2008/02/07/2156878.htm>.

K. Moran, ABC – Questions as to the Truth – Pigeon – Jandamarra's War', *The Morant,* 2013, http://themorant.wordpress.com/2013/01/20/abc-questions-as-to-the-truth-pigeon-jandamarras-war/.

Museum of Australian Democracy at Old Parliament House, http://explore.moadoph.gov.au.

National Native Title Tribunal, http://www.nntt.gov.au

Obituaries Australia, http://oa.anu.edu.au/.

The Police Gazette of Western Australia, State Library of Western Australia, http://www.slwa.wa.gov.au/find/eresources/police_gazettes.

F. Prior, 'Film Project brings history to Life', *The West Australian,* 7 August 2010, http://au.news.yahoo.com/thewest/a/-/mp/7724764/film-project-brings-history-to-life/.

J. Schembri, 'Jandamarra's War', *The Sydney Morning Herald,* 5 May 2011, http://www.smh.com.au/entertainment/tv-and-radio/jandamarras-war-thursday-may-12-20110504-1e745.html.

P. Smith, *Mistake Creek Massacre Site,* https://www.flinders.edu.au/ehl/archaeology/research-profile/current-projects/kimberley-frontier-archaeology-project/mistake-creek-massacre-site.cfm.

The Stringer, 'Jandamarra's granddaughter speaks out for women's country', 2013, http://thestringer.com.au/jandamarras-grand-daughter-speaks-out-for-womens-country-78#.Vp6zL-t0FUQ>.

The Western Australian Parliament Hansard Archive 1870 to 1995, http://www.parliament.wa.gov.au/hansard/hansard1870to1995.nsf/vwWeb1870Main.

Western Australian Police Historical Society Inc., http://www.policewahistory.org.au/.

C. Hamlyn, 'Young Aboriginal people consider jail a rite of passage, WA Chief Justice says', *ABC News,* 2015, < http://www.abc.net.au/news/2015-08-04/aboriginal-kids-see-detention-rite-of-passage-wayne-martin-says/6672462>.

Secondary Sources – Chapters, Journals, Articles, Conferences

K. Akerman, and J. Stanton, 'Riji and Jakuli: Kimberley pearl shell in Aboriginal Australia', *NT Museum of Arts and Sciences,* no. 4, 1994.

A.C. Angelo, 'Kimberleys and North-West Goldfields', *Early Days: Journal of the Royal Western Australian Historical Society,* vol. 3, part 10, 1948.

W.S. Arthur, 'Funding allocations to Aboriginal people, the Western Australia case', Canberra, Centre for Aboriginal Economic Policy Research, Australian National University, 1991.

Bibliography

K. Auty, 'Patrick Bernard O'Leary and the Forrest River Massacres, Western Australia: examining "Wodgil" and the significance of 8 June 1926', *Aboriginal History,* vol. 28, 2004, pp.122–55.

D. Black, 'The Centenary of Responsible Government in Western Australia', *Early Days: Journal of the Royal Western Australian Historical Society,* vol. 10, part. 2, 1990, pp.143–55.

D. Black and G. Bolton, *Biographical Register of Members of the Parliament of Western Australia, Volume One, 1870–1930* (revised edition), Perth, Western Australian Parliamentary History Project, 2001.

V. Blundell and R. Layton, 'Marriage, Myth and Models of Exchange in the West Kimberleys', *Mankind,* vol. 11, no. 3, 1978 , pp.231–45.

G.C. Bolton, 'The Kimberley Pastoral Industry', *University Studies in History and Economics,* vol. 11, no. 2, 1954.

G.C. Bolton and H. Pedersen, 'The Emanuels of Noonkanbah and GoGo', *Early Days: Journal of the Royal Western Australian Historical Society,* vol. 8, part 4, 1980, pp.5–21.

G.C, Bolton, 'Reflections on Oombulgurri', C. Clement (ed.), *Studies in Western Australian History,* No. 26, 2010.

R. Broome, 'Aboriginal Victims and Voyagers, Confronting Frontier Myths', *Journal of Australian Studies,* vol. 18, iss. 42, 1994, pp.70–77.

R. Broome, 'The Struggle for Australia: Aboriginal-European warfare, 1770–1930', in M. McKernan and M. Browne (eds), *Australia: Two Centuries of War and Peace,* Canberra, Australian War Memorial, 1988, chapter 4.

K. Carson and H. Idzikowska, 'The Social Production of Scottish Policing 1795–1900', in D. Hay and F. Snyder (eds), *Policing and Prosecution in Britain 1750–1850,* New York, The Clarendon Press, 1989.

S. Churches, 'Put Not Your Faith in Princes (or Courts) – Agreements Made from Asymmetrical Power Bases: the story of a promise made to Western Australia's Aboriginal people', in P. Read, G. Meyers, and B. Reece (eds), *What Good Condition? Reflections on an Australian Aboriginal Treaty 1986–2006,* Aboriginal History Monograph 13, ANU Epress, 2006, <http://press.anu.edu.au?p=15621>.

M.A. Clark and S.K. May (eds), *Macassan History and Heritage: journeys, encounters and influences,* ANU EPress, 2013, <http://epress.anu.edu.au/wp-content/uploads/2013/06/whole.pdf>.

C. Clement, 'Monotony, Manhunts and Malice: East Kimberley law enforcement, 1896–1908', *Early Days: Journal and Proceedings of the Royal Western Australian Historical Society,* vol. 10, part 1, 1989.

C. Clement, 'The Impact of Denial: an interrogation of evidence relevant to massacres at Mistake Creek', *Australian Historical Association Bulletin,* no. 96, June 2003, pp.66–77.

P. Conole, 'A Gentleman Adventurer of the WA Police', *Police Newsbeat,* no. 36, 2006.

B. De Garis, 'The First Legislative Council, 1832–1870', in D. Black (ed.),

The House on the Hill: a history of the Parliament of Western Australia, Perth, Parliament of Western Australia, 1991.

J. A. De Moor and H.L. Wesseling Leiden (ed.), 'Imperialism And War: essays on colonial wars in Asia and Africa', *Comparative Studies in Overseas History*, vol. 8, EJ Brill/Universitaire Pers Leiden, 1989.

B. Devenish, 'A Most Maligned Man', *Early Days: Journal of the Royal Western Australian Historical Society,* vol. 13, pt. 2, 2008, pp.157–72.

B. Dodsworth, '"Civic" Police and the Condition of Liberty: the rationality of governance in eighteenth century England', *Social History*, vol. 29, no. 2, 2004, pp. 199–216.

B. Dodsworth, 'The Idea of Police in Eighteenth-Century England: discipline, reformation, superintendence, c. 1780–1800', *Journal of the History of Ideas,* vol. 69, no. 4, October 2008.

M. Durack, 'Golden Days of the Kimberleys', *Walkabout*, 1 April 1936.

P.M. Durack, 'Pioneering in the East Kimberley', *Early Days: Journal of the Royal Western Australian Historical Society*, vol. 2, pt. 14, 1933, pp. 1–46.

A.P. Elkin. 'Social Organisation in the Kimberley Division of North Western Australia', *Oceania*, vol. 2, no. 3, March 1932.

A.P. Elkin, 'Totemism in North-Western Australia, The Kimberley Division', *Oceania*, vol.3, no.3, 1933.

R. Evans, 'The Country Has Another Past: Queensland and the history wars', in F. Peters-Little, A. Curthoys and J. Docker (eds), *Passionate Histories: myth, memory and Indigenous Australia*, Aboriginal History Monograph 21, Canberra, ANU Epress, 2010.

R. Evans and R. Ørsted–Jensen, "I Cannot Say the Numbers that Were killed": assessing violent mortality on the Queensland frontier', presented at 'Conflict in History', Australian Historical Association, 33rd Annual Conference, University of Queensland, 7–11 July 2014.

M. Finnane, 'Police and Politics in Australia – The Case for Historical Revision', *Australian and New Zealand Journal of Criminology*, vol. 23, no. 4, 1990, pp.218–28.

M. Finnane, 'Police Rules and the Organisation of Policing in Queensland, 1905–1916', *Australian and New Zealand Journal of Criminology*, vol. 22, no. 2, 1989, pp.95–108.

M. Finnane and S. Garton, 'The Work of Policing: social relations and the criminal justice system in Queensland 1880–1914, Part I', *Labour History,* no. 62, May 1992, pp. 52–70.

M. Finnane and S. Garton, 'The Work of Policing: social relations and the criminal justice system in Queensland 1880–1914, Part II', *Labour History*, no. 63, Nov 1992, pp.43–64.

M. Finnane and F. Paisley, 'Police Violence and the Limits of Law on a Late Colonial Frontier: the "Borroloola Case" in 1930s Australia', *Law and History Review*, vol. 28, no. 1, 2010 , pp.141–71.

M. Finnane and J. Richards, '"You'll get nothing out of it"?: the inquest, police and Aboriginal deaths in colonial Queensland', *Australian Historical Studies*, no. 123, 2004, pp.84–105.

M. Finnane, 'A Politics of Prosecution: The Conviction of Wonnerwerry and the Exoneration of Jerry Durack in Western Australia 1898', *Law in Context*, vol. 33, no. 1, 2015, pp.60–73.

R. Foster, '"Don't Mention the War": frontier violence and the language of concealment', *History Australia,* vol. 6, no. 3, 2009, pp.68.1–68.15.

S.G. Foster, 'Contra Windschuttle,' *Quadrant,* vol. 47, no. 3, March 2003.

T. Gara, 'The Flying Foam Massacre: an incident on the northwest frontier, Western Australia', in M. Smith (ed.) *Archaeology at ANZAAS*, Perth, Western Australian Museum, Anthropology Department, 1983.

A. Gill, 'Aborigines, Settlers and Police in the Kimberleys 1887–1905', *Studies in Western Australian History*, no. 1, 1977, pp.1–28.

E. Goddard and T. Stannage, 'John Forrest and the Aborigines' in B. Reece and T. Stannage (eds), 'European-Aboriginal Relations in Western Australia', *Studies in Western Australian History*, no. 8, 1984, pp.52–58.

N. Green, 'From Princes to Paupers: the struggle for control of Aborigines in Western Australia 1887–1898', *Early Days: Journal of the Royal Western Australian Historical Society*, vol. 11, no. 4, 1998, pp.447–462.

N. Green, 'Dilemmas, Dramas and Damnation in Contested History', in C. Clement (ed.), 'Ethics and the Practice of History', *Studies in Western Australian History*, no. 26, 2010, pp.203–14.

J. Harris, 'Hiding the Bodies: the Myth of the Humane Colonisation of Aboriginal Australia', *Aboriginal History*, vol. 27, 2003.

L.M. Head, 'Landscapes Socialised by Fire: post-contact changes in Aboriginal fire use in northern Australia, and implications for prehistory', *Archaeology in Oceania*, vol. 29, no. 3, 1994.

S. Hodson, 'Making a Rural Labour Force: the intervention of the state in the working lives of Nyungars in the Great Southern, 1936–1948', in C. Fox (ed.), 'Historical Refractions', *Studies in Western Australian History,* no. 14, 1993.

S. Hodson, 'Nyungars and Work: Aboriginal experiences in the rural economy of the Great Southern region of Western Australia', *Aboriginal History*, vol. 17, no. 1–2, 1993.

M.W. Hunt, 'Aboriginal Land Rights in Western Australia', *Australian Mining and Petroleum Law Journal*, vol. 30, 1985.

A. Hunter, 'John Hutt: the inconspicuous governor', *Early Days: Journal of the Royal Western Australian Historical Society,* vol. 13, no. 3, 2009, pp.309–22.

E.S. Ilbery, 'The battle of Pinjarra: the Passing of the Bibbulmun', *Early Days*, vol. 1, 1927.

M. Jebb, *Gardia Coming: collecting and interpreting Aboriginal oral sources*, unpublished, 1991.

M. Jebb, 'The Lock Hospitals Experiment: Europeans, Aborigines and venereal disease', in R. Reece and T. Stannage (eds), 'European-Aboriginal

Relations in Western Australian History', *Studies in West Australian History*, vol. 8, 1984, pp. 68–86.

C. Johnson, 'Long Live Pigeon!', *Meanjin (Aboriginal Issue)*, vol. 36, no. 4, December 1977, pp.494–507.

D. Killingray, 'Colonial Warfare in West Africa 1870–1914', in J.A. De Moor and H.L. Wesseling (eds), *Imperialism and War: essays on colonial wars in Asia and Africa, Comparative Studies in Overseas History*, vol. 8, EJ Brill/Universitaire Pers Leiden, Leiden, 1989.

H. Klaatsch, 'Some Notes on Scientific Travel Amongst the Black Population of Tropical Australia in 1904, 1905, 1906', *Australasian Association for the Advancement of Science*, Adelaide, 1907.

W.H. Lamond, 'Five Years in the Kimberley', *Early Days: Journal of the Royal Western Australian Historical Society*, vol. 7, pt. 3, 1971, pp.27–49.

J. Lunn, '"Les Races Guerrieres": racial preconceptions in the French military about West African soldiers during the First World War', *Journal of Contemporary History*, vol. 34, no. 4, Oct. 1999, pp. 517–36.

R. Lyon, 'A Glance at the Manners, and Language of the Aboriginal Inhabitants of Western Australia; With a Short Vocabulary', *Perth Gazette and Western Australian Journal*. vol. 1, no. 13, 30 March 1833, pp.51–2.

S. Macintyre, 'Reviewing the History Wars', *Labour History*, no. 85, November 2003.

G. MacKenzie, *Fossil Downs: a saga of the Kimberleys, Australia's longest droving trip*, Yeppoon, Gordon Mackenzie, c1995.

G. Marquis, 'The "Irish Model" and Nineteenth-Century Canadian Policing', *The Journal of Imperial and Commonwealth History*, vol. 25, no. 2, 1997.

L. Marsh and S. Kinnane, 'Ghost Files: the missing files of the Department of Indigenous Affairs archives', C. Choo and S. Hollbach (eds), *Studies in Western Australian History: History and Native Title*, no. 23, 2003, pp.111–27.

C. McConville, '1888 – A Policeman's Lot', in *Australia 1888: a bicentennial history bulletin for the study of Australian history centered on the year 1888*, Bulletin no. 11, May 1983.

R. McGregor, 'Law – Enforcement or Just Force? Police Actions in Two Frontier Districts', in H. Reynolds (ed.), *Race Relations in Northern Queensland*, Townsville, James Cook University, 1993.

R. McGregor, "Breed out the colour' or the importance of being white', *Australian Historical Studies*, vol. 33, no. 120, pp.286–302.

R. Moran, 'Was There a Massacre at Bedford Downs?', *Quadrant*, vol. 46, no. 11, November 2002.

A.D. Moses, 'An Antipodean Genocide? the origins of the genocidal moment in the colonization of Australia', *Journal of Genocide Research*, vol. 2, no. 1, 2000.

S. Muecke, A. Rumsey and B. Wirrunmurra [sic], 'Pigeon the Outlaw: history as texts', *Aboriginal History*, vol. 9, no. 1–2, 1985.

A. Nettelbeck, '"Equals of the White Man": prosecution of settlers for violence against Aboriginal subjects of the Crown, Colonial Western Australia,' *Law and History Review,* vol. 31, no. 2, 2013, pp.355–90.

A. Nettelbeck, 'Practices of Violence/Myths of Creation: Mounted Constable Willshire and the cultural logic of settler nationalism', *Journal of Australian Studies,* vol. 32, no. 1, 2008.

A. Nettelbeck, 'Writing and Remembering Frontier Conflict: the rule of law in 1880s central Australia', *Aboriginal History,* vol. 28, 2004.

A. Nettelbeck and R. Foster, 'Colonial Judiciaries, Aboriginal Protection and South Australia's Policy of Punishing "with Exemplary Severity"', *Australian Historical Studies,* vol. 41, no. 3, 2010.

A. Nettelbeck and R. Foster, 'Reading the Elusive Letter of the Law: policing the South Australian frontier', *Australian Historical Studies,* vol. 38, iss. 130, 2007.

C. Owen, '"The Police Appear to be a Useless Lot Up There": law and order in the East Kimberley 1884–1905', *Aboriginal History,* vol. 27, 2003, pp.105–30.

C. Owen and C. Choo, 'Deafening Silences: understanding frontier relations and the discourse of police files through Kimberley Police Records', in C. Choo and S. Hollbach (eds), *Studies in Western Australian History: History and Native Title,* no. 23, 2003, pp.128–56.

R. Paley, '"An Imperfect, Inadequate and Wretched System"? Policing London before Peel', *Criminal Justice History,* vol. 10, 1989.

S. Petrow, 'Economy, Efficiency and Impartiality: police centralisation in nineteenth century Tasmania', *Australian & New Zealand Journal of Criminology,* vol. 31, no. 3, 1998, pp.243–66.

R.H. Pilmer, *Northern Patrol: an Australian saga,* C. Clement and P. Bridge (eds), Perth, Hesperian Press, 1998.

P.E. Playford and I. Ruddock, 'Discovery of the Kimberley Goldfield', *Early Days,* vol. 9, pt. 3, 1985.

A. Redmond, and F. Skyring, 'Exchange and Appropriation: the Wurnan economy and Aboriginal land and labour at Karunjie Station, north-western Australia', in I. Keen (ed.), *Indigenous Participation in Australian Economies, Historical and anthropological perspectives,* Canberra, ANU EPress, 2010, <http://epress.anu.edu.au/apps/bookworm/view/Indigenous+Participation+in+Australian+Economies/5161/upfront.xhtml>.

A. Redmond, 'Strange Relatives: mutualities and dependencies between Aborigines and pastoralists in the Northern Kimberley', *Oceania,* vol. 75, no. 3, 2005.

R.H.W. Reece, 'Inventing Aborigines', *Aboriginal History,* vol. 11, no. 1, 1987.

H. Reynolds, 'Racial Violence in North Queensland', in B.J. Dalton (ed.), *Lectures on North Queensland History, Second Series,* Townsville, James Cook University, 1975.

H. Reynolds, 'The Breaking of the Great Australian Silence: Aborigines in Australian historiography 1955–1983', *The Trevor Reese Memorial Lecture 1984,* University of London, Institute of Commonwealth Studies, Australian Studies Centre, 30 January 1984.

H. Reynolds, 'The Unrecorded Battlefields of Queensland', *Race Relations in North Queensland*, Townsville, James Cook University, 1993.

H. Reynolds, 'Violence, the Aboriginals, and the Australian Historian', *Meanjin*, vol. 31, no. 4, 1972.

H. Reynolds, 'Violence in Australian History', in D. Chappell, P. Garbosky and H. Strang (eds), *Australian Violence: contemporary perspectives*, Australian Institute of Criminology, Canberra, 1991.

J. Richards, 'Moreton Telegraph Station 1902: the native police on Cape York Peninsula', Proceedings of the History of Crime, Policing and Punishment conference, Canberra, December 1999.

D. Ritter, 'The Fulcrum of Noonkanbah', *Journal of Australian Studies*, vol. 26, issue 75, 2002.

H. Rumley, S. Toussaint, '"For Their Own Benefit"?: a critical overview of Aboriginal policy and practice at Moola Bulla, East Kimberley, 1910–1955', *Aboriginal History*, vol. 14, no. 1, 1990, pp.80–103.

B. Scates, 'A Monument to Murder: celebrating the conquest of Aboriginal Australia', in L. Layman and T. Stannage (eds), 'Celebrations in Western Australian History', *Studies in Western Australian History*, no. 10, 1989, pp.21–31.

B. Shaw, 'Is the Pen Mightier than the Word?: a comparison between oral and written sources on the East Kimberley bushranger Major', Canberra, Aboriginal Studies Press, 1998.

T. Shellam, 'Our Natives and Wild Blacks: enumeration as a statistical dimension of sovereignty in colonial Western Australia', *Journal of Colonialism and Colonial History*, vol. 13, no. 3, 2012, pp.1–19.

C. Slaughter, 'The Aboriginal Natives of North-West Western Australia and the Administration of Justice', *Westminster Review*, vol. CLVI, no. 6, 1901, pp.411–26.

P.A. Smith, 'Into the Kimberley: the invasion of the Sturt Creek Basin (Kimberley Region, Western Australia) and evidence of Aboriginal Resistance', *Aboriginal History*, vol. 24, 2000. pp.62–74.

P.A. Smith, 'Station Camps: legislation, labour relations and rations on pastoral leases in the Kimberley region, Western Australia', *Aboriginal History*, vol. 24, 2000, pp.75–97.

G. Smithers, 'Reassuring "White Australia": a review of The Fabrication of Aboriginal History Volume One', *Journal of Social History*, vol. 37, no. 2, 2003, pp.493–505.

T. Stannage, 'The Composition of the Western Australian Parliament 1890–1911', in *University Studies in History*, vol. iv, no. 4, 1966, pp.1–37.

P. Statham, 'The First (W.A) Finnerty's – Father and Son', *Early Days*, vol. 9, pt. 2, 1984, pp.16–26.

R. Storch, 'The Old English Constabulary', *History Today*, vol. 49, no. 11, 1999.

R. Storch, 'The Plague of the Blue Locusts', *International Journal of Social History*, vol. 20, iss. 1, 1975.

M. Sturma, 'Myall Creek and the Psychology of Mass Murder', *Journal of Australian Studies,* vol. 9, iss. 16, 1985.

M. Sturma, 'Policing the Criminal Frontier in Mid-Nineteenth-Century Australia, Britain and America', in M. Finnane (ed.), *Policing in Australia Historical Perspectives,* Perth, NSW University Press, 1987.

P. Sullmann, 'Perspectives on Police and the Criminal Justice Debate', in D. Chappell and P. Wilson (eds), *The Australian Criminal Justice System,* Sydney, Butterworths, 1986.

J.J. Tobias, 'Police and the Public in the United Kingdom', in *Police Forces in History,* Sage Publications, 1975.

J.S. Turner, 'George Shenton, the Elder, 1811–1867', *Early Days: Journal of the Royal Western Australian Historical Society,* vol. 11, no. 3, 1997, pp. 379–93.

K. Windschuttle, 'The Myths of Frontier Massacres in Australian History', *Quadrant,* Vol. 44, No. 10, October 2000. Part II: 'The Fabrication of the Aboriginal Death Toll', *Quadrant,* Vol. 44, No. 11. November 2000. Part III: 'Massacre Stories and the Policy of Separatism', *Quadrant,* Vol. 44, No. 12, December 2000.

Secondary Sources – Books and Unpublished Theses

M. Allbrook, *Henry Prinsep's Empire: framing a distant colony,* ANU Press, Canberra, 2014.

M. Allbrook, *'Imperial Family': the Prinseps, Empire and colonial government in India and Australia,* PhD thesis, Griffith University, 2009.

J.A. Allen, *Sex and Secrets: crimes involving Australian women since 1880,* Melbourne, Oxford University Press, 1990.

D.M. Anderson and D. Killingray (eds), *Policing the Empire: government, authority and control, 1830–1940,* Manchester, Manchester University Press, 1991.

R.T. Appleyard and T. Manford, *The Beginning: European Discovery and Early Settlement of Swan River Western Australia,* Nedlands, UWA Press, 1979.

A. Atkinson, *The Europeans in Australia: a history, volume two: Democracy,* Melbourne, Oxford University Press, 2004.

A. Atkinson and M. Aveling, *Australians: a historical library Australians 1838,* Sydney, Fairfax, Syme and Weldon, 1987.

B. Attwood and S.G. Foster (eds), *Frontier Conflict: the Australian experience,* Canberra, National Museum of Australia, 2003.

M. Aveling, *Westralian Voices, Documents in West Australian Social History,* Nedlands, UWA Press, 1979.

J. Backhouse, *Extracts from the Letters of James Backhouse, vol. 2,* London, Harvey and Darton, 1838.

M.A. Bain, *Full Fathom Five,* Perth, Artlook Books, 1982.

M. Banton, *The Policeman and the Community,* London, Tavistock, 1964.

D.G. Barrie, *Police in the Age of Improvement: police development and the civic tradition in Scotland 1775–1865,* Devon, Willan Publishing, 2008.

D.M. Bates, *My Natives and I: Incorporating the passing of the Aborigines: A lifetime spent among the natives of Australia*, P.J. Bridge (ed.), Perth, Hesperian Press, 2004.

J.S. Battye, *The Cyclopedia of Western Australia, an historical and commercial review, descriptive and biographical facts, figures and illustrations, an epitome of progress*, Adelaide, Hussey & Gillingham, 1912.

J.S. Battye, *The History of the North West of Australia Embracing Kimberley, Gascoyne and Murchison Districts*, Perth, VK Jones, 1915.

J. Belich, *The Victorian Interpretation of Racial Conflict: the Maori, the British, and the New Zealand wars*, Montreal, McGill-Queen's University Press, 1989.

M. Bentley, *Grandfather was a Policeman: the Western Australian police force 1829–1889*, Victoria Park, Hesperian Press, 1993.

L. Benton, *Law and Colonial Cultures: legal regimes in world history, 1400–1900*, Cambridge, Cambridge University Press, 2002.

R.M. Berndt and C.H. Berndt, Ab*origines of the West; Their Past and Present*, Nedlands, UWA Press, 1979.

I. Berryman (ed.), *Swan River Letters*, Glengarry, Swan River Press, 2002.

P. Bianchi (ed.), *Canning Stock Route Royal Commission: Royal Commission to inquire into the Treatment of Natives by the Canning Exploration Party 15 January – 5 February 1908*, Carlisle, Hesperian Press, 2010.

P. Biskup, *Not Slaves, Not Citizens; The Aboriginal Problem in Western Australia 1898–1954*, St Lucia, University of Queensland Press, 1973.

J. Bohemia and B. McGregor, *Nyibayarri: Kimberley tracker*, Canberra, Aboriginal Studies Press, 1995.

G.C. Bolton, *Alexander Forrest: his life and times*, Melbourne, Melbourne University Press in association with UWA Press, 1958.

G.C. Bolton, *Land of Vision and Mirage: Western Australia since 1826*, Nedlands, UWA Press, 2008, p.85.

G.C. Bolton, *A Survey of the Kimberley Pastoral Industry from 1885 to the Present*, Master's thesis, University of Western Australia, 1953.

T. Bottoms, *The Conspiracy of Silence: Queensland's frontier killing times*, Sydney, Allen & Unwin, 2013.

E.J. Brady, *Australia Unlimited*, Melbourne, Robertson and Mullens Ltd., (n.d.).

S. Breathnach, *The Irish Police*, Dublin, Anvil Books, 1974.

P. Bridge, *Russian Jack*, Carlisle, Hesperian Press, 2002.

J. Brockman, *He Rode Alone; Being the Adventures of Pioneer Julius Brockman*, Perth, Artlook Books, 1987.

R. Broome, *Aboriginal Australians: black responses to white dominance, 1788–2001*, Sydney, Allen & Unwin, 2001.

R. Broome, *Aboriginal Australians: a history since 1788*, Sydney, Allen & Unwin, 2010.

G. Broughton, *Turn Against Home*, Brisbane, Jacaranda Press, 1965.

G. Buchanan, *Packhorse and Waterhole, With the First Overlanders to the Kimberley*, facsimile edition, Carlisle, Hesperian Press, 1984.

Bibliography

A. Calvert and L. Wells, *Journal of the Calvert Scientific Exploring Expedition, 1896–7: equipped at the request and expense of Albert F. Calvert, Esq., F.R.G.S., London, for the purpose of exploring the remaining blanks of Australia*, Carlisle, Hesperian Press, 1993.

D.W. Carnegie, *Spinifex and Sand; A Narrative of Five Years Pioneering and Exploration in Western Australia*, London, C. Arthur Pearson, 1898.

A. M. Chalarimeri, *The Man from the Sunrise Side*, Broome, Magabala Books, 2001.

D. Chappell and P. Wilson (eds), *The Australian Criminal Justice System: the mid 1980s*, Sydney, Butterworths, 1986.

C. Clement, *Australia's North-West: a study of exploration, land policy and land acquisition, 1644–1884*, PhD thesis, Murdoch University, 1991.

C. Clement, *Historical Notes Relevant to Impact Stories of the East Kimberley*, Canberra, East Kimberley Impact Assessment Project, 1989.

C. Clement, *Kimberley District Pastoral Leasing Directory, 1881–1900*, Perth, National Heritage for the Kimberley Historical Sources Project, 1993.

C. Clement, *Old Halls Creek; a town remembered*, Perth, WA National Heritage, 2000.

C. Clement, *Pre-Settlement Intrusion into the East Kimberley*, East Kimberley Impact Assessment Study, Working Paper no. 24, Canberra, Centre for Resource and Environmental Studies, ANU, 1988.

C. Clement and P. Bridge (eds), *Kimberley Scenes: sagas of Australia's last frontier*, Carlisle, Hesperian Press, 1991.

C. Clement, J. Gresham and H. McGlashan (eds), *Kimberley History: people, exploration and development*, Perth, Kimberley Society, 2012.

R. Clyne, *Colonial Blue: a history of the South Australian police force*, Adelaide, Wakefield Press, 1987.

I. Coates, *The Social Construction of the John Forrest Australian Aboriginal Collection: past and present*, unpublished honours thesis, ANU, 1989.

Y.E. Coate and K.H. Coate, *Lonely graves of Western Australia and burials at sea*, Carlisle, Hesperian Press, 1986.

R.W. Connell and T.H. Irving, *Class Structure in Australian History*, Melbourne, Longman House, 1992.

P. Conole, *Protect and Serve: a history of the Western Australian police service*, Perth, Access Press, 2002.

J. Connor, *The Australian Frontier Wars, 1788–1838*, Sydney, University of New South Wales Press, 2002.

I.M. Crawford, *The Art of the Wandjina: Aboriginal cave paintings in Kimberley, Western Australia*, London, Oxford University Press, 1968.

I.M. Crawford, *We Won the Victory: Aborigines and outsiders on the north–west coast of the Kimberley*, Fremantle, Fremantle Arts Centre Press, 2001.

J. Critchett, *A 'Distant Field of Murder': Western District frontiers 1834–1848*, Melbourne, Melbourne University Press, 1990.

T.A. Critchley, *A History of Police in England and Wales 1900–1966*, London,

Constable, 1966.

F. Crowley, *Big John Forrest 1847–1918*, Nedlands, UWA Press, 2000.

F. Crowley, *Forrest 1847–1918: apprenticeship to premiership*, St Lucia, University of Queensland Press, 1971.

P. Curtin, *Disease and Empire: the health of European troops in the conquest of Africa*, Cambridge, Cambridge University Press, 1998.

G. Davidson, J.W. McCarty and A. McLeary (eds), *Australians, 1888*, Sydney, Fairfax, Syme & Weldon Associates, 1987.

W.S. Davidson, *Havens of Refuge: a history of leprosy in Western Australia*, Nedlands, UWA Press, 1978.

K. De La Rue, *Pearl Shell and Pastures: the story of Cossack and Roebourne, and their place in the history of the North-West, from the earliest explorations to 1910*, Cossack, Cossack Project Committee, 1979.

D. Dixon (ed.), *A Culture of Corruption: changing an Australian police service*, Sydney, Hawkins Press, 1999.

M. Donaldson, *Kimberley Rock Art, Vol. 1: Mitchell Plateau Area*, Mount Lawley, Wildrocks Publications, 2012.

M. Donaldson, *Kimberley Rock Art, Vol. 2, North Kimberley*, Mount Lawley, Wildrocks Publications, 2012.

M. Donaldson, *Kimberley Rock Art, Vol. 3, Rivers and Ranges*, Mount Lawley, Wildrocks Publications, 2013.

M. Donaldson and I. Elliot (eds), F.H. Hann, *Do Not Yield to Despair; Frank Hugh Hanns exploration diaries in the arid interior of Australia 1895–1908*, Carlisle, Hesperian Press, 1998.

J. Doring (ed.), *Gwion Gwion: secret and sacred pathways of the Ngarinyin Aboriginal people of Australia*, Adelaide, Koln, Konemann, 2000.

P.S. Drew, *James Stirling, Admiral and Founding Governor of Western Australia*, Nedlands, UWA Press, 2003.

M. Durack, *Kings in Grass Castles*, London, Constable, 1959.

M. Durack, *Sons in the Saddle*, London, Constable, 1983.

J.S. Durlacher, (with an introduction by Peter Gifford), *Landlords of the Iron Shore*, Carlisle, Hesperian Press, 2013 [1900].

M.R. Dyson, *Flying Foam Massacre: a grey era in the history of the Burrup Peninsular [sic], British justice or downright vengeful bloody murder*, Karratha, CAD Centre, 2002.

M. Echenberg, *Colonial Conscripts: the Tirailleurs Sénégalais in French West Africa, 1857–1960*, Portsmouth, Heinemann, 1991.

C. Emsley, *Gendarmes and the State in Nineteenth-Century Europe*, London, Oxford University Press, 1999.

C. Emsley, *Policing and its Context 1750–1850*, Macmillan, London, 1983.

M. Enders and B. Dupont (eds), *Policing the Lucky Country*, Sydney, Hawkins Press, 2001.

R. Evans, K. Saunders, and K. Cronin, *Exclusion, Exploitation and Extermination: race relations in colonial Queensland*, St Lucia, University of Queensland Press,

1975.

R. Erickson (ed.), *The Bicentennial Dictionary of Western Australians pre 1829–1888*, vol. 1, Nedlands, UWA Press, 1988.

R. Erickson (ed.), *Dictionary of Western Australians, Free 1850–1868*, vol. 3, Nedlands, UWA Press, 1979.

M.H. Fels, *Good Men and True: the Aboriginal police of the Port Phillip district 1837–1853*, Melbourne, Melbourne University Press, 1988.

M. Finnane, 'Governing the Police', in F.B. Smith (ed.), *Ireland, England and Australia: Essays in Honour of Oliver MacDonagh*, Canberra and Cork, ANU and Cork University Press, 1990.

M. Finnane, *Police and Government: histories of policing in Australia*, Melbourne, Oxford University Press, 1994.

M. Finnane, *Policing in Australia Historical Perspectives*, NSW University Press, 1987.

M. Finnane, *Punishment in Australian Society*, Melbourne, Oxford University Press, 1997.

M. Finnane, and H. Douglas, *Indigenous Crime and Settler Law: white sovereignty after Empire*, Basingstoke, Palgrave Macmillan, 2010.

R. FitzRoy, *Narrative of the Surveying Voyages of His Majesty's Ships Adventure and Beagle Between the Years 1826 and 1836, Describing their Examination of the Southern Shores of South America, and the Beagle's Circumnavigation of the Globe. Proceedings of the Second Expedition, 1831–36, under the Command of Captain Robert Fitz-Roy, R.N.*, London, Henry Colbourn, 1839, <http://darwin-online.org.uk/content/frameset?itemID=F10.2&viewtype=text&pageseq=1>.

C.E. Flinders, *Kimberley Days and Yesterdays; A Chronicle of 45 Years in the Great Nor-West and Kimberleys of Western Australia*, unpublished, 1933.

L. Ford, *Settler Sovereignty: jurisdiction and indigenous people in America and Australia 1788–1836*, Cambridge, MA, Harvard University Press, 2010.

A. Forrest, *North West Exploration; Journal of Expedition from DeGrey River to Port Darwin*, Perth, Government Printer, 1880.

J. Forrest, *Explorations in Australia: I. Explorations in search of Dr. Leichardt and party; 2. From Perth to Adelaide, around the Great Australian Bight; 3. From Champion Bay, across the desert to the telegraph and to Adelaide, with an appendix on the condition of Western Australia*; illus. by G.F. Angas, London, Sampson Low, Marston, Low, & Searle, 1875.

K. Forrest, *The Challenge and the Chance: the colonisation and settlement of North West Australia 1861–1914*, Carlisle, Hesperian Press, 1996.

R. Foster, R Hosking and A. Nettelbeck, *Fatal Collisions: the South Australian frontier and the violence of memory*, Adelaide, Wakefield Press, 2001.

R. Foster and A. Nettelbeck, *Out of the Silence: the history and memory of South Australia's frontier wars*, Adelaide, Wakefield Press, 2012.

B. Gammage, *The Biggest Estate on Earth: how Aborigines made Australia*, Sydney, Allen & Unwin, 2011.

A. Gill, *Aspects of the Western Australian Police Force, 1887–1905*, Perth, unpublished paper, 1974.

A. Gill, *Social Conflict and Police Loyalty in Western Australia in the Late Nineteenth Century*, unpublished paper, University of Western Australia, 1981.

A. Gill, *The W.A Police Force, 1880–1910*, unpublished honours thesis, University of Western Australia, 1973.

B. Godfrey and G. Dunstall, *Crime and Empire 1840–1940; criminal justice in local and global context*, Cullompton, Willan Publishing, 2005.

A.R. Graybill, *Policing the Great Plains: rangers, mounties, and the North American frontier, 1875–1910*, Lincoln, University of Nebraska Press, 2007.

N. Green, *Broken Spears, Aboriginals and Europeans in the Southwest of Australia*, Perth, Focus Education Services, 1984.

N. Green, *The Forrest River Massacres*, Fremantle Arts Centre Press, 1995.

N. Green and S. Moon, *Far From Home: Aboriginal prisoners of Rottnest Island, 1838–1931*, Nedlands, UWA Press, 1997.

J. Gregory and J. Gothard (eds), *Historical Encyclopedia of Western Australia*, Nedlands, UWA Publishing, 2009.

M. Greenwood and T. Denton, *Jandamarra*, Sydney, Allen & Unwin, 2013.

G. Grey, *Journals of Two Expeditions of Discovery in North-West and Western Australia, During the Years 1837, 38, 39*, London, T. and W. Boone, 1841.

E. Gribble, *Forty Years with the Aborigines*, Sydney, Angus and Robertson, 1930.

E. Gribble, *The Problem of the Australian Aboriginal*, Sydney, Angus and Robertson, 1932.

J.B. Gribble, *Dark Deeds in a Sunny Land, or, Blacks and Whites in North-West Australia, 1905*, Nedlands, UWA Press, 1987.

F.W. Gunning, *Lure of the North: seventy years' memoirs of George Joseph Gooch and his pioneer friends of Western Australia*, Perth, Western Australian Newspapers, 1952.

A. Haebich, *Broken Circles, Fragmenting Indigenous Families 1800–2000*, Fremantle, Fremantle Arts Centre Press, 2000.

A. Haebich, *For Their Own Good: Aborigines and government in the Southwest of Western Australia, 1900–1940*, Nedlands, UWA Press, 1988.

S.J. Hallam, *Fire and Hearth, a study of Aboriginal usage & European usurpation in south-western Australia*, Canberra, Australian Institute of Aboriginal Studies, 1975.

V. Hanson, *The Western Way of War*, Oxford, Oxford University Press, 1989.

A. T. Harris, *Policing the City: crime and legal authority in London, 1780–1840*, History of Crime and Criminal Justice Series, Columbus, Ohio State University Press, 2004.

A. Hasluck, *Thomas Peel of Swan River*, Melbourne, Oxford University Press, 1965.

P. Hasluck, *Black Australians: a survey of native policy in Western Australia, 1829–1897*, Melbourne, Melbourne University Press, 1942.

S. Hawke, and M. Gallagher, *Noonkanbah, whose land, whose law*, Fremantle,

Fremantle Arts Centre Press, 1989.

S. Hawke, *A Town Is Born: the Fitzroy Crossing story*, Broome, Magabala Books, 2013.

A.L. Haydon, *The Trooper Police of Australia: a record of mounted police work in the Commonwealth from the earliest days of settlement to the present time*, London, A. Melrose, 1911.

B.T. Haynes, *W.A. Aborigines, 1622–1972*, Claremont, History Association of Western Australia, 1973.

J. Herlihy, *The Royal Irish Constabulary*, Dublin, Four Courts Press, 1997.

R.S. Hill, *Policing the Colonial Frontier; The Theory and Practice of Coercive Social and Racial Control in New Zealand 1767–1867*, Wellington, Government Publisher, 1986.

J. Hirst, *Sense and Nonsense in Australian History*, Melbourne, Black Inc. Agenda, 2005.

J.M. Holmes, *Australia's Open North; a study of Northern Australia bearing on the urgency of the times*, Sydney, Angus and Robertson, 1963.

K. Hopkins, *Conquerors and Slaves*, Cambridge, Cambridge University Press, 1978.

J. Host with C. Owen, *'It's Still in My Heart, This is My Country': The Single Noongar Claim History*, Perth, UWA Publishing, 2009.

S.J. Hunt, *"The Gribble Affair"; a study of Aboriginal European labour relations in the North-West Australia during the 1880s*, Honours thesis, University of Western Australia, 1978.

S.J. Hunt, *Spinifex and Hessian: women's lives in North-West Australia, 1860–1900*, Nedlands, UWA Press, 1986.

A. Hunter, *A Different Kind of 'Subject': colonial law in Aboriginal European relations in 19th century Western Australia, 1829–61*, Canberra, Australian Scholarly Publishing, 2012.

B.A. Hussainmiya, *Orang Regimen: the Malays of the Ceylon Rifle Regiment*, Bangi, Penerbit Universiti Kebangsaan Malaysia, 1990.

I. Idriess, *Man Tracks: the mounted police in Australia's Wilds*, Sydney, Angus and Robertson, 1935.

I. Idriess, *Outlaw of the Leopolds*, Sydney, Angus and Robertson, 1952.

I. Idriess, *Over the Range: sunshine and shadows in the West Kimberley*, Sydney, Angus and Robertson, 1937.

N. Jarvis, *Western Australia: an atlas of human endeavour*, Perth, Education Department of Western Australia, 1986.

M. Jebb, *Blood, Sweat and Welfare: a history of white bosses and aboriginal pastoral workers*, Nedlands, UWA Press, 2002.

M. Jebb (ed.), *Emerarra; a man of Merarra*, Broome, Magabala Books, 1996.

M. Jebb, *Isolating the 'Problem': venereal disease and Aborigines in Western Australia, 1898–1924*, Honours thesis, Murdoch University, 1987.

C. Jeffries, *The Colonial Police*, London, 1952.

C. Johnson, *Long Live Sandawarra*, Melbourne, Hyland House, 1987.

W.R. Johnstone, *The Long Blue Line: a history of the Queensland police*, Brisbane, Boolarong, 1992.

E.B. Kennedy, *The Black Police of Queensland*, London, Murray, 1902.

Kimberley Aboriginal Law and Culture Centre (eds), *New Legend: a story of law and culture and the fight for self-determination in the Kimberley*, Kimberley Aboriginal Law and Culture Centre, 2006.

Kimberley Language Resource Centre (eds), *Moola Bulla: in the shadow of the mountain*, Broome, Magabala Books, 1996.

W.B. Kimberly (ed.), *History of West Australia, A Narrative of her Past, Together With Biographies of Her Leading Men*, Melbourne, F.W. Niven, 1897.

P.P. King, *Narrative of a Survey of the Intertropical and Western Coasts of Australia: performed between the years 1818 and 1822, Volumes One and Two*, London, John Murray, 1826.

S. Kinnane, *Shadowlines*, Fremantle, Fremantle Press, 2003.

W. Lambden Owen, *Cossack Gold, The Chronicles of an Early Goldfields Warden*, Sydney, Angus and Robertson, 1933.

G.H. Lamond, *Tales of the Overland; Queensland to Kimberley in 1885*, Carlisle, Hesperian Press, 1986.

E.W. Landor, *The Bushman; or Life in a New Country*, London, R. Bentley, 1847.

R.T. Libby, *Hawke's Law: The Politics of Mining and Aboriginal Land Rights in Australia*, Nedlands, UWA, Press, 1990.

N. Loos, *Invasion and Resistance, Aboriginal –European Relations on the North Queensland Frontier 1861–1897*, Canberra, ANU Press, 1982.

J.R.B. Love, *Stone-Age Bushmen of Today; Life and Adventure among a Tribe of Savages in North-Western Australia*, London, Blackie and Son, 1936.

J. Lydon, *The Flash of Recognition: photography and the emergence of indigenous rights*, Sydney, NewSouth Publishing, 2012.

G. MacDonald, *Beyond Boundary Fences*, Carlisle, Hesperian Press, 1986.

R. Manne, *Whitewash: on Keith Windschuttle's fabrication of Aboriginal history*, Melbourne, Black Inc. Agenda, 2003.

L.R. Marchant, *Aboriginal Administration in Western Australia, 1886–1905*, Canberra, Australian Institute of Aboriginal Studies, 1981.

L.R. Marchant, *An Island unto Himself, William Dampier and New Holland*, Carlisle, Hesperian Press, 1988.

P. Marshall (ed.), *Raparapa Kularr Martuwarra: stories from the Fitzroy River drovers*, Broome, Magabala Books, 1988.

R. Marshall, *King of Kimberley: the story of a tragic injustice*, Oaklands Park, Peacock Publications, 1988.

H.G.B. Mason, *Darkest Western Australia; a treatise bearing on the habits and customs of the Aborigines and the solution of 'the native question'*, facsimile edition, Carlisle, Hesperian Press, 1980 [1909].

J. McArthur, *Policing the Colony of Western Australia 1829–1850*, unpublished Thesis, University of Western Australia, 1995.

R. McDougall, and I. Davidson, *The Roth Family: anthropology, and colonial administration,* Publications of the Institute of Archaeology, University College London, Walnut Creek, CA, Left Coast Press, 2008.

J. McGowan, *Policing the Metropolis of Scotland: a history of the police and systems of police in Edinburgh and Edinburghshire, 1770–1833,* Mussleburgh, Turlough, 2010.

R. McGregor, *Answering the Native Question: the dispossession of the Aborigines of the Fitzroy District, West Kimberley, 1880–1905,* Honours thesis, James Cook University, 1985.

R. McGregor, *Imagined Destinies: Aboriginal Australians and the doomed race theory 1880–1939,* Melbourne, Melbourne University Press, 1997.

A. McGrath, *Born in the Cattle: Aborigines in cattle country,* Sydney, Allen & Unwin, 1987.

W.T. McGrath and M.P. Mitchell (eds), *The Police Function in Canada,* Toronto, Methuen Publications, 1981.

C. McIntyre, *Suicides and Settlers, Their Place in 19th Century West Australian Social History,* Carlisle, Hesperian Press, 2008.

M. McKeough, *Rescues, Rogues and Rough Seas: 150 years of water police in Western Australia,* Fremantle, Western Australian Water Police and Police Historical Society, 2001.

W. Miller, *Cops and Bobbies: police authority in New York and London, 1830–1870* Chicago, University of Chicago Press, 1973.

E. Millet, *An Australian Parsonage or, the Settler and the Savage in Western Australia,* fascimile edition, Nedlands, UWA Press, 1980 [1872].

K. Milte, *Police in Australia: development, functions, procedures,* Sydney, Butterworths, 1977.

G.F. Moore, *Diary of Ten Years Eventful Life of an Early Settler in Western Australia and also a Descriptive Vocabulary of the Language of the Aborigines,* facsimile Edition, Nedlands, UWA Press, 1978 [1884].

K. Moran, *Pigeon,* Carlisle, Hesperian Press, 2011.

K. Moran, *Sand and Stone: cattle and conflict (Vol. 1 and 2),* Carlisle, Hesperian Press, 2009.

K. Moran, *Sand and Stone: foreign footprints: police in the Kimberley 1880–1890s,* Carlisle, Hesperian Press, 2009.

K. Moran, *Sand and Stone: a social history of Western Australia as recorded by police of the eastern frontier,* London, Frickers International Publishing, 2000.

T.R. Moreman, *The Army in India and the Development of Frontier Warfare, 1849–1947,* London, Macmillan, 1998.

E. Morris, *Austral English: a dictionary of Australasian words, phrases and usages,* Cambridge, Cambridge University Press, 2011.

E. Morrow, *The Law Provides,* London, Herbert Jenkins, 1937.

D. Mowaljarlai, *Jutta Malnic Yorro Yorro Everything Standing Up Alive: spirit of the Kimberley,* Broome, Magabala Books, 1993.

D.J. Mulvaney, *Encounters in Place: outsiders and Aboriginal Australians 1606–1985,* Brisbane, University of Queensland Press, 1989.

D.J. Mulvaney (ed.), *From the Frontier: outback letters to Baldwin Spencer*, Sydney, Allen & Unwin, 2000.

D.J. Mulvaney, and J.P. White (eds), *Australians to 1788*, Sydney, Fairfax, Syme and Weldon, 2007.

A. Nettelbeck, and R. Foster, *In the Name of the Law: William Willshire and the policing of the Australian frontier*, Adelaide, Wakefield Press, 2007.

A.O. Neville, *Australia's Coloured Minority: Its Place in the Community*, Sydney, Currawong Publishing Co, 1947.

S. Newland, *Paving the Way: a romance of the Australian bush*, London, Gay and Bird, 1893.

B. Niall, *True North: the story of Mary and Elizabeth Durack*, Melbourne, Text Publishing, 2012.

P.W. Nichols, *Police Powers in Western Australia 1829–1970*, Master's thesis, UWA, 1975.

J. Nicholson, *Kimberley Warrior: the story of Jandamarra*, Sydney, Allen & Unwin, 1997.

G.M. O'Brien, *The Australian Police Forces*, Oxford, Oxford University Press, 1960.

P. O'Farrell, '*Success and Defeat in Western Australia 1891–1907*', *Letters from Irish Australia 1825–1929*, Sydney, NSW University Press, 1994.

P. O'Farrell, *The Irish in Australia*, Sydney, NSW University Press, 1993.

N. Ogle, *The Colony of Western Australia, a manual for emigrants to that settlement or its dependencies*, London, James Fraser, 1839.

D. O'Sullivan, *The Irish Constabularies 1822–1922*, Brandon, Dingle, 1999.

K. Palmer, *Noongar People, Noongar Land: the resilience of Aboriginal culture in the south west of Western Australia*, Canberra, Aboriginal Studies Press, 2016.

S.H. Palmer, *Police and Protest in England and Ireland 1780–1850*, Cambridge, Cambridge University Press, 1990.

A.R. Pashley, *Policing Our State: a history of police stations and police officers in Western Australia 1829–1945*, Perth, Educant, 2000.

H. Pedersen, *Pigeon, an Aboriginal rebel: a study of Aboriginal European conflict in the West Kimberley, North Western Australia during the 1890s*, Honours thesis, Murdoch University, 1980.

H. Pedersen and B. Woorunmurra, *Jandamarra and the Bunuba Resistance*, Broome, Magabala Books, 1995.

D. Philips, *Crime and Authority in Victorian England: the black country 1835–1860*, London, Croom Helm, 1977.

D. Philips and R.D. Storch, *Policing Provincial England 1829–1856: the politics of reform*, London, Leicester University Press, 1999.

D. Philips and S. Davies (eds), *A Nation of Rogues, Crime, Law and Punishment in Colonial Australia*, Melbourne, Melbourne University Press, 1994.

Pigeon, dir. J. Noble, [videorecording] Film Archives collection, Filmwest, c1975.

J. Price, *The Land of Gold, The Narrative of a Journey through the West Australian Goldfields in the Autumn of 1895*, London, Sampson Low, Marston and

Bibliography

Company, 1896.

A. Ramsay, *Sir Robert Peel*, Freeport, Books for Libraries Press, 1969.

B. Reece and T. Stannage (eds), *European-Aboriginal Relations in Western Australian History*, Nedlands, UWA Press, 1984.

R.H.W. Reece, *Aborigines and Colonists: Aborigines and colonial society in New South Wales in the 1830s and 1840s*, Sydney, Sydney University Press, 1974.

G. Reid, *A Nest of Hornets*, Melbourne, Oxford University Press, 1982.

G. Reid, *A Picnic with the Natives: Aboriginal-European relations in the Northern Territory to 1910*, Melbourne, Melbourne University Press. 1990.

J.T. Reilly, *Reminiscences of Fifty Years in Western Australia*, Perth, Sands and McDougall, 1903.

E.A. Reynolds, *Before the Bobbies: the night watch and police reform in metropolitan London, 1729–1830*, Stanford, Stanford University Press, 1998

H. Reynolds, *Aborigines and Settlers: the Australian experience, 1788–1939*, Melbourne, Cassell Australia, 1972.

H. Reynolds, *Aboriginal Sovereignty: reflections on race, state, and nation*, Sydney, Allen & Unwin, 1996.

H. Reynolds, *The Forgotten Wars*, Sydney, NewSouth Publishing, 2013.

H. Reynolds, *Frontier: Aborigines, Settlers and Land*, Sydney, Allen & Unwin, 1987.

H. Reynolds, *An Indelible Stain: the question of genocide in Australia's history*, Melbourne, Viking, 2001.

H. Reynolds, *The Other Side of the Frontier: Aboriginal resistance to the European invasion of Australia*, Melbourne, Penguin Books, 1982.

H. Reynolds (ed.), *Race Relations in North Queensland*, Townsville, James Cook University, 1993.

H. Reynolds, *This Whispering in Our Hearts*, Sydney, Allen & Unwin, 1998.

H. Reynolds, *With the White People: the crucial role of Aborigines in the exploration and development of Australia*, Melbourne, Penguin, 1990.

E. Richards, J. Hudson and P. Lowe, (eds), *Out of the Desert: stories from the Walmajarri exodus*, Broome, Magabala Books, 2003.

J. Richards, *The Secret War: a true history of the Queensland native police*, St Lucia, University of Queensland Press, 2008.

A. R. Richardson, *Early Memories of the Great Nor-West and a Chapter in History of W.A.* Perth, E.S. Wigg, 1914.

T. Roberts, *Frontier Justice: a history of the Gulf Country to 1900*, St Lucia, University of Queensland Press, 2005.

F. Robinson, *The Black Resistance: an introduction to the history of the Aborigines struggle against British Colonialism*, Melbourne, Widescope, 1977.

D. R. Rose, *Hidden Histories: black stories from Victoria River Downs, Humbert River and Wave Hill stations*, Canberra, Aboriginal Studies Press, 1991.

H. Ross (ed.) and E. Bray (translator), *Impact Stories of the East Kimberley*, East Kimberley Working Paper no. 28, Canberra, East Kimberley Impact Assessment Project, 1989.

B. Rosser, *Up Rode the Troopers: the black police in Queensland*, St Lucia, University of Queensland Press, 1990.

C.D. Rowley, *Aboriginal Policy and Practice,* Canberra, ANU Press, 1971.

C.D. Rowley, *The Destruction of Aboriginal Society,* Canberra, ANU Press, 1970.

C.D. Rowley, *Recovery: the politics of Aboriginal reform,* Melbourne, Penguin, 1986.

E. Russell, *A History of the Law in Western Australia and its Development from 1829 to 1979,* Nedlands, UWA Press, 1980.

V. Ryan (ed.), *From Digging Sticks to Writing Sticks: stories of Kija women,* Perth, Catholic Education Office, 2001.

I. Shackcloth, *The Call of the Kimberleys,* Melbourne, Hallcraft Publishing, 1950.

B. Shaw (ed.), *Banggaiyerri: the story of Jack Sullivan as told to Bruce Shaw,* Canberra, Australian Institute of Aboriginal Studies, 1983.

B. Shaw, *Countrymen: the life histories of four Aboriginal men as told to Bruce Shaw,* Canberra, Australian Institute of Aboriginal Studies, 1986.

B. Shaw (ed.), *My Country of the Pelican Dreaming: the life of an Australian Aborigine of the Gadjerrong, Grant Ngabidj, 1904–1977,* Canberra, Aboriginal Studies Press, 1981.

B. Shaw (ed.), *When the Dust Come in Between; Aboriginal viewpoints in the East Kimberley prior to 1982,* Canberra, Aboriginal Studies Press, 1982.

L.E. Skinner, *Police of the Pastoral Frontier: native police 1849–1859,* Brisbane, University of Queensland Press, 1975.

W.E.H. Stanner, *White Man Got No Dreaming, Essays 1938–1973,* Canberra, ANU Press, 1979.

C.T. Stannage (ed.), *A New History of Western Australia,* Perth, UWA Press, 1981.

E.J.A. Stuart, *Land of Opportunities: being an account of the author's recent expedition to explore the Northern Territories of Australia,* London, Bodley Head, 1923.

M. Sturma, *Vice in a Vicious Society: crime and convicts in mid-nineteenth century New South Wales,* St Lucia, University of Queensland Press, 1983.

D. Taylor, *Crime, Policing and Punishment in England, 1750–1914,* London, Macmillan, 1998.

D. Taylor, *The New Police in Nineteenth Century England: crime, conflict and control,* Manchester, Manchester University Press, 1997.

N.W. Thomas, *Natives of Australia,* London, Archibald Constable & Co, 1906.

N.B. Tindale, *Aboriginal Tribes of Australia: their terrain, environmental controls, distribution, limits, and proper names with an appendix on Tasmanian tribes by Rhys Jones,* Berkeley, University of California Press, 1974.

P. Vallee, *God, Guns and Government on the Central Australian Frontier,* Canberra, Restoration, 2006.

A. Vogan, *The Black Police: a story of modern Australia,* London, Hutchinson & Co., 1890.

R. Ward, *The Australian Legend,* Melbourne, Oxford University Press, 1960.

Whispering in Our Hearts: the Mowla Bluff Massacre, dir. M. Torres, [videorecording] Australian Film Finance Corporation, 2002.

R. White and C. Alder (eds), *The Police and Young People in Australia,* Cambridge, Cambridge University Press, 1994.

K. Willey, *Boss Drover*, Adelaide, Rigby Books, 1971.

T Willing and K. Kenneally (eds), *Under a Regent Moon: a historical account of pioneer pastoralists Joseph Bradshaw and Aeneas Gunn at Marigui Settlement, Prince Margaret River, Kimberley Western Australia*, Landscope Expeditions, Department of Conservation and Land Management, 2002.

B. Wilson, *Sillitoe's Tartan in Northern Australia: a view of black and white policing in the Northern Territory, 1884 to 1935*, Honours thesis, Northern Territory University, 1996.

B. Wilson, *A Force Apart: a history of the Northern Territory police force 1870–1926*, Hong Kong, Peacock Academic Press, 2001.

K. Windschuttle, *The Fabrication of Aboriginal History: Volume One, Van Diemen's Land 1803–1947*, Sydney, Macleay Press, 2002.

K. Windschuttle, *The Fabrication of Aboriginal History, Volume Three, The Stolen Generations 1881–2008*, Sydney, Macleay Press, 2009.

N.E. Withnell Taylor, *Yeera-Mu-A Doo: a social history of the first settlement of North West Australia told through the Withnell and Hancock families 1861 to 1890*, Fremantle, Fremantle Arts Centre Press, 1980.

INDEX

www.ingramcontent.com/pod-product-compliance
Lightning Source LLC
Chambersburg PA
CBHW030854270326
41929CB00008B/417